Download Forms on Nolo.com

You can download the forms in this book at:

www.nolo.com/back-of-book/PAE.html

We'll also post updates whenever there's an important change to the law affecting this book—as well as articles and other related materials.

More Resources from Nolo.com

Legal Forms, Books, & Software

Hundreds of do-it-yourself products—all written in plain English, approved, and updated by our in-house legal editors.

Legal Articles

Get informed with thousands of free articles on everyday legal topics. Our articles are accurate, up to date, and reader friendly.

Find a Lawyer

Want to talk to a lawyer? Use Nolo to find a lawyer who can help you with your case.

25th Edition

How to
Probate an Estate in California

Attorney Lisa Fialco

TWENTY-FIFTH EDITION	MARCH 2021
Editor	BETSY SIMMONS HANNIBAL
Cover Design	SUSAN PUTNEY
Book Design	SUSAN PUTNEY
Proofreading	JOCELYN TRUITT
Index	VICTORIA BAKER
Printing	BANG PRINTING

ISSN 1940-6282 (print)
ISSN 2326-0033 (online)
ISBN 978-1-4133-2842-4 (pbk)
ISBN 978-1-4133-2843-1 (ebook)

This book covers only United States law, unless it specifically states otherwise.

Please note

We know that accurate, plain-English legal information can help you solve many of your own legal problems. But this text is not a substitute for personalized advice from a knowledgeable lawyer. If you want the help of a trained professional—and we'll always point out situations in which we think that's a good idea—consult an attorney licensed to practice in your state.

Acknowledgments

The updates in this edition reflect some of the small ways that COVID-19 has modified the probate process. The full impact on the bereaved, though, deserves sincere acknowledgment. Grieving and offering condolences carries on in different ways in times of social distancing. And nearly every interaction involved in the probate process requires adjustments in conducting business, extra patience, and empathy for the unique challenges of the times. I honor those making their way through probate now as well as those who help ease the path.

This book reflects decades of devotion by Julia Nissley, its initial author. Thanks to Betsy Simmons Hannibal for her good-natured guidance. With much appreciation to Steve, my family, friends, clients, and colleagues for their perspectives and support.

Lisa Fialco

About the Author

Lisa Fialco practices estate planning, probate, and trust law with Kelley & Farren, LLP in San Rafael, California. Her background in consumer protection motivates her commitment to demystifying estate planning and probate. Lisa is a Certified Specialist in Estate Planning, Trust, and Probate Law, certified by The State Bar of California Board of Legal Specialization. She is a graduate of Wesleyan University and the University of California, Berkeley, School of Law. She thoroughly reviewed, revised, and updated the 24th and 25th editions of *How to Probate an Estate in California.*

CAUTION

The procedures in this book are for California estates only. You cannot transfer real estate located in other states using the instructions in this book. To transfer property located outside of California, you must either learn that state's rules or consult a lawyer in the state where the property is located.

Table of Contents

Your Legal Companion for Probate

The loss of a close family member or friend can bring feelings of uncertainty and anxiety, as well as grief. While you're trying to cope and adapt to major changes, the added burden of settling the deceased person's affairs may seem overwhelming.

This book can help. *How to Probate an Estate in California* explains how the process of administering an estate works, how to do certain tasks yourself, and when to get help from a professional. It makes probate administration as easy to understand as possible, in plain English. The early chapters explain how probate works and discuss first steps. The second half of the book describes in detail how to complete specific tasks, including how to:

- complete the paperwork for a formal probate court proceeding
- deal with community property
- bypass the probate court when transferring a small estate
- handle joint tenancies, and
- much more.

You will learn that not all estates need a formal probate court proceeding. California law provides some shortcuts—methods to transfer property after a death without going to court. When there is no other way to transfer title from the deceased person to the new rightful owner, or when the estate would benefit from oversight by the court, a probate administration provides the process and the result of settling the estate.

If you are the main beneficiary and the estate is straightforward, you may be able to do much of the work yourself. Most estates, however, will require some degree of help from a professional. This may mean having an attorney represent you for the entire probate process, consulting with an attorney on one or more specific points, or getting counsel from a tax expert. Throughout the book, we point out the many situations that warrant hiring professional support.

If you have an interest in an estate, but do not plan to take an active role in handling the deceased person's affairs, this book can help you understand the process of estate administration. Learning how probate works can help you have realistic expectations about what is involved and how long it will take.

Keep in mind that this book explains how to handle the estate of someone who was a resident of California at death and who owned property in this state. If the deceased person lived elsewhere or owned real estate in another state, this book might give you some useful information about probate in California, but you will need to hire an attorney or obtain other advice to wrap up that estate.

If you're in the midst of grieving, you may wonder whether you can cope with the details and possible complexities of settling a loved one's affairs. We can only suggest that you learn about the process. In this way, you can contribute to a smooth administration, whatever your role. Take heart that your efforts will help preserve the estate and distribute it as your loved one intended. Good luck.

Get Forms, Updates, and More Online

When there are important changes to the information in this book, we'll post updates online, on a page dedicated to this book:

www.nolo.com/back-of-book/PAE.html

You'll find several of this book's forms there, as well as other useful information.

CHAPTER

1

An Overview

What Is Probate?

To many people, the term "probate" refers only to a long, drawn out, and costly legal formality that takes place after a person dies. Technically, probate means "proving the will" through a probate court proceeding. In the past, virtually every estate had to be reviewed by a judge before property could pass to those who would inherit it. Today, however, some ways to transfer property after death don't require formal court proceedings. And the term "probate" now generally describes the entire process of settling the legal and financial affairs of someone who has died.

For example, a surviving spouse or domestic partner may receive property outright without any court proceeding at all. Joint tenancy property also escapes the need for formal probate, as does property left in a trust and property in a pay on death bank account. If an estate meets the standard for a small estate, currently defined as consisting of property worth less than $166,250, it, too, can be transferred outside of formal probate. Fortunately, the paperwork necessary to actually transfer property to its new owners in the foregoing situations is generally neither time-consuming nor complicated. We discuss all of these procedures, as well as how to do a formal probate court proceeding.

The person who settles an estate usually doesn't have much choice as to which property transfer method to use. That is, whether you are required to use a formal probate or a simpler method to transfer property at death depends on how much (or little) planning the decedent (deceased person) did before death to avoid probate and how the decedent held title to the assets. This is discussed in detail as we go along.

Both formal probate and some of the other nonprobate procedures involve filing papers at a court clerk's office, usually in the county where the decedent resided at the time of death. Most probate matters don't actually require that you appear in court before a judge during the process. In fact, settling an estate through papers submitted to the court by mail or electronic filing is now the norm.

What Is Involved in Settling an Estate?

Generally, settling an estate is a continuing process that:

- determines what property is owned by the decedent
- pays the decedent's debts and taxes, if any, and
- distributes all remaining property to the appropriate beneficiaries.

When a person dies, she may own several categories of assets. Among these might be household belongings, bank accounts, vehicles, mutual funds, stocks, business interests, and insurance policies, as well as real property. All property owned by the decedent at the time of his or her death, no matter the kind or the value, is called his or her "estate."

To get this property out of the name of the decedent and into the names of the people who inherit it requires a legal bridge. There are several types of legal procedures or bridges to move different kinds of property to the new owners. Some of these are the equivalent of large suspension bridges to carry a lot of property while others are of much less use and might be more analogous to a footbridge. Lawyers often call this process "administering an estate." In this book, we refer to these procedures collectively as "settling an estate."

The estate settlement bridges may lead the property to the beneficiaries named in the deceased person's will. Or, where there is no will, state law determines the heirs, usually close relatives. And, of course, the rights of creditors are considered in the process. No matter how property is held when a person dies, it must cross an estate settlement bridge before those entitled to inherit may legally take possession. The formal court probate process is but one of these bridges. Some of the other bridges involve community property transfers, clearing title to joint tenancy property, transfer to a beneficiary designated by contract, winding up living trusts, and settling very small estates that are exempt from probate.

How Long Does It Take to Settle an Estate?

If a formal probate court procedure is required, it usually takes nine to 12 months to complete all the necessary steps. More complicated estates can take longer. On the other hand, if the decedent planned his or her estate to avoid probate, or the estate is small, or everything goes to a surviving spouse or domestic partner, then the estate may be settled in a matter of weeks by using some easier nonprobate procedures. See the checklist for formal probate in Chapter 13 for details about the typical length of a formal probate administration.

CAUTION

The procedures in this book are only for California estates. Real property and personal property (see Chapter 4 for definitions) located outside of California are not part of a California estate and cannot be transferred following the instructions in this book. To transfer property located outside of California, you will either have to familiarize yourself with that state's rules (these will be similar, but by no means identical to those in effect in California) or hire a lawyer in the state where the property is located.

What This Book Covers

Not all estates can be settled entirely by using a self-help manual. Although many California estates can be settled with the procedures described in the following chapters, some estates will require at least some formal legal assistance. Therefore, it's important to know if the estate you are dealing with has complexities beyond the scope of this book.

First, an estate that can be settled using this book (a "simple estate," for lack of a better term) is one that consists of the common types of assets, such as houses, land, a mobile home, bank accounts, household goods, automobiles, collectibles, stocks, money market funds, promissory notes, etc. More complicated assets may be more complicated to administer after death. This can include complex investments, business or partnership interests, out-of-state property, or royalties from copyrights or patents. For these assets, it may not be as easy to determine the extent of the decedent's interest in the property, relevant tax or accounting issues, or how to transfer that interest to the new owner. However, a simple estate may include unusual assets if the person settling the estate has experience in such matters or has help from an accountant or attorney along the way. When questions arise as to ownership of an asset, or when third parties make claims against the estate (as would be the case if someone threatened to sue over a disputed claim), you have a complicated situation that will require help beyond this book.

Second, for an estate to be "simple" there should be no disagreements among the beneficiaries, especially as to the distribution of the property. Certainly, dividing up a decedent's property can sometimes bring out the worst in human nature. If you face a situation with angry family members or threats of lawsuits, it is not a simple estate. To settle an estate without unnecessary delays or complications, you need the cooperation of everyone involved. If you don't have it (for example, a disappointed beneficiary or family member plans to contest the will or otherwise engage in obstructionist behavior), you will need professional help. (See Chapter 16.)

Third, and contrary to what you might think, a simple estate does not have to be small. Larger estates tend to have more complexities, may require more elaborate management of assets, and may have more at stake for potential disputes. Even so, in some circumstances even a larger estate can be simple to administer. An additional concern with a large estate is federal estate taxes, which affect estates valued over approximately $11.7 million (in 2021). Estate income tax returns may also be required. You can hire an accountant familiar with estate taxes to give advice on tax issues and prepare the necessary tax returns. We provide an overview of estate taxation in Chapter 7.

Even if you plan to get legal assistance to administer the estate—either because the estate is not simple or because you prefer to have an experienced person guiding the process—you may find this book helpful. Understanding the process will help you serve as the personal representative with confidence. Also, if you are a beneficiary, you may want to learn about the process so that you can have realistic expectations about what must be done before you get your inheritance.

TIP

This book does not cover the details of trust administration. Many people in California create a living trust to avoid a court probate procedure at their death. If the decedent set up a trust, the person named in the trust as trustee will need to follow the terms of the trust to distribute the assets of the trust. Administering a trust has its own legal requirements, which are not discussed in detail in this book.

Simple Estate Checklist

The checklist below shows basic parts in settling a simple estate in California. Each part is explained later in the book.

This list may appear a bit intimidating at first. Not every situation requires all of these parts. And some are quite straightforward. As with so many other things in life, probating a simple estate involves putting one foot in front of the other. If you understand the big picture, take it step-by-step, pay close attention to the instructions, and get professional assistance when needed, you can have a smooth and successful administration.

Important Terms in Probate

As you read through this material, you will be introduced to a number of technical words and phrases used by lawyers and court personnel. We define these as we go along, with occasional reminders. If you become momentarily confused, refer to the glossary, which follows Chapter 16.

The Gross Estate and the Net Estate

You will encounter the terms "gross estate" and "net estate" while settling an estate. The decedent's gross estate is generally the fair market value at date of death of all property that he owned or controlled. It includes everything in which the decedent had any financial interest—houses, insurance, personal effects, automobiles, bank accounts, stocks, land, businesses, and so on. It includes only the decedent's portion of the asset. How the decedent owned the property (for example, in a living trust, in joint tenancy, or as community property) may determine the decedent's portion for the purposes of the gross estate. The net estate, on the other hand, is the value of what is left after subtracting from the gross estate the total amount of any mortgages, liens, or other debts owed by the decedent at the time of death.

EXAMPLE 1: Suppose Harry died, leaving a home, a car, stocks, and some cash in the bank. To arrive at his gross estate, you would add the value of all his property without looking to see if Harry owed any money on any of it. Let's assume that Harry's gross estate was $500,000. Now, assume he had a mortgage of $150,000 against the house. This means his net estate (the value of all of his property less what he owed on it) would be worth $350,000.

EXAMPLE 2: If Diego and Louisa, husband and wife, together own as community property a house, car, and savings account having a total gross value of $800,000, and owe $100,000 in debts, the net value of their community property would be $700,000. However, if Louisa died, only one-half of their property would be included in her estate because under California community property rules, discussed in detail in Chapter 4, the other half is Diego's. Thus, Louisa's gross estate would be $400,000 and her net estate $350,000.

What's Needed to Start Settling a Simple Estate

☐ **1. Assemble Important Documents**

- Locate the will, if any, and make copies.
- Order certified copies of the death certificate.
- Locate other documents relevant to assets, including account statements, deeds, insurance policies, and beneficiary designation forms.
- Locate other important documents, including marital agreements and trusts.

☐ **2. Determine the People Involved**

- Determine who will be the estate representative.
- Determine heirs and beneficiaries and prepare a list of names, ages, and addresses.

☐ **3. Determine Assets and Creditors**

- Assemble and list assets such as properties, bank accounts, and retirement accounts.
- Determine how title is held to each asset (for example, in the decedent's name alone, in joint tenancy, in a living trust, etc.).
- Determine whether each asset is community or separate property.
- Estimate the value of each asset and, if the decedent was a co-owner, the value of the decedent's share.
- List debts and obligations.

☐ **4. Determine Procedures Required and Begin Process**

- Determine decedent's legal residence.
- Determine methods for transferring assets.
- Initiate procedures to administer estate and transfer assets. Possible procedures include:
  - terminate joint tenancies
  - transfers of some estates worth $166,250 or less without formal probate administration
  - spousal / domestic partner transfer procedures
  - formal court probate administration, and
  - trust administration.
- Pay debts having priority as soon as estate funds are available, if the estate is solvent.

☐ **5. Prepare for Taxes**

- Arrange for final income tax returns and estate fiduciary income tax returns, if required.
- Determine if requirement for federal estate tax return applies. If so, arrange to have the estate tax return prepared.

The Probate Estate

The "probate estate," quite simply, is all of the decedent's property that must go through probate. This is very likely to be less than the total amount of property the decedent owned, because if an asset already has a named beneficiary, or if title is held in a way that avoids probate, then it isn't part of the probate estate. To return to the bridge analogy discussed earlier, this means that property held in one of these ways can be transferred to the proper beneficiary using one of the alternate (nonprobate) bridges.

As a general rule, the following types of property need not be included in a probate administration:

- joint tenancy property
- life insurance with a named beneficiary other than the decedent's estate
- pension plan distributions
- property in trusts
- money in a bank account that has a named beneficiary who is to be paid on death
- individual retirement accounts (IRAs) or other retirement plans or annuities that have named beneficiaries
- community property or separate property that passes outright to a surviving spouse or domestic partner (this sometimes requires an abbreviated court procedure), and
- real estate held by a transfer on death (TOD) deed.

Put another way, the probate estate (property that must cross the formal probate bridge) consists of all property except the property that falls into the above categories. Where there has been predeath planning to avoid probate, little or no property may have to be transferred over the probate court bridge.

CAUTION

You can simplify the settlement of your own estate. Resources covering this subject are *Plan Your Estate*, by Denis Clifford (Nolo), and *8 Ways to Avoid Probate*, by Mary Randolph (Nolo). You can also find lots of good information at Nolo's Wills, Trusts & Probate Center on Nolo.com.

Overview of How to Settle an Estate in California

- Preliminary steps: Collect information and documents (Chapters 2, 3, 4).
- List assets, determine date-of-death values and figure out how title is held (Chapters 5, 6).
- File federal estate tax return (IRS Form 706): (1) if gross value of estate exceeds estate tax exclusion amount, or (2) if decedent was married and claiming deceased spouse's unused exclusion amount (Chapter 7).
- Use procedures to transfer or collect nonprobate assets:
  - Collect assets passing to named beneficiaries by beneficiary designation—such as insurance, retirement, and death benefits (Chapter 2).
  - Clear joint tenancy, pay on death, or transfer on death accounts in name(s) of survivor(s) (Chapter 10).
  - Follow trust administration procedures for assets held by trust (Chapter 12).
  - Transfer assets held held as community property with right of survivorship (Chapter 15).
  - For assets passing to surviving spouse or partner either by will or by intestate succession, confirm title to surviving spouse or partner with a Spousal or Domestic Partner Property Petition (Chapter 15).
- Transfer assets using simplified procedures for small estates if the value of the remaining estate is $166,250 or less (Chapter 11).
- If the remaining estate is greater than $166,250, or if other complications exist, initiate court probate administration to transfer assets to beneficiaries (Chapters 13, 14).

The Taxable Estate

Although this book is primarily about settling an estate, we include some mention of taxes because estates over a certain value are required to file a federal estate tax return. Therefore, you should know how to compute the value of the decedent's estate for tax purposes, which—not surprisingly—is called the "taxable estate." Keep in mind that the property that must go through probate (probate estate) is not necessarily the same as the taxable estate. Not all assets are subject to probate, but they are all counted when determining whether estate taxes must be paid. In other words, the taxable estate includes all assets in the decedent's control just prior to death. The taxable estate may include assets subject to formal probate, plus joint tenancy property, life insurance proceeds (if the decedent was the owner of the policy), death benefits, property in a living trust, and property in any other probate-avoidance device. However, if any of the assets are community property (discussed in Chapter 4), only the decedent's one-half interest is included in his or her taxable estate.

If the estate is large enough to require a federal estate tax return, any tax is computed on the net value of the decedent's property (net estate). That is, the tax is determined by the value of all property, less any debts owed by the decedent and certain other allowable deductions.

Debts and Insolvent Estates

Probate administration provides a systematic way to determine debts and the order in which to pay them. Creditors are divided into classes according to their respective priorities. (Prob. Code § 11420.) First priority is given to debts owed to the United States or to the State of California, such as various taxes. Next in priority come the required expenses to administer the probate estate (personal representative and attorneys' fees, court costs, etc.) and, after that, mortgages or other secured loans. Then funeral expenses, last illness expenses, judgment claims, and general creditors have priority, in that order. When there may not be enough money in the estate to satisfy all debts, each class is paid in full before going to the next class. For this reason, it is important to follow the correct timing for paying debts and expenses. For example, a personal representative may pay funeral expenses as soon as funds are available, but only after holding aside enough money to pay the expenses of administration.

If using small estate procedures (Chapter 11), the successors are responsible for paying the decedent's unsecured debts out of the property they receive.

An "insolvent estate" is one that does not have enough assets to pay creditors in full. Insolvent estates are subject to special rules. If the estate cannot pay a class in full, the payments are prorated.

> EXAMPLE: In the class of general debts, if Creditor One is owed $5,000 and Creditor Two is owed $10,000 and only $1,000 is left, Creditor One gets one-third of the $1,000 and Creditor Two gets two-thirds.

You must present an accounting for insolvent estates in a formal probate court proceeding. Consult an attorney if the estate is insolvent or has a complicated debt situation.

Estate Taxes

Most estates will not owe estate taxes. A person who dies in 2021 may own assets worth up to approximately $11.7 million without owing any federal estate taxes. This exclusion amount will rise with inflation. Estates having a gross value over the exclusion amount must file a federal estate tax return. The tax is computed on the net estate after certain allowable deductions have been taken.

If the net estate is under the exclusion amount, a return must still be filed if the estate has a gross value over the exclusion amount, although no tax may be owed. For example, if someone who dies in 2020 has a gross estate of $12 million and debts of $500,000, a federal estate tax return must be filed, even if the debts reduce the net value of the estate to less than the exclusion amount. Also, if the decedent was married, you may choose to file a federal estate tax return for an estate less than this amount to claim "portability" of the decedent's unused exclusion amount for the surviving spouse's estate. We discuss federal estate tax in more detail in Chapter 7.

California does not impose its own inheritance tax or estate tax. If the decedent owned property in other states, or if the recipients of property reside in other states, state estate or inheritance taxes may apply.

CAUTION

Pay taxes first. Although most estates don't have to worry about federal estate taxes, if yours is a large estate that will owe federal estate taxes, those taxes should be paid before transferring property to the people who inherit it. Many wills set aside money for the payment of taxes.

Federal and state income tax returns for the decedent's last year and sometimes for the estate (if there is a formal probate) must also be filed. (See Chapter 7.)

Do You Need an Attorney?

Being the estate representative, in itself, is an important job that can provide satisfaction of handling the decedent's estate with care. You will have responsibility for assembling assets, paying bills, managing the assets of the estate, and ultimately making distributions. The law does not require you to hire an attorney to assist you to settle an estate.

All of that said, probate is a legal process with unique rules. Hiring a lawyer who has the training and experience to maneuver through the relevant laws and procedures can make the process more smooth. Having a professional as a guide can allow you to focus on your own responsibilities with less stress.

If the estate is simple, if you have the time and desire to devote to learning the required procedures and following through, and particularly if you are the only beneficiary, you might choose to proceed without a lawyer. This book provides guidance and information on the process to help you recognize situations that may require legal assistance.

Complications that require special knowledge or handling may crop up even in an otherwise simple estate. Some examples are:

- claims against the estate by people who were left out or think they were given too little
- insolvent estates (more debts than assets)
- assets that require special handling, such as properties that will be sold, multiple owners, or business interests
- the decedent's unfinished contracts. (For example, a sale of real property begun but not completed prior to death)
- ambiguities in the will. (For example: "I give $50,000 to the poor children in the County Hospital." This would raise several problems. Does "poor" mean low income or just unfortunate enough to be in the hospital? And what did the decedent intend when it came to dividing the money? Is it to be divided among all the children in the hospital, or did the decedent intend to set up a central fund to be used to make life a little easier for all kids in the hospital?)
- substantial property given to a minor, unless legal provisions to handle this are made in the will, or
- contested claims about what property is in the estate (for example, a surviving spouse or domestic partner who claims a community property interest in property left by will to someone else).

In a probate court proceeding, standard attorneys' fees have been set by law and are based on a percentage of the gross estate (the gross value of the assets that are subjected to probate). These statutory fees set the *maximum* the attorney may charge. You may be able to negotiate for a lower fee. However, for a particularly complicated estate needing out-of-the ordinary legal services, the lawyer can seek court approval for additional compensation.

The formula for computing ordinary attorneys' fees in a formal probate court proceeding is found in California's Probate Code Section 10810. The fee is calculated as follows:

- 4% of the first $100,000 of the gross value of the probate estate
- 3% of the next $100,000
- 2% of the next $800,000
- 1% of the next $9,000,000
- 0.5% of the next $15,000,000, and
- a "reasonable amount" (determined by the court) for everything above $25,000,000.

For example, in a probate estate with a gross value of $150,000, the fee set by statute is $5,500; in an estate with a gross value of $200,000, the attorney fee is $7,000; in an estate with a gross value of $500,000, the attorney fee is $13,000; and so on. Some circumstances may allow you to negotiate a lower fee with an attorney. For example, if a probate estate contains only one piece of real property, perhaps a home worth $1,000,000, the statutory attorney fee would be $23,000, even if the home might have a substantial mortgage that reduces the decedent's equity to only $150,000. An attorney may be willing to accept a lesser fee, particularly if the estate has no complicating factors.

Attorneys' fees in a formal court proceeding are paid out of the estate after being approved by the court, usually towards the end of the probate process. Chapter 16 provides information about working with an attorney.

If an estate doesn't require formal probate because it can be settled in another way, such as a community property transfer to a surviving spouse or domestic partner, or a joint tenancy termination, a statutory fee does not apply. In these situations, an attorney will bill for his or her time at an hourly rate, which commonly varies from $250 to $450 an hour.

EXAMPLE: Returning to Harry's estate for a moment (discussed above), let's assume that Harry's will left all of his property to his daughter, Millicent, and son, Michael, and one or both of them serve as executor. If they hire a lawyer to represent and guide them as executor, the attorney's fee would be up to $13,000, computed on a gross estate of $500,000. If they, instead, proceed as executor without an attorney and also waived the executor's fee, the job could be accomplished for the cost of administration expenses only, which would amount to about $2,500 (including filing, publication, certification, and appraisal fees).

Executor's Fees

In a probate court proceeding, the court appoints a personal representative to handle the estate, called either an "executor" (if there is a will) or an "administrator" (if the decedent died without a will or without naming an executor in his or her will). This person is entitled to fees, called the estate representative's "commission." These fees are set using the same statutory formula as for the attorney; see above. The estate representative cannot be paid from the estate until approved by the court, usually towards the end of the probate process. Because the commission is subject to income tax, close family members or beneficiaries who serve as executor or administrator sometimes choose to waive the executor's or administrator's fee.

When a friend or loved one dies, the natural grief process can make administrative tasks particularly challenging. Participating in the process of settling an estate, however, sometimes becomes a tangible way to approach the grief. Whether or not you choose to get legal assistance from the start, learning about the process, organizing relevant information, and proceeding in a responsible, diligent way can honor the deceased and care for beneficiaries or heirs. This book can help with that process.

CHAPTER

2

First Steps in Settling an Estate

When someone dies, everything stops in connection with the decedent's financial affairs, and someone must step in and take charge of things until the estate is settled and the property transferred to its new owners. This person is usually called the "estate representative," or sometimes the "decedent's personal representative."

You may already know that you are going to be the estate representative if:

- you are named in the will as executor
- nobody else is named in a will and you are the closest living relative in a position to handle things, or
- you will inherit the bulk of the decedent's estate.

If that's the case, you may choose to skip or skim the first section of this chapter, which explains how the estate representative is normally chosen. But carefully read the second and third sections, which set out your responsibilities and duties as representative.

Also, before you agree to be an estate representative —and you do have a choice—carefully consider the responsibilities and the possible difficulties of managing the estate. You will need a good understanding of what the job involves to make the right decision about whether to take on the project. You have options, which include working with a lawyer, working with a corepresentative, and declining the job altogether. Plunging into the role unprepared could cause extra work and expense that could be avoided by either getting help or deciding to have another person act as estate representative.

Who Will Act as the Estate Representative?

Who will serve as estate representative depends on a number of factors, including:

- whether the will named someone to be executor
- if so, whether that person is willing and able to serve, and
- if there is no will, who among the people who have priority under the law to serve are able and willing to do the job.

About the only definite legal requirements are that the estate representative, whether formally appointed or acting informally, must be older than 18 years of age, capable of fulfilling the duties, and competent. Normally, the representative must first be appointed formally by the court before having authority to act on behalf of the estate. If urgent circumstances require you to have authority to act before the normal timeline for probate would allow—for example to preserve the estate—you can petition the court to be appointed as a special administrator. See a lawyer for assistance.

CROSS-REFERENCE

See "If Formal Probate Isn't Necessary," below, to learn about the estate representative's role if there will not be a formal probate administration.

If There Is a Will That Appoints an Executor

If the decedent left a will naming an executor or executors, normally this is who will be the estate representative unless the executor named in the will is unwilling or unable to serve. A will often nominates alternate executors to serve as the estate representative if the prior person does not or cannot serve. If a formal probate court proceeding is necessary (discussed in Chapter 6), the executor named in the will is appointed by the court and issued a formal badge of office, called "letters testamentary." If no formal probate is necessary, then the executor named in the will normally serves as the informal estate representative.

If There Is No Will

If there is no will, a court appoints an "administrator" as estate representative for the formal probate proceeding. If the estate does not require a formal probate, then no administrator is formally appointed and a close relative, often the person who inherits the bulk of the estate, serves as an informal estate representative.

Assuming probate is necessary, the probate court appoints the administrator according to a certain order of priority, with a surviving spouse or domestic partner, or a child of the decedent, usually handling the job. The administrator must be a U.S. resident. A person who has priority to serve as administrator may nominate another person to serve instead by submitting a document to the court as a part of the Petition for Probate (see Chapter 14). If the person making the nomination is a surviving spouse or domestic partner, child, grandchild, parent, brother, sister, or grandparent of the decedent, this nominee has priority after those in the same class as the person making the request. For example, if a decedent's son does not wish to be the administrator and nominates someone to serve in his place, the son's nominee does not have priority over the decedent's daughter, but would have priority over more distant relatives.

> **EXAMPLE:** Andy died a resident of California, leaving no will. His surviving relatives are four children. He leaves no surviving spouse or domestic partner. Any or all of his children are entitled to priority as administrators of his estate; if none wishes to serve as administrator, any one of them may nominate someone else—not necessarily a relative of the decedent.

The logic behind the priority system is simple. Relatives who are entitled to inherit part or all of the estate under intestate succession laws (we discuss these in Chapter 3) are entitled to priority, because lawmakers presume that a person who is entitled to receive property from the estate will most likely manage it to the best advantage of all the heirs. The following table shows the priority list for appointing an administrator, as established by Section 8461 of the Probate Code.

If the Will Appoints No Executor or an Executor Who Can't or Won't Serve

Sometimes a will does not name an executor, or names a person who has since died, or names someone who does not want to act as the estate representative.

> CAUTION
>
> **Former spouses.** If a former spouse is named as executor and the marriage was dissolved or annulled after January 1, 1985, the former spouse is prevented from serving as executor, unless the will provides otherwise. (Prob. Code § 6122.) A similar law also applies to former registered domestic partners for wills executed on or after January 1, 2002. (Prob. Code. § 6122.1.)

Priority List for Appointing an Administrator When Someone Dies Without a Will

a. Surviving spouse or domestic partner*
b. Children**
c. Grandchildren
d. Other issue (great-grandchildren, etc.)
e. Parents
f. Brothers and sisters
g. Issue of brothers and sisters
h. Grandparents
i. Issue of grandparents (uncles, aunts, first cousins, etc.)
j. Children of a predeceased spouse or domestic partner
k. Other issue of a predeceased spouse or domestic partner
l. Other next of kin
m. Parents of a predeceased spouse or domestic partner
n. Issue of parents of a predeceased spouse or domestic partner
o. Conservator or guardian of the estate of the decedent acting in that capacity at the time of death (with some limitations)
p. Public administrator
q. Creditors
r. Any other person

* For purposes of these provisions, persons qualify as domestic partners only if they have filed a Declaration of Domestic Partnership with the California Secretary of State. (Prob. Code §§ 8461 and 8462.)

** Often, one child, selected informally within the family, will serve. However, two or more children may petition to be coadministrators.

If someone named in the will does not serve as executor, then a person can request to be appointed as "administrator with will annexed" to serve as representative in the court probate proceeding. An administrator with will annexed is appointed in the same order of priority as a regular administrator, except that any person who receives property under the will has priority over those who don't. (Prob. Code § 8441.)

Any person, regardless of his or her relationship to the decedent, who takes more than 50% of the value of the estate under the will and is a resident of the United States has first priority to serve as administrator or to appoint another person to act as administrator with will annexed. If together a group of people take more than 50% under the will, then together those people can nominate someone who will then have priority over others who take under the will.

> **EXAMPLE:** Sally died a resident of California, leaving a will giving all of her property to her boyfriend, Mort. Sally's will does not name an executor. Mort is entitled to priority as administrator with will annexed because he receives all property under Sally's will, even though Sally may have surviving relatives. If Mort does not wish to serve as administrator, he may appoint anyone of his choosing to be administrator with will annexed of Sally's estate, because he is entitled to inherit more than 50% of the estate.

TIP

Distance may make it difficult to serve as estate representative. When considering whether you should serve as the estate representative, keep in mind that living far away from the county of administration could make the probate process more difficult or costly. For example, the court may have stricter bond requirements for an out-of-state personal representative. Also, the logistics of filing documents and appearing at hearings may be more complicated if you cannot personally go to the court. If you do choose to serve from a distance, you can ease these logistical hurdles by becoming very familiar with the local court practices, using a court filing service to assist with filing documents, and appearing at any necessary court hearings by telephone when allowed. Also, being represented by a local attorney can make things easier.

If It's Not Clear Who Should Be Estate Representative

In some situations, it may not be clear who will be estate representative. Here are some examples:

- The will does not name an executor and more than one person has equal priority to serve.
- The will names a business partner.
- A person with lower priority wants to serve and all persons with higher priority do not agree to that person serving.
- A person having priority to serve has a conflict of interest.
- The executor named in the will has not filed to initiate a probate within thirty days after the death without good cause for the delay.
- The will names a minor who wants to serve after turning 18 years old.
- The will does not name an executor and a non–U.S. resident is an heir.
- The person named as executor in the will or who has priority to serve is liable for abuse, neglect, or elder financial abuse against the decedent.
- Several persons with equal priority for appointment as administrator cannot agree about who should do the job.
- A bond or surety is required and cannot be obtained, for example because of bad credit.
- The surviving spouse or registered domestic partner was named in the will or has priority but was living apart from the decedent, and steps had been taken to annul or dissolve the marriage or partnership.
- Non–U.S. resident heirs want to appoint a non-California resident.

If any of these apply to your situation, or if for any other reason it's not clear to you who should be the estate representative, get advice from a probate professional.

Using a Professional Estate Representative

If the people named under the will or with priority under the law to serve as representative do not feel equipped to handle the role, the estate may have a professional do the job, either exclusively or as a corepresentative.

Professionals such as licensed professional fiduciaries, bank trust departments, trust companies, attorneys, and CPAs may serve as estate representatives.

The decedent can nominate a professional in the will. Or, if a family member or friend who is nominated does not want to serve, that person or the beneficiaries can nominate a professional to serve instead. And if the family member or friend wants to stay involved, yet wants the expertise and assistance of a professional, serving as corepresentatives may provide a good solution. Using a professional fiduciary can be particularly helpful if the estate has complicated assets—such as businesses or real estate investments—or if there are uncooperative or many beneficiaries. In such situations, an experienced fiduciary might administer the estate more swiftly and effectively than a nonprofessional.

Of course, unlike a nonprofessional family member or beneficiary who may choose to waive the fee provided under the statute, the professional services will come at a cost to the estate. But the expense of having a professional administer the estate may be well worth the benefit if a professional can maximize the value of the estate or avoid costly errors in management.

To find a professional to serve as estate representative, you can ask for recommendations from a probate attorney, accountant, bank, financial adviser, real estate professional, or others who have frequent involvement with estate administration. Here are two resources that can help you locate or research a private professional fiduciary:

- The Professional Fiduciaries Bureau within the State of California Department of Consumer Affairs licenses private professional fiduciaries and has a searchable database. See www.fiduciary.ca.gov.
- The Professional Fiduciary Association of California has a searchable listing of fiduciaries who meet educational and experience requirements set by that organization. See www.pfac-pro.org.

If you are considering nominating a professional to serve as representative or corepresentative, do some research. Speak with the professional, ask about experience with similar estates, confirm that licensing requirements are met, check references, and discuss the fee structure. Also, and sometimes as a last resort, each county has a "public administrator" that has authority to seek appointment as the personal representative if no other appropriate person is able or willing to serve to administer the estate.

If Formal Probate Isn't Necessary

Many estates do not require a formal probate court proceeding. (If you are in doubt as to whether or not probate will be required, read Chapter 6.) An increasing number of estates avoid probate as more people carefully plan their estates. Formal probate isn't necessary if most of the decedent's assets:

- were held in joint tenancy or in a trust
- pass to the surviving spouse or registered domestic partner
- pass by beneficiary designation, or
- pass in a small estate (valued under $166,250, an amount to be adjusted periodically for inflation).

SEE AN EXPERT

Get legal advice for complicated situations. Formal probate proceedings might be appropriate in some estates even when it is not required. For example, an estate might need the process and structure of the probate court to resolve complex debts or disputes among beneficiaries, even if most of the estate's property passes to a surviving spouse or registered domestic partner, through a living trust, or by beneficiary designation. If your situation shows any sign of complication, get help from an experienced probate attorney.

If there is no formal probate court proceeding, there is no court-appointed representative for the estate. This, of course, raises the question of who informally acts as the estate representative. Sometimes, even when a decedent has left most property outside of the will, there will also be a will naming an executor. In this instance, the executor named in the will usually takes over informally to help settle the estate and transfer the property. If there is no will naming an executor, a close relative or trusted friend is a logical choice—preferably one who will inherit most, or at least part, of the estate. Normally, families and friends decide this among themselves. In this situation, it is not uncommon for several people to share the responsibility, although they must coordinate their efforts to avoid complications. If there is a dispute as to who this informal estate representative should be, or if relevant people have cross purposes, see a lawyer for advice. Also, be aware that acting informally can incur liabilities, particularly if there are debts or disputes, so proceed carefully. Read more about this in "Fiduciary Duty," below.

Responsibilities of the Estate Representative

Acting as an estate representative can be a tedious job, but in most cases it doesn't require any special knowledge or training. You must be trustworthy, organized, and diligent. Throughout the process, you must stay informed of your responsibilities, follow the rules, keep good records, and communicate with everyone involved.

You can read the official requirements on Judicial Council Form DE-147, *Duties and Liabilities of Personal Representative* in Appendix B.

Organization

Organization is the best tool of anyone who wants to wind up the affairs of a deceased person efficiently and without frustrating delay. As you go along, arrange the information and material you collect in an orderly manner.

A good way to do this is to have a separate file folder for each category of information. For instance, one folder may hold unpaid bills, another may hold copies of income tax returns, another could be for official documents like the will and death certificate, and still others may be reserved for information on specific assets, such as insurance, real property, stocks, or bank accounts. Then, when you get involved in one or another of the actual steps to transfer assets described in this book, you can set up an additional folder for each (for example, formal probate or community property transfers). The folders can be kept together in one expansion file or file drawer. If you have a lot of material to organize, you might find it helpful to arrange it in the same order as the checklist in Chapter 1.

You will likely end up with a number of electronic files as well. Like hard copy records, you must keep your electronic files organized. If you feel more comfortable with either paper or electronic files, you may accumulate more of one than the other. However, some records will come to you digitally and other records you will be required to keep in hard copy. So you will almost certainly end up with a combination of both types.

You will also need to be organized about the procedural steps along the way. Maintaining one chronological file—electronic or paper—containing each document filed with or received from the court can be invaluable. Since you are presumed to know the relevant law and procedures, you should also have your reference resources handy, such as local court rules and other information from the court.

TIP

Securely store your records. You will likely collect sensitive personal information that could be used for identity theft if it ends up in the wrong hands. Keep paper records locked. Be careful about securing your computer files, protecting passwords, and backing up files. Regularly review all account activity and act quickly to report any suspected identity theft.

Fiduciary Duty

The representative, whether court appointed or acting informally, has the principal duty to protect the estate and to see that it is transferred to the rightful recipients. In other words, the representative must manage the assets in the best interests of all persons involved in the estate (this includes creditors and taxing authorities) until handing the property over to the beneficiaries.

The law does not require the representative to be an expert or to display more than ordinary care and diligence. However, the job does require the highest degree of honesty, impartiality, and diligence. This is called in law a "fiduciary duty"—the duty to act with scrupulous good faith and candor. As a fiduciary, the representative cannot speculate with estate assets and must keep all excess cash not needed to administer the estate in safe, interest-bearing insured accounts or other investments approved by the court.

If you, as an estate representative, breach your fiduciary duty, you can be personally liable for any resulting loss of value of the estate. Specifically, if you commit a wrongful act that damages the estate, you are personally financially responsible; although, if you acted reasonably and in good faith under the circumstances, the court may not hold you liable. In addition, if you advance your own interests at the expense of the estate, the court can remove you as the estate representative. Finally, if you improperly use estate money for your own needs, you will be cited to appear before the court and can be charged criminally.

Estate representatives may run into trouble in the following ways:

- causing unreasonable delays in administering the estate
- making unauthorized payments from the estate
- failing to take control over estate assets, or
- improperly selling estate assets.

If you realize that you are in over your head, get assistance from a professional as soon as possible.

In a formal probate court proceeding, the estate representative may have to post a bond (see Chapter 13) to provide a financial guarantee that he or she will carry out the fiduciary duties faithfully. Or, the decedent's will or the beneficiaries acting together may waive bond requirements, preferring to rely on the honesty of the representative.

Even so, the court may require a bond, particularly from non-California residents, for protection of possible creditors.

Note of Sanity. You may be reluctant to serve as a personal representative of an estate either with or without a lawyer, fearing that even if you make an innocent mistake, you will be held personally liable. This is unlikely in a simple estate where the assets and beneficiaries are clearly established and you scrupulously learn and follow the rules. However, if you face an estate with more substantial assets and multiple beneficiaries, you may have a legitimate cause for concern. Getting professional guidance early in the process can give you peace of mind, save time, and avoid innocent errors, so it may be well worth the expense. See Chapter 16.

Ways to Avoid Mistakes

When a personal representative runs into problems, it usually does not come from deliberate wrongdoing. Rather, unfamiliarity with the requirements, the stress of managing another person's financial affairs, and the obligations to other interested parties (beneficiaries and creditors) can catch up with the most well-intentioned personal representative. Here are some general tips to avoid mistakes:

- Secure the decedent's assets.
- Keep clear records of all transactions.
- Communicate with interested parties.
- Be diligent with deadlines.
- Learn and follow court procedures and legal requirements.
- Get help when needed.

Preliminary Duties of the Estate Representative

Whether acting formally or informally, your job as an estate representative is to take possession of the decedent's property and safeguard it until all obligations of the estate are met and the remaining assets are distributed to the proper persons. Particularly if the decedent lived alone, the residence should be made secure, and all valuables and important papers removed to a safe place. Here are some of your main preliminary responsibilities as representative, some of which you will need to do before the court gives you formal authority to act.

Determine the Residence of the Decedent

For the estate to be settled under California law, the decedent must have been a resident of this state, or owned property in California, when he or she died. When determining a decedent's residence, the court will consider where the person physically lived as well as the decedent's state of mind on the issue. That is, the court will consider whether at the time of death he or she considered California, and a particular place within this state, as his or her permanent residence. Usually, the decedent will have established some permanent ties to California, but sometimes it isn't absolutely clear what a decedent intended. Here are several factors important to making this determination:

- the length of time the decedent lived in the place
- where his or her driver's license was issued
- the location of the decedent's business assets and bank accounts, and
- the place where the decedent voted.

SEE AN EXPERT

If you are in doubt as to whether the decedent was a California resident, see an attorney.

If the decedent was a California resident, it is also necessary to determine the county of residence. Court proceedings, if required, take place through the county of the decedent's residence. Normally, where a person resides is clear enough, but occasionally, as would be the case if the decedent was ill or elderly and had moved to live with relatives or in a rest home, there may be a question as to whether he or she had changed his or her residence. If the decedent was temporarily staying in a hospital or care facility at the time of death, while intending to return to his or her usual residence, the permanent home ordinarily determines the county of residence.

If the decedent lived outside of California, yet owned property in California that needs to be administered (for example, real property), then an "ancillary" probate proceeding may need to be started in California. Ancillary probate proceedings occur in the California county where decedent's property is located. Details of bringing an ancillary probate proceeding is beyond the scope of this book. If the decedent lived outside of California, but owned property in California, get help from a California probate attorney.

What Does a Will Look Like?

In some situations, it may not be clear what document constitutes the decedent's will. A will may be handwritten, typewritten, or a filled-in preprinted form. It may or may not have a title like "Will" or "Last Will and Testament."

The basic requirement is that the document reflects the decedent's intent to transfer property upon death. A number of factors may impact the validity of a will: Does it lack the decedent's signature or the signatures of witnesses? Was it obtained by undue influence? Is there a question about the decedent's mental capacity at the time of the will? Is an original not available? If you have any questions about whether a document is a valid will, obtain legal advice.

A will may also refer to a separate list directing how tangible personal possessions, such as household belongings, are to be distributed. If so, keep your eyes out for such a list, as it will need to be filed with the court during the probate proceedings at the same time the Inventory and Appraisal is filed. (See Chapter 14.)

Locate the Will

Make a thorough search for the most recent will and any codicils that may exist. If there is no will, the decedent is said to have died "intestate," and state law determines the persons who will inherit his or her property. (See "If There Is No Will," in Chapter 3.)

Wills may be either "formal" or "holographic." A formal will is one that is signed by the decedent and at least two witnesses. Some people mistakenly believe that they have a valid will if they write (or type) their final wishes on a sheet of paper and have their signature notarized, but notarization does not make a will valid in California.

A holographic will is written and signed in the handwriting of the person making the will. A commercially printed form will that is completed in the testator's own handwriting can also be valid as a holographic will. (Prob. Code § 6111(c).)

A holographic will need not be witnessed or dated. However, if it is undated and there is another will with inconsistent provisions, the holographic will is invalid to the extent of the inconsistency, unless the time it was signed can be established by other evidence. If the decedent left any handwritten and signed document that appears to express wishes about what should happen with the decedent's assets after death, the document may be a holographic will. See a lawyer for advice if there is any question about whether a document is a will.

A codicil is a later document that supplements or modifies a will. It may also be either formal or holographic. A formal, witnessed will can have a holographic codicil. Normally, a codicil is used to make a relatively small addition, subtraction, or change in a will, as would be the case if the decedent bought or sold a piece of property that would alter the will. Sometimes, however, codicils make major changes in a will that conflict with or are inconsistent with the language of the original will so that it's difficult to understand what the decedent intended. In this situation, you would be wise to get advice from an attorney before continuing the probate process.

Most people keep their wills in a fairly obvious place, such as a desk, file cabinet, safe-deposit box, closet, or shelf. Banks allow a member of the family with a key to open a safe-deposit box in the presence of a bank officer to search for a will or burial instructions. However, nothing else may be removed until the box is officially released. (See "Examine Safe-Deposit Boxes," below.)

While it used to be common for lawyers to keep original wills for safekeeping, that is less common in California now. However, an attorney who prepared a will may have a file copy.

When you find a will, make a few photocopies, which you will need at various stages of the estate work. Be sure each page of the photocopy is complete and that the signatures are legible.

Under Probate Code Section 8200, within 30 days after being informed of the death, the original will should be lodged with the clerk of the Superior Court in the county in which the estate may be administered. To do so, you must pay a $50 fee, which is reimbursable from the estate as an expense of administration. In addition, if someone who is not named as the executor has the will, that person must also mail a copy to the named executor, and if the executor's address is not known, to a person named in the will as a beneficiary. Otherwise, you are under no obligation to provide copies of the will to anyone. After a will is admitted to probate, it becomes public record.

If you will be initiating a formal probate proceeding in the estate (see Chapter 14), check local court rules and customs to determine whether you should file the original will with the Petition for Probate or lodge it with the court before you file the petition.

TIP

If you can't find the will, a photocopy might do. If you cannot find an original will or a duplicate original (that is, a duplicate with original signatures by the testator and the witnesses), the court may accept a photocopy as a "lost" will. You may have to provide additional evidence to overcome the presumption that the decedent destroyed the will with the intent to revoke it. (Prob. Code § 6124.)

Obtain Certified Copies of the Death Certificate

When a person dies in California, an official death certificate is filed in the county health department or vital statistics office of the county where the death occurred. The death certificate provides important personal information about the deceased person, including Social Security number, date of birth, date of death, occupation, and cause of death. You will need certified copies of the death certificate to carry out many of the tasks for settling an estate—for example, collecting insurance proceeds and other death benefits, and transferring jointly owned property.

To save time and avoid arguments with bureaucrats about whether they will accept a photocopy, order plenty of certified copies. Approximately ten should be enough, but the number needed will depend on the number of insurance policies, financial institutions, and pieces of real property involved in the estate. You might order an extra or two to keep in your files; sometimes a need for a death certificate arises long after the initial estate administration.

The easiest and quickest way to obtain certified copies of the death certificate is to ask the mortuary you deal with to obtain them and add the cost to the bill. This is a common practice, and the mortuary will know how to make the arrangements.

If you need to order death certificates yourself, you can do so by contacting the vital records office in the county where the person died. It will take two weeks or more after the death for a certified copy of the death certificate to become available. In some counties, the death certificates are first available from the department of public health and then, after a period of time (approximately 60 days), from the county recorder or clerk's office. Each county has a different procedure. You can expect to pay around $21 per certified copy.

TIP

If an autopsy is required. If an autopsy is performed after the death, it may delay the final death certificate by several months. In this case, you will receive an interim death certificate that indicates the cause of death is "deferred." Financial institutions and government agencies will accept this certificate, but insurance companies will not. (They need to know the cause of death before processing claims.)

Because of concerns about identity theft, California allows only certain individuals to obtain certified copies of a death certificate. (Health & Safety Code § 103526.) If you are the executor or a close family member, however, you won't have a problem getting the documents you need.

To order, you must fill out the county's application form and submit it along with a "certificate of identity" that proves you are entitled to receive certified copies. You must sign the certificate of identity in front of a notary public. In most California counties, you can download a death certificate request form and a certificate of identity from the county website. You can also obtain the necessary forms by visiting or calling the county recorder's or clerk's office.

RESOURCE

Other options for ordering death certificates. If obtaining death certificates from the mortuary or county website is not possible or practical, you have two additional options:

Ordering online. Through www.vitalchek.com, you can obtain death certificates for most counties in California. You can order the certificate online, yet if you need certified copies, you'll still have to submit a notarized certification of identity. Expect to pay processing and shipping fees.

Ordering from the state. If three months or more have passed since the death, you can order death certificates from the California Department of Public Health. It can take a number of weeks to process a request, however, so even the state office recommends that you get death certificates from the county, if you can. If, for some reason, you must order from the state, you can find information on the Department of Public Health website at www.cdph.ca.gov.

Ascertain the Heirs and Beneficiaries

As we will discuss in more detail in Chapter 3, an heir is a person who inherits according to intestate succession laws if there is no will or alternative estate plan. A beneficiary, on the other hand, is a person who inherits under the terms of a will. If the decedent left a will, you should determine the names, ages, and mailing addresses of the beneficiaries named in the will. If any are deceased (or don't survive the decedent by any period of days specified in the will), look to the will, which may specify alternate beneficiaries. We discuss how to do this in detail in Chapter 3. Occasionally, you will find that a beneficiary has predeceased a decedent and no alternate beneficiary is listed, or that there are other problems in determining who inherits. Again, we discuss this in detail in Chapter 3.

Even with a will, if an estate must go through formal probate (we discuss this in detail in Chapter 6), information must be provided about the people who would have inherited absent a will. You must determine the names, ages (specifically, whether the person is older than or younger than age 18), and mailing addresses of the decedent's intestate heirs under law (the people who would inherit if there were no will). At first this may not make much sense; why do you need to figure out who would inherit in the absence of a will, if, in fact, there is one? The answer is simple. In a formal probate court proceeding (discussed in Chapter 14), the heirs must be listed on a Petition for Probate and notified about the proceedings, even if some or all of them inherit nothing under the terms of the will. The purpose is to let these people know that the decedent's affairs are being wound up so that they can object or otherwise participate if they wish. They rarely do unless the will is not clear or there is a reason to challenge the will.

In addition, if a decedent who died without a will was married or had a registered domestic partner and there will be a formal probate, you must list all heirs who might inherit something depending on whether the decedent's property is ultimately characterized as community or as separate property. Every person who could have an interest in the estate must be considered a possible heir. If there is no surviving spouse or domestic partner, there will be no community property, and you need list only the heirs of the separate property.

The law does not require you to make impractical and extended searches, but you must make reasonably diligent efforts to locate all heirs and beneficiaries.

Often, questioning survivors and reviewing the decedent's address book and other records is sufficient to get started. You can obtain additional information from internet searches. Chapter 14 lists other steps you may need to take to search for an heir or beneficiary.

Access Safe-Deposit Boxes

Any safe-deposit boxes in the decedent's name should be examined for assets and important papers. Particularly where the safe-deposit box may contain a will, a trust, or burial instructions, the contents should be examined soon after the death for the purpose of locating such documents. Additional time or procedures may be required to access other contents of the box. A person who has a key to a safe-deposit box held solely in the decedent's name can get access to the box by presenting to the financial institution a certified copy of the death certificate and providing reasonable proof of identity. A statement of death by the coroner, treating physician, or hospital or institution where the decedent died may substitute for a certified copy of the death certificate, if necessary.

If these requirements are met, the financial institution must permit the person with a key to open the safe-deposit box in the presence of a bank officer and make an inventory of its contents. Burial instructions and the original will may be removed for copying. No other items can be removed. Any original will found should be lodged with the clerk of the court of the county where the decedent lived and a copy should be provided to the person named as executor or beneficiary. (See "Locate the Will," above.)

Occasionally, an uninformed bank officer may attempt to deny access to a safe-deposit box, even though these necessary requirements have been met, in which case referring to Probate Code Section 331 may help bring results.

If you do not know whether the decedent had a safe-deposit box, you can inquire at his or her bank. Most banks will tell you whether or not there is a box if you present a certified copy of the death certificate. Another way to locate a safe-deposit box is to examine the decedent's bank statements. If there is a safe-deposit box rental fee shown, this could lead you to the right bank. If you already know a box exists but can't find the key, you will have to arrange for the box to be drilled. This is an administration expense that is chargeable to the estate.

Joint Tenancy

A joint tenancy safe-deposit box is generally released to the surviving joint tenant without delay. If the survivor wishes to have title to the box reregistered in the survivor's name alone, the bank will require a certified copy of the decedent's death certificate. Keep in mind that joint tenancy of the safe-deposit box does not create joint tenancy in its contents. Administration of the estate may need to include assets held in the box.

Safe-Deposit Box in Decedent's Name

Probate can be required for gaining access to contents of a safe-deposit box when the box is in the decedent's name alone. As described above, when there is no living co-owner of the box, Probate Code Section 331 permits limited access by a person in possession of the key to remove wills, trusts, and burial instructions. For other access to the contents of the box, if probate is required, the bank requires a certified copy of the death certificate and a certified copy of the estate representative's letters issued by the probate court. We show you how to get these in Chapter 14.

When no probate is required, as is the case when small estate procedures can be used, the bank will usually release the box to the heirs or beneficiaries of the estate when they present a certified copy of the decedent's death certificate and sign a declaration provided by the bank. You should also present a copy of the decedent's will if there is one. This procedure, which you can use to bypass probate in a variety of small estate situations, is discussed in Chapter 11.

Generally, small estate procedures apply to estates with assets under $166,250. Importantly, though, estates much larger than $166,250 can use small estate procedures because a lot can be excluded in this calculation—including assets passing to a surviving spouse, assets passing by joint tenancy, assets passing by beneficiary designation, vehicles, and other circumstances outlined in Probate Code Section 13050. This means, for example, that a surviving spouse or domestic partner who receives the whole estate can use the small estate affidavit to collect the safe-deposit box, no matter the size of the estate.

Collect the Decedent's Mail

If the decedent lived with relatives or friends, collecting his or her mail may not be a problem. If he or she lived alone, it is a good idea to notify the post office to have the mail forwarded to you so you may keep track of it. Assets, debts, or other important information may come to light from looking through the decedent's mail.

You should file the request in person at your local post office. The postmaster will honor forwarding instructions if provided with a certified copy of letters. If there is a delay in receiving letters, or if there is no court proceeding in which letters will be issued, the post office will usually accept a notarized statement from the individual expected to be the estate representative. For more information, call the local postmaster or 800-ASK-USPS (800-275-8777).

To reduce mail received, you may request that the deceased person's name, mailing address, and email address be placed on the national "Deceased Do Not Contact List" (DDNC). There is no charge for this service and the form is available through the USPS website or www.dmachoice.org. Beware that the form requests, but does not require, more personal information than you may feel comfortable sharing for this purpose.

Cancel Credit Cards and Subscriptions

To prevent unauthorized use of credit cards, notify all of the decedent's credit card issuers of the decedent's death, and destroy all credit cards in the decedent's name.

If the funeral home has not already done so, notify one of the three credit reporting agencies of the death. (The three agencies are Equifax, Experian, and TransUnion.) Request that the credit report reflect this notation: "Deceased. Do not issue credit." Also request a copy of the decedent's credit report, which you can use to determine any creditors who may need to be notified of the death.

Sometimes credit card companies will cancel the balance due when a cardholder is deceased if the amount owing is not substantial. It may be worthwhile to inquire about this policy. If the company does cancel the balance, it may be required to provide an IRS Form 1099-C reporting the canceled debt of $600 or more. This could have income tax consequences for the estate. If this might apply to the estate you are working on, get help from a tax professional.

Review credit card statements for recurring charges to cancel. Examples include gym memberships, music or video services, recurring charitable gifts, and subscriptions to newspapers or magazines. Be aware that canceling some online services may permanently block access to online information and data, such as emails, social media accounts, photos, videos, blogs, and other content. These policies are set by each provider in its terms of service, and tend to evolve.

If a credit card statement shows automatic billing for regular expenses such as utilities or phone service, and you want those services to continue, do not cancel the card until you have made other arrangements for payment. If the decedent had prepaid for a service—for example, for a subscription—you may be able to ask for reimbursement for any unused portion.

Manage Digital Assets

Managing the decedent's digital assets has become an increasingly important aspect of wrapping up an estate. This can include:

- maintaining or closing online accounts
- managing or terminating social media accounts
- identifying and acquiring financial assets kept or managed online
- downloading digital files, like photos stored online
- anything else required to wrap up the estate, and
- complying with requests made by the descendent in anticipation of death.

You may need to take practical steps—such as gaining access to email accounts to find important financial information. And you may need to access potentially valuable assets, such as cryptocurrency or Venmo credits. You may also do some social tasks, like "memorializing" a Facebook profile or using an email account to get the contact information for friends and family to notify of the decedent's death.

A technologically savvy decedent may have prepared for death by leaving a list of accounts and login information, (ideally) along with instructions about what to do. In that case you should be in a good position to manage the decedent's digital assets.

More commonly, however, you will have to navigate the procedures of each service provider to access information or manage social media. Evolving laws and terms of service increasingly allow family members and personal representatives to manage the online presence and digital assets of a deceased person. Privacy concerns can pose some hurdles. Beware that even if you have access to passwords, you may not have legal authority to access accounts and services. Start with the procedures offered by the "custodian" of the digital services used by the decedent—email providers, social media services (Facebook, Twitter, LinkedIn), and online data backup services (DropBox, iCloud, Google Drive). If you do not have the access you need under the terms of service of the particular provider, you may need to take more formal steps. California's Revised Uniform Fiduciary Access to Digital Assets Act provides a procedure for a personal representative to access information and terminate accounts. You will likely need to provide a written request for access or information, a certified copy of a death certificate, and proof of your authority (such as letters testamentary if the estate is going through formal probate, or a small-estate affidavit if no formal probate).

Notify Government Agencies

Notice must be given to certain public entities notifying them of the decedent's death and advising them to file any claims they may have against the estate within the time allowed by law. (Prob. Code §§ 215, 216, and 9200.) The estate representative, a beneficiary, or any person in possession of decedent's property is responsible for giving the notice.

Notice may be in letter form, as shown in the sample below. It should give the name, address, and telephone number of the personal representative, and it should include a copy of the decedent's death certificate. If a formal probate proceeding has been started, include the court title, case name, and number. The notice should be sent to any agency that might have a claim against the estate. Send two copies of the letter of notice, and ask the recipient to acknowledge receipt of the notice by signing the bottom and returning one copy to you. Enclose a self-addressed stamped envelope. If estate property is distributed before the time allowed for the public entity to file a claim, the distributees are liable to the full extent of the claim. (Prob. Code § 9203(b).)

Letter to Agency

[Name of agency] ______________________
[Address] ______________________
[City, State, Zip] ______________________
Re: ______________________, deceased

Superior Court of California, County of __________
Case No. __________

NOTICE IS HEREBY GIVEN that the above-named decedent died on __________, 20xx, and that letters (testamentary/of administration) were issued to __________ on __________, 20xx. Under Probate Code Section 9200, you are hereby requested to file any claim you may have against the decedent or the estate in the manner and within the time required by law. A copy of the decedent's death certificate is enclosed.

Date ______________________, 20xx

[Signature of Personal Representative]
[Name of Personal Representative]
[Address of Personal Representative]
[Phone Number of Personal Representative]

Receipt acknowledged by:

____
Name
____
Title
____
Agency

Franchise Tax Board

The personal representative must give notice of administration of the estate to the Franchise Tax Board within 90 days after the date "letters" are first issued to the estate representative. (Prob. Code § 9202(c).) The Franchise Tax Board has 18 months after the notice is given to file a claim for any taxes due by the decedent's estate.

Mail the notice and a copy of the letters of administration to:

Franchise Tax Board
P.O. Box 2952, MS 454
Sacramento, CA 95812-9974
Or fax to: FTB Decedent Team at 916-845-0479

Social Security Administration

If the decedent was receiving monthly Social Security benefits, you must notify Social Security that the decedent has died. Most funeral homes will report the death if provided with the decedent's Social Security number. Or, provide the notification by calling 800-772-1213 or visiting the local Social Security office. The Social Security payment for the month in which the decedent died must be returned, even if the death occurred on the last day of the month, along with any other payments issued after the decedent's death. Payments issued are for the previous month. Thus, if a recipient dies in April, the May payment must be returned.

Nearly all Social Security beneficiaries receive payments by direct deposit to their bank accounts. If payments were being deposited directly into the decedent's bank account, notify the bank to return any payments the decedent is not entitled to. It may take several weeks to stop direct deposit and such monies should be kept separate and not used by the estate.

Some Social Security recipients receive their payments loaded onto a debit card, which allows the recipient to make purchases at retail locations and receive cash back with purchases. In that case, call the phone number on the back of the card to notify Social Security of the death.

The surviving spouse or other family members may be eligible for Social Security benefits based upon the decedent's work record. This may include a one-time payment of $255 or monthly benefits. For this reason, contact Social Security as soon as possible when a recipient of Social Security benefits dies. Survivors cannot apply for benefits online, but you can find more information through www.ssa.gov.

Director of Health Care Services

If an estate representative, beneficiary, or a person in possession of property of the decedent knows or has reason to believe the decedent was receiving benefits under Medi-Cal, or was the surviving spouse or registered domestic partner of a person who received that health care, that person must notify the Director of Health Care Services of the death within 90 days of the death. The Department of Health Care Services has four months after the notice is given in which to file a claim against a decedent's estate to recover Medi-Cal expenditures for medical or nursing home care for either the decedent or the decedent's predeceased spouse or registered domestic partner. In some cases, the Department may also impose a lien on a Medi-Cal beneficiary's home to recover expenses. Many exceptions to recovery could apply, so get specific advice if the Department of Health Care Services makes a claim. (Prob. Code §§ 215, 9202(a).)

Address the notice to:

Director of Health Care Services
Estate Recovery Section
MS 4720
P.O. Box 997425
Sacramento, CA 95899-7425
For general information call 916-650-0590, or email Estate Recovery at er@dhcs.ca.gov.

Notice may also be provided to the Department of Health Care Services using an online form available through www.dhcs.ca.gov. However, the online form requests more information than the Probate Code requires to be provided for this purpose.

Victim Compensation Board

If an heir or beneficiary of the decedent is known to be in a correctional facility or has previously been confined in a prison or facility under the jurisdiction of the Department of Corrections and Rehabilitation or confined in any county or city jail, road camp, industrial farm, or other local correctional facility, the estate representative, a beneficiary, or a person in possession of the decedent's property must notify the Director of the California Victim Compensation Board. There is no requirement to do an investigation to determine whether an heir or beneficiary is or has been confined, but if this information is known, then there is an obligation to give the notice within 90 days of the decedent's death or 90 days after letters are first issued. The California Victim Compensation Board has a notification form available at https://victims.ca.gov to fill out with the required information including the name, date of birth, location, and CDCR or booking number of the decedent's heir or beneficiary. The notice and a copy of the decedent's death certificate can be submitted electronically to probate@victims.ca.gov or mailed:

California Victim Compensation Board
Revenue Recovery Branch
P.O. Box 1348
Sacramento, CA 95812-1348

The director has four months after the notice is received to pursue collection of any outstanding restitution fines or orders. (Prob. Code §§ 216 and 9202(b).)

Prepare Decedent's Final Income Tax Returns

As another early step in settling the estate, prepare for filing the decedent's final state and federal individual income tax returns if required (forms 1040–U.S. and 540–California). The returns may need to cover the period from the beginning of the tax year to the decedent's date of death. Filing an extension may also be appropriate if it is not possible to file the returns by the due dates. (We discuss this in detail in Chapter 7.) If the decedent is survived by a spouse or registered domestic partner (for California state returns), the final returns may be joint returns. A tax professional can advise you about this.

Obtain Basic Estate Information

You should learn as much about the decedent's business affairs as you can by examining all of his or her legal papers at the earliest possible time. If the decedent was not an organized person, it may take some detective work on your part to find out about the assets and liabilities. Key people in the decedent's life may have useful information. However, do not be surprised if you run into stumbling blocks getting businesses or financial institutions to disclose information before you have formal authority to act on behalf of the estate. Here are some suggestions:

- Examine bank statements, canceled checks, notes, deeds, stock certificates, insurance policies, recent tax returns, and all other tangible evidence of property.
- Contact friends, relatives, accountants, tax preparers, and business associates who may have information on the decedent's assets and debts.
- Look into whether county grantor-grantee indexes, assessor's records, or title companies can provide evidence of real property holdings.
- Go through the decedent's address book, which may list relevant professionals, such as insurance agents or financial advisers.
- Confer with the decedent's broker for information on securities held by the decedent.
- Contact the decedent's employer and, if applicable, unions or professional groups, for information about life and health insurance policies or retirement plans the decedent may have had.

Your search should include collecting and reviewing other documents that identify property of the decedent and identify ownership of the assets. Such documents may include:

- trusts
- beneficiary designation forms for retirement accounts, insurance policies, or annuities
- property agreements, such as prenuptial agreements, postnuptial agreements, and marital settlement agreements
- business or partnership documents, or
- deeds.

Keep what you find in organized files with other important estate information. Again, a convenient way to do this is to have a separate file folder for each category of information. If original documents are valuable—such as original stock certificates or savings bonds—keep the originals in a secure place and make copies for day-to-day reference.

RESOURCE

Help with records. If you need help getting organized, try *Get It Together: Organize Your Records So Your Family Won't Have To*, by Melanie Cullen and Shae Irving (Nolo). It is designed primarily as a way for people to organize their own affairs so that they will not leave a mess when they die, but it is also a fine organizational tool for an estate representative. It provides a place to list the details concerning all major assets and investments.

Studying the decedent's income tax returns can help you discover assets. For instance, if it shows the decedent received stock dividends, you will know he or she owned stock. If the tax return reports interest earned, this is a clue there are savings accounts or promissory notes, or other kinds of interest-bearing assets. The assets on prior years' returns may not still be owned at the time of the decedent's death, yet they offer clues about the decedent's finances.

Preliminary Collection of Assets

Surviving family members and other named beneficiaries may be able to collect some assets in the first weeks after the death. This is true regardless of whether the estate will require a formal probate administration. However, if an asset passes to the "estate" rather than to a particular individual, collection of the asset may need to wait until a personal representative has been appointed by the court.

Get Bank Accounts Released, If Possible

Sometimes, immediate cash may be needed to pay some obligations of the decedent, or the decedent's family may need funds for living expenses. Many people think that as soon as a person dies, all his or her cash is immediately frozen for some indefinite period. This is not necessarily true, depending on how the account was held.

Obtaining the release of cash held in the name of the decedent in banks and credit unions in California usually presents no substantial problems. The procedures for releasing bank accounts are similar to those required to release safe-deposit boxes:

- If the decedent held an account in joint tenancy with someone else, the bank will release the funds immediately to the surviving joint tenant.
- If the decedent held a bank account as trustee for another (called a "Totten trust" or a "pay on death account"), the bank will release the funds to the beneficiary if furnished with a certified copy of the decedent's death certificate.
- If the account is in the decedent's name alone, and the value of the estate is less than the amount set by law to define a "small" estate, currently $166,250, the bank should release the funds without the necessity of probate upon being presented with a certified copy of the death certificate and a form affidavit (usually provided by the bank) signed by the heirs or beneficiaries entitled to the account. There is a 40-day waiting period for this type of transfer, which is discussed in Chapter 11.
- If the account is going to a surviving spouse or domestic partner, the bank may release the account to the surviving spouse or partner without probate under Probate Code Section 13500. This could apply in a few different circumstances: (1) the account is held in the names of the decedent and the surviving spouse or domestic partner, or (2) the account is held by the decedent alone, and the decedent's will provides for such property to go to the surviving spouse or partner, or (3) if the decedent didn't leave a will but the account in the decedent's name alone is community property (in which case it would go outright to the surviving spouse or partner by the law of intestate succession—see Chapter 3). To accomplish this type of transfer, the surviving spouse or partner should submit a certified copy of the decedent's death certificate to the bank, along with a copy of the will (if there is one), and an affidavit or declaration signed by the surviving spouse or partner setting forth the facts that allow her to receive the account without probate administration. There is a 40-day waiting period for this type of transfer. Alternatively, the surviving spouse or partner may obtain a Spousal or Domestic Partner Property Order from the probate court to obtain release of the account. The procedures for obtaining this order are given in Chapter 15.
- If the account is the separate property of the decedent, the estate is over the current "small estate" amount (currently $166,250), and the account will pass to someone other than a surviving spouse or partner, probate proceedings will ordinarily be required. Before releasing the account, the bank will need a certified copy of the letters of administration issued to an estate representative appointed in a formal probate court proceeding. The procedures for obtaining the letters are detailed in Chapter 14. It usually takes about four to six weeks to obtain the letters after starting the court process.

All funds released to an estate representative in a formal probate court proceeding should normally be placed in an estate account in the name of the representative as "Executor (or Administrator) of the Estate of ______________________." If a beneficiary receives funds directly through one of the procedures discussed just above, this isn't necessary.

CAUTION

Do not access accounts online without authorization as the estate's representative. If you know how to access the decedent's bank accounts online, it may be tempting to log in and pay bills or move money around. However, it is illegal to access funds in the decedent's account before receiving authorization to do so. The account must remain untouched until released by the bank to its new owner or to the estate's representative.

Collect Life Insurance Proceeds

Life insurance claims are frequently handled directly by the beneficiary of the policy, and the proceeds are usually paid promptly. All that is usually required is a proof of death on the company's printed claim form signed by the beneficiary, a certified copy of the decedent's death certificate, and the policy itself. If you can't find the policy, ask the company for its form regarding lost policies. It's also a good idea to submit a formal request to the deceased's employer and any unions or professional groups the deceased belonged to for information about life and health insurance policies. You may discover additional policies that were in effect at the time of the decedent's death.

Always carefully examine the life insurance policy to make certain the beneficiary of the policy. Most policies name a primary beneficiary and a secondary beneficiary, meaning if the primary beneficiary predeceases the insured, the secondary beneficiary receives the proceeds. If the beneficiary is a secondary beneficiary, a certified copy of the death certificate of the primary beneficiary is also required.

If the policy does not name a beneficiary, names the "estate" as the beneficiary, or if all named beneficiaries predecease the insured, then the proceeds may be subject to probate administration or small estate procedures.

To claim life insurance benefits, notify the life insurance company that the insured has died. Notification can usually be made through the agent or group who issued the policy by telephone or through the company's website. The company will usually want the decedent's name, date of death, the number of the life insurance policy, and contact information for the beneficiary. Upon notification, the company will provide a claim form directly to the beneficiary.

Life insurance proceeds that are paid to a named beneficiary (other than the decedent's estate or personal representative) are not part of the decedent's probate estate and thus do not have to go before a probate court. The proceeds are payable under the life insurance contract, not by the terms of the decedent's will or the laws of intestate succession. However, the proceeds will be included in the decedent's taxable estate, if he or she was the owner of the policy. (We discuss ownership of life insurance in Chapter 7.) Many insurance policies do not indicate the owner of the policy, and you may have to ask the insurance company to verify this for you. It is a good idea to ask for this information when you return the claim form to the company. You should also ask the company for a copy of *Life Insurance Statement*, IRS Form 712, which must be filed with the federal estate tax return, if one is required.

How to Find Insurance Policies

If you haven't had any luck finding an insurance policy in the usual places (file cabinets, desk drawers, and so on), here are some other ways to track it down.

Look through bank statements and canceled checks. Even if you find a ten-year-old check to an insurance company, contact the company. The policy could still be in force.

Ask former employers and any union to which the person belonged. Some companies and unions provide free group life insurance coverage for employees and members; family members may not be aware of the policies.

Use a policy locator service. The National Association of Insurance Commissioners has a service to help locate benefits from insurance policies and annuity contracts. Look for the Life Insurance Policy Locator Service in the consumer section of https://eapps.naic.org/life-policy-locator.

Watch the mail (and email). Annual premium notices, policy status notices, or statements may arrive around policy anniversaries or tax time.

Collect Compensation Owed

The surviving spouse or domestic partner may collect salary or other compensation owed to the decedent. This includes unused vacation, up to $16,625 (an amount set to increase April 1, 2022 and every three years thereafter). If the employer requires formalities, you can sign and notarize an affidavit using the language from Probate Code Section 13601. This procedure can be initiated immediately after death. It does not override the rights of another rightful beneficiary (for example, through a will), yet it can be helpful to get funds quickly to those entitled to them, like a spouse or domestic partner.

Collect Annuity Benefits

If the decedent had purchased annuities naming someone to receive the benefits on his or her death, the beneficiary may obtain the benefits by submitting a certified copy of the decedent's death certificate and a completed claim form to the insurance company issuing the annuity.

Collect Social Security Benefits

If the decedent was covered by Social Security, there may be lump-sum death benefit of $255 and a monthly survivors benefit payable to the surviving spouse or dependent children. Minor children or children in college may also be entitled to benefits. To determine the rights of the estate or the heirs to Social Security benefits, contact the Social Security office in person. The surviving spouse may have various options for collecting benefits. To save time, make an appointment at the local office and be sure to bring a death certificate.

For more information, go to www.ssa.gov, where you can download booklets on the survivors benefit.

RESOURCE

More on Social Security. To get a better idea of the rights of all family members, see *Social Security, Medicare & Government Pensions*, by Joseph Matthews (Nolo).

Collect Veterans Benefits

Dependents of deceased veterans may be eligible for benefits. Information on veterans benefits may be obtained by phoning the Department of Veterans Affairs benefits hotline at 800-827-1000, or checking its website at www.va.gov. The section for family member benefits may be particularly helpful with information on help with burial costs and survivor compensation.

Collect Railroad Retirement Benefits

Death benefits and a survivors benefit may be available if the decedent was covered by the Railroad Retirement Act. If the decedent was employed by a railroad company, you should contact the nearest Railroad Retirement Board office for specific information and assistance. Call 877-772-5772 or check out the board's website at www.rrb.gov.

Collect Miscellaneous Death Benefits

Survivors are often faced with myriad forms, questionnaires, and regulations in the process of claiming certain disability and death benefits. These benefits are sometimes overlooked during mourning and then forgotten. Some examples are:

State disability income payments. If the decedent was receiving state disability benefits at the time of death, make sure all benefits were paid through the date of death and notify the California Employment Development Department.

Workers' compensation: If the decedent was receiving workers' compensation benefits at the time of death, notify the private insurance carrier who pays these benefits and make sure all benefits are paid.

Retirement or disability income from federal employment. If the decedent was a federal employee, the decedent's family or named beneficiaries may be entitled to benefits. Contact the agency where the decedent worked.

Benefits from medical insurance through decedent's employment or an association. Many employers and some unions provide group medical insurance which helps pay for medical expenses and, sometimes, funeral expenses. Make claims to cover any expenses of a last illness, and ask about any additional lump-sum death benefits.

Group life and disability income benefits. Life insurance or disability benefits may be payable through a group policy provided by the decedent's employer, union, or other organization. No one procedure to obtain the benefits will apply in all cases; you should contact the administrator of the plan offering death benefits (or the organization obligated to pay the benefits) to ask about the procedure to follow. Usually a claim form must be signed by the beneficiary and submitted with a certified copy of the decedent's death certificate. Death benefits are normally excluded from the decedent's probate estate if they are paid to a designated beneficiary (not the decedent's estate or personal representative), which means they can be collected without the approval of the probate court.

CHAPTER

3

Who Are the Heirs and Beneficiaries?

This key chapter gives you, the estate representative, information to determine what is in the decedent's estate and to figure out who is legally entitled to it. Obviously, settling any estate can't happen without this.

Fortunately, it is usually easy to figure out which beneficiaries or heirs receive which property if the decedent did one or more of the following:

- left a simple will that effectively identified the beneficiaries (often a surviving spouse, partner, children, or charities)
- died without a will in a situation where it is clear which relatives will inherit under state law (the law of intestate succession), or
- held title to the bulk of estate assets in joint tenancy, in a living trust, or so that it passes by beneficiary designation.

Life is not always this easy, however. If a will is unclear, or if the decedent died without a will and left no close relatives, or in some circumstances, if the will accidentally left out a child, spouse, or registered domestic partner, it may be more difficult to determine who inherits the decedent's property.

If it's clear from the documents who inherits the property in the estate you are dealing with, skim the material in this chapter to be sure you haven't overlooked something, and then go on to the next chapter. On the other hand, if you aren't sure who gets what property, this chapter provides important guidance.

Estate administration has a crucial purpose of getting the decedent's assets to the proper people. If you read this chapter and find that the correct distribution of the estate is not clear—or if you anticipate a dispute—get help from an attorney. Ultimately, uncertainty or disputes may require a court to make the final decision.

TIP

Registered domestic partners. California law gives registered domestic partners most of the same rights, protections, and benefits as spouses. This chapter notes the circumstances under which a registered domestic partner is entitled to inherit a portion of a partner's estate.

When this book refers to "registered domestic partners" or "domestic partners," it means partners who have registered their relationship with the State of California. Other types of domestic partnerships exist—for example, couples can sometimes register as domestic partners with a city or an employer. However those types of partnerships provide only limited rights, such as city- or employer-provided benefits. To receive the full range of rights under California law comparable to those of spouses (like the marriage-based rights, benefits, and protections described in this book), domestic partners must register their relationship with the California Secretary of State or have a valid union from another jurisdiction that is substantially equivalent to California's registered domestic partnership. Even so, domestic partners do not have the same rights as spouses under federal law. This can result in more complicated tax reporting, so get advice from a tax professional if the decedent was in a registered domestic partnership.

Where to Start

A deceased person's property is divided (after expenses are paid) among the people who are legally entitled to inherit it. Who these people are (beneficiaries or heirs) is normally decided by:

- the terms of the decedent's will
- state law (the law of intestate succession) if there is no will
- estate planning tools such as beneficiary designations, joint tenancy, or trusts set up by the decedent while still living, or, more rarely,
- state law, if a will provision turns out to be ineffective or if a few types of beneficiaries are accidentally left out of the will.

Important Terms

There are two fundamental types of estates. The estate is "intestate" if there is no will and "testate" if there is a will.

Those who inherit when the estate is intestate are called "heirs." Those who inherit under wills are termed "beneficiaries" (or, more rarely, "devisees").

The identity of the heirs who stand to inherit from an intestate estate is determined by state laws, called the laws of "intestate succession." The identity of beneficiaries who stand to inherit from a testate estate is determined, as much as possible, according to the decedent's intent as reflected in the will.

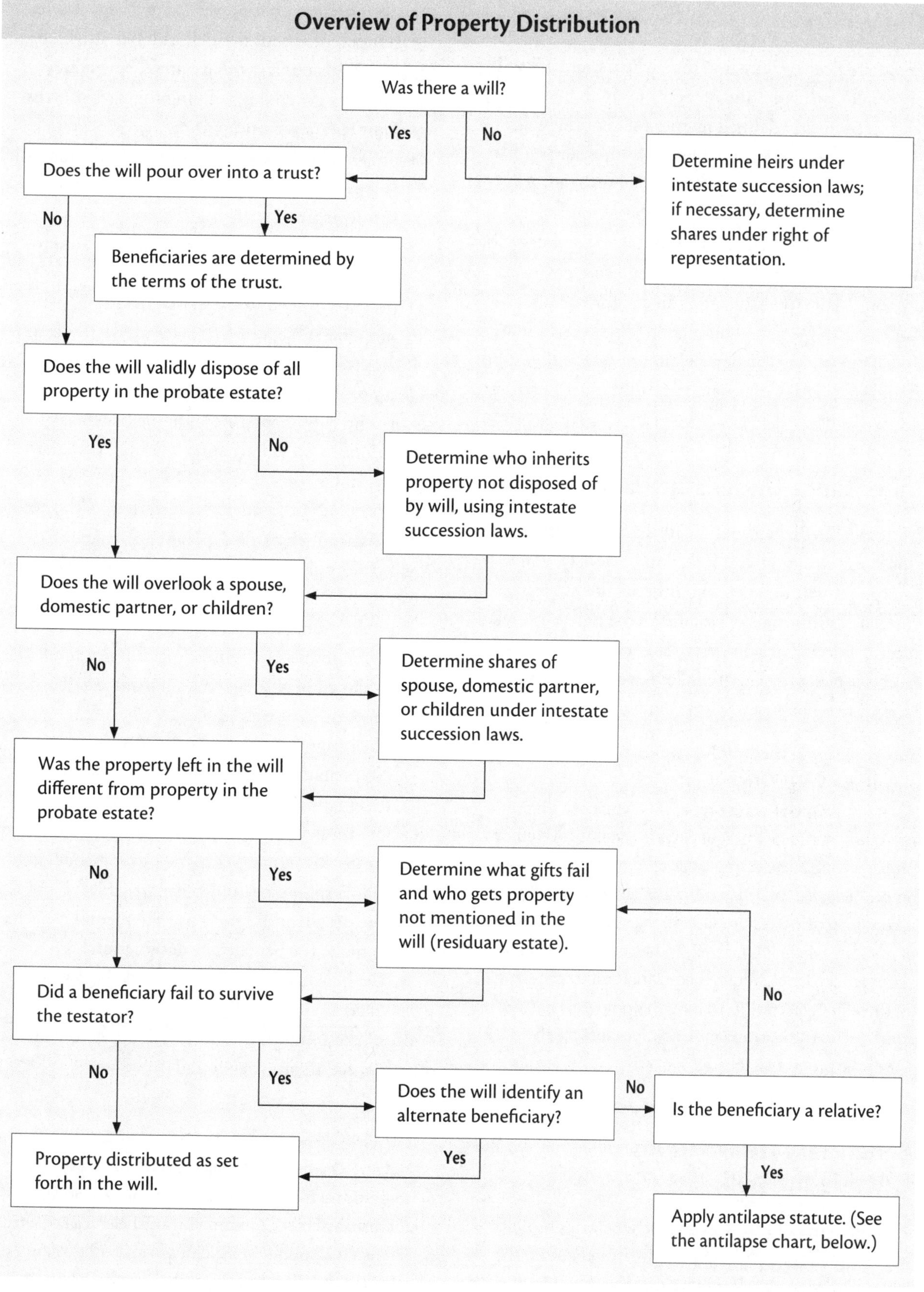
Overview of Property Distribution
Was there a will?
Yes
No
Does the will pour over into a trust?
Determine heirs under intestate succession laws; if necessary, determine shares under right of representation.
No
Yes
Beneficiaries are determined by the terms of the trust.
Does the will validly dispose of all property in the probate estate?
Yes
No
Determine who inherits property not disposed of by will, using intestate succession laws.
Does the will overlook a spouse, domestic partner, or children?
No
Yes
Determine shares of spouse, domestic partner, or children under intestate succession laws.
Was the property left in the will different from property in the probate estate?
No
Yes
Determine what gifts fail and who gets property not mentioned in the will (residuary estate).
Did a beneficiary fail to survive the testator?
No
No
Yes
Does the will identify an alternate beneficiary?
No
Is the beneficiary a relative?
Property distributed as set forth in the will.
Yes
Yes
Apply antilapse statute. (See the antilapse chart, below.)

The Will

If you are dealing with an estate where there is a will, the beneficiaries and the property for each beneficiary tend to be clearly defined by the words of the will. An obvious example would be a will that simply states, "I leave all my property to my husband, Aldo Anderson," or "I leave my real property located at 112 Visalia Street, Ukiah, California, to my husband, Aldo Anderson, and all my personal property to my son, Alan Anderson, and my daughter, Anne AndersonMcGee, in equal shares." With a will like this, determining the beneficiaries of assets should be straightforward. Otherwise, carefully read "Reading the Will," below.

Inheritance Under State Law

More people die without a will than with one. If this is the situation you face, you obviously won't interpret a will to learn who inherits the estate. Instead, California law establishes the heirs who will receive a decedent's property. The intestate succession rules are normally easy to follow; we explain them later in this chapter.

CAUTION

Out-of-state property is subject to different rules. Real estate located out of state and not covered by a probate-avoidance device— such as joint tenancy, transfer on death deeds, and living trusts—is generally distributed according to the intestate succession laws and procedures of the state where it is located. The succession laws in other states are similar to, but not necessarily exactly the same as, those in California. To transfer this property, you must comply with the laws and probate procedures of the state where the property is located.

Beneficiary Designations Outside the Will

Various types of assets pass to beneficiaries more or less automatically, without probate. In such cases, the beneficiaries were selected by the decedent either in a contract or by some other probate-avoidance arrangement. Such assets include:

- life insurance policies with named beneficiaries
- retirement accounts (such as IRA, 401(k), or 403(b) accounts) with a named beneficiary
- property covered by a living (inter vivos) trust
- joint tenancy property
- property held by spouses or registered domestic partners as community property with right of survivorship
- property in a pay on death account (Totten trust)
- property placed in a life estate, and
- property subject to a transfer on death deed.

If the estate you are concerned with is entirely made up of these types of property, you can safely skip or skim this chapter because the beneficiary designations usually determine who will take the property. In Chapter 6, you will find a summary of how these types of assets are transferred, with specific directions as to which of the "how to" chapters provide information about how to make the actual transfers.

Complications with beneficiary designations can occur in a number of circumstances, for example if:

- A named beneficiary does not survive the decedent.
- The "estate" is named as the beneficiary.
- No beneficiary is named on a beneficiary designation form.
- Community property funds were used to pay for life insurance that passes to someone other than a spouse or domestic partner.
- The decedent did not have the mental capacity to make the beneficiary designation.
- The beneficiary designation was the result of fraud or undue influence.

If any of these complications might apply to your situation, see an attorney for advice.

CAUTION

Divorce can change everything. If a spouse or domestic partner was named as the beneficiary of nonprobate assets—for example, those held in a living trust, pay on death accounts, or by joint tenancy title—those transfers will fail if, at the time of the transferor's death, the person named as beneficiary is no longer the surviving spouse or domestic partner because the couple divorced or terminated the partnership. (Prob. Code §§ 5040–5048.) If such a circumstance exists, then the asset will usually pass as if the named former spouse or domestic partner did not survive the decedent, unless the decedent clearly intended otherwise or a court order (such as a marital settlement agreement) requires otherwise. This law does not cover life insurance beneficiary designations.

To complicate matters, the U.S. Supreme Court has ruled that if the decedent named his or her former spouse as the beneficiary of an *employer-sponsored* 401(k) account, pension plan, or employer-provided life insurance policy and failed to change the beneficiary designation after the divorce, then the former spouse is entitled to the assets. (*Egelhoff v. Egelhoff*, 121 S.Ct. 1322 (2001).) The Court's decision was based on the fact that 401(k) and similar accounts, including severance plans and employee savings accounts, are governed by a federal law, the Employee Retirement Income Security Act (ERISA). That law, the Court ruled, requires the plan administrator to simply pay the proceeds to the beneficiary according to the documents—not to figure out who should get them under a particular state's law.

The bottom line is that where the former spouse or domestic partner is the designated beneficiary of an asset, that person may not be entitled to receive it. Consult a lawyer if you're not sure how to proceed.

Reading the Will

Many wills are easy to read and understand. However sometimes, what purports to be a "last will and testament" of the decedent may have bewildering language that requires deciphering. How do you unravel this sort of will to discover the identity of the intended beneficiaries and what they inherit?

Get Help With Complications

First, consider whether you should get legal advice. Some simple wills can be read and understood without specialized knowledge, but more complex wills (or the circumstances that come with them) require help from an attorney.

Get legal advice if you are not absolutely sure of what the will says, if you suspect that the words of the will may not match the decedent's intent, or if there is any dispute among people who might benefit from the will. In other words, if it's not perfectly clear what the decedent intended based on the words of the will, don't guess, get help.

As you read the will, you may notice one or more of these common problems:

- attempts to dispose of property not part of the decedent's estate (for example, a house or vehicles that were sold years ago or property held in joint tenancy)
- attempts to leave property to people who have died before the decedent, where no alternate has been named
- attempts to dispose of more than the decedent's portion of community property to someone other than the surviving spouse or domestic partner
- omissions of a child, spouse, or domestic partner from the will, or
- a former spouse or domestic partner named as an executor or beneficiary.

Further, the presence of any of these less-common situations mean that the estate administration is not simple and you will need professional help:

- Someone may have influenced or taken advantage of the decedent in the making of the will.
- Parts of the will are crossed out or have additional writing on them.
- The decedent left genetic material and there may be a child conceived after death.
- A beneficiary killed the decedent.
- Informal notes or other documents outside of the formal estate plan may show intent to make certain gifts.

When you read the will, follow the guidance below. Get help if you need it.

Prepare a List of Beneficiaries

We suggest that you start a list of the potential beneficiaries under the will. To help with this, Appendix C provides a tear-out form entitled "Who Inherits Under the Will." After you read this section and analyze the will, insert in the left-hand column the names of the people, institutions, and charities who might possibly inherit under the will. These include named beneficiaries, unnamed beneficiaries, alternate beneficiaries, and contingent beneficiaries. Most wills don't have trust provisions, but if the one you are dealing with does, list the trust beneficiaries here. We discuss trust property below. Then, list in the right-hand column the property the will says each beneficiary may inherit.

In Chapter 5, you will prepare a list of all of the decedent's property. Because the property mentioned in the will might be different from the property actually existing in the estate when the decedent died, you may wish to wait and fill in the right-hand side of the chart after you have finished the detailed list in Chapter 5.

The next section contains some sample will provisions and information to assist you in solving the routine sorts of will interpretation issues you might encounter.

Common Clauses Used in Wills to Leave Property

To begin, read the will carefully. Most wills use several distinct types of clauses to pass property. Although the syntax and jargon in these clauses vary from will to will, the purpose is to say what assets go to which people. Later sections of this chapter provide more details, where you identify each of the gifts of the will. At this point, as you prepare the list of beneficiaries, you simply want to recognize clauses that leave property.

Clauses That Leave Specific Property

One type of clause names beneficiaries of "specific" assets, such as a particular parcel of real estate, or a particular motor vehicle. (In older wills, personal property gifts were generally termed "bequests" and gifts of real estate were called "devises." Now, the term "devise" refers to giving property through a will, whether real or personal property.) Here are some examples:

> "I leave my house at 111 Apple Street, Anaheim, Orange County, to my son Keith." *(This is a specific devise of real property.)*

> "I give my 1995 green Chevrolet Camaro automobile to my nephew Michael." *(This is a specific bequest/devise of personal property.)*

As noted above, once you determine the people, institutions, and charities named to receive specific items in the will, write those names on your list. Very simple, so far.

Residuary Clause

Wills also generally have a "residuary clause," to designate a beneficiary or beneficiaries for all property that remains after all specific gifts and other gifts such as a particular amount of money have been satisfied. The clause often refers to this remaining property as the "residue." Here are some examples:

> "I give, devise, and bequeath all other property, real, personal, or mixed, not previously disposed of by this will to my son, Jasper Phillips."

> "I give all the rest, residue, and remainder of my estate to the Sierra Club, San Francisco, California."

Here again, a will usually clearly states the people, institutions, or charities named to receive the residue of an estate. Add them to your list of beneficiaries. To determine exactly what these beneficiaries get, you will first have to go through the steps outlined in Chapter 5 to determine what the decedent owned at death. Then, subtract the property left under the terms of the specific bequests and devises from the total estate. The residue is what's left.

EXAMPLE: The decedent, Tammy Rucker, died owning $50,000 cash, a 2015 Oldsmobile, a residence in San Jose, household furniture and furnishings, and personal effects. Tammy's will disposed of her property as follows:

> "I give the sum of $10,000 to my son Richard. I give my 2015 Oldsmobile automobile to my nephew Reggie. I give all the rest, residue, and remainder of my estate to my husband, John."

The residue of the estate going to John consists of the San Jose residence, the household furniture and furnishings, Tammy's personal effects, and the remaining cash ($40,000); that is, all property that was not otherwise specifically disposed of.

Trust Provisions

A trust is an arrangement where a person holds property for the benefit of another. Especially where minor children are involved, a will may leave property in a simple trust for one or more beneficiaries until the beneficiary reaches a certain age. You will know when this is happening because the magic word "trust" is used. Also, a trust may allow a surviving spouse to use trust income during life, with the principal going to the children (or other relatives or charities) when the surviving spouse dies. This structure is particularly common in blended families, where the spouses may not have the same children.

In larger estates, trusts can be used for a variety of tax planning purposes. If you are dealing with a large estate with a number of trust provisions, yours is not a simple estate, and you will need to get professional help.

Any property placed in trust goes to the person named as "trustee" (the person who cares for the property in the trust) to be held and used for the designated beneficiaries, and turned over to the beneficiaries at the specified time. Here is an example:

> "I give 50 shares of IBM stock to my executor, as trustee, to be held for the benefit of my son Joseph until his twenty-first birthday. The trustee shall hold, administer, and distribute the trust as follows." *[Instructions would be spelled out here.]*

If you discover one of these provisions in the will, you should list it under the trust section in the left-hand column of the Schedule of Assets (Chapter 5) and list the designated beneficiaries, as well as the trustee, in your beneficiary chart.

Terminology Used in Wills to Denote Groups of People

Once you identify the main clauses described above, you may be uncertain about which people the clauses include. For instance, wills commonly leave specific devises and residuary bequests to groups of people—for example, "my issue," "my children," or "my heirs."

If you encounter these types of group terms, proceed very carefully. Do not assume that you know the legal meaning of these terms—even the apparently simple term "children" may include more than you expect. Here are some definitions.

Note. You may also run into the term "right of representation" (or "per stirpes"). We deal with this concept at the end of this chapter, and it is important for both interpreting wills and for figuring out who inherits if the decedent died without a will.

Issue

> "I give one-third of the residue of my estate to my sister Clara Peters. Should Clara predecease me, this gift shall go and be distributed by right of representation to her lawful issue."

"Issue" generally means all children and their children down through the generations. Thus, a person's issue includes his or her children, grandchildren, great-grandchildren, and so on. Adopted children are considered the issue of their adopting parents, and the children of the adopted children (and so on) are also considered issue. A term often used in place of issue is "lineal descendants."

Children

> "I give the sum of $1,000 to each of the children of my two nephews, Edward Long and Charles Long, living at the date of my death."

Children include:

- biological offspring of the parent, unless they have been legally adopted by another (but see below)
- persons who were legally adopted by the parent
- children born to married spouses and registered domestic partners (these children are legally considered to be the children of both members of the couple), and
- stepchildren and other children if the relationship began during the child's minority, continued throughout both parties' lifetimes, and if it is established by clear and convincing evidence that the decedent would have adopted the person but for a legal barrier (if, for example, the child's biological parent would not consent).

When determining whether a person is a "child" of a stepparent, it is not enough that the stepparent married the biological parent—the nature of the relationship becomes important. It must be a *family* relationship like that of a parent and child. Even in cases where a family relationship existed, there must still be clear and convincing evidence that the stepparent or foster parent would have adopted the stepchild or foster child but for a legal barrier. (Prob. Code § 6454.) A stepchild or foster child who is an adult but whom the decedent did not adopt will probably not qualify as an intestate heir.

Generally, adoption severs the legal relationship between children and their biological parents. However, children who have been adopted are still considered, for purposes of inheritance, children of their biological parents if both of the following exceptional circumstances apply:

- the biological parent and the adopted child lived together at any time as parent and child, or the biological parent was married to or cohabiting with the other biological parent when the child was conceived but died before the child's birth, and
- the adoption was by the spouse of either biological parent or after the death of either biological parent. (Prob. Code § 6451.)

Parent and child relationships are covered by Probate Code Sections 6450–6455. Other potentially more complicated situations may exist. For example, children conceived after death using the decedent's genetic material, (Prob. Code § 249.5), conception through assisted reproduction (Family Code § 7613), or where a person is a presumed parent. If you have difficulty interpreting provisions that may apply to your situation, consult an attorney.

Other Family Relationships

When considering other family relationships—such as siblings, cousins, nieces, and nephews—half blood relatives, adopted relatives, relatives born outside of marriage, stepchildren, foster children, and the descendants of those people are generally considered part of the class. (Prob. Code § 21115.) For example, a gift to "siblings" includes half-sisters and half-brothers —that is, siblings who share only one biological parent.

Notice if specific definitions in the will might override the general presumptions under California law. For example, some wills define "issue" and "children" to make clear the decedent's intent for whom to include under those terms.

Heir

> "I give $10,000 to my sister Julie Lee. Should Julie predecease me, this gift shall be divided among her heirs who survive me by 45 days."

An heir is any person who inherits in the absence of a will or who is entitled by law to inherit in the event an estate is not completely disposed of under a will.

Other Confusing Language

Language used in wills can be extremely muddled. And even if the language in a will seems relatively clear, you may encounter ambiguous statements. For instance, how would you interpret this provision: "I give $15,000 to my three sons, Tom, Dick, and Harry"? Does $15,000 or $5,000 go to each one?

Start by reading the will provision in question carefully. Sometimes efforts to use formal language in a will can, instead of making matters more clear, instead make the decedent's intent more difficult to understand. Other times, what seem like extra or redundant words actually have important meaning. Pay close attention to all words and phrases and get help from an attorney if you do not know what the will means. Charting out the language can sometimes help. If you encounter strange words or suspect that several words mean the same thing, you can consult the glossary at the end of this book. Then see if the will provision makes sense. If it doesn't—which is very possible—you will need advice from an attorney.

Alternate Beneficiaries

Most wills specify who should get the property in the event a named beneficiary, or one or more of a group of beneficiaries, fails to survive the decedent. You should list these alternate beneficiaries in your chart identifying them as alternate beneficiaries. The language creating alternates is often quite straightforward:

Checklist to Identify Beneficiaries in a Will

To have a complete list of beneficiaries and possible beneficiaries, use this checklist while reviewing the will.

- ☐ 1. Locate all provisions that specifically pass property. Translate group terms (for example, "issue" or "heir") into specific persons.
- ☐ 2. Locate the clause that passes the residuary estate. As above, translate group terms into specific persons.
- ☐ 3. Locate any provisions that leave property in trust. Identify beneficiaries and trustee of the trust.
- ☐ 4. Identify alternate beneficiaries (both specifically named and group members).
- ☐ 5. Identify any contingent beneficiaries.
- ☐ 6. Identify confusing language and list possible additional beneficiaries.
- ☐ 7. Eliminate any beneficiary who would take by suggestion rather than mandatory direction.
- ☐ 8. Note on your list, next to each beneficiary, the specific section of the will and other relevant factors, such as family relationships and contingencies.

"If any of my children dies before I do, then that child's share shall pass equally to my surviving children."

"I give to my wife, Jane, all of my clothing, jewelry, furniture, books, and all property of a personal nature. In the event she predeceases me, I leave all such personal property to my sister Ella."

"I give to my son Richard my Porsche automobile, VIN __________, or, if I no longer own that automobile at my death, any automobile I own at the time of my death. Should my son predecease me, my automobile shall be left as part of my residuary estate."

Again, if the language is not straightforward, get legal advice.

Conditional Bequests

It's uncommon, but you may find bequests or devises in the will that depend on one or more conditions. That is, a will may list a different beneficiary or beneficiaries, depending on whether the specific conditions are met. In this situation, you will need to identify for your beneficiary chart both the main or primary beneficiaries and the beneficiaries who contingently stand to inherit. For example, you might find a clause leaving a house to "my three sons so long as they live in it, but if they move out, then to my sister Hannah."

Contingent and conditional gifts have long been responsible for many of the lawsuits that arise over the interpretation of wills. (In our example, who inherits if one son moves out but the others continue to live there?) If you run into one of these clauses and are unsure of who is entitled to what, talk it over with the affected family members. If everyone is reasonable and arrives at a common resolution, you may choose to continue to handle the estate settlement work yourself. However, if a dispute festers or threatens to do so, you are not dealing with a simple estate and need professional help.

Unenforceable Will Provisions

Wills sometimes contain wishes, suggestions, or unenforceable demands. As the executor or administrator of the estate, you have no duty to comply with these, although you may wish to carry out the decedent's intentions to the greatest degree possible. For instance, suppose you encounter a will that says something like this:

> "I give to my sister Bertha all my clothing, jewelry, furniture, furnishings, books, and all other property of a personal nature with the request that she give to my children as they come of age such articles as they might desire or need."

Because the clause suggests rather than mandates, it cannot be enforced, and Bertha is legally entitled to keep all of the property.

Sometimes the conditions are against the law or public policy. For example, the court would likely not enforce a gift seen as encouraging divorce.

Compare Schedule of Assets With Property Left in Will

Now that you have identified the possible beneficiaries of the will, your next job is to roughly compare the amount and character of the property the decedent actually left with the property mentioned in the will. Was the property listed in the will still owned by the deceased person at death? Will the assets cover the gifts made in the will? We give you essential information about property in Chapter 4 and show you how to identify and list the decedent's property in Chapter 5.

Sometimes this task is easy because the will doesn't give away any specific assets but instead leaves everything to beneficiaries in clearly defined portions. For example:

> "I give, devise, and bequeath all of my estate, both real and personal property, as follows: Two-thirds thereof to my wife, Mary, and one-third thereof to my son John."

However, if a decedent has left a long list of specific items to a long list of people, it can be a bit trickier. What happens, for example, if a decedent's will leaves his 2016 Ford F-150 to his son Herb, but the decedent sold it and used the money for a vacation? Does Herb get anything? Or, suppose the decedent leaves his share of his house to Herb, but later places the property in joint tenancy with his wife. Here are some general rules that apply if a person does not keep the will up-to-date and dies without owning certain assets listed in it.

Specific Gifts

A gift of a particular thing, specified and distinguished from all others of the same kind belonging to the decedent, is a specific gift. If the specific asset is not, in fact, owned by the decedent when he or she dies (or if it has been put into joint tenancy or a trust in the meantime), the gift simply fails. (Another way to say that a gift fails, is that it "lapses.") The beneficiary is not entitled to take another asset instead. Thus, in the example just above, if the decedent no longer has the 2016 Ford F-150, Herb is not entitled to any other property. But if the will said, "I give any vehicle I may own at the time of my death to my son Herb," and the decedent had sold the Ford F-150 and bought a Jeep that he still owned at his death, then Herb would inherit the Jeep.

In some circumstances, if a specific item has merely changed form, the original beneficiary may still have a claim—if, for example, a testator leaves a promissory note due him or her to a friend, and the note is paid before the testator's death, leaving easily traceable proceeds. In such a case, a court would look at the testator's intent to decide if the beneficiary should inherit from the estate.

SEE AN EXPERT

If you need to trace assets, you are not dealing with a simple estate. Normally, tracing involves looking at what was done with the proceeds of the sale of an asset to see if they are still identifiable. If the decedent sold a car and put the money in a new bank account, it's easy to trace. However, if the decedent put the money in an existing bank account with other funds, and lots of money flows in and out, tracing is generally not possible. Tracing is also not possible where it goes against the intent expressed in the document or supported by other evidence.

If you face a situation where some assets have been replaced by others between the time a will was drafted and when the decedent died, you should get professional help unless all people who stand to inherit agree to a sensible resolution that reflects the decedent's intent. In the example above, the decedent left Herb a 2016 Ford F-150 but sold it and bought a Jeep a few months before death. If everyone involved agrees that the decedent wanted Herb to have the Jeep but simply hadn't updated his will, you would be safe in honoring this intent, particularly if it is approved by the court in the case of a formal probate proceeding (see Chapter 14).

Gifts of Money

Gifts of money are called "general legacies" or "bequests" because they are not tied to specific items, but rather can be satisfied by the payment of cash. If the estate has enough cash to satisfy the terms of the will, there's no problem. However, it becomes more complicated if the will leaves a beneficiary money but insufficient cash is available when the testator dies or after debts and expenses are paid. Suppose, for instance, that a decedent's will leaves $50,000 each to two different people (call them Herb and Cathy) and there is, in fact, only $60,000 in the decedent's estate. Here is what happens:

- If the decedent has other assets in his residuary estate (that is, remaining assets have not been left to specific beneficiaries), Herb and Cathy as "named" beneficiaries of general legacies first split what money the decedent did leave, and then take assets of sufficient value from the residuary estate to make up the difference. Typically, this involves selling residuary assets, thus decreasing the amount received by the beneficiaries of the residuary estate.
- If the decedent dies leaving only $60,000 in cash (after debts and assets are paid) and no other assets, Herb and Cathy would split the $60,000 in proportion to their original shares, assuming they were either both related or both unrelated to the decedent. In our example, Herb and Cathy were willed an equal amount, so they would divide the $60,000 in half. However, if Cathy was related to the decedent and Herb was not, Cathy could receive her entire bequest ($50,000) while Herb would receive only the balance. This is because the law gives preference to a spouse, domestic partner, or relative. The relative's gift gets satisfied first, unless the will states a different intention.

Sometimes the will leaves an amount of money from a particular source—like, "$5,000 from my Wells Fargo savings account." This is called a "demonstrative" gift, which is a type of general gift. If the named source does not have the funds to fulfill the demonstrative gift, the gift comes from the general assets of the estate, unless the will says otherwise.

Be aware that if the estate does not have sufficient funds to fulfill the stated gifts in a will, the administration of the estate can become more complicated. Good communication may be important when applying these rules. Persons whose gifts cannot be fulfilled may think that the personal representative is being unfair, without understanding the legal reason for a result.

If the administration becomes complicated, proceed with caution and get legal advice.

Property Left to Someone Who Doesn't Survive the Decedent

What happens if the decedent's will leaves property to someone and that person dies before the decedent or during the will's survivorship period? Obviously, the deceased beneficiary (called a "predeceased beneficiary") receives nothing. In the great majority of instances, wills provide for this by naming an alternate beneficiary. For example: "I leave $5,000 to Mary P. if she survives me. If she does not, I leave this money to Sally P."

Most wills also require that a beneficiary survive for a period of time after the decedent (for example, 30 days). If that's the case, and if the named beneficiary does not survive the period, then the gift will lapse. If, however, the will does not specify an alternate beneficiary, and the will does not contain a survivorship period, the result will depend on the original beneficiary's relationship to the decedent. We discuss the California laws that apply in these situations below.

Deceased Beneficiary Was a Relative

If the gift was made to a relative of the decedent, or to a relative of a surviving, deceased, or former spouse or domestic partner of the decedent, the property goes to the children, grandchildren, or great-grandchildren (termed issue) of the person named to receive it, by right of representation. For this purpose, "relative" means relationship by blood or legal adoption—it doesn't include spouses. This law is called the "antilapse" statute, and is set forth in Probate Code Section 21110. The term "right of representation" refers to how shares are divided among the issue and is discussed in detail at the end of this chapter.

Deceased Beneficiary Was Not a Relative

If the beneficiary who does not survive the decedent was not a relative or a relative of a surviving or deceased spouse or domestic partner, and no alternate beneficiary was named, the gift simply lapses and is added to the residue of the estate. This means that for a predeceased beneficiary unrelated to the decedent, the predeceased beneficiary's relatives inherit nothing, and the gift passes under the terms of the will's residuary clause. This is the clause that disposes of all property not covered by a specific devise or bequest. A residuary clause usually states something like this: "I give any and all property, real, personal, or mixed, not previously disposed of by this will, to my wife, Jane."

> **EXAMPLE 1:** Bill, who never married, leaves a will that says: "I give $1,000 to my neighbor Jennie." Jennie dies before Bill, who never changed his will. Jennie receives nothing, because she's deceased. Similarly, her children or grandchildren receive nothing (unless Jennie was a relative of Bill) because under California law, the gift lapses. The $1,000 that would have gone to Jennie becomes part of the residuary estate.

> **EXAMPLE 2:** Andrew's will says, "I give $5,000 to my sister Claudia," and makes no provision for an alternative beneficiary. If Claudia dies before Andrew, Claudia's issue (children or other descendants) receive $5,000 because Claudia is related to the decedent.
>
> Even if Claudia left a will when she died, her will would have no bearing on how the $5,000 would be distributed—the money would still go to Claudia's children. On the other hand, if Andrew's will says, "I give $5,000 to my sister Claudia, but if Claudia should fail to survive me, this gift shall go to Sally," then Claudia's children and other descendants receive nothing if Sally is living.

The below diagram demonstrates how the anti-lapse laws work.

Property Left to Someone Who Dies Before Distribution

A beneficiary may survive the decedent—but die before the estate property is distributed. What happens then depends on what the will says.

If the will states that the beneficiary must survive a certain time or until the date of distribution, then the gift fails, and the property goes to the alternate beneficiary. If there's no alternate identified, it will go either to the residuary estate or to the beneficiary's descendants if the state antilapse law applies.

If the will doesn't have any stated survivorship requirement, the property is turned over to the representative of the deceased beneficiary's estate. It will go to the beneficiary's own heirs or beneficiaries. (Prob. Code §§ 11801–11802.) In this situation, put the personal representative of the deceased's beneficiary's estate on your list of beneficiaries.

When Public Policy Affects the Distribution of Property

Sometimes public policy can override a will's stated distribution provisions. This primarily occurs in three situations:

- Spouses or domestic partners who are entitled to inherit are left out of the will.
- Children who are entitled to inherit are left out of the will.
- The will was not updated after a divorce or termination of a domestic partnership.

Let's consider these areas one at a time.

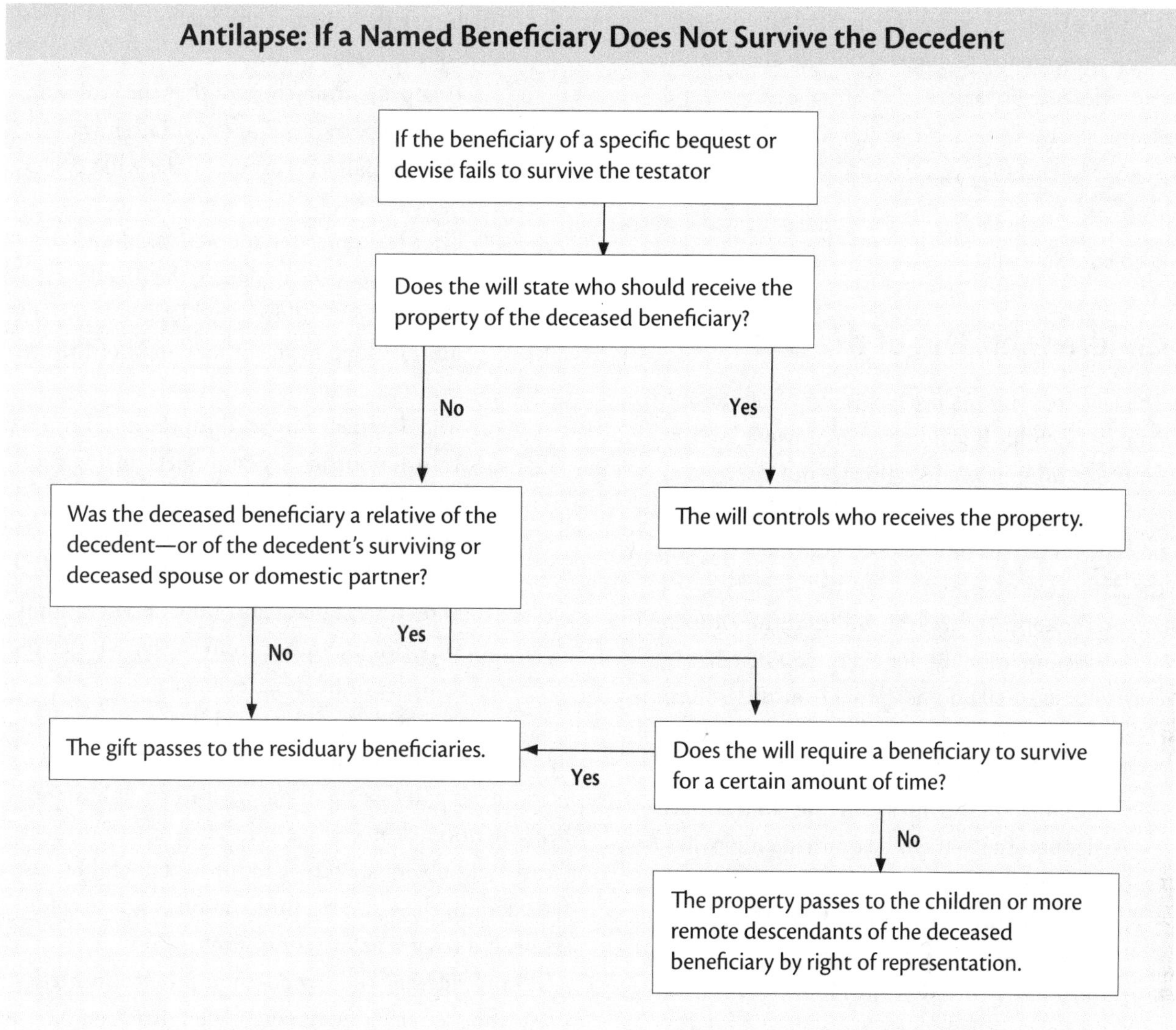

Spouse or Domestic Partner Left Out of the Will

If a person marries or enters into a registered domestic partnership after making a will and (a) doesn't provide for the new spouse or partner in the will or in a codicil (or by any other means), and (b) doesn't indicate an intention in the will to exclude the spouse or partner, and (c) dies first, then the surviving spouse or partner will be entitled to all the community and quasi-community property (the decedent's half and the one-half already owned by the surviving spouse or partner), plus up to one-half of the decedent's separate property. This is called the "statutory share" of the estate. (Prob. Code §§ 21600–21612.)

Looking at this rule from the opposite perspective, a person who married the decedent after the decedent made a will and who is not provided for in the decedent's will may claim some of the estate unless:

- the decedent intentionally omitted the spouse or partner (by language such as, "I intentionally omit any future husband")
- the decedent provided for the spouse or partner by property transfers outside the will instead (such as in a marriage contract, joint tenancy transfers, or insurance proceeds), and it can be clearly shown by statements made by the decedent, by the amount of the transfer, or by other evidence that the decedent intended the transfer to be in lieu of a will provision, or

- the omitted person made a valid written agreement waiving the right to share in the decedent's estate.

SEE AN EXPERT

Consult a lawyer if a spouse or domestic partner is left out of the will.

Children Left Out of the Will

The law does not require a parent to leave an inheritance to a child. But in some circumstances, an omitted child may have rights to an inheritance.

Some general rules apply if the decedent did not provide for one or more children in the will. (Review the definition of "children" in the Glossary.)

- If it appears from the will that the omission was intentional—for example, the will says, "I intentionally do not provide in this will for my daughter Lynn" or "I don't like my daughter Lynn and leave her nothing," or if the will simply names Lynn as a living child but leaves her nothing—then the omitted child will not inherit.
- If, at the time of writing a will, the decedent was unaware of the birth of a child, or mistakenly believed the child was dead, the omitted child will receive a share in the estate equal in value to that which the child would have received if the decedent had died without a will. Otherwise—if the decedent did know about the child when writing the will—the law assumes that the omission was intentional and the child inherits nothing.
- If the decedent fails to provide in the will for any of his or her children born or adopted after the execution of the will (and, thus, not foreseen at the time), the omitted child is entitled to receive a share in the estate equal in value to that which the child would have received had the decedent died without a will, unless one or more of the following conditions exists, in which case the omitted child does not receive a share of the estate:
  a. It appears from the will that the omission of after-born or -adopted children was intentional—for example, the will says, "I intentionally do not provide for any after-born or after-adopted children."
  b. When the will was signed, the decedent had one or more children and left substantially all the estate to the other parent of the omitted child.
  c. The decedent provided for the child by transfer outside the will (gifts during the decedent's lifetime, life insurance, joint accounts), and the intention that the transfer be in lieu of a will provision is shown by statements of the decedent (oral or written), and/or from the amount of the transfer or by other evidence.

Situations involving omitted children, covered by Probate Code Sections 21620 to 21623, can be intricate. If you face an estate where a child has not been mentioned in a will and has not otherwise been clearly and obviously provided for to that child's satisfaction, the estate administration is not simple. Consult a lawyer before continuing.

Grandchildren. The law does not protect omitted grandchildren or more remote issue (great-grandchildren) of the decedent who are living when the will is signed. If a decedent's child is deceased at the time the will was signed and the decedent failed to provide for children of that deceased child (grandchildren of the decedent), that omission is treated as intentional and the grandchildren receive nothing. However, if a child who was living when the will was made is named as a beneficiary under the will and that child dies before the decedent, leaving a child or children surviving (grandchildren of the decedent), then the grandchildren will divide the deceased child's share absent other direction in the will. We discuss how this works in "Right of Representation and Gifts to Descendants," below.

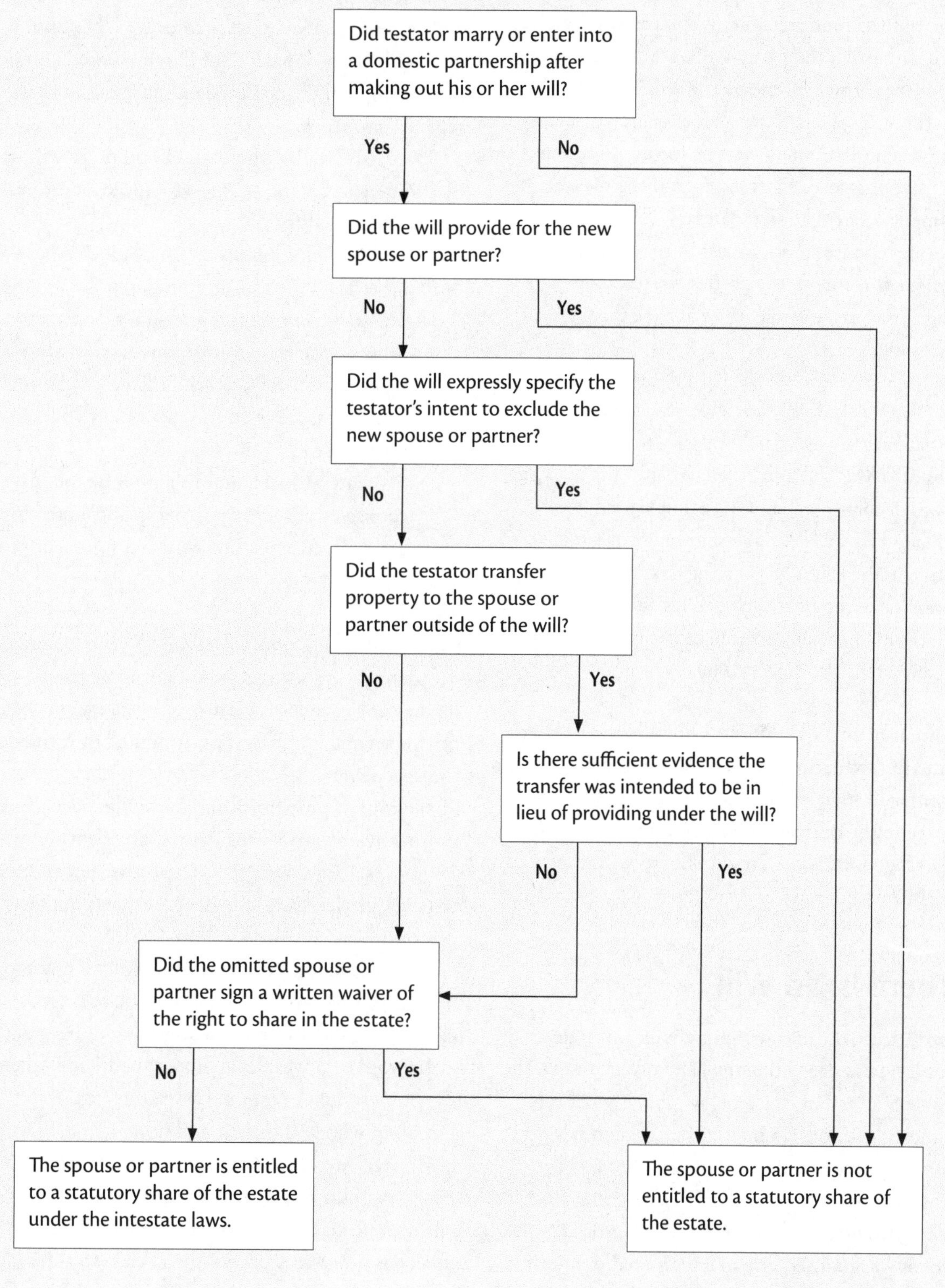
Rights of Surviving Spouse or Domestic Partner
Did testator marry or enter into a domestic partnership after making out his or her will?
Yes
No
Did the will provide for the new spouse or partner?
No
Yes
Did the will expressly specify the testator's intent to exclude the new spouse or partner?
No
Yes
Did the testator transfer property to the spouse or partner outside of the will?
No
Yes
Is there sufficient evidence the transfer was intended to be in lieu of providing under the will?
No
Yes
Did the omitted spouse or partner sign a written waiver of the right to share in the estate?
No
Yes
The spouse or partner is entitled to a statutory share of the estate under the intestate laws.
The spouse or partner is not entitled to a statutory share of the estate.

Will Not Updated After Divorce

If a decedent's will gives property to the decedent's spouse, but the marriage to that spouse was dissolved or annulled after January 1, 1985, any gift of property made to the former spouse by the will is revoked unless the will specifically provides otherwise. The estate is then distributed as if the former spouse did not survive the decedent. However, if the divorce or annulment occurred before January 1, 1985, bequests to a former spouse stand, unless in the property settlement agreement, the parties waived their rights to inherit the estate of the other at the other's death. (Prob. Code § 6122.)

> **EXAMPLE:** Harold made a will while married to Sally that gave Sally $200,000 and gave the rest of his estate to his children in equal shares. The marriage was dissolved on July 1, 1986, but Harold never made a new will. Sally gets nothing on Harold's death. The $200,000 gift to her is added to the residue of the estate going to his children. However, if the divorce had occurred before January 1, 1985, Sally would get the $200,000.

Similarly, under California's domestic partnership law, if, after executing a will, the domestic partnership is terminated, that termination revokes any gift of property to the decedent's former domestic partner. (Prob. Code § 6122.1.) This applies to wills executed after 2002.

If There Is No Will

When a decedent dies without a will, intestate succession laws determine the heirs of the estate. The Intestate Succession chart, below, shows what these laws mean. California's intestate succession laws are set out in Probate Code Sections 6400 to 6414.

The portion of the decedent's estate going to each relative first depends on (1) whether or not the decedent was married or had a registered domestic partner when he or she died and (2) whether the estate contains both community property and separate property, only community property, or only separate property. (We define and discuss community and separate property in Chapter 4.) Of course, if the decedent was not married or in a registered domestic partnership, all of the decedent's property will be separate property.

If a person dies without a will, property will be distributed according to intestate succession rules. In summary, in California:

- The surviving spouse or domestic partner inherits all community property.
- The surviving spouse or domestic partner inherits either one-third, one-half, or all of the separate property, depending on whether the decedent is survived by one or more children or other close relatives.
- Separate property not inherited by the surviving spouse or domestic partner is distributed to the children, parents, brothers and sisters, or other relatives.

The children or descendants of a predeceased spouse (who died not more than 15 years before the decedent for real property and not more than 5 years before the decedent for personal property) may also inherit separate property not inherited by family of the decedent.

To inherit property from an intestate decedent, a prospective heir must survive the decedent for at least 120 hours. Otherwise, the prospective heir is deemed to have "predeceased" the decedent, and the heirs are determined accordingly. (Prob. Code § 6403.)

If a decedent dies intestate and leaves only more distant relatives (no spouse, domestic partner, children, grandchildren, great-grandchildren, parents or their issue, or grandparents or their issue), then the property of the estate goes to the next of kin. Deciding who will inherit and how the estate will be divided involves understanding a concept called "degrees of kinship." Each generation is called a "degree." The degrees are determined by counting up to a common ancestor and then down to a decedent.

The Table of Consanguinity, below, shows the degree of different relatives. For instance, children are in the first degree, and nieces and nephews are in the third degree. Second cousins are in the sixth degree. This becomes most important when, at the closest degree of relatives, a person is both deceased and survived by more remote descendants.

SKIP AHEAD

Skip ahead to Chapter 4 if all of the known beneficiaries are alive.

Terminology. In reading this chart and the ones that come later in this section, you will see that legal terminology is often used to specifically differentiate between certain persons or classes of persons. We provide simple definitions of the most important terms in the Glossary.

Although the definition of "children" discussed above applies when determining heirs under the intestate succession laws as well as identifying beneficiaries of a will, the statute contains some special rules for intestate succession situations. A child who has been adopted may still inherit from his or her biological parents:

- if the deceased parent was married to or cohabiting with the other biological parent at the time of the child's conception and died before the child was born, or
- if the adoption was by the spouse or domestic partner of either of the biological parents or took place after the death of either biological parent.

Right of Representation and Gifts to Descendants

The concept of inheritance by right of representation (or per stirpes) can be very important in determining whether particular people will inherit property under a will (and, sometimes, by intestate succession in the absence of a will) and if so, how much.

"Right of Representation" Defined

"Right of representation" means that the descendants of a deceased beneficiary take the same share collectively that the deceased beneficiary would have taken if living at the time of the decedent's death. For instance, assume John makes a bequest to his brother Tommy, and Tommy dies before John but leaves three children of his own. Unless the will provided otherwise, Tommy's children would take the bequest by right of representation—that is, Tommy's children would equally divide Tommy's bequest.

When You Need to Understand Right of Representation and Other Distribution Options

Fortunately, most people will not have to deal with this material at all. However, if you face one of the four situations set out just below, the concept of "right of representation" will apply.

Situation 1. A will specifically leaves property to a group of beneficiaries using the words "by right of representation" or "per stirpes."

> EXAMPLE: Daisy leaves her house "to my children Myra and Andrew, but if either of them should not survive me, then to that child's children by right of representation."

Situation 2. The will provides that issue of a predeceased beneficiary should inherit the ancestor's share, but doesn't specify the method to determine the issue's shares.

> EXAMPLE: Daisy leaves her house "to my children Myra and Andrew, but if either of them should predecease me, then to their issue."

Situation 3. A will leaves property to a relative of the decedent and *both* of the following are true:

- The relative died before the decedent, or failed to survive the decedent by the time specified in the will (often 30–180 days).
- The will names no alternate beneficiary.

EXAMPLE: Albert left his sister Agnes $50,000 and made no provision for what would happen if Agnes died before he did, which she did. Who will inherit the money depends on whether she has descendants and how the right of representation is applied. If, however, Albert had left the same amount to his faithful, but not related, friend, Phil, who didn't survive Albert, the gift to Phil would lapse. The money would pass under the residuary clause of Albert's will. Because it wouldn't go to Phil's descendants, you wouldn't need to worry about right of representation.

Situation 4. There is no will, and the intestacy laws call for succession (inheritance) to descendants.

EXAMPLE: Jane dies without a will. Two of her three children survive her, as does a child of her predeceased child. The relevant intestate succession statute (Prob. Code § 6402) provides that Jane's issue (her living children and grandchild who is the child of Jane's deceased child) inherit her estate and that the grandchild takes an equal share by right of representation.

If you face one of these four situations, read on. If you don't, proceed to Chapter 4, where we discuss assessing different types of property.

Who Inherits When There Is No Will? Married or Partnered

If the decedent died without a will while married or in a registered domestic partnership, all *community property* and *quasi-community property* will go to the surviving spouse or domestic partner. This chart shows how the decedent's *separate property* is divided.

Survivor(s), in addition to spouse or domestic partner	Who gets decedent's separate property
No child or issue, parent, sibling, or issue of deceased sibling	All to spouse or domestic partner
One child, or issue of one deceased child	½ to spouse or domestic partner ½ to only child or issue of deceased child
More than one child, or one child plus issue of one or more deceased children, or issue of two or more deceased children	⅓ to spouse or domestic partner ⅔ to children or issue of deceased children
No children or their issue, but a parent or parents	½ to spouse or domestic partner ½ to parent or parents
No children or their issue, no parent, but siblings or issue of deceased siblings	½ to spouse or domestic partner ½ to issue of a parent (that is, siblings and/or issue of deceased siblings)

- "Siblings" includes half-siblings (when the decedent and the siblings share one biological or legal parent).
- Issue take equally if they are all the same degree of kinship to the decedent, but if of unequal degree, those of more remote degree take in the manner provided in Probate Code Section 240.

Who Inherits When There Is No Will? Not Married or Partnered

Survivor(s)	Who gets the decedent's property
Issue or issue of deceased children	Children or issue of deceased children
No issue, but a parent or parents	Parent or parents
No issue or parent, but issue of parent (siblings or issue of deceased siblings)	Issue of a parent (siblings and/or issue of deceased siblings)
No issue, parent, or issue of parent, but one or more grandparents or issue of grandparents (aunts, uncles, or cousins of decedent)	Grandparent(s) or issue of deceased grandparents
No issue, no parent or issue of parent, no grandparent or issue of grandparent, but a predeceased spouse or domestic partner with issue or parents or issue of parents surviving	For real property attributable to the decedent's predeceased spouse or domestic partner who died within 15 years or less of the decedent, or for personal property attributable to the decedent's predeceased spouse or domestic partner who died within 5 years or less ‡: • issue of predeceased spouse or domestic partner, or if none, then • parent(s) of the predeceased spouse or domestic partner, or if none, then • issue of deceased parent(s) of the predeceased spouse or domestic partner.
If no takers above	Next of kin of the decedent. Or, if none, State of California

- "Siblings" includes half-siblings (when the decedent and the siblings share one biological or legal parent).
- Issue take equally if they are all the same degree of kinship to the decedent, but if of unequal degree, those of more remote degree take in the manner provided in Probate Code Section 240.

‡ Probate Code § 6402.5.

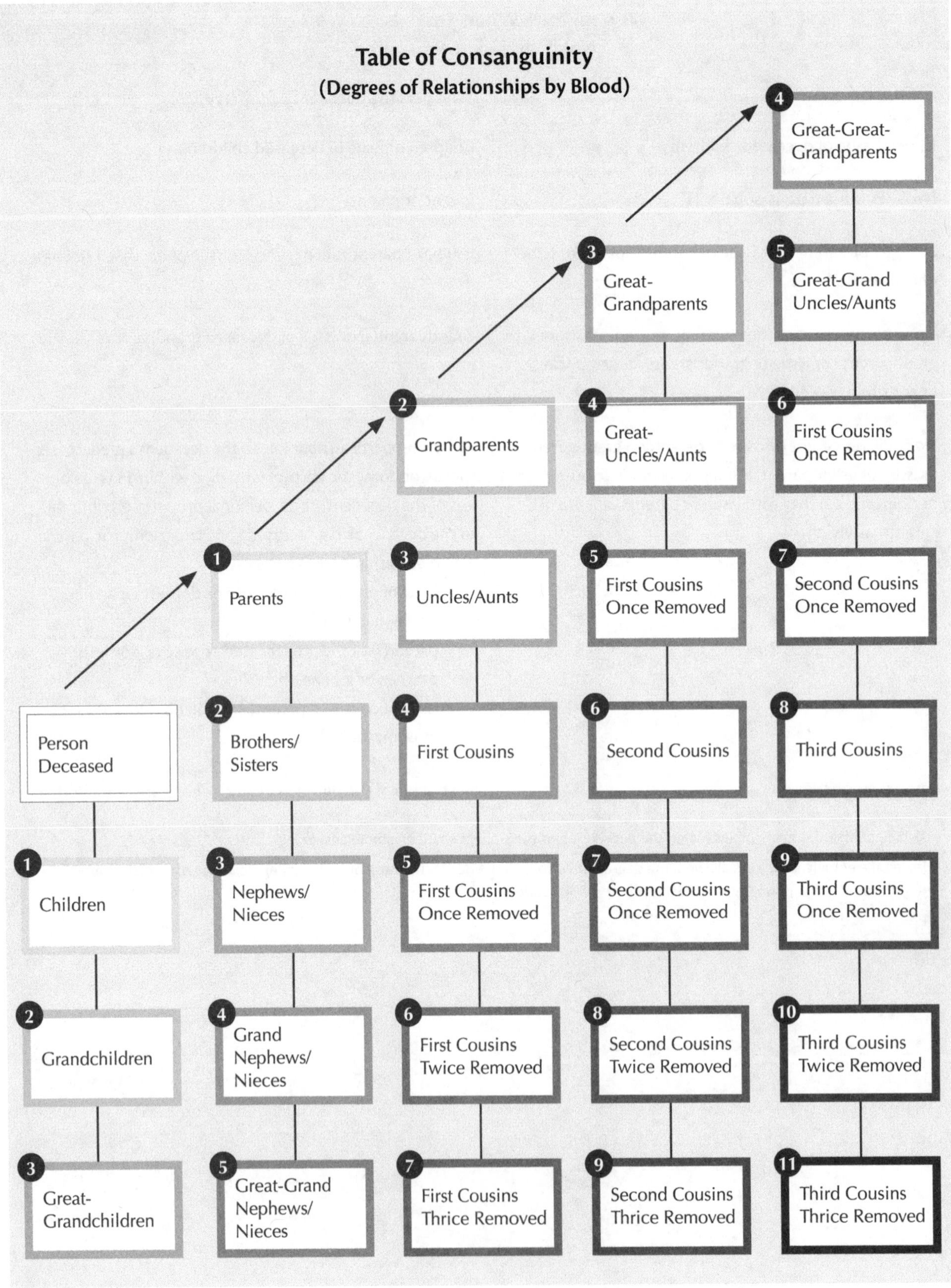
Table of Consanguinity
(Degrees of Relationships by Blood)
Person Deceased
1 Children
2 Grandchildren
3 Great-Grandchildren
1 Parents
2 Brothers/Sisters
3 Nephews/Nieces
4 Grand Nephews/Nieces
5 Great-Grand Nephews/Nieces
2 Grandparents
3 Uncles/Aunts
4 First Cousins
5 First Cousins Once Removed
6 First Cousins Twice Removed
7 First Cousins Thrice Removed
3 Great-Grandparents
4 Great-Uncles/Aunts
5 First Cousins Once Removed
6 Second Cousins
7 Second Cousins Once Removed
8 Second Cousins Twice Removed
9 Second Cousins Thrice Removed
4 Great-Great-Grandparents
5 Great-Grand Uncles/Aunts
6 First Cousins Once Removed
7 Second Cousins Once Removed
8 Third Cousins
9 Third Cousins Once Removed
10 Third Cousins Twice Removed
11 Third Cousins Thrice Removed

Three Distribution Options for Descendants

As we mentioned, there are at least three different methods or formulas for determining how descendants may inherit. Each formula can have different results, which makes it essential to apply the right formula. Make the effort to understand which one applies to the estate you are dealing with:

- Formula 1 (set out in Probate Code § 240) is used when a will provides that issue of a deceased beneficiary take but doesn't specify by what method, or when a kindred beneficiary dies before the testator, and whenever the intestate succession laws call for division to heirs (Situations 2, 3, and 4).
- Formula 2 (set out in Probate Code § 246) applies only when the will specifically calls for division by "right of representation," "per stirpes," or "by representation" (Situation 1).
- Formula 3 (set out in Probate Code § 247) applies only when the will specifically calls for "per capita" at each generation.

We discuss each of these formulas below. If the will specifically gives another formula for distribution to descendants, follow that formula.

Formula 1

When Formula 1 applies, you must first identify the closest generation of issue that has living members. The closest possible generation is that of the children. If there are no children living, go on to the grandchildren's generation, and so forth. The property is divided into equal shares at that generation. The number of shares is determined by the living members and deceased members who left issue living, of that generation. Each living member of the generation gets a share, and the issue of a deceased member take their ancestor's share, in the same manner as Formula 1.

EXAMPLE 1: Assume John died without a will and all three of his children, Bob, Bill, and Ben, survived him. The portion of his estate that would go to his children under the intestate laws would be divided equally among the children (the closest generation with a living member). It would look like this:

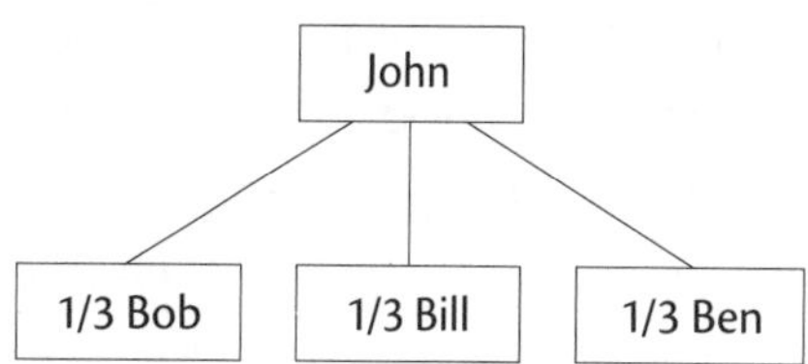

EXAMPLE 2: James makes a will and leaves his property to his children. Two of his children, Jill and Jack, are alive when James dies. One daughter, Joyce, has died before James, but after the will was signed, leaving two surviving children, Janice and Jake (James's grandchildren). James's property would be inherited as follows: Each of his surviving children (Jill and Jack) would receive one-third. The two grand-children (Janice and Jake), inheriting their deceased parent's share equally, would each receive one-sixth.

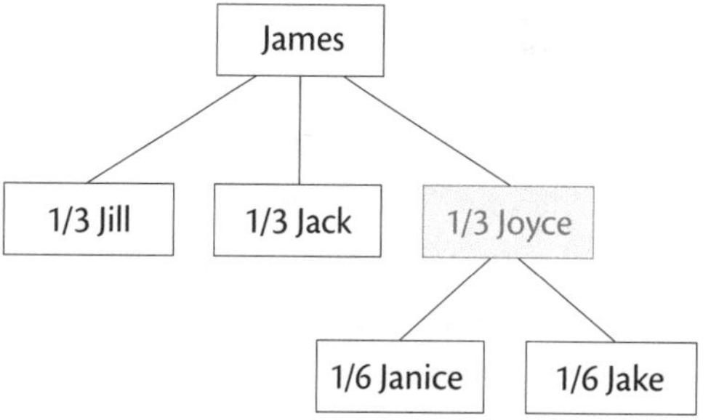

If, instead, Joyce had died before James made his will and James knew of her death, Joyce's children (James's grandchildren) would receive nothing. They would be considered "intentionally omitted" under the law. Jack and Jill would each own one-half.

EXAMPLE 3: Jeffrey makes a will and leaves all of his property to his three children, Phil, Paul, and Peter. At Jeffrey's death, Phil survives, Paul is deceased, leaving two children of his own (Sarah and Sabrina), and Peter is deceased, leaving no surviving children, but one surviving grandchild (Lew) of his own. Jeffrey's only surviving child, Phil, would receive one-third of the property. The two grandchildren, Sarah and Sabrina, would split their parent's share (one-sixth each), and the great-grandchild, Lew, would take his grandparent's share (one-third).

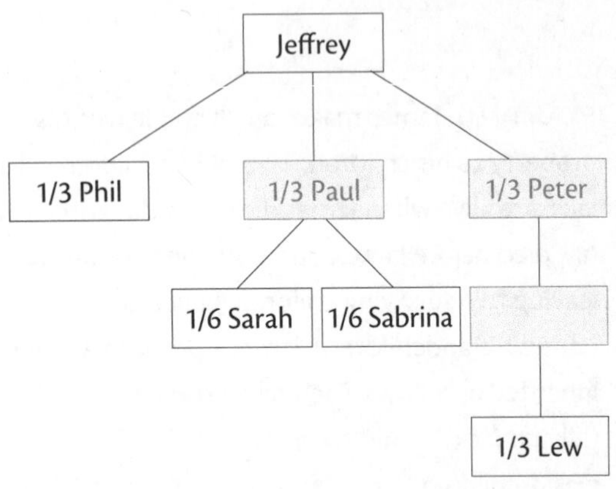

If all members in the closest degree of relationship are deceased, the property is equally divided at the next generation having a living member.

EXAMPLE 4: Angela leaves her property to her three children (Rosie, Marie, and Josefa) and none of them survives. However, Josefa leaves four children of her own, Rosie leaves two children, and Marie leaves one child. Because there are no living members in the next closest generation to Angela (that is, her children), each of the grandchildren takes an equal share (that is, one-seventh of the property).

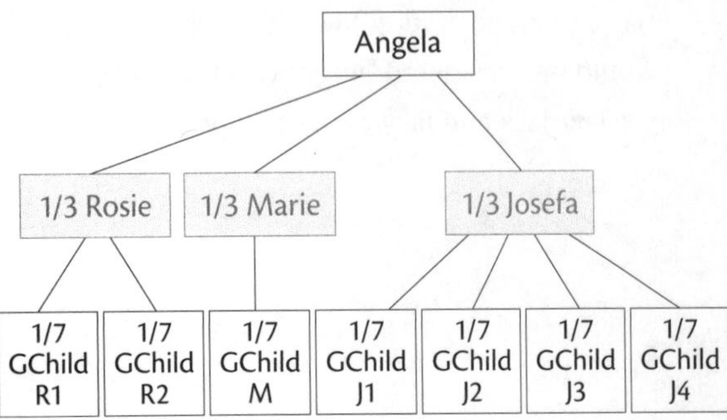

EXAMPLE 5: Suppose Rosie survived Angela. Then the other grandchildren would take only their parent's share. Thus the four grandchildren who are children of Josefa would have to split one-third of the property (one-twelfth each) while the single grandchild who is the child of Marie would inherit one-third of the property.

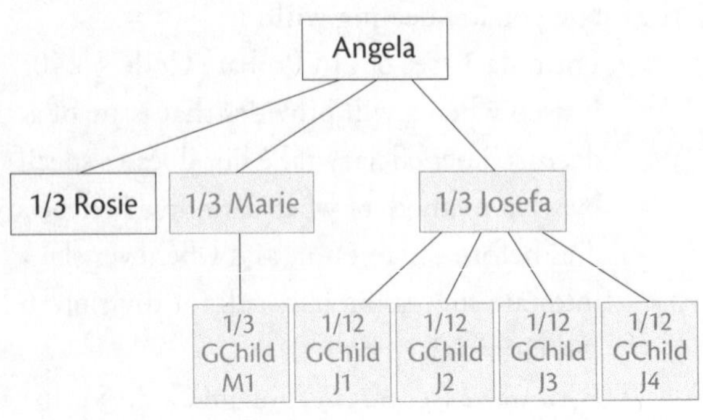

Here is a final example that demonstrates all these principles:

EXAMPLE 6: Grandpa dies without a will and leaves a childless son (Harry) and three children of a deceased daughter (Rhoda). In this situation, the estate is first divided at his children's level into two shares: one for the decedent's surviving son Harry and the other for the deceased daughter Rhoda. Harry would get half, and the three grandchildren would share the half that their mother would have had, or one-sixth each.

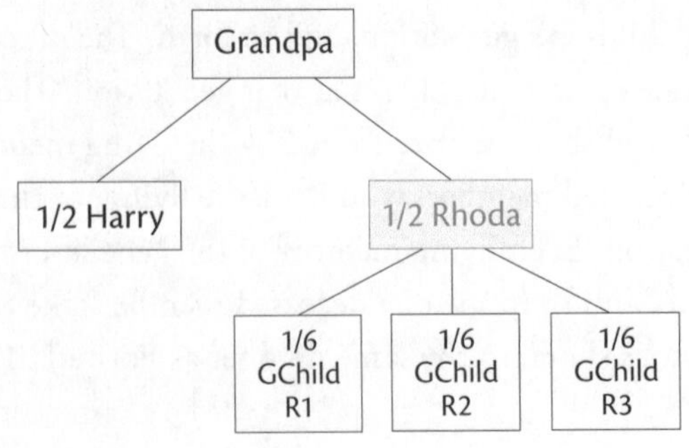

EXAMPLE 7: Suppose, however, Harry also died before Grandpa and Harry was survived by a child. In this case, the four grandchildren would each get one-fourth. Why? Because Grandpa's property is divided first at the grandchildren's level (being the generation closest to the decedent with a living member) instead of the children's level. Because the grandchildren are all in the same generation and are all living, they share equally.

EXAMPLE 8: If any of the grandchildren had also died and left surviving children (great-grandchildren of the decedent), then the deceased grandchildren's children would share the one-fourth their parent would have received.

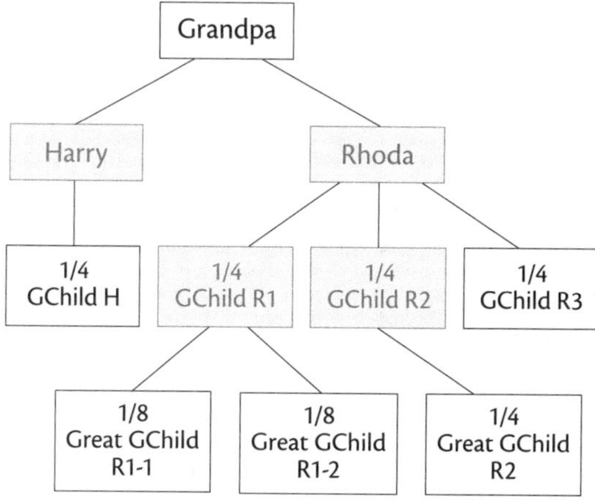

Formula 2

Formula 2 is used only if a will expressly directs that inheritance be "by right of representation," "by representation," "per stirpes," or by Probate Code Section 246. Under this system, a generation that has no living members is not ignored; the estate is always divided first at the children's generation. This can make the distribution different than it would be under Formula 1.

For example, review the right of representation chart in Example 8, above. Under Formula 1, the estate is divided first at the closest generation with living members—here, the decedent's grandchildren. The two living grandchildren take one-fourth, and each of the deceased grandchildren's shares are split among the grandchildren's children (the decedent's great-grandchildren).

If, however, Grandpa had left a will leaving his estate to his children or their issue by right of representation, the situation would be analyzed under Formula 2. The estate would be divided first at the children's level. Thus the estate would be divided in half, even though neither Harry nor Rhoda survived Grandpa. Harry's child would take Harry's one-half share. Rhoda's surviving child would take one-third of Rhoda's share (one-sixth), and the great-grandchildren would split their parent's one-sixth share.

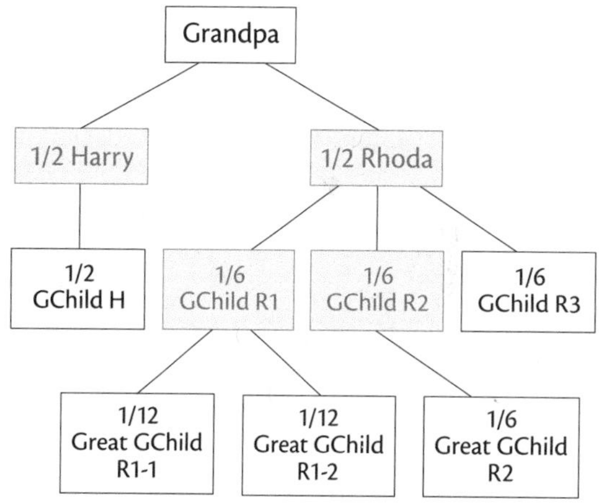

Formula 3

Formula 3 is used only if a will directs that inheritance be "per capita at each generation" or pursuant to Probate Code Section 247. Under this formula, the number of shares equals the number of living members of the nearest generation, plus the number of deceased members of that generation who have living issue. Each living member of the nearest generation receives one share, and then the remaining shares are combined and divided among the living issue of deceased members. This distribution scheme results in descendants at the same generation receiving equal amounts. This is similar to Formula 1 for the first generation receiving a share, but following generations may lead to different results.

Compare Formula 3 with Formula 1 using Example 8. Under Formula 1, the great-grandchildren's shares depend on how many siblings they have. Under Formula 3, the great-grandchildren would receive equal amounts, one sixth of the estate.

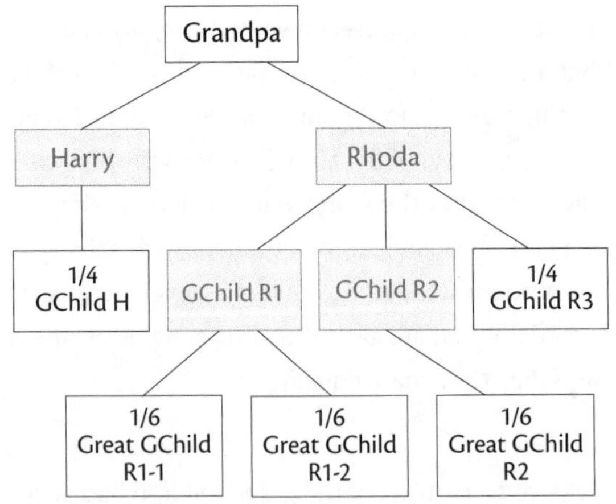

CHAPTER

4

What Is the Decedent's Estate?

To settle an estate, you must identify the decedent's property. Everything the decedent owned—from real estate, bank accounts, securities, insurance, and antiques, to furniture, art, coin collections, copyrights, cars, campers, computers, collies, and canoes—collectively makes up the estate. We specifically instruct you on how to prepare an inventory of whatever the decedent owned in the next chapter. This chapter introduces you to basic property law concepts to make sense of this inventory.

You will need to answer the following questions with respect to each item of the decedent's property:

- Is it real property (real estate) or personal property?
- How did the decedent hold title to the property —individually or jointly with someone else (for example, community property, joint tenancy, or tenancy in common)?

The answers to these questions will have a direct bearing on a few important points—the interest the decedent had in the property, who is entitled to the property, and how to transfer it to its new owner(s). Settling most estates requires at least a passing knowledge of information in this chapter. We do our best to separate simple property ownership situations from those that are more complex. You may find that if your estate qualifies for the former category, you can safely leave this chapter and go on to Chapter 5 without digesting the whole thing.

TIP

Debts owed on property. For now, don't worry about whether the decedent owed money on a particular piece of property. Once ownership rules are firmly established, you can subtract debts as part of valuing the property. (See Chapter 5.)

Real Property

"Real property" is land and things permanently affixed to land, such as houses, trees, and growing crops. If a mobile home or other structure is permanently attached to the land, it is treated as part of the real property, the same as a house. However, if the mobile home is registered with the Department of Motor Vehicles or the Department of Housing and Community Development and can be taken from place to place, it is personal property. Real property also includes condominiums, leasehold interests in most cooperatives, and underground utility installations. (Some life interests in condominiums and co-ops that do not survive the decedent are not considered real property.) A real estate lease with an unexpired term of ten years or longer, or a lease together with an option to purchase, or an oil or gas leasehold interest, is also treated as real property; any other leases are considered personal property. (Prob. Code § 10203.)

Real property is transferred to its new owners following the laws and procedures of the state in which it is located. This book covers only California real estate. To transfer real property located outside of California, you will need to find self-help information or a lawyer in that state. If the property was owned in joint tenancy with right of survivorship, you may be able to handle it yourself with some guidance. If formal probate is required on the out-of-state property, you will probably need a lawyer.

Real property is transferred from one person to another by a document. When both parties are living, this is usually done with a deed. Various kinds of deeds are used for this purpose, some of which you may have discovered among the decedent's papers. Most deeds are clearly labeled, but just in case you aren't sure whether a particular document is a deed, here are the basic elements. A deed must contain the name of the transferee (purchaser or person receiving title to the property), name of the transferor (seller or person conveying title to the property), a legal description of the property, a granting clause that says, "I hereby grant to ..." (sometimes the words "transfer" or "convey" are used), and the signature(s) of the transferor(s). Below are some of the more common deeds and what they are used for.

Grant Deed

This is the most commonly used deed in California. The grantor (seller) conveys the property, and the grantee (buyer) receives it. The grantor in a grant deed makes certain implied guarantees that the grantor owns the property and has not previously conveyed, mortgaged, or otherwise encumbered the property except as stated in the deed. A sample grant deed is shown below.

Grant Deed

RECORDING REQUESTED BY:
Thomas B. Buyer and Helen A. Buyer

AND WHEN RECORDED MAIL TO:
Name: Thomas and Helen Buyer
Address: 35 Overview Lane
City & State: San Francisco, CA
Zip: 91378

ASSESSOR'S PARCEL NO. 0028-004 SPACE ABOVE THIS LINE FOR RECORDER'S USE

GRANT DEED

The undersigned Grantor(s) declare(s) under penalty of perjury that the following is true and correct:

Documentary transfer tax is $ $70.65

☐ Computed on full value of property conveyed, or
☒ Computed on full value less value of liens and encumbrances remaining at time of sale.
☐ Unincorporated area: ☒ City of San Francisco , and

FOR A VALUABLE CONSIDERATION, receipt of which is hereby acknowledged,
George S. Seller and Mary M. Seller, husband and wife
hereby GRANT(S) to
Thomas B. Buyer and Helen A. Buyer, his husband and wife
the following described real property in the City of San Francisco , County of San Francisco State of California:
Lot 4 in Block 28, as designated on the map entitled "Twin Peaks Tract, City and County of San Francisco, State of California," filed in the Office of the Recorder of the City and County of San Francisco, State of California, on August 5, 1909 in Volume 3 of Maps, at page 8.

Dated: June 26, 1986

George S. Seller
Mary M. Seller

ACKNOWLEDGMENT

State of California)
County of San Francisco)

On June 26, 1986, before me, Nancy Notary, personally appeared George S. Seller and Mary M. Seller, who proved to me on the basis of satisfactory evidence to be the person(s) whose name(s) is/are subscribed to the within instrument and acknowledged to me that he/she/they executed the same in his/her/their authorized capacity(ies), and that by his/her/their signature(s) on the instrument the person(s), or entity upon behalf of which the person(s) acted, executed the instrument.

I certify under PENALTY OF PERJURY under the laws of the State of California that the foregoing paragraph is true and correct.

WITNESS my hand and official seal.

Signature *Nancy Notary* (SEAL)

Title Order No. **Escrow, Loan, or Attorney File No.**

MAIL TAX STATEMENTS TO PARTY SHOWN ON FOLLOWING LINE; IF NO PARTY SHOWN, MAIL AS DIRECTED ABOVE

NAME STREET ADDRESS CITY & STATE

GRANT DEED

Quitclaim Deed

This type of deed is used when the transferor makes no warranties about title, saying in effect that whatever the transferor has, the transferor is conveying. Assuming the transferor owns the property, this type of deed is just as effective to transfer ownership as is a grant deed. A sample quitclaim deed is shown in Chapter 12.

Joint Tenancy Deed

Joint tenancy is one way two or more people may own property. A "joint tenancy deed" is merely any deed that is used to convey property to two or more people as joint tenants with survivorship rights. Any grant deed or quitclaim deed can be a joint tenancy deed if it identifies the transferors (people who receive the property) specifically as joint tenants. A sample joint tenancy grant deed is shown above.

Transfer on Death Deed

Beginning January 1, 2016, owners of California property can use a "transfer on death" deed to pass their property to beneficiaries without the need for probate. The transferor completes the deed and maintains ownership and the ability to revoke the deed during life. Then at death, the property passes to the beneficiary or beneficiaries named in the deed. A sample transfer on death deed is shown below.

Deed of Trust

This type of deed is commonly used when real property is purchased and the buyer borrows part of the purchase price from a third party such as a bank or credit union. In some states this document is called a "mortgage," but "deed of trust" is the term usually used in California. When a deed of trust is given, it is normally used with a grant deed or quitclaim deed as part of a single transaction.

It works like this. A grant deed is executed by the seller to convey title to the purchaser, who becomes the owner. If the purchaser needs additional money for the purchase price, the purchaser borrows it and executes a promissory note in favor of the lender. This involves the use of a second deed, in this case a deed of trust—sometimes called a trust deed. The deed of trust, signed by the purchaser, is used to make the real estate security for money borrowed by the owner/purchaser from the bank or other lender. The trust deed is actually transferred to a third-party (neutral) trustee to hold "in trust" until the lender is paid off. The trustee is normally a title insurance company. The deed of trust becomes an encumbrance on the real property. Deeds of trust and mortgages are recorded by their owner (usually, but not always, a financial institution) at the county recorder's office where the property is located, so they will have priority over any liens on the real property that may be recorded afterwards. When the buyer has paid in full, the trustee reconveys the title using a deed of reconveyance. There may be multiple deeds of trust and deeds of reconveyance recorded on a property, particularly when refinancing occurs or a loan is transferred to another owner.

When someone dies and leaves real property subject to a mortgage or encumbrance, the real property passes to the new owner along with the encumbrance, unless the decedent's will provides otherwise. The new owner of the property then becomes responsible for making the payment on the mortgage, taxes, and so on. After the property is officially transferred, the new owner customarily notifies the person or entity collecting the mortgage payments of the name and address of the new owner. No notice to the trustee named on the deed of trust is necessary.

> **EXAMPLE:** Bruce and June want to purchase a house from Sol for $470,000, but have only $70,000 in cash for the down payment. Bruce and June borrow the balance of the purchase price from a bank that will accept the property as security for payment of the loan.
>
> Sol executes a grant deed transferring title to the residence to Bruce and June. At the same time, Bruce and June execute a promissory note payable to the bank and execute a deed of trust transferring the residence to a trustee to hold as security for the loan. Bruce and June then take the $400,000 they have borrowed, plus the $70,000 cash they already had, and give it to Sol.
>
> Bruce and June remain the owners of the property, subject to repayment of the $400,000 loan owed to the bank, which is an encumbrance against the property. In legal jargon, Bruce and June are known as trustors. The third party who holds the property subject to the deed of trust is the trustee, and the financial institution that lends the money is the beneficiary.

Transfer on Death Deed

RECORDING REQUESTED BY: **Sharon Senior** WHEN RECORDED MAIL TO: **Sharon Senior** **123 Mountain Road** **Truckee, CA 96161**	

ASSESSOR'S PARCEL NO. **12-345-67** SPACE ABOVE THIS LINE FOR RECORDER'S USE

SIMPLE TRANSFER ON DEATH (TOD) DEED
(California Probate Code Section 5642)

This document is exempt from documentary transfer tax under Rev. & Tax. Code Section 11930.
This document is exempt from preliminary change of ownership report under Rev. & Tax. Code Section 480.3.

IMPORTANT NOTICE: THIS DEED MUST BE RECORDED ON OR BEFORE 60 DAYS AFTER THE DATE IT IS SIGNED AND NOTARIZED.

Use this deed to transfer the residential property described below directly to your named beneficiaries when you die. YOU SHOULD CAREFULLY READ ALL OF THE INFORMATION ON THE OTHER PAGES OF THIS FORM. You may wish to consult an attorney before using this deed. It may have results that you do not want. Provide only the information asked for in the form. DO NOT INSERT ANY OTHER INFORMATION OR INSTRUCTIONS. This form MUST be RECORDED on or before 60 days after the date it is signed and notarized or it will not be effective.

PROPERTY DESCRIPTION

Print the legal description of the residential property affected by this deed:

LOT 7, AS SHOWN ON THE OFFICIAL MAP OF PINE FOREST AT TRUCKEE, PHASE 1, FINAL MAP NO. 01-092, RECORDED JULY 7, 1960 IN BOOK 4 OF SUBDIVISIONS AT PAGE 10.

BENEFICIARY(IES)

Print the FULL NAME(S) of the person(s) who will receive the property on your death (DO NOT use general terms like "my children") and state the relationship that each named person has to you (spouse, son, daughter, friend, etc.):

FRED M. FREEMAN, brother

TRANSFER ON DEATH

I transfer all of my interest in the described property to the named beneficiary(ies) on my death. I may revoke this deed. When recorded, this deed revokes any TOD deed that I made before signing this deed.

Sign and print your name below your printed name (your name should exactly match the name shown on your title documents):

SHARON SENIOR (name of owner)

Signature: /s/ Sharon Senior Date: **October 2, 2017**

NOTE: This deed transfers only MY ownership share of the property. The deed does NOT transfer the share of any co-owner of the property. Any co-owner who wants to name a TOD beneficiary must execute and RECORD a SEPARATE deed.

[Attached: Notary's Acknowledgment]

Joint Tenancy Grant Deed

RECORDING REQUESTED BY:
Robert Johnson and Mary Doe

AND WHEN RECORDED MAIL TO:
Name: Robert Johnson and Mary Doe
Address: 567 First Street
City & State: Los Angeles, CA
Zip: 90017

SPACE ABOVE THIS LINE FOR RECORDER'S USE

ASSESSOR'S PARCEL NO. 2345 092 086

JOINT TENANCY GRANT DEED

The undersigned Grantor(s) declare(s) under penalty of perjury that the following is true and correct:

Documentary transfer tax is $ $70.40

☒ Computed on full value of property conveyed, or
☐ Computed on full value less value of liens and encumbrances remaining at time of sale.
☐ Unincorporated area: ☒ City of Los Angeles, and

FOR A VALUABLE CONSIDERATION, receipt of which is hereby acknowledged,
JOHN SMITH and MARY SMITH
hereby GRANT(S) to
ROBERT JOHNSON and MARY DOE, as joint tenants
the following described real property in the City of Los Angeles, County of Los Angeles State of California:

Lot 101 in Tract 26834, as per map recorded in Book 691, Pages 3 to 8 of Maps, in the office of the County Recorder of said county.

Dated: June 20, 1995

John Smith
Mary Smith

ACKNOWLEDGMENT

State of California)
County of Los Angeles)

On June 20, 1995, before me, Nancy Notary, personally appeared John Smith and Mary Smith, who proved to me on the basis of satisfactory evidence to be the person(s) whose name(s) is/are subscribed to the within instrument and acknowledged to me that he/she/they executed the same in his/her/their authorized capacity(ies), and that by his/her/their signature(s) on the instrument the person(s), or entity upon behalf of which the person(s) acted, executed the instrument.

I certify under PENALTY OF PERJURY under the laws of the State of California that the foregoing paragraph is true and correct.

WITNESS my hand and official seal.

Signature *Nancy Notary* (SEAL)

Title Order No. **Escrow, Loan, or Attorney File No.**

MAIL TAX STATEMENTS TO PARTY SHOWN ON FOLLOWING LINE; IF NO PARTY SHOWN, MAIL AS DIRECTED ABOVE

NAME STREET ADDRESS CITY & STATE

JOINT TENANCY GRANT DEED

TIP

Trust transfer deeds. A "trust transfer deed" transfers a property owner's interest in a property to a trust. Property in a trust does not have to go through probate when the owner dies. Instead, the successor trustee transfers the property to trust beneficiaries following trust administration procedures. See Chapter 12.

Personal Property

All property that is not real property is "personal property." Personal property is divided into two broad categories, tangible and intangible.

Tangible Personal Property

Tangible personal property includes items you can touch, such as books, automobiles, boats, animals, clothing, household furniture, farm equipment, jewelry, machinery, motor homes, firearms, tools, antiques, and actual cash like coins or dollar bills. Tangible personal property is generally transferred following the procedures of the state in which it is located. However, in practice, many types of tangible personal property (for example, cars registered in California, jewelry, cash, etc.) are highly portable and often find their way back to the state of a person's residence at death. If this occurs in a small or medium-sized estate, there is, in practice, normally no objection to transferring the property using the small estate procedures discussed in Chapter 11.

Intangible Personal Property

Intangible personal property is abstract. It is a right to be paid money or to legally exercise some type of power (for example, stopping others from using your patented invention). It is usually represented by a paper or document that states the nature of the rights associated with it. Some examples are promissory notes, bank account statements, court judgments giving a right to receive money, mortgages, deeds of trust establishing an interest in property as security for a debt, stock or bond certificates giving an ownership interest in a corporation, securities held in book-entry form with a brokerage firm, mutual fund certificates, money market fund certificates, copyrights, patents, trademarks, and cryptocurrency. Other examples of intangible personal property include contracts giving the right to future income, as would be the case with a publishing contract granting a royalty share of income derived from the sale of a book, or a film contract providing a share of the gross receipts of a movie.

Intangible personal property is transferred under the laws and procedures of the state in which its owner resides. In other words, if a California resident dies owning stocks and bonds located in a New York safe-deposit box, has $50,000 in an Illinois bank, and has $25,000 in a money market fund headquartered in Boston, ownership of all this property (no matter where the decedent lived when it was purchased) can be transferred in California using the instructions in this book.

RELATED TOPIC

More information for couples. We discuss intangible personal property acquired by California couples before they moved to California at the end of this chapter.

What Establishes Ownership of Property?

Most valuable assets have a title document that shows who owns the property (establishes title). For instance, the owner of a savings account is shown on the paperwork establishing the account and on the account statements. Stock certificates establish title to the ownership of shares in a corporation. "Pink slips" serve as title documents for motor vehicles, motor homes, and boats. Some kinds of intangible personal property, like copyrights and patents, have documents issued by the federal government that to some extent act like certificates of title. If a decedent had executed a contract establishing a right to receive periodic payments in exchange for property or services, the contract itself shows ownership of the future income.

Title to real property, including condominiums and cooperatives, must always be in writing. It is usually represented by a deed containing a legal description of the property.

Some kinds of personal property don't have formal title slips. Nevertheless, there is usually little doubt who owns them. For instance, you can normally assume things such as clothing, books, furniture, and personal effects belonged to the decedent if they are in the decedent's possession at death and if no one steps forward to claim them.

Sometimes disputes arise as to whether the decedent made gifts prior to death. Valuable objects, such as jewelry, furs, or works of art don't come with a title document in the formal sense, but their purchase is normally accompanied by a receipt or bill of sale, which accomplishes a similar purpose. If there is no title document or bill of sale, questions of ownership can sometimes be resolved by reference to canceled checks or by contacting the seller.

You will generally find it easy to figure out what property the decedent at least claimed to own by checking in all the obvious places: Desk drawers, safe-deposit boxes, file cabinets, computer files, and the like. Watch the mail to see what bank and brokerage statements come in. Check tax returns to see sources of interest and dividend income, which may direct you to other assets. Check computer files and emails to look for information from bank or other accounts that may not mail paper statements. Also, the decedent may have digital assets, such as electronic files, digital images, e-commerce accounts, or social media accounts, some of which may have value. (See "Manage Digital Assets" in Chapter 2.)

If, as part of doing this, you find an unfamiliar document and don't know what it means, consult an expert to be sure you're not overlooking any assets or liabilities.

How Was the Decedent's Property Owned?

Property, both real and personal, may be owned either separately (the decedent owned it all) or concurrently with other persons.

The title document usually indicates who owns the property. Sometimes you need to inquire further. Bank account statements, for example, may not have all owners listed or may abbreviate ownership. You should confirm with the financial institution exactly how title is held. If a title document indicates terms such as trustee, LLC, Inc., or partnership, the underlying ownership likely requires further investigation.

Separate Property Ownership

Separate ownership simply means ownership by one person. The sole owner alone enjoys the benefits of the property, and also has responsibilities for its burdens, such as mortgages or taxes. He may dispose of his separate property by will to anyone he chooses, and if he dies without a will, the separate property goes to his heirs under intestate succession laws. All property owned by unmarried people and people not in a registered domestic partnership is separate property, except for property owned in joint tenancy (discussed below).

A married person can also own separate property. For example, property is presumed to remain separate property if the person acquired it before marriage or received it by gift or inheritance. Also, when a married couple separates, the earnings and accumulations of each spouse are separate property as of the date of permanent separation. Finally, even during marriage, the earnings of a spouse can be separate property if a written contract provides for this result and, in fact, the earner keeps the property separate. These rules for separate and community property apply to California registered domestic partners as well.

Concurrent Ownership

Concurrent ownership means ownership by two or more people at the same time. Some estates will contain assets held concurrently, but others will not. For example, if a single decedent held all of her assets in her individual name alone, then her estate will not contain assets with concurrent ownership and the types of ownership described in this section would not apply.

In California, concurrent ownership normally takes one of the following legal classifications:

- tenancy in common
- joint tenancy
- community property
- community property with right of survivorship
- partnership interests, or
- life tenancy (or life estate).

We discuss each of these just below. However, note that the information on community property ownership applies only to decedents who were married or in a registered domestic partnership at the time of death; therefore, if you are settling the estate of a single person, you can skip the discussion of community property. You also do not need to focus as much about whether or not property is community property if the decedent willed all of his property to his surviving spouse or domestic partner. Since the surviving spouse or partner gets it all anyway in this circumstance, it's usually not necessary to understand technical rules as to who owned what portion. We discuss community property ownership last because it requires more extended coverage, not because it is less important.

Tenancy in Common

This occurs when two or more people own an undivided interest in property, without an automatic right to inherit the property from each other if one owner dies. An undivided interest means a tenant in common does not own a particular separate portion of the property but rather a fractional share of the whole property. If you own a piece of land as a tenant in common with your sister, absent transfer documents stating otherwise, you each own an undivided one-half interest in the whole property. However, cotenants can own unequal shares in a property if a written contract or transfer document so provides. Thus, one cotenant may own one-tenth, another three-tenths, and a third cotenant may own the remaining six-tenths under the terms of a written agreement.

A tenancy in common is created when an ownership document states, for example, "Jill Evers and Finley Fox as Tenants in Common." In addition, whenever an ownership document does not specify that multiple owners acquired the property in joint tenancy or as community property or in a partnership, the owners hold the property as tenants in common. If any of the tenants in common dies, that person's interest is not necessarily acquired by the remaining tenants in common, but instead goes to the beneficiaries named in the deceased person's will or to the heirs of the decedent if there is no will.

Joint Tenancy

For property to be held in joint tenancy, it must be expressly stated in the deed or ownership document that the owners own it as "joint tenants" or "joint tenants with right of survivorship." The abbreviations "JTRS" or "WROS" are sometimes used for joint tenancy bank accounts. In addition, registration of a motor vehicle in the names of two people joined by "or" is treated as joint tenancy, as are certain bank accounts held in this way. U.S. savings bonds held in co-ownership form also have the same legal effect as if the words "joint tenancy" were used.

Owning property in joint tenancy means if one of the joint tenants dies, that person's interest immediately becomes the property of the remaining joint tenant(s) by operation of law. A will has no effect on joint tenancy property, nor do the laws of intestate succession have any control over who gets the property. People who own property as joint tenants always own an undivided equal interest, and all have the same rights to the use of the whole property.

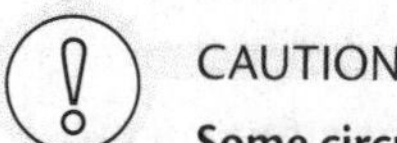

CAUTION

Some circumstances can override the survivorship of joint tenancy. Even if title shows an asset held in joint tenancy, the right of survivorship may not apply. This most commonly occurs if married joint tenants later divorce or if registered domestic partners end the partnership. Or, less commonly, if a joint tenant transferred his interest to another person. In these situations, the concurrent ownership becomes tenancy in common.

Usually, only people with a very close personal or family relationship to each other hold property this way, such as spouses, parent and child, an unmarried couple, or siblings. It isn't normally practical for others, such as business associates, to be joint tenants, because the families or other chosen beneficiaries of a joint tenant would inherit nothing in such a situation.

More than two people may be joint tenants, but this is not common. If there are three or more joint tenants and one dies, the others equally acquire the decedent's interest and still remain joint tenants.

Although joint tenancy property need not go through a formal probate proceeding, several formalities are necessary to clear the joint tenancy title to the property so that it appears in the name of the surviving tenant. We discuss how to do this in Chapter 10.

SEE AN EXPERT

Potential conflicts between joint tenancy and community property. If a decedent owned joint tenancy assets with someone other than the spouse without the other spouse's agreement, problems could arise. The surviving spouse may wish to claim a one-half community property interest in the property, rather than allow the entire property to pass to the surviving joint tenant. This concern applies equally to registered domestic partners. In this situation, get legal advice.

Sometimes a person who owns real property will execute a deed transferring title to himself or herself and another person as joint tenants. That way, when the original owner dies, the property will be transferred to the surviving joint tenant with no need for probate. When this happens, the original owner has actually made a gift of one-half of the property to the other joint tenant. Gift tax consequences may result. See Chapter 7.

Life Tenancy (Life Estate)

A life tenancy (sometimes called "life estate") is not technically co-ownership. Rather, it is ownership of property for the period of a lifetime only. Life tenancies are sometimes created to allow a person (often a spouse) to use property for the rest of the person's life and then to pass the property to another person (such as children) without needing probate proceedings. Or, a life estate can be retained by a living person to avoid probate at death.

EXAMPLE: Maxine is an elderly widow who owns a home, which she wishes to go to her son Steve upon her death. Maxine may deed the property to Steve during her lifetime, with the deed saying that "Grantor (Maxine) reserves to herself a life estate in said property." This will transfer the ownership to Steve, but subject to Maxine's life estate. It will accomplish Maxine's objective of avoiding probate of the home upon her death because she will die without ownership of the property. Her life estate will terminate at the moment of death, and the home will be owned by Steve.

Partnerships

Partnerships are another form of co-ownership. When a partner dies, the transfer of partnership property depends on the terms of the partnership agreement—and it can be quite complicated. If it looks like you're dealing with property held in partnership, get advice from an attorney.

Community Property

Married people and registered domestic partners present another subclassification as far as the concurrent ownership of property is concerned. California has community property laws that apply to property acquired during marriage or domestic partnership. At their most basic, these laws give spouses and domestic partners equal interest in property—including wages and other earned income and the property acquired with this income—they accumulate during the marriage or partnership. In other words, each spouse or domestic partner owns a one-half interest in the community property.

Any property owned before the marriage or partnership is not community property. Rather, it is the separate property of the owner. The same is true if either spouse or partner inherits or is given property during the marriage— such property remains the separate property of the person who receives it. Earnings from separate property are also separate property. Thus, if a spouse or partner acquired an apartment house prior to marriage, or inherited it or received it as a gift during the marriage or partnership, the rents from it are also usually separate property.

Certain events, however, can alter the character of property owned by spouses or partners. They can agree to change (transmute) community property into separate property, or vice versa through a written agreement signed by the person giving up interest in property. Or, they may combine their separate property and community property to such an extent that it all becomes community property. And commonly an asset (such as a family business, house, or pension) will be part community property and part separate property.

Accurately drawing the line between community property and non-community property can be fraught with complications. Before you struggle through the rest of this rather intricate material, consider whether you really need to know if the decedent owned any community property. For instance, do any of the following situations apply to your estate?

- Was the decedent neither married nor in a registered domestic partnership at the time of death? If so, he did not own any community property.
- If the decedent was married or a domestic partner, did he leave a will that gives his entire estate to his surviving spouse or partner? In this case, it is not as important to know whether the property is community or separate, since it all goes to the survivor anyway. However, you may want to clearly identify the community property if the estate might be large enough to require a federal estate tax return. This is not common. (See Chapter 7.) You may also want to account for community property if you need a court order to transfer it to the surviving spouse or partner. (See Chapter 15.)

The main reasons you will probably want to know if the decedent owned any community property include:

- If a person dies without a will (intestate), the decedent's one-half of the community property goes to the surviving spouse or partner.
- If a decedent uses a will or other estate planning device to try to transfer more than his one-half of the community property to someone other than his spouse or partner, that spouse or partner can object and claim one-half.
- If a decedent's will has different beneficiaries for separate property and community property.

Community Property With Right of Survivorship

If spouses or registered domestic partners held title to property as "community property with right of survivorship," the survivor inherits the deceased person's half-interest automatically, without probate. The property must be clearly identified on the transfer document (a real estate deed, for example) as community property with the right of survivorship. (Civ. Code § 682.1.) As with joint tenancy, divorce or termination of a domestic partnership ends the survivorship rights of the former spouse or partner.

How to Determine Whether Property Is Community or Separate

The chart below shows a step-by-step approach to determining whether any given property item is community property or separate property. Review it first for a general understanding of community property principles. Later on, when you are filling out your Schedule of Assets in Chapter 5, you will want to return and use this chart to analyze each piece of property the decedent left, unless you can conclude that all property fits into the same basic category, in which case your task will be very easy.

Many, many court cases revolve around whether assets are community property or separate property. This chart provides general guidelines. You will need specific legal advice if the result is not clear, unique facts exist, or there is a dispute.

How to Determine Whether Property Is Community or Separate

Here is a step-by-step approach to determining whether any given property item is community property or separate property.

Read it first for a general understanding of community property principles. Later on, when you are filling out your Schedule of Assets in Chapter 5, you will want to return and use this information. Follow this analysis for each asset the decedent left, unless you can conclude that it all fits into the same basic category, in which case your task will be very easy.

Many, many court cases revolve around whether assets are community property or separate property. This chart provides general guidelines. You will need specific legal advice if the result is not clear, unique facts exist, or there is a dispute.

Step 1: Is there an ownership document (deed, certificate of title, pink slip, or bank account statement) that says something like "John and Mary Doe, husband and wife," or "Andrew Ames and James Jackson, domestic partners, as community property," or "Mr. and Mrs. John Doe"? If so, the property is presumed to be community property. Go to Step 10. If not, go to Step 2.

Step 2: Does the title indicate that the decedent held the property "as separate property"? If so, the property is presumed to be separate property. Go to Step 12.

Step 3: Was the property acquired during the marriage or partnership (after the wedding or registration but prior to a permanent dissolution or termination)? If so, go to Step 4. If not, go to Step 8.

Step 4: Does the property consist of earnings (including employment fringe benefits such as insurance, pension plans, or stock options) of either spouse or partner during the marriage or partnership, gifts or inheritances to the couple jointly or property purchased with such earnings, gifts, or inheritances? If so, go to Step 10. If not, go to Step 5.

Step 5: Was the property acquired during the marriage or partnership through a gift given to just one person as an individual? If not, go to Step 6. If yes, go to Step 8.

Strictly speaking, a gift is a transfer of property without anything being paid by the person receiving it. Commonly, gifts made during marriage or partnership by one spouse or partner to the other—such as jewelry or other personal articles—are considered the separate property of the person who receives them unless the spouses or partners agree differently.

Step 6: Was the property acquired during the marriage or partnership by an inheritance of one of the spouses or partners as an individual? If not, go to Step 7. If yes, go to Step 8.

Step 7: Was the property acquired by one spouse or partner as an award in a personal injury action from an injury that occurred during the marriage or partnership? If not, go to Step 10. If yes, go to Step 8.

Step 8: Did the spouse or domestic partner who owned the property agree orally or in writing prior to January 1, 1985 to put it into community property form? (See "Actions That Change the Character of Property," below.) If so, go to Step 13. If not, go to Step 9.

Step 9: Did the spouse or partner who owned the property agree in writing after January 1, 1985 to put it into community property form? (See "Actions That Change the Character of Property," below.) If so, go to Step 13. If not, go to Step 12.

How to Determine Whether Property Is Community or Separate (continued)

Step 10: Did both spouses enter into an oral or written agreement prior to January 1, 1985 that the property be the separate property of one of them? (See "Actions That Change the Character of Property," below.) If so, go to Step 12. If not, go to Step 11.

Step 11: Did both spouses or partners agree in writing after January 1, 1985 that the property be the separate property of one of them? (See "Actions That Change the Character of Property," below.) If so, go to Step 12. If not, go to Step 13.

Step 12: Was separate property mixed with community property (lawyers call this "commingling") so that its separate nature can no longer be traced? If so, go to Step 14. If not, go to Step 15.

The most common example of commingling is when spouses or partners deposit both separate and community property in a joint bank account and make withdrawals over the years that make it impossible to characterize the funds left in the account. (See "Actions That Change the Character of Property," below.)

Step 13: Is the property a mix of community property and separate property such as a house, a contract for future payments, a family business, or a pension that was only partially earned during the marriage? (See "Property That Is a Mixture of Community and Separate Property," below.) If so, you might wish to obtain help from a lawyer or accountant in characterizing which portion of this asset is community property and which is separate property. If not, go to Step 14.

Step 14: The property should be treated as community property, which means the decedent owned only one-half of it.

Step 15: The property should be treated as separate property, owned by whichever spouse or partner acquired, inherited, or was given the property as separate property.

Actions That Change the Character of Property

In the above step-by-step analysis, we indicated that certain acts by spouses or partners could change the nature of property from community to separate and vice versa. Here we take a closer look at how this can occur.

The general rule is that the community or separate nature of property is determined by its source. However, you should understand that no matter what its source, the community or separate nature of property can be changed by actions of the spouses or partners. This is more likely to result in separate property becoming community property than the reverse, but both types of changes occur fairly frequently. Let's look at some common examples.

Commingling Assets

In general, property can change its physical form without changing its community or separate character. For instance, if one spouse uses premarriage money kept in a separate account (separate property) to buy stocks, sells the stocks, and uses the proceeds (and no other funds) to buy a house, then the house is that spouse's separate property.

Many couples, however, change the separate or community nature of their property without realizing it. One common example of this phenomenon is called "commingling." The basic commingling rule, subject to a number of technical subtleties that are beyond the scope of this book, is that if separate property assets are mixed together (commingled) with community funds so that it is impossible to trace them to their source, the formerly separate property becomes community property. If parties to an account are married or in a registered domestic partnership, contributions to the account are presumed to be community property. (Prob. Code § 5305.)

EXAMPLE: A husband and wife open a savings account during the marriage in which they deposit money they have earned during their marriage. Assume the wife receives an inheritance of $20,000, which is separate property, and deposits it into the joint account. If no withdrawals are made from the account, she can trace her $20,000 to her inheritance. However, if a number of deposits and withdrawals are made by the parties over the years and the balance dips below $20,000, she will no longer be able to trace her money and it will be treated as having been given to the community.

SEE AN EXPERT

Tracing commingled property. This subject is so complicated and confusing that it is the subject of endless litigation. If you find yourself dealing with a commingling problem, get advice from a family law attorney.

Agreements Between Spouses or Partners

The separate property of either spouse or domestic partner may be "transmuted" (changed) into community property, and community property may be transmuted into separate property of a spouse or partner by an agreement between them. It used to be that this could be accomplished through an oral agreement. For example, one spouse could have indicated to the other that the property would be community rather than separate property. Or both could have simply agreed that a community asset would become the separate property of one. However, since January 1, 1985, a change in the nature of property must be made in writing, signed by the person whose property is adversely affected. This law, however, does not apply to property whose character was changed by oral agreement prior to 1985.

Sometimes a spouse or partner may also change the character of property owned by one of them by making a gift of it to the other. For example, when a single person who owns a house gets married or enters a domestic partnership, the house is not automatically converted into community property by that fact. The house remains the separate property of the owner. However, if the owner makes a deed after marriage or registration that puts the house in the names of both spouses or partners, thereby making a gift of it, it is converted into community property.

Property That Is a Mixture of Community and Separate Property

Sometimes when property is received over a period of time and a marriage or divorce—or registration and termination of a domestic partnership—takes place during that time, it can be difficult to determine how much of the property is community property and how much is separate. Let's look at some examples of this sort of situation.

Contract Rights

It is not uncommon for high-earning executives and entertainers to receive compensation payable over a period of several years. If the right to collect the money arises—that is, if the work is done—before the marriage or partnership registration date, then any money received under such a contract is separate property, even though the payments are made during the marriage or partnership. However, if the work isn't done until after the marriage or registration, as might be the case when a sports figure or entertainer gets a large up-front payment for work to be done over several years, the money would be community property to the extent that the work needed to earn the money was performed after the marriage or partnership registration date. In other words, the test of whether the property is community normally depends on the time when the right to payment arises and not on the time when payment is actually made.

In another situation, a writer could do substantial work on, or even complete, a book during a marriage or partnership, and if the union is later dissolved, the right to future royalties would be split equally between the spouses or partners as community property, even though payment would be made after the dissolution.

SEE AN EXPERT

Get help if you need it. Sometimes it becomes extremely difficult to determine what is and isn't community property, so much so that thousands of court cases are litigated over this question every year. If any of these complications apply to your situation, see a lawyer:

- You have difficulty categorizing separate or community property.
- There is disagreement between a surviving spouse or partner and other beneficiaries or heirs.
- At the time of death, the spouses or partners were in the process of legally ending their relationship. Or the spouses or partners were living separately with the intent to end their relationship.
- The property in question was acquired by a married woman prior to 1975.

Insurance Proceeds

The extent to which proceeds from life insurance on a spouse or partner are treated as community property depends on the type of insurance and what proportion of the premiums paid for such insurance came from community funds, not necessarily on who is named as the beneficiary. In other words, the surviving spouse's or partner's community property interest in the insurance proceeds must be recognized regardless of who is named as beneficiary of the policy. For example, if a woman in a domestic partnership purchases term insurance on her life, naming her brother as beneficiary, and the premium is paid from community funds, when she dies, her partner is entitled to one-half of the proceeds of the policy and her brother is entitled to the rest.

If both spouses signed the designation form and agreed to the beneficiary, then the named beneficiary still receives the entire amount. The situation may be more complicated if the final premium of a term policy was paid with separate property. Determining the community property interest of whole or universal life policies is also more complicated where a portion of the premiums are paid with community property, because those sorts of policies have a cash value or investment fund prior to the death of the insured.

Improvements to Property

What happens when improvements are made to one type of property (community or separate) using funds that are a different type of property? For example, if one person has a separate property cabin or boat, and community property funds are used to fix it up, what happens when the decedent leaves the property to a third person? Does the surviving spouse or partner have a right to claim one-half of the value of the improvements? Similarly, if one partner uses his separate property to improve his spouse's or partner's separate property and feels unfairly treated by that person's will or alternative estate plan, what are his rights?

As you can probably gather, the law in this area can be complex. Put another way, you are dealing with an estate that isn't simple, and you need more information about the ins and outs of California marital or domestic partnership property law than we can give you here.

Pensions

A pension is regarded as compensation for services previously rendered, and a percentage of the pension right is deemed to have been earned during each year that the pensioner worked to qualify for the pension. Thus, if a pensioner worked for 15 years, then married and worked for another five years before qualifying for a pension on the basis of 20 years' service, three-fourths of the pension payments (and anything accumulated with them) would be separate property and one-fourth would be community property. If the pensioner was married for the entire employment period, pension payments are community property.

Rents and Profits

The rents and profits received on community property (interest, dividends, royalties, rents, capital gains, and so on) are community property. Rents and profits from separate property remain separate property.

Separate Property Businesses

It is often difficult to determine whether income from a separate property business in which one spouse or partner works during the marriage or partnership is community or separate property. The value of the business at the time of marriage or registration is clearly separate property. Wages paid to the person who owns the business during the marriage or partnership are clearly community property. But what about the increase in the value of the business itself? Is this just the natural growth of a separate property asset and, therefore, separate property, or is it the result of the continuing work of the spouse or partner and, therefore, community property? Often the answer to this question is some combination of the two. However, it is an area of particular difficulty, and in these situations you will need professional help to determine what is separate and what is community property.

Examples of Property Ownership

Perhaps the best way to review the material we have covered in this chapter is to examine several examples of community and separate property ownership.

Brad

Brad is single and moved to California from Nevada in 2010. While living in Nevada he inherited $50,000 from his father's estate, which he invested in a motel in Las Vegas. While living in California from 2010 until his death, he acquired 300 shares of Marvelous Corporation stock in which he took title as a joint tenant with his mother. He also purchased a Porsche and a $100,000 life insurance policy, naming his mother as beneficiary.

Since Brad was never married, all of his property is his separate property in which he has a 100% interest. His interest in the Las Vegas motel, being real property, will be transferred after his death according to Nevada procedures and excluded from his California estate. The 300 shares of Marvelous Corporation stock, being held in joint tenancy, are not subject to probate because it automatically became his mother's property on his death by right of survivorship. However, title to this property must be cleared, a procedure we discuss in Chapter 10.

The $100,000 life insurance proceeds are not subject to probate either, because Brad's mother is the named beneficiary under the policy, and the proceeds will be paid under the insurance contract entered into between Brad and the insurance company. Brad's mother needs only to send a certified copy of the death certificate and a claim form to the insurance company to collect the proceeds. The remaining asset—his Porsche—can probably be transferred using the simple affidavit procedure available for small estates, which we discuss in Chapter 11. Who gets the Porsche will depend on whether Brad left a will or died without one (intestate).

Joe and Stan

Joe and Stan registered as domestic partners on March 18, 2009 and lived in California during their entire partnership. Prior to their registration, Stan owned some valuable antiques and a $10,000 bank account. Joe owned a $20,000 promissory note secured by a deed of trust on real property located in San Diego; a boat, which he kept at Marina del Rey (in Los Angeles County); and $5,000 in a California bank savings account. During their partnership, Stan inherited 50 shares of AT&T stock from his aunt's estate. During their partnership they opened a bank account at Culver City Bank in California as tenants in common. They deposited their excess earnings into this account, plus the proceeds of the two bank accounts they each owned individually before registration, periodically making withdrawals from, and deposits into, the account. They also acquired, with their combined earnings during the partnership, a condominium located in Culver City, California, and a BMW.

When Joe dies, his estate in California is determined as follows: The boat at Marina del Rey (tangible personal property) and the $20,000 trust deed note (intangible personal property) are Joe's separate property, having been acquired before registering his partnership with Stan. The two bank accounts that Joe and Stan owned prior to registration have been commingled and are both community property, as is the Culver City Bank account, which Joe and Stan established after registration. Therefore, Stan owns a one-half interest in each of these. The AT&T stock is Stan's separate property, since he acquired it by inheritance. The antiques that Stan owned prior to registration are also his separate property. The condominium and the BMW acquired with the couple's earnings during the partnership are California community property. Thus, Joe's estate in California consists of the following:

- A 100% separate property interest in:
  - the $20,000 trust deed note, and
  - the Marina del Rey boat.
- A one-half community property interest (Stan owns the other half) in:
  - the Culver City condominium
  - the BMW, and
  - the Culver City Bank account.

Beverly and Randolph

Beverly was a scriptwriter for a large motion picture studio in Los Angeles when she married Randolph, an aspiring actor, in 1990. At the time of their marriage, Beverly owned a home in Pacific Palisades, a 1989 Mercedes-Benz automobile, and a $50,000 bank account. Also, at the time of their marriage, Beverly had completed ten of the necessary 25 years of service required to qualify for a $150,000 pension from the studio on her retirement. Beverly's daughter by a prior marriage was named contingent beneficiary of the pension.

Randolph's property at the time of their marriage consisted of an interest in a motor home, worth about $20,000, and a $5,000 savings account. Randolph was also entitled to receive residual payments from several television commercials he completed prior to their marriage, which are still rolling in at an average of $1,000 per month. Shortly after their marriage, Randolph sold his interest in the motor home, and he and Beverly pooled their money and deposited all cash in joint bank accounts, paying their expenses from the accounts and also depositing their earnings during marriage into the accounts. In 1995, they improved the Pacific Palisades residence by building a lap pool and redwood deck, at a cost of about $30,000. Since the house was Beverly's separate property, Randolph generously agreed to treat the cost of the improvements as a gift to Beverly, and did not ask for reimbursement of his one-half interest in the community funds used for the improvements.

Beverly retired from the studio in 2005 and died in 2015, after she and Randolph had been married 25 years. Their combined assets at the time of Beverly's death consisted of:

- the Pacific Palisades home
- the 1989 Mercedes-Benz automobile
- the cash in joint bank accounts of approximately $30,000
- Beverly's vested interest in her pension, and
- Randolph's rights to future residual payments from his TV commercials.

How do we know which of these assets are included in Beverly's estate? First, we know the Pacific Palisades house and Mercedes are Beverly's separate property, because she owned them prior to her marriage to Randolph. Even though the improvements to the residence were made with community funds, they took on the same character as the house (because of Randolph's gift) and are, therefore, also her separate property, along with the house. Therefore, these two assets are 100% Beverly's separate property.

Beverly's vested interest in her $150,000 pension was earned two-fifths prior to marriage and three-fifths during marriage (that is, she was married 15 of the 25 working years required to qualify for the pension). This means two-fifths of the pension ($60,000) is separate property and three-fifths ($90,000) is community property, and Randolph owns a one-half interest in the community portion, or $45,000. Randolph would have to work out an arrangement with the pension plan administrators and Beverly's daughter to receive his share. If this can't be done, then Randolph would have to see an attorney. (Of course, Randolph might not choose to claim his share and let it all go to Beverly's daughter, but he is entitled to $45,000 if he wants it.)

Beverly's separate property portion ($60,000) of the pension, plus her one-half interest in the community portion ($45,000), will go to her daughter, as the contingent beneficiary. Since the pension has named beneficiaries, it will not be subject to probate. Randolph's residual payments are his separate property, since the right to payment was earned before marriage, and they are not included in Beverly's estate. Beverly also has a one-half interest in the $25,000 in the couple's joint bank accounts. Her half interest is part of her gross estate but will not be subject to probate because the accounts were held in joint tenancy. Therefore, Beverly's estate consists of the following assets:

- the Pacific Palisades home
- the $5,000 Mercedes-Benz automobile
- a $105,000 interest in the pension, and
- a $12,500 interest in the bank accounts.

Unless Beverly has used an estate planning device, such as joint tenancy, a transfer on death deed, or a living trust, or unless Beverly has a will making Randolph the beneficiary, the home and automobile will be subject to probate in California.

Property Acquired by Couples Before They Moved to California

This section applies only if the decedent was a married Californian or registered domestic partner who acquired property during marriage or a domestic partnership prior to moving to California. The term "quasi-community property" includes all real property situated in California and all personal property, wherever located, that would have been community property if the owner had been a resident of California at the time the owner acquired it. The label is generally applied to property owned by married couples or domestic partners at the time they move to California from a non-community property state. The only exception is real property located outside of California, which is not quasi-community property. Quasi-community property is treated the same way as community property in estates of persons who die while residents of California.

California also treats community property acquired by a married couple or domestic partners while living in another community property state as community property, even though such property would not be community property in California. For instance, some community property states classify income from separate property as community property when the income is received during marriage. Although such income would be treated as separate property in California, it is treated as community property when the owner who acquired the property in such other community property state dies a resident of California.

If you have difficulty in establishing any of the decedent's out-of-state property as community or separate, you should seek the advice of an attorney.

Harry and Marsha

Harry and Marsha had only a small amount of cash between them and a few personal belongings when they were married in New York City in 1993. During their marriage, while living in New York, they acquired with their earnings an apartment building and 200 shares of XYZ Corporation stock. They moved to California in 2000, where they lived as spouses until Marsha's death. No property was acquired by either of them by gift or inheritance at any time. At the time of Marsha's death, Harry and Marsha owned the following assets:

- the apartment house in New York City, held in both their names
- 200 shares of XYZ Corporation stock, in Harry's name
- a residence in Van Nuys, California, in both names as community property
- two automobiles, one in Marsha's name and one in Harry's name, and
- a joint tenancy bank account at Union Bank in Van Nuys.

What does Marsha's estate consist of for California purposes? First of all, it doesn't include the real property (apartment house) in New York City, which will have to be transferred independently under the procedures of the state of New York. The XYZ Corporation stock is included in the California estate because it is intangible personal property. Since the stock was acquired with the combined earnings of Harry and Marsha during their marriage, it would be treated as community property in California even though the stock is in Harry's name alone and, therefore, is technically quasi-community property. The joint tenancy bank account (although obviously community property funds) is included in Marsha's estate, although it is not subject to probate and becomes Harry's property by operation of law immediately on Marsha's death. Thus, Marsha's estate in California consists of her one-half interest in the following assets:

- the 200 shares of XYZ Corporation stock
- the Van Nuys residence
- the two automobiles, and
- the Union Bank account.

CHAPTER

5

Preparing a Schedule of the Assets and Debts

By now you should have examined the necessary papers and documents and gathered sufficient information to prepare a list of all property owned by the decedent at the time of death. You will use the completed list as a worksheet in conjunction with the remaining steps required to transfer the assets and settle the estate.

To help you with this project, we have included a blank Schedule of Assets in Appendix C. The following sections contain instructions for completing the schedule. Make this schedule as thorough and accurate as possible. It will serve as your list of all property in which the decedent had any interest at death—including assets that require probate administration, as well as those that do not. Information on this schedule will help answer important questions as you proceed: What assets exist in the estate? What procedures can be used to transfer assets? Does an estate tax return need to be filed? What is the basis of assets for tax reporting purposes? Later chapters address these questions. The answers to these questions will also inform how precise the schedule needs to be. At first, focus on collecting and organizing your asset information.

You should both list the assets and briefly and carefully describe them so you can easily identify each one. A more detailed description of some items may be required on later documents, but a brief listing will do now. In addition, you should indicate for each asset, in the column provided for this purpose:

- the value of the asset as of the date of death
- how the decedent owned it (for example, as separate property, as community property, in joint tenancy, etc., see the list on the next page)
- the portion owned by the decedent and the value of the decedent's interest, and
- whether the asset is subject to formal probate or can be transferred in a simpler way. (If you are in doubt about whether a particular asset must be probated, leave this column blank until you read Chapter 6.)

The first sections of this chapter provide information and tools to assist in the process of preparing your Schedule of Assets. Then the final sections of the chapter show you how to complete the schedule, item by item. Thus, your best approach is not to try to fill in the schedule until you have read this entire chapter. Please understand, however, that this book is not designed to provide extensive coverage of California property ownership rules, a large and sometimes complex area of the law. If, after reading the previous chapter and what follows, you are still unsure about how to characterize a particular asset, see a lawyer.

Describe Each Asset

It is helpful to group assets, such as cash items, bank accounts, real property, securities, and so on, according to their general type as part of listing them on your schedule. Describe each asset briefly, including enough pertinent detail to identify it accurately. For example, a bank account might be described like this: "Personal checking account #57111; Bank of Occidental, Santa Rosa." At this point, don't worry about what percentage or type of ownership is involved, or the value of the account. Simply list every asset that might be owned by the decedent. We provide more details on how to describe particular assets in "Checklist of Property to List on Schedule of Assets," below. While the list will have a brief description, be sure to keep well organized the relevant backup documents with details.

Value Each Asset (Column A)

As well as describing each item of property, you must also determine the total date-of-death value of each asset as accurately as possible and put this amount in Column A. Here are some guidelines to help you do this. For more detail on evaluation, consult the extended discussion in "Checklist of Property to List on Schedule of Assets," below, or see an accountant.

Depending on the type of property and whether a formal probate administration is required, a probate referee may determine the exact value of the property. For now, provide exact values of items you can determine easily (for example, cash in bank accounts), and approximate values for others. Be sure to clearly note which values you estimate, so you can revise later, as you determine the exact value.

1. In placing a dollar value on an asset, the usual rule is to determine its "fair market value." The definition of fair market value is generally the price that a willing buyer would pay to a willing seller, both of them acting of their own free will and under no compulsion to buy or sell. Some assets have a definite record of value, such as stocks, bonds, and bank accounts, while others are valued by special rules, which we will discuss as we go along.
2. You should list the *gross* value of each asset in this column without regard to any liens or encumbrances against the property. In other words, for our purposes right now, do not subtract amounts owed on the property.
3. All assets and their values should be listed as of the *date of the decedent's death*, not as of the date you complete the schedule. This means that if a security is involved, you need to do a little research.

How to Determine Ownership of Property (Columns B and C)

Now you must list the manner in which the decedent owned each asset. You should insert this information in Column B. To do this, use the following abbreviations:

- separate property (SP)
- community property (CP)
- joint tenancy (JT)
- community property with right of survivorship (CPWROS)
- tenancy in common (TIC)
- life tenancy (LT), and
- pay on death or transfer on death (POD or TOD).

For mixed property (items that are part one type of property and part another), put both designations indicating the percentage share of each (for example, "one-third CP, two-thirds SP").

We describe general California property ownership rules in Chapter 4. Also, consult the extended discussion in "Checklist of Property to List on Schedule of Assets," below.

TIP

Assets held in a trust. The decedent may hold title to assets as trustee of a trust. For example, title may appear as "Lucille Chen, Trustee, Lucille Chen Living Trust." Consult the trust document to determine whether the decedent was the beneficiary of the trust. If so—as is common with a revocable living trust created to avoid probate—list the asset on the schedule of assets. If the decedent was the trustee of a trust for another person's benefit, the asset may or may not be considered a part of the decedent's estate. Get advice from an attorney.

If you have any doubt about the ownership of any item in the decedent's estate, or you want to check your conclusions, take the following steps:

Step 1. Was the decedent married or a registered domestic partner at time of death? If so, proceed to Step 2. If not, proceed to Step 3.

Step 2. Was the particular item community property or separate property? (See "How to Determine Whether Property Is Community or Separate," in Chapter 4, to help you answer this question. If the asset is a house, family business, pension, contract for future payment, or some other form of property that might be a mixture of community and separate property, also see "Property That Is a Mixture of Community and Separate Property," in Chapter 4.) As stated above, if the property was community property, put "CP" in Column B. If the property was a mixture of community property and separate property, put the respective portions in Column B (for example, "one--fourth CP, three-fourths SP"). If the title indicates "community property with right of survivorship" or "CPWROS," list CPWROS in Column B.

Step 3. Was the property held in joint tenancy—that is, jointly held with others with right of survivorship? (See "How Was the Decedent's Property Owned?" in Chapter 4.) If so, put "JT" in Column B and proceed to Step 6. If not, go to Step 4.

Step 4. Was the property held in tenancy in common—that is, jointly held with others with no right of survivorship? If so, put "TIC" in Column B and proceed to Step 6. If not, go to Step 5.

Step 5. Was the item owned solely by the decedent? If so, put "SP" in Column B. Otherwise, go to Step 6.

Step 6. Compute the share of the property owned by the decedent and put this fraction in Column C. For instance, if the decedent was married or a registered domestic partner at death, you may find that the decedent owned a one-half interest in many assets as community property. Sometimes, you may find that the decedent and the surviving spouse or partner owned (as community property or as joint tenants) a fractional interest in property with third parties. In this case, the decedent will have owned one-half of the couple's shared fractional interest. For example, if the decedent and the surviving spouse or partner owned as community property a one-fourth interest in a commercial building with several other people, the decedent's interest would be one-eighth (that is, one-half of one-fourth).

We discuss shared ownership situations in detail in Chapter 4. In most estates, determining what the decedent owned should not be a problem after you read this material. However, if the portion of the property the decedent owned is uncertain or if there is a difference of opinion between the surviving spouse or partner and a third party, get help from an attorney. (For information on finding and compensating lawyers, see Chapter 16.)

List the Value of the Decedent's Interest (Column D)

Now that we have listed all the assets, evaluated them, and determined the type of interest the decedent had in the property, it is time to insert the value of the decedent's interest in Column D. Fortunately, this is normally easy. If the decedent owned the entire asset, the dollar figure you insert here is the same as listed in Column A. (The specifics of valuing assets are described later in this chapter.)

If the decedent owned less than a full interest in any property, such as an undivided one-half interest as a tenant in common or a one-half interest as community property, include only the value of the decedent's fractional interest in Column D. For example, if the decedent owned a one-half community property interest in a residence valued at $370,000, the value of the decedent's interest in Column D is $185,000.

The total of Column D will give you the value of the decedent's gross estate to help determine if a federal estate tax return will be required. (See "Federal Estate Tax Return," in Chapter 7.)

CAUTION

Valuing joint tenancy property. If the decedent owned joint tenancy property with anyone other than the surviving spouse (federal tax laws don't apply to domestic partners), the IRS presumes (for estate tax purposes) that the decedent owned 100% of the property, so include 100% of the property's value in Column D. If the decedent, in fact, didn't contribute 100% of the purchase price of the property, you can rebut that presumption by showing that the surviving joint tenant contributed some of the purchase price.

Determine Whether Property Is a Probate or Nonprobate Asset (Column E)

In Column E, indicate whether the asset must go through formal probate (P) or will be transferred outside of formal probate and is therefore a nonprobate asset (N/P). As previewed in Chapter 1, probate assets are handled differently from nonprobate assets in settling an estate, and even some assets that are theoretically subject to probate can be transferred with no need to go to court. These are primarily assets in small estates of $166,250 or less and property that passes to a surviving spouse or domestic partner.

TIP

The dollar amount to qualify as a "small" estate will increase over time. As of January 1, 2020, to use the procedures for a small estate the value of an estate must be no larger than $166,250. On April 1, 2022 this amount will be changed to account for inflation and will continue to be adjusted by the Judicial Council every three years. To keep things simple, we reference the existing value of $166,250.

At the beginning stages of creating your schedule, enter N/P if you know that the assets are not subject to formal probate. Otherwise you may need to leave this blank until you have more information about the size of the estate and whether formal probate is required.

Let's review the distinctions between the assets that do not have to go through probate and those that do.

- **Assets not subject to probate.** Generally, nonprobate assets are those for which the beneficiary has been predetermined by reason of a contract or by law, such as life insurance proceeds, death benefits, POD accounts, property held in trust (including living trusts and savings bank trusts), and joint tenancy property. The will doesn't affect disposition of the asset.
- **Assets subject to simplified probate procedures.** Property that passes outright to a surviving spouse or domestic partner and property in small estates ($166,250 or less) can be transferred by simplified probate procedures. Because these procedures do not require a full, formal probate court proceeding, we classify these assets N/P. After you have completed your schedule and add up the total gross value of the assets, you will be able to determine whether any assets that would otherwise be subject to probate, in fact, fall in this category. See Chapters 11 and 15 to learn more about procedures for small estates and about property that passes to a surviving spouse.
- **Assets subject to formal probate.** Everything not included in the above two categories requires formal probate court proceedings before the property can be transferred.

If any of this confuses you, leave this column blank until you read Chapter 6. Chapter 6 serves as a sort of road map to the rest of the book in that it directs you to the chapter containing instructions on which property transfer procedure to follow.

List All Debts

We have also included a separate section at the end of the Schedule of Assets for listing debts and obligations owed by the decedent at the time of death. This information is not necessary for the purposes of this chapter. However, it will serve as a valuable record of these items for your future use. You'll need it to prepare the decedent's final income tax returns and, if necessary, estate income tax and federal estate tax returns. You'll also need to provide notice to creditors during a formal probate proceeding, so listing debts here can help prepare for that process.

Usually, the decedent's general debts as well as the expenses of administering the estate are paid from the general assets (residuary) of the estate, either during the formal probate administration or as part of simplified probate procedures.

However, if specific assets carry with them their own obligations (such as property taxes, mortgage payments in the case of real property, or installment payments on "secured" items, such as motor vehicles, furniture, etc.), the beneficiaries who receive these assets ordinarily assume these obligations, unless the decedent's will provides otherwise. You can check this out by carefully reading the will provision that makes the specific devise.

Checklist of Property to List on Schedule of Assets

This section discusses how to describe, evaluate, and characterize the various kinds of assets commonly found in an estate. By this time, you should have a good start on your Schedule of Assets, and the material here can help you fill in gaps. If you come across any particularly complicated assets, this may indicate that the estate is not simple and you will likely need further guidance and advice.

Cash Items

List all cash, checks, money orders, prepaid debit cards or other items that can be immediately converted to cash. The value of these items (Column A) is the face value, except for antique coins or something else of unusual value. For a decedent who is married or in a registered domestic partnership, cash items are normally community property (Column B). All items in this category are potentially subject to being transferred through a formal probate court proceeding unless they are (1) covered by a living trust or other probate-avoidance device, (2) part of a small estate, or (3) to be transferred to a surviving spouse or partner.

EXAMPLE:

Cash in decedent's possession

Uncashed checks payable to decedent:

Reimbursement check for medical expenses,
Optum Bank HSA

Refund check, Watco Corporation

Bank Accounts

Examine all bank books, statements, or other evidence as to accounts or amounts on deposit with any financial institution, such as banks, trust companies, savings and loan associations, online banks, or credit unions. Describe the type of account (checking account, savings account, savings certificate, money market account, or other), the number of the account or certificate, and the name and location of the institution where the account is held. Abbreviations used on statements may not precisely reflect title to the account. You should always verify with the bank or institution how title to the account is held.

If the decedent was married (or had a registered domestic partner) and owned a certificate of deposit as community property, you would describe it like this:

	A Total Value of Asset on Date/Death	B How Is Asset Owned?	C Portion Owned by Decedent	D Value of Decedent's Interest	E Probate or Non-probate
2. Bank Accounts					
Certificate of Deposit, No. 10235, Lighthouse Bank, Ventura, CA	20,000	CP	1/2	10,000	____*
accrued interest	150			75	

* Enter N/P if asset will pass to surviving spouse or partner using the simplified probate procedures. (See Chapter 15.) Otherwise, leave blank until you know whether you can use small estate procedures based on the size of the probate estate. (See Chapter 11.)

If the decedent wasn't married (and didn't have a registered domestic partner), or if the decedent owned an account as separate property, then you should list it like this:

	A Total Value of Asset on Date/Death	B How Is Asset Owned?	C Portion Owned by Decedent	D Value of Decedent's Interest	E Probate or Non-probate
2. Bank Accounts					
Interest-bearing checking, Mountain Credit Union, account no. 1234	5,000	SP	all	5,000	____**

** Leave blank until you know whether you can use small estate procedures based on the size of the probate estate. (See Chapter 11.)

Banks often resist giving out information about a decedent's accounts to third parties without first seeing documents issued by the court in a formal probate proceeding called "letters." This can be a problem if the decedent did not leave detailed records and you do not know if a court proceeding will be required. In this case, we suggest you contact any banks that you think the decedent may have used and present a certified copy of the death certificate. Most banks will provide information to beneficiaries if they sign a notarized affidavit 40 days after the decedent's death alleging that no probate proceeding is pending. That done, the bank will usually tell you if the decedent had bank accounts there and the value, and also if the decedent had a safe-deposit box at the bank.

Put in Column A the balance on the date of death. Savings accounts and certificates should include accrued interest to the date of death, even if not credited to the account until following the date of death. The accrued interest can be added as a separate item. The exact balances, including accrued interest, may be obtained directly from the bank or from a recent bank statement. Remember, you insert the full value in Column A, even if it is a joint account or community property account. Then, if the decedent owned only a part interest, you will insert the amount of the fraction or portion owned in Column C and the value of the fractional interest in Column D. Under Probate Code Section 5301, there is a presumption that during the lifetime of all parties a joint account is owned proportionately according to the net contributions made by each joint owner. The ownership at the death of a party depends on the specifics of the account.

POD Accounts (Also Called "Totten Trusts" or "ITF Accounts")

One can have an account that specifically designates who will inherit it, called a "pay on death" or "POD" account, or less commonly a, "Totten trust" or "in trust for (ITF)" account. These types of accounts have similar functions and effects.

The owner of the account designates with the bank someone to receive the account assets when the owner dies. The title of the account reflects the beneficiary designation. For example, the title of a POD bank account held by Mary Jones that would go to Harry Jones on her death would be "Mary Jones, POD Harry Jones." If the account is a Totten trust or ITF account, the title would be "Mary Jones, Trustee for (or ITF) Harry Jones." In either case, on the death of Mary Jones, the balance of the account automatically passes to Harry Jones, without probate procedures.

The account can be held in the name of one or more parties for one or more parties (Prob. Code §§ 80 and 5140), and may be transferred after the death of the owner by the same procedures used to terminate joint tenancy bank accounts. If the decedent owned a POD, Totten trust, or ITF account, make a notation in Column B that it is a pay on death asset (POD) and in Column E that it is a nonprobate (N/P) asset.

The balance on the date of death should be inserted in Column A. However, if community property was used to establish the account, it is a community property asset, and only one-half of its value will be owned by the decedent because the other

This example shows a POD account established using community property.

	A Total Value of Asset on Date/Death	B How Is Asset Owned?	C Portion Owned by Decedent	D Value of Decedent's Interest	E Probate or Non-probate
2. Bank Accounts					
Savings account, No. 8903, Harbor Bank, San Pedro, in sole name of decedent, POD Jon	10,000	POD(CP)	1/2	5,000	N/P

one-half belongs to the surviving spouse or domestic partner. Therefore, you would indicate in Column B that it is also community property (CP), and in Column C that the decedent owned one-half, and insert the value of the one-half interest in Column D.

Real Estate

Carefully review all deeds to real property (real estate) to verify how title is held. If there is any doubt about how title is held, a title search by a title company or searching county records may be required. On the Schedule of Assets form list the common address of the property and a simple description, such as "single family residence," "nine-unit apartment building," or "unimproved land." Including the county and Assessor's Parcel Number may be helpful for you to keep track of this important information, though it is not necessary so long as you can readily identify the property.

The value of real property takes into consideration the condition of the premises or property, the location, and recent sales prices of comparable property in the area. Assessed values shown on real property tax bills generally do not reflect the current market value and should not be used for this purpose. A private appraisal by a licensed real estate appraiser provides

Let's assume the decedent had a piece of land as separate property and owned a house with the surviving spouse or domestic partner as community property. You would list the property like this:

	A	B	C	D	E
	Total Value of Asset on Date/Death	How Is Asset Owned?	Portion Owned by Decedent	Value of Decedent's Interest	Probate or Non-probate
3. Real Property (common address, brief description)					
5 acres, unimproved grazing land,					
Alameda County	40,000	SP	all	40,000	____*
Single family residence,					
711 Hill St., Los Angeles, CA	600,000	CP	1/2	300,000	____*

*Enter N/P if asset will pass to surviving spouse or partner using the simplified probate procedures. (See Chapter 15.) Otherwise, leave blank until you know whether you can use small estate procedures based on the size of the probate estate. (See Chapter 11.)

Now assume the first piece of property was owned by decedent and a sibling as joint tenants and the second piece was decedent's separate property, which was passed to his son by use of a living (inter vivos) trust. Because the transfers do not require probate procedures, fill in the Schedule of Assets like this:

	A	B	C	D	E
	Total Value of Asset on Date/Death	How Is Asset Owned?	Portion Owned by Decedent	Value of Decedent's Interest	Probate or Non-probate
3. Real Property (common address, brief description)					
5 acres, unimproved grazing land,					
Alameda County, A8N 099B-4904-007-02	40,000	JT	1/2	20,000	N/P
Single family residence,					
711 Hill St., Los Angeles, CA	600,000	SP	all	600,000	N/P

evidence of the value of real property, and will cost a few hundred dollars. This type of appraisal may prove important for tax purposes. If a formal probate proceeding is required, you may not need a private appraisal. During a formal probate proceeding, the real property will be appraised by a probate referee at a cost of one-tenth of 1% of the value of the property. Real estate brokers familiar with the area may also provide an opinion letter of value based on comparable sales. For a rough estimate, you can check online real estate sites such as Zillow.com or Trulia.com—however, do not rely on these sites for any official valuation. If the decedent owned income-producing property, you should obtain an appraisal from an expert (unless, as mentioned above, there will be a formal probate court proceeding). An appraisal will base the value of income property on such things as capitalization of income, the kind of financing, the quality of tenants, and the effects rent control may have on such property, as well as a number of other factors, and is not something you should try to figure out on your own.

TIP

Securities in a retirement account. If the decedent held securities in a retirement account with a designated beneficiary, then the securities will be listed as part of the estate for determining the estate value, even though the retirement account is a nonprobate asset.

An appraisal may be needed as good evidence of the date-of-death value for establishing a new "stepped-up" federal income tax cost basis of the property in the hands of the new owners when computing capital gains tax, if and when the property is sold. (We discuss tax considerations briefly in Chapter 7.)

The way title is listed on a deed provides important information about the decedent's ownership and the beneficiary. Real property may be held in various forms: Single owner, joint ownership as tenants in common, joint ownership as joint tenants, or by a trustee of a trust. Certain ways of holding title also determine the beneficiary after death of the owner, such as a TOD (transfer on death) deed, community property with rights of survivorship, and joint tenancy. Provide all relevant information of this type on your asset list. Keep as backup the relevant deed(s) or other documents (such as a court order, if the property was inherited) establishing ownership.

Stocks and Bonds

Information on the type of securities the decedent owned and how the decedent held title can be obtained from examining the stock or bond certificates. However, securities are more commonly held in non-certificate form. A company, transfer agent, or brokerage firm can hold the securities in book entry form and provide regular statements reflecting the ownership. U.S. Treasury securities in non-certificate form may be registered with TreasuryDirect, the Treasury's electronic registration system. The website TreasuryDirect.gov provides access to the electronic accounts holding such U.S. Treasury securities.

Stocks should be listed by the number and type of shares (that is, common or preferred) and the name of the company issuing the shares. For preferred stock, put down the dividend rate. For bonds, put down the total gross face amount (usually in multiples of $1,000), name of the issuer, interest rate, and maturity date. For U.S. Treasury bills, list the total face amount and the maturity date. U.S. Treasury bills are issued either in a single name or in two names joined by "or." If issued in the decedent's name alone, they are included in the probate estate. If in co-ownership form, they pass to the surviving co-owner without probate; they are treated basically the same as joint tenancy assets and should be listed as such. For U.S. Series E savings bonds, list the issue date instead of the maturity date. The issue date is how the value is determined on Series E bonds. Securities that are registered in pay on death form—designated as pay-on-death (POD) or transfer on death (TOD)—may be transferred to the beneficiary on the death of the registered owner without probate.

Information on stock and bond values at the date of death can be obtained from a variety of online sources that provide historical information (such as MarketWatch.com and NASDAQ.com); however, it may take some calculations to compute the precise valuations. For now, you may want to provide only a preliminary value on the schedule of assets, marking it as an estimate.

If the estate requires probate administration, the probate referee will provide the exact date-of-death value. If the asset will pass by a nonprobate procedure, then an accurate valuation will be needed for tax reporting purposes.

If a brokerage firm held the decedent's securities, you can avoid doing calculations yourself by asking the firm to provide a date-of-death report of the decedent's holding. Or, you can contact a brokerage firm or an accountant to provide valuations for a fee. Many stock brokerage firms and accountants have an estate security valuation service for this purpose, and they can provide you with a report of all the information you need at a modest cost, based on the number of securities you want evaluated. Again, remember to insert the full value of the securities in Column A, and, if they were in co-ownership form, compute the value of the decedent's fractional interest for Column D.

If you decide to calculate the valuations yourself, the value per unit or share is the mean (midpoint) between the highest and lowest quoted selling prices

Assume you have a decedent who owned some XYZ Telephone Company preferred stock and Series E savings bonds before his marriage as separate property. After marriage, he purchased with his earnings some Transpacific Corporation stock in joint tenancy with his brother, a $5,000 Antioch Drainage System bond as community property with his wife, and a $10,000 U.S. Treasury bill in co-ownership (joint tenancy) form with his wife. Since the assets acquired after marriage are presumed to be community property (although the records don't reflect this), one-half of the decedent's interest in the Transpacific Corporation stock acquired in joint tenancy with the decedent's brother belongs to the surviving spouse. Therefore, the decedent's interest in the Transpacific stock is actually one-fourth (one-half of one-half). The surviving spouse would probably have to file a Spousal or Domestic Partner Property Petition (see Chapter 15) to claim her community property interest in this asset. The remaining two assets ($10,000 Treasury bill and Antioch Drainage System bond) are community property and are owned one-half by the decedent. In this case, your descriptions will look like this:

	A Total Value of Asset on Date/Death	B How Is Asset Owned?	C Portion Owned by Decedent	D Value of Decedent's Interest	E Probate or Non-probate
4. Securities					
Stock (name of company, type, and number of shares)					
50 shares, Transpacific common stock	16,000	JT/CP	1/4	4,000	N/P
200 shares, XYZ Telephone Company 5%					
first preferred stock, par value $100	15,000	SP	all	15,000	____*
Bonds (face amount)					
Three U.S. Series E savings bonds, face					
amount $100 each, issued July 1967	300	SP	all	300	____*
$5,000 Antioch Drainage System,					
District of Contra Costa, 2000					
Drainage bond Series B, 4½% due					
June 1, 2025	5,000	CP	1/2	2,500	____*
$10,000 U.S. Treasury bill, due					
June 30, 2027	10,000	JT	1/2	5,000	N/P

*Enter N/P if asset will pass to surviving spouse or partner using the simplified probate procedures. (See Chapter 15.) Otherwise, leave blank until you know whether you can use small estate procedures based on the size of the probate estate. (See Chapter 11.)

on the date of death. For example, if the high was 15.8 and the low was 14.2, the mean would be determined by adding these two figures together, for a total of 30, and dividing by two (2) for a mean value of 15. Then, by multiplying the unit (mean) value by the number of shares owned for each kind of stock, you will have the total value of the shares. To determine the value of bonds, divide the total gross face amount (par value) by $100 and then multiply that figure by the mean value.

Stock sold on date of death

Description of stock:

100 shares, General Motors, common

Highest selling price on date of death:	34 =	34.00
Lowest selling price on date of death:	31.5 =	31.50
		65.50

65.50 ÷ 2 = 32.75 (mean selling price per share)

32.75 × 100 (shares) = $3,275.00 (date-of-death value)

No sales on date of death (decedent died on a nontrading day)

If the decedent died on a nontrading day, such as a weekend or holiday, take the average of the mean prices on the nearest trading days. For instance, if the decedent died on a weekend, take the average of the mean prices on the Friday before and Monday after.

Description of stock:

20 shares, Natural Foods, common

Selling price on Friday (the nearest transaction date prior to death)

High: 12
Low: + 10
22 ÷ 2 = 11 (mean)

Selling price on Monday (the nearest transaction date after death)

High: 14
Low: + 12
26 ÷ 2 = 13 (mean)

The fair market value is obtained by averaging the Friday and Monday figures:

$$\frac{(11 + 13)}{2} = \$12.00$$

$12.00 × 20 (shares) = $240.00 (date-of-death value of the stock)

When the closest sales were made more than one trading day away from the date of death (that is, any day but a weekend or holiday), a slightly more complicated formula is used. The fair market value is determined by taking a weighted average of the mean price on the nearest date before the date of death and the mean price on the nearest date after the date of death. The average must be weighted inversely by the numbers of trading days between the selling dates and the valuation date.

Selling price three (3) trading days after date of death

High: 62
Low: + 60
122 ÷ 2 = 61 (mean)

The fair market value is obtained by the following computation (note that the number of trading days before date of death [2] are multiplied by the mean value of the stock on the selling date after date of death, and vice versa):

$$\frac{(3 \times 59) + (2 \times 61)}{5} = \$59.80 \text{ (unit value per share)}$$

$59.80 × 100 (shares) = $5,980 (value of shares)

Sometimes stock dividends are declared before death but not paid until after death, and these should be included in valuing the stock. For example, if a stock pays a quarterly dividend of $216 per share for the quarter ending June 30 and the decedent died on July 3 of the same year, the $216 dividend should be added to the value of the stock, even though the dividend has not been received as of the date of death.

For bonds, any accrued interest due and unpaid on the date of death should be included in the valuation. To calculate accrued interest, you compute the daily rate of interest and multiply it by the number of days since the last payment to the date of the decedent's death.

The decedent owned a $10,000 bond that pays 6% interest annually on January 1 and July 1 each year.

$10,000 bond
× .06
$600.00 (interest paid annually) ÷ 365 days = $1.64 (daily interest)

Date of death: July 15

Date of last interest payment: July 1

Days since last interest payment: 14

Accrued interest: 14 × $1.64 = $22.96

	A	B	C	D	E
	Total Value of Asset on Date/Death	How Is Asset Owned?	Portion Owned by Decedent	Value of Decedent's Interest	Probate or Non-probate
Mutual Funds (name of fund, number of shares)					
35,000 shares, Dreyfus Special Income fund, State Street Bank and Trust Co., New York	16,000	JT	1/2	8,000	N/P

For mutual funds, list the number of shares held in the fund, the name of the particular fund, and the location of the fund management firm. Frequently, share certificates for mutual funds are actually held by the fund's custodian, not by the investor. Refer to the latest statement or contact the fund management directly for information on the ownership and a description of the shares and the date-of-death value.

U.S. Savings Bonds in Co-Ownership or Beneficiary Form

U.S. savings bonds in co-ownership form will be shown registered to "John Jones or Sally Jones," as owners. Bonds registered in beneficiary form appear as "John Jones pay on death (or abbreviated "POD") to Sally Jones." John Jones is the registered owner in this case, and Sally Jones is the beneficiary. Bonds registered in co-ownership with someone, or in beneficiary form, pass to the surviving co-owner or beneficiary on the death of the co-owner or registered owner, much like a joint tenancy asset, and are not subject to probate. The surviving co-owner or beneficiary can choose to any of the following: Do nothing, redeem the savings bond, or have it reissued without the decedent's name.

Only if the present decedent is the surviving co-owner, or survives the beneficiary in the case of a POD registration, will these bonds be subject to probate, because in such cases, the present decedent is the only owner of the bonds (there being no co-owner or designated beneficiary living). Savings bonds are tax-deferred assets and subject to income taxes when redeemed.

To reissue or redeem paper savings bonds, the surviving co-owner or beneficiary should take the bonds, along with a certificate copy of the death certificate, to a local bank for assistance in preparing the forms. Or, TreasuryDirect.gov provides instructions and forms for reissuing or redeeming paper bonds through the mail.

Money Market Funds

A money market fund (as opposed to a bank money market account, which is simply a type of bank account) is a mutual fund, much like a stock market mutual fund. Instead of investing in stocks or bonds, a money market fund lends money to various entities and the interest collected is paid out as "dividends" to the depositor, who is technically a "shareholder" in the fund. The fund's latest monthly statement will show the number of shares owned (normally, shares simply reflect the dollar amount invested; so 5,000 shares means a $5,000 investment), the value of the decedent's interest in the fund, and how the decedent held title. If in doubt, contact the fund management using the information shown on the statement or on its website. Remember, even if the account is in the decedent's name alone, it may very well be community property if the decedent was married or a registered domestic partner. These accounts can also be held in joint tenancy, like other assets.

List the money market funds on the asset chart in a similar way to listing a security.

Insurance

List on the schedule only insurance policies the decedent owned. The policy itself does not always indicate the owner, and often insurance policies on the decedent's life are owned by another person, for example, a spouse or partner. (We discuss who owns insurance policies in more detail in "Federal Estate Tax Return," in Chapter 7.) If you contact the insurance company, it will provide you with a written record of the name of the owner. If the decedent was married or in a registered domestic partnership, any insurance policy may be community property if, and to the extent, the premiums were paid with community funds.

Conversely, the decedent may have owned an insurance policy on someone else's life. Strange as it may seem, such a policy is considered an asset of the decedent's estate, and the cash value of the policy on the date of the decedent's death is included in the probate estate. Usually, the cash value—as opposed to the face value—of the policy is significantly less than the face value. If the decedent had a policy on the life of someone else, contact the insurance company to verify ownership and to get a statement of the cash value of the policy on the date of the decedent's death. Upon request, the insurance company will send you a *Life Insurance Statement* (Form 712) showing what is paid in connection with policies on the decedent's life, as well as the cash value of any policies the decedent owned on the life of another.

Suppose a decedent who was married or in a registered domestic partnership owned two life insurance policies as his separate property. One is a paid-up policy on the decedent's life purchased before his marriage or partnership registration and payable to his estate, and the other is on the life of his surviving spouse or partner. Here's how to list them:

	A Total Value of Asset on Date/Death	B How Is Asset Owned?	C Portion Owned by Decedent	D Value of Decedent's Interest	E Probate or Non-probate
5. **Insurance** (name of company, policy number, name of beneficiary, name of owner)					
Policies on decedent's life					
Proceeds, Acme Insurance Policy					
No. 23456, on decedent's life,					
payable to estate as beneficiary	10,000	SP	all	10,000	____*
Policies owned by decedent on another					
Decedent's interest as owner in					
Grand Insurance Co., Policy No.					
654321, on life of decedent's					
spouse (or domestic partner)	1,500	SP	all	1,500	____*

* Enter N/P if asset will pass to surviving spouse or partner using the simplified probate procedures. (See Chapter 15.) Otherwise, leave blank until you know whether you can use small estate procedures based on the size of the probate estate. (See Chapter 11.)

What if the decedent purchased a policy on his life during his marriage or domestic partnership, without assigning ownership to anyone else and naming his daughter by a previous marriage as beneficiary? Here's how to list it:

	A Total Value of Asset on Date/Death	B How Is Asset Owned?	C Portion Owned by Decedent	D Value of Decedent's Interest	E Probate or Non-probate
5. Insurance (name of company, policy number, name of beneficiary, name of owner)					
Policies on decedent's life					
Proceeds, Beneficial Life Policy No. 45609, on decedent's life, payable to decedent's daughter, Mary	20,000	CP	1/2	10,000	N/P

In describing insurance owned by the decedent on the asset schedule, list the name of the insurance company, the policy number, and the name of the beneficiary. The value of an insurance policy on the decedent's life is the full amount of insurance proceeds paid, but the value of a policy the decedent owned on the life of another is the cash value provided by the insurance company.

Insurance proceeds on the decedent's life payable to named beneficiaries are nonprobate assets. In rare cases, the decedent's estate is the beneficiary, or no named beneficiary survives the decedent, and in this case the probate estate includes the insurance proceeds.

Retirement and Death Benefits Through Decedent's Employment

If the decedent was employed, ask the employer about any unpaid salary, pension, or survivors benefit payable. If any exist, list the name of the company paying the benefit, the name of the beneficiary, and the amount. Benefits payable to living named beneficiaries are nonprobate assets. The value of each benefit is the actual amount paid in a lump sum. If the decedent was married or in a registered domestic partnership, this is probably a community property asset.

Individual Retirement Accounts

If the decedent owned an individual retirement account (IRA), contact the institution holding the investment (bank, credit union, insurance company, or stock brokerage firm) to notify of the death, and ask for instructions on how to transfer the asset to the beneficiary. In most cases, the custodian will require a certified copy of the decedent's death certificate and it will provide paperwork to the beneficiary. An IRA is not subject to probate unless it is payable to the decedent's estate or the estate otherwise becomes the beneficiary because other named beneficiaries do not survive.

When the IRA is opened, the owner designates a beneficiary to receive the investment on the death of the owner. Usually, if the beneficiary is the surviving spouse or partner, the survivor may take ownership of the IRA. If a beneficiary has not been designated, or the named beneficiary dies before the owner, payment is made according to the plan documents, often in the following order of priority: (1) the surviving spouse or domestic partner, (2) the decedent's surviving child, or (3) the decedent's estate.

	A Total Value of Asset on Date/Death	B How Is Asset Owned?	C Portion Owned by Decedent	D Value of Decedent's Interest	E Probate or Non-probate
6. Retirement and Death Benefits (description, beneficiary, amount)					
Employee benefits					
Death Benefit, Public Employees Retirement System, payable to decedent's spouse	50,000	CP	1/2	25,000	N/P

	A Total Value of Asset on Date/Death	B How Is Asset Owned?	C Portion Owned by Decedent	D Value of Decedent's Interest	E Probate or Non-probate
Individual Retirement Accounts					
IRA Account No. 13876-2, at Superior Bank, Kelso, California, beneficiary is decedent's domestic partner	5,000	CP	1/2	2,500	N/P

Unlike most assets bequeathed at death, IRAs (except Roth IRAs) and other tax-deferred assets are subject to income taxes on withdrawal of funds because this income was not taxed before the death of the holder. Complicated rules may apply, and the rules changed effective January 1, 2020.

Beneficiaries of retirement accounts should get help from an attorney or tax professional to understand the tax consequences and required distributions.

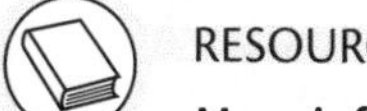

RESOURCE

More information about retirement accounts. *IRAs, 401(k)s & Other Retirement Plans: Strategies for Taking Your Money Out,* by Twila Slesnick and John C. Suttle (Nolo), explains all the options of those who inherit a retirement account.

Amounts Due to the Decedent

Add any right the decedent had to receive money from another person or entity to the schedule of assets. List any personal loans, rents, dividends, unpaid fees, salary, or commissions owed to the decedent, with the name of the payor, the amount due, and a brief description. The value of these items is generally the principal balance still owing and unpaid as of the date of death, plus the amount of any accrued but unpaid interest to that date.

If the amount owing is unlikely to be collected or not secured, this may affect the value. For instance, if the decedent made an unsecured loan to someone who refuses or is unable to pay it back, or the payments are extremely delinquent or the person cannot be located, there may not be value to the estate.

Assume Robert Morgan, the decedent, had loaned $50,000 to his son, J.P., to purchase a house, and at the time of Robert's death, J.P. had repaid $15,000. Robert was married to Ellen, and the loan is considered to be community property.

	A	B	C	D	E
	Total Value of Asset on Date/Death	How Is Asset Owned?	Portion Owned by Decedent	Value of Decedent's Interest	Probate or Non-probate
7. **Amounts Due the Decedent** (name of payor, amount)					
$50,000 promissory note of J.P. Morgan,					
dated 3/1/20xx, interest at 8%, payable					
$350 on the first of each month,					
secured by deed of trust on real					
property located at 515 Sutter Street,					
San Jose; principal balance on date					
of death: $35,000	35,000	CP	1/2	17,500	*
accrued interest	150			75	

* Enter N/P if asset will pass to surviving spouse or partner using the simplified probate procedures. (See Chapter 15.) Otherwise, leave blank until you know whether you can use small estate procedures based on the size of the probate estate. (See Chapter 11.)

The accrued interest is computed by determining the daily amount of interest on the principal balance due (that is, 0.08 × $35,000 ÷ 365 = $7.66), and multiplying this figure by the number of days from the date of the last note payment to the date of death. For instance, if the last note payment was May 1, 2020 and the decedent died on May 5, 2020, there would be five days' accrued and unpaid interest due on the date of death, or $38.30 (5 × $7.66). Online calculators for daily interest may prove helpful.

TIP

Unclaimed property. The California State Controller holds property that businesses turn over when there has been no activity to claim it for a period of time (generally three years). This can include forgotten bank accounts, uncashed checks, insurance benefits, or even wages. Conduct a search on the Controller's website at http://ucpi.sco.ca.gov to find property held in the deceased's name. You can also check for unclaimed property in other states where the decedent lived in the past.

Tangible Personal Property

Tangible personal property includes miscellaneous items of personal property. Personal effects that are not particularly valuable can be grouped together under the general heading of "furniture, furnishings, and personal effects," and given a lump-sum value. Remember, you do not consider what these items initially cost, but rather their secondhand value—and this is generally a small fraction of their original purchase price. Consulting sources such as eBay and Craigslist can help provide estimates. As an example, if you exclude specific valuable items, the value of tangible personal property in a five-room house, such as furniture and household items, would probably be around $1,000. For valuable jewelry, artwork, coin collections, antiques, musical instruments, and the like, you may obtain a private appraisal from an expert in the field. (As mentioned earlier, if the assets will go through formal probate, a court appointed referee will perform necessary appraisals, and you may not need to hire a private appraiser.) Any appraisal fees should be paid from estate assets as discussed in Chapters 13 and 14. All items in this category are usually probate items.

For a decedent who is single, your descriptions will be in the following form:

	A Total Value of Asset on Date/Death	B How Is Asset Owned?	C Portion Owned by Decedent	D Value of Decedent's Interest	E Probate or Non-probate
9. Tangible Personal Property (household furniture, furnishings, personal effects, books, jewelry, artwork, valuable collections, antiques, etc.)					
One Tiffany diamond ring, 2 carats	20,000	SP	all	20,000	**
Antique coin collection in decedent's residence	3,000	SP	all	3,000	**
Household furniture, furnishings, and personal effects	1,000	SP	all	750	**

** Leave blank until you know whether you can use small estate procedures based on the size of the probate estate. (See Chapter 11.)

Vehicles

Examine the ownership certificate (pink slip) to see the registered title to each vehicle. When multiple owners are listed joined by "and" or listed as "tenants in common," the decedent's portion does not automatically pass without probate.

However, when an ownership certificate lists multiple owners joined by "or," the Department of Motor Vehicles considers the vehicle to be in joint tenancy ownership, and it may be transferred to the surviving owner without probate. Similarly, California vehicles may be registered in TOD (transfer on death) form or joint tenancy with right of survivorship (JTRS), which means that the beneficiary inherits the vehicle without probate. (The procedures for transfer are given in Chapter 10.)

Describe automobiles by the year, make, model, and mileage. Unless the automobile is unusual (for example, antique, foreign, classic, or modified), use the *Kelley Blue Book* to estimate the value. You can get a quote online at www.kbb.com.

Business Interests

If the decedent had any interest in a business as a sole proprietor or partner or owned an interest in a closely held (private) corporation, you should list it here with the name of the business, partnership, or corporation, and the decedent's percentage ownership and manner of holding title. You may need to contact the other parties involved to obtain this information. Assets like these are valued according to many technical rules and you will need to get an estimate of the value either from an accountant or a firm that is expert in business appraisals. Some CPA firms specialize in business appraisals.

Other Assets

List here any other assets not included in the above categories. This may include cryptocurrencies, transferrable reward program benefits, and balances in PayPal or Venmo accounts. You may need an expert appraiser to determine the value of such things as copyrights or royalty interests, patents, stock options, or future residuals if the amount involved is large.

	A Total Value of Asset on Date/Death	B How Is Asset Owned?	C Portion Owned by Decedent	D Value of Decedent's Interest	E Probate or Non-probate
10. Automobiles (year, make, model)					
2015 Toyota Prius, in name of					
John Doe and Mary Doe	15,000	CP	1/2	7,500	____*
1995 Cadillac Seville, 4-door sedan,					
in name of decedent	1,000	SP	all	1,000	____*

* Enter N/P if asset will pass to surviving spouse or partner using the simplified probate procedures. (See Chapter 15.) Otherwise, leave blank until you know whether you can use small estate procedures based on the size of the probate estate. (See Chapter 11.)

Assume the decedent owned an interest in a partnership as separate property, which she left to her daughter by use of a living (inter vivos) trust, and a community property interest in a business. These would be described like this:

	A Total Value of Asset on Date/Death	B How Is Asset Owned?	C Portion Owned by Decedent	D Value of Decedent's Interest	E Probate or Non-probate
11. Business Interests (names of partnerships or family corporations, brief descriptions)					
Eureka Mining Co., a general partnership,					
500 Unity Building, Banning, CA	15,000	SP	all	15,000	N/P
"The Rori Kennel," a sole proprietorship,					
111 Bunratty Rd., Kelso, CA	70,000	CP	1/2	35,000	____*

* Enter N/P if asset will pass to surviving spouse or partner using the simplified probate procedures. (See Chapter 15.) Otherwise, leave blank until you know whether you can use small estate procedures based on the size of the probate estate. (See Chapter 11.)

	A Total Value of Asset on Date/Death	B How Is Asset Owned?	C Portion Owned by Decedent	D Value of Decedent's Interest	E Probate or Non-probate
12. Other Assets (copyrights, royalty interests, any other property not listed above)					
Copyright on book *How to Play Tennis,* published 2019 by Harvest Pub. Co., Los Angeles, annual royalties approx. $5,000 with three-year life expectancy remaining.	15,000	CP	1/2	7,500	____*
Estimated future residuals due decedent from Screen Actors Guild for services prior to death	500	SP	all	500	____*

* Enter N/P if asset will pass to surviving spouse or partner using the simplified probate procedures. (See Chapter 15.) Otherwise, leave blank until you know whether you can use small estate procedures based on the size of the probate estate. (See Chapter 11.)

Remember, you may not need to hire a private appraiser if a formal probate proceeding is required. Instead, the court-appointed probate referee will provide an appraisal. In some instances, though, having a private appraisal may be helpful to provide to the probate referee, particularly for unique assets, and a private appraisal may be appropriate for tax purposes.

Schedule of Assets for a Sample Estate

Let's look at a sample estate, the *Estate of Sybil Sample, Deceased*, and see how its Schedule of Assets would take form.

Sybil Sample married Cyrus Sample in San Jose, California, in 1984. They lived in California continuously during their marriage until Sybil's death. Sybil left all of her community and separate property to Cyrus in her will, except for her savings bonds, which she left to her cousin Alice.

At the time of marriage, Sybil owned an unimproved lot in San Bernardino County; three $500 U.S. Series E savings bonds; a savings account at Union Bank in Arcadia held in Sybil's name with her mother, Anne, listed as the POD beneficiary; and a $40,000 promissory note secured by a deed of trust on real property. Sybil also owned a $15,000 Sun Life term insurance policy on her life, naming her mother as beneficiary, on which premiums continued to be paid with her earnings during her marriage to Cyrus.

Cyrus and Sybil purchased a home and took title in both their names as husband and wife. They paid the mortgage out of community funds. Cyrus, a newspaper reporter, and Sybil, a teacher, both continued to work after marriage, depositing all of their excess earnings into a joint savings account at Pacific States Bank. During their marriage, Cyrus purchased 200 shares of AT&T stock and a 2009 Toyota Camry automobile with his earnings, taking title in his name alone. Sybil and Cyrus also invested money in Franklin Group Money Funds, a money market fund, and purchased a $10,000 Central High School District school bond, holding both of these assets as joint tenants. Cyrus also took out a $100,000

Aetna Life Insurance policy on his life during their marriage, and transferred complete ownership in the policy to Sybil. Sybil paid the premiums on the policy from her separate funds. For their anniversary in 1992, Cyrus gave Sybil a three-quarter-carat diamond ring.

At her death, Sybil also had an uncashed refund check from a hardware store and $300 in cash. She and Cyrus were owed $2,000 by Joe Swanson, to whom they had made an unsecured noninterest loan. At Sybil's death, a $5,000 pension plan death benefit became payable to Cyrus.

The Schedule of Assets for Sybil's estate is set out below. The information inserted on the schedule for each asset was determined by the following facts:

Item 1: Cash Items

The cash in Sybil's possession and the refund check are community property, having been acquired during her marriage. Thus, Sybil has a one-half interest in these items. These are technically part of her probate estate, but since Sybil left all of her community and separate property to Cyrus, they can be transferred without having to go through formal probate. (See Chapter 15.)

Item 2: Bank Accounts

The Pacific States Bank account, held in joint tenancy, passes to Cyrus outside of probate. Nevertheless, you should insert the full value of the account in Column A and the value of a one-half interest in Column D.

The savings account at Union Bank in Arcadia is a POD account, which passes to Sybil's mother as named beneficiary, without probate, on Sybil's death. The entire proceeds of the account are Sybil's separate property. She was the sole owner prior to death; she didn't transfer any percentage of ownership in the account to her mother when she made her a beneficiary, and didn't deposit any of her community property earnings in the account during marriage.

Item 3: Real Property

The residence is community property because title was acquired by Sybil and Cyrus during marriage as husband and wife, and one-half of the residence is included in Sybil's estate.

In the case of the residence, a formal probate court proceeding won't be necessary because it passes to Cyrus under Sybil's will. Cyrus can use the simplified procedure to transfer property to a surviving spouse. (See Chapter 15.)

The unimproved lot in San Bernardino is Sybil's separate property, since she owned it prior to marriage, and it is included 100% in her estate.

Item 4: Securities

Sybil owned the three U.S. Series E savings bonds prior to marriage, so they are her separate property and the current redemption value is included 100% in her estate. They will be subject to probate because they were left to cousin Alice. But because the assets subject to probate total less than $166,250 (the "small" estate limit in the year of Sybil's death), Alice may collect the bonds using a small estate affidavit and no formal probate will be required (Chapter 11). The Franklin Group Money Fund shares and the $10,000 Central High School District school bond are held in joint tenancy and, therefore, are not subject to probate. Although it is held in Cyrus's name alone, the AT&T stock is community property, because he purchased it during their marriage with community property funds, and one half of the stock is included in Sybil's estate. Because this property goes to Cyrus, no formal probate will be required. (See Chapter 15.)

Item 5: Insurance

The $15,000 Sun Life Policy that was owned by Sybil prior to her marriage was a term policy. Because she continued to pay premiums during the marriage with community property funds, the policy proceeds are community property. Therefore, even though her mother is the named beneficiary, Cyrus has a one-half vested interest in the $15,000 proceeds, which is $7,500. The policy proceeds are not subject to probate because there is a named beneficiary. In this case, you put the total value of the proceeds ($15,000) in Column A and the part owned by Sybil ($7,500) in Column D.

The $100,000 Aetna Life Policy on Cyrus's life is Sybil's separate property, and the total cash value of the policy on her date of death is included in her estate. It would be subject to formal probate except that Sybil left all of her property to Cyrus and, therefore, it qualifies for the simplified spousal transfer provisions discussed in Chapter 15. Sometimes you can transfer ownership of an insurance policy simply by furnishing the carrier with a copy of the will.

Item 6: Retirement and Death Benefits

The $5,000 pension plan death benefit, payable to Cyrus, is not subject to probate, but one-half is included in Sybil's estate as community property because it is payable by reason of her employment.

Item 7: Amounts Due to the Decedent

The $2,000 loan due from Joe Swanson is community property and one-half is included in Sybil's estate. It would be subject to formal probate except that it qualifies for the simplified spousal transfer provisions discussed in Chapter 15.

Item 8: Promissory Notes

The $40,000 promissory note owned by Sybil prior to marriage is her separate property and is included 100% in her estate. It would be subject to formal probate if it had been left to anyone but Cyrus.

Item 9: Tangible Personal Property

The household furniture and personal effects are included in Sybil's estate to the extent of her one-half community property interest. The gold diamond ring is Sybil's separate property, having been acquired as a gift, and is included 100% in her estate. Both of these would be subject to formal probate if they had not been left to a spouse.

Item 10: Automobiles

A one-half interest in the Camry is included in Sybil's estate as community property, even though Cyrus took title in his name alone. Since Cyrus inherits this vehicle anyway, nothing need be done to transfer ownership to him.

An example of the Schedule of Assets for Sybil's estate is shown below. After you review it, go on to the next chapter to see how to actually transfer the assets in Sybil's estate.

Sample Schedule of Assets

Schedule of Assets

Estate of SYBIL SAMPLE, Deceased

Description of Assets	A Total Value of Asset on Date/Death	B How Is Asset Owned?	C Portion Owned by Decedent	D Value of Decedent's Interest	E Probate or Non-probate
1. Cash Items					
Cash in decedent's possession	300	CP	1/2	150	NP[1]
Uncashed checks payable to decedent					
Refund from Abco Hardware	55.60	CP	1/2	27.80	NP[1]
2. Bank and Savings & Loan Accounts					
a. Sav. Acct. #1234, Pacific States	20,000	JT	1/2	10,000	NP[2]
Bank, San Jose (acct. int.)	150	JT	1/2	75	NP[2]
b. Sav. Acct. #0832, Union Bank	6,000	POD (SP)	all	6,000	NP[2]
Arcadia (POD for Anne) (acct. int.)	70	POD (SP)	all	70	NP[2]
3. Real Property (common address, brief description)					
a. Single-family residence, 930 Hill Street, San Jose	500,000	CP	1/2	250,000	NP[1]
b. Unimproved lot, San Bernardino County	15,000	SP	all	15,000	NP[1]
4. Securities Stock (name of company, type, and number of shares)					
200 shares AT&T common (in name of Cyrus Sample)	10,000	CP	1/2	5,000	NP[1]

Sample Schedule of Assets (continued)

	A Total Value of Asset on Date/Death	B How Is Asset Owned?	C Portion Owned by Decedent	D Value of Decedent's Interest	E Probate or Non-probate
Bonds (face amount)					
$10,000 Central High School Dist.	9,800	JT	1/2	4,900	NP[2]
bond, Series C, 4%, 12-31-15 (acc. int.)	198	JT	1/2	99	NP[2]
U.S. Savings Bonds/Treasury Bills (series, amount, date of issue)					
Three $500 U.S. Series E savings bonds, issued July 1975	7,989	SP	all	7,989	NP[3]
Mutual Funds (name of fund, number of shares)					
50,000 shares Franklin Group	50,000	JT	1/2	25,000	NP[2]
5. Insurance (name of company, policy number, name of beneficiary, name of owner)					
Policies on decedent's life					
$15,000 Sun Term Life Ins. Policy, No. 83792 (beneficiary: decedent's mother)	15,000	CP	1/2	$7,500	NP[1,2]
Policies owned by decedent on another					
$100,000 Aetna Life Policy, No. 24487	4,000	SP	all	4,000	NP[1]
6. Retirement and Death Benefits (description, beneficiary, amount)					
Employee benefits					
$5,000 School employee's pension plan	5,000	CP	1/2	2,500	NP[2]
Pension, profit-sharing, savings plans					
Social Security/Railroad Retirement					
Individual Retirement Accounts					

Sample Schedule of Assets (continued)

	A Total Value of Asset on Date/Death	B How Is Asset Owned?	C Portion Owned by Decedent	D Value of Decedent's Interest	E Probate or Non-probate
7. Amounts Due the Decedent (name of payor, amount)					
$2,000 unsecured non–interest-bearing	2,000	CP	1/2	1,000	NP[1]
loan due from Joe Swanson					
8. Promissory Note (name of payor, date, amount, balance)					
$40,000 promissory note of Mynos					
5% int., dated 7-1-80, secured					
by trust deed on real property at	35,000	SP	all	35,000	NP[1]
123 Main St., Los Angeles (acc. int.)	123.50	SP	all	123.50	NP[1]
9. Tangible Personal Property (household furniture, furnishings, personal effects, books, jewelry, artwork, valuable collections, antiques, etc.)					
a. Household furnishings and personal					
effects	1,000	CP	1/2	500	NP[1]
b. Gold ring, 3/4 carat diamond	1,500	SP	all	1,500	NP[1]
10. Automobiles (year, make, model)					
2009 Toyota Camry	4,000	CP	1/2	2,000	NP[1]
11. Business Interests (names of partnerships or family corporations, brief descriptions)					
12. Other Assets (copyrights, royalty interests, any other property not listed above)					
Total Value of Decedent's Gross Estate				$378,434.30	

1. Simplified property transfer procedures will be used to transfer the property to Cyrus. (Chapter 15.)
2. Passes through joint tenancy or POD or beneficiary designation. (Chapter 10.)
3. Small estate procedures will be used to transfer because the probate is less than $166,250. (Chapter 11.)

Sample Schedule of Assets (continued)

Deductions (for federal estate tax purposes)

a. Personal debts owed by decedent at date of death

Clark's Department Store: $1,180 (CP)	$ 590

b. Mortgages/promissory notes due

Beneficial Sav. & Loan (house loan): $98,000 (CP)	49,000

c. Expenses of estate administration

Appraisals, transfer fees, recording fees, court costs	800

d. Last illness expenses

Richard Roe, M.D., medical services	1,500
Mary Smith, nursing care	600

e. Funeral expenses

Chapel Mortuary	2,589

f. Sales contracts (automobiles, furniture, television)

C & D Financial (auto loan): $1,150 (CP)	575

Total Deductions	$ 55,654
Total Value of Decedent's Gross Estate (from previous page)	$ 378,434.30
Total Deductions (from line above)	55,654.00
Value of Decedent's Net Estate	$ 322,780.30

CHAPTER

6

How to Identify the Best Transfer Procedure

After you've figured out what the decedent owned and who will get it, the next step is to determine the best method of actually transferring the property. This chapter does not actually deal with the "how-to" of making transfers. Rather, it provides a road map to the detailed transfer instructions contained in the chapters that follow. In other words, this chapter will point you toward the most direct route to your property transfer goal.

You can use your Schedule of Assets as a guide. On that worksheet, you collected important information that will help you determine the requirements and options for transferring assets of the estate. Some estates will not need probate court involvement, and others estates will—for some or all assets. Let's briefly review the transfer rules.

SEE AN EXPERT

Note for surviving spouses and domestic partners. In many situations, property held in joint tenancy by spouses or domestic partners may be community property depending on the facts of the situation. You may transfer it either as a joint tenancy asset or you may use a Spousal or Domestic Partner Property Order (discussed in Chapter 15) to officially establish the joint tenancy property as community property. There may be favorable tax reasons to establish the property as community property. We discuss these tax rules in Chapter 7. If after reading this discussion you are still confused, see an accountant or an attorney for help.

Nonprobate Assets

Certain property of the decedent may not go through probate, either because the decedent specifically planned to avoid probate or because the decedent simply held title or designated beneficiaries in a way that avoids probate. This section lists some of the most common nonprobate assets.

The law also provides a variety of shortcut procedures that may apply. Read the next section of this chapter, "Assets That May Be Subject to Formal Probate," to help you see if, in fact, you may have to have a formal probate proceeding, or whether one or more of the simpler methods will work to transfer the property of the estate.

Joint Tenancy Assets

Assets held in joint tenancy pass to the surviving joint tenant (or tenants) by operation of law and without a probate proceeding. Chapter 10 explains how to transfer title to the surviving joint tenant (or tenants). If no joint tenant survives the decedent, then the asset may have to go through probate.

POD and TOD Assets

Assets that have a designated beneficiary generally pass to the new owners without probate. The beneficiary can transfer POD (pay on death) accounts in the same manner as joint tenancy bank accounts by using the procedures explained in Chapter 10. The beneficiary can transfer TOD (transfer on death) assets like securities, using the procedures explained in Chapter 9.

Living Trusts

Many people in California put their property in living (inter vivos) trusts to avoid probate. Any property held in a living trust created by the decedent is not subject to probate administration if the property was actually transferred to the trust, in which case title will be held in the name of the trustee. If the asset was transferred to the trust, the ownership document will show the title held something like this: "I.M. Smart, trustee of the I.M. Smart Trust." Carefully examine all title documents, such as real property deeds, bank account statements, and stock certificates to see if title is held by the trust.

Property that does not have a title document can be included in a trust just by listing it in the body of the trust document or in a document attached to and referenced by the trust document. Sometimes a document called an "assignment" is used to list non-titled property and state that it is included in the trust. Miscellaneous items of personal property can be included in a living trust in these ways.

Occasionally, a decedent may have signed a trust document, but for some reason failed to sign documents actually transferring the property to the trustee. When this happens the property may be subject to probate. Get legal assistance if the decedent created a trust, yet it appears that assets are not held by the trustee.

When the person who established a living trust dies, property held in the trust is transferred to the beneficiary (named in the trust document) by a successor trustee named in the trust. The general procedure used to transfer property subject to a living trust is set out in Chapter 12.

RESOURCE

Learn more about trust administration. Trust administration is beyond the scope of this book. To get details about trust administration and the duties of a trustee, read *The Trustee's Legal Companion: A Step-by-Step Guide to Administering a Living Trust,* by Carol Elias Zolla and Liza Hanks (Nolo). For help with California-specific rules, see a California attorney experienced in trust administration.

Revocable TOD Deeds

A revocable transfer on death (TOD) deed follows a specific format to name a beneficiary to receive the property upon the owner's death. This type of deed generally references Probate Code § 5642. To obtain legal title after the owner dies, the beneficiary need only record an affidavit indicating that the owner has died and affix a certified copy of the death certificate. (See Chapter 8.)

Transfer on death deeds allow for a simple transfer of property in many cases. However, you may need to do further research or get specific advice if you have a more complex situation. For example, the situation is not simple if:

- the property was owned in joint tenancy or as community property with the right of survivorship when the deed was signed
- the beneficiary is not specifically named
- the deed was not recorded, or
- the deed may have been revoked.

U.S. Savings Bonds in Co-Ownership or Beneficiary Form

Bonds registered with two names can avoid probate. The names may be separated by "with" (for certain electronic bonds) or "or" (for paper bonds). Bonds may also be registered as pay on death, listed with the owner followed by "POD" and the beneficiary's name.

Title passes to the surviving co-owner or beneficiary by operation of law and without probate. Your local bank can assist in redeeming bonds or reregistering the bonds in the name of the surviving owner or beneficiary. TreasuryDirect.gov also provides forms and instructions for nonprobate transfers, including redeeming or reissuing U.S. savings bonds. You will need the original bond certificates, if they exist, and a certified copy of the decedent's death certificate to handle transfer of U.S. savings bonds.

If both owners of a U.S. savings bond are deceased, then the bond is subject to probate proceedings unless a probate shortcut applies to the estate.

Life Insurance and Death Benefits Payable to Named Beneficiaries

If life insurance, retirement plans, and other death benefits payable to named beneficiaries have not already been collected, these benefits may be claimed by contacting the company or organization responsible for making payment. The company provides the necessary forms to the beneficiary or beneficiaries and will notify you of the other documents it requires (usually a certified copy of the decedent's death certificate and the policy). Instructions are in Chapter 2.

Insurance proceeds payable to the decedent's estate, as well as the cash value of any insurance policies the decedent owned on the life of another person, require probate unless the entire estate qualifies to avoid probate based on its small size (see Chapter 11) or unless the property is transferred to a surviving spouse or domestic partner (see Chapter 15).

If the decedent did not designate a beneficiary, if the beneficiary did not survive the decedent, or if the decedent named the "estate" as the beneficiary, then the asset may need to go through formal probate unless a probate shortcut applies to the estate.

Community Property With Right of Survivorship

If a married or partnered couple held title to property as "community property with right of survivorship," the survivor inherits the deceased person's half-interest automatically, without probate. The property must be clearly identified on the transfer document (a real estate deed, for example) as community property with the right of survivorship and it must have the signatures or initials of the parties accepting this form of title. (Civ. Code § 682.1.)

Transferring title to the surviving spouse or domestic partner occurs in the same manner as for joint tenancy property—for real property, an affidavit of death will be recorded with a certified copy of the death certificate. (See Chapter 8.)

Life Estates

A life estate is created when a person transfers real property to someone else but keeps the right to use the property for the rest of the transferor's life. We define life estates in Chapter 4 and discuss transfers of property held in life estates in Chapter 8.

Assets That May Be Subject to Formal Probate

The remaining assets on your schedule may have to go through formal probate. If so, court procedures will be required to transfer the assets to the heirs or beneficiaries.

Broadly speaking, if assets owned by the decedent do not pass to a beneficiary through the nonprobate mechanisms discussed in the section above, to determine whether a formal probate is necessary you will evaluate (1) if assets pass to a surviving spouse or domestic partner, and (2) the size of the remaining estate.

Community Property or Separate Property That Passes Outright to the Decedent's Surviving Spouse or Domestic Partner

SKIP AHEAD

Skip ahead. If the decedent wasn't married or in a domestic partnership at death, you can skip this and go on to the next section.

Any property—community property or separate property—that goes outright (not subject to a life estate or in a trust) to the decedent's surviving spouse or domestic partner under the terms of the decedent's will or by intestate succession in the absence of a will does not require formal probate. (Prob. Code § 13500.) Nevertheless, a court order, called a Spousal or Domestic Partner Property Order, is often required to transfer title to certain types of assets, including real property or stocks and bonds. Chapter 15 describes the simple, informal court procedure for obtaining this court order. There is no limitation on the amount or value of the assets transferred.

To find out if any of a decedent's assets fall into this category, examine the will (if there is one) to see if the decedent left the property to the surviving spouse or partner. Then, verify that such property passes to the survivor without any limitations as to ownership. If the survivor is given a qualified ownership in the property, such as in a trust, it is not eligible to be transferred in this way.

If there is no will, then all community property, plus at least a part (and sometimes all) of the decedent's separate property, if any, will go outright to the surviving spouse or domestic partner under intestate succession laws. The portion passing to the surviving spouse or partner under these laws depends on whether the decedent left any surviving children or other close relatives entitled to receive a portion of the separate property. Refer to Chapter 3 to see how a decedent's separate property is divided in the absence of a will. Again, if a court order is necessary to transfer this property, as it probably is in the case of real property or securities, see Chapter 15.

If the decedent willed interest in community property or separate property to someone other than the surviving spouse or partner, then the procedures described below will apply to that property.

Property in "Small" Estates

For many Californians, no formal probate is required. California Probate Code Sections 13000 to 13210 provide a simple way to transfer property in estates that don't exceed a total gross value of $166,250.

The Adjusted Definition of a "Small" Estate

The definition of a "small" estate for the purposes of simplified procedures is now $166,250. This dollar amount was raised from $150,000, effective January 1, 2020, and will be adjusted to account for inflation on April 1, 2022 and every three years thereafter. The Judicial Council will publish the adjusted amounts to apply for decedents who die after the date of adjustment.

Personal property in an estate valued below $166,250 may be transferred with a one-page affidavit. You may also use an affidavit procedure to transfer real property worth $55,425 or less. Title to real property up to $166,250 in value may be passed by a simple court procedure. There is a waiting period—40 days for the affidavit procedures, and six months for the simple court procedure—before you can request the transfers.

In many instances, small estate procedures may be used for estates over $166,250, because several kinds of assets aren't counted in computing the $166,250 limitation. For example, all joint tenancy property (both real and personal) is excluded, as well as all property that goes outright to a surviving spouse or domestic partner (community or separate), property passing directly by beneficiary designation, property held in a trust, and certain other property. Chapter 11 explains this simple method of transferring assets in more detail. Even if the estate you are dealing with contains assets somewhat more than $166,250, you will want to read Chapter 11 to see if the various exclusions allowed by law permit use of these simple procedures.

TIP

Do not include cotenant's interest. Keep in mind that if property is held in cotenancy form, usually expressed in a deed or on title as "tenants in common," you will consider only the decedent's portion of the property when assessing the total value of the decedent's estate.

Remaining Assets

All remaining assets that do not fall into one of the above categories require a formal probate court proceeding before title may be transferred. Generally, this includes remaining assets that are:

- not held in trust
- not held in joint tenancy
- not community or separate property going outright to the surviving spouse or domestic partner
- not passing by beneficiary designation, and
- in estates greater than $166,250 in value.

The complexity of the probate process will depend on the amount and type of the property subject to formal probate. Chapter 13 of this book provides an overview of formal probate proceedings and Chapter 14 explains how to handle the necessary paperwork for straightforward estates. While it is possible to proceed without a lawyer—particularly if the estate is simple—formal probate proceedings can be legally complicated, tedious, and time consuming. For these reasons most people choose to get professional legal support once they realize that a formal probate proceeding may be necessary. Chapter 16 provides information on getting professional help.

Examples of How Assets Are Transferred in Typical Estates

Let's return now to the estate of Sybil Sample, which we introduced in the preceding chapter. Our idea here is to illustrate the process of determining the methods used to transfer the assets of an example estate. If you review Sybil's Schedule of Assets in Chapter 5, you will find that the assets fall into the categories described above.

Joint Tenancy Assets

Sybil held three assets in joint tenancy with her husband, Cyrus: The savings account at Pacific States Bank, the $10,000 Central High School District school bond, and the 50,000 shares of Franklin Group Money Fund. These all go to Cyrus without the need for probate. Chapter 10 shows how to transfer joint tenancy assets.

POD Bank Account

The savings account at Union Bank in Arcadia (Item 2) had Sybil's mother, Anne, listed as a pay on death beneficiary. The proceeds of that account can be transferred to Anne using the procedures outlined in Chapter 10. (This is the same as for a joint tenancy account.) Because Sybil established this account prior to her marriage, Cyrus has no community property interest in it.

Insurance Payable to Named Beneficiary

The proceeds of the Sun Life Insurance policy may be paid directly to the beneficiaries by contacting the company for the necessary claim forms and submitting a certified copy of the decedent's death certificate. Since Sybil's mother, Anne, is the named beneficiary of the policy, the insurance company will pay the proceeds to Anne unless it is advised otherwise. If Cyrus wants to collect his vested community property interest in the proceeds, he must contact the insurance company and work out an arrangement with the company and Anne. If it cannot be done on this basis, Cyrus would have to see an attorney. Alternatively, Cyrus could obtain a Spousal or Domestic Partner Property Order (see Chapter 15) confirming that $7,500 of the proceeds belongs to him as his community property interest. Of course, because Cyrus gets most of the rest of the property, he might well conclude that for personal or family reasons he does not want to challenge Sybil's intent in naming Anne as beneficiary.

Pension Plan Death Benefit Payable to Named Beneficiary

The $5,000 school employee's pension plan death benefit, payable to Cyrus as named beneficiary, may be collected by Cyrus by submitting a certified copy of the death certificate to the pension plan office and asking for the necessary claim forms.

All Other Assets

The other assets on the schedule make up the part of Sybil's estate that is potentially subject to probate, unless they fall within one of the exceptions to probate discussed at the beginning of this chapter. The persons to whom these assets will pass and the method used to transfer such property depend on whether or not Sybil left a will naming beneficiaries to receive the property or whether she instead died intestate.

Sample Estates

In Chapter 5, we assumed that Sybil left a will, but here let's look at both possibilities and see what happens to the assets in each case. To make this easier, let's first divide Sybil's remaining assets into separate property and community property. If you are not sure how to do this, refer to Chapter 4.

Community Property (Sybil's one-half interest)

Cash	$150.00
Abco Hardware refund	27.80
San Jose residence	250,000.00
AT&T stock	5,000.00
Loan due from Joe Swanson	1,000.00
Household furnishings, etc.	500.00
Toyota Camry	+ 2,000.00
	$253,677.80

Separate Property (Sybil's 100% interest)	
San Bernardino lot	$15,000.00
Series E bonds	7,989.00
Aetna Life Insurance policy	4,000.00
Promissory note	35,123.50
Diamond ring	+ 1,500.00
	$63,612.50

Sybil Dies With a Will

Assume Sybil left a will leaving Cyrus all property except her savings bonds, which she left to her cousin Alice. All of the property (both community property and separate property) left to Cyrus may be transferred to him without formal probate administration using an affidavit or Spousal or Domestic Partner Property Order, obtained by using the procedures outlined in Chapter 15.

A court order is not needed to transfer ownership of every asset to Cyrus. For instance, the AT&T stock and Camry are already in his name, and since most of the other assets have no title documents, they will pass to Cyrus automatically under Probate Code Section 13500. Therefore, the only assets for which an official transfer document (the Spousal or Domestic Partner Property Order) will be required are the San Jose residence, the San Bernardino lot, and the Mynos promissory note.

Because Sybil's will left some property to someone other than Cyrus (Cousin Alice), our next step is to see what the property consists of. If it is valued under $166,250 (presuming she died in 2020), it may be transferred to the person(s) named in the will by using the affidavit procedure discussed in Chapter 11.

However, if Sybil willed property having a gross total value exceeding $166,250 to someone other than her surviving spouse, formal probate court proceedings are required before it can be transferred. Those proceedings are discussed in Chapter 14.

Sybil Dies Without a Will

If we assume Sybil died without a will, leaving Cyrus and her mother as her only heirs (there are no children), then intestate succession laws dictate that all of her community property would go outright to Cyrus and her separate property would be given one-half to Cyrus and one-half to her mother. (We show you how to figure out who inherits property in the absence of a will in Chapter 3.)

In this case, the community property and Cyrus's one-half interest in the separate property may be transferred to Cyrus without formal probate by use of a Spousal or Domestic Partner Property Order, as discussed in Chapter 15. The other one-half interest in the separate property must go through probate or, if it is valued at less than $166,250, may be transferred by the small estate procedures discussed in Chapter 11. At the close of the probate proceeding, if one is required, the court will make an order distributing a one-half interest in the separate property to Sybil's mother. If Cyrus and Sybil's mother do not wish to own a one-half interest in each separate property asset (which might not be practical in the case of the diamond ring or the Aetna Life Insurance policy), the distribution plan proposed for court approval can include another arrangement or they may make an agreement for distribution after they obtain court orders.

Estate of Cyrus Sample, Deceased

Now for further illustration, let's see what happens to Cyrus's estate when he dies approximately two years later. Assume that Cyrus did not remarry after Sybil's death and was still a resident of San Jose, California, when he died. He had two children by a previous marriage, a daughter, Sally, and a son, Michael, who survived him. Prior to his death, Cyrus disposed of some of the assets he had received from Sybil's estate, and acquired others. To avoid probate of the bulk of his estate, Cyrus executed a revocable living trust and transferred the family residence and a limited partnership interest into the trust. The trust named his brother Sam as successor trustee and Cyrus's children, Sally and Michael, to be beneficiaries after Cyrus's death.

At the time of his death, Cyrus's estate consisted of the following property:

- savings account No. 1234, Pacific States Bank, San Jose, California, having a principal balance of $20,000

- 200 shares, AT&T common stock, worth $10,000
- 10% interest in Westland Shopping Center, a limited partnership, in name of Cyrus Sample, as Trustee of the Cyrus Sample Trust, dated June 1, 20xx, valued at $200,000
- family residence, 930 Hill Street, San Jose, in the name of Cyrus Sample, as Trustee of the Cyrus Sample Trust, dated June 1, 20xx, having a value of $600,000
- $100,000 Aetna Life Insurance policy, on the life of Cyrus Sample, naming Sally and Michael as beneficiaries, and
- 2016 BMW, Model 320i sedan, having a value of $22,000.

Since Cyrus wasn't married when he died, all of his property is his separate property. His will (executed at the same time as his trust) leaves his entire estate to his two children. As we examine the transfer procedures available for the assets in Cyrus's estate, we will see that no formal probate proceedings are required to transfer the property.

First of all, the successor trustee of the Cyrus Sample Trust (Sam) can follow trust administration procedures to transfer the family residence and the partnership interest without probate to Cyrus's two children as the beneficiaries. The real property will require the preparation of a deed, signed by Sam as successor trustee, transferring the residence to Sally and Michael. The limited partnership interest will require an assignment executed by Sam, as successor trustee, assigning Cyrus's interest to Sally and Michael. As noted in Chapter 1, transfers of significant business interests should normally be handled through an attorney.

The proceeds of the Aetna Life policy will be paid to Sally and Michael, the named beneficiaries, without probate. The remaining personal property, consisting of the BMW automobile, AT&T stock, and the savings account at Pacific States Bank, all have a total gross value of $52,000. Thus, Sally and Michael, as the beneficiaries of Cyrus's will, may have each of these assets transferred to them without formal probate by using the affidavit procedure outlined in Chapter 11.

CHAPTER

7

What About Taxes?

One of the first things estate beneficiaries want to know is whether or not they have to pay taxes on the property they inherit. Usually, the answer is "no." Most estates only have to be concerned about income taxes. If, after the decedent's death, the estate assets produce enough income, they will generate an income tax bill, which will be paid either by filing an estate income tax return or by the beneficiaries who receive the income. Also, the estate representative must file the decedent's final income tax return and pay any taxes owed on income generated during the part of the tax year in which the decedent was alive.

Perhaps looming larger than income tax are the "death taxes" that most people have heard about, which are more accurately described as federal estate taxes and state inheritance and estate taxes. Most estates do not have to pay estate taxes. Federal estate tax is owed only on estates larger than approximately $11.7 million for 2021. (This amount rises with inflation.) California currently has no inheritance or estate tax.

SEE AN EXPERT

Get tax advice for outside of California. If the decedent owned property outside of California, or you are a beneficiary living outside of California, get tax advice from an attorney or tax professional.

This chapter briefly reviews the various tax returns you may have to file in settling an estate. Tax laws pertaining to estates and to beneficiaries who inherit property can be complex, especially if the estate is large or involves more than one state. If the estate you are settling has substantial assets or income to report, your best bet is to contact an accountant or attorney experienced in the area of estate taxes. An expert can advise you on how to minimize the impact of all taxes on the beneficiaries and the estate. Deadlines apply, so do not delay.

A detailed discussion of how to prepare a federal estate tax return would require another book. If an accountant or attorney prepares the return, the fee is ordinarily paid from the general assets of the estate or shared by the beneficiaries in proportion to their interests in the estate. Accounting and tax preparation fees are a deduction to the estate either on the estate's income tax returns or on the federal estate tax return, if one is required.

CAUTION

Keep up with the rules. The federal government frequently makes changes to its tax code. Do not rely on any of the dollar figures or detailed rules discussed here without checking current information from the IRS (www. irs.gov) and California Franchise Tax Board (www.ftb.ca.gov). Or, consult with a tax professional.

California Property Taxes

When a property owner dies, the transfer of ownership triggers reassessment of California property tax, unless an exclusion applies. Common exclusions from reassessment include transfers:

- between spouses or registered domestic partners, and
- between children and parents for the principal residence.

Transfers to grandchildren and cotenants may also be excluded from reassessment under certain circumstances.

Some exclusions require only a simple form to notify the county assessor of the death and of the relationship, including transfers to spouses or registered domestic partners. Other exclusions have limitations and require forms to be timely filed to claim the exclusion. Chapter 8 provides information about notifying the county assessor when a property owner dies and making claims for reassessment exclusions.

Decedent's Final Income Tax Returns

If the decedent receives more than a small amount of income in the year of death, final income tax returns may have to be filed for that year. The income levels at which returns must be filed change from year to year.

For deaths in 2019, decedents who were not married at the time of death had to file a final federal income tax return if gross income exceeded $12,200 ($13,850 if the decedent was 65 or older) for the taxable year up to the date of death. Gross income includes all income received in the form of money from property (for example, interest, dividends, or rents) as well as income from employment, pension, and other public and private benefit programs unless exempt from tax. If a married decedent was living in the same household with his or her spouse at the time of death and was eligible to file a joint return, a final federal income tax return must be filed if the combined gross income of the decedent and spouse was $24,400 or more for the entire taxable year. The cutoff is $25,700 if one spouse was 65 or older and $27,000 if both spouses were 65 or older. Returns must also be filed for other, less common reasons, such as having a net income of $400 or more from self-employment, or owing special taxes. IRS Publication 501, available at www.irs.gov, has information on who must file federal taxes.

TIP

Be on the lookout for tax information sent to the decedent via mail or email. You might see a W-2, which reports wage income. Or you might see forms in the 1099 series, which report other types of payments and income—like Form 1099-INT showing interest income, Form 1099-DIV showing dividends, or Form 1099-R showing distributions such as from pensions, annuities, or IRAs. These statements have information important for deciding whether a tax return must be filed and for completing the tax returns.

A California income tax return must be filed for California residents for 2019 if an unmarried decedent younger than age 65 had a gross income of $18,241 or more ($36,485 for married or registered domestic partner couples). If the decedent was 65 or older, the threshold is $24,341, or if one member of the married or partnered couple is 65 or older, $42,585. If both spouses or partners were 65 or older, the threshold is $48,685.

EXAMPLE 1: Molly was unmarried and 68 years old when she died in 2019. She earned a gross income of $11,000 in the year of her death. Because Molly is a single taxpayer older than 65, final income tax returns (both federal and California) do not have to be filed for Molly, except to claim a refund.

EXAMPLE 2: Jack and Jill were married, both older than 65, and earned a combined gross income of $50,000 in the year of Jack's death. Jack and Jill were entitled to file joint income tax returns. Income tax returns, both California and federal, must be filed because Jack and Jill's combined gross income for the entire taxable year exceeds the filing requirement for federal purposes and for state purposes. The joint returns will be the final year returns for Jack.

If income tax has been withheld from the decedent's wages or the decedent paid any estimated tax, you should file a final return for the decedent even if it is not required. The purpose is to obtain a refund of the taxes paid or withheld. If a refund is due, you may need to file IRS Form 1310, *Statement of Person Claiming Refund Due a Deceased Taxpayer*, with the return to claim the refund. Form 1310 isn't required if you are a surviving spouse filing a joint return with the decedent, or you are a court-appointed executor or administrator.

The due date for the decedent's final income tax returns (federal Form 1040 and California Form 540) is the same date as when the decedent was living—on or before the 15th day of the fourth month following the close of the decedent's regular tax year. This due date is usually April 15 of the year following death, unless the decedent had an accounting year different from a calendar year, which is rarely the case. (If April 15th falls on a weekend or holiday, tax returns are due the following business day.)

If the decedent died in the beginning of the year, before filing a return for the prior year, you may have to file two returns. For example, if the decedent dies on March 1, 2021 before filing returns for 2020, the personal representative of the decedent must file a return for 2020 on or before April 15, 2021. The decedent's final return (if required), for the period from January 1, 2021 to March 1, 2021 (the date of death), would be due on April 15, 2022. If, for some reason, the tax returns cannot be filed on the due date, you may apply for an extension.

Ordinarily, it is the responsibility of the executor or administrator of the estate to file the final returns and any other returns still due for the decedent. Because the final income tax returns are for the decedent, and not the estate, the estate representative prepares the returns on behalf of the decedent. In this instance, the representative signs the return on the line indicated for the taxpayer. For example, "Joan Jones, Administrator of the Estate of Anne Rose, Deceased," or "Joan Jones, Executor of the Will of Anne Rose, Deceased."

If the personal representative is the surviving spouse, the spouse should sign the return and then write in the signature area, "filing as surviving spouse." If there is no surviving spouse, administrator, or executor, it is extremely important that an accountant or the IRS be consulted before distribution of property. In this situation, the person in charge of the decedent's property should file the income tax return. Usually it is a family member or friend who stands to inherit the property who assumes the responsibility of winding up the decedent's affairs. If this is not done, those who inherit the property, or have control of it, must jointly assume responsibility for filing or appoint one of their number to take charge of the estate for this purpose; if they do not, they may be subject to penalties for willful neglect or tax evasion. The income tax return should be signed by the heirs or beneficiaries jointly (or by one of them acting on behalf of all), followed by the words "Personal Representative(s) of the Estate of Joe Brown, Deceased."

In filling out the income tax return, the decedent's name should be put on the "name" line at the top of the return, followed by the word "deceased" and the date of death. If it is a joint return, both spouses' names should be included with "deceased" after the decedents' names, such as "John Smith and Mary Smith, deceased." Also write "Deceased" across the top of the form.

TIP

Tax returns for years before year of death. Sometimes, older and less healthy persons have forgotten to prepare or file income tax returns for several years preceding death. If you suspect there may be returns due from the decedent for prior years, contact your local IRS office. Office locations and telephone numbers are listed on the IRS website at www.irs.gov. The personal representative should file any returns due for prior years and pay any taxes due before closing the estate.

The personal representative has authority to request transcripts of the decedent's past year tax returns from the IRS. Review the prior year returns and tax information if there is any question about whether the decedent properly filed returns.

An excellent source of information on this subject is IRS Publication 559, *Survivors, Executors, and Administrators*, available from the IRS website at www.irs.gov.

Fiduciary Income Tax Returns

Income received on assets in the decedent's estate after death is taxable, as is income received by an individual. Federal income tax returns must be filed if the estate has any taxable income in a tax year or if it has more than $600 in gross income per tax year. California income tax returns must be filed for a gross income of more than $10,000 per tax year or net income of more than $1,000 per tax year. The personal representative will report this income on "fiduciary income tax returns" using federal IRS Form 1041 and California FTB Form 541.

Fiduciary returns for an estate are normally required only if a formal probate court proceeding is opened and an estate representative is appointed by the court. The legal representative of the estate must have a way to report the income received on the decedent's assets during the administration of the estate until the property is distributed to the new owners. If an asset is sold during probate administration, you may need to report a capital gain on these returns. Without a formal probate, you will not have the authority to open an estate account so no income will be reported to the estate. How to report the income will be discussed below.

Fiduciary returns are due no later than the 15th day of the fourth month after the end of the estate's taxable year. The taxable year may be a fiscal year chosen by the accountant or estate representative, or a calendar year. Depending on the length of time it takes to close the estate, the first tax year may be less than 12 months. The estate is considered closed if all assets are distributed except for a reasonable amount set aside for closing expenses or unascertained liabilities.

If the probate proceeding takes less than a year, fiduciary returns are required for just the short time the estate is open, assuming the estate receives sufficient income during that period. In this case, the returns are treated as "final" returns and the beneficiaries (not the estate) pay the taxes due, if any, because all income and deductions are passed through to the beneficiaries on a "Schedule K-1" to the fiduciary tax return. However, if the estate is open more than a year (or into a new tax year, if a calendar year is being used), the first returns are called the "initial" returns, and you must file subsequent returns for each year the estate is open. Use the same forms (federal IRS Form 1041 and California FTB Form 541) for all fiduciary returns, and pay taxes due on undistributed income from the estate assets.

When a formal probate court proceeding is not required, fiduciary returns are not normally necessary. This is because property is usually transferred promptly, and the income it generates is taxed to and reported on the personal returns of the persons receiving it.

For example, income received on joint tenancy property would be reported by the surviving joint tenant(s), since they became the owner(s) of the property immediately on the death of the decedent. Income received on community or separate property passing to a surviving spouse would be reported on the surviving spouse's income tax return. Similarly, others who receive property without probate under the simple affidavit procedure used for estates no greater than $166,250 (see Chapter 11) would report income from such property on their personal income tax returns.

How to Apply for a Taxpayer Identification Number

If a probate proceeding is opened and fiduciary returns are to be filed, you should obtain a federal identification number for the estate as soon as possible. Even though the estate has no employees, the number you need is called an Employer Identification Number (EIN) and you must submit IRS Form SS-4 (*Application for Employer Identification Number*) or apply online to get one.

You can submit your application through the IRS website (www.irs.gov) and get your EIN immediately. Or get it by calling 800-829-4933. (If you call, you will need to fax a completed SS-4 to the agent.) You can download Form SS-4 from the IRS website. The IRS also processes applications by mail and fax, though it may take a couple of weeks to get your EIN through these methods.

When you get the number, notify all institutions reporting income paid on estate assets (banks, brokerage firms, etc.) and tell them to use the new number instead of the decedent's Social Security number.

Other Income Tax Returns

If the decedent was engaged in a business, it is likely that there will be other returns required, such as business tax returns, employment tax returns, and sales and use tax returns. Also, if the decedent was a shareholder in a closely held (private) corporation or a partner in a partnership, tax returns will be due. Usually, in these situations, it is appropriate to employ an accountant—often, the accountant who prepared those returns during the decedent's lifetime.

TIP

Separate fiduciary income tax returns may also be required if the decedent created a trust. For help with trust administration, see *The Trustee's Legal Companion: A Step-by-Step Guide to Administering a Living Trust*, by Carol Elias Zolla and Liza Hanks (Nolo) and obtain California-specific guidance.

Stepped-Up Tax Basis Rules for Inherited Property

Let's slow down for a moment to understand the tax status of inherited property. For example, what are the tax obligations of a person who inherits property and immediately turns around and sells it?

Normally, when property is sold for more than its cost basis, the seller must pay a capital gains tax on the difference between the sales price and its cost basis. Cost basis is generally the dollar amount that was initially paid for an asset, plus or minus certain adjustments. Rules change, however, for inherited property. For both federal and California income tax purposes, property acquired by inheritance gets a new cost basis in the hands of the new owner equal to the fair market value at the date of the decedent's death. (In limited circumstances the new cost basis is equal to the fair market value six months after the date of the decedent's death—called the "alternate valuation date." Because the alternate valuation date rarely applies, and only applies when the estate is subject to federal estate taxes, this discussion presumes that the new cost basis is the date-of-death value.) In other words, even if the property appreciated during the decedent's lifetime, the new owners do not have to pay tax on the difference between the original purchase price and the date-of-death value of the property.

> **EXAMPLE:** Morgan buys a home in 1985 for $50,000. At his death, the fair market value of the property is $350,000. The property passes under Morgan's will to his daughter, Alison. Alison's basis for the property for reporting gain or loss when it is sold is $350,000, plus or minus any adjustments during the time of Alison's ownership.

While we refer to stepped-up cost basis here, if the value of an asset is *lower* at the date of death than the decedent's cost basis, a stepped-down cost basis could apply. We focus on stepped-up cost basis because that is the more common situation.

SEE AN EXPERT

See a qualified expert if you need help with stepped-up basis.

In the case of community property for spouses, there is a substantial added tax benefit as a result of these stepped-up basis rules. This is because for state and federal income tax purposes the surviving spouse's one-half share of the community property is treated in the same manner as property the surviving spouse acquires from the deceased spouse. Thus, all community property (the decedent's and surviving spouse's shares) and all separate property included in the decedent's estate receives a new stepped-up basis equal to its fair market value as of the deceased spouse's death.

> **EXAMPLE:** Paul and Margaret purchase $50,000 worth of stock, which they hold as community property. When Paul dies, his one-half community interest in the stock passes to Margaret. The fair market value of the stock at the time of Paul's death is $75,000. Therefore, Margaret's one-half interest, as well as Paul's one-half interest, receives a stepped-up basis for California and federal income tax purposes. The basis of $75,000 will apply to determine capital gains if Margaret later sells the stock.

Many married couples hold title to their property as joint tenants to avoid probate. In the past, there has been some debate over whether property held in joint tenancy will be afforded a full step-up in its tax basis upon the death of one spouse. Usually, only the decedent's interest in joint tenancy property gets a stepped-up basis for both federal and California income tax purposes. But if joint tenancy property can be established as true community property held in joint tenancy for convenience, both the decedent's half and the surviving spouse's half may qualify for the stepped-up basis. One way to do this is to transfer the property to the surviving spouse as community property using a Spousal or Domestic Partner Property Petition, as described in Chapter 15. Get legal assistance to determine if this is possible for your situation.

Because federal tax laws do not recognize domestic partnerships, the benefits of the stepped-up basis are not currently available to domestic partners under federal law. However, they may be available under state law. Get advice from a tax professional experienced with domestic partner issues for information on the current state of the law.

Federal Estate Tax Return

A Federal Estate Tax Return (IRS Form 706) must be filed if the decedent's *gross* estate on the date of death exceeds a certain amount. This amount is the "basic exclusion amount." The exclusion amount is $11.7 million for deaths in 2021. Confirm the relevant amount for the year of death because this amount changes each year to account for inflation. And under existing law, the amount will be reduced substantially starting in 2026, dropping to $5 million, as adjusted for inflation.

Most estates don't need to file the return because most estates aren't larger than the exclusion amount. However, the estate of any married person may file a federal estate tax return anyway—for the purpose of claiming the unused exclusion amount of the deceased spouse. This is called "portability" and can help reduce or avoid estate taxes when the surviving spouse dies. We discuss portability further below.

The estate tax return is a long and detailed tax form with many schedules. Substantial penalties can apply for late or inaccurate estate tax returns. We recommend that you get professional help for preparing an estate tax return. Specific instructions for preparing an estate tax return are beyond the scope of this book. However, the information in this section will help you determine whether an estate tax return or tax advice is needed.

SKIP AHEAD

Can you skip this discussion about federal estate tax returns? If the decedent was not married, did not make substantial lifetime gifts, and had assets well below the estate tax basic exclusion amount in the year of death ($11.7 million for 2021), you can skip this section about the federal estate tax return. First confirm the current tax laws for the year of death, to be sure.

Who Needs to File?

An estate tax return is required if the gross estate, on the date of death, exceeds the federal estate tax exclusion amount (see the table below).

The Federal Estate Tax Exclusion Amount

Year of Death	Estate tax return must be filed if gross value of the estate exceeds:
2016	$5.45 million
2017	$5.49 million
2018	$11.18 million
2019	$11.4 million
2020	$11.58 million
2021	$11.7 million

The return must be filed if the gross estate is larger than the exclusion amount, even if no tax will be due. For example, if all assets are left to the surviving spouse, they are exempt from federal estate tax, as long as the spouse is a U.S. citizen. So, if a person dies leaving $12 million to a surviving spouse, the gross value of the deceased spouse's estate requires the executor to file an estate tax return, but no estate tax will be due.

Certain gifts during life are also taken into account in determining whether a federal estate tax return must be filed. Most people only make gifts up to the annual exclusion amount, and those gifts are not included in these considerations. See below for information on gifts. Get tax advice if the decedent filed any gift tax returns (IRS Form 709), or may have been required to do so, during life.

It is extremely important to understand that the gross value of an estate is used to determine whether or not a federal estate tax return is required. The actual tax, by contrast, is computed on the net value of all property owned by the decedent at death. The net estate value is arrived at by taking the total (gross) value of all of the decedent's property and subtracting such things as funeral expenses, expenses of settling the estate, any debts owed by the decedent, gifts to a spouse, and gifts to charities. (Chapter 1 explains the difference between the gross and net estate.)

Because the value of the gross estate is larger than the net estate, some estates will need to file a federal estate tax return (based on the gross estate), although no tax will be due (based on the net estate).

EXAMPLE: Anderson had a gross estate valued at $12 million when he died in 2020. A federal estate tax return must be filed because the value of the estate is over the estate tax exclusion amount for that year. However, Anderson's estate has deductions for debts (for example, a mortgage or money owed to a family member), taxes due, last illness and funeral expenses, and administration expenses (for example, attorney and accountant fees, court costs, and certification and publication fees), that bring the value of his net estate below the exclusion amount, so no estate tax is due.

Portability for Married Decedents

Even if the size of the estate does not require an estate tax return, the representative of the estate of a married decedent may choose to file an estate tax return to pass along the unused part of the exclusion amount to the surviving spouse. This is called a "portability" election and it first became available for persons dying in 2011.

If the representative of a married decedent makes the portability election on a timely filed IRS Form 706 estate tax return, the amount of the deceased spouse's unused exclusion can substantially increase the amount that the surviving spouse can pass during life or at death without incurring estate taxes.

For estates of a married decedent, get tax advice about whether it is a good idea to file a return to claim portability. The cost of preparing and filing an estate tax return may be worth the potential reduction in estate taxes at the death of the surviving spouse.

EXAMPLE: Martha and George were married and have a combined estate of $14 million. Martha dies in 2020. Martha leaves her $7 million share of the estate to her husband. Because of the marital deduction for estate taxes (meaning that an unlimited amount can be passed to a spouse without using any of the exclusion amount), Martha's estate does not use any of her $11.58 million exclusion amount. If Martha's estate timely filed an estate tax return and elected portability, then George's estate will have Martha's unused exclusion amount of $11.58 million, plus the estate tax exclusion amount at the time of George's death.

If George died in 2021, when the exclusion amount is $11.7 million, then George's estate will have the exclusion of $11.58 million claimed through portability from Martha's estate, plus his own exclusion of $11.7 million, totaling $23.28 million. Assuming that George did not remarry and his estate was $14 million, including what he inherited from Martha, his estate will not owe estate taxes because his estate is less than those combined exclusion amounts.

If Martha's estate had not elected portability, then George's estate might owe estate taxes because the $14 million value of his estate is greater than the exclusion amount for the year of his death.

Calculating the Value of the Estate for Tax Purposes

The amount of the gross estate is the total of Column D in the Schedule of Assets you prepared in Chapter 5.

The estate for federal estate tax purposes is usually not the same as the estate that goes through probate, called the probate estate. The difference is that the federal estate tax return must report all property in which the decedent had any interest. This includes property that passes outside of probate, such as joint tenancy property, pay on death accounts or other transfer on death assets, life insurance owned by the decedent, property held in living trusts, pensions, annuities, profit-sharing and death benefits, and certain gifts. The probate estate, on the other hand, is only the property that is potentially subject to formal probate administration (or small estate procedures, if those simplified procedures apply).

EXAMPLE: Ruth dies in 2021, leaving the bulk of her property to her brother. Most of the property was held in a living trust or owned in joint tenancy, so it can be transferred outside of probate. Only securities valued at $120,000 and miscellaneous personal property of little value are subject to probate. This amount qualifies as a small estate and a formal probate administration will not be required. The size of the total estate, however, is much larger. Ruth's estate has a gross value of $12 million. Because that amount is above the estate tax exclusion amount for 2021, her executor needs to file an estate tax return.

Joint Tenancy Property

Some people put their property (real estate or stocks or bank accounts, for example) in joint tenancy with someone else, to avoid probate. For example, an elderly parent may add a son or daughter to the deed to the family house as a joint tenant. In such cases, federal tax law requires that the entire joint tenancy property be included in the estate of the first owner, for estate tax purposes, if the others acquired their interests for less than full value.

One asset that's easy to overlook when you're adding up the value of the gross estate is life insurance proceeds. The decedent's taxable estate will include the proceeds of life insurance on the decedent's life if:

- the proceeds are receivable by the estate
- the proceeds are receivable by another for the benefit of the estate, or
- the decedent possessed "incidents of ownership" in the policy.

Often a person who takes out a large insurance policy will transfer ownership of the policy to someone else so the policy proceeds will not be included in the insured's taxable estate. For instance, a person may buy insurance on his own life, and then transfer ownership (including all incidents of ownership) of the policy to the beneficiary to avoid his own estate having to pay estate taxes on the proceeds upon his death.

In order for the policy proceeds not to be included in the insured's taxable estate, he must have given away complete control over the policy and he must survive the transfer by 3 years. If the decedent had the power to change beneficiaries, obtain a loan against the cash value, or surrender or cancel the policy, then the decedent possessed incidents of ownership. The policy proceeds will be included in the decedent's taxable estate at death, even if the decedent thought policy ownership had transferred to another. Gifting life insurance often results in unintended consequences, and the value of the gift may be something other than the cash value of the policy. If you are confused about this, check with the insurance company, or an accountant or attorney experienced in estate tax matters.

The taxable estate may also include taxable gifts made after December 31, 1976. Certain gifts are exempt from tax—for example, gifts to spouses, gifts to tax-exempt charities, gifts paid directly to an educational or medical institution for someone else, or gifts each year to any person of below the annual gift tax exclusion amount.

Gift Tax Annual Exclusion

Year(s)	Annual Exclusion
1998 – 2001	$10,000
2002 – 2005	$11,000
2006 – 2008	$12,000
2009 – 2012	$13,000
2013 – 2017	$14,000
2018 – 2021	$15,000

EXAMPLE: The decedent made a cash gift to a friend of $50,000 in 2007, and a gift of real property worth $150,000 to a child in 2013. The decedent also paid for tuition for her child and made gifts to charities. Only the amount of the noncharitable gifts above the gift tax exclusion amounts would be included in the taxable estate—$38,000 ($50,000 gift in 2007 less the $12,000 annual exclusion for that year) plus $136,000 ($150,000 gift in 2013 less the $14,000 annual exclusion for that year), or $174,000.

The Filing Deadline

If you need or elect to file Form 706, it is due nine months after the date of death. The IRS, however, will automatically grant your request for a six-month extension if you make your request before the original due date. Use IRS Form 4768, *Application for Extension of Time To File a Return and/or Pay U.S. Estate (and Generation-Skipping Transfer) Taxes.* You'll have to include an estimate of the tax due—and a payment. The extension of time to file is not an extension of time to pay the tax. The executor who files an estate tax return also has responsibility to provide to beneficiaries a statement of the value of assets within 30 days of filing a return.

If you have any question about whether an estate tax return should be filed—either because of the size of the estate or to elect portability for the surviving spouse—get advice and assistance early. Be prepared to provide the tax professional with detailed information on assets in the estate. Estate tax returns take time to prepare and you do not want to run up against the deadline for filing. If filing an estate tax return exclusively to claim portability, the IRS has modified the filing deadlines and such returns may be filed within two years of the date of death by following special simplified procedures (Revenue Procedure 2017-34). So even if it appears that you may have missed the nine-month deadline, get advice from an experienced tax preparer or attorney as soon as possible.

RESOURCE

More information from the IRS. You can get the federal estate tax return (Form 706) online at www.irs.gov or from an IRS office that furnishes tax information and forms. The IRS booklet of instructions for completing the federal estate tax return, called *Instructions for Form 706*, is very helpful.

Paying the Federal Tax

The federal estate tax, if any is due, must be paid in full when the return is filed. (If you apply for an extension, you'll need to pay an estimated amount of tax when you apply; the estate will still be charged interest on any unpaid tax from the due date until it is paid.) The top estate tax rate for deaths since 2013 is 40%. Consult the IRS *Instructions for Form 706* to determine the amount of tax due.

If you don't file the return by the due date (or by the extension date), the estate will be charged a penalty, in addition to interest. The penalty is 5% of the amount of the tax for each month (or part of a month) that you're late, up to a maximum of 25%.

Most wills have a provision saying all taxes are to be paid from the residue of the estate. If there is no will, or the will makes no provision and there are two or more beneficiaries, then the taxes are charged to each of the beneficiaries, according to their percentage interests. Your accountant should be able to compute the amount chargeable to each beneficiary. If there isn't enough cash to pay the taxes, the executor must sell estate property or borrow money to raise the necessary funds.

California Inheritance Tax

The California inheritance tax applies only to decedents who died on or before June 8, 1982.

One uncommon but possible occurrence is to find that real estate, usually the family home, is still held in joint tenancy with the decedent's predeceased spouse. In most cases, all that is necessary is to record an Affidavit—Death of Joint Tenant (see Chapter 10) to remove the predeceased spouse's name from the title. But if the first spouse died on or before June 8, 1982, you may also need to determine whether or not there is any tax due and to obtain a release of the tax lien on the property prior to the sale of the property.

SEE AN EXPERT

Death taxes in other states. If the decedent owned real estate outside of California, estate taxes may be owed to that state. Check with an accountant or lawyer there. Also, beneficiaries outside of California may have inheritance taxes imposed by their state on the inheritance received, and should obtain their own tax advice.

Tax Returns for Estates

Let's look at some estates that contain common situations and see what tax returns will be filed for each.

Estate of Abigail Apple

Abigail died on October 11, 2018 at the age of 66. Her gross estate of $300,000 consisted of her one-half interest in community property owned by Abigail and her husband, Alfred, who is 68. Her estate did not require probate because all of her property passed outright to Alfred either by beneficiary designation or under Abigail's will. The will names Alfred as the executor.

Abigail and Alfred received interest, dividend, and other income of $40,000 during the period of January 1, 2018 to October 11, 2018 (the date of Abigail's death), one-half of which ($20,000) was attributable to Abigail as community property.

Alfred is responsible for seeing that final income tax returns, both California and federal, are filed for Abigail for the period January 1, 2018, to October 11, 2018. They were due April 15, 2019. The returns for Abigail may or may not be joint returns with her husband, depending on which is the most advantageous way to file.

No federal estate tax return is required, because Abigail's estate is not large enough to require filing one. Alfred has decided not to file a federal estate tax return to elect portability of Abigail's unused exclusion amount for his own estate.

Fiduciary income tax returns are also not required, because Abigail's estate did not require probate. Alfred will report any future income he receives from assets in Abigail's estate on his own California and federal personal income tax returns.

Estate of Joe Brown

Joe, not married or in a registered partnership, died on March 12, 2021. The gross estate consisted of:

House	$ 800,000
Stock	550,000
Life insurance	700,000
Car	20,000
Bank account	+ 30,000
Total:	$2,100,000

Because the gross estate is less than the $11.7 million estate tax exclusion for 2021, no federal estate tax return is due for Joe's estate. However, probate court proceedings were required, and the probate court appointed his brother Jack as executor of the will. Joe had received a total of $35,000 from his employment, along with dividends and interest, for the period January 1, 2021 to March 12, 2021 (the date of death). Joe hadn't yet filed his income tax returns for 2020 when he died. The tax returns that Jack must file as executor of Joe's estate are:

- Joe's 2020 personal income tax returns, both California and federal, due April 15, 2021
- Joe's final income tax returns, both California and federal, for the period January 1, 2021 to March 12, 2021 (the date of Joe's death), due April 15, 2022, and
- Fiduciary income tax returns (California FTB Form 541 and IRS Form 1041), reporting income received during the period of probate administration on the estate assets from March 13, 2021 (the beginning of the estate's income tax year) until the estate is closed and the assets distributed to the beneficiaries.

Estate of Ralph Rambler

Reba and Ralph Rambler had been married for 35 years when Ralph died on April 20, 2020. His estate consisted of a one-half interest in the total community property he and Reba owned, as shown here:

Pacific Palisades home	$1,500,000
Santa Monica rental property	750,000
Boat	25,000
Stocks	200,000
Vacation home	600,000
Cadillac	25,000
Checking and savings accounts+	100,000
Total:	$3,200,000

Ralph's will named Reba as executor and distributed his one-half interest in the house, car, and checking and savings accounts to Reba, and the rental property and stocks to his three children. Therefore, his estate required probate administration. Reba and Ralph received income of $125,000 during the period from January 1, 2020 to April 20, 2020 (date of death), one-half of which was attributable to Ralph.

Reba is responsible for seeing that the following tax returns are filed:

- Ralph's final personal income tax returns for 2020, both California and federal. They're due April 15, 2021 and cover the period from January 1, 2020 to April 20, 2020. Reba can file a joint return for the entire year of 2020 even though Ralph died in April of that year. In the final return, Reba would include Ralph's income and deductions up to the date of his death, as well as her income and deductions for the entire year.
- Fiduciary income tax returns for Ralph's estate for the period beginning from his date of death until the estate is closed.
- Ralph's gross estate is $1.6 million (or one-half of the $3.2 million total community property), which is under the exclusion amount for the year 2020. A federal estate tax return is not required based on the size of Ralph's gross estate. However, Reba decides to file a federal estate tax return to elect portability of the unused estate tax exclusion amount. She is anticipating receiving a large inheritance from another family member and wants to increase the amount excluded from estate taxes upon her own death. The estate tax return (IRS Form 706) or an extension is due January 20, 2021; July 20, 2021 with an extension; or up to April 20, 2022 under special procedures since the return is being filed exclusively for portability.

The transfer of property upon the death of Ralph Rambler may trigger property tax reassessment for the rental property passing to the three children. Prior to Proposition 19, the children could file a Claim for Reassessment Exclusion for Transfer Between Parent and Child with the county assessor. For transfers occurring after February 15, 2021, such an exclusion may only apply for a principal residence and otherwise the property is reassessed. (See Chapter 8.)

CHAPTER

8

Transferring Title to Real Property

In California, beneficiaries legally acquire title to the decedent's real property on the date of death, but they must still take specific steps to officially document the transfer of title. In this chapter, we discuss ways to transfer the title to real property to its new owners. Some basic information about transfers applies no matter whether the real property is left in a will, passes by intestate succession, or passes outside the will via one or another of the probate-avoidance devices.

In some situations, you may be able to follow these instructions soon after the decedent dies. In other situations, you may need to first obtain authority from the court. And in some situations, the beneficiary may not learn that formal steps need to be taken to document the transfer until a title search is conducted as a part of a later sale or refinance. Handling the paperwork soon after the decedent's death can avoid surprises or complications later.

Ways to Transfer Real Estate After Death

To transfer real property belonging to a decedent, you will need to use a deed, affidavit, or court order, depending on how the decedent held title to the property and to whom it is left. For assistance with the nuts and bolts of transferring title, or if questions exist about decedent's ownership of property, consult a title company.

What Is a Title Company?

A title company provides insurance that protects property buyers against claims against the property. Part of a title company's expertise is in researching ownership and ensuring that the proper forms are used to transfer title. While one often does not purchase title insurance for transferring title upon the death of an owner, you might still ask a title company for help. For example, a title company may be able to provide information or a report about a property's current ownership—for a fee. A title company may also make common forms available. A good place to start is with the title company that provided title insurance to the decedent.

After you've completed the appropriate document to transfer title, it must be recorded in the office of the county recorder where the real property is located. (This is explained later in this chapter.)

To a Surviving Spouse or Domestic Partner

Generally, if the real property (whether community or separate) goes outright to the surviving spouse or domestic partner (either under the decedent's will or by intestate succession), you may need a Spousal or Domestic Partner Property Order, as explained in Chapter 15. If, however, the decedent's deed specifically shows title held "as community property" or "community property with right of survivorship" with the surviving spouse or partner, you may be able to clear title in the survivor's name with a simple affidavit, which is also explained in Chapter 15. Or, if the surviving spouse or domestic partner is the beneficiary of the real property through one of the probate-avoidance ways of holding title—that is, joint tenancy, a trust, a transfer on death deed, or a life estate—the surviving spouse or domestic partner can use the method listed below.

To a Surviving Joint Tenant

If title was held in joint tenancy, then you may use an Affidavit—Death of Joint Tenant, which is explained in Chapter 10, to remove the decedent's name from the title. However, for tax reasons discussed in Chapter 7, if spouses or domestic partners held title to community property in joint tenancy, the surviving spouse or partner may instead want to use the Spousal or Domestic Partner Property Order procedure explained in Chapter 15.

To Trust Beneficiaries

If the decedent held title to the property in a trust, a new deed must be prepared, usually by the successor trustee, transferring title to the beneficiaries according to the trust document. We explain the process in Chapter 12.

Affidavit – Death of Transferor (TOD Deed)

RECORDING REQUESTED BY
Name of transferee

AND WHEN RECORDED MAIL DOCUMENT
AND TAX STATEMENT TO: **Name of transferee**
Street address
City, state, zip

APN: **Parcel number**
Commonly known as: **Address of property**

SPACE ABOVE THIS LINE FOR RECORDER'S USE

[*Include if applicable:* Exempt from SB2 fee per Gov. Code Sec. 27338.1(a)(2) because recorded in connection with a transfer of real property that is a residential dwelling to an owner-occupier.]

AFFIDAVIT – DEATH OF TRANSFEROR (TOD DEED)

Person signing affidavit, of legal age, being first duly sworn, deposes and says: **Decedent's name, as written on death certificate** the decedent mentioned in the attached certified copy of Certificate of Death, is the same person as **Decedent's name, as written on deed**, the transferor under the Revocable Transfer on Death Deed dated **Date of deed** and recorded on **Date deed recorded** as Instrument No. **Recording reference number and if applicable, book/reel and page/image**, of the Official Records of **County in which deed was recorded** County, California, which named as beneficiary(ies) **Beneficiary(ies) listed on deed** and which transferred the following described property in **County where property is located** County, California:

Legal description of property

Assessor's Parcel No. ____________________

Dated: ____________________

____
Signature

____
(Type or print name of person signing affidavit)

Certificate of Notary Public

A notary public or other officer completing this certificate verifies only the identity of the individual who signed the document to which this certificate is attached, and not the truthfulness, accuracy, or validity of that document.

State of California

County of ____________________

Subscribed and sworn to (or affirmed) before me on this ____ day of __________, 20__, by ______________,

proved to me on the basis of satisfactory evidence to be the person(s) who appeared before me.

[SEAL] Signature ____________________

To Beneficiaries of a Transfer on Death Deed

If title was held by transfer on death deed (also called a "TOD deed"), you need to provide verification of the decedent's death to remove the decedent's name from the title, and replace it with the name of the beneficiary or beneficiaries. To do this, prepare an affidavit of death and record it in the county where the real estate is located, along with a certified death certificate. See the example affidavit above.

FORMS

A blank Affidavit—Death of Transferor is in Appendix C. You can download a fillable version of the form on this book's companion page at www.nolo.com/back-of-book/PAE.html.

To the Remainder Beneficiary of a Life Estate

A life estate (sometimes called a "life tenancy") is not a common form of ownership, but it deserves mention here. A life estate is ownership of property for the period of a lifetime only. Life estates are sometimes created to avoid needing probate proceedings, or to meet other estate planning goals.

> EXAMPLE: Wanda is an elderly widow who owns a home that she wishes to go to her son Steve upon her death. Wanda may deed the property to Steve during her lifetime, with the deed saying that "Grantor (Wanda) reserves to herself a life estate in said property." This will transfer the ownership to Steve, but allow Wanda full use of the property during her lifetime. This will accomplish Wanda's objective of avoiding probate of the home upon her death because she will die without ownership of the property. Her life estate will terminate at the moment of her death, and the home will be owned by Steve. Life estates are handled in much the same way as joint tenancy property on the death of the life tenant.

To clear title to real property in which there was a life estate, the owner uses the Affidavit—Death of Joint Tenant discussed in Chapter 10, and replaces the word "Joint" with the word "Life." Then the affidavit will say "Affidavit—Death of Life Tenant." Record the completed affidavit in the office of the county recorder in which the real property is located (discussed in Chapter 10), along with a certified copy of the death certificate. If other assets are subject to life estates, follow the procedures discussed in Chapter 10 for clearing joint tenancy property.

Through Formal Probate

If the decedent's interest in the real property goes to heirs or the beneficiaries of the will (other than a surviving spouse or partner), you must obtain an Order for Final Distribution through a formal probate court proceeding. The order transfers ownership to the heirs or beneficiaries, who take title as tenants in common when there is more than one person assuming ownership. Instructions for preparing an order are in Chapter 14, Step 18. However, see Chapter 11 for shortcut methods of transferring real property where the estate including real property is worth less than the small estate threshold amount, currently $166,250.

Basic Information on Recording Documents

Record documents affecting title to real property (deed, court order, affidavit, or deed of trust) in the office of the county recorder for the county in which the real property is located. However, an unrecorded document is not necessarily null or void.

Of what significance, then, is recording? Recording a deed or other document gives public notice of a person's rights in property, called "constructive notice." It informs the world of the ownership of the property and who has a mortgage on it. Once a deed is recorded, the law presumes that everyone (for example, banks, potential buyers, and title companies) has notice of this information. For example, if you buy a lot without a title search and do not check the public records yourself, you are nevertheless considered to have knowledge of whatever the records would have shown. If there is a judgment lien against the property, you are responsible for paying it even though no one ever told you about it. In other words, you had "constructive notice" of all information the recorder's office would have disclosed had you checked. This is why, when you buy a house or other real property, the title company always checks the records at the recorder's office to make sure the seller owns clear title to the property. Recording, then, is an orderly system of establishing ownership rights in, and lien rights against, property.

If a deed isn't recorded, the recorder's office will not have current property ownership information, and a person relying on the out-of-date information in good faith will be protected. For example, if you have some ownership right in property and do not record it, that right can be cut off by a competing right acquired by another person without knowledge of your right.

The recording of a document takes effect when it is received in the recorder's office along with the appropriate fee. The clerk at the recorder's office will:

1. stamp the document as received for recording at the hour and minute received
2. give the document a document or instrument number (sometimes a book and page number are used), and
3. make a copy for the recorder's records.

At that point, the document becomes a part of the "Official Records" in the recorder's office, available to anyone from the public. After a document is recorded, the recorder's office returns the original (stamped with the recording information in the top right corner) to the person named on the document to receive it—usually the one who requested the recording. Counties allow you to search for information on recorded documents on the county recorder's website. In some counties these searches provide an image of the document. If not, you may be able to order a copy directly from the county recorder or from a deed retrieval service.

You can record documents with the county recorder either in person, by mail, or using a third-party service such as a title company. Many counties now have electronic recording capabilities, but a company specifically authorized by the county must be used to record documents in this way.

To avoid having the document rejected for recording, be sure to carefully review the county's recording requirements related to signatures, formatting, fees, and other forms required for filing. The county clerk's/assessor's/recorder's (the title of the office depends on the county) has this information, as well as the appropriate forms to accompany a document being submitted for recording.

Change in Ownership Statements

Usually, a transfer of an interest in real property or a mobile home triggers a reassessment for local property tax purposes. For this reason, certain forms must be filed with local officials whenever ownership changes. The following forms are usually required when title to real property in California is transferred on the death of the owner.

Preliminary Change of Ownership Report

Whenever a deed, court order, or other document affecting title to real property is recorded, it must be accompanied by a Preliminary Change of Ownership Report, sometimes referred to as a "PCOR," or Form BOE-502-A. The PCOR provides information about the property affected by the document, the transferor and transferee, and the nature of the transfer. The county uses this information for tax purposes, so pay close attention to the instructions. Fill out the form completely, using the transferor and transferee's names as they appear on the document being recorded. Check the appropriate box in Part 1 to provide the relevant transfer information. The person receiving the property signs as the "transferee." In addition to the recording fee, a fee of $20 is charged if the form is not filed with the conveyance at the time of recordation. (Rev. & Tax. Code § 480(a).) You can get the blank form from the county assessor's office or from the county assessor's website.

Preliminary Change of Ownership Report

BOE-502-A (P1) REV. 14 (05-18)

ERNEST J. DRONENBURG, JR.
SAN DIEGO COUNTY ASSESSOR/RECORDER/COUNTY CLERK
1600 PACIFIC HIGHWAY, SUITE 103, SAN DIEGO, CA 92101
TELEPHONE (619) 531-5730

FOR RECORDER USE ONLY

PRELIMINARY CHANGE OF OWNERSHIP REPORT

To be completed by the transferee (buyer) prior to a transfer of subject property, in accordance with section 480.3 of the Revenue and Taxation Code. A *Preliminary Change of Ownership Report* must be **filed with each conveyance in the County Recorder's office for the county where the property is located.**

ASSESSOR'S PARCEL NUMBER
2346-019-014

SELLER/TRANSFEROR
Robert B. Demming, Deceased

BUYER/TRANSFEREE
John Demming

BUYER'S DAYTIME TELEPHONE NUMBER
818-123-4567

BUYER'S EMAIL ADDRESS
xxxx@gmail.com

STREET ADDRESS OR PHYSICAL LOCATION OF REAL PROPERTY
1506 Maple Street, Mission Valley, CA 92199

☐ YES ☑ NO This property is intended as my principal residence. If YES, please indicate the date of occupancy or intended occupancy. MO ___ DAY ___ YEAR ___

☐ YES ☑ NO Are you a disabled veteran or a unmarried surviving spouse of a disabled veteran who was compensated at 100% by the Department of Veterans Affairs?

MAIL PROPERTY TAX INFORMATION TO (NAME)
John Demming

MAIL PROPERTY TAX INFORMATION TO (ADDRESS)	CITY	STATE	ZIP CODE
7290 N. McDonald Ave.	San Diego	CA	91775

PART 1. TRANSFER INFORMATION *Please complete all statements.*

This section contains possible exclusions from reassessment for certain types of transfers.

YES	NO	
☐	☑	A. This transfer is solely between spouses *(addition or removal of a spouse, death of a spouse, divorce settlement, etc.).*
☐	☑	B. This transfer is solely between domestic partners currently registered with the California Secretary of State *(addition or removal of a partner, death of a partner, termination settlement, etc.).*
☑	☐	*C. This is a transfer: ☑ between parent(s) and child(ren) ☐ from grandparent(s) to grandchild(ren).
☐	☑	*D. This transfer is the result of a cotenant's death. Date of death ______
☐	☑	*E. This transaction is to replace a principal residence owned by a person 55 years of age or older. Within the same county? ☐ YES ☐ NO
☐	☑	*F. This transaction is to replace a principal residence by a person who is severely disabled as defined by Revenue and Taxation Code section 69.5. Within the same county? ☐ YES ☐ NO
☐	☑	G. This transaction is only a correction of the name(s) of the person(s) holding title to the property *(e.g., a name change upon marriage).* If YES, please explain: ______
☐	☑	H. The recorded document creates, terminates, or reconveys a lender's interest in the property.
☐	☑	I. This transaction is recorded only as a requirement for financing purposes or to create, terminate, or reconvey a security interest *(e.g., cosigner).* If YES, please explain: ______
☐	☑	J. The recorded document substitutes a trustee of a trust, mortgage, or other similar document.
		K. This is a transfer of property:
☐	☑	1. to/from a revocable trust that may be revoked by the transferor and is for the benefit of ☐ the transferor, and/or ☐ the transferor's spouse ☐ registered domestic partner.
☐	☑	2. to/from an irrevocable trust for the benefit of the ☐ creator/grantor/trustor and/or ☐ grantor's/trustor's spouse ☐ grantor's/trustor's registered domestic partner.
☐	☑	L. This property is subject to a lease with a remaining lease term of 35 years or more including written options.
☐	☑	M. This is a transfer between parties in which proportional interests of the transferor(s) and transferee(s) in each and every parcel being transferred remain exactly the same after the transfer.
☐	☑	N. This is a transfer subject to subsidized low-income housing requirements with governmentally imposed restrictions, or restrictions imposed by specified nonprofit corporations.
☐	☑	*O. This transfer is to the first purchaser of a new building containing an active solar energy system.
☐	☑	P. Other. This transfer is to ______

* Please refer to the instructions for Part 1.

Please provide any other information that will help the Assessor understand the nature of the transfer.

THIS DOCUMENT IS NOT SUBJECT TO PUBLIC INSPECTION

Preliminary Change of Ownership Report (page 2)

BOE-502-A (P2) REV. 14 (05-18)

PART 2. OTHER TRANSFER INFORMATION *Check and complete as applicable.*

A. Date of transfer, if other than recording date: 7-7-20XX

B. Type of transfer:

☐ Purchase ☐ Foreclosure ☐ Gift ☐ Trade or exchange ☐ Merger, stock, or partnership acquisition (Form BOE-100-B)

☐ Contract of sale. Date of contract: ______ ☑ Inheritance. Date of death: 7-7-20XX

☐ Sale/leaseback ☐ Creation of a lease ☐ Assignment of a lease ☐ Termination of a lease. Date lease began: ______

Original term in years *(including written options)*: ____ Remaining term in years *(including written options)*: ____

☐ Other. Please explain: ______

C. Only a partial interest in the property was transferred. ☐ YES ☑ NO If YES, indicate the percentage transferred: ______ %

PART 3. PURCHASE PRICE AND TERMS OF SALE *Check and complete as applicable.*

A. Total purchase price $ N/A

B. Cash down payment or value of trade or exchange excluding closing costs Amount $______

C. First deed of trust @ ____% interest for ____ years. Monthly payment $______ Amount $______

☐ FHA (___Discount Points) ☐ Cal-Vet ☐ VA (___Discount Points) ☐ Fixed rate ☐ Variable rate

☐ Bank/Savings & Loan/Credit Union ☐ Loan carried by seller

☐ Balloon payment $______ Due date: ______

D. Second deed of trust @ ____% interest for ____ years. Monthly payment $______ Amount $______

☐ Fixed rate ☐ Variable rate ☐ Bank/Savings & Loan/Credit Union ☐ Loan carried by seller

☐ Balloon payment $______ Due date: ______

E. Was an Improvement Bond or other public financing assumed by the buyer? ☐ YES ☐ NO Outstanding balance $______

F. Amount, if any, of real estate commission fees paid by the buyer which are not included in the purchase price $______

G. The property was purchased: ☐ Through real estate broker. Broker name: ______ Phone number: (   )

☐ Direct from seller ☐ From a family member-Relationship ______

☐ Other. Please explain: ______

H. Please explain any special terms, seller concessions, broker/agent fees waived, financing, and any other information (e.g., buyer assumed the existing loan balance) that would assist the Assessor in the valuation of your property.

PART 4. PROPERTY INFORMATION *Check and complete as applicable.*

A. Type of property transferred

☑ Single-family residence ☐ Co-op/Own-your-own ☐ Manufactured home

☐ Multiple-family residence. Number of units: ____ ☐ Condominium ☐ Unimproved lot

☐ Other. Description: (i.e., timber, mineral, water rights, etc.) ☐ Timeshare ☐ Commercial/Industrial

B. ☐ YES ☑ NO Personal/business property, or incentives, provided by seller to buyer are included in the purchase price. Examples of personal property are furniture, farm equipment, machinery, etc. Examples of incentives are club memberships, etc. Attach list if available.

If YES, enter the value of the personal/business property: $______ Incentives $______

C. ☐ YES ☑ NO A manufactured home is included in the purchase price.

If YES, enter the value attributed to the manufactured home: $______

☐ YES ☐ NO The manufactured home is subject to local property tax. If NO, enter decal number: ______

D. ☐ YES ☑ NO The property produces rental or other income.

If YES, the income is from: ☐ Lease/rent ☐ Contract ☐ Mineral rights ☐ Other: ______

E. The condition of the property at the time of sale was: ☑ Good ☐ Average ☐ Fair ☐ Poor

Please describe: ______

CERTIFICATION

I certify (or declare) that the foregoing and all information hereon, including any accompanying statements or documents, is true and correct to the best of my knowledge and belief.

SIGNATURE OF BUYER/TRANSFEREE OR CORPORATE OFFICER	DATE	TELEPHONE
▶ John Demming		(818) 123-4567
NAME OF BUYER/TRANSFEREE/PERSONAL REPRESENTATIVE/CORPORATE OFFICER (PLEASE PRINT)	TITLE	EMAIL ADDRESS
John Demming	Administrator	xxxx@gmail.com

The Assessor's office may contact you for additional information regarding this transaction.

Change in Ownership Statement—Death of Real Property Owner

BOE-502-D (P1) REV. 11 (05-18)

CHANGE IN OWNERSHIP STATEMENT
DEATH OF REAL PROPERTY OWNER

This notice is a request for a completed Change in Ownership Statement. Failure to file this statement will result in the assessment of a penalty.

ERNEST J. DRONENBURG JR., ASSESSOR
1600 PACIFIC HWY., SUITE 103
SAN DIEGO, CA 92101
TELEPHONE: (619) 531-5557

NAME AND MAILING ADDRESS
(Make necessary corrections to the printed name and mailing address)

John Demming
7290 McDonald Ave.
San Diego, CA 91775

Section 480(b) of the Revenue and Taxation Code requires that the personal representative file this statement with the Assessor in each county where the decedent owned property at the time of death. **File a separate statement for each parcel of real property owned by the decedent.**

NAME OF DECEDENT	DATE OF DEATH
Robert B. Demming	7-7-20XX

☑ YES ☐ NO Did the decedent have an interest in real property in this county? If **YES**, answer all questions. If **NO**, sign and complete the certification on page 2.

STREET ADDRESS OF REAL PROPERTY	CITY	ZIP CODE	ASSESSOR'S PARCEL NUMBER (APN)*
1506 Maple Street	Mission Valley	91775	2346-019-014

*If more than 1 parcel, attach separate sheet.

DESCRIPTIVE INFORMATION ☑ *(IF APN UNKNOWN)*

☐ Copy of deed by which decedent acquired title is attached.
☐ Copy of decedent's most recent tax bill is attached.
☐ Deed or tax bill is not available; legal description is attached.

DISPOSITION OF REAL PROPERTY ☑

☑ Succession without a will
☐ Probate Code 13650 distribution
☐ Affidavit
☐ Decree of distribution pursuant to will
☐ Action of trustee pursuant to terms of a trust

TRANSFER INFORMATION ☑ Check all that apply and list details below.

☐ Decedent's spouse
☐ Decedent's registered domestic partner
☑ Decedent's child(ren) or parent(s.) If qualified for exclusion from assessment, a *Claim for Reassessment Exclusion for Transfer Between Parent and Child* must be filed (see instructions).
☐ Decedent's grandchild(ren.) If qualified for exclusion from assessment, a *Claim for Reassessment Exclusion for Transfer from Grandparent to Grandchild* must be filed (see instructions).
☐ Cotenant to cotenant. If qualified for exclusion from assessment, an *Affidavit of Cotenant Residency* must be filed (see instructions).
☐ Other beneficiaries or heirs.
☐ A trust.

NAME OF TRUSTEE	ADDRESS OF TRUSTEE

List names and percentage of ownership of all beneficiaries or heirs:

NAME OF BENEFICIARY OR HEIRS	RELATIONSHIP TO DECEDENT	PERCENT OF OWNERSHIP RECEIVED
John Demming	Child	100%

☐ This property has been or will be sold prior to distribution. (Attach the conveyance document and/or court order).

NOTE: Sale of the property does not relieve the need to file a *Claim for Reassessment Exclusion for Transfer Between Parent and Child* if appropriate.

THIS DOCUMENT IS NOT SUBJECT TO PUBLIC INSPECTION

Change in Ownership Statement—Death of Real Property Owner (page 2)

BOE-502-D (P2) REV. 11 (05-18)

☐ YES ☑ NO Will the decree of distribution include distribution of an ownership interest in any legal entity that owns real property in this county? If **YES**, will the distribution result in any person or legal entity obtaining control of more than 50% of the ownership of that legal entity? ☐ YES ☐ NO If **YES**, complete the following section.

NAME AND ADDRESS OF LEGAL ENTITY	NAME OF PERSON OR ENTITY GAINING SUCH CONTROL

☐ YES ☑ NO Was the decedent the lessor or lessee in a lease that had an original term of 35 years or more, including renewal options? If **YES**, provide the names and addresses of all other parties to the lease.

NAME	MAILING ADDRESS	CITY	STATE	ZIP CODE

MAILING ADDRESS FOR FUTURE PROPERTY TAX STATEMENTS

NAME
John Demming

ADDRESS	CITY	STATE	ZIP CODE
7290 McDonald Ave.	San Diego	CA	91775

CERTIFICATION

I certify (or declare) under penalty of perjury under the laws of the State of California that the information contained herein is true, correct and complete to the best of my knowledge and belief.

SIGNATURE OF SPOUSE/REGISTERED DOMESTIC PARTNER/PERSONAL REPRESENTATIVE	PRINTED NAME
▶	John Demming

TITLE	DATE
Personal Representative	11/5/XX

EMAIL ADDRESS	DAYTIME TELEPHONE
xxxx@gmail.com	(818) 123-4567

INSTRUCTIONS

IMPORTANT

Failure to file a Change in Ownership Statement within the time prescribed by law may result in a penalty of either $100 or 10% of the taxes applicable to the new base year value of the real property or manufactured home, whichever is greater, but not to exceed five thousand dollars ($5,000) if the property is eligible for the homeowners' exemption or twenty thousand dollars ($20,000) if the property is not eligible for the homeowners' exemption if that failure to file was not willful. This penalty will be added to the assessment roll and shall be collected like any other delinquent property taxes and subjected to the same penalties for nonpayment.

Section 480 of the Revenue and Taxation Code states, in part:

(a) Whenever there occurs any change in ownership of real property or of a manufactured home that is subject to local property taxation and is assessed by the county assessor, the transferee shall file a signed change in ownership statement in the county where the real property or manufactured home is located, as provided for in subdivision (c). In the case of a change in ownership where the transferee is not locally assessed, no change in ownership statement is required.

(b) The personal representative shall file a change in ownership statement with the county recorder or assessor in each county in which the decedent owned real property at the time of death that is subject to probate proceedings. The statement shall be filed prior to or at the time the inventory and appraisal is filed with the court clerk. In all other cases in which an interest in real property is transferred by reason of death, including a transfer through the medium of a trust, the change in ownership statement or statements shall be filed by the trustee (if the property was held in trust) or the transferee with the county recorder or assessor in each county in which the decedent owned an interest in real property within 150 days after the date of death.

The above requested information is required by law. Please reference the following:

- Passage of Decedent's Property: Beneficial interest passes to the decedent's heirs effectively on the decedent's date of death. However, a document must be recorded to vest title in the heirs. An attorney should be consulted to discuss the specific facts of your situation.
- Change in Ownership: California Code of Regulations, Title 18, Rule 462.260(c), states in part that "[i]nheritance (by will or intestate succession)" shall be "the date of death of decedent."
- Inventory and Appraisal: Probate Code, Section 8800, states in part, "Concurrent with the filing of the inventory and appraisal pursuant to this section, the personal representative shall also file a certification that the requirements of Section 480 of the Revenue and Taxation Code either:
  (1) Are not applicable because the decedent owned no real property in California at the time of death
  (2) Have been satisfied by the filing of a change in ownership statement with the county recorder or assessor of each county in California in which the decedent owned property at the time of death."
- Parent/Child and Grandparent/Grandchild Exclusions: A claim must be filed within three years after the date of death/transfer, but prior to the date of transfer to a third party; or within six months after the date of mailing of a Notice of Assessed Value Change, issued as a result of the transfer of property for which the claim is filed. An application may be obtained by contacting the county assessor.
- Cotenant to cotenant. An affidavit must be filed with the county assessor. An affidavit may be obtained by contacting the county assessor.

This statement will remain confidential as required by Revenue and Taxation Code Section 481, which states in part: "These statements are not public documents and are not open to inspection, except as provided by Section 408."

The sample shown above reflects a transfer from a decedent to a child, using the San Diego County form. Different facts would require the form to be filled out differently to correspond to the particular situation.

Change in Ownership Statement—Death of Real Property Owner

If the decedent owned an interest in real property, file the form titled Change in Ownership Statement—Death of Real Property Owner (BOE-502d) with the assessor's office in each county where the decedent owned property. See the sample from San Diego County, above.

The assessor's office uses this form to determine whether to reassess property taxes. In formal probate proceedings, the personal representative submits this form to the assessor before or at the same time as filing the Inventory and Appraisal. In cases where formal probate is not required, such as spousal property transfers or when title is held in joint tenancy or in a trust, file the form within 150 days of the date of death. (Rev. & Tax. Code § 480(b).) Penalties may apply if the form is not filed after transferring ownership or after written request by the county assessor. You can get a copy of this form from the county assessor's office or the assessor's website.

When you submit the Change in Ownership Statement, the assessor may also require copies of the original deed, tax bill, death certificate, signed will, or letters issued by the court (if applicable). These requirements vary by county. The date of the change in ownership is the date of death, regardless of when title is actually transferred to the new owner, and the property will be reassessed as of that date unless it is excluded from reassessment (see below). Tax bills showing the date-of-death adjustments are usually sent within six months of the filing date of the Death of Real Property Owner form.

The assessor may issue supplemental assessments or corrected assessments (called "escape assessments") to catch up on assessments going back to the date of death. Depending on the time of the year of the death and when the assessor's office was notified, these assessments may come significantly after the transfer. If there will be reassessment of property taxes, check with the assessor's office before distributing all of the estate's assets to avoid surprise property tax bills later.

Proposition 19

In November 2020, California voters passed Proposition 19 which, in part, limits the ability to avoid property tax reassessment when property passes between a parent and a child or between a grandparent and a grandchild.

Prior to Proposition 19, a principal residence of any value and up to $1,000,000 of taxable value of other real property could pass between these family members without being reassessed for property tax purposes. For transfers beginning February 16, 2021, the property being transferred must be the principal residence of the transferor and must be claimed as the recipient's principal residence within one year of transfer. The exclusion will also have a value limit of the current taxable value plus $1,000,000. If the fair market value exceeds this amount, reassessment will occur for the excess amount.

As this edition goes to press, implementing guidance and relevant forms are not yet available. Check with the county assessor for up-to-date information for deaths that occur February 16, 2021 or later.

For parent-child and grandparent-child transfers that result from deaths February 15, 2021 or earlier, more generous pre-Proposition 19 rules may apply. Confirm with the county assessor how to claim the relevant exclusion.

Claim for Reassessment Exclusion

Some transfers are, or may be, excluded from reassessment, including transfers:

- to a spouse or domestic partner
- to a revocable trust

- of a principal residence between a parent and a child (including a child-in-law, stepchild, and child adopted before age 18); to qualify, the new owner must make the property their principal residence within one year of the transfer; if the fair market value of the property is greater than $1,000,000 more than the current taxable value, then the amount excluded from reassessment is limited; these rules also apply to transfers from a grandparent to a grandchild, if the grandchild's parents are deceased, and
- of a principal residence to a surviving cotenant; to qualify, the cotenants must have owned 100% of the property together as tenants in common or as joint tenants, and both must have lived in the property for one year prior to the death.

Even though these transfers are excluded from reassessment, a Preliminary Change of Ownership Report and a Change of Ownership Statement Death of Real Property Owner are still required to inform the assessor of the nature of the transaction. Specific forms are required to claim some exclusions. If the transfer occurs prior to the effective date of Proposition 19 on February 16, 2021, more generous exclusions may be available for transfers between a parent and a child and from a grandparent to a grandchild. For example, prior to Proposition 19, the exclusion could apply under certain circumstances even if the recipient did not claim the property as a principal residence.

Parent-Child Exclusion. To claim the parent-child exclusion, you must file a Claim for Reassessment Exclusion for Transfer Between Parent and Child (BOE-58-AH) with the county assessor. The recipient must also file for the homeowner's exemption or the disabled veteran's exemption within one year of the transfer. You can obtain the form from the county assessor or on the assessor's website. Passage of Proposition 19 will likely result in new forms becoming available early in 2021. The assessor may require further information about the instrument making the transfer, whether a will, a trust, or deed.

Grandparent-Grandchild. To claim the grandparent-grandchild exclusion, you must file a Claim for Reassessment Exclusion for Transfer From Grandparent To Grandchild (BOE-58-G). The recipient must also file for the homeowner's exemption or the disabled veteran's exemption within one year of the transfer. You can obtain the form from the county assessor or on the assessor's website. Passage of Proposition 19 will likely result in new forms becoming available early in 2021. Be sure to confirm that the relationship qualifies for the exclusion, because not all transfers between a grandchild and a grandparent will qualify. The transfer must be from a grandparent to a grandchild—not from a grandchild to a grandparent. Also, the parents of the grandchild must have predeceased the grandparent. Or the parent of the grandchild may still be living if that parent is an in-law of the grandparent and was either divorced from the other parent or has remarried since the other parent's death. But a daughter- or son-in-law of the grandparent who is a stepparent of the grandchild need not be deceased for the exclusion to apply. As with the parent-child exclusion, after the effective date of Proposition 19, the property must be the principal residence of both the transferor and the transferee, and the amount excluded from reassessment is limited to the current taxable value plus $1,000,000.

Time limits apply for claiming the parent-child and grandparent-grandchild exclusion from reassessment. Pay close attention to any information received from the county assessor's office, in particular any notice of supplemental or escape assessment. You may need to respond within a specific period of time.

Cotenant Exclusion. The surviving cotenant must complete an Affidavit of Cotenant Residency (BOE-58-H) to notify the assessor's office of the exclusion from reassessment.

Reassessment due to change in ownership can become complicated. Particularly where the decedent owned the property for a long time and it appreciated, the consequences of losing a reassessment exclusion can be costly for the beneficiaries. Pay attention for complications if:

- Siblings inherit property from a parent and want to receive a share different from the proportions set out in the parent's estate plan. For example, if a sibling "buys out" another sibling, the parent-child exclusion from reassessment would not apply for that transfer. But it may be possible for the transfer to be made directly from the parent's estate in a way that preserves the exclusion to the maximum extent.
- A claim for reassessment exclusion is not timely filed and the property is reassessed.

The county assessor's office and the FAQs section of the California Board of Equalization website (www.boe.ca.gov/proptaxes/faqs/changeinownership.htm) provide more information about property taxes and changes in ownership. If you have further questions, get help from an attorney.

How to Record Your Document Transferring Title

Recording a transfer document is not difficult, though it does require attention to detail. Each situation will have unique requirements, fees, and possibly additional documents required. Follow these steps:

1. Select and prepare the appropriate document from those discussed at the beginning of this chapter.
2. Follow the format requirements for recorded documents. For example, the document must leave blank the top right corner to leave space for the recorder to stamp recording information. If recording a document that does not comply (as in the case of a court order), you may need to attach a cover sheet. (See the example at the end of this chapter.) Check with the county recorder's office for specific requirements if you do not use a preprinted form.
3. Include the assessor's parcel number on the document. (You can find this number on the property tax bill.) Some printed forms of deeds and affidavits have a place to insert the number.
4. Include the name and address of the person to whom the document should be returned, and where the assessor should send property tax bills, in the upper left-hand corner. This person is usually the new owner. Printed form documents have a place for this, as a rule. In the case of court orders, however, there is usually not enough room for all the required information. Most counties require a cover page, which does have room, to be attached; a sample is shown below. You can get a cover page from the recorder's office. It is counted as a page in computing the recording fee. The name and address of either the surviving spouse or the estate representative should be typed in the upper left-hand corner as the person requesting recording. If this person is also the new owner of the real property, you may type below his or her name and address, "Mail tax statements same as above." However, if the person who requests the recording of the court order is not the new owner of the property, you should type at the bottom of the cover page of the court order the words, "Mail tax statements to: (name and address of new owner)," or the tax statements will continue to go to the old address.
5. The document you plan to record must normally be the original document. The signatures of the persons signing the document must be acknowledged by a notary public, except for joint tenancy affidavits that are subscribed and sworn to before a notary. (See Chapter 10.) However, if you record a court order, it must be a copy certified by the court clerk.
6. If the transfer is exempt from the $75 SB2 - Building Homes and Jobs Act Fee, a declaration stating the reason for the exemption must be included either on the face of the document to be recorded or on a cover sheet. Many counties offer a cover sheet for this purpose. A transfer of a residential dwelling to an owner-occupier is exempt from this fee.

Affidavit of Cotenant Residency

BOE-58-H REV. 01 (12/12)

AFFIDAVIT OF COTENANT RESIDENCY

Carmen Chu, Assessor-Recorder
Office of the Assessor-Recorder
City and County of San Francisco
1 Dr. Carlton B. Goodlett Place, Room 190
San Francisco, CA 94102
www.sfassessor.org (415) 554-5596

NAME AND MAILING ADDRESS
(Make necessary corrections to the printed name and mailing address)

Under the provisions of Revenue and Taxation Code section 62.3, if certain conditions are met, a transfer of a cotenancy interest in real property from one cotenant to the other cotenant that takes effect upon the death of one cotenant is not a change in ownership. This applies to transfers that occur on or after January 1, 2013.

The change in ownership exclusion for a transfer of an interest in real property between cotenants that takes effect upon the death of one cotenant applies as long as all of the following are met:

- The transfer is solely by and between two individuals who together own 100 percent of the real property in joint tenancy or tenancy in common.
- As a result of the death of the transferor cotenant, the deceased cotenant's interest in the real property is transferred to the surviving cotenant, resulting in the surviving cotenant owning 100 percent of the real property, and thereby terminating the cotenancy.
- For the one-year period immediately preceding the death of the transferor cotenant, both of the cotenants were owners of record.
- The real property was the principal residence of both cotenants immediately preceding the transferor cotenant's death.
- For the one-year period immediately preceding the death of the transferor cotenant, both of the cotenants continuously resided in the real property.
- The surviving cotenant must sign, under penalty of perjury, an affidavit affirming that he or she continuously resided in the real property with the deceased cotenant for the one-year period immediately preceding the date of death.

NAME OF SURVIVING COTENANT

NAME OF DECEASED COTENANT	DATE OF DEATH
STREET ADDRESS OF REAL PROPERTY	ASSESSOR'S PARCEL NUMBER (APN)

CITY, STATE, ZIP CODE

Property was eligible for: ☐ Homeowners' Exemption ☐ Disabled Veterans' Exemption

Disposition of real property:

☐ Affidavit of death of joint tenant

☐ Decree of distribution pursuant to will or intestate succession

☐ Action of trustee pursuant to terms of trust *(Attach a complete copy of trust and all amendments)*

1. Was this real property the principal residence of the deceased cotenant the one-year period prior to the date of death? ☐ Yes ☐ No

2. Was this real property the principal residence of the surviving cotenant the one-year period prior to the date of death? ☐ Yes ☐ No

3. Are there any other beneficiaries of the real property? ☐ Yes ☐ No

If yes, please list other beneficiaries: ____________________

CERTIFICATION OF COTENANT

I certify (or declare) under penalty of perjury under the laws of the State of California that the foregoing and all information hereon, including any accompanying statements or documents, is true and correct to the best of my knowledge and that I continuously resided with the decedent in this real property for the one-year period immediately preceding the decedent's date of death.

SIGNATURE OF SURVIVING COTENANT ▶	DATE
EMAIL ADDRESS	TELEPHONE NUMBER

THIS DOCUMENT IS SUBJECT TO PUBLIC INSPECTION

Sample Cover Page

RECORDING REQUESTED BY:
Jon Taylor

MAIL TAX STATEMENTS

AND WHEN RECORDED MAIL TO:
Jon Taylor
3311 – 22nd Street
Santa Monica, CA 90405

A.P.N. 123-09876

THIS SPACE FOR RECORDER'S USE ONLY

TITLE:

ORDER FOR FINAL DISTRIBUTION

This is a court-ordered conveyance or decree that is not pursuant to sale and is exempt from tax (Rev. & Tax. Code Sec. 11911).

Add the following sentence, if true, to avoid the SB2 fee:

Exempt from SB2 fee per Gov. Code Sec. 27338.1(a)(2) because recorded in connection with a transfer of real property that is a residential dwelling to an owner-occupier.

THIS PAGE ADDED TO PROVIDE ADEQUATE SPACE FOR RECORDING INFORMATION
(Additional recording fee applies)

7. A recording fee must accompany the document. Fees vary from county to county, ranging from $10 to $25 for the first page and a fee of about $3 for subsequent pages. If a clerk's certification of a court document is on the back of a page, it counts as an additional page. Additional fees may result from documents not meeting formatting requirements. Refer to the county's fee schedule or contact the recorder's office to calculate the exact amount for the recording fee.

   Depending on the county and the specific document recorded, you may also have to pay one or more of the following at the time of recording: (a) $10 "monument" fee, (b) up to $10 for the Real Estate Fraud Prosecution Trust Fund, (c) $75 "SB2 fee" per parcel, unless the document includes a statement that the transfer is exempt from this fee and cites the specific exemption. Again, get information from the county recorder's office about which fees apply.
8. When real property is sold, a documentary transfer tax is collected by the recorder's office on the recording of certain documents. Probate court orders and gifts transferring property by reason of someone's death are not subject to this tax. The following statement should appear on the cover page of the probate order: "This is a court-ordered conveyance or decree that is not pursuant to sale and is exempt from tax (Rev. & Tax. Code § 11911)." The following statement should appear on an after-death deed transfer: "This transfer is by reason of death and is exempt from documentary transfer tax (Rev. & Tax. Code § 11930)." An Affidavit—Death of Joint Tenant is also exempt from documentary transfer tax, but the document does not require a statement to this effect when the affidavit is recorded. Some counties also require a separate "Transfer Tax Affidavit" to be submitted. Check the county's rules.
9. Record the document at the county recorder's office in which the property is located. Provide a completed Preliminary Change of Ownership Report at the time of recording to avoid an additional $20 fee. Recording can be done in person or by mail or through a third-party service.

TIP

Be on the lookout for modified recording procedures due to COVID-19. Recorder's offices have modified procedures to adapt to COVID-19. Check with the county recorder to determine if in-person recording is permitted and whether an appointment is required.

SB2 - Building Homes and Jobs Act Fee

County recorders must charge an additional $75 fee at the time of recording many documents. Your document may qualify for an exemption to this fee, particularly if the transaction concerns the transfer of a "residential dwelling to an owner-occupier." For example, the $75 fee will not apply to the transfer of a home to the surviving spouse who continues to live there, or to another beneficiary who makes the property her home. Also, the fee will not exceed $225 for a single transaction. Thus, if the transaction includes more than three parcels, the exemption can be claimed for the fee beyond $225.

If an exemption to the fee applies, a statement specifically listing the relevant exemption can be included in the document itself. In the example above for a home passing to a person residing there, the deed can be prepared to include the statement (usually below the recording information and above the title to the document): "Exempt from SB2 fee per Gov. Code Sec. 27338.1(a)(2) because is a transfer of real property that is a residential dwelling to an owner-occupier or recorded concurrently in connection with a transfer of real property that is a residential dwelling to an owner-occupier." Or, a cover sheet can be used to claim the exemption.

Your county recorder's office may have unique policies related to claiming an exemption. For this reason, consider using the county's cover sheet if an exemption applies. Although using a cover sheet will add a few dollars to the recording fee, because it is an additional page to be recorded, this will allow you to avoid the $75 fee.

County Recorder
227 North Broadway
Los Angeles, CA 90012

April 10, 20xx

RE: Estate of John Doe, Deceased

Enclosed is a certified copy of the Order for Final Distribution made in the estate of the above-named decedent. Also enclosed is a Preliminary Change of Ownership Report.

Will you please record the order, and after it is recorded return it to the name and address of the person indicated in the upper left-hand corner of the first page. A check in the amount of $______ is enclosed to cover the recording fee.

Thank you for your assistance.

Sincerely,

____
(signature)

[Your name]
[Your address]
[Your phone number]

TIP

Be very careful about property transfers. Even if the recorder's office accepts the transfer document for recording, it does not verify the substance of the document. Usually any error in the transfer document will not be discovered until the new owner tries to sell or take a loan out on the property and the title company identifies an error that must be corrected to clear title. Double- and triple-check all information on the transfer document. Or work with a title company for more certainty. The decedent's title insurance policy usually covers heirs or beneficiaries, yet a beneficiary may want to have the transaction insured if the beneficiary has any concerns about receiving clear title.

Mortgages

When someone dies and leaves real property subject to a mortgage, as a rule the real property passes to the new owner along with the encumbrance, unless the decedent's will provides otherwise. The new owner of a property subject to a mortgage then becomes responsible for making the payment on the loan, taxes, and so on. After the property is officially transferred, it is customary to notify the person or entity collecting the loan payments of the name and address of the new owner.

Most home loans contain due-on-sale clauses. That means if the property is sold, the lender can demand full payment. A lender cannot, however, call the loan when title is transferred on the death of a joint tenant or by inheritance to a relative. (12 U.S.C. § 1701j-3(d).)

When the transferee is a relative of the decedent, federal law requires the mortgage to pass to the beneficiary without any changes in its terms.

TIP

Deeds of trust. Most people know the term "mortgage." But in California, the document called a "deed of trust" makes property collateral for a loan.

Reverse Mortgages

Sometimes seniors take out reverse mortgages on their homes to obtain extra cash. While this can be useful during life, at death reverse mortgages become payable in full and this big payment often causes trouble for the survivors. As the executor, you may have to make a decision about how to pay the mortgage and what to do with the home.

Do not delay in getting legal advice and communicating with the lender; time limits may apply. Some options to consider are:

- Sell the home. Any equity that's left over will pass to the estate beneficiaries.
- If the mortgage exceeds the property's value, allow the mortgage lender to foreclose. (Prob. Code § 9391.) The estate is not responsible for the difference between the loan amount and the value of the property.
- Family members can pay off the mortgage at 95% of the current appraised value of the home—the lender is required to write off the difference.
- Refinance the reverse mortgage with a traditional mortgage.

CHAPTER 9

How to Transfer Securities

Securities, including stocks, bonds, debentures, or mutual fund shares owned by a decedent, must be reregistered in the name(s) of the new owners at some point during settlement of the decedent's estate. When the assets can be transferred and who has the authority to do so depends on a number of factors—how the asset was held (which determines whether the asset passes directly to a named beneficiary or joint owner), the size of the decedent's estate (which determines whether small estate procedures can be used), and who is the beneficiary (which determines whether a surviving spouse or domestic partner can use an affidavit or court order to claim the property). Review Chapter 6 for a reminder of the various options.

These days, holding actual certificates for securities is less common than holding securities in accounts with a brokerage firm (such as Charles Schwab, Fidelity Investments, E*TRADE, and TD Ameritrade) or a transfer agent (such as Computershare and American Stock Transfer & Trust). Securities held in noncertificate form by a company, transfer agent, or brokerage firm will be transferred through that entity. Contact the entity for appropriate forms and procedures.

When certificates exist, the actual transfers, except in the case of mutual fund shares, are made by a "transfer agent," whose name and address normally appear on the face of the stock or bond certificate. Call (or check with a stock brokerage firm) for instructions and to verify the name and address of the current transfer agent.

Shares in mutual funds are transferred by the company that manages the fund. Contact the company to find out its requirements for selling, redeeming, or changing record ownership of the shares. You may get the name, address, and telephone number of the person to contact from the last monthly statement or from the brokerage company's website. Usually, the same documentation discussed in this chapter for other types of securities is required to transfer mutual funds.

Transferring title to securities involves a fair amount of detail work. Rather than tackle this project yourself, you might want to consider having a bank or stock brokerage firm handle the transfers for you. They are experienced in this area and will help with the documentation and process the transfers for a nominal charge.

TIP

Use transfer agent's forms. To transfer securities, you will likely need to fill out specific forms provided by the transfer agent. Some forms will need to be notarized or signature guaranteed. Collect forms from the transfer agent, confirm with the transfer agent that you have the appropriate forms, then fill out and sign the forms as required. Making sure that everything is in order before sending in the documents can minimize delays.

CAUTION

Taking distributions from retirement accounts may have serious tax consequences. Securities held in certain retirement accounts (401(k), IRA, or Roth IRA, for example) will be handled according to the beneficiary designations of that account. The beneficiary needs to consider carefully the tax implications of taking a distribution from the account or taking the account as an inherited or rollover IRA. Get more information from *IRAs, 401(k)s & Other Retirement Plans: Strategies for Taking Your Money Out* by John C. Suttle and Twila Slesnick (Nolo), or get help from a tax professional.

Documents Required to Transfer Securities

Several documents are required to transfer securities after a death, depending on how the securities were originally owned (and sometimes depending on whom they are transferred to).

Through Formal Probate

You will normally need a probate court order to transfer securities if the estate subject to probate exceeds the threshold for small estate procedures in effect at the time (currently $166,250), and the securities were either in the decedent's name alone or with another person as tenants in common. (The procedure for obtaining the court order is explained in Chapter 14.)

Ownership as tenants in common normally occurs when an asset is owned by two or more people, unless title is specifically held as community property, in joint tenancy, or in beneficiary form.

SKIP AHEAD

Transfers of securities to spouses and in small estates. If the securities pass outright to a surviving spouse or domestic partner, go to "To a Surviving Spouse or Domestic Partner," below. If the total estate subject to probate is under $166,250, see "Through a Small Estate Procedure," below.

When a decedent owned securities as a tenant in common with a surviving person, the decedent's interest is subject to probate and the surviving person's interest is not. Although two new certificates must be issued, one in the name of the new owner of the decedent's interest and one in the name of the surviving tenant in common, a probate court order is required only for the transfer of the decedent's shares.

> EXAMPLE: Marsha died owning 300 shares of stock as a tenant in common with her sister Clara. A new certificate for 150 shares must be issued in the name(s) of the person(s) who receive Marsha's one-half interest, and another certificate issued in the name of Clara as sole owner of the other 150 shares.

In a probate proceeding, the personal representative may choose to have securities first transferred to the estate for the administration period. This may be needed, for example, to sell securities to pay expenses of administration or to appropriately manage the assets of the estate. Or, the personal representative may choose to leave title to the securities as is during the course of administration, and then make the transfer directly to the new owner as ordered by the court. See Chapter 14.

Transferring Securities During Probate Administration - Documents to Be Submitted to the Transfer Agent

Transfer agents usually require that you submit the following documents:

- original stock certificate, bond, or debenture
- certified copy of Letters Testamentary or Letters of Administration ("letters"), certified within the prior 60 days (learn how to get these in Chapter 13)
- stock power signed by the personal representative, with the signature guaranteed (see below)
- Affidavit of Domicile, signed by the personal representative, with signature notarized (see below)
- transmittal letter requesting the transfer (if the transfer is to be made to the personal representative during the course of administration, provide the taxpayer identification number of the estate and the personal representative's address. If the transfer is to be made to the new owner to complete distribution as ordered by the court, give the name(s), Social Security number(s), and address(es) of the new owner(s) (see below).), and
- any other forms specific to the transfer agent.

To a Surviving Joint Tenant

Securities registered in joint tenancy form will usually appear as "John Brown and/or Ruth Brown, as joint tenants" or, instead of "as joint tenants," it might say "JTRS" (Joint Tenants with Right of Survivorship) or "WROS" (With Right of Survivorship). All of these terms and abbreviations mean the same thing.

It is relatively easy to transfer securities held in joint tenancy, as no probate is required. This means transfer of joint tenancy property can be done almost immediately after death.

If there are no surviving joint tenants, the stocks belong to the last joint tenant to die and will be subject to probate in that person's estate. If it has not already been done, title must still be formally transferred to the last surviving joint tenant before it is then again transferred as part of the estate. To accomplish this, the transfer agent will need a certified copy of the death certificate of the first joint tenant to die, along with the other documents listed below.

Passing Securities to Surviving Joint Tenant—Documents Required

You'll need the following:

- original stock certificate, bond, debenture, or other security
- stock power signed by surviving joint tenant(s) with signature guaranteed (see "The Stock or Bond Power," below)
- certified copy of death certificate (see Chapter 2)
- Affidavit of Domicile signed by surviving joint tenant(s), with signature(s) notarized (see "The Affidavit of Domicile," below)
- transmittal letter signed by surviving joint tenant(s) (see "The Transmittal Letter," below), and
- any other forms specific to the transfer agent.

To a Surviving Spouse or Domestic Partner

If the decedent was married or a registered domestic partner at the time of death, the decedent may have owned securities as community property. The decedent may also have owned other securities that were separate property. Remember, however, that securities can be held in the name of one person alone and still be community property, depending on when the securities were obtained. If the securities are already held in the name of the surviving spouse or partner, no transfer is required. See Chapter 4 for a detailed discussion of community property and separate property.

If the securities pass to a surviving spouse or domestic partner—whether by a will or by intestate succession—you may make the actual transfer easily with the following documents.

Passing Securities to Surviving Spouse or Domestic Partner—Documents Required

You'll need the following:

- original certificate, bond, or debenture
- stock power, signed by surviving spouse or partner, with signature guaranteed (see "The Stock or Bond Power," below)
- certified copy of Spousal or Domestic Partner Property Order (we discuss how to get this in Chapter 15)
- Affidavit of Domicile, signed by surviving spouse or partner, with signature notarized (see "The Affidavit of Domicile," below)
- transmittal letter signed by the surviving spouse or partner (see "The Transmittal Letter," below), and
- any other forms specific to the transfer agent.

Through a Small Estate Procedure

Estate property may be transferred using an affidavit when the total value of the decedent's property (in California) does not exceed $166,250, not counting property:

- owned in trust
- owned in joint tenancy
- passing to a surviving spouse or domestic partner
- passing to a designated beneficiary (including TOD or POD), or

- specifically excluded by law, such as vehicles and compensation owed to the decedent, if less than $16,625 (Prob. Code § 13050).

If the remaining value does not exceed the current threshold to be considered a "small" estate (currently $166,250), the securities may be transferred by means of an affidavit signed by the person(s) entitled to receive the securities. This procedure, which is explained in detail in Chapter 11, usually applies when the securities are registered in the decedent's name alone or as a tenant in common with another. It can also be used as a simple way of transferring community property securities to a surviving spouse or partner, if the estate is small and meets the requirements for use of this procedure.

Passing Securities Through Small Estate Procedures—Documents Required

You'll need the following:

- affidavit given pursuant to California Probate Code Section 13100, signed by person(s) entitled to receive the securities, with the signatures notarized (see Chapter 11)
- original stock certificate, bond, debenture, or mutual fund certificate
- certified copy of the decedent's death certificate (see Chapter 2)
- Affidavit of Domicile signed by person(s) entitled to the securities, with signature(s) notarized (see "The Affidavit of Domicile," below)
- transmittal letter signed by person(s) entitled to the securities (see "The Transmittal Letter," below)
- stock or bond power, signed by persons entitled to receive securities (see "The Stock or Bond Power," below), and
- any other forms specific to the transfer agent.

To Living Trust Beneficiaries

To transfer securities held by the decedent (or someone else as trustee) in a living trust, the trustee will contact the transfer agent for each security to make specific arrangements for the transfer. Usually, in this instance, the securities are held in the name of the decedent (or someone else) as trustee, and the living trust document names a successor trustee to take over on the death of the original trustee. The transfer agent will itemize the documents needed to make the transfer. Usually, a certified copy of the decedent's death certificate, a stock or bond power, and Affidavit of Domicile executed by the trustee or successor trustee are required. Sometimes the transfer agent also requests a copy of the living trust or a "certification of trust." (A certification of trust is a shorter version of the trust document that proves the existence of the trust and the trustee, but excludes some of the more personal provisions, like the names of beneficiaries.)

If a living trust was established but the securities in question were never formally transferred to it, you cannot use this procedure. You will probably need to transfer the securities under the terms of a formal probate unless they are part of a small estate or pass to the surviving spouse or domestic partner. An attorney can help you figure out the best options for your situation.

RESOURCE

Learn more about trust administration. Trustees must be aware of and fulfill the various notification, accounting, and other requirements to administer properly the trust prior to making distributions to beneficiaries. Complete instructions for trust administration are beyond the scope of this book. You can learn more about trust administration from *The Trustee's Legal Companion*, by Liza Hanks and Carol Elias Zolla (Nolo).

To Transfer on Death Beneficiaries

Ownership of stocks, bonds, and brokerage accounts can be registered as "transfer on death" to a beneficiary. Securities registered in this manner can be transferred to the beneficiary without going through probate. This is often referred to as stock registered "in beneficiary form."

A stock is registered in beneficiary form if the words "transfer on death" or "TOD" or "pay on death" or "POD" appear on the registration before the beneficiary's name and following the registered owner's name. Generally, an institution will allow you to transfer ownership to the beneficiary if you send a certified copy of the death certificate of the deceased owner and a stock power signed by the beneficiary. Confirm with the transfer agent what documents it requires. Send the required documents to the transfer agent along with a transmittal letter and the original stock ownership certificate.

CAUTION

Divorce reminder. If the decedent designated his or her spouse or partner as a transfer on death beneficiary and the couple later divorced or terminated the partnership, the former spouse or partner does not inherit. (Prob. Code § 5600.)

CAUTION

Community property. There could be complications if a married or partnered decedent held community property assets in the decedent's own name and named a transfer on death beneficiary who is not the surviving spouse or registered domestic partner. The surviving spouse or partner still has rights to his or her own community property share of the asset. If the surviving spouse and the named beneficiary are not in agreement about the result, get legal advice about how to proceed.

The Stock or Bond Power

The "stock or bond power" authorizes the actual transfer of the securities. It must be executed by a person having the authority to sign on behalf of the decedent. In each of the foregoing transfer situations, we have indicated who should sign the stock or bond power.

Most stock, bond, and mutual fund certificates have the stock or bond power printed on the back. However, a separate but very similar form is normally used, called Stock or Bond Assignment Separate From Certificate, or Irrevocable Stock or Bond Power, which you can obtain from a bank or stockbroker (many brokerage websites allow you to download this form from their sites). As you will notice in the sample just below, the form has a space to fill in the name of the employee of the transfer agent who actually transfers the stock on the books of the corporation; leave this space blank.

Because transfer agents have no means of identifying the signature of the person who signs the stock power, they usually insist that the signature be "guaranteed." This may be done by a bank officer at the bank of the person executing the stock or bond power or by a broker handling the securities transfer. In either case, the bank or brokerage office stamps the stock or bond power "Signature Guaranteed," followed by the name of the bank, trust company, or brokerage firm. The person guaranteeing the signature signs just below the stamp.

The documentation required for a signature guarantee depends on the value of the asset being transferred. Before going into a bank to request a signature guarantee, you may want to call first and explain the nature of the transaction, confirm that a person is available to provide the signature guarantee, determine the required documents, and make an appointment to come in to get the signature guarantee.

Irrevocable Stock or Bond Power

IRREVOCABLE STOCK OR BOND POWER

Account Number ______________________

FOR VALUE RECEIVED, the undersigned does (do) hereby sell, assign, or transfer to:

Name(s) of new owner(s) of stock (i.e., surviving joint tenant(s), surviving spouse, surviving domestic partner, or beneficiary(ies))

Social Security or Tax Identifying Number **Insert Social Security number of new owner(s)**

IF STOCK, COMPLETE THIS PORTION

Number of shares shares of **Type of stock (common, preferred, etc.)** stock of **Name of company** represented by Certificate(s) No. **Number of stock certificate** inclusive, standing in the name of the undersigned on the books of said company.

IF BONDS, COMPLETE THIS PORTION

Number of bonds bonds of **Issuer of bond(s)** ______________ in the principal amount of $ **Face value** No(s). **Number(s) of bond certificate(s)** ______ inclusive, standing in the name of the undersigned on the books of said company.

The undersigned does (do) hereby irrevocably constitute and appoint **Leave this blank** ______________________ attorney to transfer the said stock or bond(s), as the case may be, on the books of said company, with full power of substitution in the premises.

IMPORTANT: The signature(s) to this power must correspond with the name(s) as written upon the face of the certificate(s) or bond(s) in every particular without alteration.

Dated: ______________________

Signed by surviving joint tenant; surviving spouse or domestic partner; executor or administrator of decedent's estate; or the beneficiary(ies) entitled in the case of small estates

____

____

Person(s) Executing This Power Sign(s) Here

____

SIGNATURE GUARANTEED

The Affidavit of Domicile

The Affidavit of Domicile (sometimes called Affidavit of Residence) is required as proof that the decedent was a resident of California and not of the state in which the corporation is organized, in which case transfer taxes might be due. Many transfer agents require this affidavit as a matter of routine. Banks and stockbrokers usually have these forms on hand and it is best to use the forms they provide to minimize delays. A sample is provided below. The person signing the affidavit must do so in front of a notary public.

The Transmittal Letter

A transmittal letter should accompany the original stock and bond certificates and other documents when they are sent to the transfer agent. The transfer agent, bank, or stockbroker will usually provide an appropriate form. Below we provide a sample letter that you can adapt to various situations. Note that you must provide the name or names of the new owners of the securities, along with their addresses and Social Security numbers. If the securities are to be apportioned between two or more persons, be sure to indicate the number of shares going to each. Original certificates should be insured and sent by registered mail, return receipt requested. To protect against fraudulent transfers if the certificates were to be misdelivered, you may choose to send the original certificates separately (but at the same time) from the transfer documents.

TIP

Securities held by a custodian. If the decedent owned securities held by a stockbroker or a bank as a custodian (meaning they were not registered in the decedent's name), you should contact the broker or custodian and arrange to have them put in the name(s) of the new owner(s).

How to Sell Securities

Sometimes beneficiaries may prefer to have securities sold or liquidated, rather than have them reregistered in their names as the new owners. Be aware that there may be tax consequences for the beneficiary, depending on the change in the value of the security since the decedent's date of death. When securities are sold, the transaction is handled by a stockbroker. Selling securities requires the same documentation as needed for transferring securities. The broker will help you with the forms. If the transfer agent insists on a court order, see Chapter 14, Step 13.

Affidavit of Domicile

AFFIDAVIT OF DOMICILE

The undersigned, _ **Name of person who signs affidavit** ____________________,

being duly sworn, deposes and says:

That he/she resides at ____ **Address of person who signs affidavit** ____________________,

City of ____________________, County of ____________________,

State of ____________________, and is Executor/Administrator/Surviving Joint Tenant/Surviving Spouse/Surviving Domestic Partner of

Cross out all titles except the one that applies to your case

________ **Name of decedent** ____________________, deceased, or sole beneficiary of the Will

or Estate of said decedent, who died on ________ **Date of death** ________, 20 ____.

That at the time of death, the decedent's residence or domicile (legal residence) was

________ **Decedent's last address** ____________________

in the State of California, and has been the same for the preceding _ **Years decedent was at this address**

years, and that the decedent last voted in the State of California.

____
Executor/Administrator/Surviving Joint Tenant/
Surviving Spouse/Surviving Domestic Partner/
Beneficiary under decedent's will

Cross out all titles except the one that applies to your case

CERTIFICATE OF NOTARY PUBLIC

A notary public or other officer completing this certificate verifies only the identity of the individual who signed the document to which this certificate is attached, and not the truthfulness, accuracy, or validity of that document.

STATE OF CALIFORNIA
COUNTY OF _ **County where affidavit will be signed**

Subscribed and sworn to (or affirmed) before me on this ______ day of ____________________, 20 ______
by ____, proved to me on the basis of satisfactory evidence to be the person(s) who appeared before me.

[SEAL] Notary's Signature ______________________________

Transmittal Letter

Name and address of transfer agent

Attention: Stock Transfer Department

Re: Estate of ______________________________, Deceased

Enclosed are the following certificates registered in the names of ____________________

Names shown on original certificates

____:

Certificate Number	Type of Security	Number of Shares/ Face Amount of Bond	Name of Company or Government Entity

Fill in information from original certificates

Also enclosed are the following documents:

Use only items that apply to your case

1. Separate Stock or Bond Power
2. Certified copy of Death Certificate
3. Affidavit of Domicile
4. Certified copy of letters (certified within 60 days)
5. Notarized Affidavit Under Prob. Code § 13100
6. Certified copy of Spousal or Domestic Partner Property Order
7. [any form specifically required by the transfer agent]

Please cancel the enclosed certificates and issue new certificates as follows:

Name and Address	Social Security Number	Shares

Fill in information about new shareholders

Sincerely,

Provide your contact information

____

CHAPTER

10

Joint Tenancy Property

It's not unusual to find many of a decedent's assets held in joint tenancy. Real estate brokers, bank officers, and stockbrokers often recommend joint tenancy ownership for married couples, and sometimes for other joint owners. Many people also choose joint tenancy because joint tenancy property avoids formal court proceedings at death. Sometimes elderly or ill persons place their bank accounts in joint tenancy with a trusted relative or friend so the relative or friend can conveniently cash checks, make deposits, and carry on business for the elderly or ill person.

For our purposes, the important characteristic of joint tenancy ownership is providing a simple way to transfer ownership at death without probate. The moment one of the co-owners dies, the decedent's interest in the property shifts to the surviving joint tenant or tenants. (If there are two or more surviving joint tenants, the survivors remain joint tenants of the property.) A deceased joint tenant's creditors have no rights against property held in joint tenancy. Property held in joint tenancy doesn't pass under the provisions of the decedent's will, nor does it go to the decedent's heirs if the decedent died without a will so long as at least one joint tenant is living.

Even though joint tenancy avoids probate, a few simple formalities must be completed to remove the decedent's name from the title, deed, certificate, account, or other record of ownership if the survivors wish to hold clear title to the property. We explain how to do this here.

When the last joint tenant dies, if the asset is still held in joint tenancy, the property will be transferred as part of that person's estate. At that time, it will be subject to formal probate unless it passes to a surviving spouse or domestic partner (see Chapter 15) or passes as part of a small estate (see Chapter 11).

Where to Start

The first step is to verify that you are dealing with joint tenancy property. Examine deeds to real property and other ownership documents to make sure title is actually held in joint tenancy, and not in sole ownership, tenancy in common, or as community property. (It is also a good idea to check with a title company or the county recorder's office index for real property, because the decedent may have broken the joint tenancy prior to death without telling the other joint tenants.) Unless the title document (for example, deed, account title, or stock certificate) says "as joint tenants" or "with right of survivorship" (sometimes abbreviated as "JTRS" or "WROS"), it is probably not joint tenancy. An exception to this is a vehicle registered in the names of two people with the word "or" between their names, which is considered joint tenancy ownership as far as the Department of Motor Vehicles is concerned.

Bank accounts, stocks, bonds, and promissory notes, as well as real property, may be held in joint tenancy. A bank account held in the names of two persons connected by "or" without saying "as joint tenants" is treated as joint tenancy ownership by most banks, and the account will pass to the survivor when one of the owners dies.

Joint tenancy and estate taxes: As discussed in Chapter 7, joint tenancy property does not avoid estate taxes. Even though property held in joint tenancy is excluded from court probate procedures, it is included in the decedent's taxable estate. In addition, for property that a decedent converted while living to joint tenancy—for example, adding a joint tenant to a bank account for convenience or conveying an interest in real property to someone as a joint tenant to make it easier to transfer the property upon death—the decedent's original (whole) interest in the property is included in the taxable estate, unless a gift tax return was filed to report the transfer to the IRS or unless the other joint tenants acquired their interests for full value.

How to Clear Title to Real Property in Joint Tenancy

Real property, as we discussed in Chapter 4, is land or things permanently affixed to land, such as houses, trees, and fences. It includes condominiums and cooperatives (although some cooperatives in which the decedent's interest is a very limited one are treated as personal property), and may also include mobile homes permanently attached to land if the person who owns the mobile home also owns the land.

Step 1. Prepare an Affidavit— Death of Joint Tenant

Using an Affidavit – Death of Joint Tenant is the easiest way to clear joint tenancy title to real property, and the method most commonly used. An Affidavit – Death of Joint Tenant is a sworn statement by anyone with knowledge of the relevant facts, usually the surviving joint tenant. The affidavit states that the decedent named on the death certificate (which must be attached to the affidavit) is the same person named on the relevant existing deed to the property (quoting the decedent's name exactly as it appears on the deed) as a joint tenant. Sometimes the names on the deed and on the death certificate may be different—initials might be used on one and a given name on the other. This isn't a problem unless the names are significantly different, in which case you will have to offer proof that the decedent and the joint tenant were the same person.

FORMS

A blank Affidavit – Death of Joint Tenant is in Appendix C. You can download a fillable version of the form on this book's companion page at www.nolo.com/back-of-book/PAE.html.

A sample affidavit is shown below. Much of the information needed to complete the affidavit is obtained from the joint tenancy deed. The person completing the affidavit signs it in the presence of a notary public. If you do not have a copy of the joint tenancy deed, you can get it from the county recorder.

As mentioned above, if the decedent was the last joint tenant to die, but the interests of predeceased joint tenants were never formally ended, you must terminate the interest of all of the other joint tenant(s) in the same manner so that the record will show title passing to the last joint tenant to die. The Affidavit – Death of Joint Tenant for the prior joint tenant(s) to die may be signed by the personal representative (executor or administrator) of the estate of the last joint tenant to die.

Instructions for Filling in Affidavit— Death of Joint Tenant

In the top left-hand corner, fill in the name and address of the person to whom the document is to be returned. Usually, this is the person who signs the affidavit.

In the first blank, fill in the name of the person who will sign the affidavit.

In the next blank, fill in the name of the decedent exactly as it appears on the death certificate.

In the next two blanks, fill in the name of the decedent exactly as it appears on the joint tenancy deed, and the date of the deed.

Next, fill in the names of the person(s) who signed the joint tenancy deed.

Next, fill in the names of the persons who received the property by the joint tenancy deed.

Next, fill in information about where the joint tenancy deed is recorded: The instrument number on the deed, the date it was recorded, and the county where it was recorded. Deeds recorded before the 1980s may not have an instrument number. In this case, use the book and page number found near the recording date.

Then give the city (unless the property is in an unincorporated area) and county where the property is located, and copy the legal description of the property from the deed. Be sure to copy the legal description carefully and accurately. If the legal description will not fit in the blank, write in the blank: "See Exhibit A attached hereto," and include a separate page titled "Exhibit A" with the full legal description.

If the property is a residence passing to an owner-occupier, include a statement on the affidavit to claim an exemption to the $75 SB2 recording fee. This can be added to the affidavit below the recorder's information and above the title: "Exempt from SB2 fee per Gov. Code Sec. 27338.1(a)(2) because recorded in connection with a transfer of real property that is a residential dwelling to an owner-occupier." Or prior to recording, a cover sheet may be used for this purpose. See Chapter 8.

Sign the affidavit in front of a notary public who will ask you to swear (or affirm) that the statements you made in the affidavit are true.

Affidavit—Death of Joint Tenant

RECORDING REQUESTED BY: Mary Doe

AND WHEN RECORDED MAIL DOCUMENT
AND TAX STATEMENT TO: Mary Doe
567 First Street
Los Angeles, CA 90017

APN:
Commonly known as:

SPACE ABOVE THIS LINE FOR RECORDER'S USE

[*Include if applicable*: Exempt from SB2 fee per Gov. Code Sec. 27338.1(a)(2) because recorded in connection with a transfer of real property that is a residential dwelling to an owner-occupier.]

AFFIDAVIT—DEATH OF JOINT TENANT

Mary Doe, of legal age, being first duly sworn, deposes and says:

That Robert Steven Doe, the decedent mentioned in the attached certified copy of Certificate of Death, is the same person as Robert Doe named as one of the parties in that certain deed dated June 20, 1985, executed by John Smith and Susan Smith to Robert Doe and Mary Doe, as joint tenants, recorded on June 24, 1985 as instrument No. 85-58892, of Official Records of Los Angeles County, California, covering the following described property situated in the City of Los Angeles, County of Los Angeles, State of California:

Lot 101 of Tract 26834, as per map recorded in Book 691, Pages 3 to 8 of Maps, in the Office of the County Recorder of said county.

Assessor's Parcel No. 567-892-003-1

Dated: September 26, 20xx

Mary Doe
Signature

Mary Doe
(Type or print name of person signing affidavit)

Certificate of Notary Public

A notary public or other officer completing this certificate verifies only the identity of the individual who signed the document to which this certificate is attached, and not the truthfulness, accuracy, or validity of that document.

State of California

County of Los Angeles

Subscribed and sworn to (or affirmed) before me on this 26 day of September, 20 xx by Mary Doe, proved to me on the basis of satisfactory evidence to be the person(s) who appeared before me.

[SEAL]

Signature *Nancy Notary*

Step 2. Attach a Certified Copy of the Death Certificate

Attach a certified copy of the decedent's death certificate to the affidavit. For this purpose, a photocopy will not do. If you don't have a certified copy, see Chapter 2 for instructions on how to obtain one.

Step 3. Fill Out Preliminary Change of Ownership Report

The affidavit must be accompanied by a Preliminary Change of Ownership Report when it is recorded with the county recorder's office. You may also need to fill out a supplemental form to claim an exclusion from reassessment for property tax purposes under certain circumstances. The most common exclusions apply for transfers between a parent and child, from a grandparent to grandchild, or between cotenants. Particularly for deaths occurring after February 15, 2021, the exclusion depends on whether the property is the principal residence of the decedent and the recipient. To avoid complications, consider the rules carefully before filling out the relevant forms. (See Chapter 8.)

Step 4. Record the Affidavit With the County Recorder

Finally, record the affidavit at the county recorder's office in the county where the real property is located. This should be done as soon as possible after the death. You can bring the affidavit in person or mail it to the county recorder with a cover letter requesting that it be recorded and returned to the address indicated in the upper left-hand corner of the document. Contact the recorder's office to ascertain the amount of the recording fee. A one-page affidavit with a death certificate attached is considered two pages for recording purposes. Additional documents may be required for recording, including a Preliminary Change in Ownership Report. In some counties, the SB2 fee may be charged if an exception is not claimed. (Information on recording documents with the county recorder is in Chapter 8.) It isn't necessary to record a new deed when you record the affidavit. The purpose of the affidavit is to remove the deceased person's name from the title so ownership appears solely in the name of the survivor(s).

TIP

The Spousal or Domestic Partner Property Order alternative. If the joint tenants are spouses or registered domestic partners, a Spousal or Domestic Partner Property Order may offer another way to transfer the property to the surviving joint tenant. (See Chapter 15.) This method may be preferable if (1) the property is going to the surviving spouse or partner, and (2) the property is community property. As explained in Chapter 7, establishing (through the court order) that the joint tenancy property was, in fact, community property may have advantageous tax consequences when the property is later sold. If you are not sure which method to use, get legal advice before using the Affidavit – Death of Joint Tenant.

How to Clear Title to Securities Held in Joint Tenancy

Detailed information on how to transfer securities is in Chapter 9. Although a few different documents will be needed, you should find this process relatively simple.

How to Clear Title to Motor Vehicles and Boats Registered with the DMV and Held in Joint Tenancy

If the pink slip (ownership document) shows a vehicle or boat is registered in the names of two persons joined by "or" (for example, "Bob Smith or Sarah Lee"), this creates a joint tenancy under the Vehicle Code. If the pink slip names the decedent "and" another person (for example, "Bob Smith and Sarah Lee"), it is joint tenancy ownership only if it so states (for example, "Bob Smith and Sarah Lee, as joint tenants" or "JTRS" in place of "joint tenants").

Vehicles may also be registered in a beneficiary or TOD (transfer on death) form. In that case, the TOD beneficiary takes ownership of the vehicle without probate procedures. The transfer process is basically

Transfer of Ownership of Motor Vehicle Held in Joint Tenancy

STATE OF CALIFORNIA

55555555555 CERTIFICATE OF TITLE

AUTOMOBILE

VEHICLE ID NUMBER: JH4DB1555MS555555 | YR MODEL: 91 | MAKE: ACURA | PLATE NUMBER: 5TTT555

BODY TYPE MODEL: SD | AX | UNLADEN WEIGHT | FUEL: G | TRANSFER DATE | FEES PAID: $302 | REGISTRATION EXPIRATION DATE: 01/22/92

YR 1ST SOLD: 91 | CLASS: DT | YR | MO: WB | EQUIPMT/TRUST NUMBER | ISSUE DATE: 03/06/91

MOTORCYCLE ENGINE NUMBER | ODOMETER DATE | ODOMETER READING

REGISTERED OWNER(S)
JON DOE OR MARY DOE
1111 BERKELEY ST
OAKLEY CA 94444

FEDERAL LAW REQUIRES that you state the mileage upon transfer of ownership. Failure to complete or making a false statement may result in fines and/or imprisonment.

Odometer reading is: ______ (no tenths) which is the actual mileage of the vehicle unless one of the following statements is checked. WARNING - Mileage ☐ is not the actual mileage. ☐ Exceeds the odometer mechanical limits.

I certify under penalty of perjury under the laws of the State of California, that the signature(s) below releases interest in the vehicle and certifies to the truth and accuracy of the mileage information entered above.

Survivor dates and signs on Line 1a of front of "pink slip"

1a. ________ DATE X ________ SIGNATURE OF REGISTERED OWNER

1b. ________ DATE X ________ SIGNATURE OF REGISTERED OWNER

IMPORTANT READ CAREFULLY

Any change of Lienholder (holder of security interest) must be reported to the Department of Motor Vehicles within 10 days.

LIENHOLDER(S)

2. X ________
Signature releases interest in vehicle.

Release Date ________

014444 ET20220222

REG. 17.30 (REV 9/90)

KEEP IN A SAFE PLACE — VOID IF ALTERED

APPLICATION FOR TRANSFER BY NEW OWNER (Please print or type.)

Any change of registered owner or lienholder must be recorded with the Department of Motor Vehicles (DMV) within ten (10) days. The title, transfer fee and in most instances, use tax and a smog certificate must be presented to DMV to record the ownership change.

NEW REGISTERED OWNER

3a. TRUE FULL NAME(S) OF NEW REGISTERED OWNER(S) (LAST, FIRST, MIDDLE) AS IT APPEARS ON DRIVER'S LICENSE OR I.D. CARD

3b. ☐ AND ☐ OR (LAST, FIRST, MIDDLE)

4. STREET ADDRESS OR P.O. BOX NUMBER

5. CITY | STATE | ZIP CODE

6. MAILING ADDRESS STREET OR P.O. BOX NUMBER (DO NOT COMPLETE IF SAME AS RESIDENCE ABOVE)

7. CITY | STATE | ZIP CODE

8. FOR TRAILER COACHES ONLY – ADDRESS OR LOCATION WHERE KEPT

I certify under penalty of perjury under the laws of the State of California that the information entered by me on this document is true and correct and acknowledges the odometer mileage recorded by the seller. If there is a mailing address entered on this form, it is a valid, existing and accurate address. I consent to receive service of process at this mailing address pursuant to Civil Procedures Code Sections 415.20(b), 415.30(a) and 416.90.

9a. DATE | SIGNATURE OF NEW REGISTERED OWNER X | PURCHASE DATE

9b. DATE | SIGNATURE OF NEW REGISTERED OWNER X | PURCHASE PRICE OR IF GIFT, SO STATE

LEASED VEH. 10. ADDRESS OF NEW LESSEE IF DIFFERENT FROM LINE 4 ABOVE (WILL NOT BE PRINTED ON TITLE)

Survivor completes top portion (Lines 3a-9b) of back of "pink slip" the same as for joint tenants. The Statement of Facts (REG 256) is used to state the date and place of the owner's death and that the new owner is entitled to the vehicle as the designated beneficiary.

Automobile clubs will assist in transferring title to motor vehicles, or you may go in person to the Department of Motor Vehicles and submit the following items:

- the certified copy of the deceased joint tenant's death certificate (see Chapter 2)
- the vehicle or boat ownership certificate (pink slip) signed in the proper place on the back by the survivor
- the registration slip for the vehicle
- the $10 (for TOD transfer) or $15 transfer fee, and
- a certificate of compliance with the smog pollution control law (DMV form REG 256), unless the surviving joint tenant who is taking title is the spouse, domestic partner, child, grandparent, parent, sibling, or grandchild of the decedent.

Boat Titles

The Department of Motor Vehicles registers sailboats longer than eight feet and boats that are not registered with the U.S. Coast Guard. Different procedures apply for larger "documented" vessels holding marine certificates by the U.S. Coast Guard.

How to Clear Title to Joint Tenancy Bank Accounts (and POD Accounts)

The surviving joint tenant may continue to use a joint tenancy account. Banks will transfer a joint account or POD (pay on death) account to the survivor when presented with the following documents:

- a certified copy of the decedent's death certificate (see Chapter 2), and
- bank documentation to transfer the account to the survivor.

As with any transaction with a financial institution, confirm with the institution the specific information it will require, such as identifying information of the surviving owner.

How to Clear Title to Money Market Funds and Mutual Funds

Most money mutual funds and money market funds are held in brokerage accounts. If that is the case, the brokerage firm will remove the decedent's name from the account after the co-owner provides a certified copy of the death certificate and information to establish the account in the survivor's name and Social Security number.

Mutual funds and money market accounts not held in a brokerage account are usually transferred by the fund management instead of a transfer agent, and, as a rule, the share certificates are held by the fund's custodian instead of by the owner of the shares. Consequently, transferring these types of assets is easier than with ordinary common stocks and bonds. The best procedure is to contact the fund management directly and ask what they require to sell, redeem, or change the record ownership of the shares when the funds are held in joint tenancy. In almost all cases, a certified copy of the death certificate and identifying information of the surviving owner will be required.

How to Clear Title to U.S. Savings Bonds in Co-Ownership

To reissue or redeem paper savings bonds, the surviving owner or beneficiary should take the bonds, along with the certificate of the copy of the death certificate, to a local bank. Most banks have forms for reissuing or redeeming paper U.S. savings bonds and will assist in these transactions. TreasuryDirect.gov also provides instructions and forms for reissuing or redeeming paper bonds through the mail. If the decedent had U.S. savings bonds in a TreasuryDirect.gov account, get instructions from TreasuryDirect.gov.

CHAPTER

11

Transferring Small Estates

Overview of the Transfer Procedures for Small Estates

Estates considered "small" estates may be settled without formal probate proceedings, using relatively simple transfer procedures. What can be considered a "small" estate for this purpose is defined by California law. Currently, estates that do not exceed $166,250 can use small estate procedures. This amount, and the other values mentioned in this chapter for setting a limit on small estate proceedings, will be adjusted for inflation for decedents dying after April 1, 2022 and every three years thereafter. These small estate procedures save the beneficiaries time and money, as well as considerable stress at an already difficult time. The procedures for small estates are available regardless of whether the assets are real property or personal property, as long as:

- No probate administration proceeding is pending or has been conducted in California for the decedent's estate; or, if it has, the personal representative has consented in writing to small estate procedures. (Prob. Code §§ 13101(a)(4), 13152(a)(5), and 13200(a)(7).)
- The gross value of all real and personal property owned by the decedent in California on the date of death is no more than $166,250. (This figure is the value of the property, not counting any money owed on the property.)

Actually, the $166,250 figure is a little misleading because, as discussed more below, certain assets do not count for computing whether or not the estate falls within the allowable amount for small estate procedures. As a result, many apparently larger estates qualify to use these procedures to collect or transfer those assets that would otherwise require a formal probate court proceeding.

No published notice is required with small estate proceedings, and there are no special rules for notifying creditors as exists in a formal probate court proceeding. In most cases, small estate procedures can be completed in just a few weeks, after a 40-day waiting period (six months for small-value real estate).

Small Estate, Formal Probate, or Both?

In general, an estate will use either a formal probate proceeding or simplified transfer procedures of the type in this chapter for small estates—not both. If the size of the estate allows for small estate procedures, if no disputes exist between beneficiaries, and if no creditor problems are anticipated, then small estate procedures alone can be used. A formal probate administration may be needed for estates over $166,250 or if any of these complications exist. Also, small estate procedures are usually not appropriate if a formal probate administration proceeding is pending or anticipated.

The discussion in this chapter presumes that only small estate procedures will be used. However, the law does allow the personal representative to consent to use of these procedures if a formal probate proceeding is also occurring. This generally only occurs if the estate is opened to facilitate litigation or transfer of assets in other states. Obtain legal advice if this is the case.

There are actually three separate procedures for small estates:

- for personal property (Prob. Code §§ 13100–13116)
- for real property not exceeding $55,425 in value (Prob. Code §§ 13200–13210), and
- for real and personal property not exceeding $166,250 in value (Prob. Code §§ 13150–13158).

If the estate qualifies, anyone entitled to inherit property from the decedent, whether as a beneficiary under the will or as an heir under intestate succession laws, may obtain title or possession of the property with these abbreviated transfer procedures. (Prob. Code § 13006.)

The trustee of a living trust created by the decedent while alive may use the procedures if the estate outside of the trust qualifies as a small estate and the trust is the beneficiary under the decedent's will. In addition, a guardian, custodian, or conservator of the estate of a person who is entitled to receive property from the decedent may act on behalf of the person, and an attorney-in-fact authorized under a durable power of attorney may act on behalf of the beneficiary giving the power of attorney. (Prob. Code § 13051.)

The waiting period required by these transfer procedures is to allow creditors and legitimate claimants a chance to protect their interests in the property. The decedent's debts must be paid, and transferees who receive a decedent's property under these procedures are liable for the debts to the extent of the net value of the property received and must also file any required tax returns and pay taxes due.

CAUTION

Watch the clock. Lawsuits against a transferee must generally be commenced within one year after the date of death. (Cal. Civ. Proc. Code § 366.2.)

Transferring tangible personal property (household furniture, clothing, and keepsakes) is often handled independently by the family. When an asset has no title document and isn't worth much to begin with, it's reasonably safe and certainly efficient to simply hand it over to whomever is entitled to it under the decedent's will or under the laws of intestate succession. However, if disputes are anticipated, more formal procedures may be appropriate.

Transfer Procedures for Small Estates

Kind of Property	Procedure	Waiting Period
Personal property not exceeding $166,250 in value	Affidavit	40 days
Real property not exceeding $55,425* in value	Affidavit filed with probate court	6 months
Real and personal property not exceeding $166,250* in value	Petition filed with probate court	40 days

* This amount will be adjusted for deaths after April 1, 2022 and every three years thereafter.

How to Determine Whether You Can Use Small Estate Procedures

To find out if some or all of the decedent's assets may be transferred with these procedures, you must first compute the gross value of all property the decedent owned at death. We show you how to do this in Chapter 5. Summarized briefly, an estate's gross value is the fair market value on the date of death of all property owned by the decedent without subtracting any liens against the property, or debts or mortgages owed by the decedent.

EXAMPLE: Lily died owning stocks worth $20,000, a car with a *Blue Book* value of $8,000, a $5,000 savings account, and an apartment full of furniture and antiques worth about $20,000. This comes to a total value of $53,000. Lily owes $6,000 on her car and $5,000 on her apartment furniture. The total gross value of Lily's estate is $53,000 because the money owed on her car and furniture is not considered in computing the gross value of her estate.

Fortunately, you can ignore several types of assets in computing whether the estate's gross value meets the standards for using small estate procedures under California law—that is, $166,250 or less. (Prob. Code § 13050.) The following property isn't counted for this purpose:

- real estate outside California
- joint tenancy property (real or personal)
- property (community, quasi-community, or separate) passing outright to a surviving spouse or registered domestic partner
- life insurance, death benefits, or other assets that pass to living named beneficiaries outside of probate
- multiple-party accounts, IRAs or other assets that pass to living named beneficiaries outside of probate, and pay on death accounts
- any manufactured home, mobile home, commercial coach, floating home, or truck camper registered under the Health and Safety Code

- any vessel numbered under the Vehicle Code
- any motor vehicle, mobile home, or commercial coach registered under the Vehicle Code
- amounts due the decedent for services in the armed forces
- salary or other compensation not exceeding $16,625 (through April 1, 2022 and increasing every three years thereafter) owed the decedent, and
- property held in trust, including a living (inter vivos) trust, or in which the decedent had a life or other estate that terminated on the decedent's death.

So, in the example above, Lily's heirs wouldn't count the value of her car when they're trying to determine whether or not her estate qualifies for small estate procedures.

As you can see from the above list, if an estate has substantial joint tenancy assets, assets passing by beneficiary designation, assets held in trust, or other assets that are excluded from the calculation, it may well qualify for small estate procedures. Also, a surviving spouse or domestic partner may use small estate procedures to collect any amount of assets, so long as the value of assets not otherwise excluded from that calculation and passing to others does not exceed the small estate amount. You can use these small estate procedures to transfer many items of personal property that might otherwise require probate, such as stocks, bonds, bank accounts, or property held in storage, or even real property valued at $166,250 or less in total.

Before we look at how to transfer property using small estate procedures, let's look at some examples of situations where it can be used.

EXAMPLE 1: Curt, a single person, was a California resident when he died, leaving an estate consisting of a $10,000 savings account in a Santa Barbara bank, and stocks worth $30,000, all in Curt's name alone. His employer owed him $12,000 for his last paycheck and compensation for unused vacation. Curt also had an IRA that had a beneficiary designation form on file with the financial institution naming a charity as the beneficiary. Curt left no will, and his heirs under intestate succession laws are his parents. The IRA account will not be included in computing the value of the estate for this purpose, because accounts that pass by beneficiary designations are excluded. And the amount owed by his employer is also excluded in computing the value of the estate. Therefore, his parents may use small estate procedures to have the stocks and bank account transferred to them, because the total gross value of these two assets does not exceed $166,250. They can also collect the amounts owed by the employer.

EXAMPLE 2: Millie was a widow living in Pasadena when she died. Her will left all of her property to her three children equally. Her estate consisted of an unimproved lot in San Bernardino County having a market value of $19,950; furniture and furnishings valued around $1,000; a $5,000 bank account; and a brokerage account with bonds and securities valued at $20,000, all in her name alone. Millie also had some old furniture worth around $1,500 in a storage unit rented in Millie's name. Since the gross value of Millie's probate estate is under $166,250 ($47,450, to be exact, including the real property), Millie's children can use small estate procedures to have all of these assets, including the real property, transferred to them as the new owners. To use this procedure, the children must all act together in signing the required affidavits explained below.

EXAMPLE 3: Harry, a mechanic in Long Beach, owned the following property at the time of his death: A home, held as community property with his wife, Rita; a $20,000 joint tenancy savings account with Rita; and two automobiles worth $20,000 each. His estate also contained an interest, as tenants in common with his sister Pam, in a mountain cabin, his one-half share having a gross value of $39,500, which was acquired before his marriage to Rita. Harry's will leaves his interest in the mountain cabin to Pam, and everything else to Rita. Because the community property home passes outright to Rita under Harry's will, no matter the value (see Chapter 8 and Chapter 15 for transfer information), and the joint savings account passes to Rita as surviving joint tenant (see Chapter 10 for transfer information), those assets are not included in computing the value of the estate for the purpose of small estate procedures. The two automobiles are also not included because of the vehicle exemption (although, in this case, they could also be excluded as property passing outright to the surviving spouse). Harry's sister Pam may use small estate procedures to have Harry's interest in the mountain cabin transferred to her.

How to Transfer the Property

Three different procedures exist for transferring or clearing title to property in small estates. The methods vary depending on whether you are dealing with:

- personal property not exceeding $166,250 in value
- real property not exceeding $55,425 in value, or
- real property not exceeding $166,250 in value.

In all cases, the gross value of the decedent's assets (excluding the property described in the section above) must not exceed $166,250, and generally no formal probate proceedings are conducted for the estate.

Personal Property

Personal property includes both tangible personal property (something that can be physically held) and intangible personal property (such as bank deposits or stock). To receive personal property via this streamlined procedure, the person entitled to the property need only present an affidavit to the person, representative, corporation, or institution having custody or control of the property, or acting as a registrar or transfer agent of the property, requesting that the property be delivered or transferred to them. We've included this affidavit in Appendix C, You may see it referred to as a "small estate affidavit" or "Probate Code Section 13100 Declaration (or Affidavit.)"

When there are several assets to be transferred, they may all be included on one affidavit, or a separate affidavit may be used for each. A simple way to do this is to create one "master" copy of the affidavit of transfer, leaving out the description of the asset in Paragraph 6, and either save the file or make photocopies of the hard copy. Then, simply insert the description of each asset to be transferred on one of the copies and have it signed by the person(s) entitled to receive the asset.

To minimize confusion, prepare a separate affidavit for each holder of property, only including assets relevant to that person or entity. For example, if the decedent had ten shares of ABC Company, worth a total of $500, and a checking account at a bank with a balance of $1,000, prepare two separate affidavits: (1) for the transfer agent of ABC Company listing the 10 shares, and (2) for the bank listing the checking account.

As a rule, if more than one person is entitled to inherit an asset, all beneficiaries must sign the affidavit. In the example above, if two beneficiaries are entitled to the decedent's assets, both of the beneficiaries would sign each of the two affidavits.

CAUTION

Minors cannot sign the affidavit. If the decedent's will nominates a custodian under the Uniform Transfers to Minors Act, the custodian may sign the affidavit on behalf of the minor. If not, and the minor has no court-appointed guardian of her estate, and the amount to be distributed is not large, it may be possible for the parent having custody of the minor to sign the affidavit and receive the property on behalf of the minor if the person or entity holding the property is agreeable. Otherwise, an attorney would have to be consulted to arrange for a guardian or custodian of the minor to be appointed. (See Chapter 14.)

The form in Appendix C provides a place for the signatures to be acknowledged by a notary public. Although the Probate Code says a declaration under penalty of perjury is sufficient when dealing with personal property, many institutions require a notarized affidavit, especially when securities are involved. Check with the institution before you send in your request; it may save you the trouble of finding a notary to witness your signature.

These rules apply when using this affidavit procedure to collect or transfer personal property:

- At least 40 days must have elapsed since the death of the decedent before the affidavit or declaration is presented to the holder of the property.
- No administration proceedings (that is, a formal probate) may be pending or have been conducted for the decedent's estate.
- A certified copy of the decedent's death certificate must be attached to the affidavit.
- Evidence that the decedent owned the property —such as a stock certificate, promissory note, bank statement, storage receipt, or bill of sale—must be presented with the affidavit. This requirement protects the holder or registrar of the property, who might be liable to another person who later makes a claim to the property. If there is no evidence of ownership, the holder of the property may require an indemnity agreement or—less commonly—an indemnity bond, before handing over the property.
- Reasonable proof of identity must be furnished by the persons signing the affidavit. This requirement is satisfied if (1) the signatures on the affidavit are acknowledged by a notary public, (2) the person signing the affidavit is personally known to the holder of the property, or (3) the affidavit is signed in the presence of the holder of the property and the person who signs it presents a valid driver's license, passport, or other suitable identification.
- If the estate contains real property in California (excluding property in joint tenancy, in trust, or passing to a beneficiary by a transfer on death deed) an Inventory and Appraisal must be obtained and attached to the affidavit. The appraiser must be a probate referee who has been appointed by the state controller to appraise property in the county where the property is located. The form and procedures for preparing the Inventory and Appraisal are generally the same as in a formal probate court proceeding. (See Chapter 14, Step 14.) However, in this case, you do not have to get a court order appointing the referee. Instead you may choose the referee (appraiser) yourself. For the names and contact information of all California probate referees listed by county, go to www.sco.ca.gov/eo_probate_contact.html, or www.probatereferees.net, or contact the court clerk for a list of referees who qualify in the county of the property.

These requirements protect the holder of the property from liability on delivery of the property as requested by the affidavit. However, the person receiving the property is made personally liable for any unsecured debts of the decedent. The liability is limited to the fair market value of the property received, less the amount of any liens and encumbrances on the property.

> EXAMPLE: Marcia receives a bank account worth $500 under the terms of Eileen's will. She will use small estate procedures to collect the funds in the bank account. Marcia is liable for up to $500 of Eileen's unsecured debts (debts that don't have collateral pledged to guarantee their payment).

Anyone who falsifies information or uses the affidavit fraudulently is liable to the rightful owner in an amount three times the value of the property. The rightful owner may sue anytime within three years after the affidavit or declaration was presented to the holder of the property.

A sample affidavit is shown below, and you can find a blank affidavit in Appendix C. Here are instructions for completing it.

Item 1. Insert name of decedent, and date and place of death.

Item 2. Attach certified copy of death certificate.

Item 5. If the estate contains real property, check the first box, have property appraised by a probate referee, and attach the Inventory and Appraisal form to the affidavit. Otherwise, check the second box.

Item 6. Describe property with enough detail to be identifiable. If there is not enough space, put "See Attachment 6" and prepare a full-page attachment describing the property in detail.

Affidavit for Collection of Personal Property Under California Probate Code §§ 13100–13106

The undersigned state(s) as follows:

1. Curt Morris died on June 10, 20xx in the County of Santa Barbara, State of California.

2. At least 40 days have elapsed since the death of the decedent, as shown by the attached certified copy of the decedent's death certificate.

3. No proceeding is now being or has been conducted in California for administration of the decedent's estate.

4. The current gross fair market value of the decedent's real and personal property in California, excluding the property described in Section 13050 of the California Probate Code, does not exceed $166,250.

5. ☐ An inventory and appraisal of the real property included in the decedent's estate is attached.
   ☒ There is no real property in the estate.

6. The following property is to be paid, transferred, or delivered to the undersigned under the provisions of California Probate Code Section 13100.
   500 shares, PDQ Corporation, common stock

7. The successor(s) of the decedent, as defined in Probate Code Section 13006, is/are:
   MARY MORRIS and MICHAEL MORRIS.

8. The undersigned ☒ is/are successor(s) of the decedent to the decedent's interest in the described property, or ☐ is/are authorized under California Probate Code Section 13051 to act on behalf of the successor(s) of the decedent with respect to the decedent's interest in the described property.

9. No other person has a superior right to the interest of the decedent in the described property.

10. The undersigned request(s) that the described property be paid, delivered, or transferred to the undersigned.

I/We declare under penalty of perjury under the laws of the State of California that the foregoing is true and correct.

Dated: July 21, 20 xx

Mary Morris — Signature

1521 Elmwood Ave., Los Angeles, CA 90025 — Address

Dated: July 21, 20 xx

Michael Morris — Signature

604 Sunnyside Lane, Los Altos, CA 94022 — Address

[Attach notary certificate]

Item 7. Insert name(s) of the person(s) entitled to the property either under the decedent's will or by intestate succession. If a living trust is the beneficiary, list the name(s) of successor trustee(s) and the name of the trust (for example, "Jon Arnold, successor trustee of the Arnold Family Trust," or "Lois Taylor, successor trustee under trust agreement dated 7-20-2012").

Item 8. Check the first box if the person(s) named in Item 7 will sign the affidavit. Check the second box if a guardian, conservator, or custodian will sign the affidavit on their behalf. Include the address of the recipient, particularly if not collecting the property in person.

Here are instructions for collecting or transferring various types of personal property with an affidavit.

Securities (Stocks and Bonds)

A transfer agent of any security is required to change the registered ownership on the books of the corporation from the decedent to the new owner upon being presented with the affidavit of transfer. (Prob. Code § 13105.) Chapter 9 tells you in detail how to transfer securities. While the small estate affidavit provides authority for requesting the transfer, the transfer agent will require many additional documents to complete the transfer. The documents you should send to the transfer agent will include the following (you will find most in the appendixes):

- affidavit (of transfer), signed by the persons entitled to receive the stock, with signatures notarized
- stock or bond power, signed by the persons entitled to receive the securities, with signatures guaranteed by a bank or stock brokerage firm (see Chapter 9)
- Affidavit of Domicile, signed by the persons entitled to the securities, with signatures notarized (see Chapter 9)
- certified copy of the decedent's death certificate (see Chapter 2)
- original stock or bond certificates (see Chapter 9), and
- transmittal letter signed by the persons entitled to the securities.

As with any transfer of securities, to avoid complications, contact the transfer agent to obtain that institution's forms and confirm requirements for verifying your signature. (See Chapter 9.) Creating your own documents may not save you time or effort if the agent requires something different.

Even though you send this information, some companies, especially those out of state, may ask for certified letters testamentary, which are only provided in formal probate proceedings. Make it clear in your cover letter that no probate is being filed, and therefore no letters will be obtained. It may also be helpful to send a copy of California Probate Code Section 13105 (see Appendix A), which authorizes recovery of attorneys' fees from anyone who refuses to honor the affidavit and turn over assets.

Chapter 9 tells you where and how to send these documents.

Bank Accounts and Safe-Deposit Boxes

California banks are familiar with the procedures for transferring bank accounts and safe-deposit boxes under small estate procedures, and many of the larger institutions have their own form of affidavit. Call to find out if they do. If so, save yourself the time and use theirs. They prefer using forms they are familiar with. In any event, the following items will be required:

- affidavit (or declaration)
- certified copy of the decedent's death certificate
- documentation evidencing the ownership of accounts, and
- safe-deposit box key, if applicable.

Money Market Funds

Mutual funds and money market funds are usually transferred by the brokerage firm or fund management instead of a transfer agent, and, as a rule, the share certificates are held by the fund's custodian instead of by the owner of the shares. Consequently, transferring these types of assets is easier than with ordinary common stocks and bonds. The best procedure is to contact the fund management directly and ask what it requires to sell, redeem, or change the record ownership of the shares. In almost all cases, a certified copy of the death certificate will be required, along with the affidavit or declaration.

Motor Vehicles, Small Boats, Mobile Homes, Etc.

Title to automobiles, trailers, and other vehicles registered under the Vehicle Code may be transferred after the 40-day waiting period by means of special forms available from the Department of Motor Vehicles verifying that the deceased owner left no other property subject to probate. If more than one person has a right to the vehicle, they can agree that one person will take title and the others be reimbursed for the value of their interest. Any money owed on the vehicle is the responsibility of the new owner. To have title changed, the person entitled to the property should present the following items to the DMV:

- certificate of ownership and registration card, if available
- Affidavit for Transfer Without Probate California Vehicles or Vessels Only, DMV Form REG 5, and
- Statement of Facts, DMV Form REG 256.

The DMV explains how to transfer a vehicle without probate on its website. Go to www.dmv.ca.gov and enter "deceased" into the search field.

A similar procedure is used for manufactured homes, mobile homes, floating homes, and commercial coaches or truck campers registered under the Health and Safety Code. The transfers are handled by the Department of Housing and Community Development, which has its own form for this purpose titled, "Certificate For Transfer Without Probate," Form HCD RT 475.2. There is a 40-day waiting period before the transfer can be made. For forms and information, contact the Registration and Titling Program of California's Department of Housing and Community Development at 800-952-8356, ContactRT@hcd.ca.gov, or https://hcd.ca.gov.

Miscellaneous Personal Property

The small estate affidavit can be used to request transfer of other miscellaneous property, such as property held in storage under the decedent's name, promissory notes, or checks or money due the decedent for salary or retirement. All that is required is the affidavit describing the property and a certified copy of the decedent's death certificate. The documents should be presented to the person(s) holding the property, who should then release the property to the person(s) entitled to it.

For checks payable to the decedent received after the date of death, send the affidavit to the company or person who issued the check and request that it issue a new check made payable to the person(s) entitled to it.

Deed of Trust Notes

If the decedent was owed money, usually reflected by a promissory note, and that obligation is secured by a lien on real property (called a trust deed or deed of trust) the affidavit must be notarized and recorded in the office of the county recorder where the real property is located. (Prob. Code § 13106.5.) Chapter 8 explains how to record documents. The description in the affidavit should include the recording reference of the deed of trust or other document creating the lien, or the legal description of the real property securing the debt, or both. After it has been recorded, a copy of the affidavit should be sent to the person or entity making payments on the obligation, with the request that future payments be sent to the new owner.

Real Property Not Exceeding $55,425 in Value

If the estate contains real property not exceeding $55,425 in value (such as an unimproved lot or a portion of more valuable property), the person(s) entitled to the property may obtain title to the property by filing an Affidavit re Real Property of Small Value (DE-305) with the superior court and then recording a certified copy with the county recorder. (Prob. Code §§ 13200–13210.) The dollar amount limit for this procedure will be $55,425 for decedents who die before April 1, 2022. For deaths after that date, an adjusted amount will apply to account for inflation. Some special requirements apply to this procedure:

- The affidavit may not be filed until six months after the decedent's death.
- No probate proceedings may be pending or have been conducted in California for the estate, unless the personal representative has consented.

- A complete legal description of the real property must be included in the affidavit.
- The signature of the person or persons signing the affidavit must be notarized.
- Funeral expenses, last illness expenses, and all unsecured debts of the decedent must have been paid before the affidavit is filed.
- A certified copy of the decedent's death certificate, and a copy of the will, if any, must be attached to the affidavit.
- An appraisal by a probate referee must be attached to the affidavit showing that the gross value of all real property the decedent owned in California (excluding real property held in joint tenancy or in a living trust, property that passes by a transfer on death deed, or property that passes outright to a surviving spouse or domestic partner) does not exceed $55,425. (See "Personal Property," above, for instructions on obtaining the Inventory and Appraisal.)

When the affidavit and all attachments are complete, the original and one copy should be filed (in person or by mail) with the superior court of the county in which the decedent resided at the time of death, along with a filing fee (currently $30). If the decedent was not a California resident, the affidavit should be filed in the county in which the decedent owned real property. (See Chapter 13 on how to file court documents.) The court clerk will file the original affidavit and attachments and issue a certified copy without the attachments. To clear record title to the property in the name of the new owner, the certified copy should be recorded in the office of the county recorder of the county where the real property is located. (See Chapter 8 for instructions on how to record documents.) The affidavit (DE-305) is included in Appendix B and is available at www.courts.ca.gov/forms.htm. A sample is shown below with instructions on how to fill it in. The sample uses the facts from Example 2, above, where Millie dies leaving her property to her 3 children, including an unimproved lot.

Instructions for Preparing Affidavit re Real Property of Small Value (DE-305)

Heading

First box. Insert the name, address, and telephone number (including area code) of the person who is entitled to the property and who will sign the affidavit. If there are more than one, list the one to whom the recorded affidavit will be mailed.

Second box. Insert the name of the county and address of the superior court where the affidavit will be filed.

Third box. Insert the name of the decedent exactly as it appears on the real property deed.

The case number will be filled in by the court.

Items 1–4. Fill in the requested information.

Item 5a. Copy the legal description of the real property, taken exactly from the deed, on 8½" × 11" paper. Be sure to include the assessor's parcel number. Proofread the description carefully to make sure it is accurate. Label the page "Attachment 5a.—Legal Description" and attach it to the affidavit.

Item 5b. Indicate what percentage interest of the property the decedent owned and whether it was owned as community property or separate property. For example, you might put "an undivided one-third interest as decedent's separate property" or "an undivided one-half community property interest."

Items 6a and 6b. If the decedent left a will, check Box 6a and attach a copy of the will to the affidavit. All beneficiaries entitled to an interest in the property under the will must sign the affidavit. If there is no will, check Box 6b, and have each heir entitled to receive a portion of the property under intestate succession laws (Chapter 3) sign the affidavit.

Item 7. If the decedent had a guardian or conservator at the time of death, fill in the requested information and mail or personally deliver a copy of the affidavit to the guardian or conservator. Otherwise, check "none."

Affidavit re Real Property of Small Value (page 1)

DE-305

ATTORNEY OR PARTY WITHOUT ATTORNEY *(name, address, and State Bar number)*:
After recording return to:
Marvin Murdock
301 Green Street
Pasadena, CA 91000

TEL NO.: 560-918-0000 FAX NO.:
EMAIL ADDRESS: mmurdock1962@gmail.com
ATTORNEY FOR *(name)*: Self-represented

SUPERIOR COURT OF CALIFORNIA, COUNTY OF Los Angeles
STREET ADDRESS: 111 No. Hill Street
MAILING ADDRESS: 111 No. Hill Street
CITY AND ZIP CODE: Los Angeles, CA 90012
BRANCH NAME: Central District

FOR RECORDER'S USE ONLY

MATTER OF *(name)*:
MILLIE MURDOCK,
DECEDENT

CASE NUMBER:

AFFIDAVIT RE REAL PROPERTY OF SMALL VALUE
($55,425 or Less)

FOR COURT USE ONLY

1. Decedent *(name)*: Millie Murdock
   died on *(date)*: January 2, 20XX
2. Decedent died at *(city, state)*: Pasadena, California
3. At least **six months** have elapsed since the date of death of decedent as shown in the certified copy of decedent's death certificate attached to this affidavit. *(Attach a certified copy of decedent's death certificate.)*
4. a. [X] Decedent was domiciled in this county at the time of death.
   b. [ ] Decedent was **not** domiciled in California at the time of death. Decedent died owning real property in this county.
5. a. The **legal description** and the Assessor's Parcel Number (APN) of decedent's real property claimed by the declarant(s) are provided on an attached page labeled Attachment 5a, "Legal Description." *(Copy legal description **exactly** from deed or other legal instrument.)*
   b. Decedent's interest in this real property is as follows *(specify)*:

   100% interest

6. Each declarant is a successor of decedent (as defined in Probate Code section 13006) and a successor to decedent's interest in the real property described in item 5a, or signs this declaration on behalf of an entity that is a successor of decedent and to decedent's interest in the real property, and no other person or entity has a superior right, because each declarant or entity is:
   a. [X] *(will)* a beneficiary that succeeded to the property under decedent's will. *(Attach a copy of the will.)*
   b. [ ] *(no will)* a person who succeeded to the property under Probate Code sections 6401 and 6402.
7. Names and addresses of each guardian or conservator of decedent's estate at date of death: [X] none [ ] are as follows:*

   Names Addresses

   *(*You must mail [or serve, per Prob. Code, § 1216] a copy of this affidavit and all attachments to each guardian or conservator listed above. You may use Judicial Council form POS-030 for a proof of mailing or form POS-020 for a proof of personal service.)*
8. The **gross value** of decedent's interest in all real property located in California as shown by the attached *Inventory and Appraisal*—excluding the real property described in Probate Code section 13050 (property held in joint tenancy or as a life estate or other interest terminable upon decedent's death, property passing to decedent's spouse, property in a trust revocable by the decedent, etc.)—did not exceed $55,425 as of the date of decedent's death.

Page 1 of 2

Form Adopted for Mandatory Use
Judicial Council of California
DE-305 [Rev. January 1, 2020]

AFFIDAVIT RE REAL PROPERTY OF SMALL VALUE
($55,425 or Less)

Probate Code, § 13200
www.courts.ca.gov

Affidavit re Real Property of Small Value (page 2)

DE-305

MATTER OF *(Name):* MILLIE MURDOCK, DECEDENT	CASE NUMBER:

9. An *Inventory and Appraisal* of all of decedent's interests in **real property** in California is attached. The appraisal was made by a probate referee appointed for the county in which the property is located. *(You must prepare the Inventory on Judicial Council forms DE-160 and DE-161. You may select any probate referee appointed for the county for the appraisal. The California State Controller's Office has a list of all probate referees, shown by county on its website, and each court has a list of probate referees appointed for its county. Check with the probate referee you select or consult an attorney for help in preparing the Inventory.)*

10. No proceeding is now being or has been conducted in California for administration of decedent's estate.

11. Funeral expenses, expenses of last illness, and all known unsecured debts of the decedent have been paid. *(NOTE: You may be personally liable for decedent's unsecured debts up to the fair market value of the real property and any income you receive from it.)*

I declare under penalty of perjury under the laws of the State of California that the foregoing is true and correct.

Date: July 5, 20XX

Marvin Murdock — (TYPE OR PRINT NAME)* ▶ *Marvin Murdock* (SIGNATURE OF DECLARANT)

Date: July 5, 20XX

Milton Murdock — (TYPE OR PRINT NAME)* ▶ *Milton Murdock* (SIGNATURE OF DECLARANT)

☐ SIGNATURE OF ADDITIONAL DECLARANTS ATTACHED

*** A declarant claiming on behalf of a trust or other entity should also state the name of the entity that is a beneficiary under the decedent's will, and declarant's capacity to sign on behalf of the entity (e.g., trustee, Chief Executive Officer, etc.).**

NOTARY ACKNOWLEDGMENT *(NOTE: No notary acknowledgment may be affixed as a rider (small strip) to this page. If additional notary acknowledgments are required, they must be attached as 8-1/2-by-11-inch pages.)*

A notary public or other officer completing this certificate verifies only the identity of the individual who signed the document to which this certificate is attached, and not the truthfulness, accuracy, or validity of that document.

STATE OF CALIFORNIA, COUNTY OF *(specify):*

On *(date):* , before me *(name and title):*

personally appeared *(name(s)):*

who proved to me on the basis of satisfactory evidence to be the person(s) whose name(s) is/are subscribed to the within instrument and acknowledged to me that he/she/they executed the instrument in his/her/their authorized capacity(ies), and that by his/her/their signature(s) on the instrument the person(s), or the entity upon behalf of which the person(s) acted, executed the instrument.

I certify under PENALTY OF PERJURY under the laws of the State of California that the foregoing paragraph is true and correct.

WITNESS my hand and official seal.

(SIGNATURE OF NOTARY PUBLIC)

(NOTARY SEAL)

(SEAL)

CLERK'S CERTIFICATE

I certify that the foregoing, including any attached notary acknowledgments and any attached legal description of the property (but excluding other attachments), is a true and correct copy of the original affidavit on file in my office. *(Certified copies of this affidavit do not include the (1) death certificate, (2) will, or (3) inventory and appraisal. See Probate Code section 13202.)*

Date: Clerk, by ____________________, Deputy

DE-305 [Rev. January 1, 2020]

AFFIDAVIT RE REAL PROPERTY OF SMALL VALUE
($55,425 or Less)

Page 2 of 2

When the affidavit has been completed and signed by all beneficiaries or heirs, and the signatures notarized, make sure the following documents are attached before you file it with the probate court clerk:

- certified copy of the decedent's death certificate
- legal description of the property
- copy of the decedent's will, if any
- Inventory and Appraisal of all California real property owned by decedent, completed by the probate referee, and
- signature of additional declarant (if any), with notary acknowledgments for each declarant's signature.

Real and Personal Property Not Exceeding $166,250 in Value

If the decedent owned property in California, real and personal, not exceeding $166,250 in value, the heirs or beneficiaries of the decedent may file a petition with the superior court asking for an order determining their right to take the property without probate administration. The petition is called a Petition to Determine Succession to Real Property (DE-310) (Prob. Code §§ 13151–13152.) It is primarily for real property, but it may include a request that the court make an order determining that the petitioner has succeeded to personal property described in the petition as well. (If there is *only* personal property in the estate, this form may not be used to obtain a court order. Instead, the person(s) entitled to the property should use the Affidavit for Collection of Personal Property, discussed above.) The following requirements must be met:

- Forty days have elapsed since the decedent's death.
- No proceeding is being or has been conducted in California for administration of the decedent's estate, unless the personal representative has consented.
- The gross value of the real and personal property in the estate does not exceed $166,250 (again, not counting property excluded by Probate Code § 13050, discussed above). You must attach an Inventory and Appraisal by a probate referee of the real and personal property showing the gross value. Do not list on the Inventory any property that is excluded in determining the value of the probate estate.

Notice that this abbreviated court procedure does not require the six-month waiting period that is required for the affidavit procedure described above. Also, this abbreviated court procedure can be used to transfer real property and personal property valued under $166,250, while the affidavit procedure can only be used for real property worth $55,425 or less. Another difference between the procedures is that the court procedure can be used even if the unsecured creditors have not been paid, though the recipient may be personally liable for unsecured debts.

File the petition in the superior court of the county where the decedent resided, or if the decedent was not a California resident, in the county where the decedent owned property. As with any court proceeding, consult the local court rules and the court clerk for forms, procedures, and costs specific to your county. For example, larger counties may require a Certificate of Assignment Form, and courts vary in procedures for when to file required documents.

The following steps show you how to obtain the court order:

1. Prepare and file with the court:
   - Petition to Determine Succession to Real Property, with attachments, including completed Inventory and Appraisal (see Chapter 14, Step 14, for instructions)
   - Notice of Hearing (DE-120) (see Chapter 15, Step 3 for general instructions, include in Item 1 the title "Petition to Determine Succession to Real Property," and include notice to all people mentioned in the petition)
   - Certificate of Assignment, if required (see Chapter 14, Step 2)
   - filing fee (usually $435, confirm amount with court clerk), and
   - original will, if required (check local practice).
2. Before the hearing date on the petition:
   - mail Notice of Hearing to all persons named in the petition
   - file original Notice of Hearing, showing date of mailing

- prepare Order Determining Succession to Real Property (DE-315) (shown below)
- submit order to court clerk, if required, and
- check probate calendar notes at court (see Chapter 13).

3. After hearing:
   - submit to the court clerk Order Determining Succession to Real Property (if not provided prior to hearing), and request certified copy
   - record certified copy of order in county where real property is located (see Chapter 8)
   - submit Preliminary Change of Ownership Report to county recorder when recording order (see Chapter 8), and
   - submit forms for exemption to the SB2 fee or reassessment exclusion to county assessor/recorder, if appropriate (see Chapter 8).

See samples of the petition and order, below. The facts for this sample petition are in Example 3, above. The decedent leaves his separate property interest in a mountain cabin worth $39,500 to his sister, Pam, and other assets passing to his wife. For other instructions (for example, Notice of Hearing) see Chapter 15.

Sample Attachment to Petition to Determine Succession to Real Property

Estate of Harry Reese, deceased

PETITION TO DETERMINE SUCCESSION TO REAL PROPERTY

Attachment 11—Legal Description of Real Property:

Decedent's 100% separate property interest, acquired prior to marriage and maintained as separate property, which constitutes a one-half undivided interest, in real property situated in the County of San Bernardino, State of California, improved with a single dwelling, commonly known as 85 Pine Street, Crestline, and legally described as:

Lot 23, block 289, in Tract XYZ, per Map recorded in Book 70, Pages 91 and 92 of maps, in the office of the County Recorder of said county.

Assessor's Parcel No. 234-56-7700

Instructions for Petition to Determine Succession to Real Property (DE-310)

Caption. In the first box, enter the petitioner's name and contact information. After "Attorney for," enter "Self-represented." In the second box, fill in the court's address (including county) and branch name, if any. In the "Estate of" box, type the decedent's name, including all variations used. Check the box for "And Personal Property" only if the petition lists on the Inventory and Appraisal (DE-160) personal property in addition to real property. Leave the case number and hearing date boxes blank; the court clerk will provide this information when you file the petition.

Item 1. The petitioner (or the petitioner's guardian or conservator) is the person who is entitled to succeed to the real property under the will or by intestate succession. If there is more than one such person, list all of them as petitioners. If there isn't enough room, type "See Attachment 1" and list them on a separate 8½" × 11" paper labeled Attachment 1 and attach it to the petition.

Items 2–4. Fill in the requested information.

Item 5. If the decedent left a will, check "testate" and attach a copy of the will, labeled Attachment 5. Otherwise, check "intestate." Some counties also want the original will filed with the petition. Check local rules or ask the court clerk.

The original will may have already been submitted to the court clerk for safekeeping. If so, attach a copy of the file-stamped copy. If the original will has not yet been filed, check with the local court procedures to determine whether it should be filed before or with the petition.

Item 6. Check the first box, presuming that no proceeding is being conducted to administer the decedent's estate. If this is not the case, obtain legal advice.

Item 7. Indicate whether or not probate proceedings have begun for the decedent in another state. If the estate has proceedings in another jurisdiction, you will likely need to provide additional documentation, such as a certified copy of the letters testamentary or court order from the other jurisdiction's proceeding.

Petition to Determine Succession to Real Property (page 1)

DE-310

ATTORNEY OR PARTY WITHOUT ATTORNEY: STATE BAR NO.: NAME: Pam Reese FIRM NAME: STREET ADDRESS: 700 Harbor Way CITY: Long Beach STATE: CA ZIP CODE: 91176 TELEPHONE NO.: 213-377-7794 FAX NO.: EMAIL ADDRESS: preese1948@gmail.com ATTORNEY FOR (name): Self-represented	*FOR COURT USE ONLY*	
SUPERIOR COURT OF CALIFORNIA, COUNTY OF Los Angeles STREET ADDRESS: 111 No. Hill St MAILING ADDRESS: 111 No. Hill St CITY AND ZIP CODE: Los Angeles, CA 09912 BRANCH NAME: CENTRAL DISTRICT		
MATTER OF *(name)*: HARRY REESE, aka HARRY C. REESE DECEDENT	CASE NUMBER:	
PETITION TO DETERMINE SUCCESSION TO REAL PROPERTY ☐ **and Personal Property (Estates of $166,250 or Less)**	HEARING DATE AND TIME:	DEPT.:

1. Petitioner *(name of each person claiming an interest):*
   Pam Reese

   requests a determination that the real property ☐ and personal property described in item 11 is property passing to petitioner and that no administration of decedent's estate is necessary.
2. Decedent (*name*): HARRY REESE, aka HARRY C. REESE
   a. Date of death: April 25, 20XX
   b. Place of death *(city and state or, if outside the United States, city and country):* Long Beach, CA
3. At least 40 days have elapsed since the date of decedent's death.
4. a. ☒ Decedent was a resident of this county at the time of death.
   b. ☐ Decedent was **not** a resident of California at the time of death. Decedent died owning property in this county.
5. Decedent died ☐ intestate ☒ testate and a copy of the will and any codicil is affixed as Attachment 5 or 12a.
6. a. ☒ No proceeding for the administration of decedent's estate is being conducted or has been conducted in California.
   b. ☐ Decedent's personal representative's consent to use the procedure provided by Probate Code section 13150 et seq. is attached as Attachment 6b.
7. Proceedings for the administration of decedent's estate in another jurisdiction: a. ☒ Have **not** been commenced.
   b. ☐ Have been commenced ☐ and completed. *(Specify state, county, court, and case number):*
8. The **gross value** of decedent's interest in real and personal property located in California as shown by the *Inventory and Appraisal* attached to this petition—excluding the property described in Probate Code section 13050 (property held in joint tenancy or as a life estate or other interest terminable upon decedent's death, property passing to decedent's spouse, property in a trust revocable by decedent, etc.)—did not exceed $166,250 as of the date of decedent's death. *(Prepare and attach an* Inventory and Appraisal *as Attachment 8 (use Judicial Council forms DE-160 and DE-161 for this purpose). A probate referee appointed for the county named above must appraise all real property and all personal property other than cash or its equivalent. See Prob. Code, §§ 8901, 8902.)*
9. a. Decedent is survived by *(check items (1) or (2), and (3) or (4), and (5) or (6), and (7) or (8))*
   (1) ☒ spouse
   (2) ☐ no spouse as follows: (a) ☐ divorced or never married (b) ☐ spouse deceased
   (3) ☐ registered domestic partner
   (4) ☒ no registered domestic partner *(See Fam. Code, § 297.5(c); Prob. Code, §§ 37(b), 6401(c), and 6402.)*
   (5) ☐ child as follows: (a) ☐ natural or adopted (b) ☐ natural adopted by a third party
   (6) ☒ no child
   (7) ☐ issue of a predeceased child
   (8) ☒ no issue of a predeceased child

   b. Decedent ☐ is ☒ is not survived by a stepchild or foster child or children who would have been adopted by decedent but for a legal barrier. *(See Prob. Code, § 6454.)*

Form Adopted for Mandatory Use
Judicial Council of California
DE-310 [Rev. January 1, 2020]

PETITION TO DETERMINE SUCCESSION TO REAL PROPERTY
(Estates of $166,250 or Less)

Probate Code, § 13152
www.courts.ca.gov

Petition to Determine Succession to Real Property (page 2)

DE-310

MATTER OF (*name*): HARRY REESE, aka HARRY C. REESE DECEDENT	CASE NUMBER:

10. [x] Decedent is survived by *(complete if decedent was survived by (1) a spouse or registered domestic partner described in Prob. Code, § 37 but no issue (only a or b apply); or (2) no spouse or registered domestic partner described in Prob. Code, § 37, or issue. Check the* ***first*** *box that applies.):*
   a. [ ] A parent or parents who are listed in item 14.
   b. [x] A brother, sister, or issue of a deceased brother or sister, all of whom are listed in item 14.
   c. [ ] Other heirs under Probate Code section 6400 et seq., all of whom are listed in item 14.
   d. [ ] No known next of kin.
11. Attachment 11 contains (1) the **legal description** of decedent's real property and its Assessor's Parcel Number (APN) and [ ] a description of personal property in California passing to petitioner; (2) decedent's interest in the property; and, (3) if a petitioner's claim to the property is based on succession under Probate Code sections 6401 and 6402, facts that show the character of the property as community, separate, or quasi-community property.
12. Each petitioner is a successor of decedent (as defined in Probate Code section 13006) and a successor to decedent's interest in the real property [ ] and personal property described in item 11 because each petitioner is:
   a. [x] **(will)** A beneficiary who succeeded to the property under decedent's will.[1]
   b. [ ] **(no will)** A person who succeeded to the property under Probate Code sections 6401 and 6402.
13. The specific property interest claimed by each petitioner in the real property [ ] and personal property [ ] is stated in Attachment 13 [x] is as follows *(specify)*:
   100% interest
14. The names, relationships to decedent, ages, and residence or mailing addresses so far as known to or reasonably ascertainable by petitioner of (1) all persons named or checked in items 1, 9, and 10; (2) all other heirs of decedent; and (3) all devisees of decedent (persons designated in the will to receive any property) are listed in Attachment 14.
15. The names and addresses of all persons named as executors in decedent's will
   [x] are listed below [ ] are listed in Attachment 15 [ ] No executor is named. [ ] There is no will.

   Pam Reese, 700 Harbor Way, Long Beach, CA 91176
16. [ ] Petitioner is the trustee of a trust that is a devisee under decedent's will. The names and addresses of all persons interested in the trust, as determined in cases of future interests under paragraphs (1), (2), or (3) of subdivision (a) of Probate Code section 15804, are listed in Attachment 16.
17. [ ] Decedent's estate was under a [ ] guardianship [ ] conservatorship at decedent's death. The names and addresses of all persons serving as guardian or conservator [ ] are listed below [ ] are listed in Attachment 17.
18. Number of pages attached: 7

Date: ____________

______________________________ (TYPE OR PRINT NAME OF ATTORNEY)

▶ ______________________________ (SIGNATURE OF ATTORNEY)*

* (Signature of all petitioners also required (Prob. Code, § 1020).)

I declare under penalty of perjury under the laws of the State of California that the foregoing is true and correct.

Date: June 20, 20XX

Pam Reese (TYPE OR PRINT NAME OF PETITIONER)

▶ *Pam Reese* (SIGNATURE OF PETITIONER)[2]

______________________________ (TYPE OR PRINT NAME OF PETITIONER)

▶ ______________________________ (SIGNATURE OF PETITIONER)[2]

[ ] SIGNATURE(S) OF ADDITIONAL PETITIONERS ATTACHED

1 See Probate Code section 13152(c) for the requirement that a copy of the will be attached in certain instances. If required, include as Attachment 5 or 12a.

2 Each person named in item 1 must sign.

DE-310 [Rev. January 1, 2020] Page 2 of 2

PETITION TO DETERMINE SUCCESSION TO REAL PROPERTY
(Estates of $166,250 or Less)

Item 8. Before filing the petition, you must obtain an Inventory and Appraisal of all property required to be considered in determining whether the estate is within the $166,250 threshold. The procedure for obtaining the Inventory and Appraisal is the same as that used in a formal probate proceeding (see Chapter 14, Step 14), but in this case you may choose the state-appointed referee yourself. To find a referee, call the court for names of the referees in your county, or go to www.sco.ca.gov/eo_probate_contact.html or www.probatereferees.net. Attach the completed Inventory and Appraisal form to the petition.

Items 9 and 10. These items request information necessary to determine the decedent's heirs (people who would inherit the estate in the absence of a will). Even if the decedent left a will, you must still list the heirs. Information in Chapter 3 explains the meaning of some of the terms on the form. Read the instructions for these items carefully, because the number of boxes required to be checked can be confusing. You will check at least 4 boxes in Item 9a. Skip Item 10 if the decedent was survived by at least one child or other issue.

You can refer to the instructions for Items 5 and 6 of Step 1, Chapter 14 for additional guidance for similar sections of the Petition for Probate (DE-111).

Item 11. Put the legal description and Assessor's Parcel Number of the property (from the deed to the property) on a plain 8½" × 11" paper and label it as Attachment 11. You may also check the box and include personal property here, if it passes to the petitioner. Indicate on the attachment what interest the decedent owned. If the property is passing according to intestate succession (that is, no will) and the decedent was married, provide facts to show the character of the property as community, separate, or quasi-community property.

Item 12. Check the first box if personal property is listed in Attachment 11. If the decedent left a will, check Box 12a and attach a copy of the will. Each beneficiary entitled to receive an interest in the real property under the will must sign the petition. If there is no will, check Box 12b and have each heir of the decedent who is entitled to a portion of the property sign the petition.

Item 13. Check the first box if the petition includes personal property. List the interest in the property claimed by each petitioner. For example, if there is only one petitioner, put "100% interest." If three people are inheriting real property equally, put "Adam Doe, Barbara Doe, and Carlos Doe, each as to an undivided one-third interest." Check the appropriate box and use an attachment if needed.

Item 14. In a separate attachment, list all persons potentially interested in the estate, to give them notice of the petition. If the decedent left a will, list the name, relationship, age, and residence or mailing address of everyone (whether living or deceased) mentioned in the will as a beneficiary. Also list this information for all persons listed in Items 9 and 10 (the decedent's heirs). Before completing this item, read the instructions for Attachment 8 to the Petition for Probate (Chapter 14, Step 1). Attach this to the petition as Attachment 14.

Item 15. Check the appropriate box and list the name(s) and addresses of all executors named in the will, if any, including alternate executors. Check the box next to "No executor is named" if a will exists, but the will does not name an executor.

Item 16. If the petitioner is also the trustee of a trust that is entitled to receive property under the will, check this box and list in an attachment the names and addresses of all living persons who are potential beneficiaries of the trust. Attach this to the petition as Attachment 16.

Item 17. Skip this item if the decedent did not have a formal guardianship or conservatorship at the time of death. Otherwise, provide appropriate information.

Item 18. After you have assembled all of the attachments—including a copy of the will and any codicils, the completed Inventory and Appraisal, (DE-160), the legal description of real property, the list of interested persons, and any additional signature pages—enter the number of pages attached.

When the petition is filed with the appropriate filing fee, the clerk will give a hearing date, which is usually four to five weeks later. You will not be required to appear at the hearing unless there is a problem. At least 15 days before the hearing, written notice of the hearing must be mailed or personally

Order Determining Succession to Real Property

DE-315

ATTORNEY OR PARTY WITHOUT ATTORNEY *(name, address, and State Bar number):*
After recording, return to:

Pam Reese
700 Harbor Way
Long Beach, CA 91176

TEL NO.: 213-377-7794 FAX NO.:
EMAIL ADDRESS:
ATTORNEY FOR *(name):* Self-represented

SUPERIOR COURT OF CALIFORNIA, COUNTY OF Los Angeles
STREET ADDRESS: 111 No. Hill Street
MAILING ADDRESS: 111 No. Hill Street
CITY AND ZIP CODE: Los Angeles, CA 90012
BRANCH NAME: CENTRAL DISTRICT

FOR RECORDER'S USE ONLY

MATTER OF *(name):*
HARRY REESE, aka HARRY C. REESE
DECEDENT

CASE NUMBER:

ORDER DETERMINING SUCCESSION TO REAL PROPERTY
☐ **And Personal Property**
(Estates of $166,250 or Less)

FOR COURT USE ONLY

1. Date of hearing: 7/15/20XX Time: 9:00 a.m.
   Dept./Room: 29
   Judicial Officer *(name):*

THE COURT FINDS

2. All notices required by law have been given.
3. Decedent died on *(date):* 4/25/20XX
   a. ☒ a resident of the California county named above.
   b. ☐ a nonresident of California and owned property in the county named above.
   c. ☐ intestate. ☒ testate.
4. At least 40 days have elapsed since the date of decedent's death.
5. a. ☒ No proceeding for the administration of decedent's estate is being conducted or has been conducted in California.
   b. ☐ Decedent's personal representative has filed a consent to use the procedure provided in Probate Code section 13150 et seq.
6. The gross value of decedent's real and personal property in California, excluding property described in Probate Code section 13050, did not exceed $166,250 as of the date of decedent's death.
7. Each petitioner is a successor of decedent (as defined in Probate Code section 13006) and a successor to decedent's interest in the real ☐ and personal property described in item 9a because each petitioner is:
   a. ☒ **(will)** a beneficiary who succeeded to the property under decedent's will.
   b. ☐ **(no will)** a person who succeeded to the property under Probate Code sections 6401 and 6402.

THE COURT FURTHER FINDS AND ORDERS

8. No administration of decedent's estate is necessary in California.
9. a. The real ☐ and personal property ☐ described in Attachment 9a ☒ described as follows is property of decedent passing to each petitioner *(give* ***legal description*** *of real property).*
   An undivided one-half interest in real property in the County of San Bernardino, State of California, commonly known as 85 Pine Street, Crestline, legally described as: Lot 23, Block 789, in Tract XYZ, per Map recorded in Book 70, Pages 91 and 92 of Maps, in the office of the County Recorder of said county. APN 234-56-7890
   b. Each petitioner's **name** and specific property interest ☐ is stated in Attachment 9b. ☒ is as follows *(specify):*

   Pam Reese - 100%

10. ☐ Other orders are stated in Attachment 10.
11. Number of pages attached: 0

Date:

JUDICIAL OFFICER

☐ SIGNATURE FOLLOWS LAST ATTACHMENT

Page 1 of 1

Form Adopted for Mandatory Use
Judicial Council of California
DE-315 [Rev. January 1, 2020]

ORDER DETERMINING SUCCESSION TO REAL PROPERTY
(Estates of $166,250 or Less)

Probate Code, § 13154
www.courts.ca.gov

given to all persons listed in Items 14, 15, 16, and 17 of the petition (heirs, devisees or trustees named in the will, trust beneficiaries, and the decedent's guardian or conservator). The procedures for giving the notice of the hearing are the same as for the Spousal or Domestic Partner Property Petition (DE-221) described in Chapter 15.

Before the hearing, you should also prepare the Order Determining Succession to Real Property (DE-315) for the judge to sign to approve the petition. A sample is shown below. Some counties require the order to be submitted to the court several days *before* the hearing, so check your local court rules.

If the court approves the petition, the judge will sign the order at the hearing or shortly thereafter. When the order is signed, the person(s) entitled to the property become(s) personally liable for the unsecured debts of the decedent to the extent of the fair market value of the real property at the date of death, less liens and encumbrances. The new owner should record a certified copy of the order with the county recorder in the county where the real property is located. Chapter 8 gives instructions on how to record the order.

Instructions for Order Determining Succession to Real Property (DE-315)

Caption. Fill in the boxes at the top of the form just as you filled them in on the petition, except that you can now fill in the case number.

Item 1. Fill in date, time, and place of the hearing.

Item 3. Fill in the date of death and check the correct boxes, matching information in Items 4 and 5 of the petition.

Item 5. Check the correct boxes to match Item 6 of the petition.

Item 7. Check the correct boxes to match Item 12 of the petition.

Item 9a. Only check the first box if the petition includes personal property, in addition to real property. Fill in the legal description of real property and describe personal property, if any, exactly as listed in the petition. If there isn't enough room, check the box and put the description on a piece of paper labeled Attachment 9a.

Item 9b. Insert same information as in Item 13 of petition.

Item 10. Leave this box blank.

Item 11. Enter the number of pages attached, if any.

Box beneath judge's signature line. If you have attachments, check this box and, at the end of the last attachment page, type a place for the date and a signature line for the judge.

CHAPTER

12

How to Transfer Trust Property

People seeking to avoid the delay and expense inherent in the probate process often adopt estate planning devices such as gifts, joint tenancy transfers, and, less often, life estates to transfer their assets without a will.

Creating a living (or inter vivos) trust is another common estate planning technique used in California to avoid probate. In the trust document, the person who creates the trust, called the "settlor, "grantor," or "trustor," specifies who will manage trust assets (the "trustee") and who will receive the property (the"beneficiaries").

For example, Janet might set up a living trust for her own benefit with herself as the initial trustee. Janet names her daughter Judy as the successor trustee, and names her grandchildren as the ultimate beneficiaries of the trust. Janet would then formally transfer items of property to the trust by putting her name as the trustee of the trust on the relevant deeds, accounts, and title slips. At Janet's death, Judy acts as the successor trustee to follow trust administration procedures and ultimately transfers the remaining assets of the trust to Janet's grandchildren as beneficiaries. No probate is required to transfer trust assets.

RESOURCE

More information about living trusts. You can learn about and make your own living trusts using Nolo's Online Living Trust or *Make Your Own Living Trust*, by Denis Clifford (Nolo).

Settling the estate of a person who had a living trust can be much easier than completing a probate proceeding, which is one of the main reasons that people set up living trusts. However, administering a trust can also be quite complicated, depending on the assets involved, the specific terms of the trust, and other factors unique to the particular trust estate. While the trust administration process does not require court oversight, a successor trustee has obligations established by state law and the trust instrument.

After the death of the settlor of the living trust, the successor trustee steps in and takes charge of the assets. In general, the trustee must give appropriate notifications, pay final bills and taxes, account to beneficiaries, and then distribute the remaining trust property according to the instructions in the trust. After the trust property has been distributed and final tax returns filed, the trust ends. No formal termination document is required.

Some steps should always be taken on the death of any individual. In Chapter 2, we discuss the initial responsibilities of an estate representative. Where a decedent had assets in a living trust, the trustee may fulfill these responsibilities, instead of an executor or administrator doing so.

The discussion of this chapter cannot take the place of specific instructions for administering a trust. Rather, it provides highlights of responsibilities of a trustee and examples of key documents. Particularly if the trustee is not the sole beneficiary, a trustee takes on serious obligations that can result in personal liability for failing to administer the trust properly.

If the decedent had a living trust, the trustee should consult resources specific for trust administration and seek advice from an attorney.

RESOURCE

Learn more about administering a living trust. *The Trustee's Legal Companion*, by Liza Hanks and Carol Elias Zollo (Nolo) gives you a deeper insight into the work of a trustee.

Notifying Heirs and Beneficiaries

When the settlor of a revocable trust dies, the trust becomes "irrevocable," meaning that the terms can no longer be changed. The trustee must notify all of the trust beneficiaries and heirs of the settlor of the existence of the trust and of the right to receive a copy of the terms of the trust. (Prob. Code §§ 16060.5–16061.8.) An "heir" is any person, including the surviving spouse or registered domestic partner, who would be entitled to inherit property if the deceased person had no will. (See Chapter 3.)

The notice must provide certain information about the administration of the trust, such as contact information for the trustee and the place of trust administration. It must also inform the recipients of a time period set by law to contest the trust and use specific words printed in at least 10-point bold type.

Notification by Trustee (Prob. Code § 16061.7)

_____ **Name(s) of settlor(s) [person or persons who originally made the trust]** _____

executed the _____ **Name of trust** _____ Trust

in his/her/their capacity(ies) as Settlor(s) on _____ **Date of trust** _____, hereinafter referred to as the "Trust."

1. The name, mailing address, and telephone number of each Trustee of the Trust is set forth below:

_____

_____

_____

_____

_____

2. The address of the physical location where the principal place of administration of the Trust is located is:

_____ **Insert the address where the usual day-to-day activity of the trust is carried on—ordinarily, the trustee's residence or usual place of business.** _____

_____

_____

_____

_____

3. The terms of the Trust require disclosure of the following information:

_____ **List any additional information that is required to be given to the beneficiaries under the trust instrument and any adjustments to the original trust document or disclaimers, directions, or instructions to the trustee that affect the administration or disposition of the trust.** _____

_____

_____

_____

4. You are entitled, upon reasonable request to the Trustee, to receive from the Trustee a true and complete copy of the terms of the Trust.

5. **YOU MAY NOT BRING AN ACTION TO CONTEST THE TRUST MORE THAN 120 DAYS FROM THE DATE THIS NOTIFICATION BY THE TRUSTEE IS SERVED UPON YOU OR 60 DAYS FROM THE DATE ON WHICH A COPY OF THE TERMS OF THE TRUST IS MAILED OR PERSONALLY DELIVERED TO YOU DURING THAT 120-DAY PERIOD, WHICHEVER IS LATER.**

_____ _____

Date Trustee

Because the date the trustee serves the notice on the heir or beneficiary triggers the start of the time period to contest the trust, the trustee should have proof of the mailing. A sample "Notification by Trustee" form is shown above. A blank version is included in Appendix C.

Even after the initial notification, a trustee has ongoing responsibilities to keep beneficiaries reasonably informed of the trust and its administration. This includes providing accountings and responding to reasonable requests from a beneficiary for information related to the beneficiary's interest.

A trustee who does not make a good faith effort to comply with notice requirements and other responsibilities can be held liable for damages, including attorneys' fees and costs.

Trust Property

Sometimes you may find that the decedent signed a trust document designating certain assets to be held in trust but for some reason failed to actually transfer title into the name of the trust. As a general rule, assets not transferred to the living trust are still subject to probate. Therefore, you should carefully examine all title documents (for example, real property deeds, bank and brokerage account statements, and stock certificates) to see if title was actually transferred to the trust. If the asset was transferred to the trust, the ownership document will show title held something like this: "The I.M. Smart Trust" or "I.M. Smart, Trustee Under Declaration of Trust dated June 1, 2015." Property that doesn't have formal title documents, however, such as miscellaneous items of personal property, can be included in a living trust without being formally transferred to the trust. They need only be listed in the trust document or in an "assignment" that transfers listed property to the trust.

Often it's hard for a person to inventory every little asset owned and place it in a trust. Therefore, a "pour-over will" is sometimes used along with a trust to cover assets that have been inadvertently overlooked or left outside the trust. The pour-over will simply states that such assets are to be transferred into a specified trust at the time of the person's death. A pour-over will is treated the same as other wills, and formal probate is required if the assets covered by the will exceed $166,250. (If the decedent dies after April 1, 2022, that amount will be somewhat higher to adjust for inflation.) If such assets have a gross value under $166,250, the trustee can use the small estate procedures in Chapter 11 to transfer the assets to the trust without formal probate.

SEE AN EXPERT

Get help if you're not sure whether the property is in the trust. If property exists in the decedent's individual name, yet evidence exists that the decedent intended to hold the property in a trust, get help from an attorney. A different type of court proceeding, sometimes referred to as a Heggstad Petition or a Probate Code Section 850 Petition, may be possible to avoid probate. An attorney can help you evaluate your options.

Handling Debts and Expenses

The trustee should carefully examine the decedent's checkbooks, tax returns, and other financial records for evidence of any financial obligations the decedent may have had at death. Before distributing trust property, trustees generally withhold sufficient money to pay any legitimate debts, such as personal loans, income taxes, credit card bills, accountant's fees, doctor bills and last illness expenses (over and above amounts paid by insurance or Medicare), and funeral expenses.

In a formal probate proceeding, creditors generally must file claims within four months or the claim is barred. In the case of a trust, however, since no probate is required, creditors are not cut off at an early date, and each trust distributee is personally liable for any unpaid debts of the decedent to the extent of the value of the distribution received by that distributee. To avoid any such liability, the trustee can take advantage of a creditors' claim procedure for living trusts that operates in substantially the same way as the creditors' claim procedure for probate estates. (Prob. Code §§ 19000–19403.) The procedures are optional and would appear to be useful only in limited circumstances, such as in the case of large disputed claims against the decedent or the estate. If you have such a situation, you should contact an attorney.

How to Transfer Property Held in Trusts

After fulfilling its obligations in managing trust assets, the trustee will transfer assets to the trust beneficiaries according to the terms of the trust. The procedures used to transfer property held in a trust to the beneficiaries of the trust are similar to those used to transfer assets not held in trust.

Particularly because trust administration is not court supervised, the trustee should be sure to get legal advice to administer the trust correctly and to avoid liability. This discussion presumes that the trustee has obtained legal advice about administration of the trust and the terms of the trust allow for a simple distribution of assets.

Real Property

If real property is held in the trust, the trustee will need to prepare some documents to show the transfer of title from the trustee to the trust beneficiaries. Ordinarily, when a trustee of a revocable living trust has died, this will not be known to the title companies or others dealing with trust property. Therefore, a successor trustee should first record an Affidavit—Death of Trustee for each piece of real property held in the name of the trust so public record will show that the original trustee has died. See the sample, below. This document gives the world notice that a successor trustee is now in place. A certified copy of the original trustee's death certificate must be attached to the affidavit. The form is similar to the Affidavit—Death of Joint Tenant discussed in Chapter 10.

FORMS

A blank Affidavit – Death of Trustee is in Appendix C. You can download a fillable version of the form on this book's companion page at www.nolo.com/back-of-book/PAE.html.

To transfer title to real property from the trust to the beneficiaries named in the trust, the successor trustee must also record a deed from the trustee, to the beneficiaries. See a sample of such a deed below. The transfer to the beneficiaries is exempt from the documentary transfer tax, and the statement shown on the sample should appear on the face of the deed. If the new owner resides in the property, prior to recording you can attach a cover sheet claiming the exemption from the $75 SB2 fee. (See "SB2 Building Homes and Jobs Act Fee" in Chapter 8.) Instructions for recording the deed are given in Chapter 8. Before a title company will insure title in the names of the beneficiaries, it may require a certified copy of the death certificate of the settlor and a copy of the trust document.

Securities

For general information on how to transfer securities, see Chapter 9. As with all transfers of securities, check with the transfer agent, bank, or stockbroker for appropriate forms. The transfer agent for securities held in trust will normally require the following documents:

- certified copy of the death certificate
- copy of the trust document (if the transfer agent did not receive one when the securities were transferred into the trust)
- the original certificates for the securities
- a stock power signed by the trustee or successor trustee, with the signature guaranteed by an officer of a bank or brokerage firm
- an Affidavit of Domicile, and
- a letter of instructions for the transfer from the trustee to the beneficiaries. The letter should include the name, address, and Social Security number of each beneficiary receiving the securities.

Affidavit—Death of Trustee

RECORDING REQUESTED BY:
Fred Fiduciary

AND WHEN RECORDED MAIL DOCUMENT
AND TAX STATEMENT TO: Fred Fiduciary
20800 Circle Drive
Anywhere, CA 90000-0000

APN:

Commonly known as:

SPACE ABOVE THIS LINE FOR RECORDER'S USE

AFFIDAVIT—DEATH OF TRUSTEE

The undersigned, being of legal age, being duly sworn, deposes and says:

That I. M. Smart, the decedent mentioned in the attached certified copy of Certificate of Death, is the same person as I. M. Smart, named as Trustee in that certain Declaration of Trust dated 5-1-95, executed by I. M. Smart, as Trustor(s).

At the decedent's death, the decedent was the record owner, as Trustee of the I. M. Smart Trust, of real property commonly known as 12345 Circle Terrace, San Bernardino, California, which property was transferred to said trust and described in a deed recorded on May 10, 1995, as Instrument No. 24023, of Official Records of San Bernardino County, State of California.

The legal description of said property is as follows:

Lot 22, Block 19 of Tract 7730 as designated on the map entitled "Ramona Acres, City and County of San Bernardino, State of California," filed in the office of said county on May 5, 1903 in Volume 4 of maps at page 9.

Assessor's Parcel No.: 773-06-1996

I, Fred Fiduciary, am the named Successor Trustee under the above-referenced Trust, which was in effect at the time of the death of the decedent mentioned in Paragraph 1 above, and which has not been revoked, and I hereby consent to act as such. I declare under penalty of perjury, under the laws of the State of California, that the foregoing is true and correct.

Dated: May 17, 20xx

Fred Fiduciary
Signature

Fred Fiduciary
(Type or print name of successor trustee)

Certificate of Notary Public

A notary public or other officer completing this certificate verifies only the identity of the individual who signed the document to which this certificate is attached, and not the truthfulness, accuracy, or validity of that document.

State of California
County of San Bernardino

Subscribed and sworn to (or affirmed) before me on this 17 day of May, 20 xx by Fred Fiduciary, proved to me on the basis of satisfactory evidence to be the person(s) who appeared before me.

[SEAL] Signature *Nancy Notary*

Quitclaim Deed

RECORDING REQUESTED BY:

Betty Beneficiary

WHEN RECORDED MAIL DOCUMENT
AND TAX STATEMENTS TO:

Betty Beneficiary
12345 Circle Terrace
San Bernardino, CA 90000

The undersigned declares:

SPACE ABOVE THIS LINE FOR RECORDER'S USE

DOCUMENTARY TRANSFER TAX $ None

____ Computed on the consideration or value of property conveyed; OR

____ Computed on the consideration or value less liens or encumbrances remaining at time of sale.

This conveyance transfers title to the trust beneficiary; Grantor received nothing in return. (R & T 11911)

QUITCLAIM DEED

FOR NO CONSIDERATION, receipt of which is hereby acknowledged,

Fred Fiduciary, Successor Trustee Under Declaration of Trust dated May 1, 1995, which acquired title as I. M. Smart, Trustee,

do(es) hereby REMISE, RELEASE, AND FOREVER QUITCLAIM to Betty Beneficiary

the real property in the City of San Bernardino

County of San Bernardino, State of California, described as

Lot 22, Block 19 of Tract 7730 as designated on the map entitled "Ramona Acres, City and County of San Bernardino, State of California," filed in the office of the County Recorder of said county on May 5, 1903 in Volume 4 of Maps at page 9.

Assessor's Parcel No. 7730-06-1996

Dated: June 10, 20xx

Fred Fiduciary
Signature

A notary public or other officer completing this certificate verifies only the identity of the individual who signed the document to which this certificate is attached, and not the truthfulness, accuracy, or validity of that document.

On June 10, 20xx, before me, Nancy Notary, a notary public, personally appeared Fred Fiduciary, who proved to me on the basis of satisfactory evidence to be the person(s) whose name(s) is/are subscribed to the within instrument and acknowledged to me that he/she/they executed the same in his/her/their authorized capacity(ies), and that by his/her/their signature(s) on the instrument the person(s), or the entity upon behalf of which the person(s) acted, executed the instrument.

I certify under PENALTY OF PERJURY under the laws of the State of California that the foregoing is true and correct.

Witness my hand and official seal.

(Notary Signature) *Nancy Notary*

Bank Accounts

Title to bank accounts can usually be transferred to the successor trustee and to a beneficiary on termination of the trust by submitting to the bank a copy of the trust document and a certified copy of the death certificate.

Miscellaneous Trust Assets

For other assets held in trust, contact the principal parties involved to find out the process to have the assets transferred to the beneficiaries. In most cases, a copy of the trust document, a certified copy of the death certificate, and other proof of the trustee's authority will be required. In addition, an assignment form may be needed for assets such as a trust deed note or partnership interest. The payor on the trust deed note or the general partner of a limited partnership interest should be able to assist you.

For automobiles and other motor vehicles held in trust, the successor trustee should contact the Department of Motor Vehicles. It will provide the forms and instructions to transfer the vehicle. Start at www.dmv.ca.gov.

CHAPTER

13

An Overview of the Probate Court Process

This chapter provides an overview of what is involved in settling a simple estate through a superior (probate) court proceeding. A simple estate means there should be no complications such as disagreements among beneficiaries, questions of title to property, ambiguities in the will, substantial or disputed creditor's claims, or any other unusual or antagonistic situations—in short, nothing that requires special handling.

CROSS-REFERENCE

Chapter 1 provides a more detailed discussion of simple estates.

If you plan to be the personal representative (commonly thought of as the "executor"), after learning more about probating an estate you may decide to hire an attorney to take responsibility for preparing paperwork, staying on top of timelines and deadlines, and advising about the process. (See Chapter 16.) Or, you may decide that by following instructions carefully, you are up for the task without having an attorney guide you. If you represent yourself, you are expected to understand the relevant laws and procedures. The information in this book can help.

We suggest that you read this chapter completely before beginning the court proceeding. Then read Chapter 14, which describes conducting a court probate administration, step by step. The information in this chapter can also help you understand the process if you are a beneficiary or you have another connection to an estate.

Do You Really Need a Probate Court Proceeding?

Before you begin a probate court proceeding, you should access the decedent's assets to see if any, or even all, of them fall into categories that don't require probate. We discuss this in Chapter 6.

Probate Checklist

The checklist below sets out the tasks required in a simple probate court proceeding. Each task is explained in detail in the next chapter. You might want to refer to this checklist frequently as you proceed.

Dealing With the Probate Court

Here are the basics of what's involved in a probate court proceeding.

What Court Do You Use?

Different courts in our legal system handle different matters. A probate case is handled by the superior court of the county in which the decedent resided at the time of death, no matter where the decedent died.

For real property, that is, land and buildings, the laws of the state where real property is located will govern the transfer of that property after the decedent's death. Proceedings to have title transferred must occur in the state where the property is located. If a California resident owned real property outside of California, you will need legal advice specific to that other jurisdiction.

If a non-California resident owned property in California, there may be a probate proceeding in the state of residence as well as an "ancillary" probate proceeding in California. An ancillary probate proceeding will need some minor modifications to documents submitted to the California court. The proper court for the California proceeding will be a county in which the decedent owned real property. Because the modifications for an ancillary probate proceeding are beyond the scope of this book, and because it may be hard to know in which county you should file the California proceeding, get help from an attorney if the decedent was not a California resident yet owned real property in California.

When a superior court is dealing with a probate procedure, it is often called the "probate court." Some larger counties have specific branch courts that deal with probate proceedings. Some of those counties require filing the case with the branch court; others transfer cases to the branch court after filing. Check with the local court rules, the court's website, or the court clerk to find out where to file if the county has branch courts.

Formal Probate Court Proceeding Checklist

	Task	Time Frame or Deadline
First Month: Open Estate	☐ File Petition for Probate; obtain hearing date (Chapter 14, Steps 1 through 4)	Anytime after death
	☐ File original will and codicils, if any (Chapter 14 Step 4)	Within 30 days of death, or filed with Petition for Probate as separate filing
	☐ Publish Notice of Petition to Administer Estate (Chapter 14, Step 3)	Three times before hearing date; first publication must be at least 15 days prior to hearing
	☐ Mail Notice of Petition to Administer Estate (Chapter 14, Step 4)	At least 15 days prior to hearing date
	☐ File proof of publication and proof of mailing Notice of Petition to Administer Estate (Chapter 14, Step 3)	As early as possible before hearing date
	☐ File proof of will, if required (Chapter 14, Steps 5 and 6)	As early as possible before hearing date
	☐ Check probate calendar notes (Chapter 14, Step 9)	Prior to hearing; timing depends on county
	☐ File Order for Probate (and probate bond, if required (Chapter 14, Step 8))	Time requirements vary between counties; check with court
Letters Issued	☐ File letters and Duties and Liabilities of Personal Representative form (Chapter 14, Steps 10 and 11)	At same time or after filing Order for Probate (check local rules)
Next 4 to 5 Months: Administer Estate	☐ Apply for Taxpayer Identification Number (Chapter 7)	As early as possible after letters are issued
	☐ Notify government agencies (Chapter 14, Step 7)	Within 90 days of death
	☐ Open estate bank account (Chapter 13)	After letters are issued
	☐ Arrange for preparation of income tax returns (Chapter 7)	As soon as possible after letters are issued
	☐ Prepare Inventory and Appraisal and send to Referee (Chapter 14, Step 14)	As soon as possible after letters are issued
	☐ Mail Notice of Administration to creditors; pay debts without requiring formal claims (Chapter 14, Step 15)	Within four months after letters are issued or within 30 days after first discovering a creditor
	☐ File Change in Ownership Statement with county assessor for real property owned by decedent in California (Chapter 14, Step 14)	Prior to Inventory and Appraisal being filed with court
	☐ File Inventory and Appraisal with court (Chapter 14, Step 15)	Within four months after letters are issued
	☐ File Approval or Rejection of formal Creditors' Claims (Chapter 14, Step 14)	Before Petition for Final Distribution
	☐ File federal estate tax return if necessary (Chapter 7)	Within nine months of date of death (or within 15 months, with a timely request for extension)

Formal Probate Court Proceeding Checklist (continued)		
	Task	**Time Frame or Deadline**
Last Month: Close Estate	☐ File Petition for Final Distribution (Chapter 14, Step 16)	From four months to one year after letters are issued (within 18 months, if federal estate tax return is required)
	☐ Mail Notice of Hearing to beneficiaries (Chapter 14, Step 17)	At least 15 days prior to hearing date
	☐ File proof of mailing Notice of Hearing (Chapter 14, Step 17)	As soon as possible before hearing date on petition
	☐ File Order for Final Distribution (Chapter 14, Step 18)	Procedures vary between counties; check with court
	☐ Transfer assets and obtain receipts (Chapter 14, Step 19)	Anytime after Order for Final Distribution is signed
	☐ File receipts and Petition for Final Discharge (Chapter 14, Step 20)	After assets are distributed and all matters concluded

All superior (probate) courts follow the procedures outlined in the California Probate Code and the California Rules of Court. These documents are available online and in print. In addition, each county's superior court has special procedural rules of its own, called the "local rules." The local rules may determine when particular forms must be presented to the court, what must be included in court documents, where to call for information, and other important court-specific information. You can download each county's local rules from its court website. To find your county's superior court website, check www.courts.ca.gov.

TIP

Follow local rules to avoid frustrating errors and delays. This book does not include specific rules for each county. We recommend that you print out the local rules for the relevant county and consult those rules every step of the way. You may also want to make notes in your own copy of this book where the local rules provide specific instructions.

Who Will Represent the Estate?

The estate representative (or personal representative) represents the estate in the court proceeding. We discuss selection of the estate representative in detail in Chapter 2. To review very briefly:

- If there is a will that names an executor, that person is the estate representative.
- If there is no will (the decedent died intestate), the estate representative is called an "administrator."
- If there is a will but no executor is named, or the person named is unable to serve, the estate representative is called an "administrator with will annexed" (sometimes referred to as "administrator C.T.A.").

Even if you are the person named as executor or you are a family member, you are not required to serve as the estate representative. You may decide that you do not have the time, patience, or interest to take on this role. You can decline to serve. See Chapter 2 for options.

As a part of the court proceeding, the estate representative will be given authority by the court to act for the estate.

Commonly Used Probate Forms

Petition for Probate (DE-111)
Notice of Petition to Administer Estate (DE-121)
Proof of Subscribing Witness (used only when there is a will) (DE-131)
Proof of Holographic Instrument (used only for handwritten wills) (DE-135)
Waiver of Bond (DE-142)
Order for Probate (DE-140)
Letters (DE-150)
Duties and Liabilities of Personal Representative (DE-147)
Notice of Administration to Creditors (DE-157)
Inventory and Appraisal (DE-160)
Inventory and Appraisal (attachment) (DE-161)
Allowance or Rejection of Creditor's Claim (DE-174)
Notice of Hearing (Probate) (DE-120)
Ex Parte Petition for Final Discharge and Order (DE-295)

Local forms—these may include:

Probate Case Cover Sheet
Certificate of Assignment (for filing in branch courts)
Confidential Supplement to Duties and Liabilities (DE-147S)
Application and Order Appointing Probate Referee

Corepresentation

It is possible to have more than one person act as estate representative. If the will names two or more coexecutors and all are willing to serve, or if two or more persons wish to act as coadministrators, all must sign the Petition for Probate (DE-111). Generally all must sign the letters, and both (if two), or a majority (if three or more) must sign other papers that require the signature of the estate representative. The court will not issue separate letters. Additional signature lines may be added to the forms for this purpose.

When two or more representatives are appointed, it can sometimes complicate matters. For example:

- If one of the representatives is unavailable or absent from the state, the remaining representative(s) cannot act alone without a court order.
- Banks will not allow access to a safe-deposit box unless all representatives are present.
- Most banks will not open an estate bank account in the name of more than one representative.

Obtaining Court Forms

Virtually all documents used in a simple probate court proceeding are official forms, with the exception of the last petition and order. Above is a list of the main forms you will need, although some counties may require a few additional local forms. Consult your local rules and the local court's website.

You will find one copy of each statewide form in Appendix B. To obtain additional copies, you can photocopy the forms in the appendixes, or download them from the Judicial Council website at www.courts.ca.gov/forms.htm. When printing or copying the forms yourself, make them single-sided so that the court can easily scan them.

You may also be able to purchase a packet of the probate forms from the court.

Preparing Court Documents

Most of the forms you will need are the court-issued Judicial Council forms listed in the box above. You can get these forms in two places:

- in the appendix of this book, or
- online at www.courts.ca.gov/forms.htm.

On that website, the forms are "fillable," so that you can fill them out online and print them. You may also find it helpful to use the forms in the book as a rough draft, before entering the information in final form. If you use a form in the back of the book as your final document for filing, you'll need to fill it in using a typewriter or neat handwriting. If you do use a form from the back of the book, it's still a good idea to check the Judicial Council's website to make sure that it hasn't updated the form since the publication of this book. The form number and revision date are listed on the bottom left-hand corner of Judicial Council forms.

In the few cases where an official form is not available, you must type the entire document. Court documents must be created on 8½" × 11" white or unbleached paper, of standard quality, with lines numbered consecutively down the side. This is called pleading paper. You will find examples of documents on pleading paper in Chapter 14. Pleading paper is available at most office supply stores.

You can also use your word processing program to create the document on pleading paper. Most word processing programs have a pleading paper function built in that lets you format your paper to look like pleading paper. The program will also help you enter the text in the right places. For instructions, use the help function on your word processing program and search for "pleading."

No matter how you get your pleading paper, don't forget to check the court's local rules for specific formatting requirements and always follow these general formatting rules, which appear in the California Rules of Court (Title 2, Division 2):

- Documents must be double-spaced, (except for legal descriptions for real property, which can be single-spaced), using only one side of the paper, and each page must be numbered consecutively at the bottom.
- Each page, except for exhibits, must have a footer at the bottom containing the title of the paper, for example, Petition for Final Distribution or Order for Final Distribution.
- If attachments or exhibits are needed, they must be the same size (8½" × 11").
- All papers that belong together must be fastened at the top.
- All papers must have a standard two-hole punch at the top. (See Cal. Courts Rule 2.115.)
- The first page of all documents must be in the following form:
    - Commencing with Line 1 in the upper left-hand corner, enter the name of the petitioner, office or residence address, and telephone number.
    - Leave the space blank between Lines 1 and 7 to the right of the center of the page for the use of the clerk.
    - On or below Line 8, enter the title of the court.
    - Starting on Line 11, in the space left of the center, enter the title of the case.
    - To the right, opposite the title, put the case number.
    - Immediately below the case number, put the nature of the document (for example, "Petition for … ," "Supplement to …").

Most of the documents that must be typed are simple forms that are easy to copy from examples in the next chapter. The only document of any length that must be completely typed in a probate court proceeding is the final petition requesting distribution of the estate. A detailed sample petition is shown in Chapter 14, Step 16.

Petitions and Orders

A petition is a document that asks the court to do something. In a simple probate proceeding, you are required to file two petitions. The first requests that the court admit the will to probate (if there is a will) and that a representative (executor) be appointed. If there is no will, it only requests the appointment of the representative (administrator). The second petition requests an order closing the estate and distributing the assets to the beneficiaries.

The person who prepares and files a petition is called the "petitioner." A petitioner who acts without an attorney is identified as "Petitioner In Pro Per." This is an abbreviation for "In Propria Persona," a Latin phrase meaning you're representing yourself without a lawyer. You can simply use the term "Self-represented" on court forms where the attorney's name would otherwise appear.

If the court approves a petition, it will issue an order to that effect. Court orders are usually prepared by the petitioner and presented to the court for the judge's signature before or at the time of the hearing on the petition. Some courts allow the order to be submitted after the hearing date, so always check local rules.

Verifications

All statements in petitions should be verified at the end of the document by the petitioner. The verification paragraph is usually as follows:

> "I declare under penalty of perjury under the laws of the State of California that the foregoing, including any attachments, is true and correct. Executed this ____________ day of ____________________, 20___, at ______________________________________, California."

The verification has the same effect as a sworn statement or an affidavit witnessed by a notary, so that a personal appearance in court is not necessary. All court forms have the verification printed on them, if one is required. If you have to type a document that needs to be verified, be sure to include the verification. For instance, a supplement to a petition must be verified in the same manner as the petition. Always be sure to insert the date when the verification is signed, and the location where it is signed—it's easy to overlook this.

Filing Court Documents in Hardcopy

To file court documents, either mail them or present them in person to the clerk's office at the county courthouse. As a general rule, it is a good idea to include two copies of all documents in addition to the original, because some courts require them. The court always keeps the original document; any copies not needed will be returned to you. When you file your papers by mail, always keep a copy of each for your records in case the others get lost, and always include a stamped, self-addressed envelope so the court will return your conformed (stamped "filed" by the clerk) copies.

If you choose to file by mail, consult the local rules and contact the court clerk to confirm the following information:

- how many copies to provide, in addition to the original documents
- the required filing fee and methods of payment accepted
- mailing address for the court
- how to receive filed documents back from the court, such as a self-addressed stamped envelope, and
- any other rules or requirements for filing by mail.

When you file the first petition, the court clerk stamps it with a case number that you'll use on every other court document you prepare. In addition, each petition is given a hearing date. This is the time and date the court will decide whether or not it will approve the petition. As discussed below, even though a specific date, time, and location are assigned, a personal appearance may not be required.

TIP

Check with the court first. Court procedures for submitting filings are changing as a result of COVID-19. Check with the clerk's office before attempting to file. An appointment may be required for filing in person.

Electronic Filing

Some courts have adopted electronic filing (e-filing) as a means of handling paperwork more efficiently. Procedures vary from county to county. Some courts encourage e-filing for civil litigation, but not for probate cases. Other courts may require e-filing by attorneys, but not by self-represented parties. Each court provides specific information about e-filing on its website. Generally, to file electronically you must register with the court's electronic service provider. The provider will file your papers and in some cases may advance court fees for reimbursement later as a convenience.

Check your county court's website for information about e-filing in your county.

Filing Fees

The court charges a filing fee whenever a document is filed that requires a court hearing. In a simple probate proceeding, the filing fee is $435 for the Petition for Probate and another $435 for the Petition for Final Distribution. Most courts also collect an additional $30 court reporter fee. (San Francisco,

San Bernardino, and Riverside may also charge a "construction surcharge," so be sure to check the court's website or call the clerk in these counties to determine the correct amount.)

Certified Copies

A certified copy of a court document is one that has been certified by the clerk as a true and correct copy of the original document on file with the court. You may need certified copies during the administration process; you can order them from the court for a nominal fee. The court's website will have the fee schedule or you can contact the court clerk for the exact amount.

Beginning the Probate Process

A probate proceeding may begin at any time after someone dies. There is no specific time limit or deadline. In most cases, however, the process is initiated as soon as possible.

Filing the Probate Petition

You start the probate proceeding by filing a petition with the clerk of the superior court in the county where the decedent resided at the time of death, no matter where the decedent died. (Prob. Code § 7051.) For more information, see "Determine the Residence of the Decedent" in Chapter 2.

The person requesting to be appointed the estate representative (either the executor, administrator, or administrator with will annexed) files the probate petition. This person is called "the petitioner." From now on, we will assume you are the petitioner and will be the estate representative.

If there's a will, the original is lodged separately with the court clerk and a copy is attached to the petition. A copy of the death certificate is not required. The petition asks the court to admit the will (if any) to probate and appoint someone to act as estate representative. The petition also gives the court certain information, such as the names of the decedent's heirs, the beneficiaries in the will, where the decedent lived, what kind of property the decedent owned, approximate value of estate property, and where and when the decedent died.

The court clerk gives the petition a hearing date, which should be not less than 15 or more than 30 days after it is filed. (Prob. Code § 8003(a).) In reality, the hearing date may be set further out from the filing date to accommodate court scheduling. In most situations there is no opposition to the petition; it is automatically approved and the representative appointed without anyone having to appear in court.

It is a good idea to file your first papers in person, especially if you're lodging an original will. You may then pick up forms from that court for filing future documents and also get information about local court rules and procedures at the same time. Particularly with court procedures adapting to COVID-19, check with the clerk's office before attempting to file in person.

TIP

For urgent matters, a special administrator can act quickly. If urgent matters require someone to have authority to act on behalf of the estate before the normal timeline for a hearing on a probate petition, you can request that the court appoint a special administrator. This can be particularly important when assets of the estate are at risk, a business of the decedent needs to be continued, or a dispute delays the proceedings. "I want things to happen faster," in itself, usually does not justify a request for a special administrator. The local rules for the court may provide guidance on the types of requests the court will consider. See a lawyer for assistance.

The Independent Administration of Estates Act

The probate petition will likely request that the court grant you permission to handle the estate under the Independent Administration of Estates Act. (Prob. Code §§ 10400–10600.)

CAUTION

You cannot use the simplified procedures allowed by the Independent Administration of Estates Act if the decedent's will prohibits its use. This almost never happens, but if the will prohibits the use of the Independent Administration of Estates Act, you can still do your own probate using the procedures outlined in the next chapter. You will not, however, be able to pay creditors' claims or sell estate property without prior court approval. Obtaining court approval to pay formal creditors' claims is simple and merely requires submitting the original claim and a copy to the court asking that it be approved for payment and that a conformed copy be returned to you. Selling real property without the authority of the Independent Administration of Estates Act is more involved. It requires special documents and procedures not covered in this book. See "Sales of Estate Property," below.

This Act is designed especially for simple estates (regardless of size) where there are no disputes among the beneficiaries. It allows the representative to do many things without having to obtain prior permission from the court. This is referred to as administering an estate "without court supervision." If all of the heirs and beneficiaries have a cooperative attitude toward the representative, settling the estate under the Act will save a lot of time and paperwork.

You may ask for either "full authority" or "limited authority" under the Act. "Full authority" means you have *all* of the powers granted by the Act. "Limited authority" means you have all of the powers *except* the power to (a) sell real property, (b) exchange real property, (c) grant an option to purchase real property, or (d) borrow money with the loan secured by an encumbrance upon real property. (Prob. Code § 10403.)

If you are granted either full or limited authority, you may do the following without court approval or notifying the beneficiaries:

- allow, pay, reject, or contest any claim by or against the estate
- sell listed securities
- make repairs or improvements to estate property
- sell perishable or depreciating property
- accept a deed in lieu of foreclosure, and
- pay taxes and expenses of administration.

Generally, however, you must obtain approval from the court to buy estate property yourself, exchange estate property for your own property, or pay or compromise your own claims against the estate, unless you are also the sole beneficiary, or all known beneficiaries have consented to the transaction. (Prob. Code § 10501.) Before taking any of these actions, check the requirements carefully.

Many other powers are granted to a personal representative who has authority to administer the estate without court supervision. (Prob. Code §§ 10550–10564.) However, the actions described above are usually the most helpful.

Other actions may be taken without court supervision by giving prior notice, called Notice of Proposed Action (DE-165), to beneficiaries whose interests will be affected. The purpose of the notice is to give the beneficiaries a chance to object. Actions that require such notice are listed in Probate Code Sections 10510–10538. Those that may come up in simple estates are:

- selling or exchanging real estate (a bond may be required by the court when real estate is sold for cash under this procedure, unless the will waives bond)
- selling or exchanging nonperishable personal property
- leasing real estate for a term in excess of one year
- investing funds of the estate (other than in banks and savings and loan accounts, or direct obligations of the United States or the State of California maturing in one year or less)
- completing a contract entered into by the decedent to convey real or personal property
- borrowing money, executing a mortgage or deed of trust, or giving other security (Only a personal representative who has "full authority" under the Act may borrow money with the loan secured by an encumbrance on real property.)
- abandoning tangible personal property, if the value is less than the cost to collect or maintain it, and
- making preliminary distributions (such as tangible property or cash gifts less than $10,000), in limited circumstances.

A sample of the Notice of Proposed Action (DE-165) is shown in Chapter 14. It includes a space for the recipient to object or consent to the proposed action. A person who fails to object to a proposed action cannot have a court review the action later.

At least 15 days before the proposed action would be taken, a copy of the notice must be mailed to or personally served on all persons whose interest would be affected. The notice must be given by someone who is older than 18 and does not have an interest in the estate, and proof of the mailing or personal service is usually filed with the court. A sample form is included in the next chapter, with instructions.

If the proposed action involves selling or granting an option to buy real estate, the notice must include the material terms of the sale and any payment that is to be made to a broker or agent.

Persons entitled to receive notice forms may waive, in writing, their right to notice. They must use a Waiver of Notice of Proposed Action (DE-166), which is available on the California courts website (www.courts.ca.gov/forms.htm). The waiver can apply to all actions taken by the personal representative or only certain actions specified on the form. Persons who should have received notice may also consent to an action that has already been taken.

The Notice of Petition to Administer Estate

When you file the probate petition to start the court proceeding, the court clerk assigns a hearing date. Notice of the time, date, and place of the hearing must then be given to all heirs, beneficiaries, creditors, and persons who may be interested in the estate. This gives them an opportunity to appear at the hearing and assert their rights, if they wish to do so.

Notice is given in two ways:

- publishing a Notice of Petition to Administer Estate (DE-121) in a newspaper in the city where the decedent lived at the time the decedent died (or where the decedent left property, if not a California resident), and
- mailing notice of the hearing date to all heirs, beneficiaries, and alternate executors, as well as other persons mentioned in the will or a codicil, within 15 days of the hearing date.

Procedures vary in different court districts as to who arranges for the preparation, publication, and mailing of the notice. In some counties, the petitioner does all the work, while in others the court clerk and the newspaper do everything. However, seeing that the notice is properly given is your responsibility, even if the job is delegated to a newspaper. We discuss this in more detail in Chapter 14.

The Notice of Petition to Administer Estate also advises interested persons that they may serve you with a written request for notice of the filing of all documents or just certain documents, such as the Inventory and Appraisal or Petition for Distribution. The request is made on the Request for Special Notice (DE-154). A person or business with a possible claim against the estate—a disgruntled heir or a funeral director, for example—may file such a request. Medi-Cal will file a request if it files a claim for reimbursement of the cost of health services that were provided to the decedent or a predeceased spouse. If a Request for Special Notice is filed, a copy will be sent to you, and you must notify the interested person in writing when a petition or the Inventory and Appraisal has been filed, and also when a Notice of Proposed Action is given, and send the interested person a copy of the document. We explain how to do this in the next chapter.

Proving the Will

If there is a will, it must be "proven" in a probate court hearing (unless it is a "self-proving" will—see "Self-Proving Wills and Codicils," below). To prove a will, it must be shown either that (1) the decedent signed it in front of witnesses, declaring that it was the decedent's will, or (2) the witnesses understood it was the decedent's will. You do this by finding the witnesses and having them sign a declaration to this effect. The declaration is a simple court form with a photocopy of the will attached showing the signature of the witnesses and the filing stamp of the court clerk. We provide a sample in Step 5 of the next chapter.

If the decedent left a holographic will (an unwitnessed will in which the signature and material provisions are in the decedent's handwriting), you need a declaration from someone who knows the decedent's handwriting and who will verify that the will was written by the decedent. A commercially printed form will is a valid holographic will if a statement of testamentary intent is in the testator's own handwriting. (Prob. Code § 6111(c).) Any person having knowledge of the decedent's handwriting may sign the declaration, even if that person stands to inherit all or a part of the estate. This declaration is also a simple court form, and is shown in Step 6 of the next chapter.

Self-Proving Wills and Codicils

Many formal wills and codicils are self-proving, meaning you won't need to get a declaration from the witnesses. A self-proving will or codicil is one signed by the witnesses under penalty of perjury declaring the document was executed according to law. (Prob. Code § 8220.) If the paragraph preceding the signature of the witnesses is in the following basic form, it is usually sufficient to prove the will or codicil, if no one appears to contest the probate.

If, however, someone questions the validity of the will during the probate proceeding, the court may require evidence beyond this clause. Some courts always require a written declaration by at least one witness, regardless of whether or not the original will is self-proving, so find out your court's requirements.

Lost Will

You do not need to have the original, signed will to admit the decedent's will to probate. However if the original, signed will is not available, it is considered a "lost" will and the terms of the will need to be proved in some other way. If a copy of the original document exists, that is often the easiest way to provide the terms of the will. Otherwise, there must be other evidence of the substance of the will. If the decedent had the original will and it cannot be found, then you must also provide evidence that the decedent did not intend to revoke the will. If no one contests the will, usually a statement by someone with knowledge of the relevant facts will be sufficient. The Petition for Probate (DE-111) has specific items related to proving a lost will.

Sample of Self-Proving Clause of Will

Each of us declares under penalty of perjury under the laws of the State of California that the following is true and correct:

a. On the date written below, the maker of this Will declared to us that this instrument was the maker's Will and requested us to act as witnesses to it;
b. We understand this is the maker's Will;
c. The maker signed this Will in our presence, all of us being present at the same time;
d. We now, at the maker's request, and in the maker's presence, sign below as witnesses;
e. We believe the maker is of sound mind and memory;
f. We believe that this Will was not procured by duress, menace, fraud or undue influence;
g. The maker is age 18 or older; and
h. Each of us is now age 18 or older, is a competent witness, and resides at the address set forth after his or her name.

Date:____________________

Witness Signature ____________________

Witness Name ____________________

Witness Address ____________________

Witness Signature ____________________

Witness Name____________________

Witness Address ____________________

Probate Calendar Notes or "Tentative Rulings"

After you file the petition, a court employee who specializes in probate procedures, called a "probate examiner" reviews it to see if it contains all necessary information and to see if it conforms to certain requirements, such as whether notice has been properly given (Chapter 14, Step 9) or whether the petition is properly signed and verified. Probate calendar notes, sometimes called "Tentative Rulings," are notations made by the probate examiner on the calendar sheets after the petition has been reviewed.

If there are no defects, the examiner enters the words "Recommended for Approval" or "RFA," which means that no court appearance is necessary and the petition will be approved routinely. If a problem exists or if the examiner requires more information, the examiner makes a note about what is required before approval can be granted. Some courts publish a list of commonly used abbreviations, to help decipher the notes.

Look on the website or call the probate department of the court where you filed your papers well in advance of the hearing to find out how the notes are provided. In many counties, you can view them on the court's website.

Sometimes the court posts notes or tentative rulings at the courthouse the day before the hearing, or provides a recorded message you can call.

If the petition isn't preapproved, contact one of the "clearing attorneys" or probate examiners to get more information about any problems or open issues. Most probate examiners in larger counties are extremely busy and do not take telephone calls or are available only at certain times. But some can be contacted by email at an address given on the court's website. Courts in smaller districts are usually very helpful.

While it can be frustrating to have problems pointed out, understand that the court personnel want the procedures to work smoothly. Carefully follow the guidance provided by the probate examiner. You can correct most defects with additional paperwork. Do not be surprised if a hearing is postponed to allow time to correct the problem. If you cannot easily resolve matters raised by the probate examiner at this stage, you may need help from an attorney.

Supplements to the Petition

If the probate calendar notes indicate that additional information is required, or corrections should be made, you may prepare a supplement to the petition providing the necessary information and file it before the hearing date. (See instructions in Chapter 14, Step 9.)

Correcting information on a petition that is already filed with the court is a lot of extra work and it sometimes requires notice to be given again. If you can't get the petition approved in time for the hearing, the court will continue it to a new date (usually a number of weeks later) to give you time to do whatever is necessary to have it approved. Some courts have a rule that a matter may be continued only once, and others take the petition "off calendar" if it is continued three times. If a petition is marked "off calendar," rather than given a new date, this means the court has removed the petition from its calendar of cases and it has lost jurisdiction to act on the petition. However, this is not as bad as it sounds. All you need to do is request a new hearing date when you are ready and start over by giving notices of the hearing when the hearing on the petition is reset.

Telephone and Videoconference Court Appearances

In most counties you may now appear at a court hearing by telephone or videoconference, instead of in person. All telephone appearances are arranged in advance by an independent vendor called "CourtCall." It charges a fee for each appearance and you must make arrangements in advance. For more information visit www.courtcall.com or call 888-882-6878. The option to participate remotely, including by videoconference, has expanded substantially during the COVID-19 state of emergency. It may even be required. Check with your county to determine the procedures available.

Probate Bonds

Before being appointed by the court as executor or administrator, you must ordinarily post a bond (a sum of money or insurance policy) as insurance that you will faithfully perform your duties as representative, unless bond is waived in the decedent's will. Most wills include this waiver provision.

If the will doesn't waive the bond, all beneficiaries under the will, or heirs if there is no will, may waive the bond as long as they are all adults and competent. Use the Waiver of Bond by Beneficiary or Heir (DE-142/DE-111 (A3-e)) and attach it to the Petition for Probate when it is filed with the court. The waivers can usually be obtained easily in a simple estate where the beneficiaries are all friendly. The form is shown in Chapter 14.

Even if bond is waived in the will, the court may still impose a bond if it sees a need. Some courts require at least a minimum bond (around $10,000), even if written waivers are obtained. Check your local rules. Following are some situations where a bond may be required:

- One of the beneficiaries is a minor and therefore not qualified to sign a waiver of bond.
- The will names two or more persons to serve as executors and all do not serve, and the will does not waive bond for fewer than the number specified.
- The executor or administrator resides outside of California.
- The executor named in a will that waives bond does not qualify, and an administrator with the will annexed is appointed instead.

When the estate is represented by an attorney, probate bonds are most often obtained from authorized surety companies. With "limited" independent administration authority, the amount of the bond is fixed at the value of all the personal property plus the probable annual gross income from all property (including real property) in the estate. In contrast, if "full" independent administration authority is requested, the value of the decedent's net interest in real property is included in fixing the amount of bond.

Most surety companies will not provide a bond for self-represented personal representatives, although some will provide a bond for a representative who is working with a legal document assistant. If you cannot get a bond from a corporate surety, individuals may act as sureties instead, subject to the following limitations:

- At least two individual sureties must be used.
- The amount of the bond must be not less than twice the value of the personal property and twice the value of the probable annual income from the real and personal property.
- You may not be one of the sureties.
- The individuals must be California residents and either "householders" or owners of real property in California.
- Each individual's net worth (after debts) must be at least the amount of the bond in real or personal property, or both, in California. But if the bond is greater than $10,000, and one individual's net worth does not meet this requirement, the collective net worth must do so.

Blocked Accounts

In lieu of bond, or to reduce the amount of bond required, alternate security can be provided by putting estate assets beyond your immediate control, to be released only on court order. (Prob. Code § 8483.) For instance, you may:

- Deposit estate money in an insured account in a financial institution in California. (Prob. Code § 9700.)
- Deposit estate securities (stocks and bonds) or other estate assets (for example, jewelry, fine art, and precious metals) with a trust company. (Prob. Code [section symbol] 9701.) Most, but not all, banks are authorized trust companies.

Arrangements for the deposits may be made before or after the Petition for Probate is filed. The request that the blocked account be allowed is made by checking the appropriate box on the Petition for Probate (Item 2d). The money, securities, or other assets deposited are then excluded from the computation of the amount of bond required. This task is easier if the securities or money are already on deposit with an authorized bank; otherwise it might be difficult to obtain possession of the assets before the representative is appointed by the court. Alternatively, you may allege in the petition that the money or other property will be deposited with an authorized institution promptly after you are appointed representative, subject to withdrawal only upon court order. In any event, a written receipt from the depository, including the statement that withdrawals will not be allowed except on court order, must be obtained and filed with the court—use Judicial Council form MC-356.

To sum up, if bond is not waived in the will or if there is no will, you should obtain written waivers of bond forms from all adult heirs or beneficiaries and attach them to the petition for probate. In addition, you may request authorization in the petition to deposit some or all of the estate's personal property and funds not needed for estate expenses in blocked accounts with an authorized bank or trust company. If the court still imposes a bond, it should be minimal. If you cannot obtain a bond, you may be able to obtain an individual surety instead.

Order for Probate and Letters

When the court approves the petition, you must prepare and send in an Order for Probate (DE-140) for the judge's signature. The order appoints the estate representative, admits the will to probate, and usually appoints a probate referee to appraise the estate assets. After the order is signed, the court will issue "letters" to you. This document is your badge of office as estate representative. The original of the letters stays in the court file, and certified copies are supplied to you when you need evidence that you are authorized to act on behalf of the estate. Sometimes even after the order is signed, the letters may be delayed until all required documents, such as proof of any required bond, have been filed with the court.

"Letters testamentary" are issued to an executor, "letters of administration" are issued to an administrator, and "letters of administration with will annexed" (or "letters of administration C.T.A.") are issued to an administrator with will annexed. They each amount to the same thing.

Probate Register/Case Summary

Every court keeps a journal page for each probate case, which carries information on everything that happens in the court proceeding, such as when a petition or order has been filed, the hearing date on a petition, whether the petition is approved, if bond is required, and when the estate inventory is filed. This information is often available on the court's website. and is usually called the "Register of Actions." Some courts also have images of filed documents available online.

If you are interested, you may be able to go to the courthouse and examine the probate register as well as some probate files. These records have traditionally been open to the public, and you may find the information helpful. However, the COVID-19 pandemic reduced the availability of the walk-in service of the probate courts, so confirm your court's current procedures before going to the courthouse.

Taking Care of the Estate During Probate

One of your primary duties is to take good care of estate property while the probate process chugs along. This section discusses some of the tasks involved.

Probate Referee/Inventory and Appraisal

The court will appoint a "probate referee" to value (or appraise) the noncash assets in the estate as of date of the decedent's death.

Procedures vary between counties on how and when the referee is appointed. In some counties, the referee's name, address, and telephone number are stamped on your copy of the Petition for Probate when it is filed, or later on the Order for Probate.

Some counties require you to file a special form requesting that a probate referee be appointed, so ask the court whether it follows this procedure. The referee is paid a fee set by statute of one-tenth of 1% of the total value of the noncash assets appraised (minimum of $75), not to exceed $10,000. The referee is also allowed to be reimbursed for expenses such as mileage, mapping, and photos if real property is inspected. The referee does not appraise money or other cash assets where the value is clearly established.

You will describe the probate assets on Inventory and Appraisal (DE-160). You are responsible for preparing the form, which has two attachments. You can prepare the attachments using Inventory and Appraisal Attachment (DE-161).

Cash items are described on Attachment No. 1, and noncash assets are described on Attachment No. 2. Nonprobate property, such as joint tenancy property, property held in trust, or insurance proceeds payable to a named beneficiary, is not included. Also, property passing outright to a surviving spouse or domestic partner and transferred by means of a Spousal or Domestic Partner Property Petition (see Chapter 15) should not be included. When you have completed the form, send it to the probate referee who will insert the appraised values on Attachment No. 2 and return it to you for filing with the court. The Inventory and Appraisal, showing the referee's appraisals, must be filed with the court within four months after letters are issued. If not, some courts require the representative to appear and explain why it has not been filed, so you should start preparing the inventory as early as possible. Guidelines are in Chapter 14.

Change in Ownership Report

If the inventory includes real estate in California, a change of ownership report (death of real property owner) must be filed with the county assessor of each county in which real property is situated. (See Chapter 8.) To show that this requirement has been met, check the applicable box at Item 5 on the inventory form, stating that the change of ownership report has been filed, or that no filing is required because the decedent did not own real property in California.

TIP

Creditors or debt collectors may attempt to collect the decedent's debts from family members. Family members other than spouses typically are not obligated to pay a deceased relative's debts from their own assets. And a probate administration provides specific procedures for creditors to make claims from the estate. Be aware of your obligations, if any, for the debt before making any promises to pay. Specific rules govern communications of debt collectors, so seek more information on your rights if you feel like a debt collector is being unfair, abusive, or deceptive.

Handling Debts and Creditors' Claims

Anyone who winds up a deceased person's affairs through a probate administration must see that all legitimate debts are paid. You may pay debts in response to a formal claim by a creditor or in response to a legitimate bill.

At the formal level, the Notice of Petition to Administer Estate (DE-121) published in the newspaper gives legal notice to all creditors to file their claims within four months after issuance of your letters. In addition, you must use the Notice of Administration to Creditors (DE-157) form to give notice to all known or reasonably ascertainable creditors within four months after the letters are issued. You must continue to give notice as you become aware of new creditors. While you must make reasonable efforts to identify all debts, the law does not require you to make an intensive search for creditors. Creditors must file claims with the court and serve the claims upon the personal representative for the claims to be valid. Creditors use the court's Creditor's Claim form (DE-172) for this purpose. Uncomplicated estates tend to have few formal claims submitted.

CAUTION

If new creditors turn up. If you first acquire knowledge of the claim during the last 30 days of the period or after the four-month period has run, the notice must be mailed within 30 days after acquiring knowledge. This is explained in more detail in the next chapter.

The second level at which claims are made is the informal one, where bills keep coming to the decedent's last address. The usual ordinary expenses can be taken care of with a minimum of paperwork. Probate Code Section 10552 allows you to pay debts at your discretion without court approval or without requiring a formal claim if you have obtained independent administration authority and if the estate is solvent. In addition, when there has been a written demand for payment, Probate Code Section 9154 allows you to pay debts incurred by the decedent before death within 30 days after the claim period ends without requiring a formal claim, unless for some reason you dispute the amount or legitimacy of the debt.

SEE AN EXPERT

Complicated debts. If the decedent was heavily in debt or there are complicated or large disputed claims against the estate, you should get help from an attorney.

How to Handle Assets During Administration

After letters are issued there is a four-month waiting period before the estate may be closed and distributed, during which the creditors are allowed to file their claims. During this time, the personal representative must preserve assets of the estate. Review carefully the form Duties and Liabilities of Personal Representative (DE-147), particularly the section "Managing the Estate's Assets," and obtain appropriate advice if needed. Here are some suggestions on how to treat various types of assets during this period.

Bank Accounts

All accounts in the decedent's name (including out-of-state bank accounts) should be transferred to estate accounts in your name as the estate representative. Contrary to what many people believe, bank accounts in the name of a deceased person are not frozen for long periods of time. Banks will release the funds to you as the estate representative if you present a certified copy of your letters.

All money received during the administration of the estate (such as stock dividends) should be deposited into the estate checking account. The decedent's debts and expenses of administration (such as court costs and publication fees) should be paid from the estate account. Keep an accurate record of each payment or disbursement, indicating the reason for the payment and the date. For each deposit, keep a record of the source of the funds and the date received. This detailed information on receipts and disbursements will be needed to prepare an accounting of estate administration and the estate's income tax returns, if they are required.

If the estate checking account has more cash than you need to pay estate expenses, transfer the excess to insured interest-bearing accounts (Prob. Code § 9652) or invest it in government obligations maturing in five years or less or in direct obligations of the State of California maturing in one year or less. (Prob. Code § 9730.) Be sure not to mix any of your personal funds with the estate's funds. If it is necessary to pay estate expenses with your personal funds, you may later reimburse yourself from the estate. However, you should keep accurate records of such transactions.

Important. The estate is a separate taxpayer, and before opening the estate account most banks will require you to obtain a taxpayer identification number. After you have obtained letters, apply for the number as soon as possible online or on form SS-4 (*Application for Employer Identification Number*), available from the Internal Revenue Service. The same taxpayer identification number for the estate is used for state income tax purposes. See Chapter 7 for instructions on how to obtain the number.

Rent/Tangible Personal Property

If the decedent rented rather than owned a residence, you must decide whether or not to:

- pay additional rent on the decedent's apartment to safeguard the contents
- store the items at the estate's expense, or
- permit the beneficiaries to take possession of items to which they are presumptively entitled, pending administration. (Prob. Code § 9650(c).)

In most instances, the last alternative is preferable and usually not objectionable as long as the items are not of unusual value, no problems are anticipated, and you obtain a receipt. Keep in mind, however, that it is the duty of the estate representative to protect estate property, so proceed with caution and care.

If rented premises are to be vacated, you should immediately contact the landlord and give the required notice—usually 30 days—and arrange for a refund of any security deposit. If a long-term lease is involved, you should give prompt written notice and move out. The landlord has the duty to try to rerent the property. Assuming the landlord accomplishes this at the same or a higher rent, or reasonably could have done so, the estate is off the hook for additional rent from the day of the new rental. (If you have more questions about mitigation of damages, see *California Tenants' Rights*, by Janet Portman and J. Scott Weaver (Nolo).)

Vehicles

If the decedent owned a motor vehicle (auto, motor home, motorcycle, etc.) in the decedent's name alone, the identity of the person entitled to it is not in doubt (either under the will or by intestate succession), and it is clear there will be no objections, then the vehicle may be transferred to the new owner prior to the closing of the estate. (Veh. Code § 5910.) However, you or the new owner should make sure there is adequate insurance coverage to eliminate any chance that a claim could be made against the estate based on a subsequent accident. Although the Vehicle Code does not specifically permit it, a transfer on the signature of the representative is normally honored by the Department of Motor Vehicles if submitted with a certified copy of your letters. Motor vehicles can be transferred only to licensed drivers.

If the vehicle is owned in joint tenancy with someone else, it may be transferred by the procedures outlined in Chapter 10. If money is owed on the vehicle, this obligation is normally assumed by the new owner, unless the decedent's will says otherwise.

If none of the beneficiaries wants the vehicle, it is probably wise to sell it quickly, as a depreciating asset, to avoid the expense of caring for it during administration of the estate.

Stocks and Bonds

The easiest way to handle stocks and bonds is to leave them in the decedent's name and transfer them to the beneficiaries on final distribution of the estate. Dividend checks and checks for interest on bonds or debentures will, of course, be made payable to the decedent, but you can endorse the checks and deposit them to the estate bank account. Usually, there is no problem with the checks being honored.

Sales of Estate Property

Sometimes it may be necessary or desirable to sell some estate assets before the estate is closed to raise cash to pay debts or to avoid the expense of caring for the property during probate. Selling property may also facilitate distribution of an asset, as when beneficiaries do not wish to own fractional interests in an asset, such as a one-third interest in a car or a one-half interest in a stamp collection. Property may be sold during probate administration and distribution made in cash, if the beneficiaries agree.

If you have authority to administer the estate under the Independent Administration of Estates Act, you may sell estate property (real or personal) for cash or on credit, and for the price you determine, subject to the following rules.

Depreciating Personal Property

Personal property that will depreciate in value, or that will cause loss or expense to the estate if retained, may be sold without prior court approval and without prior notice to any person interested in the estate. Automobiles and furniture are frequently sold under this provision. In addition, if the cost of collecting, maintaining, and safeguarding tangible personal property would exceed its fair market value (for example, junk cars and garage sale leftovers), you may abandon or otherwise dispose of the property after giving written notice to the persons whose interest in the estate would be affected by the proposed action—usually the beneficiary of the will or an heir if no will. The minimum notice period is ten days by mail or five days by personal delivery. If an affected person objects in writing within that period, you can demand that the objecting person take the property into possession at their own expense for safekeeping. (Prob. Code § 9788.)

Securities, Stocks, and Bonds

Securities listed on a stock or bond exchange may be sold for cash at the best price on the stock exchange without notifying the beneficiaries in advance or obtaining prior court approval. (Prob. Code §§ 10537 and 10200.) Despite this authority, some transfer agents may refuse to transfer title without a court order. In such case, the next chapter shows a simple way to obtain the order.

Other Personal Property

You may sell other personal property without prior court approval as well, but (except for property noted above) you must first give a Notice of Proposed

Action (DE-165) to the beneficiaries whose interest will be affected by the sale. See "Beginning the Probate Process," above, and Chapter 14, Step 13 to learn more about this notice procedure.

Real Estate

An estate representative who has full authority under the Independent Administration of Estates Act may also sell real estate without court supervision. In this case, the sale procedure is virtually the same as in other real estate sales. A special form of the listing agreement with a licensed real estate broker should be used to comply with probate rules. You will sign the required documents as the estate representative in the place of the decedent, upon furnishing a certified copy of your letters. Another special requirement is that a Notice of Proposed Action (DE-165) must be given 15 days before the sale date to all persons whose interests will be affected. The court is not involved in any other way. The more complicated requirements that apply to sales of real estate through a probate court proceeding, such as publication of notice of sale and court approval of the sale price and of agent's and broker's commissions, do not apply to sales under the Independent Administration of Estates Act. You may sell the property at a price and on terms you find acceptable. (Prob. Code § 10503.) The Notice of Proposed Action must, however, include the material terms of the transaction, including the sale price and commission paid an agent or broker.

We recommend that the title company be notified in advance that the sale will be made without court supervision. Usually, the title company will want assurance that the notice has been given properly and will require a certified copy of the letters.

If you don't have full independent administration authority, selling real property during probate is more complicated. The sale must be confirmed by the court, and you must file a Report of Sale and Petition for Order Confirming Sale of Real Property (DE-260). The procedure is a cumbersome and detailed process that is not covered in this book. It may be better to wait and have the beneficiary sell the property after probate is closed, if possible. If you must sell the property during probate, consult Chapter 18 of *California Decedent Estate Practice* (CEB), a useful resource that is available in most law libraries.

Income Taxes

You should contact an accountant early in the proceedings to arrange for preparation of the decedent's final state and federal income tax returns. Of course, you can do the paperwork yourself, but the moderate fee you will pay to have an experienced person do the work is probably worth the trouble and risk of liability you save.

In addition, if the estate remains open long enough, it may receive enough income to require the filing of income tax returns for the estate. These are called fiduciary income tax returns. An accountant may advise you in this regard. (Income taxes are discussed in more detail in Chapter 7.)

Federal Estate Tax Return

If the value of all the decedent's property (this includes probate assets, joint tenancy property, insurance proceeds when the decedent owned the policy at death, death benefits, and property in trust) is high enough, a federal estate tax return will have to be prepared and filed within nine months of the date of death. (See Chapter 7.)

Even if the size of the estate does not require a federal estate tax return, you may elect to file the return if a spouse survives the decedent. A timely filed estate tax return is required to elect portability of the deceased spouse's unused applicable exclusion amount. This can reduce the estate taxes otherwise owed in the surviving spouse's estate.

Real and Personal Property Taxes

Probate Code Section 9650 requires the personal representative to pay all taxes on the property in the representative's possession during administration of the estate.

Preliminary Distributions

If the closing of the estate will be delayed for some reason, such as tax problems or delays in selling property, you may obtain a court order allowing distribution of a portion of the assets before the estate is ready to be finally closed. This allows the beneficiaries to enjoy all or a portion of their inheritance before final distribution.

To obtain the order, you must file a Petition for Preliminary Distribution with the court. You may request distribution of certain specific gifts or a pro rata distribution of a percentage of the estate. Generally, you must wait until the four-month claim period ends; however, the court will allow distribution two months after letters are issued if the distributees post a bond. Because most estates are ready to close after the claim period ends, we do not provide details on how to make preliminary distributions. Specific guidelines are given in the CEB publication *California Decedent Estate Practice*, Chapter 25, available in most law libraries.

Probate Code Section 10520 permits limited preliminary distributions without a court order if the representative has authority under the Independent Administration of Estates Act and: (1) if the creditor's claim period has expired, and (2) the distribution can be made without loss to creditors or injury to the estate.

The following property can be distributed under this provision after giving a Notice of Proposed Action:

- estate income
- tangible personal property not exceeding $50,000 in value, and
- cash gifts under a will that do not exceed $10,000 to any one person.

Family Protections

Certain family members have special rights to help buffer the consequences after a death. The specific procedures are beyond the scope of this book, yet the book mentions them so you can seek further information and assistance if needed.

Possession of family home and set aside of other property for the family. A surviving spouse or registered domestic partner and minor children of the decedent may remain in possession of the family home and household furniture at least until 60 days after an inventory is filed in the estate, or for longer if approved by the court. (Prob. Code § 6500-6501.) These family members may also petition the court to set apart the home and/or other property for their benefit. The court will consider the needs of the surviving spouse and minor children, any encumbrances on the property, the claims of creditors, the needs of other heirs or beneficiaries of the decedent, and the intent of the decedent. These protections may result in property being set apart for the family members either temporarily, or permanently, possibly in a different manner than would result from applying the terms of the will or the rules of intestate succession. (Prob. Code § 6510-6528.)

Family allowance during administration. Sometimes family members need financial assistance while the estate is being administered. There are procedures to claim a family allowance for funds from the estate during this time. This is most commonly applied for a surviving spouse or registered domestic partner, minor children of the decedent, and incapacitated adult children who were dependent on the decedent. But the court also has the discretion to grant an allowance from the estate for other adult children or parents of the decedent who depended on the decedent for support. (Prob. Code § 6540-6545.) The procedures for granting or authorizing a family allowance may depend on whether the personal representative has authority under the Independent Administration Estates Act (Prob. Code § 10535), and who seeks the allowance. A family allowance has priority over most other claims, so can be an important protection for family members in an insolvent estate.

Small estate set aside. If the size of the net estate does not exceed $85,900, the entire estate can be set aside for the surviving spouse or domestic partner and minor children. (Prob. Code § 6600-6615.) The net estate value for this purpose takes into consideration liens and encumbrances and does not include the home if set aside under Probate Code § 6520. The dollar amount will be adjusted for inflation on April 1, 2022 and every three years thereafter. This right to a set aside effectively gives priority to the surviving spouse or domestic partner and minor children, over the priority interests of people who would inherit through a will. To claim the small estate set aside, a petition must be filed with the court, either with the petition for administration of the estate or any time before the order for final distribution of the estate. The recipient is generally liable for the decedent's debts, so the timing of when a creditor may file a claim could be a factor in when to file for a small estate set aside.

Closing the Estate

When you've taken care of all the debts and claims made on the estate and filed all the right papers, you're ready to ask the court to wind up the probate and distribute the balance of the assets to the beneficiaries.

Petition for Final Distribution

You may take steps to close the estate any time after the expiration of the creditor's claim period (four months from the date letters are issued) if:

- All debts and taxes have been paid or sufficiently secured.
- No problems prevent closing the estate.

If you've worked steadily on each of the steps described above, you should be ready to close a simple estate within six to seven months from the time you filed the petition to open the estate.

CAUTION

Do not delay. You must file a status report or the Petition for Final Distribution within one year after letters have issued (or 18 months, if a federal estate tax return is required). Unless there are specific reasons the estate must stay open, file the Petition for Final Distribution within this time period to avoid a substantial amount of paperwork and further delay.

To get authority to close the estate, you must file a Petition for Final Distribution with the court, showing that the estate is in a condition to be closed and requesting that distribution be made to the beneficiaries. This final petition is not an official form; you must create it according to special rules. (See Chapter 14, Step 16.) A sample of the petition, which may be adapted to your circumstances, is shown in Chapter 14 with instructions on how to prepare it. After the petition is filed, set for hearing, and approved, the court will sign an Order for Final Distribution.

Representative's Compensation

As estate representative you are entitled to compensation for services, sometimes referred to as "commissions," paid out of the estate assets. (Prob. Code § 10800.) You may request or waive the compensation in the Petition for Final Distribution. The amount is based on the gross value of the probate estate (probate assets only, not joint tenancy or trust property or life insurance proceeds). Here is how it is computed:

4% of the first $100,000
3% of the next $100,000
2% of the next $800,000
1% of the next.................. $9,000,000
0.5% of the next.............$15,000,000
"reasonable amount" for
everything above........ $25,000,000

The statutory fee is generally the maximum fee unless "extraordinary" fees are requested and approved. For example, the personal representative could request special fees for running a business, litigation related to the estate, selling property, and preparing tax returns.

If you are the sole beneficiary, you may choose not to claim the compensation, since you will receive all the estate anyway. However, if there are several beneficiaries and you have done all the work, you may be more inclined to claim the compensation to which you are entitled. You may also request less than the statutory amount, if you choose. Apart from the compensation, you can also obtain reimbursement from the estate for expenses such as travel (depending on local rules) by listing the items on the Petition for Final Distribution. Compensation paid to you is treated as taxable income and you must report it on your personal tax return. You can take compensation only after it's approved by the court.

TIP

Payment of attorneys' fees. If you have hired an attorney to represent you as the estate representative, payment to the attorney will be made from estate assets only after authorized in a court order. Attorney compensation will usually be requested in the Petition for Final Distribution. Attorney compensation is separate and in addition to compensation for the estate representative. Attorney compensation for ordinary services is limited to the statutory commission schedule, the same as for the representative's commission. If extraordinary compensation is justified, it must be requested and approved by the court prior to being paid.

Waiver of Accounting

Ordinarily, when you file a Petition for Final Distribution, the court requires a detailed accounting of all monies or other items received, and all monies paid out, during administration. However, the accounting requirement may be avoided when all persons entitled to receive property from the estate have executed a written waiver of accounting. Probate Code Section 10954 describes the conditions for obtaining waivers.

A waiver of accounting simplifies the closing of the estate. When all beneficiaries are friendly, there is usually no problem in obtaining the waiver. Informally providing records of the estate administration, such as bank account statements, may give beneficiaries comfort to waive the requirement for a formal accounting. The waivers may be signed by the following persons:

- any beneficiary who is an adult and competent
- if the distributee is a minor, by a person authorized to receive money or property belonging to the minor—parent, guardian (attach a certified copy of Letters of Guardianship), or custodian named in the will (see Chapter 14, Step 16)
- if the distributee is a conservatee, by the conservator (attach a certified copy of Letters of Conservatorship)
- if the distributee is a trust, by the trustee who has filed a written Consent to Act as Trustee
- if the distributee is an estate, by the personal representative (attach a certified copy of letters), or
- by an attorney-in-fact for the distributee.

We show you how to get the accounting waived in the next chapter in the instructions for Paragraph 16 of the Petition for Final Distribution.

A Waiver of Accounting is not required if adequate provision has been made for satisfaction in full of the person's interest. (Prob. Code § 10954(a)(2).) For example, if a will leaves each of the decedent's grandchildren a specified cash gift, and the estate has enough money to pay those gifts, a waiver is not required of the grandchildren. Similarly, if a will leaves only $1 to someone (possibly a disgruntled relative who might refuse to sign a waiver), and the estate can pay it, a waiver is not required.

Distributions to Minors

Special rules apply for distributions to a person younger than age eighteen (18), depending on the amount of the gift and provisions of the will. (Prob. Code § 3413.) If a minor beneficiary is entitled to receive noncash estate assets worth more than $10,000, a court-appointed guardian may be needed for the minor's estate, unless a custodian was named in the decedent's will to receive the property on behalf of the minor. Although minors can receive title to real estate, they cannot convey valid title if the property is sold. One alternative is to wait to sell until the minor becomes 18. If not, a guardian may be appointed for the minor's estate in a separate court proceeding.

Transferring the Assets

After the court signs the Order for Final Distribution (Chapter 14, Step 18), the property may be transferred to the beneficiaries. This is relatively easy with most assets. All beneficiaries must sign a receipt for the assets they receive, which you will file with the court along with another form requesting that you be discharged from your duties as estate representative. This concludes the court proceeding. See Chapter 14, Steps 19 and 20.

CHAPTER

14

Conducting a Simple Probate Proceeding

Now that you have a general idea from Chapter 13 of what a probate court proceeding involves, this chapter will tell you what you need to do. It provides samples of forms, with detailed explanations of how to complete them.

Appendix B of this book contains most of the court forms. You can use these tear-out forms as your official forms, or you can use them for notes before preparing the final document for use. You can also download current forms from the California Judicial Council's website at www.courts.ca.gov/forms.htm. Most of the relevant forms are listed under the category of "Probate—Decedents Estates." After you download a form, you can either fill it out on your computer and then print the completed form, or you can print out a blank copy and fill in the information by hand, printing neatly in blue or black ink. (See Chapter 13.) Carefully read and follow the instructions that come with each form.

If you've hired an attorney to help you with your duties as personal representative, then the attorney will likely complete the forms instead of you. However, using this chapter to follow along the steps will help you do your job with confidence.

TIP

Consult the court rules every step of the way. Before filing any documents, consult the local rules and California Rules of Court. Courts publish these rules to set expectations about specific requirements that, if not followed, can cause delays.

TIP

Check information from the court clerk first. Before you head to the court (or the post office) to file your Petition for Probate (DE-111), review the local probate court's website carefully and contact the court clerk to find out if your court requires any additional forms to be filed along with DE-111. For example, some courts require you to submit Forms DE-147 and DE-147S (Duties and Liabilities of Personal Representatives with supplement) along with your Petition for Probate.

If you're not sure what number to call, call the main number for the county's superior court and ask for the probate clerk or probate department. When you get the right number, write it in your files—you're likely to need it again at some point.

Step 1: Prepare the Petition for Probate

The Petition for Probate (DE-111) initiates the court probate proceeding. It requests that the court admit the will (if there is one) to probate and appoint a representative to administer the estate. Be sure all attachments are full-sized sheets (8½" × 11").

Box 1 (Attorney or Party Without Attorney). Insert in the upper left-hand corner box your name and address as the petitioner and proposed personal representative of the estate. You will find this general format on all court forms. After the words "Attorney For," enter "Self-represented," as shown in the sample form. This means that you are acting as your own attorney. Instead, you could enter "Petitioner in pro per" or "Petitioner in pro se" which also mean that you represent yourself.

Box 2 (Name and Address of Court). Enter the name of the county and the street address of the court. The county will be the one where the decedent resided at the time of death. (See "What Court Do You Use?" in Chapter 13 for more on how to determine the correct county and court.)

Box 3 (Estate of). Enter the name of the decedent, including all name variations under which the decedent held property. All of these names should be carried forward to all probate documents filed with the court. If the decedent used more than one name, put the name used most often for legal purposes followed by "aka" ("also known as") and then the other names used for business purposes. For example, if John Doe held most of his property in that name but had several bank accounts and a car registration under Jack Doe and John L. Doe, you would insert "John Doe, aka Jack Doe, aka John L. Doe." Use a similar format if the decedent had prior last names, such as "Jane Storm, aka Jane Merryweather, aka Jane Merryweather Storm."

Box 4 (Petition for). You will have to work your way carefully through this section after the words "Petition for." Usually at least two boxes will be checked, and possibly up to four boxes, depending on the circumstances.

Petition for Probate (page 1)

DE-111

ATTORNEY OR PARTY WITHOUT ATTORNEY: STATE BAR NO.:
NAME: Billy M. Kidd
FIRM NAME:
STREET ADDRESS: 1109 Sky Blue Mountain Trail
CITY: Billings STATE: MT ZIP CODE: 48906
TELEPHONE NO.: 715-555-6408 FAX NO.:
E-MAIL ADDRESS: billy@gmail.com
ATTORNEY FOR (*name*): Self-represented

FOR COURT USE ONLY

SUPERIOR COURT OF CALIFORNIA, COUNTY OF LOS ANGELES
STREET ADDRESS: 111 No. Hill St
MAILING ADDRESS: 111 No. Hill St
CITY AND ZIP CODE: Los Angeles, CA 90012
BRANCH NAME: CENTRAL DISTRICT

ESTATE OF (*name*): ANABELLE KIDD, aka ANABELLE O.KIDD,
DECEDENT

PETITION FOR [x] **Probate of** [ ] **Lost Will and for Letters Testamentary**
[ ] **Probate of** [ ] **Lost Will and for Letters of Administration with Will Annexed**
[ ] **Letters of Administration**
[ ] **Letters of Special Administration** [ ] **with general powers**
[x] **Authorization to Administer Under the Independent Administration of Estates Act** [ ] **with limited authority**

CASE NUMBER:

HEARING DATE AND TIME: DEPT.:

1. Publication will be in (*specify name of newspaper*): Santa Monica Daily Press
   a. [ ] Publication requested.
   b. [x] Publication to be arranged.
2. **Petitioner** (*name each*):
   Billy M. Kidd

   requests that
   a. [x] decedent's will and codicils, if any, be admitted to probate.
   b. (*name*): Billy M. Kidd be appointed
      (1) [x] executor
      (2) [ ] administrator with will annexed
      (3) [ ] administrator
      (4) [ ] special administrator [ ] with general powers

      and Letters issue upon qualification.
   c. [x] full [ ] limited authority be granted to administer under the Independent Administration of Estates Act.
   d. (1) [x] bond not be required for the reasons stated in item 3e.
      (2) [ ] $ bond be fixed. The bond will be furnished by an admitted surety insurer or as otherwise provided by law. (*Specify reasons in Attachment 2 if the amount is different from the maximum required by Prob. Code, § 8482.*)
      (3) [ ] $ in deposits in a blocked account be allowed. Receipts will be filed. (*Specify institution and location*):
3. a. Decedent died on (*date*): 6-18-xx at (*place*): Santa Monica, California
      (1) [x] a resident of the county named above.
      (2) [ ] a nonresident of California and left an estate in the county named above located at (*specify location permitting publication in the newspaper named in item 1*):
   b. [ ] Decedent was a citizen of a country other than the United States (*specify country*):
   c. Street address, city, and county of decedent's residence at time of death (*specify*):
      950 Euclid Street, Santa Monica, Los Angeles County, California 90403

Form Adopted for Mandatory Use
Judicial Council of California
DE-111 [Rev. July 1, 2017]

PETITION FOR PROBATE
(Probate—Decedents Estates)

Probate Code, §§ 8002, 10450;
www.courts.ca.gov

Petition for Probate (page 2)

DE-111

ESTATE OF *(name)*: ANABELLE KIDD, aka ANABELLE O.KIDD, DECEDENT	CASE NUMBER:

3. d. **Character and estimated value of the property of the estate** *(complete in all cases)*:
   - (1) Personal property: $48,500.00
   - (2) Annual gross income from
     - (a) real property: $ None
     - (b) personal property: $ 3,400.00
   - (3) **Subtotal** *(add (1) and (2))*: $ 51,900.00
   - (4) Gross fair market value of real property: $ 400,000.00
   - (5) (Less) Encumbrances: ($ 95,000.00)
   - (6) Net value of real property: $ 305,000.00
   - (7) **Total** *(add (3) and (6))*: $ 356,900.00

   e. (1) [x] Will waives bond. [ ] Special administrator is the named executor, and the will waives bond.
   (2) [ ] All beneficiaries are adults and have waived bond, and the will does not require a bond. *(Affix waiver as Attachment 3e(2).)*
   (3) [ ] All heirs at law are adults and have waived bond. *(Affix waiver as Attachment 3e(3).)*
   (4) [ ] Sole personal representative is a corporate fiduciary or an exempt government agency.

   f. (1) [ ] Decedent died intestate.
   (2) [x] Copy of decedent's will dated: 7-1-xx [ ] codicil dated *(specify for each)*:

   are affixed as Attachment 3f(2). *(Include typed copies of handwritten documents and English translations of foreign-language documents.)*
   [x] The will and all codicils are self-proving (Prob. Code, § 8220).
   (3) [ ] The original of the will and/or codicil identified above has been lost. *(Affix a copy of the lost will or codicil or a written statement of the testamentary words or their substance in Attachment 3f(3), and state reasons in that attachment why the presumption in Prob. Code, § 6124 does not apply.)*

   g. **Appointment of personal representative** *(check all applicable boxes)*:
   (1) Appointment of executor or administrator with will annexed:
   - (a) [x] Proposed executor is named as executor in the will and consents to act.
   - (b) [ ] No executor is named in the will.
   - (c) [ ] Proposed personal representative is a nominee of a person entitled to Letters. *(Affix nomination as Attachment 3g(1)(c).)*
   - (d) [ ] Other named executors will not act because of [ ] death [ ] declination [ ] other reasons *(specify)*:

     [ ] Continued in Attachment 3g(1)(d).

   (2) Appointment of administrator:
   - (a) [ ] Petitioner is a person entitled to Letters. *(If necessary, explain priority in Attachment 3g(2)(a).)*
   - (b) [ ] Petitioner is a nominee of a person entitled to Letters. *(Affix nomination as Attachment 3g(2)(b).)*
   - (c) [ ] Petitioner is related to the decedent as *(specify)*:

   (3) [ ] Appointment of special administrator requested. *(Specify grounds and requested powers in Attachment 3g(3).)*
   (4) [ ] Proposed personal representative would be a successor personal representative.

   h. Proposed personal representative is a
   (1) [ ] resident of California.
   (2) [x] nonresident of California *(specify permanent address)*:

   1109 Sky Blue Mountain Trail, Billings, Montana 48906

   (3) [x] resident of the United States.
   (4) [ ] nonresident of the United States.

DE-111 [Rev. July 1, 2017] **PETITION FOR PROBATE (Probate—Decedents Estates)** Page 2 of 4

Petition for Probate (page 3)

DE-111

ESTATE OF *(name)*: ANABELLE KIDD, aka ANABELLE O.KIDD, DECEDENT	CASE NUMBER:

4. [x] Decedent's will does not preclude administration of this estate under the Independent Administration of Estates Act.

5. a. Decedent was survived by *(check items (1) or (2), and (3) or (4), and (5) or (6), and (7) or (8))*
   - (1) [ ] spouse.
   - (2) [x] no spouse as follows:
     - (a) [ ] divorced or never married.
     - (b) [x] spouse deceased.
   - (3) [ ] registered domestic partner.
   - (4) [x] no registered domestic partner. *(See Fam. Code, § 297.5(c); Prob. Code, §§ 37(b), 6401(c), and 6402.)*
   - (5) [x] child as follows:
     - (a) [x] natural or adopted.
     - (b) [ ] natural adopted by a third party.
   - (6) [ ] no child.
   - (7) [ ] issue of a predeceased child.
   - (8) [x] no issue of a predeceased child.

   b. Decedent [ ] was [x] was not survived by a stepchild or foster child or children who would have been adopted by decedent but for a legal barrier. *(See Prob. Code, § 6454.)*

6. *(Complete if decedent was survived by (1) a spouse or registered domestic partner but no issue (only* ***a*** *or* ***b*** *apply), or (2) no spouse, registered domestic partner, or issue. (Check the* ***first*** *box that applies):*
   - a. [ ] Decedent was survived by a parent or parents who are listed in item 8.
   - b. [ ] Decedent was survived by issue of deceased parents, all of whom are listed in item 8.
   - c. [ ] Decedent was survived by a grandparent or grandparents who are listed in item 8.
   - d. [ ] Decedent was survived by issue of grandparents, all of whom are listed in item 8.
   - e. [ ] Decedent was survived by issue of a predeceased spouse, all of whom are listed in item 8.
   - f. [ ] Decedent was survived by next of kin, all of whom are listed in item 8.
   - g. [ ] Decedent was survived by parents of a predeceased spouse or issue of those parents, if both are predeceased, all of whom are listed in item 8.
   - h. [ ] Decedent was survived by no known next of kin.

7. *(Complete only if no spouse or issue survived decedent.)*
   - a. [ ] Decedent had no predeceased spouse.
   - b. [ ] Decedent had a predeceased spouse who
     - (1) [ ] died not more than 15 years before decedent and who owned an interest in **real property** that passed to decedent,
     - (2) [ ] died not more than five years before decedent and who owned **personal property** valued at $10,000 or more that passed to decedent, *(If you checked (1) or (2), check only the* ***first*** *box that applies):*
       - (a) [ ] Decedent was survived by issue of a predeceased spouse, all of whom are listed in item 8.
       - (b) [ ] Decedent was survived by a parent or parents of the predeceased spouse who are listed in item 8.
       - (c) [ ] Decedent was survived by issue of a parent of the predeceased spouse, all of whom are listed in item 8.
       - (d) [ ] Decedent was survived by next of kin of the decedent, all of whom are listed in item 8.
       - (e) [ ] Decedent was survived by next of kin of the predeceased spouse, all of whom are listed in item 8.
     - (3) [ ] neither (1) nor (2) apply.

8. Listed on the next page are the names, relationships to decedent, ages, and addresses, so far as known to or reasonably ascertainable by petitioner, of (1) all persons mentioned in decedent's will or any codicil, whether living or deceased; (2) all persons named or checked in items 2, 5, 6, and 7; and (3) all beneficiaries of a trust named in decedent's will or any codicil in which the trustee and personal representative are the same person.

Petition for Probate (page 4)

DE-111

ESTATE OF *(name)*: ANABELLE KIDD, aka ANABELLE O.KIDD, DECEDENT	CASE NUMBER:

8. Name and relationship to decedent	Age	Address
Mary Kidd Clark, daughter	Adult	789 Main Street, Venice CA 90410
Billy M. Kidd, son	Adult	1109 Sky Blue Mountain Trail, Billings, Montana 48906
Jon Kidd, son (predeceased decedent 4-5-82)		
Carson Kidd, grandson (son of Jon Kidd)	Adult	711 Valley Road, Owens, California 98455
Calvin Kidd, spouse (predeceased decedent 11-3-08)		
Pat Garret, alternate executor	Adult	25 So. Corral Street, Santa Fe, New Mexico 57256
Albertine Terreux, non-relative	Adult	17 Rue Madeleine, Paris, France
Consulate of France	n/a	8350 Wilshire Blvd., Los Angeles, California 90035

☐ Continued on Attachment 8.

9. Number of pages attached: 3

Date:

(TYPE OR PRINT NAME OF ATTORNEY) ▶ (SIGNATURE OF ATTORNEY) *

* (Signatures of all petitioners are also required. All petitioners must sign, but the petition may be verified by any one of them (Prob. Code, §§ 1020, 1021; Cal. Rules of Court, rule 7.103).)

I declare under penalty of perjury under the laws of the State of California that the foregoing is true and correct.

Date: July 5, 20xx

Billy M. Kidd ▶ Billy M. Kidd

(TYPE OR PRINT NAME OF PETITIONER) (SIGNATURE OF PETITIONER)

▶

(TYPE OR PRINT NAME OF PETITIONER) (SIGNATURE OF PETITIONER)

Signatures of additional petitioners follow last attachment.

Petition for Probate (Attachment 3e)

Estate of Anabelle Kidd, aka Anabelle O. Kidd, deceased

Petition for Probate

Attachment 3e - Waiver of Bond

Petitioner has personal knowledge of the decedent's financial affairs. The current known liabilities of the estate consist of last illness expenses in the total amount of $4,300 and there are sufficient probate assets to guarantee payment of these expenses. There are no known other unsecured creditors, contingent liabilities or tax liabilities, and the estate is solvent. Therefore, petitioner requests that no bond be required while he is serving as personal representative.

- If the original, signed will is not available, yet you will submit a copy or other evidence of a will, you will check the box before the word "Lost" on the appropriate line. (See Chapter 13.) Read on to see which line you will use. Otherwise, read the first two lines as if the word "Lost" were not there.
- If there is a will and you are the executor named in the will, check the box before "Probate of [ ] Lost Will and for Letters Testamentary." Again, the word "Lost" only applies if the box before that word is checked.

  If there is a will but no executor is named, or the named executor is unable or unwilling to act and no coexecutor or successor is named, you will petition to serve as "administrator with will annexed." Check the box at the beginning of the second line, before "Probate of [ ] Lost Will and for Letters of Administration with Will Annexed."

  If there is no will, check the box before "Letters of Administration."

  Leave the box before "Letters of Special Administration" blank.
- Check the next to last box, which says "Authorization to Administer Under the Independent Administration of Estates Act." Make sure the will doesn't prohibit this. (See Chapter 13.) Even if it does, you can probably still use the procedures outlined in this chapter, but you shouldn't check the box requesting authorization to use independent administration procedures.

  Be aware that some courts refuse to give full independent authority to self-represented estate representatives. Check local policy to avoid delays and extra work.

  Unless real property of the estate will be sold during probate, we recommend you also check the last box, before the words "with limited authority." This means you request all of the powers granted by the Independent Administration of Estates Act except the power to sell, or otherwise deal with, real property. If you do need to sell real property during probate, see Step 13.

  If you request full authority and the estate contains real property, the court may require you to post a bond for the value of the cash that would be received on the sale of the real property, unless bond is waived in the decedent's will. Some courts require such a bond even if the heirs and beneficiaries have all filed written waivers.

Item 1. This item pertains to publication of the Notice of Petition to Administer Estate (DE-121), which is discussed in Step 3, below. Selecting the proper newspaper is very important. The best way to handle this is to first check local rules, and then, if necessary, ask the court clerk for the names of newspapers of general circulation, if any, in the city where the decedent lived at the time of death. Then contact the newspaper to make arrangements for publication of the notice. Most newspapers are familiar with the requirements. Ask if they will prepare and file the required affidavit giving proof of the publication with the court. If not, you will have to do it yourself. (See Step 3.) You pay the newspaper publication fee in advance, which can be $200 or more. Fees vary by newspaper, so you can compare fees if you have the choice of multiple newspapers. Weekly newspapers, for example, may cost less but their limited publishing dates may make time tight to comply with the notice requirements before the hearing. After you have determined the newspaper you will use, enter the newspaper's name in Item 1, and check Box 1b indicating that publication is being arranged for.

Item 2. Enter your name, as petitioner, on this line. If there are multiple petitioners, enter all names.

Item 2a. If there is a will, check this box.

Item 2b. Check the first box and, on the same line, enter your name and the name of any other petitioners (that is, if you will have a coexecutor or coadministrator). Check Box (1), (2), or (3), whichever applies to your situation. (See Chapter 13 if you are in doubt.) Leave Box (4) blank.

Item 2c. If the estate contains real property that will be sold during probate, check the box requesting full authority under the Act. Otherwise, check the second box requesting limited authority. This must be consistent with the box checked above in the "Petition for" section.

Receipt and Agreement by Depository

Name:
Address:

Telephone No.:

Petitioner, Self-represented

SUPERIOR COURT OF CALIFORNIA

COUNTY OF ____________

Estate of	) No.____________
(name of decedent),	) RECEIPT AND AGREEMENT BY
deceased.	) DEPOSITORY (Prob. Code
____________	) § 541.1)

The undersigned acknowledges receipt from ____________ ____________, personal representative of the estate of the above-named decedent, of the following items of personal property:

a. 200 shares of Miracle Corporation common stock

b. Cash in sum of $12,000

The undersigned agrees that the foregoing cash and securities will be held by the undersigned for the personal representative, and will permit withdrawals only upon express order of the above-entitled court.

DATE: ____________, 20____

WESTERN STATES BANK

By:____________

(authorized officer)

Item 2d. You probably won't have to post a bond if all beneficiaries or all heirs waive the bond, or if the will waives the requirement of a bond, unless the court orders otherwise. (See Chapter 13.) Assuming you will be able to get waivers (if bond isn't waived by the will), check Box (1), which says "bond not be required." If it is preferable to deposit assets into a blocked account to avoid or reduce the amount of a bond, check Box (3) and fill in the name and address of the institution.

It is not always possible to obtain possession of the decedent's assets before being appointed representative and receiving letters. Arrangements can be made in advance by allowing a bank or trust company to retain on deposit money already in its possession. Or, the deposit may also be made after the Order for Probate is signed but before the letters are issued. Either alternative results in a bond in a reduced amount.

You must obtain a written receipt from the depository acknowledging its agreement that it will not allow any withdrawals except on court order. (Prob. Code § 8401(b).) The receipt should be filed with the court either with the petition or after letters are issued, depending on when the deposit is made. The sample receipt shown below is accepted in most courts.

Item 3a. Enter the date and city and state of the decedent's death, and check the appropriate box under Item 3a. You must file the petition in the county of the decedent's residence in California, wherever the place of death. (See Chapter 13.) If the decedent was not a resident of California, file the petition in the California county where the decedent left real property or tangible personal property in California. If the decedent was a resident of the county in which you are filing your petition, check Box (1). If not a resident of California but the decedent left real or tangible personal property here, check Box (2) and enter the address of the property.

Item 3b. If the decedent was a citizen of a country other than the United States, check the box for Item 3b and enter the country.

Item 3c. Enter the street address, city, and county where the decedent lived at the time of death. (See Chapter 2, "Determine the Residence of the Decedent.")

Item 3d. Enter the estimated value of the property of the probate estate. (Use the estimate from the Schedule of Assets—see Chapter 5.) Enter the value of personal property (Item 3d(1)) plus the gross fair market value of real property (Item 3d(4)). Enter the amount of any encumbrances on the real property (Item 3d(5)). List the annual gross income from real property and personal property (Item 3d(2)). Complete the calculations (Items 3d(3), (6), and (7)). Remember that personal property includes all assets that are not real property—for example, stocks, bank accounts, and household items. Include only property subject to probate administration. (See Chapter 5, particularly Column E of the Schedule of Assets). If any of the assets are community property, under most circumstances include only the decedent's one-half interest. (See Chapter 4.) This information is used to determine the amount of bond, when one is required.

Item 3e. If the will waives the requirement of a bond, on line (1) check the first box and leave the second one blank. If it doesn't waive bond, but does not specifically state that bond is required, check Box (2) and attach a Waiver of Bond as Attachment 3e(2) (as shown below) signed by each beneficiary named in the will. If there is no will, check Box (3) and attach a Waiver of Bond signed by each heir as Attachment 3e(3). Leave Box (4) blank.

In addition, when a waiver of bond is requested, some courts (for example, Los Angeles, San Diego, and San Francisco) require a statement by the petitioner regarding knowledge of any creditors of the decedent and the amount of any debts. The Attachment 3e shown at the end of our sample petition, above, may be revised to conform to your situation. We recommend this information be included in all petitions requesting that bond be waived. Even so, the court may require a bond.

Item 3f. If the decedent did not leave a will, check Box (1). If the decedent died with a will, check Box (2), enter the date of the will, and attach a copy of the will, labeled Attachment 3f(2), to your petition. If there are any codicils, check the box before "codicil dated," enter those dates, and attach a copy of the codicil. If the will is holographic (handwritten by the decedent), prepare an accurate typed copy and attach it along with a photocopy of the handwritten will as Attachment 3f(2).

Waiver of Bond by Heir or Beneficiary

DE-142/DE-111(A-3e)

ATTORNEY OR PARTY WITHOUT ATTORNEY: STATE BAR NO.:	FOR COURT USE ONLY
NAME: Billy M. Kidd FIRM NAME: STREET ADDRESS: 1109 Sky Blue Mountain Trail CITY: Billings STATE: MT ZIP CODE: 48906 TELEPHONE NO.: 715-555-6408 FAX NO.: E-MAIL ADDRESS: ATTORNEY FOR (*name*): Self-represented	
SUPERIOR COURT OF CALIFORNIA, COUNTY OF LOS ANGELES STREET ADDRESS: 111 North Hill Street MAILING ADDRESS: 111 North Hill Street CITY AND ZIP CODE: Los Angeles, CA 90012 BRANCH NAME: Central District	
ESTATE OF (*Name*): **ANABELLE KIDD, aka ANABELLE O. KIDD** , DECEDENT	
WAIVER OF BOND BY HEIR OR BENEFICIARY [x] **Attachment 3e to *Petition for Probate****	CASE NUMBER:

NOTICE: READ PARAGRAPHS A–G BEFORE YOU SIGN

A. A bond is a form of insurance to replace assets that may be mismanaged or stolen by the executor or administrator (the estate's **personal representative**). The cost of the bond is paid from the assets of the estate.

B. A bond may not be required if the decedent's will admitted to probate waives a bond and the court approves.

C. If the decedent's will does not waive bond, or if the decedent died without a will, the law ordinarily requires the personal representative to give a bond approved and ordered by the court. However, all persons eligible to receive a share of the estate may waive the requirement of a bond. If they all waive bond and the court approves, the personal representative will NOT have to give a bond.

D. **If bond is not ordered by the court, and the estate suffers loss because the personal representative fails to properly perform the duties of the office, the loss or some part of it may not be recoverable from the personal representative. If so, your share of the estate may be partly or entirely lost.**

E. You may waive the requirement of a bond by signing this form and delivering it to the petitioner for appointment of a personal representative or to the petitioner's attorney. Your waiver cannot be withdrawn after the court appoints the personal representative without requiring a bond. However, if you sign a waiver of bond, you may later petition the court to require a bond.

F. A guardian ad litem or other legal representative with specific authority under law to waive bond must sign for a minor, an incapacitated person, an unascertained beneficiary, or a designated class of persons who are not ascertained or not yet in being. See Judicial Council forms DE-350 and DE-351 and Probate Code section 1003.

G. **If you do not understand this form, do not sign it until you have asked a lawyer (who is independent of the lawyer for the proposed personal representative) to explain it to you.**

WAIVER

1. **I have read and understand paragraphs A through G above.**
2. **I understand that before signing this form, I am free to consult with a lawyer of my choice concerning the possible consequences to me of waiving bond.**
3. **I understand that I do not have to waive bond to allow the estate administration to begin or proceed, or to receive my share of the estate.**
4. **I WAIVE the posting of bond in this estate by** *(name of personal representative):* **Billy M. Kidd**

Date: July 1, 20xx

Mary Kidd Clark
(TYPE OR PRINT NAME OF BENEFICIARY (AND AUTHORIZED SIGNER, IF BENEFICIARY IS NOT AN INDIVIDUAL))

▶ *Mary Kidd Clark*
(SIGNATURE)

(This form may be filed as an independent form (as form DE-142) OR as Attachment 3e(2) (will) or Attachment 3e(3) (intestacy) to the* Petition for Probate *(form DE-111) (as form DE-111(A-3e).)

Form Adopted for Mandatory Use
Judicial Council of California
DE-142/DE-111(A-3e) [Rev. July 1, 2017]

WAIVER OF BOND BY HEIR OR BENEFICIARY
(Probate—Decedents Estates)

Probate Code, § 8481
www.courts.ca.gov
Page____ of ____

Nomination: Attachment 3g(1)(c)

Estate of ____________________, deceased

Attachment 3g(1)(c) to Petition for Probate

NOMINATION OF ADMINISTRATOR WITH WILL ANNEXED

The person named as executor in the decedent's will predeceased the decedent, and the undersigned, being beneficiaries of more than one-half of the estate, hereby nominate ____________________________, a resident of the State of California and over the age of majority, as administrator of the decedent's estate with the will annexed.

DATED: ____________, 20__

____

____

Nomination - Attachment 3g(1)(c)

Declination: Attachment 3g(1)(d)

Estate of ____________________, deceased

Attachment 3g(1)(d) to Petition for Probate

DECLINATION

The undersigned, named as executor in the decedent's will, hereby declines to act and renounces all right to receive Letters Testamentary herein.

DATED: ______________, 20__

____

____

Declination - Attachment 3g(1)(d)

Nomination: Attachment 3g(2)(b)

Estate of ______________________, deceased

Attachment 3g(2)(b) to Petition for Probate

NOMINATION OF ADMINISTRATOR

The undersigned, ______________________, surviving spouse of the above-named decedent, hereby nominates ____________________________, a resident of the State of California and over the age of majority, to serve as administrator of the estate of the deceased.

DATED: ______________, 20__

____

____

Nomination - Attachment 3g(2)(b)

If the witnessed will and all codicils are self-proving (that is, language in the will makes further verification by the witnesses unnecessary), check the box under Item 3f(2) that indicates this. See Chapter 13 for an explanation of self-proving wills and codicils. Be sure to check if your county accepts self-proving wills. Otherwise, you must file a Proof of Subscribing Witness form (discussed in Step 5) before the hearing date on your petition.

If the original wills or codicils are not available, check the box for Item 3f(3). You will need to provide evidence of the terms of the lost will or codicil—usually a copy of the signed document—as well as reasons to believe that decedent did not intend to destroy or revoke the original will. (See "Lost Will" in Chapter 13.) Attach a copy of the will or codicil and a statement of relevant facts as Attachment 3f(3).

Item 3g(1). The boxes under Section (1) of Item 3g apply only if the decedent left a will. If there is no will, skip Section (1) and go to Section (2) under Item 3g.

Complete Item 3g(1) as follows:

- If the will names you as executor, check Box (a).
- If the will does not name an executor, check Box (b).
- If the executors named in the will are unable or unwilling to act (due to death, illness, declining to act, or another reason), check Box (d), indicating the reason by checking one of the additional boxes that follow. Then prepare either a Declination to Act signed by the person who declines to serve (as shown below) or check Box (d) and provide the reason why the named executor cannot act. Attach the signed declination to the petition as Attachment 3g(1). (See Chapter 2 for the rules governing how an administrator with will annexed is chosen under these circumstances.) If you are petitioning as the executor named in the will, and a person named with higher priority than you or a person named as your coexecutor cannot act, check Box (a) as well as Box (d).
- If a person named in the will as executor declines to serve and nominates you as the personal representative, check Box (c), and attach a nomination as Attachment 3g(1)(c). The wording of the nomination should be similar to the sample nomination (Attachment 3g(2)(b), for intestate situations) shown above. Use Item 3g(1)(d), too, to explain why the named executor will not serve (unless the nominated person and the named executor will serve together).

Item 3g(2). Complete Section (2) under Item 3g if the decedent died without a will. Review the discussion in "Who Will Represent the Estate?" in Chapter 13, before completing Section (2). If you are entitled by priority to be administrator, check Box (a). Provide a statement as Attachment 3g(2)(a) explaining your relationship to the decedent and how you have priority—for example "Petitioner is the only sibling of the decedent, and decedent had no surviving spouse or domestic partner, child, grandchild, or parent." If someone who would otherwise have priority to be administrator instead nominates you to serve, check Box (b) and attach a nomination as Attachment 3g(2)(b), as shown in the sample above. If you, as the proposed administrator, are related to the decedent, check Box (c) and indicate the relationship, in addition to checking either Box (a) or Box (b).

Items 3g(3) and 3g(4). Leave these boxes blank.

Item 3h. You will check two boxes in this section. Check either Box (1) or Box (2), depending on whether or not you are a resident of California. Include your permanent address if you are a nonresident of California. Also check either Box (3) or Box (4), depending on whether or not you are a resident of the United States. A person does not have to be a resident of California to be an administrator, but must be a resident of the United States. An executor named in the will may reside anywhere.

Item 4. Before checking this box, read the will to make sure it does not prohibit you from using the procedures of the Independent Administration of Estates Act. Wills rarely prohibit this. See the comments in Chapter 13 regarding this situation.

Note on Items 5, 6, and 7. These items request information necessary to determine the decedent's heirs (people who inherit the estate in the absence of a will). Even if the decedent left a will, you must still list the heirs. Before completing these sections, carefully review Chapter 3, which gives detailed information on how to determine the heirs of a decedent. Chapter 3 also explains the meaning of certain common legal terminology, such as issue, predeceased spouse, and child.

Item 5a. You will check at least four boxes in this section. Follow the instructions carefully because it's easy to miss a necessary box. Check Box (1) if the decedent left a surviving spouse. If no spouse, check Box (2) and one of the next boxes indicating whether divorced, never married, or spouse deceased. Check Box (3) if the decedent is survived by a registered domestic partner. If not, check Box (4). Check Box (5) if the decedent left surviving children, and then indicate (by checking one or both of the boxes below) whether any child is natural or adopted, or natural adopted by a third party. "Natural" means biological. (See Chapter 3 for a definition of child as it pertains to each of these situations.) If there are no children, check Box (6). If the decedent had a child who died before the decedent (a predeceased child), and the predeceased child left issue (child, grandchild, or great-grandchild) who are now living, check Box (7). If there are no issue of a predeceased child now living, check Box (8).

Item 5b. Check the first box only if you know that the decedent had a parent-child relationship (as defined in Chapter 3) with a stepchild or foster child. You are required to give such persons notice of the probate proceeding. Otherwise, check the second box.

Many attorneys recommend that notice be served on all known stepchildren or foster children, whether or not you reasonably believe they might have had a parent-child relationship with the decedent, as described in Probate Code Section 6454.

Item 6. If decedent is survived by any issue (children, grandchildren, and so on), skip Item 6. Otherwise, one box should be checked. To determine which one to check, read these two options and follow the one that fits your situation:

Option One

If the decedent is survived by a spouse or domestic partner, then only Box a or b applies:

Box 6a. If the decedent is survived by a spouse or domestic partner and a parent or parents, check this box.

Box 6b. If there is a surviving spouse or domestic partner, no surviving parents, but surviving siblings or issue of deceased siblings (such as nieces, nephews, or their descendants), check this box.

Option Two

If the decedent left no spouse or domestic partner and no children or issue of deceased children (grandchildren, etc.), then check the first box under Item 6 that applies:

Box 6a. If there is a parent (or parents) surviving, check Box a and no other.

Box 6b. If no parents are living, but there are descendants of deceased parents living (siblings of the decedent, or their descendants), then check Box b only.

Box 6c. If the decedent is survived by a grandparent or grandparents, but none of the people listed for Boxes a and b, check this box.

Box 6d. If there are issue of the decedent's grandparents surviving (uncles, aunts, or cousins of the decedent), but none of the people listed in Boxes a through c, check Box d.

Box 6e. This box applies if the decedent had a predeceased spouse or domestic partner (a spouse or domestic partner who died before the decedent while married or partnered to the decedent) whose issue (children, grandchildren, etc.) are living. In this case (if Boxes a, b, c, and d do not apply), check Box e.

Box 6f. If Boxes a through e do not apply, check Box f if relatives survive. You will need to determine the next of kin by reviewing the charts in Chapter 3.

Box 6g. This box applies if a parent or parents of a predeceased spouse or domestic partner or their issue (brothers, sisters, nieces, nephews, and so on) are living.

Box 6h. Check this box if no prior box applies and there is no known next of kin.

Item 7. This section is for determining distribution of real and personal property when there is a predeceased spouse or domestic partner. Complete Item 7 in all cases where the decedent left no surviving spouse, domestic partner, or issue. Check Box a if the decedent did not have a predeceased spouse or domestic partner. Or, check Box b if the decedent had a predeceased spouse or domestic partner. If you check Box b, then continue to the subsections.

If there is no valid will, and the decedent is not survived by a spouse, domestic partner, or issue, Probate Code Section 6402.5 provides that property inherited from a predeceased spouse or domestic partner may pass by intestate succession to relatives of the predeceased spouse or domestic partner. The rules apply differently depending on whether the inherited property is real property or personal property, and depending on how long the decedent survived the predeceased spouse or domestic partner. Under Item 7b:

- Check Box (1) if the decedent inherited real property from a spouse or domestic partner who died less than 15 years before the decedent, or
- Check Box (2) if the decedent inherited personal property totaling $10,000 from a spouse or domestic partner who died not more than five years before the decedent.
- Check Box (3) if neither Box (1) nor Box (2) applies.

If you checked either Box (1) or Box (2), then continue to check the first applicable lettered box ((a), (b), etc.) that applies and list the relatives of the predeceased spouse or domestic partner under Item 8, below.

The heirs determined under Probate Code Section 6402.5 have priority over the heirs in Item 6.

EXAMPLE: Joe and Ruth owned a home together as community property when they were married. Ruth died, leaving her half interest in the house to Joe. Joe never had children; Ruth had a child from a previous marriage. After Ruth died, Joe did not remarry and did not have any children. When Joe dies without a will 14 years after Ruth's death, the one-half interest in the house that was Ruth's goes to Ruth's child. (Even if Joe left a will, you would be required to list Ruth's child in the petition as a possible intestate heir along with the beneficiaries in the will. If Joe's will is later admitted to probate as his valid will and the will gives the property to someone else, Ruth's child does not inherit anything.)

Item 8: List the name, relationship, age, and residence or mailing address of everyone mentioned in the decedent's will and codicils (if any), whether as a beneficiary, whether living or deceased, plus all persons checked in Items 2, 5, 6, and 7, above. If you list second-generation heirs, also list the relevant deceased ancestor of the prior generation, and state the deceased ancestor's relationship to the decedent. You are not required to make impractical and extended searches, but you must make reasonably diligent efforts to ascertain all heirs and beneficiaries of the decedent. (Prob. Code § 8002(a)(3).) You should also list all alternate executors named in the will, if any. Each living person listed in Item 8 will be mailed a notice of the hearing on the petition. Persons not related to the decedent by blood or marriage or adoption are designated as "not related." You can show their ages as either "under 18" or "over 18." This alerts the court to the possible need of a guardian if assets will be distributed to a minor.

Generally, don't use an "in care of" address. If more than one person in a household is listed, each should get a separate notice—including all minors who live at the same address.

When listing persons named in the decedent's will and codicils, here are some things you should watch for to make sure you list everyone the court will require:

1. If any of the beneficiaries named in the will or codicil died before the decedent, list the deceased beneficiary's name, relationship to the decedent, and approximate date of death, if known. If the predeceased beneficiary was related to the decedent (kindred), then list the deceased beneficiary's issue, if any (that is, children, grandchildren, etc.), specifically identifying them as "child of…." The reason for this is that the issue of a predeceased beneficiary who was kindred of the decedent may inherit the predeceased beneficiary's share of the estate. (See Chapter 3.) If the predeceased beneficiary had no issue, state that. For example, "Robert Jones (predeceased decedent on 12-5-11; no surviving issue)."
2. If an heir or will beneficiary dies after the decedent, and a personal representative has been appointed for that person, list the name of the deceased heir or beneficiary with a notation that the person is deceased, followed by the name and address of the personal representative. For example, "John Doe (postdeceased decedent on March 17, 2016)/ Jack Smith, Executor,

123 Main Street, Sun City, CA 90000." If no personal representative has been appointed, list the beneficiary name as deceased and note that no personal representative has been appointed. When this is the case, notice should be sent to the beneficiaries of the postdeceased heir or beneficiary, or to other persons entitled to that person's interest in the decedent's estate. (See California Rule of Court, Rule 7.51.)

3. If the will has a pour-over provision, meaning that property passes to a trust, list each trustee of that trust as a beneficiary of the will. If the trustee and the personal representative are the same person, you must also list the names and addresses of all the beneficiaries of the trust so they will receive notice. In addition, you must state whether the trust was executed after, before, or concurrently with the execution of the will, and whether or not the trust was later revoked. (Prob. Code § 6300.)
4. If the decedent's will or codicil makes a gift to a nonrelative who died before the decedent, then the gift lapses or goes to an alternate beneficiary identified by the will. (See Chapter 3.) It is not necessary to list the deceased beneficiary's issue, because they will not inherit anything. However, be sure to list any alternate beneficiaries named in the will. For instance, if the will contains this provision: "I give my stamp collection to my friend Sam. In the event Sam predeceases me, I give my stamp collection to my friend John," Sam should be listed as a deceased beneficiary (if he died before the decedent), and John should be listed as the alternate beneficiary.
5. If the will requires any beneficiary to survive the decedent for a certain period of time and that time has not yet passed, list by name the contingent beneficiary. For example: "I give all my jewelry to my sister Mary if she survives me for a period of six months. In the event my sister Mary does not survive me for a period of six months, I give all of my jewelry to my niece, Ellen." In this case, you should list Ellen as a contingent beneficiary who will inherit the jewelry in the event Mary does not survive for six months following the decedent's death. It isn't necessary to label Ellen as a contingent beneficiary; her name and address will merely be included with the other beneficiaries.
6. List any person named as a beneficiary in the will even if subsequently deleted in a codicil. For example, if paragraph four of the will says, "I give $5,000 to my brother, Robert," and a later codicil says, "I delete paragraph four of my will in its entirety," then Robert should be listed in Item 8. The reason for this is that if the codicil is proven to be invalid, Robert would inherit the $5,000.
7. You should list any executor named in the will who is not joining in the petition. For example, if the will names two persons to act as executors and only one signs the petition requesting to be appointed, then list the other person in Item 8 as a person interested in the estate. If the will lists alternate executors, list them as well. Executors who were named in any earlier wills should also be listed. Again, there is no need to identify them as "nonpetitioning coexecutor" or "alternate executor."
8. If the will refers to people only by category, such as "my children," "my issue," or "my brother's children," list the names of all people in this category in Item 8 and specify their relationship. For instance, if the will gives property to "my brother's children," then you would list them by name and specify their relationship as "child of decedent's brother Alfred." See Chapter 3 for definitions of the more commonly used group terms, especially if your situation involves adopted children, stepchildren, or foster children.
9. If it appears that property may pass to a citizen of a foreign nation, you must list the consul of that nation in Item 8 and give notice of the filing of the petition as a formality. For example, if the will leaves property to Françoise Terreux, a French citizen, you would list Françoise as the beneficiary, giving her address, and you would also list the French consul and its local address. The county clerk may provide a list of local

foreign consular offices. You may also be able to get the relevant contact information from the U.S. Department of State website. Or, try an online search for "foreign consular offices in the U.S." If an heir or beneficiary is a U.S. citizen merely residing in a foreign country, you do not have to list the foreign consul. In this latter case, you should indicate that the beneficiary is a U.S. citizen.

10. If any beneficiary or heir is a minor, list the child and the person (or persons) who has custody of the minor. Give notice to each.
11. Beneficiaries that are organizations must also be listed and given notice.

When You Can't Locate an Heir or Beneficiary

If you can't find the address for an heir or beneficiary, you must prepare a "Declaration of Diligent Search" to let the court know what steps you have taken to locate the person. California Rules of Court, Rule 7.52 contains the requirements. Prepare the declaration and attach it to the petition. The petition should state the name of the missing person, last known address, approximate date when the person was last known to reside there, the efforts you made to locate the person, and any facts that explain why you cannot obtain the person's address. A "diligent search" requires that you search for the person using obvious sources of information, such as:

- relatives, friends, acquaintances, and employers of the missing person and of the decedent
- last known address
- telephone directories
- online directories, and
- the real and personal property indexes at the recorder's and assessor's office in the county where the person was last known or believed to reside.

When the court reviews the declaration with the petition, it will either decide that enough has been done to find the person, or it will tell you what else you need to do to give the person notice of the court proceeding.

12. If the will lists a beneficiary or executor by an inaccurate or outdated name, list the current name and add in parentheses: "(named in the will as ______________________________)."

Item 9. Fill in the number of pages of attachments.

Signature and Verification. The petitioner must sign the petition on page 4 near the bottom. Type or print the petitioner's name on the line at the left, and be sure to fill in the date above. If there are two petitioners, both must sign. Leave the signature line for the attorney blank or put "not applicable." All court forms should be signed in blue ink, not black, so the originals can be distinguished from copies.

Step 2: Prepare the Certificate of Assignment

This is a local form required in some, but not all, counties that have branch courts. Branch courts are usually found in larger counties. These smaller courts in outlying districts serve the same function as the main court. The form requests that the court assign the probate matter to the main court or a particular branch court because the decedent resided within the district. The local rules for the county will tell you if a specific form is required. Also, confirm whether there are any case-tracking forms required by your court. This information can be obtained on the court's website or by contacting the clerk's office.

Step 3: Prepare the Notice of Petition to Administer Estate

When you file the Petition for Probate (DE-111), the court clerk assigns it a hearing date. Notice of the time and date of the hearing must then be given to certain persons. If the notice is not properly given, the petition will not be approved, so give careful attention to these procedures. You must give the notice using the Notice of Petition to Administer Estate (DE-121) form in two ways. Instructions for completing the form appear below. You will prepare the form, but will not publish or mail it until after filing the petition and obtaining the hearing date (see Step 4).

Certificate of Assignment – Los Angeles Superior Court (page 1)

TITLE OF CASE	CASE NUMBER

PROBATE CASE COVERSHEET AND CERTIFICATE OF GROUNDS FOR ASSIGNMENT TO DISTRICT

This form is required for all new probate cases filed in the Los Angeles Superior Court.

Step 1: In the "Type of Action" column below, select **one** type of action that best describes the nature of this case by checking a box.

Step 2: Across from the "Type of Action" you selected, place an "X" in the column that corresponds to the reason for your choice of district. Note that you may only select from the boxes that are not shaded.

TYPE OF ACTION (check one) ▼	District where one or more parties resides	District where proposed conservatee, person w/o capacity or minor resides nor or proposed conservatee resides	District where petitioner resides	District where decedent resided	Decedent, conservatee or minor not CA resident but property is in district	Principal place of trust administration (Probate Code § 17002)	Other statutory authority (list statute): ___ Or may be filed in Central Dist. per LASC Rule 2.3(b)
Decedent's Estate							
□ Petition – Letters of Administration (Initial) [3069]							
□ Petition – Letters of Special Admin w/Gen Powers (Initial) [3070]							
□ Petition – Letters of Special Admin w/o Gen Powers (Initial) [3071]							
□ Petition – Probate of Lost Will (Initial) [3074]							
□ Petition – Probate of Will (Initial) [3075]							
Conservatorship							
□ Petition – Appoint Conservator of Estate – Attend/Nominate (Initial) [3303] *(Note: The proposed conservatee will appear at the hearing and has nominated the proposed conservator.)*							
□ Petition – Appoint Conservator of Estate Only (Initial) [3046]							
□ Petition – Appoint Conservator of Person Only (Initial) [3047]							
□ Petition – Appoint Conservator of Person & Estate (Initial) [3048]							
□ Petition – Appoint Ltd Conservator of Person/Person & Estate (Initial) [3198]							
Guardianship							
□ Petition – Appoint Guardian of Estate Only (Initial) [3049]							
□ Petition – Appoint Guardian of Person Only (Initial) [3051]							
□ Petition – Appoint Guardian of Person & Estate (Initial) [3050]							
Trust							
□ Accounting – Trust (Initial) [3229]							
□ Notice – Initial Trust Filing & Notice to Creditors [3038]							
□ Petition – Special Needs Trust (Initial) [3297]							
□ Petition – Trust/Pursuant Prob Code Sec 17200 (Initial) [3076]							
Minor's Compromise							
□ Petition – Approve Minor's Compromise (Initial) [3058]							
□ Petition – Approve Minor's Compromise (Expedited) [3154]							

Certificate of Assignment – Los Angeles Superior Court (page 2)

TYPE OF ACTION (check one) ▼	District where one or more parties resides	District where proposed conservatee, person w/o capacity or minor resides nor or proposed conservatee resides	District where petitioner resides	District where decedent resided	Decedent, conservatee or minor not CA resident but property is in district	Principal place of trust administration (Probate Code § 17002)	Other statutory authority (list statute):___ Or may be filed in Central Dist. per LASC Rule 2.3(b)
Other Probate Matters							
Other Probate With At Least One Hearing							
□ Petition – Advance Health Care Directive (Initial) [3044]							
□ Petition – Appoint Successor Custodian/CUTMA (Initial) [3052]							
□ Petition – Authority to Give Medical Consent w/o Conservatorship (Initial) [3059]							
□ Petition – Determine Succession to Real Property (Initial) [3301]							
□ Petition – Establish Fact of: □ Birth [3065], □ Death [3066], or □ Marriage [3067]							
□ Petition – Release of Decedent's Remains (Initial) [3077]							
□ Petition – Spousal/Domestic Partner Property (Initial) [3179]							
□ Petition – Transaction Where Spouse Lacks Capacity (Initial) [3082]							
□ Petition – Tuberculosis Matter [3083]							
□ Other Probate matter (specify): ____________							
Other Probate With No Hearing							
□ Affidavit – Real Property of Small Value - Prob Code Sec 13200 [3001]							
□ Petition – Order Setting Aside Estate of Small Value (Prob Code Sec 6602) [3292]							
□ Petition – Summary Probate (Public Administrator) [3081]							

Step 3: Select the appropriate district:

□ Central □ North (Antelope Valley)

The undersigned hereby certifies that the above entitled matter is properly filed for assignment to the ____________ District of the Los Angeles Superior Court pursuant to the California Probate Code and Rule 2.3 of this court for the reason checked above. I declare under penalty of perjury under the laws of the State of California that the foregoing is true and correct and that this declaration was executed on ____________.
(Date)

____
(Signature of Attorney or Self-Represented Party)

Step 4: Indicate if person filing this petition will require an interpreter:

□ Yes □ No

If yes, what language? ____________________

Certificate of Assignment – Los Angeles Superior Court (page 3)

Step 5: The following information is required for the proposed conservatee, ward, trustor or decedent. Please check the appropriate box for the subject of this case:

□ Conservatee □ Trustor □ Other: ___________

□ Ward (minor in a guardianship case) □ Decedent

Does the subject of this Petition require an interpreter?

□ Yes □ No

If yes, what language?______________________________

First Name	Last Name	Middle Name	Suffix
A.K.A(s)			
Email Address:			
Cell Phone (For Text Messaging):			
I accept service and notices to be delivered to me by [ ] Email [ ] Cell Phone			
Home Address:			
Street			Apt./Suite/Unit #
City		State	Zip Code
Mailing Address: (□ *same as above*)			
Street			Apt./Suite/Unit #
City		State	Zip Code
IDENTIFICATION (For Minors)			
Gender: Male Female		Date of Birth: (mm/dd/yyyy) ____/_____/______	

With changes in procedures resulting from COVID-19, courts may require specific additional information added to the notice. For example, the notice may require specific information about how to attend a hearing remotely or to state objections. Check the local rules and procedures.

Published Notice

Arrange to publish the notice in a newspaper of general circulation in the city where the decedent resided at the time of death (or, if the decedent was a nonresident of California, where the decedent owned property). If there is no such newspaper, or if the decedent did not reside in a city, publish the notice in a newspaper of general circulation that is circulated in the area of the county in which the decedent lived or owned property. (Prob. Code § 8121.) The published notice gives a general notice to creditors and any other persons who may be interested in the estate. (Step 15 explains how to give individual written notice to certain known creditors.) To find the right newspaper, check the local rules or ask the court clerk. If you have a choice, call the newspaper to find out price and publication schedule. You may be surprised at the difference in cost among newspapers. Daily papers are usually the most expensive. As long as the newspaper has been approved by the county, you may pick the least expensive and still meet the legal requirement.

In some counties, including Los Angeles, the court clerk will deliver the notice to the newspaper for publication. If the clerk does not, you will have to see that the newspaper gets a copy of the Notice of Petition to Administer Estate (DE-121) once the petition has been filed and a hearing date set.

The newspaper will publish the notice three times before the date of the court hearing, and the absolute deadline for the first publication is 15 days before the date of the hearing. Three publications in a newspaper published once a week or more often, with at least five days between the first and last publication dates, not counting those dates, are sufficient. Most newspapers are familiar with the publication rules.

Be sure to check the published notice for accuracy as to the case number, title of the notice, dates of publication, and wording. For example, a notice is defective and void if it does not show the name of the court. Also, be sure the notice states that the petition requests authority to administer the estate under the Independent Administration of Estates Act (unless, of course, you have not requested the authority). The wording of the published notice must follow exactly the words on the Notice of Petition to Administer Estate, including the wording of the boxes checked and the filled-in blanks.

After the notice is published, you must file a proof of publication with the court before the hearing date on the petition. Most newspapers have their own form. It must contain a copy of the notice and show the date of its first publication.

Find out if the newspaper will file the proof of publication directly with the court; otherwise, you will have to file it. To avoid delays, follow the local court procedures for having the proof of publication filed far enough in advance of the hearing date for the court's review.

Checklist for Publication of Notice of Petition to Administer Estate

- ✓ Publish the notice in a newspaper of general circulation in the city where the decedent resided at the time of death (or where the decedent owned property, if nonresident). If there is no such newspaper or if the decedent didn't reside in a city or if the property isn't in a city, publication may be made in a newspaper of general circulation that is circulated in the area of the county in which the decedent lived or left property.
- ✓ Publish the notice three times before the date of the court hearing. The first publication must be at least 15 days before the hearing date.
- ✓ Publish the notice three times in a newspaper that is published once a week or more often, with at least five days between the first and last publication dates, not counting those dates.
- ✓ File proof of the publication (by way of an affidavit from the newspaper) with the court before the hearing date on the petition.
- ✓ If the petition requests authority to administer the estate under the Independent Administration of Estates Act, the notice must specify this.

Mailed Notice

Mail the Notice of Petition to Administer Estate by first class mail to all heirs and beneficiaries and other persons named in Item 8 of the petition (see Step 1, Item 8, above) at least 15 days before the hearing date. Although we describe here how to fill out the notice form, the mailing of the notice won't occur won't occur until after the petition is filed and a hearing date set by the court.

Other Ways to Give Notice

Providing notice by first class mail is most common and has the most straightforward requirements. Notice may instead be given by personal delivery or electronic delivery, provided that special requirements are met. If notice is given by personal delivery, that is, handing the notice to the recipient, proof of service will be reported using Judicial Council form DE-120(P). Electronic delivery may only be used where the recipient has expressly agreed to accept electronic service and has provided appropriate notice to you and has filed it with the court. Because the Notice of Petition to Administer Estate occurs at the very start of the probate administration, for our purposes here, we will presume that electronic delivery is not available. If the relevant parties do want to use electronic delivery, carefully investigate the requirements and procedures.

The notice doesn't have to be mailed to the petitioner or anyone joining in the petition, nor to creditors. The notice mailed to creditors uses a different form, discussed in Step 15.

The person doing the mailing must sign a declaration under penalty of perjury on the form, giving proof of the mailing which is filed with the court prior to the hearing. The petitioner cannot mail the notice. Another adult who does not have interest in the estate can sign and mail the form.

Procedures vary in the different court districts as to who prepares the Notice of Petition to Administer Estate and who completes the mailing and publication of the notice. In some circumstances, the legal newspaper may prepare the notice, mail it, prepare and file proof of mailing, publish the notice, and also prepare and file the proof of publication directly with the court. In most circumstances, the petitioner has responsibility to make sure these tasks occur.

Ask the court clerk and/or the newspaper how it is handled in your county. To be safe, you may prepare the notice according to the instructions below, leaving the case number and date of hearing blank, and submit the original and as many copies as you will need for mailing (plus an extra one to be stamped by the court and returned to you for your records) to the court clerk when you file your petition. The clerk will either insert the date of hearing on the notices and return them to you, or notify you of the hearing date by stamping or writing it on your copy of the petition. In some counties, the petitioner is required to fill in the date of hearing according to certain days of the week when such matters are heard in that court. If this is the case, the clerk will advise you. If you pick a date, be sure you give yourself enough time to do the newspaper publication and mail the notice 15 days prior to the hearing.

It is your responsibility to see that the notice is published and mailed, and that proof of the publication and mailing is filed with the court, no matter what procedure is followed.

Instructions for Preparing Notice of Petition to Administer Estate (DE-121)

Heading. Fill in same information as on the Petition for Probate (DE-111). In the last box of the heading (opposite the case number), be sure to enter all names by which the decedent was known.

Item 1. Fill in decedent's name and all variations.

Item 2. Your name goes here. Insert the name of the county on the second line.

Item 3. Put in the name of the personal representative(s).

Item 4. If there is a will, check this box. If not, leave it blank.

Item 5. If you are requesting independent administration authority, check this box. This should match what is requested in the petition, both in the heading and Item 2c.

Item 6. Leave this blank until the court clerk gives you this information.

Item 10. Check the first box and enter your name, address, and telephone number where indicated.

Notice of Petition to Administer Estate (page 1)

DE-121

ATTORNEY OR PARTY WITHOUT ATTORNEY *(Name, State Bar number, and address):*
Billy M. Kidd
1109 Sky Blue Mountain Trail
Billings, Montana 48906
TELEPHONE NO.: 715-555-6408 FAX NO. *(Optional):*
E-MAIL ADDRESS *(Optional):*
ATTORNEY FOR *(Name):* Self-represented

FOR COURT USE ONLY

SUPERIOR COURT OF CALIFORNIA, COUNTY OF
STREET ADDRESS: 111 No. Hill St
MAILING ADDRESS: 111 No. Hill St
CITY AND ZIP CODE: Los Angeles, CA 90012
BRANCH NAME: CENTRAL DISTRICT

ESTATE OF *(Name):*
ANABELLE KIDD, aka ANABELLE O. KIDD, DECEDENT

NOTICE OF PETITION TO ADMINISTER ESTATE OF
(Name): Anabelle Kidd, aka Anabelle O. Kidd

CASE NUMBER: BP 14813

1. To all heirs, beneficiaries, creditors, contingent creditors, and persons who may otherwise be interested in the will or estate, or both, of *(specify all names by which the decedent was known):*
Anabelle Kidd, aka Anabelle O. Kidd, deceased
2. A **Petition for Probate** has been filed by *(name of petitioner):* Billy M. Kidd
in the Superior Court of California, County of *(specify):* LOS ANGELES
3. The Petition for Probate requests that *(name):* Billy M. Kidd
be appointed as personal representative to administer the estate of the decedent.
4. [X] The petition requests the decedent's will and codicils, if any, be admitted to probate. The will and any codicils are available for examination in the file kept by the court.
5. [X] The petition requests authority to administer the estate under the Independent Administration of Estates Act. (This authority will allow the personal representative to take many actions without obtaining court approval. Before taking certain very important actions, however, the personal representative will be required to give notice to interested persons unless they have waived notice or consented to the proposed action.) The independent administration authority will be granted unless an interested person files an objection to the petition and shows good cause why the court should not grant the authority.
6. **A hearing on the petition will be held in this court as follows:**
a. Date: July 25, 20xx Time: 9:30 A.M. Dept.: A Room:
b. Address of court: [X] same as noted above [ ] other *(specify):*
7. **If you object** to the granting of the petition, you should appear at the hearing and state your objections or file written objections with the court before the hearing. Your appearance may be in person or by your attorney.
8. **If you are a creditor or a contingent creditor of the decedent,** you must file your claim with the court and mail a copy to the personal representative appointed by the court within the **later** of either (1) **four months** from the date of first issuance of letters to a general personal representative, as defined in section 58(b) of the California Probate Code, or (2) **60 days** from the date of mailing or personal delivery to you of a notice under section 9052 of the California Probate Code.
Other California statutes and legal authority may affect your rights as a creditor. You may want to consult with an attorney knowledgeable in California law.
9. **You may examine the file kept by the court.** If you are a person interested in the estate, you may file with the court a *Request for Special Notice* (form DE-154) of the filing of an inventory and appraisal of estate assets or of any petition or account as provided in Probate Code section 1250. A *Request for Special Notice* form is available from the court clerk.
10. [X] Petitioner [ ] Attorney for petitioner *(name):* Billy M. Kidd
(Address): 1109 Sky Blue Mountain Trail
Billings, Montana 48906
(Telephone): 715-555-6408

NOTE: If this notice is published, print the caption, beginning with the words NOTICE OF PETITION TO ADMINISTER ESTATE, and do not print the information from the form above the caption. The caption and the decedent's name must be printed in at least 8-point type and the text in at least 7-point type. Print the case number as part of the caption. Print items preceded by a box only if the box is checked. Do not print the italicized instructions in parentheses, the paragraph numbers, the mailing information, or the material on page 2.

Page 1 of 2

Form Adopted for Mandatory Use
Judicial Council of California
DE-121 [Rev. January 1, 2013]

NOTICE OF PETITION TO ADMINISTER ESTATE
(Probate—Decedents' Estates)

Probate Code, §§ 8100, 9100
www.courts.ca.gov

Notice of Petition to Administer Estate (page 2)

DE-121

ESTATE OF *(Name):* Anabelle Kidd, aka Anabelle O. Kidd DECEDENT	CASE NUMBER: BP 14813

PROOF OF SERVICE BY MAIL

1. I am over the age of 18 and not a party to this cause. I am a resident of or employed in the county where the mailing occurred.
2. My residence or business address is *(specify):*
   2328 - 20th Street, Santa Monica, California 90405
3. I served the foregoing *Notice of Petition to Administer Estate* on each person named below by enclosing a copy in an envelope addressed as shown below **AND**
   a. [X] **depositing** the sealed envelope with the United States Postal Service on the date and at the place shown in item 4, with the postage fully prepaid.
   b. [ ] **placing** the envelope for collection and mailing on the date and at the place shown in item 4 following our ordinary business practices. I am readily familiar with this business's practice for collecting and processing correspondence for mailing. On the same day that correspondence is placed for collection and mailing, it is deposited in the ordinary course of business with the United States Postal Service, in a sealed envelope with postage fully prepaid.
4. a. Date mailed: July 8, 20xx b. Place mailed *(city, state):* Santa Monica, California
5. [ ] I served, with the *Notice of Petition to Administer Estate,* a copy of the petition or other document referred to in the notice.

I declare under penalty of perjury under the laws of the State of California that the foregoing is true and correct.

Date: July 8, 20xx

Hilton Waller — (TYPE OR PRINT NAME OF PERSON COMPLETING THIS FORM)

Hilton Waller — (SIGNATURE OF PERSON COMPLETING THIS FORM)

NAME AND ADDRESS OF EACH PERSON TO WHOM NOTICE WAS MAILED

	Name of person served	Address *(number, street, city, state, and zip code)*
1.	Mary Kidd Clark	789 Main Street Venice, California 90410
2.	Carson Kidd	711 Valley Road Owens, California 98455
3.	Pat Garret	25 So. Corral Street Santa Fe, New Mexico 57256
4.	Albertine Terreaux	17 Rue Madeleine Paris, France
5.	Consulate of France	8350 Wilshire Boulevard Los Angeles, California 90035
6.		

[ ] Continued on an attachment. *(You may use form DE-121(MA) to show additional persons served.)*

Assistive listening systems, computer-assisted real-time captioning, or sign language interpreter services are available upon request if at least 5 days notice is provided. Contact the clerk's office for *Request for Accommodations by Persons With Disabilities and Order* (form MC-410). (Civil Code section 54.8.)

Page 2

Fill in the decedent's name and the case number at the top. Complete the Proof of Service by Mail as follows:

Item 2. Fill in the address of the person who mails the notice. The person mailing the notice cannot be the petitioner.

Item 3. Check Box a if the notice was mailed directly by the individual. Box b pertains to businesses (usually law firms) where the notice has been placed for mailing along with other business correspondence on the date and place shown.

Item 4. Fill in date of mailing, and the city and state where mailed.

Item 5. You don't have to check this box unless you prefer to mail a copy of the Petition for Probate (DE-111) along with the notice.

Enter the name of the person who mails the notice, and the date, where indicated. The person who mails the notice should sign the original after the copies of the notice have been mailed. In the space at the bottom of the form, enter the names and addresses of all persons to whom a copy of the notice was mailed. This will be everyone listed in Item 8 of the petition. When the notice is deposited in the mail mailing is complete and the period of notice is not extended. (Prob. Code § 1215(e)).

If you need additional space to show persons served, check the box near the bottom and use the attachment sheet Attachment to Notice to Petition to Administer Estate (DE-121(MA)), provided in Appendix B.

Step 4: File Your Petition for Probate

After you've completed and signed the Petition for Probate (DE-111), you're ready to get it and some other documents ready for your first trip to the courthouse.

TIP

Confirm the court's procedures. To save time and frustration, review the local rules and consult with the court clerk to determine the local court procedures for lodging the will and filing the Petition for Probate. These procedures vary by county and may differ from what this book describes.

Check Petition for Probate for Accuracy and Make Copies

Review the petition carefully to make sure the appropriate schedules are attached and all the proper boxes are checked. If there is a will, attach a copy of it and any codicils to the petition as "Attachment 3f(2)." Make sure all other attachments are properly numbered. It is also important that the signatures on the copies be clear and legible. Make three copies of the petition.

Make Copies of Will and Codicils

Make a few copies of the will and each codicil, if any (and a typed transcript if either is handwritten), for your files. The court will keep the original will once it has been lodged or filed. If the will is not self-proving, you must also obtain either (1) a copy made by the clerk's office *after* the original will is filed, showing the clerk's file stamp and the probate case number, or (2) a copy that has been certified by the court clerk. This is required to prove the will (Step 5).

Make Copies of Notice of Petition to Administer Estate

Make enough copies of the Notice of Petition to Administer Estate (DE-121) to mail to all persons listed in Item 8 of the petition, plus an extra copy for your file. (If the newspaper mails the notice, you don't have to do this.)

File the Petition and the Original Will and Codicils

Submit the original and two copies of the petition to the court by mail or in person. One copy will be stamped "filed" by the clerk and returned to you, and the other will be for the legal newspaper to pick up addresses for mailing Notices to the heirs and beneficiaries, if the newspaper mails the notices. Keep one copy for your files.

The original will and codicils, if any, are filed with the court at the same time you file the petition if they were not previously lodged with the court for safekeeping. These documents are presented separately, in their original form, and do not require any preparation for filing. You can file these documents in person or through the mail. If you mail them to the court, include a cover letter such as the one shown below. Send the original will by certified mail. Be sure to include a self-addressed, stamped envelope for the court to return your conformed copies, and be sure to keep a file copy of everything you send to the court for your records. You'll need to include a check for the filing fee (see below), so call the court clerk to find out the amount.

Sample Cover Letter

July 5, 20xx

CERTIFIED MAIL - RETURN RECEIPT REQUESTED

Clerk of the Superior Court
1735 Main Street
Santa Monica, CA 90401

Re: Estate of Anabelle Kidd, Deceased:

Enclosed are the following documents:

1. Petition for Probate (DE-111)
2. Notice of Petition to Administer Estate (DE-121)
3. Original Will, plus a copy
4. Probate Case Cover Sheet, and
5. Check in the amount of $__________.

Please file the original documents with the court and return the extra copies, conformed, in the enclosed stamped, self-addressed envelope, advising me of the time and date of the hearing.

Thank you for your assistance.

Sincerely,

Billy M. Kidd
Billy M. Kidd
1109 Sky Blue Mountain Trail
Billings, MT 48906
715-555-6408

Pay the Filing Fee

You must pay an initial filing fee, currently $435, when you file the Petition for Probate (DE-111). Some courts have surcharges and charge more, so call the court to verify the amount. Make your check payable to the "Clerk of the Superior Court."

The filing fee should come out of the estate assets as an expense of administration. If it is necessary for you (or someone else) to advance the fee from personal funds, reimbursement may be made from the estate's assets as soon as an estate bank account is opened. (See Chapter 13.)

SKIP AHEAD

Go through Step 5 only if the decedent left a formal typed will. If the will is a holographic one—that is, in the decedent's handwriting—go on to Step 6. If the decedent did not leave a will—go on to Step 7.

Step 5: Complete a Proof of Subscribing Witness

A Proof of Subscribing Witness (DE-131) is required only if the decedent left a formal typed and witnessed will or codicil that does not have a self-proving clause. In other words, if a will or codicil has a self-proving clause, a Proof of Subscribing Witness is not required. A self-proving will contains language that makes verification by witnesses unnecessary. (See "Self-Proving Wills and Codicils" in Chapter 13.)

A Proof of Subscribing Witness is a declaration by one of the witnesses to the will (and/or codicil) that it was signed and witnessed according to the requirements of the law.

Only one proof is required to prove a will or codicil if no one contests the validity of the documents. If there are any codicils, prepare a separate proof form for each. Attach a conformed copy of the will (or codicil) showing the court clerk's filing stamp (or a certified copy) to the Proof of Subscribing Witness. (You should have this as a result of filing the will in Step 4, above.) The signature on the copies of the will should be clear and legible.

Proof of Subscribing Witness

DE-131

ATTORNEY OR PARTY WITHOUT ATTORNEY *(Name, state bar number, and address)*: TELEPHONE AND FAX NOS.: FOR COURT USE ONLY

Use same heading as on petition

ATTORNEY FOR *(Name)*:

SUPERIOR COURT OF CALIFORNIA, COUNTY OF

STREET ADDRESS:

MAILING ADDRESS:

CITY AND ZIP CODE:

BRANCH NAME:

ESTATE OF *(Name)*:

DECEDENT

PROOF OF SUBSCRIBING WITNESS

CASE NUMBER:

Fill in case number

Fill in all that apply

1. I am one of the attesting witnesses to the instrument of which Attachment 1 is a photographic copy. I have examined Attachment 1 and my signature is on it.
   a. ☐ The name of the decedent was signed in the presence of the attesting witnesses present at the same time by
      (1) ☐ the decedent personally.
      (2) ☐ another person in the decedent's presence and by the decedent's direction.
   b. ☐ The decedent acknowledged in the presence of the attesting witnesses present at the same time that the c[...] was signed by
      (1) ☐ the decedent personally.
      (2) ☐ another person in the decedent's presence and by the decedent's direction.
   c. ☐ The decedent acknowledged in the presence of the attesting witnesses present at the same time that the i[...] signed was decedent's
      (1) ☐ will.
      (2) ☐ codicil.

Attach copy of filed will or codicil as Attachment 1

Select one

2. When I signed the instrument, I understood that it was decedent's ☐ will ☐ codicil.
3. I have no knowledge of any facts indicating that the instrument, or any part of it, was procured by duress, menace, fraud, or undue influence.

I declare under penalty of perjury under the laws of the State of California that the foregoing is true and correct.

Date: Date signed

Signature of witness

(TYPE OR PRINT NAME) (SIGNATURE OF WITNESS)

Type name of witness

ATTORNEY'S CERTIFICATION

(Check local court rules for requirements for certifying copies of wills and codicils)

Leave this section blank if you are not a California attorney

[...]n active member of The State Bar of California. I declare under penalty of perjury under the laws of the State of California that [...]ment 1 is a photographic copy of every page of the ☐ will ☐ codicil presented for probate.

(TYPE OR PRINT NAME) (SIGNATURE OF ATTORNEY)

[...]n Approved by the [...] Council of California
DE-131 [Rev. January 1, 1998]
Mandatory Form [1/1/2000]

PROOF OF SUBSCRIBING WITNESS
(Probate)

Probate Code, § 8220

Declaration re Execution of Will (page 1)

Name:
Address: **Name, address, and telephone number**

Telephone No.:

Petitioner, Self-represented

SUPERIOR COURT OF CALIFORNIA

COUNTY OF **Name of county**

Estate of	) No.____________
____________	) Hearing date:________ **Date, place, and time of hearing**
	) Department:________ Time:________
deceased.	) DECLARATION RE EXECUTION OF WILL

The undersigned, **Name of person who signs affidavit**, hereby declares:

1. I am the petitioner in the above-entitled proceeding.

2. The decedent's will, dated **Date of will** ______, ______, presented for probate herein, of which Exhibit "A" attached hereto is a true and correct copy, was signed at the end by **Names of all witnesses** ________, ____________ and ____________, as witnesses to its execution.

3. After reasonable search and inquiry, I have been unable to locate any of these witnesses to obtain evidence that the will was executed in all particulars as required by law.

Declaration re Execution of Will (page 2)

4. I mailed letters to each of the witnesses at the addresses shown in the will, requesting that each sign and return to me an affidavit of Proof of Subscribing Witness; however, the envelopes were returned as "not deliverable as addressed" and "unable to forward." I was unable to locate the witnesses through the phone directories or online searches. I have no knowledge of any person who knows any of these witnesses or their whereabouts.

Customize to explain efforts to locate the witnesses

5. I am ___ **Relation to decedent of person signing affidavit (for example, "the son," "the daughter," or "a close friend")** ___ of the decedent and I have personal knowledge of her handwriting and signature which I acquired by having seen her write and having received handwritten documents in the mail purporting to be from the decedent. I have examined Exhibit "A," which is a true and correct copy of what purports to be the decedent's will, and in my opinion the name subscribed on the signature line was signed by the decedent personally.

I declare under penalty of perjury under the laws of the State of California that the foregoing is true and correct and that this declaration was executed on ___ **Date signed** ___, 20___ at ___ **Place signed** ___, California.

___ **Signature of person making declaration** ___

2.

Declaration re Execution of Will

When you have completed the proof form, mail it to the witness and ask that it be signed and returned to you. Enclose a self-addressed, stamped envelope for the convenience of the witness. After one Proof of Subscribing Witness is signed, file it with the court. These documents should be on file as far in advance of the hearing date as possible, and in compliance with local rule requirements. If you get more than one Proof of Subscribing Witness, keep the extras as a reserve.

The following comments refer to certain items on the Proof of Subscribing Witness that may need further explanation:

Item 1. Attach a conformed (or certified) copy of the will to the Proof of Subscribing Witness, showing the filing stamp of the court clerk and the probate case number. Label it Attachment 1 at the bottom of the first page. If there are any codicils, attach a separate Proof of Subscribing Witness for each one, and attach a copy of the codicil, labeled Attachment 1, at the bottom of the first page of the codicil.

Item 1a. If the decedent signed the will or codicil personally in the presence of the witnesses, check Box 1a and Box (1). In rare instances, wills are signed by someone else for the decedent because the decedent for some reason could not sign it (for instance, the decedent was unable to write because of a stroke). If this is the case, check Box (2).

Item 1b. If the decedent didn't sign in the presence of the witnesses, but acknowledged to the witnesses that he or she personally signed the will or codicil, check Box b and Box (1). If the decedent acknowledged to the witnesses that another person signed for the decedent at the decedent's direction and in the decedent's presence, then check Box (2).

Item 1c. Check Box 1c and the additional box under Item 1c that indicates whether the document is the decedent's will or codicil.

Item 2. If the Proof of Subscribing Witness is for the decedent's will, check the first box. If it is for a codicil, check the second box.

The witness must sign and date the form. To the left of the signature line, enter the witness's name and address. Leave the "Attorney's Certification" part of the form blank.

What happens if all the witnesses have died or can't be found? Don't worry; the will is still good. However, you must prepare a declaration like the one just above, which describes your efforts and inability to locate any of the witnesses (or which states that they are dead) and a statement "proving" the handwriting of the decedent. The wording in our sample is usually sufficient to prove handwriting in the absence of evidence to the contrary. Anyone having personal knowledge of the decedent's handwriting can make a sworn statement proving it is the decedent's handwriting. Since you (the petitioner) are probably a relative or close friend, you may be a suitable person to do this.

The sample we have provided may be modified to suit your particular situation. For instance, Paragraph 4 may be reworded to add additional information showing your efforts to locate the witnesses, and you may add (or omit) from Paragraph 5 any facts that explain why you are qualified to prove the decedent's handwriting. Be sure to attach a certified or file-stamped copy of the will as Exhibit A.

Step 6: Complete a Proof of Holographic Instrument

If the will is a holographic will—that is, in the decedent's handwriting—someone who can prove the decedent's handwriting must sign a Proof of Holographic Instrument (DE-135). Anyone, including you (the petitioner), who has personal knowledge of the decedent's handwriting can sign this form, even someone who will receive all or part of the estate by reason of the holographic will. Attach a clear copy of the handwritten will to the form, and label it Attachment 4 at the bottom of the first page. A sample of the form, with instructions for filling it in, is shown below.

This form is also used in cases where the decedent made handwritten changes on a typewritten or printed will.

Proof of Holographic Instrument

DE-135

ATTORNEY OR PARTY WITHOUT ATTORNEY (Name, state bar number, and address): TELEPHONE AND FAX NOS.:	FOR COURT USE ONLY
ATTORNEY FOR (Name):	
SUPERIOR COURT OF CALIFORNIA, COUNTY OF STREET ADDRESS: MAILING ADDRESS: CITY AND ZIP CODE: BRANCH NAME:	
ESTATE OF (Name): DECEDENT	
PROOF OF HOLOGRAPHIC INSTRUMENT	CASE NUMBER: **Fill in case number**

Use same heading as on petition

Fill in all that apply

1. I was acquainted with the decedent for the following number of years *(specify)*:

2. ☐ I was related to the decedent as *(specify)*:

3. I have personal knowledge of the decedent's handwriting which I acquired as follows:
   a. ☐ I saw the decedent write.
   b. ☐ I saw a writing purporting to be in the decedent's handwriting and upon which decedent acted or was charged. It was *(specify)*:

   c. ☐ I received letters in the due course of mail purporting to be from the decedent in response to letters I addressed and mailed to the decedent.
   d. ☐ Other *(specify other means of obtaining knowledge)*:

4. I have examined the attached copy of the instrument, and its handwritten provisions were written by and the instrument was signed by the hand of the decedent. *(Affix a copy of the instrument as Attachment 4.)*

Attach copy of holographic will as Attachment 4

I declare under penalty of perjury under the laws of the State of California that the foregoing is true and correct.

Date: **Date signed**

Enter name of person who will sign proof
(TYPE OR PRINT NAME)

Signature of person who will sign proof

(ADDRESS)

ATTORNEY'S CERTIFICATION

(Check local court rules for requirements for certifying copies of wills and codicils)

Leave this section blank if you are not a California attorney

I am an active member of The State Bar of California. I declare under penalty of perjury under the laws of the State of California that Attachment 4 is a photographic copy of every page of the holographic instrument presented for probate.

Date:

(TYPE OR PRINT NAME) (SIGNATURE OF ATTORNEY)

Form Approved by the Judicial Council of California
DE-135 [Rev. January 1, 1998]
Mandatory Form [1/1/2000]

PROOF OF HOLOGRAPHIC INSTRUMENT
(Probate)

Probate Code, § 8222

Step 7: Notify Government Agencies

You can take some of the actions in this step soon after the decedent's death, while others will wait until after the court process begins and letters are issued.

If you know or have reason to believe the decedent was receiving health care under Medi-Cal, or was the surviving spouse or registered domestic partner of someone who did, you must send a notice within 90 days of the death to the Director of Health Care Services advising that office of the decedent's death and providing the office with a death certificate. (Prob. Code § 9202(a).) The Department of Health Care Services has four months after notice is given to file a claim for repayment of benefits.

If the personal representative knows that an heir or beneficiary is or has previously been in a prison or facility under the jurisdiction of the Department of Corrections and Rehabilitation or its Division of Juvenile Facilities or confined in any county or city jail, road camp, industrial camp, industrial farm, or other local correctional facility, the personal representative must give notice of the decedent's death, and the name, date of birth, CDRC or booking number, and the location of the decedent's heir or beneficiary to the Director of the California Victim Compensation and Government Claims Board within 90 days after letters are issued. (Prob. Code §§ 216 and 9202(b).) The director of the board has four months after notice is received to pursue collection of any outstanding restitution fines or orders. The notice should be addressed to the director at his Sacramento office and provide a copy of the death certificate, the name of the probate court and the case number.

In addition, you must give notice of administration of the estate to the Franchise Tax Board within 90 days after letters are issued. Send a copy of the letters of administration. (Prob. Code § 9202 (c)). To expedite processing, the notice may be faxed to: FTB Decedent Team (916) 845-0479. There is no special form for giving the notices. (See Chapter 2 for a sample letter.) Be sure to provide a copy of the decedent's death certificate.

Step 8: Prepare Your Order for Probate

You must prepare an Order for Probate (DE-140) and submit it to the court for the signature of the judge. The purpose of the Order for Probate is to admit the will (if any) to probate and appoint an estate representative.

Some counties require the order to be in the hands of the court well before the hearing date so it may be examined before the judge signs it. In other counties, including Los Angeles, the order may be submitted on or after the date of the hearing. If you are unsure of the procedure followed by the court in your area, it is good practice to provide it to the court as early as possible after filing the petition and before the hearing date. You may mail the Letters Testamentary or Letters of Administration you have prepared and, for those counties that require it, the Application for Appointment of Probate Referee at the same time. (See Steps 10, 11, and 12.)

How to Fill Out the Order for Probate (DE-140)

Caption. Fill in your name, address, the court's name, and case number, as you have on your other court papers.

Order for Probate. Indicate whether an executor or administrator is being appointed. Also indicate that you petitioned for authority (full or limited) under the Independent Administration of Estates Act.

Item 1. Fill in the date, time, location, and judge for the court hearing. Call the court for the name of the judge, or leave it blank.

Item 2. Fill in the date of death for Item 2b and check the correct box about residence. Indicate whether there was a will (testate) or not (intestate). If there is a will, fill in the date of the will and any codicils. For the date the will was admitted to probate, put the date of the court hearing.

Item 3. Fill in your name and check the appropriate box. This will be consistent with Item 2b of the Petition for Probate (DE-111). Leave Item 3d blank.

Item 4. Check Box a if you petitioned for full authority to use the Independent Administration of Estates Act; check Box b if you asked for limited authority. This will be consistent with Item 2c of the Petition for Probate (DE-111).

Order for Probate

DE-140

ATTORNEY OR PARTY WITHOUT ATTORNEY *(Name, state bar number, and address)*: TELEPHONE AND FAX NOS.: 715-555-6408

Billy M. Kidd
1109 Sky Blue Mountain Trail
Billings, Montana 48906

ATTORNEY FOR *(Name)*: Self-represented

FOR COURT USE ONLY

SUPERIOR COURT OF CALIFORNIA, COUNTY OF LOS ANGELES
STREET ADDRESS: 111 No. Hill Street
MAILING ADDRESS: 111 No. Hill Street
CITY AND ZIP CODE: Los Angeles, CA 90012
BRANCH NAME: CENTRAL DISTRICT

ESTATE OF *(Name)*: ANABELLE KIDD, aka ANABELLE O. KIDD, DECEDENT

ORDER FOR PROBATE

ORDER APPOINTING [X] Executor [ ] Administrator with Will Annexed [ ] Administrator [ ] Special Administrator

[X] Order Authorizing Independent Administration of Estate
[X] with full authority [ ] with limited authority

CASE NUMBER: BP 14813

WARNING: THIS APPOINTMENT IS NOT EFFECTIVE UNTIL LETTERS HAVE ISSUED.

1. Date of hearing: 7-25-20xx Time: 9:30 A.M. Dept./Room: A Judge:

THE COURT FINDS

2. a. All notices required by law have been given.
   b. Decedent died on *(date)*: June 18, 20xx
      (1) [X] a resident of the California county named above.
      (2) [ ] a nonresident of California and left an estate in the county named above.
   c. Decedent died
      (1) [ ] intestate
      (2) [X] testate
      and decedent's will dated: July 1, 1980 and each codicil dated:
      was admitted to probate by Minute Order on *(date)*: July 25, 20xx

THE COURT ORDERS

3. *(Name)*: Billy M. Kidd
   is appointed **personal representative:**
   a. [X] executor of the decedent's will
   b. [ ] administrator with will annexed
   c. [ ] administrator
   d. [ ] special administrator
      (1) [ ] with general powers
      (2) [ ] with special powers as specified in Attachment 3d(2)
      (3) [ ] without notice of hearing
      (4) [ ] letters will expire on *(date)*:

   and letters shall issue on qualification.
4. a. [X] **Full authority** is granted to administer the estate under the Independent Administration of Estates Act.
   b. [ ] **Limited authority** is granted to administer the estate under the Independent Administration of Estates Act (there is no authority, without court supervision, to (1) sell or exchange real property or (2) grant an option to purchase real property or (3) borrow money with the loan secured by an encumbrance upon real property).
5. a. [X] Bond is not required.
   b. [ ] Bond is fixed at: $ to be furnished by an authorized surety company or as otherwise provided by law.
   c. [ ] Deposits of: $ are ordered to be placed in a blocked account at *(specify institution and location)*:
      and receipts shall be filed. No withdrawals shall be made without a court order. [ ] Additional orders in Attachment 5c.
   d. [ ] The personal representative is not authorized to take possession of money or any other property without a specific court order.
6. [X] *(Name)*: is appointed probate referee.

Date:

JUDGE OF THE SUPERIOR COURT

7. Number of pages attached: [ ] SIGNATURE FOLLOWS LAST ATTACHMENT

Form Approved by the Judicial Council of California DE-140 [Rev. January 1, 1998] Mandatory Form [1/1/2000]

ORDER FOR PROBATE

Probate Code, §§ 8006, 8400

Supplement to Petition for Probate of Will

John J. Smith
202 Park Street
Los Angeles, California 90087
Telephone: 213-555-8754
Petitioner, Self-represented

SUPERIOR COURT OF CALIFORNIA

FOR THE COUNTY OF LOS ANGELES

Estate of	No. BP 394860
DOROTHY JANE SMITH aka DOROTHY SMITH aka DOROTHY J. SMITH	SUPPLEMENT TO PETITION FOR PROBATE OF WILL AND FOR LETTERS TESTAMENTARY
deceased.	5/30/20xx, 9:15 A.M., Dept. 5

The undersigned is the petitioner in the above-entitled proceeding. As a supplement to Paragraph 8 of the Petition for Probate of Will and for Letters Testamentary on file herein, the undersigned alleges as follows:

Carol Brown, daughter of the decedent, is the same person named as Carol Marie Smith in paragraph FIRST of the decedent's will.

I declare under penalty of perjury under the laws of the State of California that the foregoing is true and correct and that this declaration is executed on May 27, 20xx at Los Angeles, California.

John J. Smith

This supplement corrects the following problem: The decedent's daughter, Carol Brown, was married after the will was made, and was listed as an heir in the petition under her married name. Because she was named in the will under her birth name, the court wanted proof that Carol Marie Smith was the same person and not someone else who was inadvertently omitted as an heir.

Bond (Personal) on Qualifying (page 1)

Name:
Address:

Telephone No.:

Petitioner, Self-represented

SUPERIOR COURT OF CALIFORNIA
COUNTY OF ____________________

Estate of (name of decedent), deceased	NO. BOND (PERSONAL) ON QUALIFYING

I, (name of representative), as principal and (name of first surety), and (name of second surety), as sureties, are bound to the State of California in the sum of $__________. We bind ourselves, our heirs, executors, and administrators, jointly and severally, to pay in event of breach of this bond.

This bond is being executed under an order of the Superior Court of California for ______________________________ County, made on ______________, 20____, by which (name of representative) was appointed (executor/administrator) of the estate of the above-named decedent, and letters (testamentary/of administration) were directed to be issued to (name of representative) on executing a bond under the laws of California.

Bond (Personal) on Qualifying (page 2)

If ________________, as ________________, faithfully executes the duties of the trust according to the law, this obligation shall become void; otherwise, it will remain in effect.

DATED:__________ ______________________________
(Name of Representative)

DATED:__________ ______________________________
(Name of First Surety)

DATED:__________ ______________________________
(Name of Second Surety)

DECLARATION OF SURETIES

________________ and ________________, the sureties named in the above bond state, each for himself/herself, declare that he/she is a householder or property owner and resides within said state and is worth the sum of $________ over and above all his debts and liabilities, exclusive of property exempt from execution.

Signed and dated at ________________, California, on ____________, 20___. I declare under penalty of perjury under the laws of the State of California that the foregoing is true and correct.

____
(First Surety)

____
(Address of First Surety)

____
(Second Surety)

____
(Address of Second Surety)

Item 5. Check Box a if bond is waived. If bond is required, check Box b and fill in the amount. If cash is to be deposited in a blocked account, check Box c and fill in the amount, and name and address of the depository. (You must file a receipt for the deposit with the court either before or shortly after letters are issued. Some banks and trust companies request a certified copy of the Order for Probate naming them as depository.)

Item 6. Check this box and the court will complete it.

Leave the rest of the form blank.

Step 9: Obtain and Respond to the Probate Calendar Notes and Hearing

As discussed in Chapter 13, probate calendar notes (sometimes called "tentative rulings") are shorthand terms used by the court's probate examiners to indicate whether a petition will be approved on the date of the hearing or if you must answer or correct a question or problem.

This step involves first determining how and when you will check the probate calendar notes, and then actually checking the notes at the appropriate time. Be aware that, depending on the specific circumstances and the court, preparing and submitting documents identified in Step 10, Step 11, and/or Step 12 may happen in the time period prior to the probate notes being issued. Planning ahead may help you to have the greatest opportunity to have a favorable tentative ruling prior to the hearing date.

Many courts now list probate calendar notes on their websites. Consult the local rules or the court clerk to learn the procedures for checking the notes and to determine how far in advance of the hearing the notes may be available. In some counties, the probate clerk or probate examiner will call you to advise of problems identified.

The probate examiner may provide instructions about information you need to provide or procedures you need to follow. Follow these instructions carefully. If you need to provide additional information, you must either appear at the hearing personally or file a "supplement" to the petition. If a supplement is required, it must be typed and verified (under penalty of perjury) by the petitioner in the same way as the original petition. Insert the hearing date on the right-hand side under the title of the document. (See the sample below.) You may need to take the supplement to the court personally for it to be filed in time to have the petition approved on the hearing date. Delivering courtesy copies to the probate examiner can be helpful in getting matters approved, and is required by some courts. If filing a supplement just prior to a hearing, make sure the court clerk is aware of the timing so the supplement will be placed in the case file in time for the hearing. Answering questions at the hearing is often another way to cure defects and, generally, is not intimidating.

If the probate calendar notes indicate bond is required, you must file the bond before the court issues the letters. (See "Probate Bonds" in Chapter 13 for how to arrange for bond.) In this case, the Order for Probate may be issued before letters are issued. A sample of a bond that may be used for personal sureties is shown above. Remember, when personal sureties are used, the bond must be for twice the amount required. Contact the court in advance and consult local rules to determine what evidence, if any, of net worth the sureties will have to show.

In many counties, on the day before the hearing, you can look at a list posted on the court's website or call a number and listen to a recording of all the petitions granted without requiring a court appearance. If your case is not pregranted, follow the procedures established by that court to find out what the problem is and how to correct it.

On the date set for the hearing, the court will act on the petition and the related documents (Steps 8, 10, and 12). Normally, attendance is not required at the actual hearing. The hearing does provide an opportunity for any interested person to be heard, such as to make an objection. If attending the hearing is desired or required, appearing by phone or video may be possible. Check local court procedures ahead of time. Occasionally a person will object to the petition, for example if the person wants to challenge the validity of the will or the appropriateness of the personal representative. If this happens, you may need legal assistance. If you need time to get an attorney, you may ask the court for a continuance to delay the hearing.

If all goes according to plan, the court will sign the Order for Probate on the date of the hearing and issue letters. You are then set to administer the estate.

Step 10: Prepare the Letters

After the judge signs the Order for Probate appointing you as the estate representative, the court will issue to you the "letters" that confirm your appointment. You must prepare ahead of time the letters that the court will issue to you.

Letters Testamentary or Letters of Administration are both prepared on the same form (DE-150). Instructions and a sample form are shown below. You may sign the letters prior to the hearing date and send them to the court at the same time you mail the Order for Probate, as discussed in Step 8.

You should order at least one certified copy of the letters by enclosing a check payable to the "Clerk of Superior Court" in an amount sufficient to cover the court's certification fees, usually around $25 for each certified copy. Call the court for the exact amount or look it up on the court's website. You can pick up the certified copies from the court in person after the hearing. Or you can provide a self-addressed stamped envelope to have the court mail it to you.

The certified copies are usually needed right away to transfer bank accounts from the decedent's name to that of the estate. You may order additional certified copies now or later, if you need them. In some counties, your signature on the letters must not be dated prior to the date you filed your petition.

How to Fill Out the Letters (DE-150)

Caption. Fill in your name, address, the court's name, and case number, as you have on your other court papers.

Letters. Check "testamentary" if there is a will, or the box under that if you are administrator with will annexed. Check "of administration" if there is no will.

Item 1. If there is no will, go to Item 2. If there is a will, check the first box and enter the name of the representative below it. Then check either Box a or b, and go to Item 3.

Item 2. If there is no will, enter the name of the administrator and check Box a.

Item 3. Check the first box and then indicate whether you petitioned for full or limited authority under the Independent Administration of Estates Act.

Item 4. If possession of bank accounts or other assets has been blocked by the court, check this box.

Leave the rest of this half blank.

Affirmation. Check Box 2 and sign the form, and fill in the date and city.

Step 11: Prepare a Duties and Liabilities of Personal Representative

The Duties and Liabilities of Personal Representative (DE-147) provides a summary of your responsibilities as personal representative. You must read it, fill out and sign the acknowledgment of receipt, and file it before the court will issue the letters. Check with your county's local probate rules to see if you are required to file the addendum to this form, the Confidential Supplement to Duties and Liabilities of Personal Representative (DE-147S). This is a form where you list your date of birth and driver's license number. In courts where this form is required, the clerk will file it separately so that it does not become a public record. Samples of the Duties and Liabilities and the Confidential Supplement are shown below, and blank copies are in Appendix B.

Step 12: Prepare the Application Appointing Probate Referee

All noncash assets must be appraised by a probate referee appointed by the court. In most counties, and in the branch courts in Los Angeles, you don't have to submit a separate document to request appointment of a referee; the court does it automatically. In the Central District in Los Angeles County and some other counties, a separate form must be used to request appointment of a referee. Check with your local court to see if you must file a form to have a referee appointed.

Letters

DE-150

ATTORNEY OR PARTY WITHOUT ATTORNEY (Name, state bar number, and address): TELEPHONE AND FAX NOS.: 715-555-6408

Billy M. Kidd
1109 Sky Blue Mountain Trail
Billings, Montana 48906

ATTORNEY FOR (Name): Self-represented

FOR COURT USE ONLY

SUPERIOR COURT OF CALIFORNIA, COUNTY OF LOS ANGELES
STREET ADDRESS: 111 No. Hill Street
MAILING ADDRESS: 111 No. Hill Street
CITY AND ZIP CODE: Los Angeles, CA 90012
BRANCH NAME: CENTRAL DISTRICT

ESTATE OF (Name): ANABELLE KIDD, aka ANABELLE O. KIDD, DECEDENT

LETTERS
[X] TESTAMENTARY [ ] OF ADMINISTRATION
[ ] OF ADMINISTRATION WITH WILL ANNEXED [ ] SPECIAL ADMINISTRATION

CASE NUMBER: BP 14813

LETTERS

1. [X] The last will of the decedent named above having been proved, the court appoints (name): Billy M. Kidd
   a. [X] executor.
   b. [ ] administrator with will annexed.
2. [ ] The court appoints (name):
   a. [ ] administrator of the decedent's estate.
   b. [ ] special administrator of decedent's estate
      (1) [ ] with the special powers specified in the *Order for Probate*.
      (2) [ ] with the powers of a general administrator.
      (3) [ ] letters will expire on (date):
3. [X] The personal representative is authorized to administer the estate under the Independent Administration of Estates Act [X] **with full authority**
   [ ] **with limited authority** (no authority, without court supervision, to (1) sell or exchange real property or (2) grant an option to purchase real property or (3) borrow money with the loan secured by an encumbrance upon real property).
4. [ ] The personal representative is not authorized to take possession of money or any other property without a specific court order.

WITNESS, clerk of the court, with seal of the court affixed.

(SEAL)

Date:

Clerk, by

(DEPUTY)

AFFIRMATION

1. [ ] PUBLIC ADMINISTRATOR: No affirmation required (Prob. Code, § 7621(c)).
2. [X] INDIVIDUAL: **I solemnly affirm** that I will perform the duties of personal representative according to law.
3. [ ] INSTITUTIONAL FIDUCIARY (name):

   I solemnly affirm that the institution will perform the duties of personal representative according to law. I make this affirmation for myself as an individual and on behalf of the institution as an officer.
   (Name and title):
4. Executed on (date): July 20, 20xx
   at (place): Santa Monica, California.

Billy M. Kidd
(SIGNATURE)

CERTIFICATION

I certify that this document is a correct copy of the original on file in my office and the letters issued by the personal representative appointed above have not been revoked, annulled, or set aside, and are still in full force and effect.

(SEAL)

Date:

Clerk, by

(DEPUTY)

Form Approved by the Judicial Council of California DE-150 [Rev. January 1, 1998] Mandatory Form [1/1/2000]

LETTERS (Probate)

Probate Code, §§ 1001, 8403, 8405, 8544, 8545; Code of Civil Procedure, § 2015.6

Duties and Liabilities of Personal Representative (page 1)

DE-147

ATTORNEY OR PARTY WITHOUT ATTORNEY (*Name, state bar number, and address*): Billy M. Kidd 1109 Sky Blue Mountain Trail Billings, Montana 48906 TELEPHONE NO.: 715-555-6408 FAX NO. (*Optional*): E-MAIL ADDRESS (*Optional*): ATTORNEY FOR (*Name*): Self-represented	FOR COURT USE ONLY
SUPERIOR COURT OF CALIFORNIA, COUNTY OF LOS ANGELES STREET ADDRESS: 111 No. Hill Street MAILING ADDRESS: 111 No. Hill Street CITY AND ZIP CODE: Los Angeles, CA 90012 BRANCH NAME: CENTRAL DISTRICT	
ESTATE OF (*Name*): ANABELLE KIDD, aka ANABELLE O. KIDD, DECEDENT	
DUTIES AND LIABILITIES OF PERSONAL REPRESENTATIVE and Acknowledgment of Receipt	CASE NUMBER: BP 14813

DUTIES AND LIABILITIES OF PERSONAL REPRESENTATIVE

When the court appoints you as personal representative of an estate, you become an officer of the court and assume certain duties and obligations. An attorney is best qualified to advise you about these matters. You should understand the following:

1. MANAGING THE ESTATE'S ASSETS

a. **Prudent investments**
You must manage the estate assets with the care of a prudent person dealing with someone else's property. This means that you must be cautious and may not make any speculative investments.

b. **Keep estate assets separate**
You must keep the money and property in this estate separate from anyone else's, including your own. When you open a bank account for the estate, the account name must indicate that it is an estate account and not your personal account. Never deposit estate funds in your personal account or otherwise mix them with your or anyone else's property. Securities in the estate must also be held in a name that shows they are estate property and not your personal property.

c. **Interest-bearing accounts and other investments**
Except for checking accounts intended for ordinary administration expenses, estate accounts must earn interest. You may deposit estate funds in insured accounts in financial institutions, but you should consult with an attorney before making other kinds of investments.

d. **Other restrictions**
There are many other restrictions on your authority to deal with estate property. You should not spend any of the estate's money unless you have received permission from the court or have been advised to do so by an attorney. You may reimburse yourself for official court costs paid by you to the county clerk and for the premium on your bond. Without prior order of the court, you may not pay fees to yourself or to your attorney, if you have one. If you do not obtain the court's permission when it is required, you may be removed as personal representative or you may be required to reimburse the estate from your own personal funds, or both. You should consult with an attorney concerning the legal requirements affecting sales, leases, mortgages, and investments of estate property.

2. INVENTORY OF ESTATE PROPERTY

a. **Locate the estate's property**
You must attempt to locate and take possession of all the decedent's property to be administered in the estate.

b. **Determine the value of the property**
You must arrange to have a court-appointed referee determine the value of the property unless the appointment is waived by the court. You, rather than the referee, must determine the value of certain "cash items." An attorney can advise you about how to do this.

c. **File an inventory and appraisal**
Within four months after Letters are first issued to you as personal representative, you must file with the court an inventory and appraisal of all the assets in the estate.

Page 1 of 2

Form Adopted for Mandatory Use
Judicial Council of California
DE-147 [Rev. January 1, 2002]

DUTIES AND LIABILITIES OF PERSONAL REPRESENTATIVE (Probate)

Probate Code, § 8404

Duties and Liabilities of Personal Representative (page 2)

ESTATE OF *(Name):* ANABELLE KIDD, DECEDENT	CASE NUMBER: BP 14813

d. File a change of ownership
At the time you file the inventory and appraisal, you must also file a change of ownership statement with the county recorder or assessor in each county where the decedent owned real property at the time of death, as provided in section 480 of the California Revenue and Taxation Code.

3. NOTICE TO CREDITORS

You must mail a notice of administration to each known creditor of the decedent within four months after your appointment as personal representative. If the decedent received Medi-Cal assistance, you must notify the State Director of Health Services within 90 days after appointment.

4. INSURANCE

You should determine that there is appropriate and adequate insurance covering the assets and risks of the estate. Maintain the insurance in force during the entire period of the administration.

5. RECORD KEEPING

a. Keep accounts
You must keep complete and accurate records of each financial transaction affecting the estate. You will have to prepare an account of all money and property you have received, what you have spent, and the date of each transaction. You must describe in detail what you have left after the payment of expenses.

b. Court review
Your account will be reviewed by the court. Save your receipts because the court may ask to review them. If you do not file your accounts as required, the court will order you to do so. You may be removed as personal representative if you fail to comply.

6. CONSULTING AN ATTORNEY

If you have an attorney, you should cooperate with the attorney at all times. You and your attorney are responsible for completing the estate administration as promptly as possible. **When in doubt, contact your attorney.**

NOTICE: 1. This statement of duties and liabilities is a summary and is not a complete statement of the law. Your conduct as a personal representative is governed by the law itself and not by this summary.
2. If you fail to perform your duties or to meet the deadlines, the court may reduce your compensation, remove you from office, and impose other sanctions.

ACKNOWLEDGMENT OF RECEIPT

1. I have petitioned the court to be appointed as a personal representative.
2. My address and telephone number are *(specify):* 1109 Sky Blue Mountain Trail
Billings, MT 48906
Tel # 715-555-6408
3. I acknowledge that I have received a copy of this statement of the duties and liabilities of the office of personal representative.

Date: JULY 20, 20xx

Billy M. Kidd ▶ *Billy M. Kidd*

(TYPE OR PRINT NAME) (SIGNATURE OF PETITIONER)

Date:

▶

(TYPE OR PRINT NAME) (SIGNATURE OF PETITIONER)

CONFIDENTIAL INFORMATION: If required to do so by local court rule, you must provide your date of birth and driver's license number on supplemental Form DE-147S. (Prob. Code, § 8404(b).)

Confidential Supplement to Duties and Liabilities of Personal Representative

CONFIDENTIAL **DE-147S**

ESTATE OF *(Name)*:	CASE NUMBER:
ANABELLE KIDD, DECEDENT	BP 14813

CONFIDENTIAL STATEMENT OF BIRTH DATE AND DRIVER'S LICENSE NUMBER

(Supplement to *Duties and Liabilities of Personal Representative* (Form DE-147))

*(NOTE: This supplement is to be used if the court by local rule requires the personal representative to provide a birth date and driver's license number. Do **not** attach this supplement to Form DE-147.)*

This separate *Confidential Statement of Birth Date and Driver's License Number* contains confidential information relating to the personal representative in the case referenced above. This supplement shall be kept separate from the *Duties and Liabilities of Personal Representative* filed in this case and shall not be a public record.

INFORMATION ON THE PERSONAL REPRESENTATIVE:

1. Name: Billy M. Kidd
2. Date of birth: 7-11-54
3. Driver's license number: BO 8339025 State: Montana

TO COURT CLERK:
THIS STATEMENT IS **CONFIDENTIAL**. DO NOT FILE
THIS CONFIDENTIAL STATEMENT IN A PUBLIC COURT FILE.

Form Adopted for Mandatory Use
Judicial Council of California
DE-147S [New January 1, 2001]

CONFIDENTIAL SUPPLEMENT TO DUTIES AND LIABILITIES OF PERSONAL REPRESENTATIVE
(Probate)

Probate Code, § 8404

Step 13: Prepare Notice of Proposed Action, If Necessary

After letters are issued, you must wait four months before you may close the estate. This gives creditors time to file claims against the estate. During this period, you will take care of such things as estate bank accounts, tax returns, and the estate inventory.

You may also find it necessary to perform some of the acts allowed by the Independent Administration of Estates Act (discussed in Chapter 13). Some of these require a Notice of Proposed Action (DE-165). In particular, the sale of estate property usually requires a Notice of Proposed Action, with some exceptions as discussed in Chapter 13. Most courts want the original action notice and any waiver or consent obtained filed with the court with proof that it was given to all interested persons. Instructions for filling out the notice and a sample notice are shown below with a proof of service. Although using the Judicial Council form itself is not required, using that form will help you provide the required information.

"Interested persons" are those whose interest in the estate would be affected by the proposed action. For example, if real property is to be sold, give notice to all persons entitled to inherit an interest in the property. A beneficiary receiving only a cash gift or other specific property is not entitled to notice. Give notice to anyone who has filed a Request for Special Notice with the court, regardless of whether that person is entitled to any part of the property.

How to Fill Out a Notice of Proposed Action (DE-165)

Caption. Fill in your name, address, the court's name, and case number, as on other court papers. Do not check the boxes for Objection or Consent; those boxes are used by the person receiving the notice.

Item 1. Enter the name of executor or administrator.

Item 2. Check the box that indicates whether you were granted full or limited authority under the Independent Administration of Estates Act.

Item 3. Fill in the date of the proposed action, which must be at least 15 days after the date of this notice, unless all interested persons sign the consent on page two. Describe the action with a reasonably specific description if there is room, or check the box if you describe it in an attachment.

Item 4. Check this box if the proposed action is a real estate transaction. Make sure that the description in Item 3 includes the required information listed in Item 4a. Either provide the value determined by the probate referee in Item 4b, or check the "No inventory yet" box.

Item 5. Fill in your name and address.

Item 7. Fill in your name, your phone number, your name (again), and the date. Sign your name on the signature line.

Sale of Real Property

When real property is sold under the Independent Administration of Estates Act, the title company will require the following documents:

- copy of the Notice of Proposed Action (DE-165), with a proof of mailing showing that the notice was given within the time period required, and
- certified copy of your letters.

Sale of Securities

You may want to sell securities during probate to raise cash or to facilitate distribution to multiple beneficiaries. You should contact a stockbroker or the transfer agent to handle the sale. (See Chapter 9 on the documentation required.) No prior court approval is necessary, and no Notice of Proposed Action (DE-165) is required to sell securities over the counter or when listed on an established stock or bond exchange when sold for cash. (Prob. Code §§ 10200(e)(2) and 10537(b)(1).) If a transfer agent nevertheless insists on a court order, you may file a short form with the court called Ex Parte Petition for Authority to Sell Securities (DE-270) and obtain the order without a court hearing. A sample is shown above. Here are instructions for preparing it.

Letter to Court

July 12, 20xx

Clerk of the Superior Court
Probate Department
111 No. Hill St.
Los Angeles, California 90012

Re: Estate of ANABELLE KIDD, deceased
Case No. BP 14813
Hearing Date: July 25, 20xx

Enclosed are the original and one copy of the following documents:

1. Notice of Petition to Administer Estate (DE-121) (with proof of service by mail)
2. Order for Probate
3. Letters, and
4. Duties and Liabilities of Personal Representative.

Please file the original documents with the court and return the extra copies, conformed, in the enclosed stamped, self-addressed envelope.

Once issued, please return one certified copy of letters. A check is enclosed to cover your certification fees. Thank you for your assistance.

Sincerely,

Billy M. Kidd
Billy M. Kidd
1109 Sky Blue Mountain Trail
Billings, MT 48906
715-555-6408

Notice of Proposed Action (page 1)

DE-165

ATTORNEY OR PARTY WITHOUT ATTORNEY *(Name, state bar number, and address)*: TELEPHONE AND FAX NOS.:
Billy M. Kidd 715-555-6408
1109 Sky Blue Mountain Trail
Billings, Montana 48906

ATTORNEY FOR *(Name)*: Self-represented

FOR COURT USE ONLY

SUPERIOR COURT OF CALIFORNIA, COUNTY OF LOS ANGELES
STREET ADDRESS: 111 No. Hill Street
MAILING ADDRESS: 111 No. Hill Street
CITY AND ZIP CODE: Los Angeles, CA 90012
BRANCH NAME: CENTRAL DISTRICT

ESTATE OF *(Name)*:
ANABELLE KIDD, aka
ANABELLE O. KIDD, DECEDENT

NOTICE OF PROPOSED ACTION
Independent Administration of Estates Act
☐ **Objection** ☐ **Consent**

CASE NUMBER: BP 14813

NOTICE: If you do not object in writing or obtain a court order preventing the action proposed below, you will be treated as if you consented to the proposed action and you may not object after the proposed action has been taken. If you object, the personal representative may take the proposed action only under court supervision. An objection form is on the reverse. If you wish to object, you may use the form or prepare your own written objection.

1. The personal representative (executor or administrator) of the estate of the deceased is *(names)*:

   Billy M. Kidd

2. The personal representative has authority to administer the estate without court supervision under the Independent Administration of Estates Act (Prob. Code, § 10400 et seq.)
   a. ☒ with **full authority** under the act.
   b. ☐ with **limited authority** under the act (there is no authority, without court supervision, to (1) sell or exchange real property or (2) grant an option to purchase real property or (3) borrow money with the loan secured by an encumbrance upon real property).

3. **On or after** *(date)*: August 20, 20xx, the personal representative will take the following action without court supervision *(describe in specific terms here or in Attachment 3)*:
   ☐ The proposed action is described in an attachment labeled Attachment 3.

The Executor will sell the real property located at 9560 Euclid Street, Santa Monica, California, for a total sales price of $395,000, all cash. Buyer to obtain own financing. Property to be sold as is, and seller will not make any repairs nor provide any warranty on house and other structures on lot. Sales price includes all built-in appliances. Seller to pay broker's commission of 6% of sales price, allocated as follows: 3% to Exceptional Real Estate and 3% to J. F. Realty. Seller to furnish buyer at seller's expense a California Land Title Association policy issued by Commonwealth Land Title Insurance. County transfer tax and documentary transfer fee to be paid by seller.

4. ☒ **Real property transaction** *(Check this box and complete item 4b if the proposed action involves a sale or exchange or a grant of an option to purchase real property.)*
   a. The material terms of the transaction are specified in item 3, including any sale price and the amount of or method of calculating any commission or compensation to an agent or broker.
   b. $ is the value of the subject property in the probate inventory. ☒ No inventory yet.

NOTICE: A sale of real property without court supervision means that the sale will NOT be presented to the court for confirmation at a hearing at which higher bids for the property may be presented and the property sold to the highest bidder.

(Continued on reverse)

Form Approved by the Judicial Council of California
DE-165 [Rev. January 1, 1998]
Mandatory Form [1/1/2000]

NOTICE OF PROPOSED ACTION
Objection—Consent
(Probate)

Probate Code, § 10580 et seq.

Notice of Proposed Action (page 2)

ESTATE OF *(Name)*: ANABELLE KIDD, DECEDENT	CASE NUMBER: BP 14813

5. **If you OBJECT to the proposed action**
   a. **Sign** the objection form below and deliver or mail it to the personal representative at the following address *(specify name and address)*: Billy M. Kidd
   1109 Sky Blue Mountain Trail, Billings, Montana 48906
   OR
   b. **Send** your own written objection to the address in item 5a. *(Be sure to identify the proposed action and state that you object to it.)*
   OR
   c. **Apply** to the court for an order preventing the personal representative from taking the proposed action without court supervision.
   d. **NOTE**: Your written objection or the court order must be received by the personal representative before the date in the box in item 3, or before the proposed action is taken, whichever is later. If you object, the personal representative may take the proposed action only under court supervision.
6. **If you APPROVE the proposed action**, you may sign the consent form below and return it to the address in item 5a. If you do not object in writing or obtain a court order, you will be treated as if you consented to the proposed action.
7. **If you need more INFORMATION, call** *(name)*: Billy M. Kidd
   (telephone): 715-555-6408

Date: August 3, 20xx

Billy M. Kidd — Billy M. Kidd
(TYPE OR PRINT NAME) — (SIGNATURE OF PERSONAL REPRESENTATIVE OR ATTORNEY)

OBJECTION TO PROPOSED ACTION

☐ **I OBJECT** to the action proposed in item 3.

NOTICE: Sign and return this form (both sides) to the address in item 5a. The form must be received before the date in the box in item 3, or before the proposed action is taken, whichever is later. *(You may want to use certified mail, with return receipt requested. Make a copy of this form for your records.)*

Date:

(TYPE OR PRINT NAME) — (SIGNATURE OF OBJECTOR)

CONSENT TO PROPOSED ACTION

☐ **I CONSENT** to the action proposed in item 3.

NOTICE: You may indicate your *consent* by signing and returning this form (both sides) to the address in item 5a. If you do not object in writing or obtain a court order, you will be treated as if you consented to the proposed action.

Date:

(TYPE OR PRINT NAME) — (SIGNATURE OF CONSENTER)

DE-165 [Rev. January 1, 1998]

NOTICE OF PROPOSED ACTION
Objection—Consent
(Probate)

Page two

Proof of Service

BILLY M. KIDD
1109 Sky Blue Mountain Trail
Billings, Montana 48906

Telephone: 715-555-6408
Petitioner, Self-represented

SUPERIOR COURT OF CALIFORNIA

FOR THE COUNTY OF LOS ANGELES

Estate of ANABELLE KIDD, aka ANABELLE O. KIDD deceased.	CASE NO. BP 14813 PROOF OF SERVICE BY MAIL OF NOTICE OF PROPOSED ACTION

STATE OF MONTANA, COUNTY OF BILLINGS;

I am a resident of the county aforesaid; I am over the age of eighteen years and not a party to the within entitled action; my business address is: 1809 - G Street, Billings, Montana.

On August 3, 20xx, I served the attached NOTICE OF PROPOSED ACTION on the interested parties by placing a true copy thereof enclosed in a sealed envelope with postage thereon fully prepaid in the United States mail at Billings, Montana, addressed as follows:

Mary Kidd Clark, 789 Main Street, Venice, California 90410

Carson Kidd, 711 Valley Road, Owens, California 98455

I declare under penalty of perjury under the laws of the State of California that the foregoing is true and correct.

DATED: August 10, 20xx

Mary Smith
Mary Smith

Proof of Service by Mail of Notice of Proposed Action

Ex Parte Petition for Authority to Sell Securities and Order (page 1)

DE-270, GC-070

ATTORNEY OR PARTY WITHOUT ATTORNEY *(Name, state bar number, and address)*: TELEPHONE AND FAX NOS.:

Billy M. Kidd 715-555-6408
1109 Sky Blue Mountain Trail
Billings, Montana 48906

ATTORNEY FOR *(Name)*: Self-represented

FOR COURT USE ONLY

SUPERIOR COURT OF CALIFORNIA, COUNTY OF Los Angeles
STREET ADDRESS: 111 No. Hill Street
MAILING ADDRESS: 111 No. Hill Street
CITY AND ZIP CODE: Los Angeles, CA 90012
BRANCH NAME: CENTRAL DISTRICT

ESTATE OF *(Name)*: ANABELLE KIDD, aka ANABELLE O. KIDD

[X] DECEDENT [ ] CONSERVATEE [ ] MINOR

EX PARTE PETITION FOR AUTHORITY TO SELL SECURITIES AND ORDER

CASE NUMBER: BP 14813

1. **Petitioner** *(name of each; see footnote[1] before completing)*: Billy M. Kidd

   is the [X] personal representative [ ] conservator [ ] guardian of the estate and requests a court order authorizing sale of estate securities.

2. a. The estate's securities described on the reverse should be sold for cash at the market price at the time of sale on an established stock or bond exchange, or, if unlisted, the sale will be made for not less than the minimum price stated on the reverse.
   b. [ ] Authority is given in decedent's will to sell property; **or**
   c. [X] The sale is necessary to raise cash to pay
      (1) [ ] debts
      (2) [ ] legacies
      (3) [ ] family allowance
      (4) [ ] expenses
      (5) [ ] support of ward
      (6) [X] other *(specify)*: To avoid distribution of undivided interests
   d. [X] The sale is for the advantage, benefit, and best interests of the estate, and those interested in the estate.
   e. Other facts pertinent to this petition are as follows:
      (1) [X] Special notice has not been requested.
      (2) [ ] Waivers of all special notices are presented with this petition.
      (3) [X] No security to be sold is specifically bequeathed.
      (4) [ ] Other *(specify)*:

Date:

* (Signature of all petitioners also required (Prob. Code, § 1020).)

▶ (not applicable)
(SIGNATURE OF ATTORNEY *)

I declare under penalty of perjury under the laws of the State of California that the foregoing is true and correct.

Date: September 12, 20xx

Billy M. Kidd
(TYPE OR PRINT NAME)

▶ *Billy M. Kidd*
(SIGNATURE OF PETITIONER)

(TYPE OR PRINT NAME)

▶
(SIGNATURE OF PETITIONER)

[1] Each personal representative, guardian, or conservator must sign the petition.

(Continued on reverse)

Ex Parte Petition for Authority to Sell Securities and Order (page 2)

ESTATE OF *(Name)*: ANABELLE KIDD, deceased	CASE NUMBER: BP 14813

LIST OF SECURITIES

Number of shares or face value of bonds	Name of security	Name of exchange *(when required by local rule)*	Recent bid asked *(when required by local rule)*	Minimum selling price
300 shares	Macy's Inc., common	NYSE		

ORDER AUTHORIZING SALE OF SECURITIES

THE COURT FINDS the sale is proper.

THE COURT ORDERS

The ☐ personal representative ☐ guardian ☐ conservator is authorized to sell the securities described above upon the terms and conditions specified. Notice of hearing on the petition is dispensed with.

Date:

____

JUDGE OF THE SUPERIOR COURT

☐ SIGNATURE FOLLOWS LAST ATTACHMENT

DE-270, GC-070 [Rev. January 1, 1998]

EX PARTE PETITION FOR AUTHORITY TO SELL SECURITIES AND ORDER

Page two

If the will gives you, as executor, authority to sell property, check Box 2b. Otherwise, you must state the necessity for the sale in Item 2c. In many counties you may simply allege that the sale is made to avoid distribution of undivided interests. Check Item 2d and indicate in Item 2e whether requests for special notice are on file. If a special notice on file requests special notice of either all matters or petitions for the sale of property (see the box checked under Item 2 of the Request for Special Notice form), then you should only proceed if the interested person will submit a document waiving the request for special notice. If the stock is not specifically bequeathed, check Item 2e(3). If the stock is specifically bequeathed, say so in Item 2e(4) and attach the written consent of the beneficiaries.

On the reverse side of the form, list the correct name of each company, the precise number of shares or bonds to be sold, and the name of the exchange on which the security is traded, if so traded. Another column is provided for inserting recent "bid" and "asked" quotations for a security that is traded but not on an established exchange. If a security is traded on an exchange, the minimum selling price need not be stated. Otherwise, a minimum price should be provided that is approximately 10% below current trading prices to allow for fluctuations between the time the order is obtained and the time the stock is sold. If mutual fund shares are to be redeemed, insert in the minimum-selling-price column a statement that "the shares will be redeemed by the issuer for the net asset value per share on the date of redemption."

When the petition is ready to file, check with the court to find out its procedures for obtaining ex parte orders. It is usually advisable to file the petition in person to obtain the order quickly, rather than mail it to the court. Once the order has been signed, obtain one certified copy for each issuer listed in the petition.

Step 14: Prepare the Inventory and Appraisal

On this important form, you list all of the decedent's property that is subject to probate in California. The noncash assets listed on the Inventory and Appraisal (DE-160) must be appraised by a probate referee who has been appointed by court order. (For information on the appointment of the probate referee, see Step 12.) All probate assets are appraised as of the date of death.

General Instructions

You must file the inventory of the probate assets within four months after letters are issued. (Prob. Code § 8800.) Some courts (for example, Riverside County) strictly enforce this rule, so we recommend that the inventory be prepared as soon as possible on the form shown below. The description of the probate assets will follow the same general format as on the Schedule of Assets you prepared (Chapter 5), with these additional requirements:

1. If the decedent owned only a partial interest in an asset (for example, a one-half or one-third interest with others), indicate this in the beginning of your description. For example, a "one-half interest in promissory note secured by deed of trust ..." or a "one-third interest in real property located at ...." Make clear in the description that the decedent owned only a part interest; otherwise the referee will appraise the asset at its full value, which would be incorrect.
2. List only assets subject to probate that were owned at the date of death.
3. Provide the full *legal description* of all real property, and for each property you must also include the assessor's parcel number, which you can find on the property's tax bill.

4. For a mortgage or deed of trust secured by real property (that is, an amount that is owed to the decedent, not an amount owed by the decedent), include the recording reference or, if not recorded, a legal description of the real property. (Caution: If an encumbrance on real property is unrecorded, you should immediately see an attorney to take steps to make an estate's lien claim a matter of record.)
5. Indicate whether the property is community, quasi-community, or separate property of the decedent. If community property passes outright to the surviving spouse or domestic partner, it doesn't require probate (unless the surviving spouse or partner wishes the property to be probated) and is not listed on the inventory. (See Chapter 15.) If the decedent willed his or her one-half interest in community property to someone else, however, it is listed.

The Inventory and Appraisal (DE-160) is fairly short. This is because the assets are listed on separate attachment sheets stapled to the first page of the inventory. These attachments (Inventory and Appraisal Attachment, DE-161) should list everything owned by the decedent at the time of death, except joint tenancy property, property held in trust (including living trusts), pay on death accounts, death benefits, and retirement plan or insurance proceeds payable to named beneficiaries. (You do, however, list insurance proceeds or death benefits payable to the estate.) Number and describe each asset separately and fully, as shown in the samples below. Don't be afraid to call the referee and ask how to list a certain asset. Further information and instructions are available in *The Probate Referee Guide*, published by the California Probate Referee's Association and available for download at www.probatereferees.net.

The first attachment (Attachment 1) is for assets for which the value is certain and which will be appraised by the personal representative. Under Probate Code Section 8901, such assets include:

- money and checks, drafts, or money orders issued on or before the date of death that can be immediately converted to cash
- checks issued after the date of death for wages, or for refunds of tax and utility bills, and Medicare, medical insurance, and other health care reimbursements and payments
- bank accounts and certificates of deposit
- money market funds or accounts, including a brokerage cash account, and
- insurance proceeds or retirement fund benefits payable in a lump sum to the estate.

Specifically describe and number each item consecutively, as in our example below. Insert the date-of-death value of each item in the column at the right, and show an overall total at the end.

List all other property on Attachment 2, with the values left blank so the referee may fill in the appraisals. Our sample of Attachment 2 shows how to describe many noncash assets. The referee doesn't normally examine household items and personal effects, which means you should include an estimate of the value of these items in a cover letter when you forward the inventory to the referee. They are usually grouped together as one item and valued at what they would bring at a yard sale or if sold to someone who purchases household goods. In other words, they are not worth much. The referee will usually accept your suggested valuation, if it seems reasonable, and will insert it as the appraised value.

Instructions for the Inventory and Appraisal (DE-160)

Heading. In the large block titled "Inventory and Appraisal," check the box that says "Final." The other boxes are checked when a filing a partial, supplemental, or corrected inventory. However, in a simple estate, the initial inventory is usually the final inventory. In unusual circumstances, additional assets may be discovered after the filing of an inventory, in which case a supplemental inventory may be filed (checking the appropriate box) with separate attachments describing the additional assets. Send a supplemental inventory to the referee for processing in the same way as the initial inventory.

Insert the date of death in the small box in the lower right corner of the heading.

Item 1. Fill in the total value of assets listed on Attachment 1.

Inventory and Appraisal (page 1)

DE-160/GC-040

ATTORNEY OR PARTY WITHOUT ATTORNEY *(Name, state bar number, and address)*:

Billy M. Kidd
1109 Sky Blue Mountain Trail
Billings, Montana 48906

TELEPHONE NO.: 715-555-6408 FAX NO. *(Optional)*:
E-MAIL ADDRESS *(Optional)*:
ATTORNEY FOR *(Name)*: Self-represented

FOR COURT USE ONLY

SUPERIOR COURT OF CALIFORNIA, COUNTY OF LOS ANGELES
STREET ADDRESS: 111 No. Hill Street
MAILING ADDRESS: 111 No. Hill Street
CITY AND ZIP CODE: Los Angeles, CA 90012
BRANCH NAME: CENTRAL DISTRICT

ESTATE OF *(Name)*: ANABELLE KIDD, aka ANABELLE O. KIDD

[X] DECEDENT [ ] CONSERVATEE [ ] MINOR

INVENTORY AND APPRAISAL

[ ] **Partial No.:** [ ] **Corrected**
[X] **Final** [ ] **Reappraisal for Sale**
[ ] **Supplemental** [X] **Property Tax Certificate**

CASE NUMBER: BP 14813

Date of Death of Decedent ~~or of Appointment of Guardian or Conservator:~~ 6-18-20xx

APPRAISALS

1. Total appraisal by representative, guardian, or conservator (Attachment 1): $ $38,590.38
2. Total appraisal by referee (Attachment 2): $

TOTAL: $

DECLARATION OF REPRESENTATIVE, GUARDIAN, CONSERVATOR, OR SMALL ESTATE CLAIMANT

3. Attachments 1 and 2 together with all prior inventories filed contain a true statement of [X] all [ ] a portion of the estate that has come to my knowledge or possession, including particularly all money and all just claims the estate has against me. I have truly, honestly, and impartially appraised to the best of my ability each item set forth in Attachment 1.
4. [ ] No probate referee is required [ ] by order of the court dated *(specify)*:
5. **Property tax certificate.** I certify that the requirements of Revenue and Taxation Code section 480
   a. [ ] are not applicable because the decedent owned no real property in California at the time of death.
   b. [X] have been satisfied by the filing of a change of ownership statement with the county recorder or assessor of each county in California in which the decedent owned property at the time of death.

I declare under penalty of perjury under the laws of the State of California that the foregoing is true and correct.

Date: August 28, 20xx

Billy M. Kidd ▶ *Billy M. Kidd*

(TYPE OR PRINT NAME; INCLUDE TITLE IF CORPORATE OFFICER) (SIGNATURE)

STATEMENT ABOUT THE BOND

(Complete in all cases. Must be signed by attorney for fiduciary, or by fiduciary without an attorney.)

6. [X] Bond is waived, or the sole fiduciary is a corporate fiduciary or an exempt government agency.
7. [ ] Bond filed in the amount of: $ [ ] Sufficient [ ] Insufficient
8. [ ] Receipts for: $ have been filed with the court for deposits in a blocked account at *(specify institution and location)*:

Date: August 28, 20xx

Billy M. Kidd ▶ *Billy M. Kidd*

(TYPE OR PRINT NAME) (SIGNATURE OF ATTORNEY OR PARTY WITHOUT ATTORNEY)

Inventory and Appraisal (page 2)

DE-160/GC-040

ESTATE OF *(Name):* ANABELLE KIDD [X] DECEDENT [ ] CONSERVATEE [ ] MINOR	CASE NUMBER: BP 14813

DECLARATION OF PROBATE REFEREE

9. I have truly, honestly, and impartially appraised to the best of my ability each item set forth in Attachment 2.
10. A true account of my commission and expenses actually and necessarily incurred pursuant to my appointment is:

Statutory commission: $
Expenses *(specify):* $
TOTAL: $

I declare under penalty of perjury under the laws of the State of California that the foregoing is true and correct.

Date:

(TYPE OR PRINT NAME) ▶ (SIGNATURE OF REFEREE)

INSTRUCTIONS

(See Probate Code sections 2610-2616, 8801, 8804, 8852, 8905, 8960, 8961, and 8963 for additional instructions.)

1. See Probate Code section 8850 for items to be included in the inventory.
2. If the minor or conservatee is or has been during the guardianship or conservatorship confined in a state hospital under the jurisdiction of the State Department of Mental Health or the State Department of Developmental Services, mail a copy to the director of the appropriate department in Sacramento. (Prob. Code, § 2611.)
3. The representative, guardian, conservator, or small estate claimant shall list on Attachment 1 and appraise as of the date of death of the decedent or the date of appointment of the guardian or conservator, at fair market value, moneys, currency, cash items, bank accounts and amounts on deposit with each financial institution (as defined in Probate Code section 40), and the proceeds of life and accident insurance policies and retirement plans payable upon death in lump sum amounts to the estate, except items whose fair market value is, in the opinion of the representative, an amount different from the ostensible value or specified amount.
4. The representative, guardian, conservator, or small estate claimant shall list in Attachment 2 all other assets of the estate which shall be appraised by the referee.
5. If joint tenancy and other assets are listed for appraisal purposes only and not as part of the probate estate, they must be separately listed on additional attachments and their value excluded from the total valuation of Attachments 1 and 2.
6. Each attachment should conform to the format approved by the Judicial Council. *(See Inventory and Appraisal Attachment* (form DE-161/GC-041) and Cal. Rules of Court, rules 2.100—2.119.)

DE-160/GC-040 [Rev. January 1, 2007] **INVENTORY AND APPRAISAL** **Page 2 of 2**

Attachment 1

DE-161, GC-041

ESTATE OF (Name):	CASE NUMBER:
ANABELLE KIDD, deceased	BP 14813

INVENTORY AND APPRAISAL
ATTACHMENT NO.: 1

(In decedents' estates, attachments must conform to Probate Code section 8850(c) regarding community and separate property.)

Page: 1 of: 1 total pages.
(Add pages as required.)

Item No.	Description	Appraised value
1.	SEPARATE PROPERTY	$
	1. Cash in decedent's possession at time of death	26.39
	2. Checking Account No. 145 778, Westside National Bank, Los Angeles; balance at date of death	1,366.49
	3. Certificate of Deposit No. 3459, Central Savings and Loan Association, Santa Monica Branch	
	Principal balance on date of death	20,000.00
	Accrued interest to date of death	143.00
	4. Uncashed check dated 6-12-20xx from Jon Harrad payable to decedent	500.00
	5. Refund of security deposit, Safe Storage	250.00
	6. Magazine refund from Fortune Magazine	10.50
	7. Merrill Lynch Ready Assets Trust, Account No. 063-215-29235	6,294.00
	8. Proceeds of Acme Insurance, Policy No. 54377, payable to decedent's estate	10,000.00
	Total Attachment 1	$38,590.38

Form Approved by the Judicial Council of California
DE-161, GC-041 [Rev. January 1, 1998]
Mandatory Form [1/1/2000]

INVENTORY AND APPRAISAL ATTACHMENT

Probate Code, §§ 301, 2610-2613, 8800-8920, 10309

Attachment 2

DE-161, GC-041

ESTATE OF (Name):	CASE NUMBER:
ANABELLE KIDD, deceased	BP 14813

INVENTORY AND APPRAISAL
ATTACHMENT NO.: 2

(In decedents' estates, attachments must conform to Probate Code section 8850(c) regarding community and separate property.)

Page: 1 of: 1 total pages.
(Add pages as required.)

Item No.	Description	Appraised value
1.	SEPARATE PROPERTY	$
1.	Real property in the city of Santa Monica, County of Los Angeles, State of California, described as Lot 11 in Block 9 of Tract 5721, as per map recorded in Book 63, page 31 of Maps in the office of the County Recorder of said county. Commonly known as 9560 Euclid Street, Santa Monica, improved with a single dwelling. A.P.N. 3467-047-379	______
2.	One-third (1/3) interest as tenant in common with co-owners John Smith and Mary Smith, in real property in the County of Contra Costa, described as Section 3, Township 20 North, Range 3 East (unimproved land) A.P.N. 4562-34-5770	______
3.	300 shares, Macy's, Inc., common stock	______
4.	75 shares, BestCo, Inc., $3 Cumulative, convertible preferred stock	______
5.	Five $100 U.S. Series E bonds, issued June 1975	______
6.	$10,000 promissory note of June 1, 1999, to decedent by David Hudson, unsecured, payable interest only at 7%	______
7.	Decedent's interest as owner in Great Life Insurance Co. Policy No. 365678 on life of decedent's daughter	______
8.	Decedent's 50% interest in Valueless Mining Co., a limited partnership	______
9.	Antique silver teapot, marked "Sheffield, 1893"	______
10.	2002 Chevrolet Camaro automobile	______
11.	Household furniture, furnishings, and personal effects located at decedent's residence	______
	Total Attachment 2	______

Form Approved by the Judicial Council of California
DE-161, GC-041 [Rev. January 1, 1998]
Mandatory Form [1/1/2000]

INVENTORY AND APPRAISAL ATTACHMENT

Probate Code, §§ 301, 2610-2613, 8800-8920, 10309

Change in Ownership Statement—Death of Real Property Owner (page 1)

BOE-502-D (P1) REV. 10 (06-17) ASSR-176 (REV. 8-17)

CHANGE IN OWNERSHIP STATEMENT
DEATH OF REAL PROPERTY OWNER

This notice is a request for a completed Change in Ownership Statement. Failure to file this statement will result in the assessment of a penalty.

JEFFREY PRANG
ASSESSOR

COUNTY OF LOS ANGELES • OFFICE OF THE ASSESSOR
500 WEST TEMPLE STREET ROOM 205
LOS ANGELES, CA 90012-2770 • Telephone 213.974.3441
Email: helpdesk@assessor.lacounty.gov
Website: assessor.lacounty.gov
Si desea ayuda en Español, llame al número 213.974.3211

NAME AND MAILING ADDRESS
(Make necessary corrections to the printed name and mailing address)

Billy M. Kidd
1109 Sky Blue Mountain Trail
Billings, Montana 48906

Section 480(b) of the Revenue and Taxation Code requires that the personal representative file this statement with the Assessor in each county where the decedent owned property at the time of death. **File a separate statement for each parcel of real property owned by the decedent.**

NAME OF DECEDENT	DATE OF DEATH
Anabelle Kidd	June 18, 20XX

☑ YES ☐ NO Did the decedent have an interest in real property in this county? If **YES**, answer all questions. If **NO**, sign and complete the certification on page 2.

STREET ADDRESS OF REAL PROPERTY	CITY	ZIP CODE	ASSESSOR'S PARCEL NUMBER (APN)*
9560 Euclid Street	Santa Monica	90404	3467-047-375

*If more than 1 parcel, attach separate sheet.

DESCRIPTIVE INFORMATION ☑ *(IF APN UNKNOWN)*

☐ Copy of deed by which decedent acquired title is attached.
☐ Copy of decedent's most recent tax bill is attached.
☐ Deed or tax bill is not available; legal description is attached.

DISPOSITION OF REAL PROPERTY ☑

☐ Succession without a will
☐ Probate Code 13650 distribution
☐ Affidavit of death of joint tenant
☑ Decree of distribution pursuant to will
☐ Action of trustee pursuant to terms of a trust

TRANSFER INFORMATION ☑ Check all that apply and list details below.

☐ Decedent's spouse ☐ Decedent's registered domestic partner

☑ Decedent's child(ren) or parent(s.) If qualified for exclusion from assessment, a *Claim for Reassessment Exclusion for Transfer Between Parent and Child* must be filed (see instructions).

☑ Decedent's grandchild(ren.) If qualified for exclusion from assessment, a *Claim for Reassessment Exclusion for Transfer from Grandparent to Grandchild* must be filed (see instructions).

☐ Cotenant to cotenant. If qualified for exclusion from assessment, an *Affidavit of Cotenant Residency* must be filed (see instructions).

☐ Other beneficiaries or heirs.

☐ A trust.

NAME OF TRUSTEE	ADDRESS OF TRUSTEE

List names and percentage of ownership of all beneficiaries or heirs:

NAME OF BENEFICIARY OR HEIRS	RELATIONSHIP TO DECEDENT	PERCENT OF OWNERSHIP RECEIVED
Mary Kidd Clark	Daughter	One-third
Billy M. Kidd	Son	One-third
Carson Kidd	Grandson	One-third

☑ This property has been or will be sold prior to distribution. (Attach the conveyance document and/or court order).

NOTE: Sale of the property does not relieve the need to file a *Claim for Reassessment Exclusion for Transfer Between Parent and Child* if appropriate.

THIS DOCUMENT IS NOT SUBJECT TO PUBLIC INSPECTION

Change in Ownership Statement—Death of Real Property Owner (page 2)

BOE-502-D (P2) REV. 10 (06-17) ASSR-176 (REV. 8-17)

☐ YES ☑ NO Will the decree of distribution include distribution of an ownership interest in any legal entity that owns real property in this county? If **YES**, will the distribution result in any person or legal entity obtaining control of more than 50% of the ownership of that legal entity? ☐ YES ☐ NO If **YES**, complete the following section.

NAME AND ADDRESS OF LEGAL ENTITY	NAME OF PERSON OR ENTITY GAINING SUCH CONTROL

☐ YES ☑ NO Was the decedent the lessor or lessee in a lease that had an original term of 35 years or more, including renewal options? If **YES**, provide the names and addresses of all other parties to the lease.

NAME	MAILING ADDRESS	CITY	STATE	ZIP CODE

MAILING ADDRESS FOR FUTURE PROPERTY TAX STATEMENTS

NAME
Billy M. Kidd

ADDRESS	CITY	STATE	ZIP CODE
1109 Sky Blue Mountain Trail	Billings	MT	48906

CERTIFICATION

I certify (or declare) under penalty of perjury under the laws of the State of California that the information contained herein is true, correct and complete to the best of my knowledge and belief.

SIGNATURE OF SPOUSE/REGISTERED DOMESTIC PARTNER/PERSONAL REPRESENTATIVE	PRINTED NAME
▶ *Billy M. Kidd*	Billy M. Kidd

TITLE	DATE
Executor	9-10-20XX

EMAIL ADDRESS	DAYTIME TELEPHONE
xxxx@gmail.com	(715) 555-6000

INSTRUCTIONS

Failure to file a Change in Ownership Statement within the time prescribed by law may result in a penalty of either $100 or 10% of the taxes applicable to the new base year value of the real property or manufactured home, whichever is greater, but not to exceed five thousand dollars ($5,000) if the property is eligible for the homeowners' exemption or twenty thousand dollars ($20,000) if the property is not eligible for the homeowners' exemption if that failure to file was not willful. This penalty will be added to the assessment roll and shall be collected like any other delinquent property taxes and subjected to the same penalties for nonpayment.

Section 480 of the Revenue and Taxation Code states, in part:

(a) Whenever there occurs any change in ownership of real property or of a manufactured home that is subject to local property taxation and is assessed by the county assessor, the transferee shall file a signed change in ownership statement in the county where the real property or manufactured home is located, as provided for in subdivision (c). In the case of a change in ownership where the transferee is not locally assessed, no change in ownership statement is required.

(b) The personal representative shall file a change in ownership statement with the county recorder or assessor in each county in which the decedent owned real property at the time of death that is subject to probate proceedings. The statement shall be filed prior to or at the time the inventory and appraisal is filed with the court clerk. In all other cases in which an interest in real property is transferred by reason of death, including a transfer through the medium of a trust, the change in ownership statement or statements shall be filed by the trustee (if the property was held in trust) or the transferee with the county recorder or assessor in each county in which the decedent owned an interest in real property within 150 days after the date of death.

The above requested information is required by law. Please reference the following:

- Passage of Decedent's Property: Beneficial interest passes to the decedent's heirs effectively on the decedent's date of death. However, a document must be recorded to vest title in the heirs. An attorney should be consulted to discuss the specific facts of your situation.
- Change in Ownership: California Code of Regulations, Title 18, Rule 462.260(c), states in part that "[i]nheritance (by will or intestate succession)" shall be "the date of death of decedent."
- Inventory and Appraisal: Probate Code, Section 8800, states in part, "Concurrent with the filing of the inventory and appraisal pursuant to this section, the personal representative shall also file a certification that the requirements of Section 480 of the Revenue and Taxation Code either:
  (1) Are not applicable because the decedent owned no real property in California at the time of death
  (2) Have been satisfied by the filing of a change in ownership statement with the county recorder or assessor of each county in California in which the decedent owned property at the time of death."
- Parent/Child and Grandparent/Grandchild Exclusions: A claim must be filed within three years after the date of death/transfer, but prior to the date of transfer to a third party; or within six months after the date of mailing of a Notice of Assessed Value Change, issued as a result of the transfer of property for which the claim is filed. An application may be obtained by contacting the county assessor.
- Cotenant to cotenant. An affidavit must be filed with the county assessor. An affidavit may be obtained by contacting the county assessor.

This statement will remain confidential as required by Revenue and Taxation Code Section 481, which states in part: "These statements are not public documents and are not open to inspection, except as provided by Section 408."

Item 2. The total value of the assets appraised by the referee on Attachment 2 will be filled in by the referee. The total of Attachment 1 and Attachment 2 will also be completed by the referee.

Item 3. Check the first box, before "all" as indicated on the sample form, unless you are filing a partial or supplemental inventory, in which case you should check the next box to indicate that the inventory only reflects a portion of the estate.

Item 4. Check the first box only if all assets are Attachment 1 assets that do not need to be appraised by a referee. The second box applies if the appointment of the referee has been waived by the court and is usually left blank.

Item 5. If the decedent owned real property in California, you must file a Change in Ownership Statement—Death of Real Property Owner with the county assessor's office. The statement is filed in the county where the real property is located. (See Chapter 8.) Passage of title by inheritance is considered a change in ownership, generally requiring a reassessment for property tax purposes, unless the real property goes to a surviving spouse, surviving domestic partner, or, in certain circumstances, the decedent's children, grandchildren or cotenants.

Even if the property will not be reassessed, you must still file the Change in Ownership Statement.

Each county has its own form based on Board of Equalization form BOE-502-D, which may be obtained on the county assessor's website or by calling the county assessor's office. However, most accept forms furnished by other counties. See the sample provided.

When the Inventory and Appraisal is filed, the personal representative must certify that either a Change in Ownership Statement has been filed or that the decedent owned no real property in California at the time of death. (Prob. Code § 8800(d).) Do this by checking the applicable box in Item 5.

Items 6, 7, and 8. Complete the Statement About the Bond section on every Inventory and Appraisal. Whether you complete this section before or after you send the form to the probate referee will depend upon whether or not bond is required. Check the box for Item 6 if the Order for Probate signed by the court indicates at Item 5a that bond is not required.

Letter to Probate Referee

September 15, 20xx

Mr. Frank Adams
California Probate Referee
7856 Third Street
West Los Angeles, CA 90410

Re: Estate of Anabelle Kidd, Deceased
Los Angeles County Superior Court
Case No. BP 14813

Dear Mr. Adams:

Enclosed is the Order for Probate showing that you have been appointed by the Court to appraise the assets in the above estate.

Enclosed are the original and one copy of the Inventory and Appraisal. Please appraise the assets listed on Attachment 2 and return to me for filing with the Court.

The approximate date-of-death value of the household furniture, furnishings, and personal effects was $350.

Should you require any additional information, please contact me at the address and phone number indicated below.

Thank you for your assistance.

Sincerely,
Billy M. Kidd
Billy M. Kidd
1109 Sky Blue Mountain Trail
Billings, MT 48906
715-555-6408

If bond was required on the Order for Probate at Item 5b, check Box 7 and fill in the amount of the bond. You cannot determine whether the bond is sufficient until after the probate referee appraises the inventory, so you may need to wait to complete the remainder of this section. When you receive the appraised inventory from the probate referee, check to make sure that the amount of the bond is sufficient. The two boxes in Item 7 that say "sufficient" or "insufficient" are for this purpose. To be sufficient, the amount of the bond should be equal to the value of all of the personal property plus the annual estimated income from real and personal property in the estate (or twice this amount if personal sureties are used), excluding cash or other personal property deposited in blocked accounts. If bond is insufficient, an additional bond will be required by the court. (See Chapter 13.) If blocked accounts were established, check Box 8 and fill in the information.

Forward the Inventory and Appraisal with the appropriate attachments to the probate referee. The referee will fill in the second page of the form. In your cover letter, include additional information about unusual assets to help with the appraisals. For instance, in the case of income property or business interests, the referee will probably need operating statements for at least the last three years (usually the handiest source is the decedent's income tax returns). If the inventory contains real property that is subject to depreciation for income tax purposes, the referee will appraise the land and improvements separately, if requested to do so, so the new owner can later justify a new basis for depreciation.

The referee will complete the appraisals, insert the values of the assets appraised, enter information about commission and expenses at Item 10, sign the Inventory and Appraisal on page two, and return it to you within 60 days for filing with the court.

When the inventory is prepared, submitted to the probate referee, received back from the probate referee, and before filing it with the court, the estate representative signs it under oath after Item 5. (If there is more than one estate representative, each representative must sign.) The estate representative also needs to sign the Statement About the Bond after Item 8.

If you disagree with the appraised value, contact the probate referee prior to filing the Inventory and Appraisal with the court. In many counties, the inventory must be filed in duplicate. If the referee did not insert the total of Attachments 1 and 2 under Item 2, do this yourself. When you file the Inventory and Appraisal, also file with the court any writing by the decedent that directs how tangible personal property should be distributed. (Prob. Code § 6132.)

TIP

Try to resolve appraisal concerns informally. While formal procedures do exist to challenge an appraised value, many times the issue can be resolved informally by providing additional information to the probate referee.

CAUTION

Sending copies to others. Under Probate Code Section 8803, you must mail a copy of the Inventory and Appraisal to anyone who has requested special notice within 15 days after the inventory is filed with the court. The Judicial Council form DE-120 may be modified for this purpose, to show that it is a Notice of Filing the Inventory and Appraisal. See Step 3 for general information on mailing notice.

Unique Assets

Appraisal of unique items, such as coin or art collections, sometimes requires expertise beyond that of most probate referees. If the decedent owned a unique, artistic, unusual, or special item of tangible personal property, you have the option of having it appraised by an independent expert instead of a probate referee. (Prob. Code §§ 8904 and 8905.)

If you want to do that, prepare a separate and additional Attachment 1 for the independent expert. On that Attachment 1, list all items to be appraised by the expert, and have the expert sign a declaration in the following form:

Declaration of Independent Expert

I have truly, honestly, and impartially appraised, to the best of my ability, each item set forth in this Attachment 1.

I declare under penalty of perjury under the laws of the State of California that the foregoing is true and correct.

Date: ______________________

____
(Type or print name)

____
(Signature of independent expert)

Another more common option for unique items is to provide the probate appraiser with an appraisal from a reliable source, such as a dealer or other expert. The probate appraiser will often then consider that information in valuing the asset.

Step 15: Notify Creditors and Deal With Creditors' Claims and Other Debts

As estate representative, you must handle the decedent's debts. If you have authority to administer the estate under the Independent Administration of Estates Act, you may allow, pay, reject, contest, or compromise any claim against the estate without court supervision and without first giving a Notice of Proposed Action. (Prob. Code §§ 10552(a) and (b).)

Generally, creditors' claims are debts and obligations of the decedent that were due and unpaid as of the date of death and funeral expenses. Expenses and obligations incurred *after* the date of death, such as court filing fees, certification fees, and expenditures necessary to protect estate property, are administration expenses and don't require formal claims. Formal claims are also not required for tax bills, secured debts such as mortgages on real property, or judgments secured by recorded liens.

CAUTION

Notify all mortgage lenders. If the decedent owned a house or other real estate that was acquired with a "money purchase" loan (that is, a loan used to buy the real property), the loan is a "nonrecourse" loan. That means the lender has no recourse against the decedent's other assets. The lender can only go after the real estate that secures the loan. If, however, the decedent refinanced the loan, it is no longer a money purchase loan, and the lender can attach the decedent's other assets to pay off the debt. For this reason, many attorneys recommend giving a written Notice of Administration to Creditors (see below) to all lenders who hold mortgages on real property in the estate.

SEE AN EXPERT

Paying debts and claims is subject to many technical rules. If the estate you are settling involves large debts or claims other than the usual expenses, get the advice of an attorney.

Written Notice to Creditors

The personal representative must give actual written notice to all known or reasonably ascertainable creditors. (Prob. Code § 9050.) The written notice is in addition to the published notice discussed in Step 3. It is given on a Notice to Creditors (DE-157), which advises the creditor how and where to file a claim. A sample is shown below.

Here are the rules on when claims may be filed (Prob. Code §§ 9051 and 9100):

- You must give the notice to all known or reasonably ascertainable creditors within four months after the date letters are first issued to the personal representative. All creditors so notified must file their claims within the four-month period.
- If a creditor is discovered only during the last 30 days of the four-month period, or *after* the four- month period has expired, you must give notice to that creditor within 30 days after discovery of the creditor. That creditor then has 60 days from the date notice is given to file a claim.
- If a creditor does not receive notice and only discovers that he has a claim after the four-month period has expired, the creditor may petition the court to file a late claim under Probate Code Section 9103. A late claim cannot be allowed after one year from the date of death. (Civ. Proc. Code § 366.2.)

Generally, claims are barred from payment if they are not filed within these time frames. In limited cases, a distributee of an estate may be liable for a claim if the creditor was known or reasonably ascertainable and the personal representative did not give the creditor written Notice of Administration. (Prob. Code § 9392.) Actions against a distributee must be commenced within one year of the date of death.

A personal representative is not liable to a creditor for failure to give written notice to that creditor unless the failure was in bad faith. The burden of proving bad faith is on the person seeking to impose liability. (Prob. Code § 9053.)

Notice to Creditors (page 1)

DE-157

NOTICE OF ADMINISTRATION
OF THE ESTATE OF

ANABELLE KIDD, aka Anabelle O. Kidd
(NAME)

DECEDENT

NOTICE TO CREDITORS

1. *(Name):* Billy M. Kidd
(Address): 1109 Sky Blue Mountain Trail
Billings, Montana 48906

(Telephone): 715-555-6408

is the **personal representative** of the **ESTATE OF** *(name):* Anabelle Kidd, who is deceased.

2. The personal representative HAS BEGUN ADMINISTRATION of the decedent's estate in the
   a. **SUPERIOR COURT OF CALIFORNIA, COUNTY OF** ***(specify):***
   STREET ADDRESS: 111 No Hill Street
   MAILING ADDRESS: 111 No Hill Street
   CITY AND ZIP CODE: Los Angeles, CA 90012
   BRANCH NAME: CENTRAL DISTRICT
   b. Case number *(specify):* BP 14813

3. You must FILE YOUR CLAIM with the court clerk (address in item 2a) AND mail or deliver a copy to the personal representative before the **last to occur** of the following dates:
   a. **four months** after *(date):* July 25, 20xx, the date letters (authority to act for the estate) were first issued to a general personal representative, as defined in subdivision (b) of section 58 of the California Probate Code, **OR**
   b. **60 days** after *(date):* August 2, 20xx, the date this notice was mailed or personally delivered to you.

4. LATE CLAIMS: If you do not file your claim within the time required by law, you must file a petition with the court for permission to file a late claim as provided in Probate Code section 9103. Not all claims are eligible for additional time to file. See section 9103(a).

EFFECT OF OTHER LAWS: Other California statutes and legal authority may affect your rights as a creditor. You may want to consult with an attorney knowledgeable in California law.

WHERE TO GET A CREDITOR'S CLAIM FORM: If a *Creditor's Claim* (form DE-172) did not accompany this notice, you may obtain a copy of the form from any superior court clerk or from the person who sent you this notice. You may also access a fillable version of the form on the Internet at *www.courts.ca.gov/forms* under the form group Probate—Decedents' Estates. A letter to the court stating your claim is *not* sufficient.

FAILURE TO FILE A CLAIM: Failure to file a claim with the court and serve a copy of the claim on the personal representative will in most instances invalidate your claim.

IF YOU MAIL YOUR CLAIM: If you use the mail to file your claim with the court, for your protection you should send your claim by certified mail, with return receipt requested. If you use the mail to serve a copy of your claim on the personal representative, you should also use certified mail.

Note: To assist the creditor and the court, please send a blank copy of the *Creditor's Claim* form with this notice.

(Proof of Service by Mail on reverse)

Page 1 of 2

Form Adopted for Mandatory Use
Judicial Council of California
DE-157 [Rev. January 1, 2013]

NOTICE OF ADMINISTRATION TO CREDITORS
(Probate—Decedents' Estates)

Probate Code, §§ 9050, 9052
www.courts.ca.gov

Notice to Creditors (page 2)

DE-157

ESTATE OF *(Name):* ANABELLE KIDD, aka Anabelle O. Kidd DECEDENT	CASE NUMBER: BP 14813

[Optional]

PROOF OF SERVICE BY MAIL

1. I am over the age of 18 and not a party to this cause. I am a resident of or employed in the county where the mailing occurred.
2. My residence or business address is *(specify)*:
   25 Sutter Street, Billings, Montana 48906
3. I served the foregoing *Notice of Administration to Creditors* [✓] and a blank *Creditor's Claim* form* on each person named below by enclosing a copy in an envelope addressed as shown below AND
   a. [✓] **depositing** the sealed envelope with the United States Postal Service with the postage fully prepaid.
   b. [ ] **placing** the envelope for collection and mailing on the date and at the place shown in item 4 following our ordinary business practices. I am readily familiar with the business's practice for collecting and processing correspondence for mailing. On the same day that correspondence is placed for collection and mailing, it is deposited in the ordinary course of business with the United States Postal Service in a sealed envelope with postage fully prepaid.
4. a. Date of deposit: August 2, 20xx b. Place of deposit *(city and state):*

I declare under penalty of perjury under the laws of the State of California that the foregoing is true and correct.

Date:

August 2, 20xx ▶ ____________________

(TYPE OR PRINT NAME) (SIGNATURE OF DECLARANT)

NAME AND ADDRESS OF EACH PERSON TO WHOM NOTICE WAS MAILED

	Name of person	Address *(number, street, city, state, and zip code)*
1.	Bullocks Wilshire	P.O. Box 19807 Los Angeles, CA 90002
2.	Jon Harrad	1206 19th Street Santa Monica, CA 90047
3.	Sullivan's Catering	11560 Lincoln Boulevard Marina del Rey, CA 90408
4.	Springs Ambulance Service	P.O. Box 2349 Santa Monica, CA 90405
5.	Bankamericard Visa	P.O. Box 1848 - Terminal Annex Los Angeles, CA 90007
6.		
7.		
8.		

[ ] List of names and addresses continued in attachment. *(You may use form POS-30(P) to show additional persons to whom a copy of this notice was mailed. Do not use page 2 of this form or form POS-030(P) to show that you personally delivered a copy of this notice to a creditor. You may use forms POS-020 and POS-020(P) for that purpose.)*

*** NOTE:** *To assist the creditor and the court, please send a blank copy of the* Creditor's Claim *(form DE-172) with the notice.*

DE-157 [Rev. January 1, 2013] **NOTICE OF ADMINISTRATION TO CREDITORS (Probate—Decedents' Estates)** Page 2 of 2

Creditor's Claim (page 1)

DE-172

ATTORNEY OR PARTY WITHOUT ATTORNEY (*Name, state bar number, and address*): TELEPHONE AND FAX NOS.:
Michael Sullivan 310-555-6632
11560 Lincoln Boulevard
Marina del Rey, California 90488

ATTORNEY FOR (*Name*): Self-represented

FOR COURT USE ONLY

SUPERIOR COURT OF CALIFORNIA, COUNTY OF Los Angeles
STREET ADDRESS: 111 No. Hill Street
MAILING ADDRESS: 111 No. Hill Street
CITY AND ZIP CODE: Los Angeles, CA 90012
BRANCH NAME: CENTRAL DISTRICT

ESTATE OF (*Name*):
ANABELLE KIDD, aka ANABELLE O. KIDD DECEDENT

CREDITOR'S CLAIM

CASE NUMBER: BP 14813

You must file this claim with the court clerk at the court address above before the LATER of (a) four months after the date letters (authority to act for the estate) were first issued to the personal representative, or (b) sixty days after the date the *Notice of Administration* was given to the creditor, if notice was given as provided in Probate Code section 9051. You must also mail or deliver a copy of this claim to the personal representative and his or her attorney. A proof of service is on the reverse.
WARNING: Your claim will in most instances be invalid if you do not properly complete this form, file it on time with the court, and mail or deliver a copy to the personal representative and his or her attorney.

1. Total amount of the claim: $ 347.00
2. Claimant (*name*): Michael Sullivan
   a. [X] an individual
   b. [ ] an individual or entity doing business under the fictitious name of (*specify*):
   c. [ ] a partnership. The person signing has authority to sign on behalf of the partnership.
   d. [ ] a corporation. The person signing has authority to sign on behalf of the corporation.
   e. [ ] other (specify):
3. Address of claimant (*specify*):
   11560 Lincoln Boulevard, Marina del Rey, CA 90488
4. Claimant is [X] the creditor [ ] a person acting on behalf of creditor (*state reason*):
5. [ ] Claimant is [ ] the personal representative [ ] the attorney for the personal representative.
6. I am authorized to make this claim which is just and due or may become due. All payments on or offsets to the claim have been credited. Facts supporting the claim are [X] on reverse [X] attached.

I declare under penalty of perjury under the laws of the State of California that the foregoing is true and correct.

Date: August 15, 20xx

Michael Sullivan ▶ *Michael Sullivan*
(TYPE OR PRINT NAME AND TITLE) (SIGNATURE OF CLAIMANT)

INSTRUCTIONS TO CLAIMANT

A. On the reverse, itemize the claim and show the date the service was rendered or the debt incurred. Describe the item or service in detail, and indicate the amount claimed for each item. Do not include debts incurred after the date of death, except funeral claims.
B. If the claim is not due or contingent, or the amount is not yet ascertainable, state the facts supporting the claim.
C. If the claim is secured by a note or other written instrument, the original or a copy must be attached (*state why original is unavailable.*) If secured by mortgage, deed of trust, or other lien on property that is of record, it is sufficient to describe the security and refer to the date or volume and page, and county where recorded. (*See Prob. Code, § 9152.*)
D. Mail or take this original claim to the court clerk's office for filing. If mailed, use certified mail, with return receipt requested.
E. Mail or deliver a copy to the personal representative and his or her attorney. Complete the *Proof of Mailing or Personal Delivery* on the reverse.
F. The personal representative or his or her attorney will notify you when your claim is allowed or rejected.
G. Claims against the estate by the personal representative and the attorney for the personal representative must be filed within the claim period allowed in Probate Code section 9100. See the notice box above.

(Continued on reverse)

Form Approved by the Judicial Council of California
DE-172 [Rev. January 1, 1998]
Mandatory Form [1/1/2000]

CREDITOR'S CLAIM
(Probate)

Probate Code, §§ 9000 et seq., 9153

Creditor's Claim (page 2)

ESTATE OF *(Name)*: Anabelle Kidd, a.k.a. Anabelle O. Kidd DECEDENT	CASE NUMBER: BP 14813

FACTS SUPPORTING THE CREDITOR'S CLAIM
[X] **See attachment** ***(if space is insufficient)***

Date of item	Item and supporting facts	Amount claimed
6-10-20xx	Food and service provided decedent per attached statement	$347.00
	TOTAL:	**$** 347.00

PROOF OF [X] **MAILING** [ ] **PERSONAL DELIVERY TO PERSONAL REPRESENTATIVE**
(Be sure to mail or take the original to the court clerk's office for filing)

1. I am the creditor or a person acting on behalf of the creditor. At the time of mailing or delivery I was at least 18 years of age.
2. My residence or business address is *(specify)*:
   11560 Lincoln Blvd., Marina del Rey, Calif.
3. I mailed or personally delivered a copy of this *Creditor's Claim* to the personal representative as follows *(check either a or b below)*:
   a. [X] **Mail**. I am a resident of or employed in the county where the mailing occurred.
      (1) I enclosed a copy in an envelope AND
         (a) [X] **deposited** the sealed envelope with the United States Postal Service with the postage fully prepaid.
         (b) [ ] **placed** the envelope for collection and mailing on the date and at the place shown in items below following our ordinary business practices. I am readily familiar with this business' practice for collecting and processing correspondence for mailing. On the same day that correspondence is placed for collection and mailing, it is deposited in the ordinary course of business with the United States Postal Service in a sealed envelope with postage fully prepaid.
      (2) The envelope was addressed and mailed first-class as follows:
         (a) Name of personal representative served: Billy M. Kidd
         (b) Address on envelope: 1109 Sky Blue Mountain Trail
             Billings, Montana 48906
         (c) Date of mailing: August 15, 20xx
         (d) Place of mailing *(city and state)*: Marina del Rey, CA 90488
   b. [ ] **Personal delivery**. I personally delivered a copy of the claim to the personal representative as follows:
      (1) Name of personal representative served:
      (2) Address where delivered:
      (3) Date delivered:
      (4) Time delivered:

I declare under penalty of perjury under the laws of the State of California that the foregoing is true and correct.

Date: August 15, 20xx

Michael Sullivan
(TYPE OR PRINT NAME OF CLAIMANT)

Michael Sullivan
(SIGNATURE OF CLAIMANT)

DE-172 [Rev. January 1,1998]

CREDITOR'S CLAIM
(Probate)

Page two

TIP

Collect and examine all itemized bills and statements that have been sent to the decedent. If bills are legitimate and the estate has sufficient assets, you may be able to save time and paperwork by paying them under the provisions of Probate Code Section 10552 or Section 9154, without giving written notice or requiring a formal claim, as discussed below.

Written notice should be given to all creditors, or potential creditors, who can be identified through reasonably diligent efforts. For your protection, make a thorough search of the decedent's files and records for evidence of any obligation or potential liability the decedent may have had at death. Look for such things as outstanding loans, mortgages, promissory notes, disputed bills, pending or anticipated lawsuits where the decedent is or could be a defendant, and outstanding judgments against the decedent.

For each possible creditor, make a list of the name of the individual, corporation, or other entity, the mailing address, the account number, and any other information relevant to the debt or obligation. Each creditor on this list should receive a written Notice of Administration to Creditors (DE-157) and should be required to file a formal creditor's claim—Creditor's Claim (DE-172). This task can be simplified by preparing a master copy of the notice, filling in all relevant information except the date in Item 3b, and making several copies. Also make a copy of the Creditor's Claim (DE-172) to provide to each creditor.

When you're ready to mail the notice, fill in the date before sending it to the creditor, and have a disinterested person mail the copies of the notice along with a blank Creditor's Claim, and complete the proof of mailing on page two. In some counties, the original notice(s) should be filed with the court.

How to Fill Out the Notice of Administration to Creditors (DE-157)

Caption. Fill in the decedent's name.

Item 1. Fill in the name, address, and phone number of the executor or administrator and the name of the decedent.

Item 2. Fill in the address and branch name of the court and the case number.

Item 3. In the first box, put the date letters were issued. In the second box, put the date you are mailing the notice.

Proof of Service. Have a disinterested person mail copies of the notice to creditors and fill out and sign the Proof of Service on page two of the original notice. Check the box in Item 3 if including a copy of the Creditor's Claim. Keep the original notice(s) until you are ready to close the estate. You may need to file them with the court when you file the Petition for Final Distribution.

Bills You May Pay Without a Claim or Giving Written Notice

Under Probate Code Section 9154, a written demand for payment, such as an itemized bill or statement, may be treated as an established claim if it's received within four months after letters are issued. You can pay these debts without requiring a formal creditor's claim if they're bona fide debts and paid in good faith, and the estate is solvent. If the estate is insolvent, there is an order of priority for payment set by law in Probate Code Section 11420.

As a practical matter, in simple estates it's easier to pay ordinary expenses such as utility bills, account balances, doctor or other medical bills, funeral expenses, property taxes and income taxes, and other clearly proper debts without giving written notice or requiring a formal claim as long as you're sure no one will object to the payment. Just remember these requirements: (1) You must have received a written demand for payment within four months after letters were issued, (2) the debt must be justly due, (3) the amount you pay must take into account any previous payments or offsets, (4) payment must be made within 30 days after the four-month period that begins with issuance of your letters, and (5) the estate must be solvent.

Formal Creditors' Claims

The published Notice of Petition to Administer Estate (DE-121) advises creditors how and when to file claims. Subject to the few exceptions discussed in

"Written Notice to Creditors," above, a creditor must file a formal Creditor's Claim (DE-172) directly with the court within four months after letters are issued, or 60 days after notice was mailed or delivered to the creditor, whichever is later. The creditor must also serve the creditor's claim on the personal representative within the four-month period or within 30 days of the filing of the claim, whichever is later.

Few formal claims, if any, are filed in uncomplicated estates. Usually, you just receive bills addressed to the decedent's last address, because many creditors don't know of the death.

A sample Creditor's Claim is shown above.

Claim by Personal Representative

If you, as personal representative, have paid any of the decedent's debts from your personal funds (funeral expenses or utility bills, for example), or have any other claim against the estate, you must file a Creditor's Claim (DE-172) with the court. Attach copies of canceled checks or other evidence of payment. A claims examiner will review the claim, and the court's approval or rejection will be endorsed on the Allowance or Rejection of Creditor's Claim (DE-174) (discussed below), which you should submit with the claim when it is filed. After the court has approved the claim, you pay yourself the amount allowed out of estate funds.

As stated previously, payment of administrative expenses such as court filing fees don't require formal claims. You may be reimbursed for these expenses from the estate bank account immediately after your appointment.

Allowance or Rejection of Creditors' Claims

If formal claims are filed, you must allow, reject, or partially allow each one. You prepare an Allowance or Rejection of Creditor's Claim (DE-174) to let the creditor and the court know what action you've taken on the claim. You file the original form with the court (with a copy of the claim attached) and provide a copy to the creditor and the creditor's attorney, if any. The mailing or personal delivery to the creditor must be done by a disinterested adult, who afterwards must complete the proof of mailing or personal delivery on page two of the original form before it's filed. If you have authority to administer the estate under the Independent Administration of Estates Act, no further court action is required; however, if you don't have independent powers, the court must review your action and endorse its allowance or rejection on the original form.

You should examine each Creditor's Claim carefully to make sure (1) it's signed and dated,the debt was incurred or the service was rendered before the date of death, and (2) the claim was filed within the four-month claim period or within 60 days after written notice was given. Otherwise, it may be defective and not be an allowable claim. If the defect is minor and you have authority to administer the estate under the Independent Administration of Estates Act, you may choose to use the Notice of Proposed Action (DE-165) to inform interested parties of your intended action. Claims generally may not be paid when filed after the one-year statute of limitations of Code of Civil Procedure Section 366.2.

If you receive a creditor's claim for a debt you question for some reason (for example, the amount is too high or the service rendered wasn't satisfactory), you may reject the claim in whole or in part. A creditor who refuses to accept the amount you allow has 90 days from the date of the rejection within which to file suit against the estate. If the suit is not filed within such time, the claim is barred forever. If the creditor files suit, you'll need an attorney. Whenever a claim is rejected, you must wait three months from the date of rejection before filing a petition to close the estate.

Payment of Claims

Claims for funeral expenses, last illness expenses, and wage claims that have been allowed and approved should be paid promptly as soon as there are sufficient funds in the estate, after retaining enough to pay administration expenses and debts owed to the United States or California. (Prob. Code § 11421.)

Allowance or Rejection of Creditor's Claim (page 1)

DE-174

ATTORNEY OR PARTY WITHOUT ATTORNEY *(Name, State Bar number, and address):*
Billy M. Kidd
1109 Sky Blue Mountain Trail
Billings, Montana 48906

TELEPHONE NO.: 715-555-6408 FAX NO. *(Optional):*
E-MAIL ADDRESS *(Optional):*
ATTORNEY FOR *(Name):* Self-represented

FOR COURT USE ONLY

SUPERIOR COURT OF CALIFORNIA, COUNTY OF Los Angeles
STREET ADDRESS: 111 No. Hill Street
MAILING ADDRESS: 111 No. Hill Street
CITY AND ZIP CODE: Los Angeles, CA 90012
BRANCH NAME: CENTRAL DISTRICT

ESTATE OF *(Name):* ANABELLE KIDD, aka ANABELLE O. KIDD, DECEDENT

ALLOWANCE OR REJECTION OF CREDITOR'S CLAIM

CASE NUMBER: BP 14813

NOTE TO PERSONAL REPRESENTATIVE

Attach a copy of the creditor's claim to this form. If approval or rejection by the court is not required, do not include any pages attached to the creditor's claim.

PERSONAL REPRESENTATIVE'S ALLOWANCE OR REJECTION

1. Name of creditor *(specify):* Michael Sullivan
2. The claim was filed on *(date):* August 15, 20xx
3. Date of first issuance of letters: July 25, 20xx
4. Date of *Notice of Administration*: August 2, 20xx
5. Date of decedent's death: June 18, 20xx
6. Estimated value of estate: $356,900
7. Total amount of the claim: $347.00
8. [x] Claim is allowed for: $347.00 *(The court must approve certain claims before they are paid.)*
9. [ ] Claim is rejected for: $ *(A creditor has 90 days to act on a rejected claim.* See box below.)*
10. Notice of allowance or rejection given on *(date):* August 20, 20xx
11. [x] The personal representative is authorized to administer the estate under the Independent Administration of Estates Act.

Date: August 20, 20xx

Billy M. Kidd
(TYPE OR PRINT NAME OF PERSONAL REPRESENTATIVE)

▶ *Billy M. Kidd*
(SIGNATURE OF PERSONAL REPRESENTATIVE)

NOTICE TO CREDITOR ON REJECTED CLAIM

From the date that notice of rejection is given, you must act on the rejected claim (e.g., file a lawsuit) as follows:

1. **Claim due:** within 90 days* after the notice of rejection.
2. **Claim not due:** within 90 days* after the claim becomes due.

***The 90-day period mentioned above may not apply to your claim because some claims are not treated as creditors' claims or are subject to special statutes of limitations, or for other legal reasons. You should consult with an attorney if you have any questions about or are unsure of your rights and obligations concerning your claim.**

COURT'S APPROVAL OR REJECTION

12. [ ] Approved for: $
13. [ ] Rejected for: $

Date:

SIGNATURE OF JUDICIAL OFFICER

14. Number of pages attached: ________ [ ] SIGNATURE FOLLOWS LAST ATTACHMENT

(Proof of Mailing or Personal Delivery on reverse)

Page 1 of 2

Form Adopted for Mandatory Use
Judicial Council of California
DE-174 [Rev. January 1, 2009]

ALLOWANCE OR REJECTION OF CREDITOR'S CLAIM
(Probate—Decedents' Estates)

Probate Code, § 9000 et seq., 9250-9256, 9353

Allowance or Rejection of Creditor's Claim (page 2)

DE-174

ESTATE OF (Name): ANABELLE KIDD, aka ANABELLE O. KIDD, DECEDENT	CASE NUMBER: BP 14813

PROOF OF [x] MAILING [ ] PERSONAL DELIVERY TO CREDITOR

1. At the time of mailing or personal delivery I was at least 18 years of age and **not a party** to this proceeding.
2. My residence or business address is *(specify):* 25 Sutter Street, Billings, MT 48906
3. I mailed or personally delivered a copy of the *Allowance or Rejection of Creditor's Claim* as follows *(complete either a or b)*:

   a. [x] **Mail.** I am a resident of or employed in the county where the mailing occurred.

   (1) I enclosed a copy in an envelope AND

   (a) [x] **deposited** the sealed envelope with the United States Postal Service with the postage fully prepaid.

   (b) [ ] **placed** the envelope for collection and mailing on the date and at the place shown in items below following our ordinary business practices. I am readily familiar with this business's practice for collecting and processing correspondence for mailing. On the same day that correspondence is placed for collection and mailing, it is deposited in the ordinary course of business with the United States Postal Service in a sealed envelope with postage fully prepaid.

   (2) The envelope was addressed and mailed first-class as follows:

   (a) Name of creditor served: Michael Sullivan

   (b) Address on envelope: 11560 Lincoln Boulevard
Marina del Rey, CA 90488

   (c) Date of mailing:

   (d) Place of mailing *(city and state):*

   b. [ ] **Personal delivery.** I personally delivered a copy to the creditor as follows:

   (1) Name of creditor served:

   (2) Address where delivered:

   (3) Date delivered:

   (4) Time delivered:

I declare under penalty of perjury under the laws of the State of California that the foregoing is true and correct.

Date: August 20, 20xx

Samantha Long
(TYPE OR PRINT NAME OF DECLARANT)

▶ Samantha Long
(SIGNATURE OF DECLARANT)

Strictly speaking, you're not required to pay any other claims without a court order. However, this rule isn't strictly observed where the personal representative has independent administration authority. You may safely pay other allowed and approved claims as long as (1) the time for filing or presenting claims has not expired, (2) the estate is solvent and there is cash available for payment, and (3) no one having an interest in the estate is going to challenge the payment. If the claim is based on a written contract, interest accrues at the rate and in accordance with the contract. (Prob. Code § 11423.)

If the Department of Health Care Services has filed a claim for the cost of Medi-Cal services, you must ordinarily pay the full claim before probate closes. If the estate doesn't have enough cash, but does contain real estate, the Department may agree to let property be distributed, but with a lien against the estate. Contact the Department if you run into difficulty paying the debt. The rules for Medi-Cal recovery are complex and changing; consider getting help from an attorney.

How to Fill Out the Allowance or Rejection of Creditor's Claim (DE-174)

Caption. Fill in your name, address, the court's name, and case number, as you have on your other court papers.

Items 1-7. Fill in the requested information (most of it is on the Creditor's Claim (DE-172)). Leave Item 2 blank if you don't know when the claim was filed with the court. Item 6 may be the same as provided as Item 3d(7) of the Petition for Probate.

Items 8 and 9. Fill in the amount you are approving or rejecting.

Item 10. Enter the date you mail this form to the creditor.

Item 11. Check the box if you are authorized to administer the estate under the Independent Administration of Estates Act.

Print your name, and date and sign the form. Leave the rest of the front page blank.

Proof of Service. Whoever mails or gives the form to the creditor should fill out and sign the Proof of Service on page two of the original of the form, after a copy is sent to the creditor. Then you file the original with the court.

Step 16: Prepare the Petition for Final Distribution

After the creditor's claim period has expired (four months from the issuance of letters), you may file a petition with the court requesting an order distributing the assets to the beneficiaries—if the estate is in a condition to be closed. You must file the Petition for Final Distribution within one year after letters have issued (or 18 months if a federal estate tax return is required in the estate). If the estate is not ready to be closed by that time, you must file a status report showing the condition of the estate, the reasons why the estate cannot be distributed and closed, and an estimate of the time needed to close administration of the estate. Check local court procedures.

Following is a checklist of the requirements to help you determine whether or not the estate is ready to be closed:

1. The creditor's claim period has expired.
2. All creditor's claims have been allowed and approved and paid or sufficiently secured. If any were rejected, the time to file suit on the rejected claims must have expired. (See Step 15, above.)
3. All expenses of administration, including charges for legal advertising, bond premiums, and probate referee's fees, have been paid.
4. All taxes have been paid, or payment secured.

If you do not have enough information to complete all tax returns but the estate is otherwise ready to close, you may request a cash reserve to cover payment of any taxes that may be due. For example, if the decedent died early in the year and received enough income for that year to require a final income tax return, you have the option of either filing the decedent's final income tax return before filing the Petition for Final Distribution and paying the tax (assuming you have the required information), or you may wait and file the return after the end of the calendar year and request a sufficient reserve from distribution to pay the estimated taxes.

Petition for Final Distribution (page 1)

BILLY M. KIDD
1109 Sky Blue Mountain Trail
Billings, Montana 48906

Telephone: 715-555-6408
Petitioner, self-represented

SUPERIOR COURT OF CALIFORNIA

FOR THE COUNTY OF LOS ANGELES

Estate of	) CASE NO. BP 14813
ANABELLE KIDD, aka ANABELLE O. KIDD	) PETITION FOR FINAL DISTRIBUTION ON WAIVER OF ACCOUNTING (**Add if applicable:** AND FOR ALLOWANCE OF STATUTORY COMPENSATION TO PERSONAL REPRESENTATIVE)
	) (Prob. Code §§ 10400-10406, 10954, 11600-11642)
deceased.	) Hearing Date:) Time:) Department:) Judge:

Petitioner, BILLY M. KIDD, as personal representative of the estate of the above-named decedent, states:

1. ANABELLE KIDD, aka ANABELLE O. KIDD, died testate (**or** intestate) on June 18, 20xx, a resident of the county named above. Petitioner was appointed personal representative of decedent's estate and letters were issued to petitioner on August 20, 20xx.

2. Notice of death was timely published. Petitioner made a thorough search of decedent's files and records for evidence of any obligation or potential liability the decedent may have had at death. No reasonably

Petition for Final Distribution (page 2)

ascertainable creditors were found beyond those who submitted bills in the ordinary course, all of which were paid within the four-month claim period, and therefore specific notice of administration under Probate Code Section 9050 was not required. (**Or, if applicable:** Actual notice of administration under Probate Code Section 9050 was given to each known or reasonably ascertainable creditor, except those within the class described in Probate Code Section 9054. The notices are on file herein with proof of service. Attached as Exhibit "A" is a list of all creditors who were given notice, including the date notice was mailed.) More than four (4) months have elapsed since letters were first issued (**Add, if applicable:** and more than 60 days have elapsed since the last notice of administration was given.) The time for filing claims has expired.

3. The decedent did not receive Medi-Cal benefits, nor was the decedent the surviving spouse or registered domestic partner of a person who received Medi-Cal benefits, and notice to the Director of Health Care Services is not required.

(or)

3. Notice of this proceeding with a copy of the decedent's death certificate was mailed to the Director of Health Care Services on _______________, 20___.

4. No heir or beneficiary is known to be held or previously confined in a prison or facility under the jurisdiction of the Department of Corrections and Rehabilitation or is confined in any county or city jail, road camp, industrial farm or other local correctional facility and notice to the Director of California Victim Compensation Board is not required.

(or)

Petition for Final Distribution (page 3)

4. Notice of this proceeding with a copy of the decedent's death certificate as well as information concerning the heir or beneficiary as required by Probate Code § 216 was mailed to the Director of California Victim Compensation and Government Claims Board on ________________, 20__.

5. Notice to the Franchise Tax Board was given on ________________, 20__; a copy of which is attached as Exhibit "A."

6. No claims were filed against the estate.

(or)

6. Exhibit "B" to this petition lists all claims filed against the estate, including the name of the claimant, the nature of the claim, amount of the claim, the date filed, and the action taken. (**Add, if applicable:** The date of service of notice of rejection of each rejected claim is also stated. Petitioner has no knowledge of any suit having been filed on any rejected claim and no service of process has been served upon petitioner. The time to file suit has expired.) All debts paid were legally enforceable claims against the estate.

7. Certain debts were paid under the provisions of Probate Code Section 9154, without formal claims having been filed. All such creditors made a written demand for payment within four months after letters were issued. The debts were justly due, were paid in good faith within 30 days after expiration of the four-month claim period, the amounts paid were net payments or setoffs. The estate is solvent.

8. All debts of the decedent and of the estate and all administration expenses, including charges for legal advertising, (add if applicable: bond premiums), and probate referee's fees have been paid and the estate is in a condition to be closed.

9. An Inventory and Appraisal of the estate assets was filed, showing the value of the estate to be $ ________________.

3

PETITION FOR FINAL DISTRIBUTION ON WAIVER OF ACCOUNTING

Petition for Final Distribution (page 4)

10. The estate was administered under the Independent Administration of Estates Act. No independent acts were performed that required a Notice of Proposed Action.

(or)

10. The estate was administered under the Independent Administration of Estates Act. Petitioner performed the following actions without court supervision, after having given a Notice of Proposed Action if required:

a. Petitioner sold the decedent's residence at 9560 Euclid Street, Santa Monica, to John A. Buyer on September 1, 20xx for the sales price of $395,000. Notice of Proposed Action was given to Mary Kidd Clark and Carson Kidd, who, in addition to Petitioner, are all persons whose interest was affected by the sale, and no objections were received. The original notice is on file herein, with proof of service.

b. Petitioner sold the decedent's Chevrolet automobile to Willy Worthy, without notice, for cash in the sum of $8,000. Said automobile would have depreciated in value and caused expense to the estate by being kept.

c. To avoid the expense of storing the decedent's household furniture, furnishings, and personal effects, petitioner allowed the beneficiaries to take possession of the items they were presumptively entitled to, as authorized by Probate Code Section 9650(c), and the remaining items were sold without notice at public sales, for cash. Said property would have caused expense to the estate by being kept and it was in the best interests of the estate that it be disposed of promptly.

11. All income tax returns due by the decedent or the estate as of the date of this petition have been filed and the taxes paid. **Note: If all income taxes not paid, add:** except returns for the tax year(s) of (describe). Petitioner will request a reserve from distribution to pay all taxes in full.)

12. No estate taxes are owed in this estate.

4

PETITION FOR FINAL DISTRIBUTION ON WAIVER OF ACCOUNTING

Petition for Final Distribution (page 5)

(or)

12. Federal estate taxes will be owed by the estate and have not yet been paid. Petitioner believes that estate taxes will not exceed $__________, and petitioner will request a sufficient reserve from distribution to pay all estate taxes in full.

13. The assets on hand, including their community or separate character, are set forth in Exhibit "C."

14. The names, present addresses, ages, and relationship to the decedent of all persons entitled to receive property of the estate and the plan of distribution are set forth in Exhibit "D."

15. No requests for special notice have been filed in this matter.

(or)

15. The following person(s) filed a request for special notice in this matter:

Name	Address
[list name]	[list address]

16. Petitioner waives the filing of a final account. **Add, if appropriate:** Waivers of Account by the remaining beneficiaries are attached as Exhibits "E," etc.)

17. Petitioner waives any right to statutory compensation.

(or)

17. Petitioner's statutory compensation is computed as follows:

Amount of Inventory and Appraisal [list final appraised value]

4% on first	$100,000.00	=	$4,000.00
3% on next	$100,000.00	=	$3,000.00
2% on next	[list relevant amount greater than $200,000]	=	[calculate amount]
	Total compensation	=	$[enter calculated total]

Petition for Final Distribution (page 6)

18. Petitioner requests authorization to withhold $________ for closing expenses (**Add, if applicable:** and as a reserve for payment of income taxes or other liabilities that may hereafter be determined to be due from the estate.)

19. No compensation has been paid from estate assets to the representative or to an attorney for the representative.

20. There is no family or affiliate relationship between the representative and any agent hired by the representative during the administration of the estate.

Add, if estate contains cash:

21. Petitioner has kept all cash invested in interest-bearing accounts or other investments authorized by law, except what was needed to administer estate.

Add, if applicable:

22. The estate contained real property and a change of ownership report was filed with the county assessor in the county where the real property is located.

WHEREFORE, petitioner prays that the administration of the estate be brought to a close without the requirement of an accounting; that all reported acts and proceedings of petitioner as herein set forth be confirmed and approved; (**Add, if applicable:** that petitioner be authorized to retain $________ for closing expenses and to pay liabilities, and to deliver the unused part to the beneficiaries of the estate without further court order after the closing expenses have been paid;) (**Add, if applicable:** that Billy M. Kidd be allowed $________ as statutory compensation; that distribution of the estate in petitioner's hands and any other property of the decedent or the estate not now known or

Petition for Final Distribution (page 7)

discovered be made to the persons entitled to it, as set forth in the petition, and the Court make such further Orders as may be proper.

DATED: December 10, 20xx

Billy M. Kidd

BILLY M. KIDD, Petitioner

Attach verification page as last page after exhibits

Verification

Verification

I, the undersigned, the petitioner and personal representative of the estate of the above-named decedent, declare that I have read the foregoing Petition for Final Distribution on Waiver of Accounting and the requests designated therein and know its contents. I declare that the petition, including all attachments, is true to my knowledge, except as to matters in it stated on my own information and belief, and as to those matters I believe it to be true.

I declare under penalty of perjury under the laws of the State of California that the foregoing is true and correct and that this declaration was executed on ______ **Date signed** ______, 20____ at ______ **Place signed** ___________, California.

______ **You sign here** ______
Petitioner

Petition for Final Distribution Exhibit "A"

ESTATE OF ANABELLE KIDD, DECEASED

EXHIBIT "A"

Creditors Given Notice of Administration

(Probate Code Sec. 9050)

Creditor	Date of Service of Notice
Springs Ambulance Service	8-2-20xx
Michael Sullivan	8-2-20xx
Bankamericard Visa	8-2-20xx
Bullock's Wilshire	8-2-20xx
John Harrad	8-2-20xx

Petition for Final Distribution Exhibit "B"

ESTATE OF ANABELLE KIDD, DECEASED

EXHIBIT "B"

Creditors' Claims

Claimant	Nature of Claim	Amount of Claim	Date Filed	Date of Service of Notice of Rejection or Date Paid
Wilshire Medical Center	Last illness expense	$237.50	9-4-20xx	Paid 10-15-20xx
Michael Sullivan	Food and services provided decedent	347.00	8-15-20xx	Paid 10-15-20xx
Harry's Auto Shop	Auto services - (previously paid by decedent)	150.00	8-23-20xx	Rejected on 8-31-20xx
Bankamericard Visa	Account balance	789.56	8-23-20xx	Paid 8-31-20xx

Federal *estate* taxes may also be paid from a cash reserve, if the estate is large enough to require a federal estate tax return and it has not yet been finalized. The estate's final fiduciary income tax returns are always filed *after* the estate is closed and distributed. You do not have to request a tax reserve for the final fiduciary returns, because the income and deductions are passed through to the beneficiaries. Tax matters are discussed in Chapter 7.

Besides taxes that may be paid after distribution, the petition should also request a reserve for miscellaneous closing expenses such as the cost of transferring securities, certifying and recording copies of the Order for Final Distribution, fees for preparation of income tax returns, and reasonable storage, delivery, and shipping costs for distribution of tangible personal property to a distributee.

There is no official form for the Petition for Final Distribution. You will need to type it, following the sample and customizing for your particular circumstance and local rule requirements. This document reports to the court the actions taken during administration, the current status of the estate, and a request for court authorization to distribute the estate.

Note that alternative paragraphs listed address different situations. Use only the provisions that fit your situation, which you can determine after reading the notes below keyed to each numbered provision. If you omit any of the paragraphs in the example (which may be likely, depending on your situation) be sure to renumber the paragraphs. Also, letter all exhibits consecutively, without skipping any letters.

CAUTION

Special local requirements. The samples we provide should be acceptable for most counties. However, most courts have requirements of their own for the preparation of petitions and orders, so be sure to carefully read the local probate rules. You might even examine some probate files at the courthouse for specific examples.

To prepare the Petition for Final Distribution, you will need the numbered court paper or "pleading paper" that we discussed in Chapter 13. Review the instructions in that section before you begin. Here are a few key points:

- The title of the court must start on or below Line 8.
- The title of the estate usually starts on Line 11 on the left side of the paper, as shown.
- On the right side, enter the case number assigned to you when you filed your first petition, as shown in our sample.
- Double-space the body of the petition so each typewritten line is opposite one of the numbers on the left side of the paper. Also, be sure to keep within the margins.

Here are some guidelines for preparing the petition:

Heading. Under the case number, type in the title of the petition as shown. The title must include what the petition requests; in some cases the petition requests more than final distribution. The sample provided presumes that an accounting has been waived. Add the words in parentheses if you will request compensation as the personal representative. (If distribution will be made to a trust established by the will, add "AND DISTRIBUTION TO TESTAMENTARY TRUST.") Some courts (for example, Riverside County) require that the applicable Probate Code sections be shown under the title. Under that, type in a space for the time and place of the hearing.

The body of the petition starts on the next numbered line after your heading.

Paragraph 1. Indicate whether the decedent died testate (with a will) or intestate (without a will). It's good practice to include the date letters were issued.

Paragraph 2. If you gave a written Notice to Creditor to any creditor (see Step 15), use the alternate language in parentheses. For some counties, such as Los Angeles, you must also file the notices and the proof of service, and attach a schedule of all creditors who were given notice, listing the date of the notice. (Remember, if the notice was given during the last 30 days of the four-month period, the claims period doesn't expire until 60 days after that last notice was given.)

Paragraphs 3 and 4. Use whichever language applies.

Paragraph 5. Insert the date notice was given to the Franchise Tax Board. Some courts also require you to file a letter from the Franchise Tax Board in response to the notice.

Paragraph 6. If no formal claims were filed, use the first Paragraph 6. If formal claims were filed with the court, use the second Paragraph 6 and list the claims and relevant details in an exhibit. (If the accounting is waived, you do not have to list debts paid without formal claims under Probate Code § 9154.)

If there were rejected claims, add the wording in parentheses.

Paragraph 7. When debts are paid without formal claims, as in most estates, include this paragraph. Such debts usually do not have to be listed if an accounting is waived, but some courts may require it.

Paragraph 8. In a simple estate, debts and expenses of administration, except for closing expenses, will be paid before filing the Petition for Final Distribution. Include this paragraph to report to the court that the estate is in a position to be closed.

Paragraph 9. Fill in the total appraised value of the estate inventory. Get this figure from the Inventory and Appraisal. (See Step 14.) Be sure to include the final appraised value of all assets in the estate, particularly if you completed partial, supplemental, or corrected Inventory and Appraisal forms. If multiple Inventory and Appraisal forms were filed, provide a simple explanation of the filing date of the forms that reflect the final appraised value.

Paragraph 10. If you performed any actions without court supervision under the Independent Administration of Estates Act, especially those that require a Notice of Proposed Action, list and describe them here. Ordinary steps taken in administering the estate and in caring for and preserving the estate assets, such as making ordinary repairs, paying taxes and other expenses, terminating a lease, or storing personal property, need not be listed. However, describe major transactions that substantially affect or alter the property in the estate and the assets that remain on hand for distribution. For instance, if property was sold or additional assets were acquired, describe these actions. Some examples are shown in our sample petition. Others might be:

> "Sold 100 shares of General Oil Corp. common stock, for cash on an established stock exchange."

> "Invested funds of the estate in a $10,000 U.S. Treasury Bond, series 2000, due August 15, 20xx."

> "Continued the operation of the decedent's business known as 'John's Auto Repair Shop,' to preserve the interest of the estate and those persons interested in the business."

> "Executed a $5,000 promissory note, dated January 7, 20xx, interest at 10%, all due and payable January 7, 20xx, secured by deed of trust on real property of the estate located at 1801 Cove Street, Seaside, California."

If a Notice of Proposed Action was given, most counties require that the original be filed with the court (before or at the same time as the Petition for Final Distribution) with a proof of mailing attached, or the consent of the parties shown on the form. A proof of mailing may be typed separately, as shown in Step 13.

Paragraphs 11 and 12. Include these two required paragraphs to show the condition of the estate.

In **Paragraph 11,** add the last sentence shown in parentheses, if this applies to your situation. (See Chapter 13.)

Paragraph 13. The petition must have a schedule attached to it describing in detail all property in the probate estate that is to be distributed. Some counties also require the description to include the appraised value and total balance on hand. (See Exhibit "C," below.) There is no need to explain the difference between property included in the Inventory and Appraisal and the property on hand if an accounting is waived and actions taken under the Independent Administration of Estates Act are listed. If there is real property, provide the legal description, common address, and assessor's parcel number. With the exception of the cash remaining on hand, the value of the assets listed in the petition—if local rules require it to be included—will be the same as the appraised value shown on the Inventory and Appraisal (Step 14, above). This is called the "carry value." If any of the assets have been sold, they will not be listed on this schedule because they are not "on hand" for distribution. Instead, the cash received from the sale will be in the estate's bank account. The amount of cash on hand will be whatever is left in the estate account (both checking and savings) reasonably close to the date you prepare the petition. Any assets that have been acquired since the estate was opened will also be included in the schedule. Cash or other personal property held in blocked accounts should be so indicated, with the name of the depository given. The court order will then direct the depository to distribute the property to the beneficiaries on the closing of the estate.

Paragraph 14. Attach another schedule naming all persons who are entitled to receive property from the estate, showing their addresses, ages, relationship to the decedent, and the amount of property each will receive. The schedule will vary somewhat, depending on whether or not there is a will.

- **When there is no will.** The schedule must list all the heirs who are entitled to the estate according to the laws of intestate succession (as explained in Chapter 3), and the share (fraction) each will receive. Usually, you don't have to itemize the property going to each heir, because each will merely receive a proportionate share of each and every asset. However, some counties (for example, San Diego) require a separate distribution schedule specifically describing the assets going to each distributee. If any heir is deceased, be sure to indicate this and show the date of death, and then list the issue of the deceased heir. A sample of a schedule for an intestate estate is shown below (Example 2).
- **When there is a will.** The decedent's will determines how the property is to be distributed. Therefore, you must set out the will provisions and list all of the beneficiaries and the property they receive. The easiest way to do this is to simply quote the paragraphs in the will that say who receives what. After that, list the beneficiaries' names, addresses, ages ("over 18" or "under 18"), and relationship to the decedent, and what they will receive from the estate. Persons who are not related to the decedent are listed as "not related." (See Example 1, below.)

  As we discussed in Chapter 3, occasionally it is difficult to determine how the property is to be distributed, and you may have some doubt as to how to proceed. This might be the case if the will gives away a lot more than the decedent had, or if a beneficiary under a will predeceased the decedent (or didn't survive the number of days required by the will) and there is no alternate beneficiary. In this situation, your best bet is to consult a lawyer. (See Chapter 16 for guidance on how to hire lawyers.)

  If the will directs that one person receives everything, or to several persons in equal shares, this schedule will be much like the one in an intestate estate where each beneficiary receives a percentage, or fraction. Many wills direct that specific gifts be given to certain persons, such as, "I give $1,000 to John, and I give my antique blue china dishes to Mary, and the remainder of my estate to my daughter, Jane." Unless the will provides otherwise, the specific gifts must normally be paid or distributed first. Whatever property is left is called the "remainder" or "residue" of the estate. If it should so happen that no residue is left after making the specific gifts, then the person or persons entitled to the residue are simply out of luck, *unless there is a provision in the will to prevent this from happening.*

  Examples 1 and 3, below, show how this schedule might be prepared for a testate estate (one having a will).

  A specific gift (for example, "I give my 200 shares of IBM stock to Jane") carries with it income on the property from the date of death, less taxes and other expenses attributable to the property during administration. (Prob. Code § 12002.) Also, unless a will provides otherwise, gifts for a specific amount of money receive interest one year after the date of death if not paid within that time. (Prob. Code § 12003.) To compute the interest, see Probate Code Section 12001. Most simple estates are closed within a year and don't have to deal with this requirement.

  Example 4, below, shows how you would prepare the distribution schedule if the will makes only specific gifts of property and does not contain a provision disposing of the residue of the estate. The property not disposed of by the will passes to the decedent's heirs under intestate succession laws (discussed in Chapter 3). Therefore, it passes one-third to each of the two brothers, and the children of the deceased sister share the one-third their mother would have inherited, or one-sixth each. Albert, the decedent's nephew, doesn't receive anything because the decedent disposed of the Pontiac automobile before his death.

Petition for Final Distribution Exhibit "C"

Estate of Anabelle Kidd, Deceased

Exhibit "C"

Assets on Hand

SEPARATE PROPERTY	Carry Value
1. One-third (1/3) interest as tenant in common with co-owners John and Mary Smith, in real property in the County of Contra Costa, described in Section 3, Township 20 North, Range 3 East; unimproved land, Assessor's Parcel No. 4562-34-5770	$5,000.00
2. 300 shares, Macy's, Inc. common stock	6,000.00
3. 75 shares, Bestco, Inc. $3 Cumulative, convertible preferred stock	1,500.00
4. Five $100 U.S. Series E bonds, issued June 1975	500.00
5. $10,000 promissory note of June 1, 1999, to decedent by David Hudson, unsecured, interest at 7%, payable interest only	10,000.00
6. Decedent's interest as owner in Great Life Insurance Company Policy No. 36678	1,300.00
7. Decedent's 50% interest in Valueless Mining Co., a Limited Partnership	250.00
8. Antique silver teapot, marked "Sheffield, 1893"	90.00
9. Household furniture, furnishings, and personal effects located at decedent's residence	350.00
10. Cash on deposit in checking Account No. 345 778, Westside National Bank, Los Angeles	140,000.00
11. Certificate of Deposit No. 3459, Central Savings and Loan Association, Santa Monica Branch	200,000.00
	$364,990.00

Petition for Final Distribution Exhibit "D" (example 1)

Estate of Anabelle Kidd, Deceased

Exhibit "D"

Beneficiaries Under Decedent's Will and Proposed Distribution

1. The decedent's will disposes of her estate as follows:

   "I give to my friend, ALBERTINE TERREUX, that certain silver teapot marked 'Sheffield, 1893.'

   "I give, devise, and bequeath all the rest, residue, and remainder of my property, of whatsoever kind and character and wheresoever situated, to my husband, CALVIN KIDD. If my husband should predecease me, then in that event I give the residue of my estate to my three children, MARY KIDD CLARK, BILLY M. KIDD, and JON KIDD, in equal shares. If any of my children should predecease me, then that child's share shall go to his or her then living lawful issue, by right of representation."

2. The decedent's husband, CALVIN KIDD, predeceased the decedent. The decedent's son JON KIDD also predeceased the decedent, and under the terms of the decedent's will his share of the estate passes to his son, CARSON KIDD.

3. Petitioner proposes to distribute the estate on hand as follows:

Name and Address	Age	Relationship	Share
Albertine Terreux 17 Rue Madeleine Paris, France	Adult	Not related	Silver teapot marked "Sheffield, 1893"
Mary Kidd Clark 789 Main Street Venice, California 90410	Adult	Daughter	1/3 Residue
Billy M. Kidd 1109 Sky Blue Mountain Trail Billings, Montana 48906	Adult	Son	1/3 Residue
Carson Kidd 711 Valley Road Owens, California 98455	Adult	Grandson	1/3 Residue

Petition for Final Distribution Exhibit "D" (example 2)

Estate of Bonnie Doe, Deceased

Exhibit "D"

Heirs of Decedent and Proposed Distribution

Decedent's heirs at law and the respective shares to which they are entitled are:

Name and Address	Age	Relationship	Share
Robert Doe 100 Ocean Avenue Santa Monica, CA 90000	Over 18	Son	1/2
Mary Smith (Deceased January 10, 1986)		Daughter	
Margaret Smith 1022 - 10th Street Culver City, CA 90000	Over 18	Granddaughter (daughter of Mary Smith)	1/4
William Smith 123 Main Street Los Angeles, CA 90000	Over 18	Grandson (son of Mary Smith)	1/4

Petition for Final Distribution Exhibit "D" (example 3)

Estate of John Doe, Deceased

Exhibit "D"

Beneficiaries Under Decedent's Will
And
Proposed Distribution

1. The decedent's will disposes of this estate as follows:

"I hereby give, devise, and bequeath all of my estate, of every kind and character, to my wife, JANE DOE.

"Should my wife, JANE DOE, predecease me or fail to survive a period of six months following my death, then and in that event, I give, devise, and bequeath the sum of $1,000 to my daughter, MARY CLARK, I hereby give, devise, and bequeath all the rest, residue, and remainder of my estate, both real and personal of whatsoever kind and character and wheresoever situated to my son, ROBERT DOE.

"In the event either of my said two children shall predecease me, or fail to survive a period of six months following my death, then I direct that the share which would otherwise have been paid to that child distributed be to my surviving child."

2. The decedent's wife, JANE DOE, predeceased the decedent. The decedent's daughter, MARY CLARK, and the decedent's son, ROBERT DOE, survived the decedent for six months and are now living.

Name and Address	Age	Relationship	Share
Mary Clark 789 Main Street Venice, California 90000	Over 18	Daughter	$1,000
Robert Doe 21 Kelley Court Santa Ana, CA 90000	Over 18	Son	100% Residue

Petition for Final Distribution Exhibit "D" (example 4) (page 1)

Estate of Susan Jones, Deceased

Exhibit "D"

Beneficiaries Under Decedent's Will
And
Proposed Distribution

1. The decedent's Will disposes of her estate as follows:

   "FIRST, I give my collection of tennis trophies to my niece, Eileen.

   SECOND, I give my 1984 Pontiac automobile to my nephew, Albert.

   THIRD, I give my household furniture, furnishings, and personal effects, and artwork to my brother Mark.

   FOURTH, I give my condominium located at 2009 Sagebrush Circle in Palm Springs, to my brother Ron.

   FIFTH, I give the sum of $10,000 to my sister, Mary."

2. Petitioner, as personal representative of the estate, did not come into possession of the 1984 Pontiac automobile referred to in Article Second of the decedent's Will, and said property was not among the assets of the decedent's estate.

3. The decedent's sister, Mary Smith, predeceased the decedent on January 3, 1996. Accordingly the gift of $10,000 given to Mary Smith in Article Fifth of the Will should be distributed to Mary Smith's surviving issue, her daughter Betty Smith and her son James Smith, in equal shares.

4. Included among the assets of the decedent's estate were 200 shares of Miracle Corporation stock and a 2014 Buick automobile. The decedent's Will does not dispose of these assets, and under the laws of intestate succession such property should be distributed to the decedent's heirs at law whose names, ages, and relationships are set forth below.

5. Proposed Distribution:

Name and Address	Age	Relationship	Share
Mark Jones 21 Paseo St. Cathedral City, CA 90000	Over 18	Brother	Household furniture, furnishings, personal effects, and artwork, plus 1/3 interest as an heir at law in 200 shares of Miracle Corporation stock and a 2014 Buick automobile

Petition for Final Distribution Exhibit "D" (example 4) (page 2)

Estate of Susan Jones, Deceased

Ron Jones 89 Thermal Dr. Apt. 8 Needles, CA 90000	Over 18	Brother	Condominium at 2009 Sagebrush Circle, Palm Springs, plus 1/3 interest as an heir at law in 200 shares of Miracle Corporation stock and a 2014 Buick automobile
Mary Smith, deceased	Sister		
Eileen Jones 1835 Navajo Circle Palm Springs, CA 90000	Under 18	Niece	Trophies
Betty Smith 10 Acorn St. Sun City, CA 90000 (daughter of Mary Smith)	Over 18	Niece	$5,000 plus 1/6 interest as an heir at law in 200 shares of Miracle Corporation stock and a 2014 Buick automobile
James Smith 10 Acorn St. Sun City, CA 90000 (son of Mary Smith)	Over 18	Nephew	$5,000 plus 1/6 interest as an heir at law in 200 shares of Miracle Corporation stock and a 2014 Buick automobile

Petition for Final Distribution Exhibit "D" (example 5) (page 1)

Estate of Laura Smith, Deceased

Exhibit "D"

Beneficiaries Under Decedent's Will
and Proposed Distribution

1. The decedent's Will disposes of her estate as follows:

"THIRD, I hereby give:

A. My nephew, ARTHUR JONES, the sum of $5,000. If he should predecease me, this gift shall lapse and become part of the residue of my estate.

B. My niece, FRIEDA JONES, the sum of $5,000. If she should predecease me, this gift shall lapse and become part of the residue of my estate.

C. I give, devise, bequeath all the rest, residue, and remainder of my estate, both real and personal and wherever situated, to my children, SHARON SMITH, SALLY SMITH, and LINDA SMITH, in equal shares. All of my children are over the age of twenty-one (21) as of the date of this will, with the exception of LINDA. It is my wish that the portion of my estate bequeathed and devised to LINDA be held in trust by ALEXANDER BROWN, as Trustee, to be held, administered, and distributed in accordance with the following provisions.

1. I direct that my Trustee provide for the health, education, welfare, and support, and other needs of LINDA, so long as she is living and is under age thirty-five (35). The Trustee shall pay to or apply for her benefit, as much of the net income and principal of the trust as in the Trustee's discretion he deems necessary, after taking into consideration to the extent the Trustee deems advisable any other income or resources she may possess. Any unexpended income shall be added to the principal.

2. When LINDA for whom a share has been so allocated in trust attains the age of twenty-five (25), the Trustee shall distribute to the said child one-half (1/2) of the principal of such child's trust as then constituted; when said child attains age thirty-five (35) the Trustee shall distribute to said child the undistributed balance of her trust.

3. To carry out the purpose of the trust created for LINDA and subject to any limitations stated elsewhere in this will, the Trustee is vested with the following powers with respect to

Petition for Final Distribution Exhibit "D" (example 5) (page 2)

Estate of Laura Smith, Deceased

EXHIBIT "D" - PAGE 2

the trust estate and any part of it, in addition to those powers now or hereafter conferred by law:

a. To continue to hold any property including shares of the Trustee's own stock, and to operate at the risk of the trust estate any business that the Trustee receives or acquires under the trust as long as the Trustee deems advisable;

b. To manage, control, grant options on, sell (for cash or on deferred payments), convey, exchange, partition, divide, improve, and repair trust property;

c. To borrow money, and to encumber or hypothecate trust property by mortgage, deed of trust, pledge, or otherwise;

4. If LINDA dies before becoming entitled to receive distribution of her share of the estate, the undistributed balance of her portion shall be distributed to her issue, if any, by right of representation, and if none then to my surviving children in equal shares."

2. Proposed Distribution:

Name and Address	Age	Relationship	Share
Arthur Jones 35 Berkeley Square, No. 6 Newhall, California	Adult	Nephew	$5,000
Frieda Jones 3885 Overlook Drive Ojai, California	Adult	Niece	$5,000
Sharon Smith 2332 - 20th Street Santa Monica, California	Adult	Daughter	1/3 residue
Sally Smith 1139 Oak Avenue Ocean Park, California	Adult	Daughter	1/3 residue
Alexander Brown 477 Palisades Park Drive Brentwood Park, California	Adult	Trustee	1/3 residue

3. Alexander Brown has consented to act as Trustee, and a Consent to Act as Trustee and Waiver of Accounting by Alexander Brown is attached to this petition.

Consent to Act as Trustee and Waiver of Accounting

Name:
Address:

Telephone No.:

Petitioner in pro per

SUPERIOR COURT OF CALIFORNIA
COUNTY OF ____________________

Estate of	) NO. ____________
	)
MARY BROWN,	) CONSENT TO ACT AS TRUSTEE AND
	)
deceased	) WAIVER OF ACCOUNTING
____________________	)

The undersigned, named in the Will of the above-named decedent to act as Trustee of the testamentary trust provided for therein, hereby consents to act as Trustee and waives the filing and settlement of a final account by the estate representative.

DATED:__________, 20__

____

Declination to Act as Trustee

Name:
Address:

Telephone No.:

Petitioner in pro per

SUPERIOR COURT OF CALIFORNIA
COUNTY OF ____________________

Estate of) NO. ____________
)
__________, aka) DECLINATION TO ACT AS TRUSTEE
)
__________,)
)
deceased)
____________________)

The undersigned, being nominated by name to act as Trustee of the trust created under the decedent's will, does hereby decline to act as Trustee.

DATED: __________, 20__

____

- **When the will contains a trust.** If the will distributes property in trust for one or more of the beneficiaries, the proposed distribution schedule will list the trustee as a beneficiary, showing the amount distributed to the trust. You do not have to list the trust beneficiaries, nor the property they each receive from the trust. But if the personal representative of the estate and the trustee are the same person, list the beneficiaries of the trust, too, because you must send the notice of petition to the trust beneficiaries in this circumstance. The distribution schedule must also quote the language in the will providing for the trust and the trust provisions. Wills containing trusts are usually many pages long, which in turn makes this exhibit longer. Example 5 shows you an abridged sample of a distribution schedule for a will that contains a simple trust.

  A Consent to Act as Trustee and Waiver of Accounting signed by the trustee must be attached to the petition or filed separately before the hearing date. In some counties, if the personal representative and the trustee are the same person, any Waiver of Accounting must be signed by the trust beneficiaries rather than the trustee. Check local rules.

  If the trustee named in the will declines to act, you will have to file a Declination to Act as Trustee in addition to the successor trustee's Consent to Act. Samples are shown above. If no trustee or successor trustee named in the will can serve, you will likely need the assistance of an attorney to have a trustee appointed.

Distribution to Minors (Under 18)

Usually, you cannot safely distribute property to a minor unless a guardian has been appointed for the minor's estate. However, there are exceptions if the amount to be distributed is small, the decedent's will names a custodian to receive the minor's property, or the minor has a court-appointed guardian. Here are some guidelines.

Minor Has a Court-Appointed Guardian

If a guardian is appointed for the minor's estate, you may distribute the minor's property to the guardian. In this case, add a paragraph to the body of the petition in Paragraph 15 in the following basic form:

> __*(Name of minor)*__, one of the beneficiaries, is a minor, and petitioner proposes to distribute the property belonging to the minor to __*(name of guardian)*__ as guardian of the minor's estate. A copy of Letters of Guardianship issued to the guardian is attached as Exhibit ___.

The Decedent's Will Names a Custodian to Receive Minor's Property

If there is no guardian for the minor's estate, but the decedent nominated a custodian in the will (or in some other document) to receive the minor's property, then the personal representative may transfer the property to that person. The property will be held for the benefit of the minor under the California Uniform Gifts to Minors Act or the California Uniform Transfers to Minors Act.

Specific language must be used when transferring title to the property to the custodian, for example, "John Doe, as Custodian for Mary Doe, under the California Uniform Transfers to Minors Act." Any type of property may be transferred under the California Uniform Transfers to Minors Act. The custodian has certain duties with respect to the custodial property, such as keeping records of all transactions regarding the property, including information necessary for the minor's tax return, and making them available for inspection. The custodian also has certain powers with respect to the management of the custodial property.

A custodianship created in this way ends when the minor reaches age 18, unless the will allows for a later age, up to age 25. A custodianship can be created for a beneficiary who is already older than 18 if the will provides that the custodianship continues until a later age. The laws governing transfers under the Uniform Transfers to Minors Act are set out in Probate Code Sections 3900 to 3925.

Declaration re Distribution to a Minor

Name:
Address:

Telephone Number:
Petitioner, Self-represented

SUPERIOR COURT OF CALIFORNIA

FOR THE COUNTY OF ____________________

Estate of) NO. ____________________
)
____________________) DECLARATION UNDER SECTION 3401 OF
deceased.) THE CALIFORNIA PROBATE CODE
__________________________)

The undersigned declares:

I am a parent of ___________________, a minor, who is a distributee of the estate of the above-named decedent. I am entitled to the custody of the minor. The total estate of the minor, including the money or other property to be paid or delivered from the above estate, does not exceed five thousand dollars ($5,000) in value. I acknowledge my obligation to hold the property received from the above estate in trust for the minor and to account to the minor for the management of this property when the minor reaches the age of majority.

I declare under penalty of perjury under the laws of the State of California that the foregoing is true and correct. Executed this _____ day of ___________________, 20___.

____

DECLARATION

When making a distribution to a custodian nominated by the decedent to receive a minor's property, add the following paragraph to Paragraph 15 of the petition:

> Petitioner proposes to distribute the property belonging to *(name of minor)*, a minor, to *(name of custodian)* as custodian for the minor until age *(age specified in the will, up to age 25, or if no age specified, 18)* under the California Uniform Transfers to Minors Act, as authorized by the decedent's will. A consent to act as custodian, signed by *(name of custodian)*, is attached hereto as Exhibit ___.

Attach as an exhibit the consent document. The consent should be a simple statement, signed and dated by the custodian, such as:

> I hereby consent to act as custodian for *(name of minor)*, under the California Uniform Transfers to Minors Act.

Minor's Estate Does Not Exceed $5,000

If there is no appointed guardian, and the decedent did not nominate a custodian to receive the minor's property but the total estate of the minor (that is, what the minor already owns plus what's being inherited) does not exceed $5,000, then money or other personal property belonging to the minor may be delivered to a parent of the minor. The parent can hold the property in trust for the minor until the minor reaches age 18.

To accomplish this, attach a declaration signed by the parent under oath (under penalty of perjury) to the petition attesting to the fact that the total estate of the minor, including the money or other property delivered to the parent, does not exceed $5,000 in value. A sample declaration is shown above. In this situation, add the following paragraph to Paragraph 15 of the petition:

> *(Name of minor)*, one of the beneficiaries entitled to receive property of the estate, is a minor. The total estate of the minor does not exceed $5,000, and petitioner proposes to distribute the property belonging to the minor to the minor's parent, *(name of parent)*, to be held in trust for the benefit of the minor until age 18, pursuant to Probate Code §§ 3400–3401. A declaration signed by *(name of parent)* attesting to the fact that the total estate of the minor, including the money or other property to be paid or delivered to the parent, does not exceed $5,000 in value, is attached hereto as Exhibit ___.

Property to Be Distributed Does Not Exceed $10,000

If the minor has no guardian of the estate and the decedent did not nominate a custodian, but the property to be transferred does not exceed $10,000 in value, the personal representative may, under certain conditions, designate another adult as custodian under the California Uniform Transfers to Minors Act. This is true even if the will contains no express authorization for such a distribution or if the decedent died intestate. (Prob. Code § 3906.) The conditions are:

- The personal representative must consider the transfer to be in the best interests of the minor, and
- The will must not prohibit the transfer or contain provisions inconsistent with such a transfer.

If you wish to make this type of transfer, we suggest adding a paragraph in substantially the following form to Paragraph 15 of the petition:

> *(Name of minor)*, one of the beneficiaries entitled to receive property of the estate, is a minor. The minor does not have a guardian of the estate appointed, nor did the decedent designate a guardian or custodian to receive property belonging to the minor The property to be distributed to *(name of minor)* does not exceed a value of $10,000, and petitioner, in the capacity as personal representative of the decedent's estate, considers it to be in the best interest of the minor to transfer the property belonging to the minor to *(name of custodian)*, the minor's *(state relationship, for example, parent, adult sister)*, as custodian for *(name of minor)* under the California Uniform Transfers to Minors Act to hold without bond until the minor attains the age of 18 years, pursuant to the provision of Probate Code § 3906. [*Add, if the decedent left a will:* The custodianship is not prohibited by or inconsistent with the terms of the decedent's will or any other governing instrument.] *(Name of custodian)* has consented to act as custodian and written consent is attached hereto as Exhibit ___.

Prepare a consent as described, above.

Petition for Final Distribution—Exhibit "E"

Name:
Address:

Telephone Number:
Petitioner, Self-represented

SUPERIOR COURT OF CALIFORNIA
FOR THE COUNTY OF __ Name of county ________

Estate of Name of estate as it appears on petition deceased.	NO. __ Case number ________ WAIVER OF ACCOUNTING

The undersigned, __ Name of beneficiary who will sign waiver ____, beneficiary of the Estate of the above-named decedent, hereby waives the filing and settlement of a final account.

DATED:__ Date signed ________

________ Name of beneficiary ________

EXHIBIT E

Property to Be Distributed Consists of Money

If the minor has no guardian of the estate and money is to be distributed to the minor, the court may order that the money be deposited in an insured account in a financial institution in California, or in a single-premium deferred annuity, subject to withdrawal only upon authorization of the court. (Prob. Code § 3413.) In this situation, you may add the following paragraph to Paragraph 15 of the petition:

> The cash distribution to *(name of minor)* should be deposited in an account at *(name of institution)*, subject to withdrawal only on order of the court.

You should contact the bank or trust company in advance to make arrangements for the deposit. A similar form of receipt and agreement to be signed by the depository is shown under Item 2d of the instructions for preparing the Petition for Probate.

Other Types of Property Distributed to a Minor

In the absence of a guardian or designated custodian for the minor's estate, transfer of other types of property to a minor must normally be authorized by the court. However, transfer to a custodian under the California Uniform Transfers to Minors Act may still be made if the court approves the transfer. If you are faced with this situation, we suggest you see an attorney to handle the transfer for you.

Paragraph 15. Include appropriate paragraph. You will send both notice and a copy of the petition to anyone who has requested special notice. See Step 17.

Paragraph 16. This paragraph waives the requirement of an accounting. (See Chapter 13.) When the accounting is waived, the representative does not have to prepare a detailed list of receipts and disbursements during probate administration, which makes the closing of the estate much easier. All beneficiaries or heirs receiving property from the estate must sign waivers before the court will allow the accounting to be waived. The document to use, called Waiver of Accounting, is shown as Exhibit "E" to the sample petition. If you are the sole beneficiary, you may waive the accounting by a statement in the petition as shown in Paragraph 16. If there are other beneficiaries, either attach a separate waiver for each one, or all of the beneficiaries may sign one waiver.

If the custodian, guardian, conservator, or personal representative of an estate will receive property for a beneficiary, have that person sign the waiver and not the beneficiary.

Persons who receive property as surviving joint tenants, as named beneficiaries under the decedent's life insurance policies, do not have to sign waivers. When the will names a trust as a beneficiary, the persons who receive property through that trust do not have to sign waivers, except in some counties when the personal representative and the trustee are the same person.

If a beneficiary is hesitant to sign the waiver, sometimes providing information such as bank statements or other records of the estate administration informally may overcome the beneficiary's reluctance. If any beneficiary or heir will not sign the waiver, you may need additional assistance to prepare an accounting. Courts have specific requirements for presenting accountings. Instructions for preparing an accounting are beyond the scope of this book. If a beneficiary or heir does not sign the waiver because of concerns about the administration of the estate, contact a lawyer for assistance.

Paragraph 17. This paragraph refers to the compensation to which you are entitled as estate representative. (See Chapter 13.) If you waive your compensation, use the first paragraph. If you claim compensation, use the second paragraph and fill in the computation based on the total Inventory and Appraisal amount. If the amount is greater than $1,000,000, you will need to add additional lines to the sample to compute the relevant compensation. If you claim compensation, also be sure that the title of the petition used in the heading reflects this.

Paragraph 18. Use this paragraph when there are other beneficiaries besides the estate representative and there is cash available for distribution. The court will authorize funds to be withheld to cover closing expenses and other liabilities that may be due after the estate is closed. This saves the representative from the chore of collecting expenses from the distributees after distribution. If the estate contains no cash, do not include this paragraph.

Some courts require additional information when requesting a reserve of more than a nominal amount—either determined as a percentage of the estate or a set amount, depending on the county. Consult the local court rules.

Transmittal Letter

> County Clerk
>
> (Address)
>
> RE: Estate of ______________________
> Case No. ______________________
>
> Enclosed are the following items:
>
> 1. Original and one copy of the Petition for Final Distribution in the above estate. Please file the original petition and return the extra copy to me, conformed, in the enclosed stamped, self-addressed envelope.
> 2. Original and __________ copies of Notice of Hearing. Please fill in the date, time, and place of the hearing and return all copies to me for processing.
> 3. Check payable to your order in the amount of $435, as the filing fee.
>
> Thank you for your assistance.
>
> Sincerely,
>
> (Name)
>
> ______________________
>
> (Signature)
> (Address)
> (Phone number)

Paragraphs 19, 20, 21, and 22. Include any of these paragraphs that apply. In Paragraph 20, "family" means a relationship by blood or marriage, and "affiliate" generally means an entity that directly or indirectly controls the estate representative. (Prob. Code § 1064(c).) If the estate contains no cash, omit Paragraph 21 or revise it to state that there was no cash to invest. If the estate did not contain real property, omit Paragraph 22.

Final Paragraph. Include this final paragraph, called the "prayer," which requests that the court approve the petition and direct distribution as set forth therein. The last sentence is called the "omnibus clause," which directs distribution of after-discovered property. (Prob. Code § 11642(a).) After-discovered property vests as of the date of the Order for Final Distribution, and the omnibus clause avoids the reopening the proceeding when property is discovered after the order is signed.

Filing the Petition for Final Distribution

After you have completed the Petition for Final Distribution, prepare it for filing by following these steps:

1. Sign and date it at the end, and don't forget to also sign and date the verification page.
2. Make two copies, one for your file and one to send to the court with the original. Staple the original and the copies at the top in at least two places. (Note: Most counties now scan probate documents and don't want the originals stapled, but want them paper-clipped or binder clipped instead, so check with the court on this.) The original should be two-hole punched at the top, as well.
3. Provide the original and one copy to the court, either in person, using a filing service, or mailing with a transmittal letter in the form shown in the sample above. Provide a self-addressed stamped envelope. You will also prepare and enclose a Notice of Hearing (Probate), which is discussed in Step 17 below.
4. A filing fee, currently $435, is required when the petition is filed. Make the check payable to "Clerk of Superior Court."

Step 17: Prepare Notice of Hearing

Mail the Notice of Hearing (DE-120) for the Petition for Final Distribution at least 15 days before the date of hearing to the following persons:

- if there is a will, to all the beneficiaries affected
- if there is no will, to all heirs who succeed to the estate
- if any portion of the estate escheats to the State of California, to the Attorney General in Sacramento
- to anyone who has requested special notice (send a copy of the petition, too)
- if a distributee is a trustee of a trust, to the trustee
- if the trustee is also the personal representative, to certain trust beneficiaries (Prob. Code § 1208), and
- if a court has appointed a guardian or conservator for a distributee, the guardian or conservator, as well as the distributee.

If you are the sole beneficiary, a Notice of Hearing is unnecessary; you don't have to send notice to yourself. Alternate beneficiaries named in the will also aren't given notice unless they receive property from the estate.

Particular notice requirements also exist for less frequent situations, such as when there was a change in personal representative or attorney in the course of probate administration, when a beneficiary's whereabouts are unknown, or when an estate is insolvent.

The notice is given on Notice of Hearing - Decedent's Estate or Trust (DE-120), shown below. In many counties, you must prepare the notice ahead of time and send it to the court when you file the petition so the court clerk may insert the date of the hearing on the notice and return it to you. In some counties (Los Angeles, for example), you don't have to send in the notice form when you file the petition. Instead, the date of the hearing is stamped or written on the petition form by the court clerk. You then must fill in this date on the Notice of Hearing. Some counties require the notice to be submitted with the petition even though notice is not required, such as when the petitioner is also the sole distributee. Inquire locally as to the required procedure. In some counties, you will make a copy of the notice for each beneficiary, plus an extra one to be stamped and returned to you for your file. For some courts, you will submit the original and one copy, and once you receive the filed copy back from the court you will then make a copy for each beneficiary. Confirm your local court's practices.

Also confirm whether the local court has special notice requirements to advise of remote hearing procedures.

Caption. Fill in your name, address, the court's name, and case number, as you have on your other court papers.

Item 1. Fill in your name and title (executor, administrator), and that you have filed a Petition for Final Distribution on Waiver of Accounting. If the petition requests statutory compensation, be sure to add this to the title. The title on the notice must match the title of the petition.

Item 2. Fill in the requested information about the hearing. If the street address of the court is not shown in the caption, enter the street address at the right side of the box.

On page two of the form, fill in the name of the estate and the case number, and mark the boxes for "Estate of" and "Decedent." Leave the top section (Clerk's Certificate of Posting/Mailing) blank. Complete the Proof of Service by Mail the same way as on page two of the Notice of Petition to Administer Estate (explained in Step 3). Check the box for Item 5 if you provide a copy of the petition along with the notice. It can be a good idea to provide a copy of the petition so the relevant people have the details, though it is not required. In the space at the bottom, enter the name and address of everyone who is entitled to notice. A copy should be mailed to each of these persons. The person who mails the notice should fill in and sign the Proof of Service on the original notice (or one of the copies, if the court kept the original), after all copies are sent. Before the hearing, file the original proof of mailing with the court. If you choose to have notice personally delivered, use form DE-120(P), instead.

Notice of Hearing (page 1)

DE-120

ATTORNEY OR PARTY WITHOUT ATTORNEY STATE BAR NUMBER:
NAME: Billy M. Kidd
FIRM NAME:
STREET ADDRESS: 1109 Sky Blue Mountain Trail
CITY: Billings STATE: MT ZIP CODE: 48906
TELEPHONE NO.: 715-555-6408 FAX NO.:
EMAIL ADDRESS:
ATTORNEY FOR (name): Self-represented

FOR COURT USE ONLY

SUPERIOR COURT OF CALIFORNIA, COUNTY OF LOS ANGELES
STREET ADDRESS: 111 No. Hill Street
MAILING ADDRESS: 111 No. Hill Street
CITY AND ZIP CODE: Los Angeles, CA 90012
BRANCH NAME: CENTRAL DISTRICT

[X] ESTATE OF *(name)*: [ ] IN THE MATTER OF *(name)*:
Anabelle Kidd, aka
Anabelle O. Kidd [X] DECEDENT [ ] TRUST [ ] OTHER

NOTICE OF HEARING—DECEDENT'S ESTATE OR TRUST

CASE NUMBER: BP14813

This notice is required by law. You are not required to appear in court, but you may attend the hearing and object or respond if you wish. If you do not respond or attend the hearing, the court may act on the filing without you.

1. NOTICE is given that *(name)*: Billy M. Kidd
(fiduciary or representative capacity, if any): Executor
has filed a petition, application, report, or account *(specify complete title and briefly describe)*:*

A Petition for Final Distribution on Waiver of Accounting and for Allowance of Statutory Compensation to Personal Representative

[ ] The filing is a report of the status of a decedent's estate administration made under Probate Code section 12200. See the NOTICE below.

Please refer to the filed documents for more information about the case. *(Some documents filed with the court are confidential.)*

2. A HEARING on the matter described in 1 will be held as follows:

Hearing Date → Date: December 30, 20xx Time: 9:30 A.M.
Dept.: A Room:
Name and address of court, if different from above:

NOTICE
If the filing described in 1 is a report of the status of a decedent's estate administration made under Probate Code section 12200,
YOU HAVE THE RIGHT TO PETITION FOR AN ACCOUNTING UNDER SECTION 10950 OF THE PROBATE CODE.

Requests for Accommodations
Assistive listening systems, computer-assisted real-time captioning, or sign language interpreter services are available if you ask at least five days before the hearing. Contact the clerk's office or go to *www.courts.ca.gov/forms* for *Request for Accommodations by Persons With Disabilities and Response* (form MC-410). (Civ. Code, § 54.8.)

* Do **not** use this form to give notice of a petition to administer an estate (see Prob. Code, § 8100, and use form DE-121), notice of a hearing in a guardianship or conservatorship case (see Prob. Code, §§ 1511 and 1822, and use form GC-020), or notice of a hearing on a petition to determine a claim to property (see Prob. Code, § 851, and use form DE-115/GC-015).

Page 1 of 2

Form Adopted for Mandatory Use
Judicial Council of California
DE-120 [Rev. January 1, 2020]

NOTICE OF HEARING—DECEDENT'S ESTATE OR TRUST

Probate Code, §§ 1211, 1215, 1220, 1230, 12201, 17100, 17203
www.courts.ca.gov

Notice of Hearing (page 2)

DE-120

[X] ESTATE OF *(name)*: [ ] IN THE MATTER OF *(name)*: Anabelle Kidd, aka Anabelle O. Kidd, [X] DECEDENT [ ] TRUST [ ] OTHER	CASE NUMBER: BP14813

CLERK'S CERTIFICATE OF POSTING

1. I certify that I am not a party to this cause.
2. A copy of the foregoing *Notice of Hearing—Decedent's Estate or Trust*
   a. was posted at *(address)*:

   b. was posted on *(date)*:

Date: Clerk, by ______________________, Deputy

PROOF OF SERVICE BY MAIL*

1. I am over the age of 18 and not a party to this cause. I am a resident of or employed in the county where the mailing occurred.
2. My residence or business address is *(specify)*: 1809 - G Street, Billings, Montana 30400
3. I served the foregoing *Notice of Hearing—Decedent's Estate or Trust* on each person named below by enclosing a copy in an envelope addressed as shown below AND
   a. [X] **depositing** the sealed envelope on the date and at the place shown in item 4 with the U.S. Postal Service with the postage fully prepaid.
   b. [ ] **placing** the envelope for collection and mailing on the date and at the place shown in item 4 following our ordinary business practices. I am readily familiar with this business's practice for collecting and processing correspondence for mailing. On the same day that correspondence is placed for collection and mailing, it is deposited in the ordinary course of business with the U.S. Postal Service in a sealed envelope with postage fully prepaid.
4. a. Date mailed: December 14, 20xx
   b. Place mailed *(city, state)*: Billings, Montana
5. [ ] I served with the *Notice of Hearing—Decedent's Estate or Trust* a copy of the petition or other document referred to in item 1 of the Notice.

I declare under penalty of perjury under the laws of the State of California that the foregoing is true and correct.

Date: December 14, 20xx

Mary Smith
(TYPE OR PRINT NAME)

Mary Smith
(SIGNATURE)

NAME AND ADDRESS OF EACH PERSON TO WHOM NOTICE WAS MAILED

	Name	Address *(street & number, city, state, zip code)*
1.	Mary Kidd Clark	789 Main Street, Venice, California 90410
2.	Carson Kidd	711 Valley Road, Owens, California 98455
3.	Albertine Terreux	17 Rue Madeleine, Paris, France
4.	Consulate of France	8350 Wilshire Blvd., Los Angeles, CA 90035
5.		

[ ] Continued on an attachment. *(You may use* Attachment to Notice of Hearing Proof of Service by Mail, *form DE-120(MA)/GC-020(MA), for this purpose.)*

* Do **not** use this form for proof of personal service. You may use form DE-120(P) to prove personal service of this Notice.

Step 18: Prepare Order for Final Distribution

You will have to prepare the Order for Final Distribution and provide it to the court for the judge's signature. When you send the order, enclose a transmittal letter modeled on the one in Step 16, above. If real estate is being transferred, ask the court to return a certified copy of the order so you can record it, and include a check for the certification fee (call the court to find out the amount). Some courts require the order to be submitted a number of days before the hearing date. Check local rules.

The sample order shown below should fulfill the requirements of most courts, and may be modified to conform to your particular situation. The first paragraph must include the date, time of hearing, department number, and the judge's name. If you don't know the judge's name, you can leave a blank space and the court will fill it in. The order must always list in detail the property to be distributed to each person.

CAUTION

Local rules may determine what information must be included in the order. For example, only some counties (like San Diego) require the appraisal value of the property to be listed. Also, some counties (like San Bernardino) require that you include the address of all beneficiaries. Double-check your local rules to find out what your court requires.

In the case of real property, provide the legal description and assessor's parcel number. Be sure to proofread the legal description, comparing it with the deed to the property, to make sure it is accurate, since the order will be recorded with the county recorder's office as evidence of the transfer of ownership. To make sure it's right, have one person read aloud from the deed while another reads the description in the order carefully. Or, if you have a legible copy of the legal description on a deed, title insurance report, or homestead declaration, you can photocopy the document, cut out the legal description, tape it onto the order, and photocopy the whole document.

The persons receiving specific gifts of property are always listed first, and those receiving the assets making up the balance of the estate (residue) are described after that. Don't include any of the specific gifts in the residue. No riders or exhibits may be attached to any court order, at least three lines of text must appear before the judge's signature on the last page, and nothing should appear after the signature of the judge.

If property will be distributed to a trust created by the will, you must set out the terms of the trust in full, again, in the Order for Final Distribution, changing the wording to the present tense and the third person. For example, "my daughter" should be changed to "decedent's daughter," or "I direct that my Trustee provide ..." should be changed to "The Trustee shall provide ...." Based on Example 5 of the exhibit for Paragraph 13 of the Petition for Final Distribution, this is what the order would recite:

IT IS FURTHER ORDERED that the following property shall be and the same is hereby distributed as follows:

To ARTHUR JONES, the sum of $5,000;

To FRIEDA JONES, the sum of $5,000;

All the rest, residue, and remainder of the estate, hereinafter more particularly described, together with any and all other property not now known or discovered which may belong to the decedent or her estate, or in which the decedent or her estate may have an interest, is hereby distributed as follows:

To SHARON SMITH, one-third (1/3) thereof;

To SALLY SMITH, one-third (1/3) thereof;

To ALEXANDER BROWN, as Trustee, one-third (1/3) thereof in trust for decedent's daughter, LINDA SMITH, to be held, administered, and distributed in accordance with the following provisions:

The Trustee shall provide for the health, education, welfare, and support, and other needs of LINDA, so long as she is living and is younger than age thirty-five (35). The Trustee shall pay to or apply for her benefit, as much of the net income and principal of the trust as in the Trustee's discretion ... (etc.).

Order for Final Distribution (page 1)

BILLY M. KIDD
1109 Sky Blue Mountain Trail
Billings, Montana 48906

Telephone: 715-555-6408
Petitioner, Self-represented

SUPERIOR COURT OF CALIFORNIA

FOR THE COUNTY OF LOS ANGELES

Estate of ANABELLE KIDD, aka ANABELLE O. KIDD, deceased.	CASE NO. BP 14813 ORDER FOR FINAL DISTRIBUTION ON WAIVER OF ACCOUNTING [AND FOR ALLOWANCE OF STATUTORY COMPENSATION TO PERSONAL REPRESENTATIVE] Hearing Date: 12-30-20xx Time: 9:30 A.M. Department A

BILLY M. KIDD, as personal representative of the estate of the above-named decedent, having filed a Petition for Final Distribution on Waiver of Accounting, and the report and petition coming on this day, December 30, 20xx, regularly for hearing at 9:30 A.M. in Dept. A of the above-entitled Court, the Court, after examining the petition and hearing the evidence, finds that due notice of the hearing of the petition has been regularly given as prescribed by law; that all of the allegations of the petition are true; that the assets described in this decree of distribution comprise the entire estate on hand for distribution; that no federal estate taxes were due from the estate; that all taxes due and

Order for Final Distribution (page 2)

payable by said estate have been paid or are adequately secured; and that said report and petition should be approved and distribution ordered as prayed for.

IT IS THEREFORE ORDERED by the Court that notice to creditors has been given as required by law; that the personal representative has in his possession belonging to said estate the assets described herein; that said report and petition are approved; (**Add, if applicable:** that the personal representative is authorized to retain $________ as a reserve for closing expenses and to pay liabilities and to deliver the unused portion to the beneficiaries of the estate without further court order;) (**Add, if applicable:** and that the personal representative is hereby authorized to pay to **Insert: himself or herself** the sum of $________, hereby allowed as statutory compensation.)

IT IS FURTHER ORDERED that the decedent's will disposes of the estate as follows: **Quote dispositive provisions of the will verbatim. If there is no will, leave paragraph out.**

IT IS FURTHER ORDERED that the following property shall be and the same is hereby distributed as follows:

To ALBERTINE TERREUX, the decedent's antique silver teapot, marked "Sheffield, 1893"; Appraised Value: $90.00

All the rest, residue, and remainder of the estate, hereinafter more particularly described, together with any other property of the estate not now known or discovered which may belong to the estate, or in which the decedent or the estate may have an interest, is hereby distributed to MARY KIDD CLARK, BILLY M. KIDD, and CARSON KIDD, in equal shares.

The residue of the estate, insofar as is now known, consists of the following property:

Order for Final Distribution (page 3)

		Carry Value
1.	One-third (1/3) interest as tenant in common with co-owners John and Mary Smith, in real property in the County of Contra Costa, described as Section 3 Township 20 North, Range 3 East. Unimproved land. Assessor's Parcel No. 4562-34-5770.	**Include if required by local rules.** $ 5,000.00
2.	300 shares, Macy's, Inc. Common stock	$ 6,000.00
3.	75 shares, Bestco, Inc., $3 Cumulative, convertible preferred stock	$ 1,500.00
4.	Five $100 U.S. Series E bonds, issued June 1975	$ 500.00
5.	$10,000 promissory note of June 1, 1999, to decedent by David Hudson, unsecured, interest at 7%, payable interest only	$ 10,000
6.	Decedent's interest as owner in Great Life Insurance Company Policy No. 36678	$ 1,300.00
7.	Decedent's 50% interest in Valueless Mining Co., a Limited Partnership	$ 250.00
8.	Household furniture, furnishings, and personal effects located at decedent's residence	$ 350.00
9.	Cash on deposit in checking Account No. 345 778, Westside National Bank, Los Angeles	$140,000.00
10.	Certificate of Deposit No. 3459, Central Savings and Loan Association, Santa Monica Branch	$200,000.00

DATED:______________________, 20___

____

JUDGE OF THE SUPERIOR COURT

3.

ORDER FOR FINAL DISTRIBUTION

If the will leaves property to an already existing trust, then the order should list the trustee and the name of the trust:

> To ______________________________, Trustee, ____________________, Trust dated ______________, the following: (describe property).

If property will be distributed to a minor, here are some examples of the wording that may be used:

> To ______________________________, the parent of ______________________________, a minor, the sum of $5,000 to hold in trust for the minor until the minor's majority.

> To ______________________________, as Custodian for ______________________________, a minor, under the California Uniform Transfers to Minors Act, the following property: (describe property).

If a beneficiary or heir cannot be located, identify in the petition the alternate distributees. The alternate distributees are those persons who would have received the property if the missing person had died before the decedent. If the missing beneficiary or heir does not claim the property within the time set by law—five years—then the alternate beneficiaries or heirs are entitled to the property. You may need additional advice about how to either hold the property for the five-year period, or deposit the property with the county treasurer.

> The property that is to be distributed to ______________________________, who cannot be located, shall be distributed to the following persons who would be entitled to distribution under the decedent's will (or under the laws of intestate succession) if ______________________________ does not claim his or her share in the manner and within the time allowed by law: (list alternate person(s) who would be entitled to distribution, and the share to which each person would be entitled).

Step 19: Transfer the Assets and Obtain Court Receipts

Although the signed Order for Final Distribution is proof in itself of a beneficiary's right to property from an estate, the estate representative must still see that title is transferred in the case of certain types of assets.

You will prepare a formal receipt, typed on numbered pleading paper, to be signed by each person who receives property in the Order for Final Distribution. The receipt should list the property received by the distributee, as shown below. If real property is being distributed, the personal representative must file a statement that identifies the date and place or location of the recording of the Order for Final Distribution. (Prob. Code § 11753.) This is typed on the Ex Parte Petition for Final Discharge (DE-295), shown below.

Cost Basis Data. As discussed in Chapter 7, assets passing to beneficiaries usually carry a new, stepped-up income tax basis, which is the appraised value on the date of death (inventory value), not the date when the assets are distributed. Beneficiaries should be advised of the income tax basis of each asset they receive. The cost basis data can be shown on the court receipt as the "Carry Value," or provided in a separate letter. If an estate tax return has been filed, special rules and deadlines for reporting the cost basis apply.

Missing Beneficiaries. If you can't locate a beneficiary who is entitled to receive a cash gift, you may deposit the money, in the name of the beneficiary, with the county treasurer. (Prob. Code § 11850.) When you deposit the funds, provide a certified copy of the court order for distribution. Obtain a receipt from the county treasurer. If the beneficiary turns up, the beneficiary can claim the money by petitioning the probate court. And if the beneficiary does not turn up within five years, then the alternate beneficiary named in the Petition for Final Distribution can claim the money by petitioning the probate court. If the gift is other personal property that remains unclaimed for a year, you may need to seek a court order to have the property sold and the proceeds deposited with the county treasurer. (Prob. Code § 11851.)

Sample Deed

Recording requested by:
Billy M. Kidd, and when
recorded mail this deed
and tax statements to:

Billy M. Kidd
1109 Sky Blue Mountain Trail
Billings, Montana 48906

This is a court-ordered conveyance that is not pursuant to sale and is excluded from documentary transfer tax (R & T 11911).

DEED TO REAL PROPERTY

The undersigned, BILLY M. KIDD, as executor of the will of ANABELLE KIDD, deceased, pursuant to authority in the Order for Final Distribution made in the matter of the Estate of ANABELLE KIDD, aka ANABELLE O. KIDD, deceased, Case No. BP14813, on April 13, 20xx, in the Superior Court of California, for the County of Los Angeles, does hereby convey to MARY KIDD CLARK, BILLY M. KIDD, and CARSON KIDD, each as to a 11.11% interest as tenants in common with co-owners John and Mary Smith, without any representation, warranty, or covenant of any kind, express or implied, all right, title, interest, and estate of the decedent at the time of death and all right, title, and interest that the estate may have subsequently acquired in the real property situated in the County of Contra Costa, State of California, described as follows:

Section 3 Township 20 North, Range 3 East. Unimproved land.

Assessor's Parcel No. 4562-34-5770

Dated: May 25, 20xx

Billy M. Kidd
BILLY M. KIDD,
Executor of the Will of Anabelle Kidd, deceased

(notarial acknowledgment)

Real Property

You can transfer real property by (1) recording the order for distribution, or (2) preparing a deed that documents a transfer from the personal representative to the beneficiary. You may prefer to record a deed, rather than recording the order, because the order contains many other details about the estate.

To transfer title using the Order for Final Distribution, obtain a certified copy of the order from the court and record it in the county in which the property is located. The order must include a legal description of the property and the assessor's parcel number. You may need to include a cover sheet with appropriate information prior to filing. (See Chapter 8 for information about how to record documents with the recorder's office.)

As an alternative, you may prepare an executor's or administrator's deed to transfer title. The deed should contain a reference to the representative's authority to convey title, and a limitation on representations, warranties, and covenants. The sample shown above can be adapted to your situation.

You will need to prepare a Preliminary Change in Ownership Report to record the deed or order. (See Chapter 8.)

Promissory Notes

You should endorse over and deliver promissory notes to the distributee together with any deed of trust, pledge, or other security, and a copy of the Order for Final Distribution. The endorsement may be typed on the note in substantially the following form:

> __*(Name of city)*__, California, __*(date)*__, 20__.
> For value received, I hereby transfer and assign to __*(name of beneficiary)*__ all right, title, and interest of __*(name of decedent)*__ at the time of his/her death in the within note [*add, if applicable:* and the deed of trust securing the same, so far as the same pertains to said note, without recourse].
>
> Executor/Administrator of the Estate of
> ______________________, deceased.

Stocks and Bonds

Stocks and bonds should be transferred as discussed in Chapter 9. When stock shares must be divided among two or more persons and the shares do not come out even, an extra share may be distributed to one person and an equivalent amount of cash distributed to the other(s). For example, if 25 shares of stock were to be divided among three beneficiaries, one would receive nine shares, and two would receive eight shares plus extra cash in the amount equal to the extra share. Lay out the distribution plan in the Petition for Final Distribution. The court may require the written consent of each interested beneficiary when the distribution plan does not split each asset in proportion.

Mutual Funds and Money Market Funds

Transferring record ownership of mutual funds and money market funds is usually handled by the fund custodian. Therefore, the easiest way to deal with these assets is to contact the fund management directly (the monthly statement should tell you the address) and ask what is required to transfer or redeem the shares.

Tangible Personal Property

Items of tangible personal property, such as household furnishings, and other personal effects, usually have no record of title and require only physical delivery. Reasonable storage, delivery, and shipping costs for distribution of such items are chargeable to the estate.

Automobiles, Motor Vehicles, and Small Boats

The Department of Motor Vehicles will help in the transfer of title to these assets. Usually, this requires the representative to endorse the certificate of title (pink slip) as "owner" and present a certified copy of letters and pay a transfer fee. Submit to the DMV a Notice of Transfer and Release of Liability (DMV form REG 147). The new owner must apply for the transfer using the endorsed Certificate of Title and completing the Application for Transfer by New Owner on the reverse side. The insurance company should be notified of the change in ownership as well.

Cash in Blocked Accounts

Cash or other assets that were placed in blocked accounts to reduce bond will be released if you present the bank or institution holding the assets, with a certified copy of the Order for Final Distribution. The assets can then be distributed to the beneficiaries.

Step 20: Request Discharge From Your Duties

After you've delivered all property to the persons who are entitled to it, you may request that the court discharge you from your duties as the estate representative. The court form for this purpose is titled Ex Parte Petition for Final Discharge and Order (DE-295). "Ex parte" means without a hearing. The petition and order are on the same form, with the order for final discharge at the bottom. Instructions and a sample form are shown below.

Some courts require all receipts to be filed at the same time and some courts also require a copy of the court order for final distribution. This is to make it easier for the probate examiners to make sure there is a receipt from everybody.

If everything is in order, the judge will sign the order on the bottom of the form, discharging you as the representative, and this concludes the court proceeding. If you had to post a bond while serving as representative, be sure to send a copy of the Ex Parte Petition for Final Discharge and Order, once signed by the court officer, to the bonding company to terminate the bond.

In many instances, you will wait at least a year after distribution before filing for discharge because you will have winding-up duties to fulfill—for example, signing fiduciary income tax returns, handling tax reserves, and transferring assets. If there is a surety bond, however, every effort should be made to get the Ex Parte Petition for Final Discharge and Order signed before the next premium is due. When a signed copy of the discharge comes back from the court, you should send a copy to the bonding company with a request that the bond be canceled and any unearned premium be refunded to the representative. (Surety bond premiums are not refundable for the first year. After the first year, a pro rata portion is refundable.) If there is a refund, it should be divided among the residuary beneficiaries.

Caption. Fill in your name, address, and court's name, and case number, as on your other court forms.

Item 1. Check the first box and insert the date the Order for Final Distribution was signed by the court.

Item 2a. If personal property was distributed, check this box and provide receipts as noted.

Item 2b. If no personal property was distributed, check this box.

Item 2c. If real property was distributed, check this box and insert the recording information. The recording information will be stamped on the top right corner of the document (either the Order for Final Distribution or the deed) after being recorded. Most counties also have an online searchable index of recorded documents you can use to confirm the information, sometimes called a "Grantor/Grantee Index." You may also be able to get this information from contacting the recorder's office.

Item 2d. If no real property was distributed, check this box.

Item 2e. If the estate representative is the sole distributee, check this box, indicating no receipt is required.

Item 2f. Leave this box blank.

Item 3. Sign and date the form.

Complete the section at the bottom, under "Order for Final Discharge," by inserting the name of the personal representative where indicated and checking the appropriate box below. The date and signature line will be completed by the court officer issuing the order.

Court Receipt

Name:
Address:

Telephone Number:
Petitioner, Self-represented

SUPERIOR COURT OF THE STATE OF CALIFORNIA

FOR THE COUNTY OF LOS ANGELES

Estate of ________________ ________________ deceased.	) NO. ______________)) RECEIPT OF DISTRIBUTEE)))

The undersigned hereby acknowledges receipt from ______________ ______________, as personal representative of the estate of the above-named decedent, of the following listed property:

Cash in the sum of $______________;

1/3 interest in 200 shares of Miracle Corporation stock;

2014 Buick automobile; and

Household furniture, furnishings, personal effects, and artwork.

The undersigned acknowledges that the above property constitutes all of the property to which the undersigned is entitled pursuant to the Order for Final Distribution made in the above estate on ______________, 20___.

Dated: ______________, 20___

____

RECEIPT ON DISTRIBUTION

Ex Parte Petition for Final Discharge and Order

DE-295/GC-395

ATTORNEY OR PARTY WITHOUT ATTORNEY *(Name, State Bar number, and address):*
Billy M. Kidd
1109 Sky Blue Mountain Trail
Billings, Montana 48906

TELEPHONE NO.: 715-555-6408 FAX NO. *(Optional):*
E-MAIL ADDRESS *(Optional):*
ATTORNEY FOR *(Name):* Self-represented

FOR COURT USE ONLY

SUPERIOR COURT OF CALIFORNIA, COUNTY OF LOS ANGELES
STREET ADDRESS: 111 No. Hill Street
MAILING ADDRESS: 111 No. Hill Street
CITY AND ZIP CODE: Los Angeles, CA 90012
BRANCH NAME: CENTRAL DISTRICT

[X] ESTATE [ ] CONSERVATORSHIP [ ] GUARDIANSHIP OF
(Name): ANABELLE KIDD, aka ANABELLE O. KIDD,
[X] DECEDENT [ ] CONSERVATEE [ ] MINOR

EX PARTE PETITION FOR FINAL DISCHARGE AND ORDER

CASE NUMBER: BP 14813

1. Petitioner is the [X] personal representative [ ] conservator [ ] guardian of the estate of the above-named decedent, conservatee, or minor. Petitioner has distributed or transferred all property of the estate as required by the final order [ ] and all preliminary orders for distribution or liquidation filed in this proceeding on *(specify date each order was filed):* December 30, 20xx

2. All required acts of distribution or liquidation have been performed as follows *(check all that apply):*
   a. [X] All personal property, including money, stocks, bonds, and other securities, has been delivered or transferred to the distributees or transferees as ordered by the court. The receipts of all distributees or transferees are now on file or are filed with this petition. Conformed copies of all receipts previously filed are attached on Attachment 2.
   b. [ ] No personal property is on hand for distribution or transfer.
   c. [X] Real property was distributed or transferred. The order for distribution or transfer of the real property; the personal representative's, conservator's, or guardian's deed; or both, were recorded as follows *(specify documents recorded, dates and locations of recording, and document numbers or other appropriate recording information):*
   The Order for Final Distribution was recorded January 10, 20xx in Contra Costa County as Document NO. 05-123456.
   d. [ ] No real property is on hand for distribution or transfer.
   e. [ ] No receipts are required because Petitioner is the sole distributee.
   f. [ ] The minor named above attained the age of majority on *(date):*

3. Petitioner requests discharge as personal representative, conservator, or guardian of the estate.

I declare under penalty of perjury under the laws of the State of California that the foregoing is true and correct.

Date: 3-5-20xx

Billy M. Kidd — (TYPE OR PRINT NAME OF PETITIONER)
Billy M. Kidd — (SIGNATURE OF PETITIONER)

ORDER FOR FINAL DISCHARGE

THE COURT FINDS that the facts stated in the foregoing *Ex Parte Petition for Final Discharge* are true.

THE COURT ORDERS that *(name):* Billy M. Kidd
is discharged as [X] personal representative [ ] conservator [ ] guardian of the estate of the above-named decedent, conservatee, or minor, and sureties are discharged and released from liability for all acts subsequent hereto.

Date:

JUDICIAL OFFICER
[ ] SIGNATURE FOLLOWS LAST ATTACHMENT.

Page 1 of 1

Form Adopted for Mandatory Use
Judicial Council of California
DE-295/GC-395
[New January 1, 2006]

EX PARTE PETITION FOR FINAL DISCHARGE AND ORDER
(Probate—Decedents' Estates and Conservatorships and Guardianships)

Probate Code, §§ 2100, 2627, 2631, 11753, 12250;
www.courtinfo.ca.gov

CHAPTER

15

Handling Property That Passes Outright to the Surviving Spouse or Domestic Partner

Fortunately for a surviving spouse or registered domestic partner, all property inherited outright by the decedent's surviving spouse or registered domestic partner may pass to the survivor without formal probate. (Prob. Code § 13500.) There is no limitation on the amount or value of the assets transferred under simplified procedures for a surviving spouse or partner. This includes community property, separate property, and quasi-community property. Quasi-community property is property acquired by couples outside California that would have been community property if acquired in California. It is treated just like community property. (See Chapter 4.)

Read This First

The procedures described in this chapter do not apply to all marriages, all partnerships, or all property situations. First determine if these simplified procedures may apply, or not.

Marriage. You can use these procedures if, at the time of death, the decedent was legally married.

Domestic partnerships. You can use these procedures if, at the time of death, the decedent was in a partnership registered with the California Secretary of State or validly formed in another jurisdiction under laws substantially equivalent to a California domestic partnership. The procedures in this chapter do not apply to domestic partnerships registered with only a city, county, employer, or other non-state entity.

Relationships in the process of ending. Do not use these procedures if, at the time of death, the decedent's marriage or domestic partnership was in the process of being dissolved or terminated. In this situation, get help from an attorney.

Complex estates. If the estate has complications with creditors, investors, or strained family relations, these procedures may not be the best option. Get help from an attorney.

Read more about these limitations in "When to Use These Procedures," on this page. If you have any concerns about whether to apply these procedures, see a lawyer for personalized advice.

An Overview of These Simplified Procedures

A surviving spouse or domestic partner will normally have no problem acquiring assets that don't have official title documents, such as household furniture and personal effects. However, title companies, stock transfer agents, and others won't turn over property to the survivor without some kind of official document establishing that the property really belongs to the survivor. Not surprisingly, they want assurance that the survivor's position is valid.

Different documents are used, depending on the type of property involved. For community real property, a simple form affidavit can usually be used. For other property, the surviving spouse or partner can obtain a Spousal or Domestic Partner Property Order from the superior court. This chapter shows you how to use each method.

TIP

If you can't use these simplified procedures, the surviving spouse or registered domestic partner may take advantage of certain family protections allowed through formal probate administration. This can include a family allowance for support from the estate during administration, continuing possession of the home after the decedent's death, set-aside of the home or other property, and set-aside of a small estate (that is, not exceeding a net value of $85,900). See Family Protections in Chapter 13 for more information.

When to Use These Procedures

The simplified procedures outlined in this chapter should not be used in complex property situations. They apply only to simple estates with assets such as houses, cars, household goods, bank accounts, stocks, bonds, mutual funds, promissory notes, personal belongings, and antiques. If there are complex investments, large or complex claims by creditors, or strained family relations, or if the decedent owned an interest in a business (with the possible exception of a small sole proprietorship), the surviving spouse or partner should consult an attorney.

To qualify as a surviving spouse or surviving domestic partner, the survivor must have been either legally married to the decedent or in a registered domestic partnership at the time of death. The procedures discussed in this chapter apply only to property that goes *outright* to a surviving spouse or partner, either under the deceased's will or by intestate succession. If any of the decedent's property passes to the surviving spouse or partner under a "qualified" form of ownership, formal probate is usually required. Qualified ownership means there is some sort of limitation on the ownership—for example, property that passes to the surviving spouse or partner and someone else as joint tenants or tenants in common, or under a trust that gives the surviving spouse or partner only a lifetime right to use the property.

If the will merely has a survivorship period, such as, "I leave my entire estate to my wife, providing she survives me for 30 days," this is not considered a qualified interest. If the surviving spouse or domestic partner survives for the required period, the property may be transferred by the procedures described in this chapter and without a full probate administration.

These shortcut procedures to transfer property to a surviving spouse or domestic partner also will not work if the decedent willed all or part of the interest in the community property or separate property to someone else.

Here are a couple of examples of will provisions that necessitate probate:

> I leave my husband a life estate in my interest in our home in Montebello. Upon my husband's death, I leave my interest in said property to my two granddaughters, Holly and Celeste.

The husband is given a life estate (a qualified ownership) in the home; because it doesn't pass outright to him as surviving spouse, it will require probate.

> I leave my residence at 18865 Navajo Circle, Indio, to my son, Raymond. I leave the sum of $50,000 to my daughter, Elsa. I leave the residue of my estate to my husband, Anthony.

Because the decedent's interest in the residence in Indio and the $50,000 do not pass to the decedent's surviving spouse, a probate proceeding will be required for these assets. However, the assets contained in the residue of the estate, which pass outright to the decedent's husband, Anthony, can be transferred without formal probate administration using the abbreviated spousal procedures described here.

TIP

Small estate note. Remember, if the total gross value of the decedent's real and personal property that is willed to someone else (or passes to someone else under intestate succession) is less than $166,250, or the amount that applies in the year of death, it may be possible to use the transfer procedures outlined in Chapter 11. A surviving spouse or domestic partner may use small estate procedures even if the amount passing to that person exceeds $166,250. This is because any amount passing to a surviving spouse or domestic partner gets left out of the calculation when figuring the value for the purpose of whether an estate is small enough to use these procedures.

Creditors' Claims

The surviving spouse or partner is responsible for any debts chargeable against community or separate property received using these procedures. The creditor can enforce the debt against the surviving spouse or partner as it could have been enforced against the decedent. Normally, such claims must be brought within one year after the date of death. (Code of Civil Procedure Section 366.2).

When formal probate proceedings are used, however, most creditors' claims are cut off four months after probate is begun (exceptions to this rule are discussed in Chapter 14). In most estates, because no (or very few) creditors even present claims in the first place, using the spousal procedures outlined in this chapter will cause no problems. If, however, after examining the decedent's affairs you anticipate the possibility of substantial creditors' claims against the estate, consider putting the property through formal probate. It will give you peace of mind knowing that creditors cannot bring any claims after the deadlines have passed.

If the deceased spouse's or partner's estate goes through a formal probate proceeding, under Probate Code Section 11444, the debts are characterized as separate or community property and are allocated to the separate or community property of the parties accordingly. More detailed rules apply in particular situations. When there is an issue as to whether a debt should be paid from community property or a decedent's separate property, you should consult an attorney.

Community Versus Separate Property

If a will gives a decedent's entire estate to a spouse or partner, it is not crucial to know the character of the property for the purposes of making the transfer. However, in other instances, before going ahead with these unsupervised transfer procedures in the estate you are settling, you must know whether the decedent's property is community property or separate property, and of course, you must be sure the survivor is entitled to inherit it. How to classify property as community or separate is discussed in detail in Chapter 4. Read that chapter before continuing. How to identify who will inherit property, whether or not there is a will, is covered in Chapter 3.

If classifying property or interpreting the will is not simple and clear, get advice from an attorney. These issues, by their very nature, may involve the interests of different people, and having a lawyer can help you proceed in a way that may minimize disputes.

Collecting Compensation Owed the Decedent

A surviving spouse or partner (or the guardian or conservator of the estate of the surviving spouse or partner) may collect salary or other compensation owed by an employer for personal services of the decedent, including compensation for unused vacation, by presenting the employer with a Declaration for Collection of Compensation Owed to Deceased Spouse, or Registered Domestic Partner. An example of the blank form is shown below. On this book's companion page, you can download a digital version of the form; see Appendix C. The digital version also provides direction for filling in each blank line.

The procedure may be used immediately if the surviving spouse or partner is entitled to the compensation under the decedent's will or intestate succession. The procedure may be used regardless of the size of the estate; however, the amount collected cannot exceed $16,625, total, from all employers of the decedent. (Prob. Code § 13600.) If some compensation has already been received by the surviving spouse or partner from an employer, disclose that amount in subsequent declarations so the total amount claimed under this procedure does not exceed $16,625. The maximum amount that can be collected under these procedures will be adjusted by the Judicial Council on April 1, 2022 and every three years thereafter. If a guardian or conservator presents the declaration on behalf of the spouse or domestic partner, proof of formal appointment to that position must also be provided.

The person signing the declaration must provide reasonable proof of identity. If you sign the declaration in the presence of the employer and either the employer knows you or you provide a current driver's license or certain other identity documents (listed in Probate Code Section 13104), that will provide the proof. Or, if you do not sign the declaration in front of the employer, you can instead provide a certificate of acknowledgment by a notary public as proof of identity. The notary public can provide the certificate of acknowledgment.

A surviving spouse or partner using these procedures may be liable to someone with greater right to the payment received, for example if a probate proceeding is later initiated and the funds are needed for creditors' claims.

Collecting compensation in this way should be straightforward. If it's not, an employer that unreasonably refuses to pay the compensation due may be liable for reasonable attorneys' fees incurred by the surviving spouse or partner.

Affidavit for Transferring Community Real Property

A surviving spouse or partner has a 40-day waiting period before being able to sell, lease, mortgage, or otherwise dispose of any community real property—a provision that allows others (creditors, or anyone else who claims an interest in the property) to file their claims against it. If someone else does claim an interest in the real property, you should see a lawyer.

For community real property, most title insurance companies will accept a simple form affidavit to clear title in the name of the surviving spouse or partner. See the sample Affidavit—Death of Spouse or Domestic Partner, below. To use such an affidavit, the deed to the property must clearly show that title was held as community property; that is, the deed must show ownership in the names of the parties as "community property," as "domestic partners," or as "husband and wife." The affidavit cannot be used for community property held in joint tenancy or in the decedent's name alone. In those situations, use the Death of Joint Tenant affidavit (see Chapter 10) or Spousal or Domestic Partner Property Petition procedures (see "The Spousal or Domestic Partner Property Petition," below).

It is a good idea to check with the title company involved in the relevant transaction before preparing the affidavit, since the title company may have specific requirements, or it may provide its own form.

Firefighters and Police Officers

If the decedent was a firefighter or peace officer, replace Paragraphs 5 through 8 in the sample below with the following:

"The decedent was a firefighter or peace officer described in subdivision (a) of Section 22820 of the Government Code. Sections 13600 to 13605, inclusive, of the California Probate Code require that the earnings of the decedent, including compensation for unused vacation, be paid promptly to the affiant or declarant."

Survivorship Community Property

If the spouses or partners held title to real estate as "community property with right of survivorship," the property automatically passes to the survivor, without probate court involvement. To change title to the survivor's name, the survivor should prepare and record an affidavit called Affidavit—Death of Spouse or Domestic Partner—Survivorship Community Property. A sample is shown below and a downloadable blank form is in Appendix C. You'll find instructions for completing each blank line on the downloadable version of the form.

You can get much of the information you need to complete the affidavit from the original deed—the one that transferred the property to the parties as community property with the right of survivorship.

In the top left-hand corner, fill in the name and address of the person to whom the document is to be returned. Usually, this is the survivor, who signs the affidavit.

In the first blank, fill in the name of the surviving spouse or partner, who will sign the affidavit.

In the next blank, fill in the name of the deceased spouse or partner.

In the next two blanks, fill in the name of the deceased spouse or partner as it appears on the deed, and the date of the deed.

After "executed by," fill in the names of the persons who signed the deed.

Next, fill in the names of the spouses or partners as stated on the deed.

Next, fill in information about where the deed is recorded: The number on the deed, the date it was recorded, the book and page where it was recorded, and the county.

Then give the city and county where the property is located, and copy—carefully and exactly—the legal description of the property from the deed. Also fill in the Assessor's Parcel Number (APN).

Sign the affidavit in front of a notary public.

Declaration for Collection of Compensation Owed to Deceased Spouse or Domestic Partner

Declaration for Collection of Compensation Owed to Deceased Spouse or Domestic Partner

(California Probate Code Sections 13600-13606)

I, ____, declare as follows:

1. ____
   died on ____________________, _______ at _______. and at the time of death was a resident of California.

2. ☐ I am the surviving spouse of the decedent.
   ☐ I am the surviving domestic partner of the decedent.
   ☐ I am the guardian or conservator of the estate of the surviving spouse of the decedent.
   ☐ I am the guardian or conservator of the estate of the surviving domestic partner of the decedent.

3. The surviving spouse/domestic partner of the decedent is entitled to the earnings of the decedent under the decedent's will or by intestate succession and no one else has a superior right to the earnings.

4. No proceeding is now being or has been conducted in California for administration of the decedent's estate.

5. Sections 13600 to 13605, inclusive, of the California Probate Code require that the earnings of the decedent, including compensation for unused vacation, not in excess of sixteen thousand six hundred twenty five dollars ($16,625) net, be paid promptly to me.

6. Neither the surviving spouse/domestic partner nor anyone acting on behalf of the surviving spouse/ domestic partner, has a pending request to collect compensation owed by another employer for personal services of the decedent under Sections 13600 to 13605, inclusive, of the California Probate Code.

7. Neither the surviving spouse/domestic partner nor anyone acting on behalf of the surviving spouse/ domestic partner has collected any compensation owed by an employer for personal services of the decedent under Sections 13600 to 13605 of the California Probate Code [*add if applicable: except the sum of ________________ dollars ($____________) that was collected from __________*].

8. I request that I be paid the salary or other compensation owed by you for personal services of the decedent, including compensation for unused vacation, not to exceed sixteen thousand six hundred twenty five dollars ($16,625) net [*add if applicable: less the amount of ________________ dollars ($____________), that was previously collected*].

I declare under penalty of perjury under the laws of the State of California that the foregoing is true and correct.

____________________ ____________________________________
Date Signature

Affidavit—Death of Spouse or Domestic Partner (page 1)

RECORDING REQUESTED BY:
Mary Doe

AND WHEN RECORDED MAIL DOCUMENT
AND TAX STATEMENT TO:
Mary Doe
567 First Street
Los Angeles, CA 90017

APN: 123-456-789-1

Commonly known as:
567 First Street
Los Angeles, CA 90017

SPACE ABOVE THIS LINE FOR RECORDER'S USE

Exempt from SB2 fee per Gov. Code Sec. 27338.1(a)(2) because recorded in connection with a transfer of real property that is a residential dwelling to an owner-occupier.

AFFIDAVIT – Death of Spouse or Domestic Partner

By Surviving Spouse or Registered Domestic Partner Succeeding to Title to Community Property
(California Probate Code Section 13540)

Mary Doe of legal age, being first duly sworn, deposes and says:

That Robert Amos Doe, the decedent mentioned in the attached certified copy of Certificate of Death, is the same person as Robert A. Doe, named as one of the parties in that certain Grant Deed dated December 15, 20XX, executed by Lee Johnson to Mary Doe and Robert A. Doe as community property, recorded on December 16, 20XX as Instrument No. 01-99999 of Official Records of Los Angeles County, California, in the following described real property:

> Lot 135, Tract 8932, County of Los Angeles, State of California, as per map recorded in Book 74, page 28 of maps, in the office of the County Recorder of said county.

That at the time of the death of the decedent, Mary Doe was the spouse of the decedent.

That the above-described property has been at all times since acquisition considered the community property of Mary Doe and the decedent.

That more than forty (40) days have passed since the decedent's death.

That the above-described property has not passed to someone other than Mary Doe under the decedent's will or by intestate succession.

That the property has not been disposed of in trust under the decedent's will.

That the decedent's will does not limit Mary Doe to a qualified ownership.

That, with respect to the above-described property, there has not been nor will there be an election filed pursuant to California Probate Code Section 13502 or 13503 in any probate proceeding.

That this Affidavit is made for the protection and benefit of the surviving spouse; her successors, assigns, and personal representatives; and all other parties hereafter dealing with or who may acquire an interest in the above-described property.

Dated: February 3, 20XX

Mary Doe
Mary Doe

Affidavit—Death of Spouse or Domestic Partner (page 2)

Certificate of Notary Public

A notary public or other officer completing this certificate verifies only the identity of the individual who signed the document to which this certificate is attached, and not the truthfulness, accuracy, or validity of that document.

State of California

County of Los Angeles

Subscribed or affirmed before me on this 3rd day of February, 20xx

by Mary Doe proved to me on the basis of satisfactory evidence to be the person(s) who appeared before me.

[SEAL]

Nate Notary
Notary Public

Affidavit—Death of Spouse or Domestic Partner—Survivorship Community Property

RECORDING REQUESTED BY:

Mary Doe

AND WHEN RECORDED MAIL DOCUMENT
AND TAX STATEMENT TO:

Mary Doe
567 First St
Los Angeles, CA 90017

APN:

Commonly known as:

SPACE ABOVE THIS LINE FOR RECORDER'S USE

[*Include if applicable*: Exempt from SB2 fee per Gov. Code Sec. 27338.1(a)(2) because recorded in connection with a transfer of real property that is a residential dwelling to an owner-occupier.]

AFFIDAVIT—DEATH OF SPOUSE OR DOMESTIC PARTNER—SURVIVORSHIP COMMUNITY PROPERTY

Mary Doe, of legal age, being first duly sworn, deposes and says:

That Robert Doe, the decedent mentioned in the attached certified copy of Certificate of Death, is the same person as Robert Doe, named as one of the parties in the deed dated July 20, 20xx, executed by John Smith and Susan Smith to Mary Doe and Robert Doe, as community property with right of survivorship, recorded on July 21, 20xx as Instrument No. 01-59237, of Official Records of Los Angeles County, California, covering the following described property situated in the City of Los Angeles, County of Los Angeles, State of California:

Lot 101 of Tract 26834, as per map recorded in Book 691, pages 3 to 8 of Maps, in the Office of the County Recorder of said county.

Assessor's Parcel No. 567-892-003-1

February 3, 20xx
Dated

Mary Doe
Signature

Mary Doe
(Type or print name of person signing affidavit)

Certificate of Notary Public

A notary public or other officer completing this certificate verifies only the identity of the individual who signed the document to which this certificate is attached, and not the truthfulness, accuracy, or validity of that document.

State of California

County of Los Angeles

Subscribed and sworn to (or affirmed) before me on this 3 day of February, 20 xx by Mary Doe, proved to me on the basis of satisfactory evidence to be the person(s) who appeared before me.

[SEAL]

Notary Public Nancy Notary

Possible Complications

Names don't match. The affidavit states that the decedent named on the death certificate (which must be attached to the affidavit) is the same person named on the deed that transferred the property to the parties as survivorship community property. If the names on the deed and on the death certificate are different—for example, initials are used on one and a given name on the other—it isn't a problem. In that case, you will have to show that the two names identified the same person. If there are significant differences in the name, further explanation may be required.

Both spouses or partners have died. If you are dealing with the estate of the second spouse or partner to die, but the interest of the first spouse or partner was never formally ended, you must first terminate the interest of the first spouse or partner so that the record will show title held solely in the name of the last surviving owner. The survivorship community property affidavit for the first to die should be signed by the executor or administrator of the estate of the last surviving spouse or partner, and recorded as discussed below.

Attach a Death Certificate

Attach a certified copy of the decedent's death certificate to the affidavit. If you don't have a certified copy of the certificate of death, see Chapter 2 for instructions on how to get one.

Fill Out Preliminary Change of Ownership Report

All documents that transfer real property must be accompanied by a Preliminary Change of Ownership Report when they are recorded, or an additional $20 recording fee may apply. See Chapter 8.

Record the Affidavit With the County Recorder

The final step is to record the affidavit at the county recorder's office in the county where the real property is located. Do this as soon as possible after the death. Mail it to the county recorder with a cover letter requesting that it be recorded and returned to the address indicated in the upper left-hand corner of the document. Look at the recorder's office fee schedule or call to find out the amount of the recording fee. A one-page affidavit with a death certificate attached is considered two pages for recording purposes. If the property is a residential property passing to an owner-occupier, a cover sheet to claim the exemption to the $75 SB2 fee should be added. See Chapter 8.

It isn't necessary to record a new deed when you record the affidavit. The affidavit has the purpose of removing the deceased spouse's or partner's name from the title so ownership appears solely in the name of the survivor.

The Spousal or Domestic Partner Property Petition

In other situations where a court order is required, a slightly more involved procedure is required for real property and certain other assets. This involves the surviving spouse or partner (or the personal representative if the surviving spouse or partner is deceased, or conservator if the survivor is incapacitated) filing a Spousal or Domestic Partner Property Petition (DE-221) with the superior court in the county of the decedent's residence (or in the county where the property is located, if the decedent was not a California resident). This petition is appropriate for the following types of property:

- Real property held in the names of the parties in joint tenancy or where the deed does not indicate the manner in which title is held, or real property held in the name of the decedent alone, or in the name of the decedent with a third party. Absent a court order in a formal probate proceeding, the title company will want a Spousal or Domestic Partner Property Order specifying that the property belongs to the surviving spouse or partner before it will insure title, unless the deed says title is held by the parties as community property, in which case the affidavit discussed above may be used instead.

- Securities, stocks, and bonds that are in the names of the parties as "community property" or as "tenants in common," or are held in the name of the decedent alone. The stock transfer agent will require a Spousal or Domestic Partner Property Order before transferring title to the securities.
- Trust deed notes or promissory notes payable to the decedent alone, or to the decedent and the surviving spouse or partner. The person or entity making payment on the notes will normally require evidence in the form of a court order before making payments to the new owner. In the case of a trust deed note, a certified copy of the Spousal or Domestic Partner Property Order should be recorded in the county where the real property securing the note is located as evidence of the transfer of ownership.
- Vehicles held in the name of the decedent alone, or in the names of the decedent and the surviving spouse or partner if their names are not joined by "or." The DMV has many simple transfer documents for vehicles and it is worthwhile to check with the DMV before applying for a court order authorizing the transfer. However, if you have to file a Spousal or Domestic Partner Property Petition for other assets anyway, it is no more trouble to add the vehicle to the petition.
- Bank accounts in the name of the decedent alone, or in the name of the decedent and spouse or partner as community property or as tenants in common. Since banks sometimes follow different procedures, you should check with the bank first to see if the transfer can be made without a court order. If so, you may be able to avoid having to obtain the court order to transfer a bank account.

CAUTION

If you claim that property held in joint tenancy is community property. When you do this, the petition must explain the way in which the property was converted to community property and give the date. If the decedent and the surviving spouse or partner changed joint tenancy property to community property after December 31, 1984, it must be based on an agreement signed by both spouses or partners (Civ. Code §§ 5110.710–5110.740, now Fam. Code §§ 850–853), and the court will require that a copy of the document, showing signatures, be attached to the petition. If the joint tenancy property was acquired before January 1, 1985, it may be proved that it is community property either by a writing or other supporting facts (for example, that there was an oral agreement between the spouses or partners) that must be set forth in the petition. (See example of Attachment 7b to petition below.)

Spousal or Domestic Partner Property Petition, (DE-221) is a Judicial Council of California form, that describes the property and gives facts to support the surviving spouse's or partner's claim. Several schedules are attached to the form. One schedule describes the survivor's one-half interest in community property (the half already owned by the survivor), which the court is requested to "confirm" as belonging to the surviving spouse or partner. Another schedule describes the decedent's one-half interest in community property and the decedent's 100% interest in any separate property that the court is requested to transfer to the surviving spouse or partner.

If probate court proceedings are required to transfer other assets (meaning if a Petition for Probate has been or will be filed), the Spousal or Domestic Partner Property Petition must be filed separately, yet using the same case number as the probate proceeding.

Once filed, the court will set the petition for hearing. A notice of the hearing must then be mailed to certain people established by law (close relatives, others interested in the estate, etc., as explained in Step 3, below) at least 15 days prior to the hearing. An appearance in court is not usually required, unless someone objects to the petition. Consult with a lawyer if you anticipate a challenge to the petition.

Property Petition Checklist

Each item in the checklist is discussed below. Most forms needed for this procedure are included in the appendixes at the back of this book. We recommend that you review Chapter 13 on court procedures before you begin. Consult the local court rules for specific procedures and requirements.

Prepare and file with the court:

- ☐ Spousal or Domestic Partner Property Petition.
- ☐ Notice of Hearing, if required.
- ☐ Certificate of Assignment, if required (see Chapter 14, Step 2).
- ☐ Filing fee (if no probate administration).
- ☐ Original will (filed for safekeeping).

Before the hearing date on the petition:

- ☐ Mail Notice of Hearing.
- ☐ File original Notice of Hearing that shows date of mailing.
- ☐ Prepare Spousal or Domestic Partner Property Order.
- ☐ File Spousal or Domestic Partner Property Order, if required.
- ☐ Check probate calendar notes (see Chapter 13).

After hearing:

- ☐ File Spousal or Domestic Partner Property Order.
- ☐ Record Spousal or Domestic Partner Property Order in counties where real property (or real property securing trust deed notes) is located.
- ☐ Transfer assets to surviving spouse or partner.

If everything is in order, and there are no objections, the court will routinely approve the petition and grant an order declaring that the property "passes to" and "belongs to" the surviving spouse or partner. If the decedent's will requires the surviving spouse or partner to survive for a specified period of time (for example, 30 days, 90 days, or 180 days), you must wait to file the petition because the court will not order property transferred until the expiration of the required survivorship period. Once obtained, the court order is used as the official document to transfer or clear title to the property, and no further proceedings are required. The entire procedure takes one to two months.

Step 1: Prepare the Spousal or Domestic Partner Property Petition

Caption boxes. In the first box, enter the petitioner's name, address, and telephone number. After "Attorney for," enter "Self-represented." In the second box, fill in the court's address (including county) and branch name, if any. In the "Estate of" box, enter the decedent's name, including all variations used. Under that, check either the "Spousal" or "Domestic Partner" box, depending on your situation. Leave the case number and hearing information boxes blank; the court clerk will give you a case number when you file the petition.

Item 1. Usually the surviving spouse or partner is the petitioner. However, the personal representative of the survivor's estate (executor or administrator in a formal probate proceeding), may be the petitioner if the spouse or partner survived the decedent but then died, or a conservator acting on behalf of the surviving spouse or partner may be the petitioner if the survivor is incapacitated. In this case, a copy of court-issued letters evidencing the appointment must be attached to the petition.

Items 1a and 1b. Box 1a, which should always be checked, refers to the decedent's one-half interest in community property or quasi-community property, or the decedent's 100% interest in separate property, that the petitioner contends should be transferred to the surviving spouse or partner without probate administration. Box 1b refers only to the one-half interest in community property that is already owned by the surviving spouse or partner. This box is usually checked to request that the one-half interest in the community property be "confirmed" as belonging to the survivor. If the decedent didn't own any community property, don't check Box 1b.

Spousal or Domestic Partner Property Petition (page 1)

DE-221

ATTORNEY OR PARTY WITHOUT ATTORNEY *(Name, State Bar number, and address)*:

Mary Doe
1022 Ninth Street
Santa Monica, CA 90403

TELEPHONE NO.: (213) 365-4084 FAX NO. *(Optional)*:

E-MAIL ADDRESS *(Optional)*:

ATTORNEY FOR *(Name)*: Self-represented

FOR COURT USE ONLY

SUPERIOR COURT OF CALIFORNIA, COUNTY OF LOS ANGELES

STREET ADDRESS: 111 No. Hill Street

MAILING ADDRESS: 111 No. Hill Street

CITY AND ZIP CODE: Los Angeles, CA 90012

BRANCH NAME: Central District

ESTATE OF *(Name)*:

JOHN DOE, aka JOHN C. DOE DECEDENT

CASE NUMBER:

HEARING DATE:

DEPT.: TIME:

[X] **SPOUSAL** [ ] **DOMESTIC PARTNER PROPERTY PETITION**

1. **Petitioner** *(name)*: Mary Doe **requests**
   a. [X] determination of property passing to the surviving spouse or surviving registered domestic partner without administration (Fam. Code, § 297.5, Prob. Code, § 13500).
   b. [X] confirmation of property belonging to the surviving spouse or surviving registered domestic partner (Fam. Code, § 297.5, Prob. Code, §§ 100, 101).
   c. [ ] immediate appointment of a probate referee.
2. Petitioner is
   a. [X] surviving spouse of the decedent.
   b. [ ] personal representative of *(name)*: , surviving spouse.
   c. [ ] guardian or conservator of the estate of *(name)*: , surviving spouse.
   d. [ ] surviving registered domestic partner of the decedent.
   e. [ ] personal representative of *(name)*: , surviving registered domestic partner.
   f. [ ] conservator of the estate of *(name)*: , surviving registered domestic partner.
3. Decedent died on *(date)*: July 14, 20xx
4. Decedent was
   a. [X] a resident of the California county named above.
   b. [ ] a nonresident of California and left an estate in the county named above.
   c. [ ] intestate [X] testate and a copy of the will and any codicil is affixed as Attachment 4c. *(Attach copies of will and any codicil, a typewritten copy of any handwritten document, and an English translation of any foreign-language document.)*
5. a. *(Complete in all cases)* The decedent is survived by
      (1) [ ] no child. [X] child as follows: [X] natural or adopted [ ] natural, adopted by a third party.
      (2) [X] no issue of a predeceased child. [ ] issue of a predeceased child.
   b. Decedent [ ] is [X] is not survived by a stepchild or foster child or children who would have been adopted by decedent but for a legal barrier. *(See Prob. Code, § 6454.)*
6. *(Complete only if no issue survived the decedent. Check **only** the **first** box that applies.)*
   a. [ ] The decedent is survived by a parent or parents who are listed in item 9.
   b. [ ] The decedent is survived by a brother, sister, or issue of a deceased brother or sister, all of whom are listed in item 9.
7. Administration of all or part of the estate is not necessary for the reason that all or a part of the estate is property passing to the surviving spouse or surviving registered domestic partner. The facts upon which petitioner bases the allegation that the property described in Attachments 7a and 7b is property that should pass or be confirmed to the surviving spouse or surviving registered domestic partner are stated in Attachment 7.
   a. [X] Attachment 7a[1] contains the legal description *(if real property add Assessor's Parcel Number)* of the deceased spouse's or registered domestic partner's property that petitioner requests to be determined as having passed to the surviving spouse or partner from the deceased spouse or partner. This includes any interest in a trade or business name of any unincorporated business or an interest in any unincorporated business that the deceased spouse or partner was operating or managing at the time of death, subject to any written agreement between the deceased spouse or partner and the surviving spouse or partner providing for a non pro rata division of the aggregate value of the community property assets or quasi-community assets, or both.

[1] See Prob. Code, § 13658 for required filing of a list of known creditors of a business and other information in certain instances. If required, include in Attachment 7a.

Page 1 of 2

Form Adopted for Mandatory Use
Judicial Council of California DE-221
[Rev. January 1, 2014]

SPOUSAL OR DOMESTIC PARTNER PROPERTY PETITION
(Probate—Decedents Estates)

Family Code, § 297.5;
Probate Code, § 13650

Spousal or Domestic Partner Property Petition (page 2)

ESTATE OF *(Name)*: John Doe, aka John C. Doe DECEDENT	CASE NUMBER:

7. b. [X] Attachment 7b contains the legal description *(if real property add Assessor's Parcel Number)* of the community or quasi-community property petitioner requests to be determined as having belonged under Probate Code sections 100 and 101 and Family Code section 297.5 to the surviving spouse or surviving registered domestic partner upon the deceased spouse's or partner's death, subject to any written agreement between the deceased spouse or partner and the surviving spouse or partner providing for a non pro rata division of the aggregate value of the community property assets or quasi-community assets, or both.

8. There [ ] exists [X] does not exist a written agreement between the deceased spouse or deceased registered domestic partner and the surviving spouse or surviving registered domestic partner providing for a non pro rata division of the aggregate value of the community property assets or quasi-community assets, or both. *(If petitioner bases the description of the property of the deceased spouse or partner passing to the surviving spouse or partner or the property to be confirmed to the surviving spouse or partner, or both, on a written agreement, a copy of the agreement must be attached to this petition as Attachment 8.)*

9. The names, relationships, ages, and residence or mailing addresses so far as known to or reasonably ascertainable by petitioner of (1) all persons named in decedent's will and codicils, whether living or deceased, and (2) all persons checked in items 5 and 6 [X] are listed below [ ] are listed in Attachment 9.

Name and relationship	Age	Residence or mailing address
Jane Doe, Daughter	Adult	1022 Ninth Street Santa Monica, CA 90403

10. The names and addresses of all persons named as executors in the decedent's will and any codicil or appointed as personal representatives of the decedent's estate [X] are listed below [ ] are listed in Attachment 10 [ ] none

Mary Doe, 1022 Ninth Street, Santa Monica, CA 90405
(Petitioner herein)

11. [ ] The petitioner is the trustee of a trust that is a devisee under decedent's will. The names and addresses of all persons interested in the trust who are entitled to notice under Probate Code section 13655(a)(2) are listed in Attachment 11.

12. A petition for probate or for administration of the decedent's estate
    a. [ ] is being filed with this petition.
    b. [ ] was filed on *(date)*:
    c. [X] has not been filed and is not being filed with this petition.

13. Number of pages attached: 3

Date:

(not applicable)
(TYPE OR PRINT NAME)

▶ ______________________
(SIGNATURE OF ATTORNEY)

I declare under penalty of perjury under the laws of the State of California that the foregoing is true and correct.

Date: July 28, 20xx

Mary Doe
(TYPE OR PRINT NAME)

▶ Mary Doe
(SIGNATURE OF PETITIONER)

Item 1c. Although it is usually not required for these proceedings, this item gives you the option of requesting that the court appoint a probate referee to appraise the noncash assets listed in the petition. The referee charges a fee of one-tenth of 1% of the value of all noncash assets. Some counties require the filing of an Inventory and Appraisal before hearing a Spousal or Domestic Partner Property Petition, so check local practice. Unless the court requires it, however, it shouldn't be necessary to have a referee appointed.

You may choose, however, to have a probate referee appointed to appraise property for tax purposes if you do not obtain the date-of-death value in another way (like through a professional real estate appraisal or securities valuation). The date-of-death values of stocks and bonds can also be determined yourself from widely available sources (see Chapter 5).

You should have an official record of the date-of-death value of appreciated property, because all of the decedent's separate property and both halves of the community property receive a new federal income tax basis equal to the date-of-death value of the asset. For assets that have appreciated, this reduces the amount of capital gains tax owing, if and when the property is sold. (See Chapter 7.) The basis rules for both halves of community property are not available to domestic partners, because federal tax laws do not recognize domestic partnerships in the same way as marriages.

Some people rely on a letter from a real estate broker, supported by a list of recent comparable sales in the area, to establish fair market value. Private appraisers may charge from $350 to $500 to appraise residential real property, while many probate referees will appraise assets outside of a court proceeding for the same fee charged in a probate matter (for example, one-tenth of 1% of the value of the asset). Find a listing of probate referees by county on the California State Controller's website, www.sco.ca.gov/eo_probate_contact.html.

If you request the appointment of a probate referee in the court proceeding, the referee's name, address, and telephone number are stamped on the conformed copy of the petition when it is filed. You must then prepare an Inventory and Appraisal with the attachments describing the property, following the procedures outlined in Chapter 14 for formal probate court proceedings, and forward it to the referee, who will appraise the assets and return it to you for filing with the court prior to the hearing. Ordinarily, if you have a probate referee appraise the assets, you will not get the appraised inventory back in time to file it with the court prior to the hearing date (usually four to six weeks from the day you file your petition), which means you will have to request that the court continue the hearing to a later date. A phone call to the court may accomplish this, or follow procedures specific to the court. The appraised value of each asset will be shown in the Spousal or Domestic Partner Property Order, thereby providing an official record for future use.

Item 2. Check Box 2a if the surviving spouse is the petitioner, which is usually the case. However, if the petitioner is the personal representative of the surviving spouse's estate, check Box 2b. Box 2c is to be checked if the petition is filed by a conservator or guardian of the surviving spouse.

Check Box 2d if the decedent's domestic partner is the petitioner. If the petitioner is the personal representative of the surviving partner's estate, check Box 2e. Check Box 2f only if the petition is filed by a conservator of the estate of the domestic partner.

If you check Box 2b, 2c, 2e, or 2f, include the name of the surviving spouse or domestic partner.

CAUTION

Powers of Attorney. If the surviving spouse or partner signed a Durable Power of Attorney to cover other financial affairs, the person acting as agent under such a power may not be able to file a Spousal or Domestic Partner Property Petition on behalf of the surviving spouse or partner. See an attorney if the surviving spouse or partner is still living but is unable to file the petition and no conservator has been appointed.

Item 3. Fill in the date of death.

Item 4a or 4b. Check the box that applies.

Item 4c. If the decedent died without a will, check the first box. If the decedent left a will, check the second box and be sure to attach a copy of the will (and any codicils) to the petition as Attachment 4c. If the will (or codicil) is handwritten, also attach an exact typewritten version. You must also lodge the original will for "safekeeping" when you submit the petition, unless it has been filed in another case.

Item 5a. If there are no surviving children, check the first box after (1). If the decedent is survived by a child or children, check the second box after (1) and then check one or more of the additional boxes on the same line indicating whether the child is natural, adopted, or adopted by a third party.

If the decedent had a child or children who died before the decedent (predeceased child) leaving a child or children or grandchildren (issue) living, check the second box after (2). If not, check the first box.

Item 5b. Check the first box in Item 5b if the decedent had a foster child or stepchild that the decedent would have adopted but for a legal barrier. If not, check the second box. (See Chapter 3 for a discussion of parent and child relationships.)

Item 6. Complete this section only if the deceased spouse or partner left no children, grandchildren, or great-grandchildren (issue) surviving. Only one of the two boxes should be checked. If there are surviving parents, check Box 6a, and list them in Item 9, below. If there are no parents, but a surviving brother, sister, children, or grandchildren of a predeceased brother or sister, check Box 6b and list their names, addresses, and ages under Item 9, below.

Items 7a and 7b. Boxes 7a and 7b correspond to Boxes 1a and 1b. Check Box 7a. Then, if you checked Box 1b, also check Box 7b. You will prepare two separate attachments on plain white, letter-size paper. If you do not check Boxes 1b and 7b, then you will not prepare the second attachment. Attachment 7a should list and describe the decedent's interest in community or separate property that passes outright to the surviving spouse or partner. The decedent's interest in community property should be shown as 50%, and in separate property 100%. (See sample below.) Attachment 7b is practically the same, except that it should list only the surviving spouse's or partner's 50% interest in community property. Be sure to describe the property fully, as shown in the sample below, indicating whether it is community property or separate property. Pay particular attention to the legal description for real estate; identify the property exactly as it is shown on the real property deed. A copy of the deed showing vesting at the decedent's death must also be attached.

Community property held in joint tenancy may be included in the attachments if you wish to have a court order finding the joint tenancy property to be community property. As we mentioned earlier, the court order may help establish a new cost basis for both halves of community property that joint tenancy property would not otherwise receive. (See Chapter 7.)

If the decedent owned an interest in a going trade or business, additional information, including a list of creditors, is required, and the surviving spouse or partner should have the help of an attorney.

Attachment 7. Here the court requires an attachment giving information to support the surviving spouse's or partner's contention that the property listed in Attachments 7a and 7b is community property or separate property and why it should pass to, or be confirmed as belonging to, the surviving spouse or partner. A sample of Attachment 7 that may be adapted to your particular situation is shown below. The sample below shows a Spousal Property Petition. For a Domestic Partner Property Petition, use "partner(s)" or "domestic partner(s)" instead of "husband and wife," "spouse," or "spousal," where appropriate. Local court rules in some counties list specific requirements. Normally, to establish that property is community property, most courts require the following information:

- date and place of marriage or registration of the domestic partnership
- description and approximate value of any real or personal property owned by decedent on the date of marriage or registration (This tells the court whether the decedent owned a substantial amount of separate property prior to the marriage or registration of the domestic partnership. Property acquired after the date of marriage or registration through the combined efforts of the parties will be presumed to be community property, absent evidence to the contrary.)
- decedent's occupation at time of marriage or registration
- decedent's net worth at time of marriage or registration.

Attachment 7a

Estate of John Doe, Deceased

Spousal or Domestic Partner Property Petition

Attachment 7a

Legal description of the deceased spouse's or registered domestic partner's property having passed to the surviving spouse or partner from the deceased spouse or partner:

Community Property:

Decedent's undivided one-half (50%) interest in the following community property assets:

1. Real property, improved with a single dwelling and separate garage, commonly known as 1022 Ninth Street, Santa Monica, California, standing in the name of John Doe and Mary Doe, husband and wife as joint tenants, legally described as Lot 23, Block 789, in Tract ZYZ, per map recorded in Book 73, Pages 91-94 of Maps, records of Los Angeles County. Assessor's I.D. No. 435-22-477.

2. $25,000 trust deed note of Robert Smith, dated October 1, 1997, payable to John Doe and Mary Doe, interest at 6%, payable $400 per month, principal and interest, secured by deed of trust dated October 1, 1997, recorded October 25, 1997 as Instrument No. 3645 in Book T5553, Page 578, covering real property in the City of Santa Monica, County of Los Angeles, State of California, described as:

    Lot 231 of Tract No. 1234, in the City of Santa Monica, County of Los Angeles, State of California, as per map recorded in Book 29, Pages 33 to 37 inclusive of Maps, in the office of the County Recorder of said County. Assessor's I.D. No. 345-35-588.

3. 454 shares of W.R. Grace Company common stock (held in the name of the decedent, acquired as community property).

Separate property:

A 100% interest in the following separate property assets:

4. 200 shares of XYX Corporation common stock.

5. 50% interest in Desert Sands West, a limited partnership.

Attachment 7b

Estate of John Doe, Deceased

Spousal or Domestic Partner Property Petition

Attachment 7b

Legal description of the community or quasi-community property to be confirmed as having belonged to the surviving spouse or registered domestic partner upon the deceased spouse's or partner's death:

Community Property:

Petitioner's undivided one-half (50%) interest in the following community property assets:

1. Real property, improved with a single dwelling and separate garage, commonly known as 1022 Ninth Street, Santa Monica, California, standing in the name of John Doe and Mary Doe, husband and wife as joint tenants, legally described as Lot 23, Block 789, in Tract ZYZ, per map recorded in Book 73, Pages 91-94 of Maps, records of Los Angeles County. Assessor's I.D. No. 435-22-477.

2. $25,000 trust deed note of Robert Smith, dated October 1, 1997, payable to John Doe and Mary Doe, interest at 6%, payable $400 per month, principal and interest, secured by deed of trust dated October 1, 1997, recorded October 25, 1997 as Instrument No. 3645 in Book T5553, Page 578, covering real property in the City of Santa Monica, County of Los Angeles, State of California, described as:

    Lot 231 of Tract No. 1234, in the City of Santa Monica, County of Los Angeles, State of California, as per map recorded in Book 29, Pages 33 to 37 inclusive of Maps, in the office of the County Recorder of said County. Assessor's I.D. No. 345-35-588.

3. 454 shares of W.R. Grace Company common stock (held in the name of the decedent, acquired as community property).

Attachment 7

Estate of John Doe, Deceased

Spousal or Domestic Partner Property Petition

Attachment 7

The facts in support of allegation that property listed as Items 1, 2, and 3 of Attachments 7a and 7b is community property that should pass or be confirmed to the surviving spouse or registered domestic partner are:

1. Petitioner and decedent were married on July 10, 1960 in New York City. They remained married and continuously lived together as husband and wife from 1960 to the date of decedent's death.

2. At the time of the marriage decedent owned no real property and the value of the personal property then owned by the decedent was no more than Five Hundred Dollars ($500.00). Decedent was not indebted at the time to any significant extent, and his net worth was approximately Five Hundred Dollars ($500.00).

3. Decedent's occupation at the time of marriage was that of a bookkeeper.

4. Decedent and his surviving spouse first came to California in 1965, and their net worth at the time was no more than a few thousand dollars.

5. During the marriage, the decedent inherited 200 shares of XYZ Corporation common stock and a 50% interest in Desert Sands West, a Limited Partnership, from his mother, Jane Doe, who died in Los Angeles County in 1963. Said stock and partnership interest, described as Items 4 and 5 of Attachment 7a are the decedent's separate property. Decedent did not receive any other property by inheritance nor any property of significant value by way of gift.

6. The real property described in Item 1 of Attachments 7a and 7b was acquired in 1969 by the decedent and his surviving spouse as joint tenants. Decedent and his surviving spouse had no written agreement concerning their property, but at all times it was understood and orally agreed between them that all property they acquired during their marriage, notwithstanding the form of conveyance by which the property was taken or acquired, including all property held in the name of either spouse alone or in their names as joint tenants, would be and remain their community property.

Under the terms of Article Fourth of the decedent's Will, a copy of which is attached hereto as Attachment 4c, the decedent devised his entire estate outright to his wife. Accordingly, the separate property listed as Items 4 and 5 of Attachment 7a passes to decedent's surviving spouse, Mary Doe, petitioner herein.

- description, approximate value, and date of receipt of any property received by decedent after date of marriage or registration by gift, bequest, devise, descent, proceeds of life insurance, or joint tenancy survivorship; these assets are the decedent's separate property (unless they have been commingled with other assets or converted to community property by an agreement between the parties)
- identification of any property received by decedent under any of the devices listed directly above that is still a part of this estate
- if claim is based on any document, a photocopy showing signatures (Normally, these would be the decedent's will, a deed to real property showing title held as community property, or a written agreement between the parties.)
- date decedent first came to California, and
- any additional facts upon which claim of community property is based; here you may add anything of significance that would support a claim by the surviving spouse or partner to community property, such as a commingling of community and separate property, or actions by the parties showing an intention to treat property either as community property or separate property.

For separate property, you should provide the following information:

- If the separate property passes outright to the surviving spouse or partner under the decedent's will, the paragraph number in the will. (See example of Attachment 7.)
- If there is no will, how the surviving spouse's or partner's share of the separate property is computed under intestate succession law. (See Chapter 3.) For example, if the decedent is survived by two children as well as the surviving spouse or partner, put:

> The decedent died without a will, and is survived by two children in addition to the surviving spouse. Under the laws of intestate succession, the surviving spouse is entitled to receive one-third of the decedent's separate property.

Item 8. Under Probate Code Section 13651(a), you must disclose whether or not there was a written agreement between the decedent and the surviving spouse or partner that provides for a "non pro rata" division of the aggregate value of the community or quasi-community property. If one exists it was probably prepared by an attorney. If the decedent had one of these agreements, check the first box and attach a copy. Otherwise check the second box. Note: If the decedent and the surviving spouse or partner signed a written agreement concerning the character of their property (that is, describing it as community or separate), attach that agreement to the petition as Attachment 8.

Item 9. This section is for listing all persons potentially interested in the estate so they may be given notice of the filing of the petition. If the decedent left a will, you must list here the name, relationship, age, and residence or mailing address of everyone mentioned in the decedent's will or codicil as a beneficiary, whether living or deceased. Include any organization identified in the will or codicil as a beneficiary, too. In addition, the name, relationship, age, and residence of all persons checked in Items 5 and 6 of the petition should be listed (these are the decedent's heirs under intestate succession laws). Even if the surviving spouse or partner claims the entire estate, the heirs must be given notice, to give them an opportunity to present any adverse claims. Often, the heirs are the same as the beneficiaries named in the will; if so, you need list each person only once. Persons not related to the decedent by blood are described as "not related." Ages may be shown as either "under eighteen" or "over eighteen." For a detailed explanation of the persons who should be included in this listing, see Item 8 of the instructions for preparing the Petition for Probate in Chapter 14, Step 1. If you don't have enough room for all the names, prepare an attachment in the same format and attach it to the petition as Attachment 9.

Item 10. List here the names and addresses of all persons named as executors in the decedent's will (or appointed as executors or administrators, if a probate proceeding is pending). If there is enough space on the petition to list them, check the first box. Otherwise, check the second box and prepare a separate list and attach it to the petition as

Attachment 10. If the surviving spouse or partner is the executor or administrator, you should also list your name here. If the will does not list an executor, or if there is no will, check the last box, before the word "none."

Item 11. Check this box if the decedent left a will and the executor or administrator with will annexed is the trustee of a trust that is entitled to receive property under the will. Prepare a list of the names and addresses of all beneficiaries of the trust, including those who will become a beneficiary in the future upon the occurrence of a future event (for example, upon the death of the surviving spouse). Attach the list as Attachment 11.

Item 12. If a petition for probate or for administration of the decedent's estate is required, check the appropriate box and fill in the filing date of the petition.

Item 13. Enter the number of pages attached, including the copy of the will, the deed, and any other attachments.

Signatures. Sign the petition as petitioner where indicated, and be sure to fill in the date. Leave the signature line for the attorney blank, or enter "Not applicable."

Step 2: File the Petition

Make one copy for your files, and another copy if local court rules require the petition to be filed in duplicate. Read the petition over carefully to make sure all the required boxes are checked. If there is a will, don't forget to attach a copy to the petition.

The petition, along with the other required documents, should be filed with the court clerk's office in the superior court of the county in which the decedent resided (or in the county where the property is located, if the decedent was not a resident of California), in person or by mail. Prepare a Certificate of Assignment, if necessary.

This form is normally required if you file your papers in a county that has branch courts. (See Chapter 14 on probate court procedures for instructions on how to fill it in.)

The filing fee, if required, will be $435 or more. Some counties have surcharges, so confirm the exact amount. The check should be made payable to the clerk of the superior court in the county where you file your papers. Most courts accept personal checks, but verify this before you mail your papers. Credit cards may be accepted, but confirm whether additional fees apply. A separate filing fee is not required if a probate administration is filed at the same time or is already proceeding.

The sample form letter shown below may be adapted to your particular situation when mailing the petition and other documents to the court for filing. Not all items listed in the form letter will apply in all situations, so include only those that apply to your particular estate. Be sure to include a self-addressed, stamped envelope so the court clerk will return conformed (file stamped) copies of your documents to you.

Letter to Court

August 16, 20xx

Clerk of Superior Court
Probate Department
1725 Main Street
Santa Monica, CA 90402

RE: Estate of John Doe, Deceased

Enclosed are the following documents:

1. Original and two copies of Spousal or Domestic Partner Property Petition (DE-221)
2. Original and four copies of Notice of Hearing (DE-120)
3. Original and one copy of Certificate of Assignment
4. Filing fee of $__________.

Please file the original documents with the court and return the extra copies to me, conformed with your filing stamp, indicating the case number and time and date of the hearing on the petition. A stamped, self-addressed envelope is enclosed for your convenience.

Thank you for your assistance.

Sincerely,

Mary Doe
Mary Doe
1022 Ninth Street
Santa Monica, CA 90403

RELATED TOPIC

Probate note. When the Spousal or Domestic Partner Property Petition is joined with a Petition for Probate, notice of the hearing may be combined with the Notice of Petition to Administer Estate given in the probate proceedings. In this case, wording is added to the Notice of Petition to Administer Estate to indicate that the hearing is on the Spousal or Domestic Partner Property Petition as well as the Petition for Probate, and that a copy of the Spousal or Domestic Partner Property Petition (if required) was mailed with the notice. (We show you how to do this in Chapter 14.) Some counties, however, require separate notice for the Spousal or Domestic Partner Property Petition, so check local rules.

Step 3: Mail and File a Notice of Hearing

When you file the petition, the court clerk will establish a hearing date, and all persons listed in Items 9 and 10 of the petition (except the petitioner) must be given notice of the time, date, and place of the hearing. Use Notice of Hearing (DE-120) for this purpose. The person filing the petition is responsible for preparing the notice form and seeing that notice is properly given. A copy of the notice is shown above, with instructions on how to fill it in. You will find a blank Notice of Hearing in Appendix B.

In some counties, the Notice of Hearing must be submitted to the court when you file the petition. The court clerk fills in the time and date of the hearing on the original copy, plus any extra copies, and returns them with your conformed copy of the petition in the stamped, self-addressed envelope you provided. Some courts keep the original and return only the copies. In other counties, the petitioner must choose a hearing date according to when such matters are heard on the court calendar. Check with the court where you file your papers for the procedures it follows. If you pick a date, be sure to allow enough time to give the required 15 days' notice to the required people.

When the Notice of Hearing is completed, with the time, date, and place of the hearing, mail a copy (not the original) 15 days prior to the hearing date to all the persons, other than the petitioner, named in Item 9 and Item 10 of the petition. The mailing must be done by someone older than 18 years of age who is not a person interested in the estate. Thus, the notice cannot be mailed by the surviving spouse or partner, any of the heirs or beneficiaries, or others named in Item 9 or 10 of the petition. After the notice is mailed, the person giving the notice must complete the declaration on page two of the original copy of the notice, giving proof of the mailing. Notice may also be given by personal delivery, in which case a different form, Proof of Personal Service of Notice of Hearing—Decedent's Estate (DE-120(P)) will be used instead. For more about service of notice, see Chapter 14, Step 17.

You can provide a copy of the petition to the recipients with the Notice of Hearing; however, doing so is not required.

File the original notice (or a copy, if the court kept the original) with the Proof of Service by Mail (or, Proof of Personal Service), with the court prior to the hearing date.

Page 1

Heading. Fill in the same information as on the Spousal or Domestic Partner Property Petition. Check the box before "Estate of," enter the name of the decedent, and check the box before "Decedent." Insert the case number.

Item 1. Enter your name on the first line. On the second line, enter representative capacity from Item 2 of the petition, if the petitioner is not the surviving spouse or domestic partner of the decedent. On the third line enter "Spousal Property Petition" or "Domestic Partner Property Petition."

Item 2. Fill in the date, time, and place of the hearing and address of the court, if different from the court's mailing address listed in the heading.

Notice of Hearing (page 1)

DE-120

ATTORNEY OR PARTY WITHOUT ATTORNEY STATE BAR NUMBER:
NAME: Mary Doe
FIRM NAME:
STREET ADDRESS: 1022 Ninth Street
CITY: Santa Monica STATE: CA ZIP CODE: 90403
TELEPHONE NO.: 213-365-4084 FAX NO.:
EMAIL ADDRESS: mdoe1955@gmail.com
ATTORNEY FOR (name): Self-represented

FOR COURT USE ONLY

SUPERIOR COURT OF CALIFORNIA, COUNTY OF LOS ANGELES
STREET ADDRESS: 111 No. Hill Street
MAILING ADDRESS: 111 No. Hill Street
CITY AND ZIP CODE: Los Angeles, CA 90012
BRANCH NAME: CENTRAL DISTRICT

[x] ESTATE OF *(name):* [ ] IN THE MATTER OF *(name):*
John Doe, aka John C. Doe
[x] DECEDENT [ ] TRUST [ ] OTHER

NOTICE OF HEARING—DECEDENT'S ESTATE OR TRUST

CASE NUMBER: BP 4084

This notice is required by law. You are not required to appear in court, but you may attend the hearing and object or respond if you wish. If you do not respond or attend the hearing, the court may act on the filing without you.

1. NOTICE is given that *(name):* Mary Doe
(fiduciary or representative capacity, if any):
has filed a petition, application, report, or account *(specify complete title and briefly describe):**

Spousal Property Petition

[ ] The filing is a report of the status of a decedent's estate administration made under Probate Code section 12200. See the NOTICE below.
Please refer to the filed documents for more information about the case. *(Some documents filed with the court are confidential.)*

2. A HEARING on the matter described in 1 will be held as follows:

Hearing Date → Date: August 24, 20XX Time: 9:30 a.m.
Dept.: Dept. A Room:
Name and address of court, if different from above:

NOTICE
If the filing described in 1 is a report of the status of a decedent's estate administration made under Probate Code section 12200,
YOU HAVE THE RIGHT TO PETITION FOR AN ACCOUNTING UNDER SECTION 10950 OF THE PROBATE CODE.

Requests for Accommodations
Assistive listening systems, computer-assisted real-time captioning, or sign language interpreter services are available if you ask at least five days before the hearing. Contact the clerk's office or go to *www.courts.ca.gov/forms* for *Request for Accommodations by Persons With Disabilities and Response* (form MC-410). (Civ. Code, § 54.8.)

* Do **not** use this form to give notice of a petition to administer an estate (see Prob. Code, § 8100, and use form DE-121), notice of a hearing in a guardianship or conservatorship case (see Prob. Code, §§ 1511 and 1822, and use form GC-020), or notice of a hearing on a petition to determine a claim to property (see Prob. Code, § 851, and use form DE-115/GC-015).

Page 1 of 2

Form Adopted for Mandatory Use
Judicial Council of California
DE-120 [Rev. January 1, 2020]

NOTICE OF HEARING—DECEDENT'S ESTATE OR TRUST

Probate Code, §§ 1211, 1215, 1220, 1230, 12201, 17100, 17203
www.courts.ca.gov

Notice of Hearing (page 2)

DE-120

[x] ESTATE OF *(name):* [ ] IN THE MATTER OF *(name):* John Doe, aka John C. Doe [x] DECEDENT [ ] TRUST [ ] OTHER	CASE NUMBER: BP 4084

CLERK'S CERTIFICATE OF POSTING

1. I certify that I am not a party to this cause.
2. A copy of the foregoing *Notice of Hearing—Decedent's Estate or Trust*
   a. was posted at *(address):*

   b. was posted on *(date):*

Date: Clerk, by ______________________, Deputy

PROOF OF SERVICE BY MAIL*

1. I am over the age of 18 and not a party to this cause. I am a resident of or employed in the county where the mailing occurred.
2. My residence or business address is *(specify):*

   2332-20th Street, Santa Monica, CA 90405

3. I served the foregoing *Notice of Hearing—Decedent's Estate or Trust* on each person named below by enclosing a copy in an envelope addressed as shown below AND
   a. [x] **depositing** the sealed envelope on the date and at the place shown in item 4 with the U.S. Postal Service with the postage fully prepaid.
   b. [ ] **placing** the envelope for collection and mailing on the date and at the place shown in item 4 following our ordinary business practices. I am readily familiar with this business's practice for collecting and processing correspondence for mailing. On the same day that correspondence is placed for collection and mailing, it is deposited in the ordinary course of business with the U.S. Postal Service in a sealed envelope with postage fully prepaid.
4. a. Date mailed: August 7, 20XX
   b. Place mailed *(city, state):* Santa Monica, California
5. [ ] I served with the *Notice of Hearing—Decedent's Estate or Trust* a copy of the petition or other document referred to in item 1 of the Notice.

I declare under penalty of perjury under the laws of the State of California that the foregoing is true and correct.

Date: August 7, 20XX

Laura Jones
(TYPE OR PRINT NAME)

▶ *Laura Jones*
(SIGNATURE)

NAME AND ADDRESS OF EACH PERSON TO WHOM NOTICE WAS MAILED

	Name	Address *(street & number, city, state, zip code)*
1.	Jane Doe	1022 Ninth Street, Santa Monica, CA 90403
2.		
3.		
4.		
5.		

[ ] Continued on an attachment. *(You may use* Attachment to Notice of Hearing Proof of Service by Mail, *form DE-120(MA)/GC-020(MA), for this purpose.)*

* Do **not** use this form for proof of personal service. You may use form DE-120(P) to prove personal service of this Notice.

Page 2

Heading. Fill in the name of the decedent and case number. Check the boxes for "Estate of" and "Decedent." Leave the next section (Clerk's Certificate of Posting/ Mailing) blank.

Proof of Service by Mail. Complete this section in the same way as page two of the Notice of Administration (explained in Chapter 14, Step 3). In the space at the bottom, list the name and address of each person to whom a copy of the notice was mailed. (This must be everyone listed in Items 9 and 10 of the petition, except the petitioner.) If you provide a copy of the petition with the Notice of Hearing, check the box for Item 5.

Step 4: Prepare Your Spousal or Domestic Partner Property Order

The purpose of filing a Spousal or Domestic Partner Property Petition (DE-221) is to obtain an official document from the court stating that the property described in the petition belongs to the surviving spouse or partner. That official document is the Spousal or Domestic Partner Property Order (DE-226). The petitioner has the responsibility to prepare the order for the judge's signature.

A sample order is shown below.

Instructions for Filling Out the Spousal or Domestic Partner Property Order (DE-226)

Caption boxes. Fill in as you did on the Spousal or Domestic Partner Property Petition. Include the case number.

Item 1. Fill in date, time, and department (courtroom) of hearing as it appears on your Notice of Hearing.

Item 3. Fill in the relevant information and check the appropriate boxes, as in Items 3 and 4 of the petition.

Item 4. Fill in the name of the surviving spouse or domestic partner and check the appropriate box.

Items 5a and 7a. Check Box 5a and prepare an Attachment 5a describing the decedent's 50% interest in the community property and any separate property that passes outright to the surviving spouse or domestic partner. To do this, you can use Attachment 7a of your petition; just change the title to "Spousal or Domestic Partner Property Order" and "Attachment 5a." For Item 7a, prepare Attachment 7a, which will describe only the surviving spouse's or partner's 50% interest in the community property. You can modify what was Attachment 7b of your petition.

Just be sure to:

- change the title to "Spousal or Domestic Partner Property Order"
- change the name of the attachment to "Attachment 7a," and
- for courts that do not permit attachments after the judge's signature, add a line for the date and signature of the judge, as shown in our example.

The attachments should be on plain white paper, the same size as the petition, and the property described the same way as in the petition.

Items 5b and 7b. These items refer to attachments "for further order respecting transfer of the property to the surviving spouse or surviving domestic partner." Such orders are required only in unusual circumstances. In most estates you can leave this blank.

Item 6. This section applies only to a trade or business owned by a decedent.

Item 8. If during the proceedings it has been ascertained that some part of the property described in the petition does not pass to or belong to the surviving spouse or partner, check this box. (This means the property will be subjected to probate administration, unless the entire estate is worth less than $166,250, or the relevant limit for small estate procedures. See Chapter 11.)

Item 9. Leave this box blank.

Item 10. Check the box, add up pages of attachments, and fill in.

Some counties, such as Los Angeles, do not permit attachments to a court order after the judge's signature. Because you will have at least one or two attachments, this means you should check the box at the bottom of the Spousal or Domestic Partner Property Order and then type lines at the bottom of the last page attached to the order for the judge's

Spousal or Domestic Partner Property Order

DE-226

ATTORNEY OR PARTY WITHOUT ATTORNEY *(name, address, and State Bar number)*:
After recording, return to:
Mary Doe
1022 Ninth Street
Santa Monica, CA 90403

TEL NO.: 213-365-4084 FAX NO. (optional):
E-MAIL ADDRESS *(optional)*:
ATTORNEY FOR (name): Self-represented

SUPERIOR COURT OF CALIFORNIA, COUNTY OF Los Angeles
STREET ADDRESS: 111 No. Hill Street
MAILING ADDRESS: 111 No. Hill Street
CITY AND ZIP CODE: Los Angeles, CA 90012
BRANCH NAME: Central District

FOR RECORDER'S USE ONLY

ESTATE OF *(Name)*: JOHN DOE, aka JOHN C. DOE, DECEDENT

CASE NUMBER: BP4084

[X] SPOUSAL [ ] DOMESTIC PARTNER PROPERTY ORDER

FOR COURT USE ONLY

1. Date of hearing: 8-24-20xx Time: 9:30 a.m.
   Dept.: 29 Room:

THE COURT FINDS

2. All notices required by law have been given.
3. Decedent died on *(date)*: July 14, 20xx
   a. [X] a resident of the California county named above.
   b. [ ] a nonresident of California and left an estate in the county named above.
   c. [ ] intestate. [X] testate.
4. Decedent's [X] surviving spouse [ ] surviving registered domestic partner is *(name)*: Mary Doe

THE COURT FURTHER FINDS AND ORDERS

5. a. [X] The property described in Attachment 5a is property passing to the surviving spouse or surviving registered domestic partner named in item 4, and no administration of it is necessary.
   b. [ ] See Attachment 5b for further order(s) respecting transfer of the property to the surviving spouse or surviving registered domestic partner named in item 4.
6. [ ] To protect the interests of the creditors of (business name):

   an unincorporated trade or business, a list of all its known creditors and the amount owed each is on file.
   a. [ ] Within *(specify)*: days from this date, the surviving spouse or surviving registered domestic partner named in item 4 shall file an undertaking in the amount of $
   b. [ ] See Attachment 6b for further order(s) protecting the interests of creditors of the business.
7. a. [X] The property described in Attachment 7a is property that belonged to the surviving spouse or surviving registered domestic partner under Family Code section 297.5 and Probate Code sections 100 and 101, and the surviving spouse's or surviving domestic partner's ownership upon decedent's death is confirmed.
   b. [ ] See Attachment 7b for further order(s) respecting transfer of the property to the surviving spouse or surviving domestic partner.
8. [ ] All property described in the *Spousal or Domestic Partner Property Petition* that is not determined to be property passing to the surviving spouse or surviving registered domestic partner under Probate Code section 13500, or confirmed as belonging to the surviving spouse or surviving registered domestic partner under Probate Code sections 100 and 101, shall be subject to administration in the estate of decedent. [ ] All of such property is described in Attachment 8.
9. [ ] Other *(specify)*:

   [ ] Continued in Attachment 9.
10. Number of pages attached: 1

Date:

JUDICIAL OFFICER

[X] SIGNATURE FOLLOWS LAST ATTACHMENT

Page 1 of 1

Form Adopted for Mandatory Use
Judicial Council of California
DE-226 [Rev. January 1, 2015]

SPOUSAL OR DOMESTIC PARTNER PROPERTY ORDER (Probate—Decedents Estates)

Family Code, § 297.5;
Probate Code, § 13656
www.courts.ca.gov

Attachment 7a

Estate of John Doe, Deceased

Spousal or Domestic Partner Property Order

Attachment 7a

Legal description of property confirmed as belonging to surviving spouse:

Community Property:

Undivided one-half (50%) interest in the following community property assets:

1. Real property, improved with a single dwelling and separate garage, commonly known as 1022 Ninth Street, Santa Monica, California, standing in the name of John Doe and Mary Doe, husband and wife as joint tenants, legally described as Lot 23, Block 789, in Tract ZYZ, per map recorded in Book 73, Pages 91-94 of Maps, records of Los Angeles County. Assessor's I.D. No. 435-22-477.

2. $25,000 trust deed note of Robert Smith, dated October 1, 1997, payable to John Doe and Mary Doe, interest at 6%, payable $400 per month, principal and interest, secured by deed of trust dated October 1, 1997, recorded October 25, 1997 as Instrument No. 3645 in Book T5553, Page 578, covering real property in the City of Santa Monica, County of Los Angeles, State of California, described as:

    Lot 231 of Tract No. 1234, in the City of Santa Monica, County of Los Angeles, State of California, as per map recorded in Book 29, Pages 33 to 37 inclusive of Maps, in the office of the County Recorder of said County. Assessor's I.D. No. 345-35-588.

3. 454 shares of W.R. Grace Company common stock (held in the name of the decedent, acquired as community property).

Dated: ______________________, 20____

____

Judge of the Superior Court

signature and the date, as shown in our example of Attachment 7a. (We do not show an example of Attachment 5a to the order, inasmuch as it is the same as Attachment 7a to the petition, except for the title.)

In most counties, if the petition is unopposed, the Spousal or Domestic Partner Property Order will be signed without an appearance in court by anyone. Because of this, some counties require the order to be submitted to the court for review a certain number of days prior to the hearing date. In other counties, the order may be sent in after the hearing date for the judge's signature, so you should check local practice.

Letter to Court

September 1, 20xx

Clerk of the Superior Court
1500 Main Street
Santa Monica, CA 90402

RE: Estate of John Doe, Deceased
Case No. : ________________
Hearing Date : ________________

Enclosed is a Spousal or Domestic Partner Property Order (DE-226) in the above-entitled matter.

When the order is signed and filed, please return one certified copy to me in the enclosed stamped, self-addressed envelope. A check in the amount of ______, made payable to Clerk of Superior Court, is enclosed to cover your certification fees.

Thank you for your assistance.
Sincerely,
Mary Doe
Mary Doe
1022 Ninth Street
Santa Monica, CA 90403

In either case, after the judge signs the Spousal or Domestic Partner Property Order and after the hearing, you will need one certified copy of the order for each issue of security to be transferred and one certified copy of the order to record in each county in which any item of real property is located. You can request these certified copies when you send in the order, or afterwards, depending on the county procedures. A sample cover letter for mailing the order and requesting a certified copy is shown below. You can find specific certification fees on the court's website or by contacting the court clerk's office.

How to Transfer the Assets to the Surviving Spouse or Partner

As a reminder, providing a Spousal or Domestic Partner Property Order may not be needed in all circumstances to transfer assets to the surviving spouse or registered domestic partner. Assuming the Spousal or Domestic Partner Property Order has been signed by the judge, you are ready to transfer property that requires the formality of a court order. Here is how you do it.

Real Property

Title to real property is transferred by recording a certified copy of the Spousal or Domestic Partner Property Order in the office of the county recorder for each county where the real property is located. If there are several items of real property in one county, you need record only one certified copy of the order in that county. See Chapter 8 on how to record documents with the county recorder.

Securities

Send the transfer agent the following items by registered mail, insured, for each issue:

- certified copy of Spousal or Domestic Partner Property Order
- stock power signed by the surviving spouse or partner, with signature guaranteed

- original stock or bond certificates
- Affidavit of Domicile, and
- transmittal letter, giving instructions.

See Chapter 9 on how to transfer securities, where to get the forms, and how to fill them in.

Promissory Notes and Trust Deed Notes

Usually, if the surviving spouse or partner notifies the person making payments on the note that the note is now the sole property of the surviving spouse or partner (or owned by the surviving spouse or partner with another), and furnishes the payor with a certified copy of the Spousal or Domestic Partner Property Order, the payor will update records and make future checks payable to the new owner. The surviving spouse or partner should keep a certified copy of the order with other important papers as evidence of ownership of any promissory notes. If the note is secured by a deed of trust on real property, recording a certified copy of the order in the county in which the property described in the deed of trust is located will establish a record of transfer to the new owner.

Automobiles

The surviving spouse or partner should go in person to the Department of Motor Vehicles to transfer title to any community property automobiles or other motor vehicles. Upon being presented with the Certificate of Ownership (pink slip) and a copy of the Spousal or Domestic Partner Property Order, the DMV will provide the survivor with the required forms to complete the transfer of title.

Bank Accounts

You can usually transfer bank accounts into the name of the surviving spouse or partner without loss of interest simply by submitting a certified copy of the Spousal or Domestic Partner Property Order to the bank with a request that the account or accounts be transferred.

Money Market Funds and Mutual Funds

Present the fund management with a certified copy of the Spousal or Domestic Partner Property Order, and it will transfer ownership in these types of assets to the surviving spouse or partner.

Miscellaneous Assets

You can usually transfer tangible personal property held by third parties, as well as other property interests such as partnership and joint venture interests, by presenting a certified copy of the court order to the persons having possession or control over the property.

CHAPTER

16

If You Need Expert Help

Wrapping up a deceased person's estate can be a daunting and complicated task. You don't have to do it without professional help.

If you are the only beneficiary of a simple estate, you may try to work through the probate process yourself. After all, if you have some missteps or the process takes a bit longer, it mostly impacts you. However, most estates and most estate representatives benefit from getting help from professionals who do this work every day. You have several options to get the help you need—from hiring an attorney from the beginning to assist with administering the estate, to getting support for certain tasks. This final chapter explains when to get help, helps you figure out what kind of help you need, and provides guidance about working with and paying the professionals you hire.

Deciding to Get Help

Keep in mind that your role as estate representative is important and often time-consuming, even if you get help from an attorney or other professionals. The estate representative has ultimate responsibility for the estate during the period of administration—which usually involves tasks as mundane as clearing out the refrigerator and as important as writing checks and signing deeds to distribute the assets. The more organized, prepared, and diligent you are in your duties as estate representative, the more you minimize delays, reduce unnecessary costs, and make the experience as smooth as possible for yourself and the estate's beneficiaries. Wisely enlisting professionals may make the most of your own efforts.

TIP

You can decline to serve. If you do not have the time to devote to the managing the estate, if the estate is very complicated, if you anticipate disputes among interested parties, or for any other reason, you may decide that you do not want to serve as estate representative at all. See Chapter 2 for options about who will serve as estate representative in your place.

What Kind of Help Do You Need?

As the estate representative, you have options for how to get the help you may need from professionals.

Situations that Require Hiring an Attorney

If the estate has several beneficiaries or obvious complexities, your need for professional guidance may be apparent from the outset. Or, even a seemingly straightforward and simple estate can have quirks that become unexpectedly complicated.

Seek the advice or assistance of an attorney if you find yourself in any of the following situations:

- Someone challenges your right to settle the estate.
- The decedent resided outside of California and has property in California.
- The will is ambiguous.
- The will gives away property that is no longer owned by the decedent.
- A named beneficiary does not survive the decedent, and the will does not provide an alternate beneficiary.
- An heir or beneficiary can't be located.
- A would-be beneficiary contests the will or otherwise interferes with settlement of the estate.
- The estate includes complicated assets, such as a business or non-California property.
- Separate and community property of a married couple are commingled, and you don't know how to distribute the decedent's property.
- A creditor files a large disputed claim against the estate.
- A beneficiary challenges how you manage the estate.

Advice from a professional will allow you to assess the complexity of the situation to determine how to proceed.

Having an Attorney Represent the Estate Representative

Most personal representatives hire a probate attorney to represent them for the entire probate administration from start to finish. The attorney guides them through the estate administration process, prepares the necessary paperwork, provides advice on legal issues, and interacts with the court and other parties. This is often a wise choice. It can provide peace of mind and allow the personal representative to focus on the tasks at hand of administering the estate without needing to learn all of the ins and outs of the legal process.

Other Arrangements With Attorneys

If you know you need help, but you don't want a lawyer to represent you from start to finish, you may be able to find an attorney who is willing to either provide consultation on an as-needed basis or allow you to take on additional responsibilities to reduce fees.

Also, you can change your mind about hiring an attorney. If you choose not to hire a probate attorney at the beginning, do not delay in seeking assistance if you get stuck or if the estate ends up having complexities. Any delay in getting help will likely cause the administration to be more complicated, time consuming, and costly to resolve. Even if you start to administer a simple estate on your own without complication, you may want involvement from an attorney towards the end of the process when it comes time to seek court approval for distribution of the estate.

If you do make a unique arrangement, good communication between you and the attorney will be vital, so that the attorney can provide you with appropriate advice and so that you each have a clear understanding of each person's responsibilities and expectations.

Hiring Other Professionals for Specific Tasks

You may need help from other types of experts with specific tasks outside of your experience or comfort. For example, a tax accountant will be able to assist you with estate tax or income tax concerns. This is particularly important if an estate tax return may be filed, either because of the size of the estate or to claim advantages for the surviving spouse's estate. Even if you file your own income tax returns, preparing the final income tax returns for the decedent or the decedent's estate may require expertise from a professional tax preparer. A real estate agent can be involved in the sale of real property. A bookkeeper can help keep finances organized. You may use a document filing service for filing papers with the court. And a title company can research title issues and prepare real property documents. If you work with a probate attorney, you and the attorney together will assemble others on your team. If you do not work with an attorney, you may need to enlist the help of these other professionals during the course of the estate administration.

Using a Legal Document Assistant

If the estate is without complication and you want to do all of the work yourself *except the paperwork for probate administration*, you may be able to hire a nonlawyer "legal document assistant" to help with just that part of the job.

California law authorizes legal document assistants to prepare forms for consumers who wish to handle their own legal work. Legal document assistants are often experienced paralegals. Many of them operate independent offices, so customers can go to them directly instead of hiring a lawyer.

Legal document assistants don't offer legal advice. You are responsible for making decisions about how to proceed and for providing the information to fill out the papers. They can prepare your papers and file them with the court for you.

Most legal document assistants specialize in one or two areas; for example, some handle only divorce paperwork, and others just do bankruptcy or eviction papers. Be sure to use one who is experienced in probate paperwork.

Working With an Attorney

If you decide to hire an attorney, you'll need to find a qualified attorney that meets your needs and the needs of the estate. Here are some tips about finding a good lawyer and establishing a good working relationship with the lawyer you hire.

Finding a Lawyer

Looking for a lawyer who meets your needs may seem like a daunting task, particularly after the death of a loved one. However, finding a good fit in terms of experience, personality, and fees may make the difference in your overall satisfaction with the estate administration. If the decedent had a will prepared by an attorney, you may choose to start by communicating with that person, who will already have familiarity with the situation. But you are not obligated to do so.

As a general rule, you will be better off using a lawyer who specializes to some extent in probate matters. Many attorneys devote a part of their practice to probate and will do a competent job while charging fairly for the services. However, because this area is so specialized, you simply can't expect much creative help from someone who doesn't work regularly with these matters.

Certified specialists. Some lawyers who practice in the area of probate law are certified as specialists in estate planning, trust, and probate law by the State Bar of California Board of Legal Specialization. While certification is a mark of an attorney who has met standards for specialized education, knowledge, and experience in the field, other well-qualified and seasoned probate attorneys do not acquire this specialization certification. Consider using the list of certified specialists in your area to assist in your search for an attorney. On the website of The State Bar of California, you can search for a list of certified Estate Planning, Trust & Probate Law specialists in your county (www.calbar.ca.gov/Public/Need-Legal-Help).

Personal, professional, or public referrals. A good way to find a suitable attorney may be through a friend or some trusted person who has had a satisfactory experience with a similar matter. Or, you could ask for recommendations from a trusted professional who may work with probate attorneys, such as an accountant, tax preparer, real estate agent, banker, or social worker. You might also take a look at reviews on sites like Yelp.com, but take these public reviews with a grain of salt, as you won't have any objective information about the reviewers or their circumstances.

Bar association referrals. Local bar associations often have referral services that provide the names and practice areas of member attorneys. View these referrals as a resource, not as a recommendation. Be sure to ask about the screening process for attorneys and do your own investigation about the experience of any referral.

Lawyer directories. Online lawyer directories allow you to search for a lawyer by region and topic. For example, most lawyer directories allow you to search for a probate attorney in any city in California. From this perspective, lawyer directories are attractive because they are easy to use and provide well-honed results. However, keep in mind that most lawyer directories are essentially paid advertisements. Attorneys pay fees to have their profiles to appear in search results. This fact is *not* a condemnation of the lawyer directories or the lawyers who advertise in them, but do not confuse a lawyer's profile with a recommendation for that lawyer. As with each of these resources, you will still need to take the time to vet and interview any lawyer you find through a lawyer directory.

RESOURCE

Looking for a lawyer? Asking for a referral to an attorney from someone you trust can be a good way to find legal help. Also, two sites that are part of the Nolo family, Lawyers.com and Avvo.com, provide comprehensive and free lawyer directories. These directories allow you to search by location and area of law, and list detailed information about and reviews of lawyers. You can find them at www.lawyers.com/find-a-lawyer and www.avvo.com/find-a-lawyer.

Prepaid legal services. If your employer or union offers a prepaid legal services plan that offers you a free or low-cost consultation with a lawyer, take advantage of it. But remember that you need to talk to someone experienced in probate law and practice. Because maximum attorneys' fees for probate administration are set by statute, the prepaid legal services may not necessarily provide additional value, so do not feel locked in by the offerings of the prepaid legal service.

TIP

Consider the attorney's location. You might choose to use an attorney in the county where the decedent resided, so the attorney is more familiar with that court's local practices. Or, you might choose to use a lawyer close to you to make it easier to have in-person appointments. No matter where the attorney works, the attorney must be licensed in California and should be experienced with probate administration. Talk with any prospective lawyer about options where distance from the court or from you may be a factor.

After you have the names of a few attorneys that might be a good match, look them up on the California State Bar website (www.calbar.ca.gov) to confirm that each attorney is licensed in California and to view any disciplinary record.

Next, call each attorney or the attorney's law office and state your situation. Ask a few questions to get a general sense of the attorney's experience and the office's procedures for taking on new matters. Do not expect to get advice during the preliminary call. If you want advice on a particular problem, find out if the lawyer is willing to see you to discuss it.

When you find an attorney who may meet your needs, make an appointment to discuss your situation personally. Be ready to pay for this consultation, and bring all relevant documents and information with you when you go so that your time and money are well spent.

Information a Lawyer Will Need

When you hire an attorney, you will likely need to provide certain key information about the estate. This includes:

- any estate planning documents—will, trust, and beneficiary designation forms
- contact information for individuals listed in the will, or if a will does not exist, a list of the heirs
- a simple family tree of the decedent, showing the closest surviving family members and their relationship to the decedent
- information about current and previous marriages or registered domestic partnerships
- death certificate
- what the decedent owned—types of assets, how title was held, and approximate value
- debts owed, and
- information on any potential complications—disputes among family members, for example.

Do not worry if you do not have everything available right away. The attorney may ask you to fill out a questionnaire and to provide additional information as the administration proceeds. Keep documents and information well organized from the start.

Lawyers' Fees

Standard fees for a lawyer representing the personal representative in a court probate proceeding from start to finish are set by California statute as a percentage of the gross value of the property subject to probate. (See Chapter 1.)

You can, depending on the circumstances, negotiate with the attorney for the estate to pay a lump sum or an hourly rate instead, so long as the amount will not exceed the statutory fee. For example, if the value of the estate is large, yet the estate is otherwise simple, an hourly rate may be appropriate. Typical hourly fees range from $250–500, depending on the lawyer's experience and the location.

In a probate administration, the statutory fee for the attorney is generally the maximum fee, unless "extraordinary" fees are requested and approved by the court for services above and beyond the usual tasks. Examples of services that may warrant additional fees include those related to challenges to the will, litigation to benefit the estate, selling property, defending the representative, or coordinating out-of-state assets.

Settling an estate may include procedures other than a formal probate administration—such as transferring nonprobate assets, transfers to a surviving spouse or partner without probate, and trust administration. The fees for services related to those procedures are usually provided on an hourly basis, or sometimes based on a flat fee set by the attorney.

It's always a good idea to get your fee agreement with the lawyer in writing, to avoid misunderstandings. If it is reasonably foreseeable that you will end up paying more than $1,000 for legal fees and costs, the agreement between you and the lawyer must be in writing. (This law doesn't apply if you have hired the lawyer for similar services before, or for the statutory fee for a probate administration.) The contract must state the hourly rate and other standard fees that may apply, the general nature of the services to be provided, and the responsibilities of both you and the attorney—for example, you may be responsible for paying out-of-pocket court fees as the case progresses. (Bus. & Prof. Code § 6148(a).)

Bills sent by the attorney can't contain just a bare amount due; they must state the rate or other method of arriving at the total. If you are billed for costs and expenses, the bill must clearly identify them. If you haven't gotten a bill in a month, you may ask for one, and the lawyer must provide it within 10 days. (Bus. & Prof. Code § 6148(b).)

If the lawyer represents you in a probate administration as the estate representative, the lawyer will be paid with estate funds. You will not pay from your personal accounts. Attorneys' fees cannot be paid from the estate until approved by the court, usually towards the end of the estate administration.

Tips for Working With Attorneys or Other Professionals

When you hire a professional to assist you, these tips can help you to work well together for a smooth administration.

- Keep organized so you can provide information easily when requested.
- Don't be afraid to say if you don't understand instructions or information provided to you.
- Know when you are supposed to check in and the expected next steps.
- Ask questions before taking action.
- Keep a list of questions that can wait, rather than asking each question piecemeal. But if something seems important, don't delay.
- Share preferences for communications—phone, email, mail—and find out the preferences of others on your team.
- Be clear about who's doing what. For example, who will communicate with beneficiaries, what information will you provide to appraisers, how will bookkeeping be handled, and who will arrange for the preparation of tax returns.
- Avoid the temptation to be penny-pinching with professionals' fees. Fees paid by the estate to professionals may save time and frustration.
- Let others on your team know if you will not be available at any time during the estate administration process.
- If the relationship does not seem to be working, express your concerns and work with the professional to find a solution.

Glossary

Abatement. Cutting back certain gifts under a will when necessary to create a fund to meet expenses, pay taxes, satisfy debts, or to have enough to take care of other bequests that are given priority under law or under the will.

Ademption. The failure of a specific gift of property left in a will because the property is no longer owned by the testator at the time of death.

Administrator. The title given to the person who is appointed by the probate court, when there is no will, to collect assets of the estate, pay its debts, and distribute the rest to the appropriate beneficiaries.

Administrator With Will Annexed. Sometimes termed "Administrator CTA," this title is given to the administrator when there is a will but the will either fails to nominate an executor or the named executor is unable to serve.

Adopted Child. Any person, whether an adult or a minor, who is legally adopted as the child of another in a court proceeding.

Affidavit. A voluntary written statement of facts that is signed under oath before a notary public (or other officer having authority to administer oaths) by any person having personal knowledge of the facts. Affidavits are used instead of live testimony to support the facts contained in a petition or other document submitted in the course of the probate process.

Antilapse Statute. A statute that prevents certain dispositions to relatives in a will from failing in the event the beneficiary predeceases the testator. See "Lapse."

Appraiser. A person possessing expertise in determining the market or fair value of real or personal property. The probate court appoints an appraiser, called a "probate referee," to place a value on assets as of the date of death for purposes of estate administration and taxes.

Attestation. The act of witnessing the signing of a document by another, and the signing of the document as a witness. Thus, a will requires both the signature by the person making the will and attestation by at least two witnesses.

Beneficiary. A person (or organization) receiving benefits under a legal instrument such as a will, trust, or life insurance policy. Except when very small estates are involved, beneficiaries of wills only receive their inheritance after the will is examined and approved by the probate court. Beneficiaries of trusts and life insurance policies receive their benefits usually without a court proceeding.

Bequeath. The first-person legal term used to leave someone personal property through a will, for example, "I bequeath my antique car collection to my brother David."

Bequest. The legal term used to describe personal property left in a will.

Bond. A document guaranteeing that a certain amount of money will be paid to the victim if a person occupying a position of trust does not carry out legal and ethical responsibilities. Thus, if an executor, trustee, or guardian who is bonded (covered by a bond) wrongfully deprives a beneficiary of property (say, by taking it on a one-way trip to Las Vegas), the bonding company will replace it, up to the limits of the bond. Bonding companies, which are normally divisions of insurance companies, issue a bond in exchange for an annual premium. Because the cost of any required bond is paid out of the estate, most wills provide that no bond shall be required.

Children. Children are: (1) the biological offspring, unless they have been legally adopted by another, (2) persons who were legally adopted, (3) children born to married spouses and registered domestic partners are the children of both members of the couple; and (4) stepchildren and foster children if the relationship began during the person's minority, continued throughout the parties' joint lifetimes, and it is established by clear and convincing evidence that the decedent would have adopted the person but for a legal barrier.

Class. A group of beneficiaries or heirs that is designated only by status—for example, "children" or "issue." A class member is anyone who fits in the category.

Codicil. A supplement or addition to a will. It may explain, modify, add to, subtract from, qualify, alter, restrain, or revoke provisions in the will. Because a codicil changes a will, it must be executed with the same formalities as a will. When admitted to probate, it forms a part of the will.

Collateral. Property pledged as security for a debt.

Community Property. Very generally, all property acquired by a couple after marriage (or after registering as domestic partners) and before permanent separation, except for gifts to and inheritances by one spouse or partner only, or unless the nature of property has been changed by agreement between the spouses or partners. Assets purchased during the marriage or partnership with the income earned by either spouse or partner during the marriage or partnership are usually community property, unless the spouses or partners have entered into an agreement to the contrary. Property purchased with the separate property of a spouse or partner is separate property, unless it has been given to the community by gift or agreement. If separate property and community property are mixed together (commingled) in a bank account and expenditures are made from this bank account, the goods purchased will usually be treated as community property.

Community Property With Right of Survivorship. Property co-owned by a married couple (or by registered domestic partners) that is clearly identified, on the title document, as "community property with right of survivorship." When one spouse or partner dies, the surviving spouse or partner inherits the deceased's half-interest without probate administration.

Conditional Bequest. A bequest that passes only under certain specified conditions or upon the occurrence of a specific event. For example, if you leave property to Aunt Millie provided she is living in Cincinnati when you die, and otherwise to Uncle Al, you have made a conditional bequest.

Conformed Copy. A copy of a document filed with the court that has been stamped with the filing date by the court clerk.

Consanguinity. An old-fashioned term referring to the relationship enjoyed by people who have a common ancestor. Thus, consanguinity exists between brothers and sisters but not between husbands and wives.

Contingent Beneficiary. Any person entitled to property under a will in the event one or more prior conditions are satisfied. For example, if Eli is entitled to take property under a will on the condition that Harry does not survive the testator, Eli is a contingent beneficiary. Similarly, if Ellen is named to receive a house only in the event her mother, who has been named to receive the house, does not live there, Ellen is a contingent beneficiary.

Creditor. For probate purposes, a creditor is any person or entity to whom the decedent was liable for money at the time of death, and any person or entity to whom the estate owes money (say a taxing authority, funeral home, etc.).

CTA. An abbreviation for the Latin phrase "cum testamento annexo," meaning "with the will annexed." Thus, an administrator who is appointed to serve in a context where a will exists but no executor was either named or able to serve is termed an administrator CTA or administrator with will annexed.

Decedent. For probate purposes, the person who died with or without a will. The "decedent's estate" refers to assets the decedent owned at the time of death.

Decree. A court order or judgment.

Deductions. Items that cause the value of the estate to be reduced for purposes of calculating taxes. They include the decedent's debts, expenses associated with a last illness, funeral expenses, taxes, and costs of administration (for example, court filing fees, certification fees, bond premiums, fees for public notices, etc.).

Deed. A document that transfers ownership of real property, and includes the person(s) making the transfer, the new owner(s), and a description of the property transferred. There are many types of deeds, including quitclaim deeds (a naked transfer of the property ownership without any guarantees), grant deeds (a transfer of ownership including certain guarantees, including the fact that the person making the transfer has the power to do so), as well as joint tenancy deeds, and transfer on death deeds.

Deed of Trust. A special type of deed (similar to a mortgage) that places legal title to real property in the hands of one or more trustees as security for repayment of a loan. Thus, if Isabel borrows $100,000 to buy a house, she will sign a deed of trust in favor of the designated trustees, who will retain the deed of trust until the loan has been paid off. Sometimes homes carry more than one deed of trust—one executed as security for a loan to buy the house and another (termed the "second deed of trust") executed at a later time as security for another loan (for example, for home improvement).

Devise. Real or personal property that is transferred under the terms of a will. Previously, the term referred only to real property.

Devisee. A person or entity who receives real or personal property under the terms of a will.

Discharge. The court order releasing the administrator or executor from any further duties regarding a probate estate. This typically occurs when the duties have been completed but can also happen earlier if the executor or administrator wishes to withdraw.

Distributee. Someone who receives property from an estate.

Domestic Partners. The members of a couple who have officially registered their relationship with a state, county, city, or employer. Couples who use a Declaration of Domestic Partnership to register their relationship with the California Secretary of State are California Registered Domestic Partners.

Encumbrances. Debts (for example, taxes, mechanic's liens, and judgment liens) and loans (for example, mortgages, deeds of trust, and security interests) that use property as collateral for payment of the debt or loan are considered to encumber the property because they must be paid off before clear title to the property can pass from one owner to the next. Generally, the value of a person's ownership in such property (called the "equity") is measured by the market value of the property less the sum of all encumbrances.

Equity. The difference between the fair market value of real and personal property and the amount owed on it, if any.

Escheat. A legal doctrine under which property belonging to a deceased person with no beneficiaries or heirs passes to the state.

Estate. Generally, the property idea person owns at death. There are different ways to measure an estate, depending on whether determining tax obligations (taxable estate), probate avoidance (probate estate), net worth (net estate), or total value of assets (gross estate).

Estate Planning. The process of planning for death and possible incapacity. Estate planning allows a person to specify who has authority manage personal and financial affairs when needed. It also allows a person to establish who will inherit property, and to do so in a way that minimizes court involvement and expense.

Estate Taxes. See "Federal Estate Taxes."

Executor/Executrix. The person specified in a will to manage the estate, deal with the probate court, and distribute assets as the will has specified. If there is no will, or no executor nominated under the will, the probate court will appoint such a person, who is then called the administrator of the estate.

Expenses of Administration. The expenses incurred by an executor or administrator in carrying out the terms of a will or in administering an estate. These include probate court fees, and fees charged by the executor or administrator, attorney, accountant, and appraiser.

Fair Market Value. That price for which an item of property would be purchased by a willing buyer, and sold by a willing seller, both knowing all the facts and neither being under any compulsion to buy or sell. All estates are appraised for their fair market value, and taxes are computed on the basis of the estate's net fair market value.

Federal Estate Tax. Tax imposed by the federal government on property as it passes from a deceased person to those who inherit. For deaths in 2021, only estates over $11.7 million, taking into consideration lifetime gifts, can pass without being subject to federal estate tax. In addition, assets can pass to a surviving spouse or charitable organizations without being subject to federal estate tax.

Gift. Property passed to others for no return or substantially less than its actual market value is considered a gift when the giver (donor) is still alive, and a bequest, legacy, or devise when left by a will.

Gross Estate. The total value of property owned by a person, without regard to debts, liens, or expenses.

Heir. A person who is entitled by law to inherit in the event an estate is not completely disposed of under a will, and sometimes refers to any person or entity named as a beneficiary in a will.

Heir at Law. A person entitled to inherit under intestate succession laws.

Holographic Will. A will in which the signature and material provisions are in the handwriting of the person making it. Any statement of testamentary intent contained in a holographic will may be either in the testator's own handwriting or as part of a commercially printed form will. Holographic wills are valid in California.

Inheritance Tax. A tax imposed on someone who inherits property. California no longer has a state inheritance tax. See Chapter 7.

Intangible Personal Property. Personal property that does not assume a physical form but that derives its value from the rights and powers that it gives to its owner. Thus, stock in a corporation, the right to receive a pension, and a patent or copyright are all examples of intangible personal property. Intangible personal property is, as a matter of law, deemed to be located where the decedent resides at the time of the decedent's death, even if, in fact, a title slip (for example, a stock or bond certificate) is physically located elsewhere.

Inter Vivos Trusts. See "Living Trust."

Intestate. A person who dies without having made a will dies "intestate." The laws governing intestate succession govern distribution of the estate.

Intestate Succession. The method by which property is distributed when a person fails to leave a will or otherwise transfer the estate at death. In such cases, California law provides that the property be distributed in certain shares to the closest surviving relatives. Generally, property goes to the surviving spouse or registered domestic partner, children, parents, siblings, nieces and nephews, and next of kin, in that order. In California, intestate succession rules can be different depending on whether separate or community property is involved (see Chapter 3). The intestate succession laws are also used in the event children are unintentionally overlooked in the will or if the beneficiary named to inherit the residuary estate predeceases the testator and there is no alternate.

Inventory. A list of property owned by the decedent at death and subject to a probate proceeding. During probate administration the inventory is filed with the court to establish the assets governed by the court proceeding.

Issue. A term generally meaning all biological children and their children down through the generations. Thus, a person's issue includes that person's children, grandchildren, great-grandchildren, and so on. Adopted children are considered the issue of their adopting parents and the children of the adopted children (and so on) are also considered issue. A term often used in place of issue is "lineal descendants."

Joint Tenancy. A way to hold title to jointly owned real or personal property. When two or more people own property as joint tenants, when one owner dies, the other joint tenants automatically become owners of the deceased owner's share. Thus, if a parent and child own a house as joint tenants, and the parent dies, the child automatically becomes full owner. Because of this "right of survivorship," a joint tenancy interest in property does not go through probate administration so long as at least one joint tenant survives. Instead, title passes directly to the surviving joint tenant(s).

Kindred. All persons described as relatives of the decedent under the California Probate Code.

Lapse. The failure of a gift of property left in a will because when the testator dies the beneficiary is deceased and no alternate has been named. California has a statute (termed an "antilapse" statute) that prevents gifts to relatives from lapsing unless the relative has no heirs.

Lawful Issue. The phrase was once used to distinguish between legitimate and illegitimate children (and their issue). Now, the phrase means the same as "issue" and "lineal descendant."

Legacy. An old legal word meaning a transfer of personal property by will. The more common term for this type of transfer is "bequest" or "devise."

Letters of Administration. The formal instrument of authority granted by the probate court that designates an administrator of an estate and authorizes the administrator to carry out the required duties.

Letters Testamentary. The formal instrument of authority given to an executor by the probate court, empowering the executor to carry out the executor's duties.

Life Estate. Interest in real estate that lasts for only as long as the interest holder lives. The ownership passes to someone else after the life-estate holder's death.

Lineal Descendants. Persons who are in the direct line of descent from an ancestor, such as children, grandchildren, and great-grandchildren. The term does not include nondescendant relatives such as siblings, nieces and nephews, and cousins.

Living Trust. A trust that remains in the control of the trust maker during that person's life. Property in a living trust normally passes to trust beneficiaries at the death of the trust's creator without the involvement of the probate court.

Marriage. A specific status conferred on a couple by the state. In California, it is necessary to file papers with a county clerk and have a marriage ceremony conducted by authorized individuals in order to be married, unless there is a valid marriage in another state.

Minor. In California, any person younger than 18 years of age.

Net Estate. The value of all property owned at death less liabilities.

Next of Kin. The closest living relatives of a decedent, under the California law governing intestate succession.

Personal Effects. Belongings of a personal nature, such as clothes and jewelry.

Personal Property. All items, both tangible and intangible, that are considered susceptible to ownership and that are not real property. For example, household possessions, stock, and cash. Property in an estate may be treated differently depending on whether it is considered personal or "real."

Personal Representative. The generic title applied to the person who is authorized to act on behalf of the decedent's estate. Almost always, this person is either the executor or administrator, depending on whether or not the decedent had a will.

Per Stirpes. A Latin term meaning that a beneficiary inherits through a deceased ancestor by right of representation. In real life, the term is normally used in wills to control the way property should be divided if a named beneficiary is not living, yet is survived by children. See Chapter 3.

Petition. A document filed with a court requesting a court order. In the probate context, an initial petition filed with the probate court requests that the estate be probated; a subsequent petition may request court permission for the personal representative to take certain actions in managing the estate, including making distributions; and a final request to discharge the executor or administrator from the duties of probate.

Predeceased Beneficiary. A person named as a beneficiary of the decedent who died either before the decedent died or before the end of the survivorship period.

Predeceased Domestic Partner. A person who died while in a domestic partnership with the decedent.

Predeceased Spouse. A person who died while married to the decedent.

Pretermitted Heir. A child, spouse, or domestic partner who, under certain circumstances, is not mentioned in the will and who the court believes was accidentally overlooked when the testator made the will. This typically occurs when a child has been born or adopted after the will was made.

Because state law presumes that persons want their children to inherit, the failure to provide for a child in a will is considered unintentional unless there is evidence of an intent to disinherit. Mentioning a child in the will and then not providing for that child is considered sufficient evidence of intent to disinherit in California. If the court determines that an heir was pretermitted, that heir is entitled to receive the same share of the estate that the heir would have received had the testator died intestate.

Probate. Generally, the process by which: (1) the authenticity of a will (if any) is established, (2) an executor or administrator is granted authority to act for the estate, (3) debts and taxes are paid, (4) heirs are identified, and (5) property in the probate estate is distributed according to the will or intestate succession laws.

Probate Estate. All the assets owned at death that require some form of legal proceeding before title may be transferred to the proper heirs. Property that passes automatically at death (property in a trust, life insurance proceeds, property in a "pay on death" account, or property held in joint tenancy) is not in the probate estate.

Public Administrator. A publicly appointed person who handles the administration of an estate when no other person has been appointed as executor or administrator. This usually occurs when there are no known heirs.

Quasi-Community Property. Property acquired by a husband and wife or registered domestic partners during their marriage or registered partnership while residing outside California that would have been community property had it been acquired in California. California law treats it the same as community property. In essence, this means that in assessing whether or not a decedent's property is community property, the residence of the decedent when the property was acquired is irrelevant. An important exception: Real property located outside California is not considered quasi-community property.

Real Property. Land, things affixed to the land such as trees and crops, buildings, stationary mobile homes and cabins are termed real property. All property that is not real property is termed personal property. See "Personal Property."

Registered Domestic Partners. See "Domestic Partners."

Residence. The physical location that a person considers and treats as home, both presently and for the indefinite future. For example, although members of Congress typically spend most of their time in Washington, D.C., they generally consider the states they come from as their residences. With rare exceptions, a person may have only one residence. Usually the laws of the state of a decedent's residence apply to administration of the decedent's estate, with the exception of certain property located in other states.

Residuary Estate. All the property contained in the probate estate except for property that has been specifically and effectively left to designated beneficiaries.

Right of Representation. When the descendants of a deceased person take the same share collectively that the deceased person would have taken if living at the time of a decedent's death. See "Per Stirpes."

Self-Proving Will. A will that is executed in a way that allows the court to accept it as the true will of the decedent without further proof.

Separate Property. In the probate context, all property owned by a California decedent that is not considered community or quasi-community property. Separate property generally includes all property acquired by the decedent before marriage or domestic partnership and after a legal separation or dissolution, property acquired by separate gift or inheritance at any time, property acquired from separate property funds, and property that has been designated separate property by agreement of the spouses or partners.

Small Estate. A general term for an estate that has a low enough value to qualify for simplified probate procedures.

Specific Bequest. A specific item, distinguished from all others of the same kind belonging to the testator, that is designated in the will as going to a specific beneficiary. If the specific item is no longer in the estate when the decedent dies, the bequest fails. Thus, if John leaves his 1954 Mercedes to Patricia in his will, and when John dies the 1954 Mercedes is long gone, Patricia doesn't receive John's current car or the cash equivalent of the Mercedes.

Succession. The act of acquiring title to property when it has not been disposed of by will. Thus, when Abbie receives her mother's coin collection through "succession," she gets it under the intestate laws rather than as a beneficiary under a will.

Surviving Domestic Partner. A person who was in a domestic partnership with the decedent when the decedent died.

Surviving Spouse. A person who was married to the decedent when the decedent died.

Tangible Personal Property. Personal property that takes a tangible form, such as automobiles, furniture, and heirlooms. Although items such as stock ownership and copyrights may be represented in the form of paper certificates, the actual property is not in physical form and is therefore considered intangible personal property. See "Intangible Personal Property."

Taxable Estate. The fair market value of all assets owned by a decedent at date of death (gross estate) less certain allowable deductions, such as debts of the decedent, last illness and funeral expenses, and expenses of administering the decedent's estate (attorneys' fees, court costs, and newspaper publication fees).

Tenancy in Common. The ownership of property by two or more persons in such a manner that each has an undivided interest in the whole and each can pass that interest to heirs/beneficiaries instead of to the other owners (as is the case with joint tenancy). Also, unlike joint tenancies, the ownership shares need not be equal.

Testamentary Disposition. A disposition of property in a will.

Testate. Having left a will. For example, if Marc dies having made a will, he is said to have died testate.

Testator. One who has made a will; one who dies leaving a will.

Transfer Agent. A representative of a corporation who is authorized to transfer ownership of a corporation's stock from one person to another. An executor or administrator must use a transfer agent when passing title to a decedent's stock to an heir or beneficiary.

Trust. A legal arrangement under which one person or institution (called a "trustee") controls property given by another person (termed a "trustor," "grantor," or "settlor") for the benefit of a third person (called a "beneficiary"). The property itself is sometimes termed the "corpus" of the trust or the "trust estate." See "Living Trust."

Uniform Transfer on Death Securities Registration Act. A law adopted by the State of California that allows you to name someone to inherit your stocks, bonds, or brokerage accounts without probate. When you register your ownership, you make a request to take ownership in what's called "beneficiary form." The beneficiary has no rights to the stock while you are alive, but on your death, the beneficiary can claim the securities without probate.

Uniform Transfers to Minors Act. A set of statutes adopted by the California legislature that provides a way for someone to give or leave property to a minor by appointing a "custodian" to manage the property for the minor. It is common for wills to appoint a custodian for property left to minors by the will.

Will. A legal document in which the will maker names beneficiaries for property, names an executor, sets up property management for young beneficiaries, and provides other instructions that take effect when the will maker dies.

Judicial Council Forms

You can download all Judicial Council forms at **www.courts.ca.gov/forms.htm**

DE-111	Petition for Probate
DE-120	Notice of Hearing
DE-121	Notice of Petition to Administer Estate
DE-121(MA)	Attachment to Notice of Petition to Administer Estate
DE-131	Proof of Subscribing Witness
DE-135	Proof of Holographic Instrument
DE-140	Order for Probate
DE-142	Waiver of Bond by Heir or Beneficiary
DE-147	Duties and Liabilities of Personal Representative
DE-147S	Confidential Supplement to Duties and Liabilities of Personal Representative
DE-150	Letters
DE-157	Notice of Administration to Creditors
DE-160	Inventory and Appraisal
DE-161	Inventory and Appraisal Attachment
DE-165	Notice of Proposed Action
DE-172	Creditor's Claim
DE-174	Allowance or Rejection of Creditor's Claim
DE-221	Spousal or Domestic Partner Property Petition
DE-226	Spousal or Domestic Partner Property Order
DE-270	Ex Parte Petition for Authority to Sell Securities and Order
DE-295	Ex Parte Petition for Final Discharge and Order
DE-305	Affidavit re Real Property of Small Value ($55,425 or Less)
DE-310	Petition to Determine Succession to Real Property (Estates of $166,250 or Less)
DE-315	Order Determining Succession to Real Property (Estates of $166,250 or Less)

ESTATE OF *(name)*: DECEDENT	CASE NUMBER:

3. d. **Character and estimated value of the property of the estate** *(complete in all cases)*:
   (1) Personal property: $
   (2) Annual gross income from
   (a) real property: $
   (b) personal property: $
   (3) **Subtotal** *(add (1) and (2))*: $ ________________
   (4) Gross fair market value of real property: $
   (5) (Less) Encumbrances: ($ ________________)
   (6) Net value of real property: $ ________________
   (7) **Total** *(add (3) and (6))*: $ ________________

e. (1) ☐ Will waives bond. ☐ Special administrator is the named executor, and the will waives bond.
(2) ☐ All beneficiaries are adults and have waived bond, and the will does not require a bond. *(Affix waiver as Attachment 3e(2).)*
(3) ☐ All heirs at law are adults and have waived bond. *(Affix waiver as Attachment 3e(3).)*
(4) ☐ Sole personal representative is a corporate fiduciary or an exempt government agency.

f. (1) ☐ Decedent died intestate.
(2) ☐ Copy of decedent's will dated: ☐ codicil dated *(specify for each)*:

are affixed as Attachment 3f(2). *(Include typed copies of handwritten documents and English translations of foreign-language documents.)*
☐ The will and all codicils are self-proving (Prob. Code, § 8220).

(3) ☐ The original of the will and/or codicil identified above has been lost. *(Affix a copy of the lost will or codicil or a written statement of the testamentary words or their substance in Attachment 3f(3), and state reasons in that attachment why the presumption in Prob. Code, § 6124 does not apply.)*

g. **Appointment of personal representative** *(check all applicable boxes)*:
(1) Appointment of executor or administrator with will annexed:
(a) ☐ Proposed executor is named as executor in the will and consents to act.
(b) ☐ No executor is named in the will.
(c) ☐ Proposed personal representative is a nominee of a person entitled to Letters. *(Affix nomination as Attachment 3g(1)(c).)*
(d) ☐ Other named executors will not act because of ☐ death ☐ declination
☐ other reasons *(specify)*:

☐ Continued in Attachment 3g(1)(d).

(2) Appointment of administrator:
(a) ☐ Petitioner is a person entitled to Letters. *(If necessary, explain priority in Attachment 3g(2)(a).)*
(b) ☐ Petitioner is a nominee of a person entitled to Letters. *(Affix nomination as Attachment 3g(2)(b).)*
(c) ☐ Petitioner is related to the decedent as *(specify)*:

(3) ☐ Appointment of special administrator requested. *(Specify grounds and requested powers in Attachment 3g(3).)*
(4) ☐ Proposed personal representative would be a successor personal representative.

h. Proposed personal representative is a
(1) ☐ resident of California.
(2) ☐ nonresident of California *(specify permanent address)*:

(3) ☐ resident of the United States.
(4) ☐ nonresident of the United States.

ESTATE OF *(name)*: DECEDENT	CASE NUMBER:

4. ☐ Decedent's will does not preclude administration of this estate under the Independent Administration of Estates Act.
5. a. Decedent was survived by *(check items (1) or (2), and (3) or (4), and (5) or (6), and (7) or (8))*
   (1) ☐ spouse.
   (2) ☐ no spouse as follows:
      (a) ☐ divorced or never married.
      (b) ☐ spouse deceased.
   (3) ☐ registered domestic partner.
   (4) ☐ no registered domestic partner. *(See Fam. Code, § 297.5(c); Prob. Code, §§ 37(b), 6401(c), and 6402.)*
   (5) ☐ child as follows:
      (a) ☐ natural or adopted.
      (b) ☐ natural adopted by a third party.
   (6) ☐ no child.
   (7) ☐ issue of a predeceased child.
   (8) ☐ no issue of a predeceased child.

   b. Decedent ☐ was ☐ was not survived by a stepchild or foster child or children who would have been adopted by decedent but for a legal barrier. *(See Prob. Code, § 6454.)*
6. *(Complete if decedent was survived by (1) a spouse or registered domestic partner but no issue (only* ***a*** *or* ***b*** *apply), or (2) no spouse, registered domestic partner, or issue. (Check the* ***first*** *box that applies):*
   a. ☐ Decedent was survived by a parent or parents who are listed in item 8.
   b. ☐ Decedent was survived by issue of deceased parents, all of whom are listed in item 8.
   c. ☐ Decedent was survived by a grandparent or grandparents who are listed in item 8.
   d. ☐ Decedent was survived by issue of grandparents, all of whom are listed in item 8.
   e. ☐ Decedent was survived by issue of a predeceased spouse, all of whom are listed in item 8.
   f. ☐ Decedent was survived by next of kin, all of whom are listed in item 8.
   g. ☐ Decedent was survived by parents of a predeceased spouse or issue of those parents, if both are predeceased, all of whom are listed in item 8.
   h. ☐ Decedent was survived by no known next of kin.
7. *(Complete only if no spouse or issue survived decedent.)*
   a. ☐ Decedent had no predeceased spouse.
   b. ☐ Decedent had a predeceased spouse who
      (1) ☐ died not more than 15 years before decedent and who owned an interest in **real property** that passed to decedent,
      (2) ☐ died not more than five years before decedent and who owned **personal property** valued at $10,000 or more that passed to decedent, *(If you checked (1) or (2), check only the* ***first*** *box that applies):*
         (a) ☐ Decedent was survived by issue of a predeceased spouse, all of whom are listed in item 8.
         (b) ☐ Decedent was survived by a parent or parents of the predeceased spouse who are listed in item 8.
         (c) ☐ Decedent was survived by issue of a parent of the predeceased spouse, all of whom are listed in item 8.
         (d) ☐ Decedent was survived by next of kin of the decedent, all of whom are listed in item 8.
         (e) ☐ Decedent was survived by next of kin of the predeceased spouse, all of whom are listed in item 8.
      (3) ☐ neither (1) nor (2) apply.
8. Listed on the next page are the names, relationships to decedent, ages, and addresses, so far as known to or reasonably ascertainable by petitioner, of (1) all persons mentioned in decedent's will or any codicil, whether living or deceased; (2) all persons named or checked in items 2, 5, 6, and 7; and (3) all beneficiaries of a trust named in decedent's will or any codicil in which the trustee and personal representative are the same person.

ESTATE OF *(name)*: DECEDENT	CASE NUMBER:

8. Name and relationship to decedent | Age | Address

☐ Continued on Attachment 8.

9. Number of pages attached: ________

Date:

_______________________________ (TYPE OR PRINT NAME OF ATTORNEY)

▶ _______________________________ (SIGNATURE OF ATTORNEY) *

* (Signatures of all petitioners are also required. All petitioners must sign, but the petition may be verified by any one of them (Prob. Code, §§ 1020, 1021; Cal. Rules of Court, rule 7.103).)

I declare under penalty of perjury under the laws of the State of California that the foregoing is true and correct.

Date:

_______________________________ (TYPE OR PRINT NAME OF PETITIONER)

▶ _______________________________ (SIGNATURE OF PETITIONER)

_______________________________ (TYPE OR PRINT NAME OF PETITIONER)

▶ _______________________________ (SIGNATURE OF PETITIONER)

Signatures of additional petitioners follow last attachment.

ATTORNEY OR PARTY WITHOUT ATTORNEY STATE BAR NUMBER:	FOR COURT USE ONLY
NAME:	
FIRM NAME:	
STREET ADDRESS:	
CITY: STATE: ZIP CODE:	
TELEPHONE NO.: FAX NO.:	
EMAIL ADDRESS:	
ATTORNEY FOR (*name*):	
SUPERIOR COURT OF CALIFORNIA, COUNTY OF	
STREET ADDRESS:	
MAILING ADDRESS:	
CITY AND ZIP CODE:	
BRANCH NAME:	
☐ ESTATE OF *(name):* ☐ IN THE MATTER OF *(name):*	
☐ DECEDENT ☐ TRUST ☐ OTHER	
NOTICE OF HEARING—DECEDENT'S ESTATE OR TRUST	CASE NUMBER:

This notice is required by law. You are not required to appear in court, but you may attend the hearing and object or respond if you wish. If you do not respond or attend the hearing, the court may act on the filing without you.

1. NOTICE is given that *(name):*
   (fiduciary or representative capacity, if any):
   has filed a petition, application, report, or account *(specify complete title and briefly describe):**

   ☐ The filing is a report of the status of a decedent's estate administration made under Probate Code section 12200. See the NOTICE below.

   Please refer to the filed documents for more information about the case. *(Some documents filed with the court are confidential.)*

2. A HEARING on the matter described in 1 will be held as follows:

Hearing Date	Date:	Time:	Name and address of court, if different from above:
	Dept.:	Room:	

NOTICE

If the filing described in 1 is a report of the status of a decedent's estate administration made under Probate Code section 12200,

YOU HAVE THE RIGHT TO PETITION FOR AN ACCOUNTING UNDER SECTION 10950 OF THE PROBATE CODE.

Requests for Accommodations

Assistive listening systems, computer-assisted real-time captioning, or sign language interpreter services are available if you ask at least five days before the hearing. Contact the clerk's office or go to *www.courts.ca.gov/forms* for *Request for Accommodations by Persons With Disabilities and Response* (form MC-410). (Civ. Code, § 54.8.)

* Do **not** use this form to give notice of a petition to administer an estate (see Prob. Code, § 8100, and use form DE-121), notice of a hearing in a guardianship or conservatorship case (see Prob. Code, §§ 1511 and 1822, and use form GC-020), or notice of a hearing on a petition to determine a claim to property (see Prob. Code, § 851, and use form DE-115/GC-015).

(b) If the evidence of ownership is not presented to the holder pursuant to subdivision (a), the holder may require, as a condition for the payment, delivery, or transfer of the property, that the person presenting the affidavit or declaration provide the holder with a bond or undertaking in a reasonable amount determined by the holder to be sufficient to indemnify the holder against all liability, claims, demands, loss, damages, costs, and expenses that the holder may incur or suffer by reason of the payment, delivery, or transfer of the property. Nothing in this subdivision precludes the holder and the person presenting the affidavit or declaration from dispensing with the requirement that a bond or undertaking be provided and instead entering into an agreement satisfactory to the holder concerning the duty of the person presenting the affidavit or declaration to indemnify the holder.

(Enacted Stats 1990 ch 79 § 14 (AB 759), operative July 1, 1991.)

§ 13103. Inventory and appraisal of real property

If the estate of the decedent includes any real property in this state, the affidavit or declaration shall be accompanied by an inventory and appraisal of the real property. The inventory and appraisal of the real property shall be made as provided in Part 3 (commencing with Section 8800) of Division 7. The appraisal shall be made by a probate referee selected by the affiant or declarant from those probate referees appointed by the Controller under Section 400 to appraise property in the county where the real property is located.

(Enacted Stats 1990 ch 79 § 14 (AB 759), operative July 1, 1991.)

§ 13104. Proof of identity

(a) Reasonable proof of the identity of each person executing the affidavit or declaration shall be provided to the holder of the decedent's property.

(b) Reasonable proof of identity is provided for the purposes of this section if both of the following requirements are satisfied:
   (1) The person executing the affidavit or declaration is personally known to the holder.
   (2) The person executes the affidavit or declaration in the presence of the holder.

(c) If the affidavit or declaration is executed in the presence of the holder, a written statement under penalty of perjury by a person personally known to the holder affirming the identity of the person executing the affidavit or declaration is reasonable proof of identity for the purposes of this section.

(d) If the affidavit or declaration is executed in the presence of the holder, the holder may reasonably rely on any of the following as reasonable proof of identity for the purposes of this section:
   (1) An identification card or driver's license issued by the Department of Motor Vehicles of this state that is current or was issued during the preceding five years.
   (2) A passport issued by the Department of State of the United States that is current or was issued during the preceding five years.
   (3) Any of the following documents if the document is current or was issued during the preceding five years and contains a photograph and description of the person named on it, is signed by the person, and bears a serial or other identifying number:
      (A) A passport issued by a foreign government that has been stamped by the United States Immigration and Naturalization Service.
      (B) A driver's license issued by a state other than California.
      (C) An identification card issued by a state other than California.
      (D) An identification card issued by any branch of the armed forces of the United States.

(e) For the purposes of this section, a notary public's certificate of acknowledgment identifying the person executing the affidavit or declaration is reasonable proof of identity of the person executing the affidavit or declaration.

(f) Unless the affidavit or declaration contains a notary public's certificate of acknowledgment of the identity of the person, the holder shall note on the affidavit or declaration either that the person executing the affidavit or declaration is personally known or a description of the identification provided by the person executing the affidavit or declaration.

(Enacted Stats 1990 ch 79 § 14 (AB 759), operative July 1, 1991.)

§ 13105. Transfer of property to successor

(a) If the requirements of Sections 13100 to 13104, inclusive, are satisfied:
   (1) The person or persons executing the affidavit or declaration as successor of the decedent are entitled to have the property described in the affidavit or declaration paid, delivered, or transferred to them.
   (2) A transfer agent of a security described in the affidavit or declaration shall change the registered ownership on the books of the corporation from the decedent to the person or persons executing the affidavit or declaration as successor of the decedent.

(b) If the holder of the decedent's property refuses to pay, deliver, or transfer any personal property or evidence thereof to the successor of the decedent within a reasonable time, the successor may recover the property or compel its payment, delivery, or transfer in an action brought for that purpose against the holder of the property. If an action is brought against the holder under this section, the court shall award reasonable attorney's fees to the person or persons bringing the action if the court finds that the holder of the decedent's property acted unreasonably in refusing to pay, deliver, or transfer the property to them as required by subdivision (a).

(Enacted Stats 1990 ch 79 § 14 (AB 759), operative July 1, 1991.)

§ 13106. Protection of transferor from liability

(a) If the requirements of Sections 13100 to 13104, inclusive, are satisfied, receipt by the holder of the decedent's property of the affidavit or declaration constitutes sufficient acquittance for the payment of money, delivery of property, or changing registered ownership of property pursuant to this chapter and discharges the holder from any further liability with respect to the money or property. The holder may rely in good faith on the statements in the affidavit or declaration and has no duty to inquire into the truth of any statement in the affidavit or declaration.

(b) If the requirements of Sections 13100 to 13104, inclusive, are satisfied, the holder of the decedent's property is not liable for any taxes due to this state by reason of paying money, delivering property, or changing registered ownership of property pursuant to this chapter.

(Enacted Stats 1990 ch 79 § 14 (AB 759), operative July 1, 1991.)

ATTORNEY OR PARTY WITHOUT ATTORNEY: STATE BAR NO.:	FOR COURT USE ONLY
NAME:	
FIRM NAME:	
STREET ADDRESS:	
CITY: STATE: ZIP CODE:	
TELEPHONE NO.: FAX NO.:	
E-MAIL ADDRESS:	
ATTORNEY FOR (*name*):	
SUPERIOR COURT OF CALIFORNIA, COUNTY OF	
STREET ADDRESS:	
MAILING ADDRESS:	
CITY AND ZIP CODE:	
BRANCH NAME:	
ESTATE OF (*name*): DECEDENT	
PETITION FOR ☐ **Probate of** ☐ **Lost Will and for Letters Testamentary** ☐ **Probate of** ☐ **Lost Will and for Letters of Administration with Will Annexed** ☐ **Letters of Administration** ☐ **Letters of Special Administration** ☐ **with general powers** ☐ **Authorization to Administer Under the Independent Administration of Estates Act** ☐ **with limited authority**	CASE NUMBER:
	HEARING DATE AND TIME: DEPT.:

1. Publication will be in (*specify name of newspaper*):
   a. ☐ Publication requested.
   b. ☐ Publication to be arranged.
2. **Petitioner** (*name each*):

   requests that
   a. ☐ decedent's will and codicils, if any, be admitted to probate.
   b. (*name*): be appointed
      (1) ☐ executor
      (2) ☐ administrator with will annexed
      (3) ☐ administrator
      (4) ☐ special administrator ☐ with general powers
      and Letters issue upon qualification.
   c. ☐ full ☐ limited authority be granted to administer under the Independent Administration of Estates Act.
   d. (1) ☐ bond not be required for the reasons stated in item 3e.
      (2) ☐ $ bond be fixed. The bond will be furnished by an admitted surety insurer or as otherwise provided by law. (*Specify reasons in Attachment 2 if the amount is different from the maximum required by Prob. Code, § 8482.*)
      (3) ☐ $ in deposits in a blocked account be allowed. Receipts will be filed. (*Specify institution and location*):

3. a. Decedent died on (*date*): at (*place*):
      (1) ☐ a resident of the county named above.
      (2) ☐ a nonresident of California and left an estate in the county named above located at (*specify location permitting publication in the newspaper named in item 1*):

   b. ☐ Decedent was a citizen of a country other than the United States (*specify country*):
   c. Street address, city, and county of decedent's residence at time of death (*specify*):

Form Adopted for Mandatory Use
Judicial Council of California
DE-111 [Rev. July 1, 2017]

PETITION FOR PROBATE
(Probate—Decedents Estates)

Probate Code, §§ 8002, 10450;
www.courts.ca.gov

California Probate Code §§ 13100–13106

Affidavit Procedure for Collection or Transfer of Personal Property

§ 13100. Estates not exceeding $166,250; authorization to act without procuring letters of administration or awaiting probate

Excluding the property described in Section 13050, if the gross value of the decedent's real and personal property in this state does not exceed one hundred sixty-six thousand two hundred fifty dollars ($166,250), as adjusted periodically in accordance with Section 890, and if 40 days have elapsed since the death of the decedent, the successor of the decedent may, without procuring letters of administration or awaiting probate of the will, do any of the following with respect to one or more particular items of property:

(a) Collect any particular item of property that is money due the decedent.

(b) Receive any particular item of property that is tangible personal property of the decedent.

(c) Have any particular item of property that is evidence of a debt, obligation, interest, right, security, or chose in action belonging to the decedent transferred, whether or not secured by a lien on real property.

(Stats.1990, c. 79 (A.B.759), § 14, operative July 1, 1991. Amended by Stats.1996, c. 86 (A.B.2146), § 4; Stats.1996, c. 862 (A.B.2751), § 34; Stats.2011, c. 117 (A.B.1305), § 4; Stats.2019, c. 122 (A.B.473), § 5, eff. Jan. 1, 2020.)

§ 13101. Affidavit or declaration; contents; requirements; attachments

(a) To collect money, receive tangible personal property, or have evidences of a debt, obligation, interest, right, security, or chose in action transferred under this chapter, an affidavit or a declaration under penalty of perjury under the laws of this state shall be furnished to the holder of the decedent's property stating all of the following:

(1) The decedent's name.

(2) The date and place of the decedent's death.

(3) "At least 40 days have elapsed since the death of the decedent, as shown in a certified copy of the decedent's death certificate attached to this affidavit or declaration."

(4) Either of the following, as appropriate:

(A) "No proceeding is now being or has been conducted in California for administration of the decedent's estate."

(B) "The decedent's personal representative has consented in writing to the payment, transfer, or delivery to the affiant or declarant of the property described in the affidavit or declaration."

(5) "The current gross fair market value of the decedent's real and personal property in California, excluding the property described in Section 13050 of the California Probate Code, does not exceed [Insert dollar amount specified in subdivision (g) of Section 13101 of the California Probate Code].

(6) A description of the property of the decedent that is to be paid, transferred, or delivered to the affiant or declarant.

(7) The name of the successor of the decedent (as defined in Section 13006 of the California Probate Code) to the described property.

(8) Either of the following, as appropriate:

(A) "The affiant or declarant is the successor of the decedent (as defined in Section 13006 of the California Probate Code) to the decedent's interest in the described property."

(B) "The affiant or declarant is authorized under Section 13051 of the California Probate Code to act on behalf of the successor of the decedent (as defined in Section 13006 of the California Probate Code) with respect to the decedent's interest in the described property."

(9) "No other person has a superior right to the interest of the decedent in the described property."

(10) "The affiant or declarant requests that the described property be paid, delivered, or transferred to the affiant or declarant."

(11) "The affiant or declarant affirms or declares under penalty of perjury under the laws of the State of California that the foregoing is true and correct."

(b) Where more than one person executes the affidavit or declaration under this section, the statements required by subdivision (a) shall be modified as appropriate to reflect that fact.

(c) If the particular item of property to be transferred under this chapter is a debt or other obligation secured by a lien on real property and the instrument creating the lien has been recorded in the office of the county recorder of the county where the real property is located, the affidavit or declaration shall satisfy the requirements both of this section and of Section 13106.5.

(d) A certified copy of the decedent's death certificate shall be attached to the affidavit or declaration.

(e) If the decedent's personal representative has consented to the payment, transfer, or delivery of the described property to the affiant or declarant, a copy of the consent and of the personal representative's letters shall be attached to the affidavit or declaration.

(f) If the decedent dies on or after April 1, 2022, the list of adjusted dollar amounts, published in accordance with subdivision (c) of Section 890, in effect on the date of the decedent's death, shall be attached to the affidavit or declaration.

(g) (1) If the decedent dies prior to April 1, 2022, the dollar amount for paragraph (5) of subdivision (a) is one hundred sixty-six thousand two hundred fifty dollars ($166,250).

(2) If the decedent dies on or after April 1, 2022, the dollar amount for paragraph (5) of subdivision (a) is the adjusted dollar amount, published in accordance with subdivision (c) of Section 890, in effect on the date of the decedent's death.

(Stats.1990, c. 79 (A.B.759), § 14, operative July 1, 1991. Amended by Stats.1991, c. 1055 (S.B.271), § 36; Stats.1996, c. 86 (A.B.2146), § 5; Stats.1996, c. 862 (A.B.2751), § 35; § 5 Stats.2011, c. 117 (A.B.1305), § 5; Stats.2019, c. 122 (A.B.473), § 6, eff. Jan. 1, 2020.)

§ 13102. Presenting decedent's evidence of ownership

(a) If the decedent had evidence of ownership of the property described in the affidavit or declaration and the holder of the property would have had the right to require presentation of the evidence of ownership before the duty of the holder to pay, deliver, or transfer the property to the decedent would have arisen, the evidence of ownership, if available, shall be presented with the affidavit or declaration to the holder of the decedent's property.

☐ ESTATE OF *(name):* ☐ IN THE MATTER OF *(name):* ☐ DECEDENT ☐ TRUST ☐ OTHER	CASE NUMBER:

CLERK'S CERTIFICATE OF POSTING

1. I certify that I am not a party to this cause.
2. A copy of the foregoing *Notice of Hearing—Decedent's Estate or Trust*
   a. was posted at *(address):*

   b. was posted on *(date):*

Date: Clerk, by ______________________, Deputy

PROOF OF SERVICE BY MAIL*

1. I am over the age of 18 and not a party to this cause. I am a resident of or employed in the county where the mailing occurred.
2. My residence or business address is *(specify):*
3. I served the foregoing *Notice of Hearing—Decedent's Estate or Trust* on each person named below by enclosing a copy in an envelope addressed as shown below AND
   a. ☐ **depositing** the sealed envelope on the date and at the place shown in item 4 with the U.S. Postal Service with the postage fully prepaid.
   b. ☐ **placing** the envelope for collection and mailing on the date and at the place shown in item 4 following our ordinary business practices. I am readily familiar with this business's practice for collecting and processing correspondence for mailing. On the same day that correspondence is placed for collection and mailing, it is deposited in the ordinary course of business with the U.S. Postal Service in a sealed envelope with postage fully prepaid.
4. a. Date mailed:
   b. Place mailed *(city, state):*
5. ☐ I served with the *Notice of Hearing—Decedent's Estate or Trust* a copy of the petition or other document referred to in item 1 of the Notice.

I declare under penalty of perjury under the laws of the State of California that the foregoing is true and correct.

Date:

______________________ (TYPE OR PRINT NAME) ▶ ______________________ (SIGNATURE)

NAME AND ADDRESS OF EACH PERSON TO WHOM NOTICE WAS MAILED

	Name	Address *(street & number, city, state, zip code)*
1.		
2.		
3.		
4.		
5.		

☐ Continued on an attachment. *(You may use* Attachment to Notice of Hearing Proof of Service by Mail, *form DE-120(MA)/GC-020(MA), for this purpose.)*

* Do **not** use this form for proof of personal service. You may use form DE-120(P) to prove personal service of this Notice.

ATTORNEY OR PARTY WITHOUT ATTORNEY *(Name, State Bar number, and address)*:	FOR COURT USE ONLY
TELEPHONE NO.: FAX NO. *(Optional)*:	
E-MAIL ADDRESS *(Optional)*:	
ATTORNEY FOR *(Name)*:	
SUPERIOR COURT OF CALIFORNIA, COUNTY OF	
STREET ADDRESS:	
MAILING ADDRESS:	
CITY AND ZIP CODE:	
BRANCH NAME:	
ESTATE OF *(Name)*: DECEDENT	
NOTICE OF PETITION TO ADMINISTER ESTATE OF *(Name)*:	CASE NUMBER:

1. To all heirs, beneficiaries, creditors, contingent creditors, and persons who may otherwise be interested in the will or estate, or both, of *(specify all names by which the decedent was known)*:
2. A **Petition for Probate** has been filed by *(name of petitioner)*:
   in the Superior Court of California, County of *(specify)*:
3. The Petition for Probate requests that *(name)*:
   be appointed as personal representative to administer the estate of the decedent.
4. ☐ The petition requests the decedent's will and codicils, if any, be admitted to probate. The will and any codicils are available for examination in the file kept by the court.
5. ☐ The petition requests authority to administer the estate under the Independent Administration of Estates Act. (This authority will allow the personal representative to take many actions without obtaining court approval. Before taking certain very important actions, however, the personal representative will be required to give notice to interested persons unless they have waived notice or consented to the proposed action.) The independent administration authority will be granted unless an interested person files an objection to the petition and shows good cause why the court should not grant the authority.
6. **A hearing on the petition will be held in this court as follows:**

a. Date:	Time:	Dept.:	Room:

   b. Address of court: ☐ same as noted above ☐ other *(specify)*:

7. **If you object** to the granting of the petition, you should appear at the hearing and state your objections or file written objections with the court before the hearing. Your appearance may be in person or by your attorney.
8. **If you are a creditor or a contingent creditor of the decedent,** you must file your claim with the court and mail a copy to the personal representative appointed by the court within the **later** of either (1) **four months** from the date of first issuance of letters to a general personal representative, as defined in section 58(b) of the California Probate Code, or (2) **60 days** from the date of mailing or personal delivery to you of a notice under section 9052 of the California Probate Code.
   Other California statutes and legal authority may affect your rights as a creditor. You may want to consult with an attorney knowledgeable in California law.
9. **You may examine the file kept by the court.** If you are a person interested in the estate, you may file with the court a *Request for Special Notice* (form DE-154) of the filing of an inventory and appraisal of estate assets or of any petition or account as provided in Probate Code section 1250. A *Request for Special Notice* form is available from the court clerk.
10. ☐ Petitioner ☐ Attorney for petitioner *(name)*:

    (Address):

    (Telephone):

NOTE: If this notice is published, print the caption, beginning with the words NOTICE OF PETITION TO ADMINISTER ESTATE, and do not print the information from the form above the caption. The caption and the decedent's name must be printed in at least 8-point type and the text in at least 7-point type. Print the case number as part of the caption. Print items preceded by a box only if the box is checked. Do not print the italicized instructions in parentheses, the paragraph numbers, the mailing information, or the material on page 2.

ESTATE OF *(Name):* DECEDENT	CASE NUMBER:

PROOF OF SERVICE BY MAIL

1. I am over the age of 18 and not a party to this cause. I am a resident of or employed in the county where the mailing occurred.
2. My residence or business address is *(specify)*:
3. I served the foregoing *Notice of Petition to Administer Estate* on each person named below by enclosing a copy in an envelope addressed as shown below **AND**
   a. ☐ **depositing** the sealed envelope with the United States Postal Service on the date and at the place shown in item 4, with the postage fully prepaid.
   b. ☐ **placing** the envelope for collection and mailing on the date and at the place shown in item 4 following our ordinary business practices. I am readily familiar with this business's practice for collecting and processing correspondence for mailing. On the same day that correspondence is placed for collection and mailing, it is deposited in the ordinary course of business with the United States Postal Service, in a sealed envelope with postage fully prepaid.
4. a. Date mailed: b. Place mailed *(city, state)*:
5. ☐ I served, with the *Notice of Petition to Administer Estate,* a copy of the petition or other document referred to in the notice.

I declare under penalty of perjury under the laws of the State of California that the foregoing is true and correct.

Date:

(TYPE OR PRINT NAME OF PERSON COMPLETING THIS FORM) ▶ (SIGNATURE OF PERSON COMPLETING THIS FORM)

NAME AND ADDRESS OF EACH PERSON TO WHOM NOTICE WAS MAILED

	Name of person served	Address *(number, street, city, state, and zip code)*
1.		
2.		
3.		
4.		
5.		
6.		

☐ Continued on an attachment. *(You may use form DE-121(MA) to show additional persons served.)*

Assistive listening systems, computer-assisted real-time captioning, or sign language interpreter services are available upon request if at least 5 days notice is provided. Contact the clerk's office for *Request for Accommodations by Persons With Disabilities and Order* (form MC-410). (Civil Code section 54.8.)

DE-121(MA)

ESTATE OF *(Name):* DECEDENT	CASE NUMBER:

ATTACHMENT TO NOTICE OF PETITION TO ADMINISTER ESTATE—PROOF OF SERVICE BY MAIL

(This attachment is for use with form DE-121.)

NAME AND ADDRESS OF EACH PERSON TO WHOM NOTICE WAS MAILED

No.	Name of person served	Address *(number, street, city, state, and zip code)*
____		
____		
____		
____		
____		
____		
____		
____		
____		
____		
____		
____		

ATTORNEY OR PARTY WITHOUT ATTORNEY *(Name, state bar number, and address)*:	TELEPHONE AND FAX NOS.:	*FOR COURT USE ONLY*
ATTORNEY FOR *(Name)*:		
SUPERIOR COURT OF CALIFORNIA, COUNTY OF STREET ADDRESS: MAILING ADDRESS: CITY AND ZIP CODE: BRANCH NAME:		
ESTATE OF *(Name)*: DECEDENT		
PROOF OF SUBSCRIBING WITNESS		CASE NUMBER:

1. I am one of the attesting witnesses to the instrument of which Attachment 1 is a photographic copy. I have examined Attachment 1 and my signature is on it.
   a. ☐ The name of the decedent was signed in the presence of the attesting witnesses present at the same time by
      (1) ☐ the decedent personally.
      (2) ☐ another person in the decedent's presence and by the decedent's direction.
   b. ☐ The decedent acknowledged in the presence of the attesting witnesses present at the same time that the decedent's name was signed by
      (1) ☐ the decedent personally.
      (2) ☐ another person in the decedent's presence and by the decedent's direction.
   c. ☐ The decedent acknowledged in the presence of the attesting witnesses present at the same time that the instrument signed was decedent's
      (1) ☐ will.
      (2) ☐ codicil.

2. When I signed the instrument, I understood that it was decedent's ☐ will ☐ codicil.

3. I have no knowledge of any facts indicating that the instrument, or any part of it, was procured by duress, menace, fraud, or undue influence.

I declare under penalty of perjury under the laws of the State of California that the foregoing is true and correct.

Date:

.... (TYPE OR PRINT NAME)

▶ ______________________________ (SIGNATURE OF WITNESS)

.... (ADDRESS)

ATTORNEY'S CERTIFICATION

(Check local court rules for requirements for certifying copies of wills and codicils)

I am an active member of The State Bar of California. I declare under penalty of perjury under the laws of the State of California that Attachment 1 is a photographic copy of every page of the ☐ will ☐ codicil presented for probate.

Date:

.... (TYPE OR PRINT NAME)

▶ ______________________________ (SIGNATURE OF ATTORNEY)

DE-135

ATTORNEY OR PARTY WITHOUT ATTORNEY *(Name, state bar number, and address):* TELEPHONE AND FAX NOS.:	FOR COURT USE ONLY
ATTORNEY FOR *(Name):*	
SUPERIOR COURT OF CALIFORNIA, COUNTY OF STREET ADDRESS: MAILING ADDRESS: CITY AND ZIP CODE: BRANCH NAME:	
ESTATE OF *(Name):* DECEDENT	
PROOF OF HOLOGRAPHIC INSTRUMENT	CASE NUMBER:

1. I was acquainted with the decedent for the following number of years *(specify)*:

2. ☐ I was related to the decedent as *(specify)*:

3. I have personal knowledge of the decedent's handwriting which I acquired as follows:
   a. ☐ I saw the decedent write.
   b. ☐ I saw a writing purporting to be in the decedent's handwriting and upon which decedent acted or was charged. It was *(specify)*:

   c. ☐ I received letters in the due course of mail purporting to be from the decedent in response to letters I addressed and mailed to the decedent.
   d. ☐ Other *(specify other means of obtaining knowledge)*:

4. I have examined the attached copy of the instrument, and its handwritten provisions were written by and the instrument was signed by the hand of the decedent. *(Affix a copy of the instrument as Attachment 4.)*

I declare under penalty of perjury under the laws of the State of California that the foregoing is true and correct.

Date:

. . . . ▶ ______________________________

(TYPE OR PRINT NAME) (SIGNATURE)

. . . .

(ADDRESS)

ATTORNEY'S CERTIFICATION

(Check local court rules for requirements for certifying copies of wills and codicils)

I am an active member of The State Bar of California. I declare under penalty of perjury under the laws of the State of California that Attachment 4 is a photographic copy of every page of the holographic instrument presented for probate.

Date:

. . . . ▶ ______________________________

(TYPE OR PRINT NAME) (SIGNATURE OF ATTORNEY)

DE-140

ATTORNEY OR PARTY WITHOUT ATTORNEY *(Name, state bar number, and address)*: TELEPHONE AND FAX NOS.:	FOR COURT USE ONLY
ATTORNEY FOR *(Name)*:	
SUPERIOR COURT OF CALIFORNIA, COUNTY OF STREET ADDRESS: MAILING ADDRESS: CITY AND ZIP CODE: BRANCH NAME:	
ESTATE OF *(Name)*: DECEDENT	
ORDER FOR PROBATE **ORDER APPOINTING** ☐ **Executor** ☐ **Administrator with Will Annexed** ☐ **Administrator** ☐ **Special Administrator** ☐ **Order Authorizing Independent Administration of Estate** ☐ **with full authority** ☐ **with limited authority**	CASE NUMBER:

WARNING: THIS APPOINTMENT IS NOT EFFECTIVE UNTIL LETTERS HAVE ISSUED.

1. Date of hearing: Time: Dept./Room: Judge:

THE COURT FINDS

2. a. All notices required by law have been given.
   b. Decedent died on *(date)*:
      (1) ☐ a resident of the California county named above.
      (2) ☐ a nonresident of California and left an estate in the county named above.
   c. Decedent died
      (1) ☐ intestate
      (2) ☐ testate
      and decedent's will dated: and each codicil dated:
      was admitted to probate by Minute Order on *(date)*:

THE COURT ORDERS

3. *(Name)*:
   is appointed **personal representative:**
   a. ☐ executor of the decedent's will
   b. ☐ administrator with will annexed
   c. ☐ administrator
   d. ☐ special administrator
      (1) ☐ with general powers
      (2) ☐ with special powers as specified in Attachment 3d(2)
      (3) ☐ without notice of hearing
      (4) ☐ letters will expire on *(date)*:

   and letters shall issue on qualification.
4. a. ☐ **Full authority** is granted to administer the estate under the Independent Administration of Estates Act.
   b. ☐ **Limited authority** is granted to administer the estate under the Independent Administration of Estates Act (there is no authority, without court supervision, to (1) sell or exchange real property or (2) grant an option to purchase real property or (3) borrow money with the loan secured by an encumbrance upon real property).
5. a. ☐ Bond is not required.
   b. ☐ Bond is fixed at: $ to be furnished by an authorized surety company or as otherwise provided by law.
   c. ☐ Deposits of: $ are ordered to be placed in a blocked account at *(specify institution and location)*:
      and receipts shall be filed. No withdrawals shall be made without a court order. ☐ Additional orders in Attachment 5c.
   d. ☐ The personal representative is not authorized to take possession of money or any other property without a specific court order.
6. ☐ *(Name)*: is appointed probate referee.

Date:

JUDGE OF THE SUPERIOR COURT

☐ SIGNATURE FOLLOWS LAST ATTACHMENT

7. Number of pages attached: _____

ATTORNEY OR PARTY WITHOUT ATTORNEY: STATE BAR NO.:	FOR COURT USE ONLY
NAME:	
FIRM NAME:	
STREET ADDRESS:	
CITY: STATE: ZIP CODE:	
TELEPHONE NO.: FAX NO.:	
E-MAIL ADDRESS:	
ATTORNEY FOR *(name)*:	
SUPERIOR COURT OF CALIFORNIA, COUNTY OF	
STREET ADDRESS:	
MAILING ADDRESS:	
CITY AND ZIP CODE:	
BRANCH NAME:	
ESTATE OF *(Name)*: , DECEDENT	
WAIVER OF BOND BY HEIR OR BENEFICIARY ☐ **Attachment 3e to *Petition for Probate****	CASE NUMBER:

NOTICE: READ PARAGRAPHS A–G BEFORE YOU SIGN

A. A bond is a form of insurance to replace assets that may be mismanaged or stolen by the executor or administrator (the estate's **personal representative**). The cost of the bond is paid from the assets of the estate.

B. A bond may not be required if the decedent's will admitted to probate waives a bond and the court approves.

C. If the decedent's will does not waive bond, or if the decedent died without a will, the law ordinarily requires the personal representative to give a bond approved and ordered by the court. However, all persons eligible to receive a share of the estate may waive the requirement of a bond. If they all waive bond and the court approves, the personal representative will NOT have to give a bond.

D. **If bond is not ordered by the court, and the estate suffers loss because the personal representative fails to properly perform the duties of the office, the loss or some part of it may not be recoverable from the personal representative. If so, your share of the estate may be partly or entirely lost.**

E. You may waive the requirement of a bond by signing this form and delivering it to the petitioner for appointment of a personal representative or to the petitioner's attorney. Your waiver cannot be withdrawn after the court appoints the personal representative without requiring a bond. However, if you sign a waiver of bond, you may later petition the court to require a bond.

F. A guardian ad litem or other legal representative with specific authority under law to waive bond must sign for a minor, an incapacitated person, an unascertained beneficiary, or a designated class of persons who are not ascertained or not yet in being. See Judicial Council forms DE-350 and DE-351 and Probate Code section 1003.

G. **If you do not understand this form, do not sign it until you have asked a lawyer (who is independent of the lawyer for the proposed personal representative) to explain it to you.**

WAIVER

1. **I have read and understand paragraphs A through G above.**
2. **I understand that before signing this form, I am free to consult with a lawyer of my choice concerning the possible consequences to me of waiving bond.**
3. **I understand that I do not have to waive bond to allow the estate administration to begin or proceed, or to receive my share of the estate.**
4. **I WAIVE the posting of bond in this estate by** *(name of personal representative):*

Date:

_______________________________ ▶ _______________________________

(TYPE OR PRINT NAME OF BENEFICIARY (AND AUTHORIZED SIGNER, IF BENEFICIARY IS NOT AN INDIVIDUAL)) (SIGNATURE)

(This form may be filed as an independent form (as form DE-142) OR as Attachment 3e(2) (will) or Attachment 3e(3) (intestacy) to the* Petition for Probate *(form DE-111) (as form DE-111(A-3e).)

ATTORNEY OR PARTY WITHOUT ATTORNEY (*Name, state bar number, and address*):	FOR COURT USE ONLY
TELEPHONE NO.: FAX NO. (*Optional*):	
E-MAIL ADDRESS (*Optional*):	
ATTORNEY FOR (*Name*):	
SUPERIOR COURT OF CALIFORNIA, COUNTY OF	
STREET ADDRESS:	
MAILING ADDRESS:	
CITY AND ZIP CODE:	
BRANCH NAME:	
ESTATE OF (*Name*): DECEDENT	
DUTIES AND LIABILITIES OF PERSONAL REPRESENTATIVE and Acknowledgment of Receipt	CASE NUMBER:

DUTIES AND LIABILITIES OF PERSONAL REPRESENTATIVE

When the court appoints you as personal representative of an estate, you become an officer of the court and assume certain duties and obligations. An attorney is best qualified to advise you about these matters. You should understand the following:

1. MANAGING THE ESTATE'S ASSETS

a. Prudent investments
You must manage the estate assets with the care of a prudent person dealing with someone else's property. This means that you must be cautious and may not make any speculative investments.

b. Keep estate assets separate
You must keep the money and property in this estate separate from anyone else's, including your own. When you open a bank account for the estate, the account name must indicate that it is an estate account and not your personal account. Never deposit estate funds in your personal account or otherwise mix them with your or anyone else's property. Securities in the estate must also be held in a name that shows they are estate property and not your personal property.

c. Interest-bearing accounts and other investments
Except for checking accounts intended for ordinary administration expenses, estate accounts must earn interest. You may deposit estate funds in insured accounts in financial institutions, but you should consult with an attorney before making other kinds of investments.

d. Other restrictions
There are many other restrictions on your authority to deal with estate property. You should not spend any of the estate's money unless you have received permission from the court or have been advised to do so by an attorney. You may reimburse yourself for official court costs paid by you to the county clerk and for the premium on your bond. Without prior order of the court, you may not pay fees to yourself or to your attorney, if you have one. If you do not obtain the court's permission when it is required, you may be removed as personal representative or you may be required to reimburse the estate from your own personal funds, or both. You should consult with an attorney concerning the legal requirements affecting sales, leases, mortgages, and investments of estate property.

2. INVENTORY OF ESTATE PROPERTY

a. Locate the estate's property
You must attempt to locate and take possession of all the decedent's property to be administered in the estate.

b. Determine the value of the property
You must arrange to have a court-appointed referee determine the value of the property unless the appointment is waived by the court. You, rather than the referee, must determine the value of certain "cash items." An attorney can advise you about how to do this.

c. File an inventory and appraisal
Within four months after Letters are first issued to you as personal representative, you must file with the court an inventory and appraisal of all the assets in the estate.

ESTATE OF *(Name):* DECEDENT	CASE NUMBER:

d. File a change of ownership
At the time you file the inventory and appraisal, you must also file a change of ownership statement with the county recorder or assessor in each county where the decedent owned real property at the time of death, as provided in section 480 of the California Revenue and Taxation Code.

3. NOTICE TO CREDITORS

You must mail a notice of administration to each known creditor of the decedent within four months after your appointment as personal representative. If the decedent received Medi-Cal assistance, you must notify the State Director of Health Services within 90 days after appointment.

4. INSURANCE

You should determine that there is appropriate and adequate insurance covering the assets and risks of the estate. Maintain the insurance in force during the entire period of the administration.

5. RECORD KEEPING

a. Keep accounts
You must keep complete and accurate records of each financial transaction affecting the estate. You will have to prepare an account of all money and property you have received, what you have spent, and the date of each transaction. You must describe in detail what you have left after the payment of expenses.

b. Court review
Your account will be reviewed by the court. Save your receipts because the court may ask to review them. If you do not file your accounts as required, the court will order you to do so. You may be removed as personal representative if you fail to comply.

6. CONSULTING AN ATTORNEY

If you have an attorney, you should cooperate with the attorney at all times. You and your attorney are responsible for completing the estate administration as promptly as possible. **When in doubt, contact your attorney.**

NOTICE: 1. This statement of duties and liabilities is a summary and is not a complete statement of the law. Your conduct as a personal representative is governed by the law itself and not by this summary.
2. If you fail to perform your duties or to meet the deadlines, the court may reduce your compensation, remove you from office, and impose other sanctions.

ACKNOWLEDGMENT OF RECEIPT

1. I have petitioned the court to be appointed as a personal representative.

2. My address and telephone number are *(specify):*

3. I acknowledge that I have received a copy of this statement of the duties and liabilities of the office of personal representative.

Date:

(TYPE OR PRINT NAME) ▶ (SIGNATURE OF PETITIONER)

Date:

(TYPE OR PRINT NAME) ▶ (SIGNATURE OF PETITIONER)

CONFIDENTIAL INFORMATION: If required to do so by local court rule, you must provide your date of birth and driver's license number on supplemental Form DE-147S. (Prob. Code, § 8404(b).)

ESTATE OF *(Name)*: DECEDENT	CASE NUMBER:

CONFIDENTIAL STATEMENT OF BIRTH DATE AND DRIVER'S LICENSE NUMBER

(Supplement to *Duties and Liabilities of Personal Representative* (Form DE-147))

(NOTE: This supplement is to be used if the court by local rule requires the personal representative to provide a birth date and driver's license number. Do ***not*** *attach this supplement to Form DE-147.)*

This separate *Confidential Statement of Birth Date and Driver's License Number* contains confidential information relating to the personal representative in the case referenced above. This supplement shall be kept separate from the *Duties and Liabilities of Personal Representative* filed in this case and shall not be a public record.

INFORMATION ON THE PERSONAL REPRESENTATIVE:

1. Name:
2. Date of birth:
3. Driver's license number: State:

TO COURT CLERK:
THIS STATEMENT IS **CONFIDENTIAL**. DO NOT FILE
THIS CONFIDENTIAL STATEMENT IN A PUBLIC COURT FILE.

ATTORNEY OR PARTY WITHOUT ATTORNEY *(Name, state bar number, and address)*:	TELEPHONE AND FAX NOS.:	*FOR COURT USE ONLY*
ATTORNEY FOR *(Name)*:		
SUPERIOR COURT OF CALIFORNIA, COUNTY OF STREET ADDRESS: MAILING ADDRESS: CITY AND ZIP CODE: BRANCH NAME:		
ESTATE OF *(Name)*: DECEDENT		
LETTERS ☐ **TESTAMENTARY** ☐ **OF ADMINISTRATION** ☐ **OF ADMINISTRATION WITH WILL ANNEXED** ☐ **SPECIAL ADMINISTRATION**		CASE NUMBER:

LETTERS

1. ☐ The last will of the decedent named above having been proved, the court appoints *(name)*:

   a. ☐ executor.
   b. ☐ administrator with will annexed.

2. ☐ The court appoints *(name)*:

   a. ☐ administrator of the decedent's estate.
   b. ☐ special administrator of decedent's estate
      (1) ☐ with the special powers specified in the *Order for Probate*.
      (2) ☐ with the powers of a general administrator.
      (3) ☐ letters will expire on *(date)*:

3. ☐ The personal representative is authorized to administer the estate under the Independent Administration of Estates Act ☐ **with full authority** ☐ **with limited authority** (no authority, without court supervision, to (1) sell or exchange real property or (2) grant an option to purchase real property or (3) borrow money with the loan secured by an encumbrance upon real property).

4. ☐ The personal representative is not authorized to take possession of money or any other property without a specific court order.

WITNESS, clerk of the court, with seal of the court affixed.

(SEAL)

Date:

Clerk, by

(DEPUTY)

AFFIRMATION

1. ☐ PUBLIC ADMINISTRATOR: No affirmation required (Prob. Code, § 7621(c)).

2. ☐ INDIVIDUAL: **I solemnly affirm** that I will perform the duties of personal representative according to law.

3. ☐ INSTITUTIONAL FIDUCIARY *(name)*:

   I solemnly affirm that the institution will perform the duties of personal representative according to law.
   I make this affirmation for myself as an individual and on behalf of the institution as an officer.
   (Name and title):

4. Executed on *(date)*:
   at *(place)*: , California.

(SIGNATURE)

CERTIFICATION

I certify that this document is a correct copy of the original on file in my office and the letters issued by the personal representative appointed above have not been revoked, annulled, or set aside, and are still in full force and effect.

(SEAL)

Date:

Clerk, by

(DEPUTY)

NOTICE OF ADMINISTRATION
OF THE ESTATE OF

____

(NAME)

DECEDENT

NOTICE TO CREDITORS

1. *(Name):*
   (Address):

   (Telephone):

   is the **personal representative** of the **ESTATE OF** *(name):* , who is deceased.

2. The personal representative HAS BEGUN ADMINISTRATION of the decedent's estate in the
   a. **SUPERIOR COURT OF CALIFORNIA, COUNTY OF** *(specify):*
      STREET ADDRESS:
      MAILING ADDRESS:
      CITY AND ZIP CODE:
      BRANCH NAME:
   b. Case number *(specify):*

3. You must FILE YOUR CLAIM with the court clerk (address in item 2a) AND mail or deliver a copy to the personal representative before the **last to occur** of the following dates:
   a. **four months** after *(date):* [ ] , the date letters (authority to act for the estate) were first issued to a general personal representative, as defined in subdivision (b) of section 58 of the California Probate Code, **OR**
   b. **60 days** after *(date):* [ ] , the date this notice was mailed or personally delivered to you.

4. LATE CLAIMS: If you do not file your claim within the time required by law, you must file a petition with the court for permission to file a late claim as provided in Probate Code section 9103. Not all claims are eligible for additional time to file. See section 9103(a).

EFFECT OF OTHER LAWS: Other California statutes and legal authority may affect your rights as a creditor. You may want to consult with an attorney knowledgeable in California law.

WHERE TO GET A CREDITOR'S CLAIM FORM: If a *Creditor's Claim* (form DE-172) did not accompany this notice, you may obtain a copy of the form from any superior court clerk or from the person who sent you this notice. You may also access a fillable version of the form on the Internet at *www.courts.ca.gov/forms* under the form group Probate—Decedents' Estates. A letter to the court stating your claim is *not* sufficient.

FAILURE TO FILE A CLAIM: Failure to file a claim with the court and serve a copy of the claim on the personal representative will in most instances invalidate your claim.

IF YOU MAIL YOUR CLAIM: If you use the mail to file your claim with the court, for your protection you should send your claim by certified mail, with return receipt requested. If you use the mail to serve a copy of your claim on the personal representative, you should also use certified mail.

Note: To assist the creditor and the court, please send a blank copy of the *Creditor's Claim* form with this notice.

(Proof of Service by Mail on reverse)

ESTATE OF *(Name)*: DECEDENT	CASE NUMBER:

[Optional]

PROOF OF SERVICE BY MAIL

1. I am over the age of 18 and not a party to this cause. I am a resident of or employed in the county where the mailing occurred.
2. My residence or business address is *(specify)*:

3. I served the foregoing *Notice of Administration to Creditors* ☐ and a blank *Creditor's Claim* form* on each person named below by enclosing a copy in an envelope addressed as shown below AND
   a. ☐ **depositing** the sealed envelope with the United States Postal Service with the postage fully prepaid.
   b. ☐ **placing** the envelope for collection and mailing on the date and at the place shown in item 4 following our ordinary business practices. I am readily familiar with the business's practice for collecting and processing correspondence for mailing. On the same day that correspondence is placed for collection and mailing, it is deposited in the ordinary course of business with the United States Postal Service in a sealed envelope with postage fully prepaid.
4. a. Date of deposit: b. Place of deposit *(city and state)*:

I declare under penalty of perjury under the laws of the State of California that the foregoing is true and correct.

Date:

(TYPE OR PRINT NAME) ▶ (SIGNATURE OF DECLARANT)

NAME AND ADDRESS OF EACH PERSON TO WHOM NOTICE WAS MAILED

	Name of person	Address *(number, street, city, state, and zip code)*
1.		
2.		
3.		
4.		
5.		
6.		
7.		
8.		

☐ List of names and addresses continued in attachment. *(You may use form POS-30(P) to show additional persons to whom a copy of this notice was mailed. Do not use page 2 of this form or form POS-030(P) to show that you personally delivered a copy of this notice to a creditor. You may use forms POS-020 and POS-020(P) for that purpose.)*

*** NOTE:** *To assist the creditor and the court, please send a blank copy of the* Creditor's Claim *(form DE-172) with the notice.*

ATTORNEY OR PARTY WITHOUT ATTORNEY *(Name, state bar number, and address):*	FOR COURT USE ONLY
TELEPHONE NO.: FAX NO. *(Optional):*	
E-MAIL ADDRESS *(Optional):*	
ATTORNEY FOR *(Name):*	
SUPERIOR COURT OF CALIFORNIA, COUNTY OF	
STREET ADDRESS:	
MAILING ADDRESS:	
CITY AND ZIP CODE:	
BRANCH NAME:	
ESTATE OF *(Name):* ☐ DECEDENT ☐ CONSERVATEE ☐ MINOR	
INVENTORY AND APPRAISAL	CASE NUMBER:
☐ **Partial No.:** ☐ **Corrected** ☐ **Final** ☐ **Reappraisal for Sale** ☐ **Supplemental** ☐ **Property Tax Certificate**	Date of Death of Decedent or of Appointment of Guardian or Conservator:

APPRAISALS

1. Total appraisal by representative, guardian, or conservator (Attachment 1): $
2. Total appraisal by referee (Attachment 2): $

TOTAL: $

DECLARATION OF REPRESENTATIVE, GUARDIAN, CONSERVATOR, OR SMALL ESTATE CLAIMANT

3. Attachments 1 and 2 together with all prior inventories filed contain a true statement of ☐ all ☐ a portion of the estate that has come to my knowledge or possession, including particularly all money and all just claims the estate has against me. I have truly, honestly, and impartially appraised to the best of my ability each item set forth in Attachment 1.
4. ☐ No probate referee is required ☐ by order of the court dated *(specify):*
5. **Property tax certificate.** I certify that the requirements of Revenue and Taxation Code section 480
   a. ☐ are not applicable because the decedent owned no real property in California at the time of death.
   b. ☐ have been satisfied by the filing of a change of ownership statement with the county recorder or assessor of each county in California in which the decedent owned property at the time of death.

I declare under penalty of perjury under the laws of the State of California that the foregoing is true and correct.

Date:

(TYPE OR PRINT NAME; INCLUDE TITLE IF CORPORATE OFFICER) ▶ (SIGNATURE)

STATEMENT ABOUT THE BOND

(Complete in all cases. Must be signed by attorney for fiduciary, or by fiduciary without an attorney.)

6. ☐ Bond is waived, or the sole fiduciary is a corporate fiduciary or an exempt government agency.
7. ☐ Bond filed in the amount of: $ ☐ Sufficient ☐ Insufficient
8. ☐ Receipts for: $ have been filed with the court for deposits in a blocked account at *(specify institution and location):*

Date:

(TYPE OR PRINT NAME) ▶ (SIGNATURE OF ATTORNEY OR PARTY WITHOUT ATTORNEY)

ESTATE OF *(Name)*: ☐ DECEDENT ☐ CONSERVATEE ☐ MINOR	CASE NUMBER:

DECLARATION OF PROBATE REFEREE

9. I have truly, honestly, and impartially appraised to the best of my ability each item set forth in Attachment 2.
10. A true account of my commission and expenses actually and necessarily incurred pursuant to my appointment is:
    Statutory commission: $
    Expenses *(specify)*: $
    TOTAL: $

I declare under penalty of perjury under the laws of the State of California that the foregoing is true and correct.

Date:

(TYPE OR PRINT NAME) ▶ (SIGNATURE OF REFEREE)

INSTRUCTIONS

(See Probate Code sections 2610-2616, 8801, 8804, 8852, 8905, 8960, 8961, and 8963 for additional instructions.)

1. See Probate Code section 8850 for items to be included in the inventory.
2. If the minor or conservatee is or has been during the guardianship or conservatorship confined in a state hospital under the jurisdiction of the State Department of Mental Health or the State Department of Developmental Services, mail a copy to the director of the appropriate department in Sacramento. (Prob. Code, § 2611.)
3. The representative, guardian, conservator, or small estate claimant shall list on Attachment 1 and appraise as of the date of death of the decedent or the date of appointment of the guardian or conservator, at fair market value, moneys, currency, cash items, bank accounts and amounts on deposit with each financial institution (as defined in Probate Code section 40), and the proceeds of life and accident insurance policies and retirement plans payable upon death in lump sum amounts to the estate, except items whose fair market value is, in the opinion of the representative, an amount different from the ostensible value or specified amount.
4. The representative, guardian, conservator, or small estate claimant shall list in Attachment 2 all other assets of the estate which shall be appraised by the referee.
5. If joint tenancy and other assets are listed for appraisal purposes only and not as part of the probate estate, they must be separately listed on additional attachments and their value excluded from the total valuation of Attachments 1 and 2.
6. Each attachment should conform to the format approved by the Judicial Council. *(See Inventory and Appraisal Attachment* (form DE-161/GC-041) and Cal. Rules of Court, rules 2.100—2.119.)

ESTATE OF *(Name)*:	CASE NUMBER:

INVENTORY AND APPRAISAL
ATTACHMENT NO.: _____

(In decedents' estates, attachments must conform to Probate Code section 8850(c) regarding community and separate property.)

Page: _________ of: _________ total pages.
(Add pages as required.)

Item No.	Description	Appraised value
1.		$

DE-165

ATTORNEY OR PARTY WITHOUT ATTORNEY *(Name, state bar number, and address)*:	TELEPHONE AND FAX NOS.:	*FOR COURT USE ONLY*
ATTORNEY FOR *(Name)*:		
SUPERIOR COURT OF CALIFORNIA, COUNTY OF STREET ADDRESS: MAILING ADDRESS: CITY AND ZIP CODE: BRANCH NAME:		
ESTATE OF *(Name)*:	DECEDENT	
NOTICE OF PROPOSED ACTION **Independent Administration of Estates Act** ☐ **Objection** ☐ **Consent**		CASE NUMBER:

NOTICE: If you do not object in writing or obtain a court order preventing the action proposed below, you will be treated as if you consented to the proposed action and you may not object after the proposed action has been taken. If you object, the personal representative may take the proposed action only under court supervision. An objection form is on the reverse. If you wish to object, you may use the form or prepare your own written objection.

1. The personal representative (executor or administrator) of the estate of the deceased is *(names)*:

2. The personal representative has authority to administer the estate without court supervision under the Independent Administration of Estates Act (Prob. Code, § 10400 et seq.)
   a. ☐ with **full authority** under the act.
   b. ☐ with **limited authority** under the act (there is no authority, without court supervision, to (1) sell or exchange real property or (2) grant an option to purchase real property or (3) borrow money with the loan secured by an encumbrance upon real property).

3. **On or after** *(date)*: ☐, the personal representative will take the following action without court supervision *(describe in specific terms here or in Attachment 3)*:
   ☐ The proposed action is described in an attachment labeled Attachment 3.

4. ☐ **Real property transaction** *(Check this box and complete item 4b if the proposed action involves a sale or exchange or a grant of an option to purchase real property.)*
   a. The material terms of the transaction are specified in item 3, including any sale price and the amount of or method of calculating any commission or compensation to an agent or broker.
   b. $ is the value of the subject property in the probate inventory. ☐ No inventory yet.

NOTICE: A sale of real property without court supervision means that the sale will NOT be presented to the court for confirmation at a hearing at which higher bids for the property may be presented and the property sold to the highest bidder.

(Continued on reverse)

ESTATE OF *(Name)*: DECEDENT	CASE NUMBER:

5. **If you OBJECT to the proposed action**
   a. **Sign** the objection form below and deliver or mail it to the personal representative at the following address *(specify name and address)*:

   OR
   b. **Send** your own written objection to the address in item 5a. *(Be sure to identify the proposed action and state that you object to it.)*
   OR
   c. **Apply** to the court for an order preventing the personal representative from taking the proposed action without court supervision.
   d. **NOTE**: Your written objection or the court order must be received by the personal representative before the date in the box in item 3, or before the proposed action is taken, whichever is later. If you object, the personal representative may take the proposed action only under court supervision.

6. **If you APPROVE the proposed action**, you may sign the consent form below and return it to the address in item 5a. If you do not object in writing or obtain a court order, you will be treated as if you consented to the proposed action.

7. **If you need more INFORMATION, call** *(name)*:
   (telephone):

Date:

. . . .
(TYPE OR PRINT NAME)

▶ ______________________________
(SIGNATURE OF PERSONAL REPRESENTATIVE OR ATTORNEY)

OBJECTION TO PROPOSED ACTION

☐ **I OBJECT** to the action proposed in item 3.

NOTICE: Sign and return this form (both sides) to the address in item 5a. The form must be received before the date in the box in item 3, or before the proposed action is taken, whichever is later. *(You may want to use certified mail, with return receipt requested. Make a copy of this form for your records.)*

Date:

. . . .
(TYPE OR PRINT NAME)

▶ ______________________________
(SIGNATURE OF OBJECTOR)

CONSENT TO PROPOSED ACTION

☐ **I CONSENT** to the action proposed in item 3.

NOTICE: You may indicate your *consent* by signing and returning this form (both sides) to the address in item 5a. If you do not object in writing or obtain a court order, you will be treated as if you consented to the proposed action.

Date:

. . . .
(TYPE OR PRINT NAME)

▶ ______________________________
(SIGNATURE OF CONSENTER)

DE-172

ATTORNEY OR PARTY WITHOUT ATTORNEY *(Name, state bar number, and address):* TELEPHONE AND FAX NOS.: ATTORNEY FOR *(Name):*	*FOR COURT USE ONLY*
SUPERIOR COURT OF CALIFORNIA, COUNTY OF STREET ADDRESS: MAILING ADDRESS: CITY AND ZIP CODE: BRANCH NAME:	
ESTATE OF *(Name):* DECEDENT	
CREDITOR'S CLAIM	CASE NUMBER:

You must file this claim with the court clerk at the court address above before the LATER of (a) four months after the date letters (authority to act for the estate) were first issued to the personal representative, or (b) sixty days after the date the *Notice of Administration* was given to the creditor, if notice was given as provided in Probate Code section 9051. You must also mail or deliver a copy of this claim to the personal representative and his or her attorney. A proof of service is on the reverse.
WARNING: Your claim will in most instances be invalid if you do not properly complete this form, file it on time with the court, and mail or deliver a copy to the personal representative and his or her attorney.

1. Total amount of the claim: $
2. Claimant *(name):*
   a. ☐ an individual
   b. ☐ an individual or entity doing business under the fictitious name of *(specify):*
   c. ☐ a partnership. The person signing has authority to sign on behalf of the partnership.
   d. ☐ a corporation. The person signing has authority to sign on behalf of the corporation.
   e. ☐ other (specify):
3. Address of claimant *(specify):*
4. Claimant is ☐ the creditor ☐ a person acting on behalf of creditor *(state reason):*
5. ☐ Claimant is ☐ the personal representative ☐ the attorney for the personal representative.
6. I am authorized to make this claim which is just and due or may become due. All payments on or offsets to the claim have been credited. Facts supporting the claim are ☐ on reverse ☐ attached.

I declare under penalty of perjury under the laws of the State of California that the foregoing is true and correct.

Date:

(TYPE OR PRINT NAME AND TITLE) ▶ (SIGNATURE OF CLAIMANT)

INSTRUCTIONS TO CLAIMANT

A. On the reverse, itemize the claim and show the date the service was rendered or the debt incurred. Describe the item or service in detail, and indicate the amount claimed for each item. Do not include debts incurred after the date of death, except funeral claims.
B. If the claim is not due or contingent, or the amount is not yet ascertainable, state the facts supporting the claim.
C. If the claim is secured by a note or other written instrument, the original or a copy must be attached *(state why original is unavailable.)* If secured by mortgage, deed of trust, or other lien on property that is of record, it is sufficient to describe the security and refer to the date or volume and page, and county where recorded. *(See Prob. Code, § 9152.)*
D. Mail or take this original claim to the court clerk's office for filing. If mailed, use certified mail, with return receipt requested.
E. Mail or deliver a copy to the personal representative and his or her attorney. Complete the *Proof of Mailing or Personal Delivery* on the reverse.
F. The personal representative or his or her attorney will notify you when your claim is allowed or rejected.
G. Claims against the estate by the personal representative and the attorney for the personal representative must be filed within the claim period allowed in Probate Code section 9100. See the notice box above.

(Continued on reverse)

ESTATE OF *(Name)*: DECEDENT	CASE NUMBER:

FACTS SUPPORTING THE CREDITOR'S CLAIM

☐ **See attachment *(if space is insufficient)***

Date of item	Item and supporting facts	Amount claimed
	TOTAL:	$ 0.00

PROOF OF ☐ MAILING ☐ PERSONAL DELIVERY TO PERSONAL REPRESENTATIVE

(Be sure to mail or take the original to the court clerk's office for filing)

1. I am the creditor or a person acting on behalf of the creditor. At the time of mailing or delivery I was at least 18 years of age.
2. My residence or business address is *(specify)*:
3. I mailed or personally delivered a copy of this *Creditor's Claim* to the personal representative as follows *(check either a or b below)*:

   a. ☐ **Mail**. I am a resident of or employed in the county where the mailing occurred.

   (1) I enclosed a copy in an envelope AND

   (a) ☐ **deposited** the sealed envelope with the United States Postal Service with the postage fully prepaid.

   (b) ☐ **placed** the envelope for collection and mailing on the date and at the place shown in items below following our ordinary business practices. I am readily familiar with this business' practice for collecting and processing correspondence for mailing. On the same day that correspondence is placed for collection and mailing, it is deposited in the ordinary course of business with the United States Postal Service in a sealed envelope with postage fully prepaid.

   (2) The envelope was addressed and mailed first-class as follows:

   (a) Name of personal representative served:

   (b) Address on envelope:

   (c) Date of mailing:

   (d) Place of mailing *(city and state)*:

   b. ☐ **Personal delivery**. I personally delivered a copy of the claim to the personal representative as follows:

   (1) Name of personal representative served:

   (2) Address where delivered:

   (3) Date of mailing:

   (4) Time delivered:

I declare under penalty of perjury under the laws of the State of California that the foregoing is true and correct.

Date:

_______________________________	▶ _______________________________
(TYPE OR PRINT NAME OF CLAIMANT)	(SIGNATURE OF CLAIMANT)

ATTORNEY OR PARTY WITHOUT ATTORNEY *(Name, State Bar number, and address):*	FOR COURT USE ONLY
TELEPHONE NO.: FAX NO. *(Optional):*	
E-MAIL ADDRESS *(Optional):*	
ATTORNEY FOR *(Name):*	
SUPERIOR COURT OF CALIFORNIA, COUNTY OF	
STREET ADDRESS:	
MAILING ADDRESS:	
CITY AND ZIP CODE:	
BRANCH NAME:	
ESTATE OF *(Name):* DECEDENT	
ALLOWANCE OR REJECTION OF CREDITOR'S CLAIM	CASE NUMBER:

NOTE TO PERSONAL REPRESENTATIVE

Attach a copy of the creditor's claim to this form. If approval or rejection by the court is not required, do not include any pages attached to the creditor's claim.

PERSONAL REPRESENTATIVE'S ALLOWANCE OR REJECTION

1. Name of creditor *(specify):*
2. The claim was filed on *(date):*
3. Date of first issuance of letters:
4. Date of *Notice of Administration*:
5. Date of decedent's death:
6. Estimated value of estate: $
7. Total amount of the claim: $
8. ☐ Claim is allowed for: $ *(The court must approve certain claims before they are paid.)*
9. ☐ Claim is rejected for: $ *(A creditor has 90 days to act on a rejected claim.* See box below.)*
10. Notice of allowance or rejection given on *(date):*
11. ☐ The personal representative is authorized to administer the estate under the Independent Administration of Estates Act.

Date:

(TYPE OR PRINT NAME OF PERSONAL REPRESENTATIVE) ▶ (SIGNATURE OF PERSONAL REPRESENTATIVE)

NOTICE TO CREDITOR ON REJECTED CLAIM

From the date that notice of rejection is given, you must act on the rejected claim (e.g., file a lawsuit) as follows:

1. **Claim due:** within 90 days* after the notice of rejection.
2. **Claim not due:** within 90 days* after the claim becomes due.

***The 90-day period mentioned above may not apply to your claim because some claims are not treated as creditors' claims or are subject to special statutes of limitations, or for other legal reasons. You should consult with an attorney if you have any questions about or are unsure of your rights and obligations concerning your claim.**

COURT'S APPROVAL OR REJECTION

12. ☐ Approved for: $
13. ☐ Rejected for: $

Date:

SIGNATURE OF JUDICIAL OFFICER

☐ SIGNATURE FOLLOWS LAST ATTACHMENT

14. Number of pages attached: ______

(Proof of Mailing or Personal Delivery on reverse)

ESTATE OF *(Name):* DECEDENT	CASE NUMBER:

PROOF OF ☐ MAILING ☐ PERSONAL DELIVERY TO CREDITOR

1. At the time of mailing or personal delivery I was at least 18 years of age and **not a party** to this proceeding.

2. My residence or business address is *(specify):*

3. I mailed or personally delivered a copy of the *Allowance or Rejection of Creditor's Claim* as follows *(complete either a or b)*:

   a. ☐ **Mail.** I am a resident of or employed in the county where the mailing occurred.
      (1) I enclosed a copy in an envelope AND
         (a) ☐ **deposited** the sealed envelope with the United States Postal Service with the postage fully prepaid.
         (b) ☐ **placed** the envelope for collection and mailing on the date and at the place shown in items below following our ordinary business practices. I am readily familiar with this business's practice for collecting and processing correspondence for mailing. On the same day that correspondence is placed for collection and mailing, it is deposited in the ordinary course of business with the United States Postal Service in a sealed envelope with postage fully prepaid.
      (2) The envelope was addressed and mailed first-class as follows:
         (a) Name of creditor served:
         (b) Address on envelope:
         (c) Date of mailing:
         (d) Place of mailing *(city and state):*

   b. ☐ **Personal delivery.** I personally delivered a copy to the creditor as follows:
      (1) Name of creditor served:
      (2) Address where delivered:
      (3) Date delivered:
      (4) Time delivered:

I declare under penalty of perjury under the laws of the State of California that the foregoing is true and correct.

Date:

_______________________________ (TYPE OR PRINT NAME OF DECLARANT)

▶ _______________________________ (SIGNATURE OF DECLARANT)

ATTORNEY OR PARTY WITHOUT ATTORNEY *(Name, State Bar number, and address)*: TELEPHONE NO.: FAX NO. *(Optional)*: E-MAIL ADDRESS *(Optional)*: ATTORNEY FOR *(Name)*:	*FOR COURT USE ONLY*
SUPERIOR COURT OF CALIFORNIA, COUNTY OF STREET ADDRESS: MAILING ADDRESS: CITY AND ZIP CODE: BRANCH NAME:	
ESTATE OF *(Name)*: DECEDENT	CASE NUMBER: HEARING DATE:
☐ **SPOUSAL** ☐ **DOMESTIC PARTNER PROPERTY PETITION**	DEPT.: TIME:

1. **Petitioner** *(name)*: **requests**
   a. ☐ determination of property passing to the surviving spouse or surviving registered domestic partner without administration (Fam. Code, § 297.5, Prob. Code, § 13500).
   b. ☐ confirmation of property belonging to the surviving spouse or surviving registered domestic partner (Fam. Code, § 297.5, Prob. Code, §§ 100, 101).
   c. ☐ immediate appointment of a probate referee.
2. Petitioner is
   a. ☐ surviving spouse of the decedent.
   b. ☐ personal representative of *(name)*: , surviving spouse.
   c. ☐ guardian or conservator of the estate of *(name)*: , surviving spouse.
   d. ☐ surviving registered domestic partner of the decedent.
   e. ☐ personal representative of *(name)*: , surviving registered domestic partner.
   f. ☐ conservator of the estate of *(name)*: , surviving registered domestic partner.
3. Decedent died on *(date)*:
4. Decedent was
   a. ☐ a resident of the California county named above.
   b. ☐ a nonresident of California and left an estate in the county named above.
   c. ☐ intestate ☐ testate and a copy of the will and any codicil is affixed as Attachment 4c. *(Attach copies of will and any codicil, a typewritten copy of any handwritten document, and an English translation of any foreign-language document.)*
5. a. *(Complete in all cases)* The decedent is survived by
      (1) ☐ no child. ☐ child as follows: ☐ natural or adopted ☐ natural, adopted by a third party.
      (2) ☐ no issue of a predeceased child. ☐ issue of a predeceased child.
   b. Decedent ☐ is ☐ is not survived by a stepchild or foster child or children who would have been adopted by decedent but for a legal barrier. *(See Prob. Code, § 6454.)*
6. *(Complete only if no issue survived the decedent. Check* ***only*** *the* ***first*** *box that applies.)*
   a. ☐ The decedent is survived by a parent or parents who are listed in item 9.
   b. ☐ The decedent is survived by a brother, sister, or issue of a deceased brother or sister, all of whom are listed in item 9.
7. Administration of all or part of the estate is not necessary for the reason that all or a part of the estate is property passing to the surviving spouse or surviving registered domestic partner. The facts upon which petitioner bases the allegation that the property described in Attachments 7a and 7b is property that should pass or be confirmed to the surviving spouse or surviving registered domestic partner are stated in Attachment 7.
   a. ☐ Attachment 7a[1] contains the legal description *(if real property add Assessor's Parcel Number)* of the deceased spouse's or registered domestic partner's property that petitioner requests to be determined as having passed to the surviving spouse or partner from the deceased spouse or partner. This includes any interest in a trade or business name of any unincorporated business or an interest in any unincorporated business that the deceased spouse or partner was operating or managing at the time of death, subject to any written agreement between the deceased spouse or partner and the surviving spouse or partner providing for a non pro rata division of the aggregate value of the community property assets or quasi-community assets, or both.

[1] See Prob. Code, § 13658 for required filing of a list of known creditors of a business and other information in certain instances. If required, include in Attachment 7a.

ESTATE OF *(Name)*: DECEDENT	CASE NUMBER:

7. b. ☐ Attachment 7b contains the legal description *(if real property add Assessor's Parcel Number)* of the community or quasi-community property petitioner requests to be determined as having belonged under Probate Code sections 100 and 101 and Family Code section 297.5 to the surviving spouse or surviving registered domestic partner upon the deceased spouse's or partner's death, subject to any written agreement between the deceased spouse or partner and the surviving spouse or partner providing for a non pro rata division of the aggregate value of the community property assets or quasi-community assets, or both.

8. There ☐ exists ☐ does not exist a written agreement between the deceased spouse or deceased registered domestic partner and the surviving spouse or surviving registered domestic partner providing for a non pro rata division of the aggregate value of the community property assets or quasi-community assets, or both. *(If petitioner bases the description of the property of the deceased spouse or partner passing to the surviving spouse or partner or the property to be confirmed to the surviving spouse or partner, or both, on a written agreement, a copy of the agreement must be attached to this petition as Attachment 8.)*

9. The names, relationships, ages, and residence or mailing addresses so far as known to or reasonably ascertainable by petitioner of (1) all persons named in decedent's will and codicils, whether living or deceased, and (2) all persons checked in items 5 and 6 ☐ are listed below ☐ are listed in Attachment 9.

Name and relationship	Age	Residence or mailing address

10. The names and addresses of all persons named as executors in the decedent's will and any codicil or appointed as personal representatives of the decedent's estate ☐ are listed below ☐ are listed in Attachment 10 ☐ none

11. ☐ The petitioner is the trustee of a trust that is a devisee under decedent's will. The names and addresses of all persons interested in the trust who are entitled to notice under Probate Code section 13655(a)(2) are listed in Attachment 11.

12. A petition for probate or for administration of the decedent's estate
    a. ☐ is being filed with this petition.
    b. ☐ was filed on *(date)*:
    c. ☐ has not been filed and is not being filed with this petition.

13. Number of pages attached: ________

Date:

________________________________ ▶ ________________________________
(TYPE OR PRINT NAME) (SIGNATURE OF ATTORNEY)

I declare under penalty of perjury under the laws of the State of California that the foregoing is true and correct.

Date:

________________________________ ▶ ________________________________
(TYPE OR PRINT NAME) (SIGNATURE OF PETITIONER)

ATTORNEY OR PARTY WITHOUT ATTORNEY *(name, address, and State Bar number):*
After recording, return to:

TEL NO.: FAX NO. (optional):
E-MAIL ADDRESS *(optional):*
ATTORNEY FOR (name):

SUPERIOR COURT OF CALIFORNIA, COUNTY OF
STREET ADDRESS:
MAILING ADDRESS:
CITY AND ZIP CODE:
BRANCH NAME:

FOR RECORDER'S USE ONLY

ESTATE OF *(Name):*

DECEDENT

CASE NUMBER:

☐ **SPOUSAL** ☐ **DOMESTIC PARTNER PROPERTY ORDER**

FOR COURT USE ONLY

1. Date of hearing: Time:
   Dept.: Room:

THE COURT FINDS

2. All notices required by law have been given.
3. Decedent died on *(date):*
   a. ☐ a resident of the California county named above.
   b. ☐ a nonresident of California and left an estate in the county named above.
   c. ☐ intestate. ☐ testate.
4. Decedent's ☐ surviving spouse ☐ surviving registered domestic partner
   is *(name):*

THE COURT FURTHER FINDS AND ORDERS

5. a. ☐ The property described in Attachment 5a is property passing to the surviving spouse or surviving registered domestic partner named in item 4, and no administration of it is necessary.
   b. ☐ See Attachment 5b for further order(s) respecting transfer of the property to the surviving spouse or surviving registered domestic partner named in item 4.
6. ☐ To protect the interests of the creditors of (business name): ,
   an unincorporated trade or business, a list of all its known creditors and the amount owed each is on file.
   a. ☐ Within *(specify):* days from this date, the surviving spouse or surviving registered domestic partner named in item 4 shall file an undertaking in the amount of $
   b. ☐ See Attachment 6b for further order(s) protecting the interests of creditors of the business.
7. a. ☐ The property described in Attachment 7a is property that belonged to the surviving spouse or surviving registered domestic partner under Family Code section 297.5 and Probate Code sections 100 and 101, and the surviving spouse's or surviving domestic partner's ownership upon decedent's death is confirmed.
   b. ☐ See Attachment 7b for further order(s) respecting transfer of the property to the surviving spouse or surviving domestic partner.
8. ☐ All property described in the *Spousal or Domestic Partner Property Petition* that is not determined to be property passing to the surviving spouse or surviving registered domestic partner under Probate Code section 13500, or confirmed as belonging to the surviving spouse or surviving registered domestic partner under Probate Code sections 100 and 101, shall be subject to administration in the estate of decedent. ☐ All of such property is described in Attachment 8.
9. ☐ Other *(specify):*

   ☐ Continued in Attachment 9.
10. Number of pages attached:

Date:

JUDICIAL OFFICER
☐ SIGNATURE FOLLOWS LAST ATTACHMENT

ATTORNEY OR PARTY WITHOUT ATTORNEY *(Name, state bar number, and address)*: TELEPHONE AND FAX NOS.: ATTORNEY FOR *(Name)*:	***FOR COURT USE ONLY***
SUPERIOR COURT OF CALIFORNIA, COUNTY OF STREET ADDRESS: MAILING ADDRESS: CITY AND ZIP CODE: BRANCH NAME:	
ESTATE OF *(Name)*: ☐ DECEDENT ☐ CONSERVATEE ☐ MINOR	
EX PARTE PETITION FOR AUTHORITY TO SELL SECURITIES AND ORDER	CASE NUMBER:

1. **Petitioner** *(name of each; see footnote[1] before completing)*:

   is the ☐ personal representative ☐ conservator ☐ guardian of the estate and requests a court order authorizing sale of estate securities.

2. a. The estate's securities described on the reverse should be sold for cash at the market price at the time of sale on an established stock or bond exchange, or, if unlisted, the sale will be made for not less than the minimum price stated on the reverse.
   b. ☐ Authority is given in decedent's will to sell property; **or**
   c. ☐ The sale is necessary to raise cash to pay
      (1) ☐ debts
      (2) ☐ legacies
      (3) ☐ family allowance
      (4) ☐ expenses
      (5) ☐ support of ward
      (6) ☐ other *(specify)*:

   d. ☐ The sale is for the advantage, benefit, and best interests of the estate, and those interested in the estate.
   e. Other facts pertinent to this petition are as follows:
      (1) ☐ Special notice has not been requested.
      (2) ☐ Waivers of all special notices are presented with this petition.
      (3) ☐ No security to be sold is specifically bequeathed.
      (4) ☐ Other *(specify)*:

Date:

* (Signature of all petitioners also required (Prob. Code, § 1020).)

▶ ______________________________
(SIGNATURE OF ATTORNEY *)

I declare under penalty of perjury under the laws of the State of California that the foregoing is true and correct.

Date:

. . . . ▶ ______________________________
(TYPE OR PRINT NAME) (SIGNATURE OF PETITIONER)

. . . . ▶ ______________________________
(TYPE OR PRINT NAME) (SIGNATURE OF PETITIONER)

[1] Each personal representative, guardian, or conservator must sign the petition.

(Continued on reverse)

ESTATE OF (*Name*):	CASE NUMBER:

LIST OF SECURITIES

Number of shares or face value of bonds	Name of security	Name of exchange (*when required by local rule*)	Recent bid asked (*when required by local rule*)	Minimum selling price

ORDER AUTHORIZING SALE OF SECURITIES

THE COURT FINDS the sale is proper.

THE COURT ORDERS

The ☐ personal representative ☐ guardian ☐ conservator is authorized to sell the securities described above upon the terms and conditions specified. Notice of hearing on the petition is dispensed with.

Date:

JUDGE OF THE SUPERIOR COURT

☐ SIGNATURE FOLLOWS LAST ATTACHMENT

ATTORNEY OR PARTY WITHOUT ATTORNEY *(Name, State Bar number, and address):*	*FOR COURT USE ONLY*
TELEPHONE NO.: FAX NO. *(Optional):* E-MAIL ADDRESS *(Optional):* ATTORNEY FOR *(Name):*	
SUPERIOR COURT OF CALIFORNIA, COUNTY OF STREET ADDRESS: MAILING ADDRESS: CITY AND ZIP CODE: BRANCH NAME:	
☐ ESTATE ☐ CONSERVATORSHIP ☐ GUARDIANSHIP OF *(Name):* ☐ DECEDENT ☐ CONSERVATEE ☐ MINOR	
EX PARTE PETITION FOR FINAL DISCHARGE AND ORDER	CASE NUMBER:

1. Petitioner is the ☐ personal representative ☐ conservator ☐ guardian of the estate of the above-named decedent, conservatee, or minor. Petitioner has distributed or transferred all property of the estate as required by the final order ☐ and all preliminary orders for distribution or liquidation filed in this proceeding on *(specify date each order was filed):*

2. All required acts of distribution or liquidation have been performed as follows *(check all that apply):*
   a. ☐ All personal property, including money, stocks, bonds, and other securities, has been delivered or transferred to the distributees or transferees as ordered by the court. The receipts of all distributees or transferees are now on file or are filed with this petition. Conformed copies of all receipts previously filed are attached on Attachment 2.
   b. ☐ No personal property is on hand for distribution or transfer.
   c. ☐ Real property was distributed or transferred. The order for distribution or transfer of the real property; the personal representative's, conservator's, or guardian's deed; or both, were recorded as follows *(specify documents recorded, dates and locations of recording, and document numbers or other appropriate recording information):*
   d. ☐ No real property is on hand for distribution or transfer.
   e. ☐ No receipts are required because Petitioner is the sole distributee.
   f. ☐ The minor named above attained the age of majority on *(date):*

3. Petitioner requests discharge as personal representative, conservator, or guardian of the estate.

I declare under penalty of perjury under the laws of the State of California that the foregoing is true and correct.

Date:

____________________________ ▶ ____________________________

(TYPE OR PRINT NAME OF PETITIONER) (SIGNATURE OF PETITIONER)

ORDER FOR FINAL DISCHARGE

THE COURT FINDS that the facts stated in the foregoing *Ex Parte Petition for Final Discharge* are true.

THE COURT ORDERS that *(name):*

is discharged as ☐ personal representative ☐ conservator ☐ guardian of the estate of the above-named decedent, conservatee, or minor, and sureties are discharged and released from liability for all acts subsequent hereto.

Date:

____

JUDICIAL OFFICER

☐ SIGNATURE FOLLOWS LAST ATTACHMENT.

Form Adopted for Mandatory Use
Judicial Council of California
DE-295/GC-395
[New January 1, 2006]

EX PARTE PETITION FOR FINAL DISCHARGE AND ORDER
(Probate—Decedents' Estates and Conservatorships and Guardianships)

Probate Code, §§ 2100, 2627, 2631, 11753, 12250;
www.courtinfo.ca.gov

DE-305

ATTORNEY OR PARTY WITHOUT ATTORNEY *(name, address, and State Bar number):*
After recording return to:

TEL NO.: FAX NO.:
EMAIL ADDRESS:
ATTORNEY FOR *(name):*

SUPERIOR COURT OF CALIFORNIA, COUNTY OF
STREET ADDRESS:
MAILING ADDRESS:
CITY AND ZIP CODE:
BRANCH NAME:

FOR RECORDER'S USE ONLY

MATTER OF *(name):*

DECEDENT

CASE NUMBER:

AFFIDAVIT RE REAL PROPERTY OF SMALL VALUE
($55,425 or Less)

FOR COURT USE ONLY

1. Decedent *(name):*
   died on *(date):*
2. Decedent died at *(city, state):*
3. At least **six months** have elapsed since the date of death of decedent as shown in the certified copy of decedent's death certificate attached to this affidavit. *(Attach a certified copy of decedent's death certificate.)*
4. a. ☐ Decedent was domiciled in this county at the time of death.
   b. ☐ Decedent was **not** domiciled in California at the time of death. Decedent died owning real property in this county.
5. a. The **legal description** and the Assessor's Parcel Number (APN) of decedent's real property claimed by the declarant(s) are provided on an attached page labeled Attachment 5a, "Legal Description." *(Copy legal description **exactly** from deed or other legal instrument.)*
   b. Decedent's interest in this real property is as follows *(specify):*
6. Each declarant is a successor of decedent (as defined in Probate Code section 13006) and a successor to decedent's interest in the real property described in item 5a, or signs this declaration on behalf of an entity that is a successor of decedent and to decedent's interest in the real property, and no other person or entity has a superior right, because each declarant or entity is:
   a. ☐ (*will*) a beneficiary that succeeded to the property under decedent's will. *(Attach a copy of the will.)*
   b. ☐ (*no will*) a person who succeeded to the property under Probate Code sections 6401 and 6402.
7. Names and addresses of each guardian or conservator of decedent's estate at date of death: ☐ none ☐ are as follows:*

   Names Addresses

   *(*You must mail [or serve, per Prob. Code, § 1216] a copy of this affidavit and all attachments to each guardian or conservator listed above. You may use Judicial Council form POS-030 for a proof of mailing or form POS-020 for a proof of personal service.)*
8. The **gross value** of decedent's interest in all real property located in California as shown by the attached *Inventory and Appraisal*—excluding the real property described in Probate Code section 13050 (property held in joint tenancy or as a life estate or other interest terminable upon decedent's death, property passing to decedent's spouse, property in a trust revocable by the decedent, etc.)—did not exceed $55,425 as of the date of decedent's death.

MATTER OF *(Name):* DECEDENT	CASE NUMBER:

9. An *Inventory and Appraisal* of all of decedent's interests in **real property** in California is attached. The appraisal was made by a probate referee appointed for the county in which the property is located. *(You must prepare the Inventory on Judicial Council forms DE-160 and DE-161. You may select any probate referee appointed for the county for the appraisal. The California State Controller's Office has a list of all probate referees, shown by county on its website, and each court has a list of probate referees appointed for its county. Check with the probate referee you select or consult an attorney for help in preparing the Inventory.)*

10. No proceeding is now being or has been conducted in California for administration of decedent's estate.

11. Funeral expenses, expenses of last illness, and all known unsecured debts of the decedent have been paid. *(NOTE: You may be personally liable for decedent's unsecured debts up to the fair market value of the real property and any income you receive from it.)*

I declare under penalty of perjury under the laws of the State of California that the foregoing is true and correct.

Date:

(TYPE OR PRINT NAME)* ▶ (SIGNATURE OF DECLARANT)

Date:

(TYPE OR PRINT NAME)* ▶ (SIGNATURE OF DECLARANT)

☐ SIGNATURE OF ADDITIONAL DECLARANTS ATTACHED

*** A declarant claiming on behalf of a trust or other entity should also state the name of the entity that is a beneficiary under the decedent's will, and declarant's capacity to sign on behalf of the entity (e.g., trustee, Chief Executive Officer, etc.).**

NOTARY ACKNOWLEDGMENT *(NOTE: No notary acknowledgment may be affixed as a rider (small strip) to this page. If additional notary acknowledgments are required, they must be attached as 8-1/2-by-11-inch pages.)*

A notary public or other officer completing this certificate verifies only the identity of the individual who signed the document to which this certificate is attached, and not the truthfulness, accuracy, or validity of that document.

STATE OF CALIFORNIA, COUNTY OF *(specify):*

On *(date):* , before me *(name and title):*

personally appeared *(name(s)):*

who proved to me on the basis of satisfactory evidence to be the person(s) whose name(s) is/are subscribed to the within instrument and acknowledged to me that he/she/they executed the instrument in his/her/their authorized capacity(ies), and that by his/her/their signature(s) on the instrument the person(s), or the entity upon behalf of which the person(s) acted, executed the instrument.

I certify under PENALTY OF PERJURY under the laws of the State of California that the foregoing paragraph is true and correct.

WITNESS my hand and official seal.

(SIGNATURE OF NOTARY PUBLIC)

(NOTARY SEAL)

(SEAL)

CLERK'S CERTIFICATE

I certify that the foregoing, including any attached notary acknowledgments and any attached legal description of the property (but excluding other attachments), is a true and correct copy of the original affidavit on file in my office. *(Certified copies of this affidavit do not include the (1) death certificate, (2) will, or (3) inventory and appraisal. See Probate Code section 13202.)*

Date: Clerk, by ______________________, Deputy

ATTORNEY OR PARTY WITHOUT ATTORNEY: STATE BAR NO.:	FOR COURT USE ONLY
NAME: FIRM NAME: STREET ADDRESS: CITY: STATE: ZIP CODE: TELEPHONE NO.: FAX NO.: EMAIL ADDRESS: ATTORNEY FOR (*name*):	
SUPERIOR COURT OF CALIFORNIA, COUNTY OF STREET ADDRESS: MAILING ADDRESS: CITY AND ZIP CODE: BRANCH NAME:	
MATTER OF (*name*): DECEDENT	CASE NUMBER:
PETITION TO DETERMINE SUCCESSION TO REAL PROPERTY ☐ **and Personal Property (Estates of $166,250 or Less)**	HEARING DATE AND TIME: DEPT.:

1. Petitioner *(name of each person claiming an interest):*

   requests a determination that the real property ☐ and personal property described in item 11 is property passing to petitioner and that no administration of decedent's estate is necessary.

2. Decedent (*name*):
   a. Date of death:
   b. Place of death *(city and state or, if outside the United States, city and country):*
3. At least 40 days have elapsed since the date of decedent's death.
4. a. ☐ Decedent was a resident of this county at the time of death.
   b. ☐ Decedent was **not** a resident of California at the time of death. Decedent died owning property in this county.
5. Decedent died ☐ intestate ☐ testate and a copy of the will and any codicil is affixed as Attachment 5 or 12a.
6. a. ☐ No proceeding for the administration of decedent's estate is being conducted or has been conducted in California.
   b. ☐ Decedent's personal representative's consent to use the procedure provided by Probate Code section 13150 et seq. is attached as Attachment 6b.
7. Proceedings for the administration of decedent's estate in another jurisdiction: a. ☐ Have **not** been commenced.
   b. ☐ Have been commenced ☐ and completed. *(Specify state, county, court, and case number):*
8. The **gross value** of decedent's interest in real and personal property located in California as shown by the *Inventory and Appraisal* attached to this petition—excluding the property described in Probate Code section 13050 (property held in joint tenancy or as a life estate or other interest terminable upon decedent's death, property passing to decedent's spouse, property in a trust revocable by decedent, etc.)—did not exceed $166,250 as of the date of decedent's death. *(Prepare and attach an* Inventory and Appraisal *as Attachment 8 (use Judicial Council forms DE-160 and DE-161 for this purpose). A probate referee appointed for the county named above must appraise all real property and all personal property other than cash or its equivalent. See Prob. Code, §§ 8901, 8902.)*
9. a. Decedent is survived by *(check items (1) or (2), and (3) or (4), and (5) or (6), and (7) or (8))*
   (1) ☐ spouse
   (2) ☐ no spouse as follows: (a) ☐ divorced or never married (b) ☐ spouse deceased
   (3) ☐ registered domestic partner
   (4) ☐ no registered domestic partner *(See Fam. Code, § 297.5(c); Prob. Code, §§ 37(b), 6401(c), and 6402.)*
   (5) ☐ child as follows: (a) ☐ natural or adopted (b) ☐ natural adopted by a third party
   (6) ☐ no child
   (7) ☐ issue of a predeceased child
   (8) ☐ no issue of a predeceased child
   b. Decedent ☐ is ☐ is not survived by a stepchild or foster child or children who would have been adopted by decedent but for a legal barrier. *(See Prob. Code, § 6454.)*

MATTER OF *(name)*: DECEDENT	CASE NUMBER:

10. ☐ Decedent is survived by *(complete if decedent was survived by (1) a spouse or registered domestic partner described in Prob. Code, § 37 but no issue (only a or b apply); or (2) no spouse or registered domestic partner described in Prob. Code, § 37, or issue. Check the* ***first*** *box that applies.)*:
   a. ☐ A parent or parents who are listed in item 14.
   b. ☐ A brother, sister, or issue of a deceased brother or sister, all of whom are listed in item 14.
   c. ☐ Other heirs under Probate Code section 6400 et seq., all of whom are listed in item 14.
   d. ☐ No known next of kin.

11. Attachment 11 contains (1) the **legal description** of decedent's real property and its Assessor's Parcel Number (APN) and ☐ a description of personal property in California passing to petitioner; (2) decedent's interest in the property; and, (3) if a petitioner's claim to the property is based on succession under Probate Code sections 6401 and 6402, facts that show the character of the property as community, separate, or quasi-community property.

12. Each petitioner is a successor of decedent (as defined in Probate Code section 13006) and a successor to decedent's interest in the real property ☐ and personal property described in item 11 because each petitioner is:
   a. ☐ **(will)** A beneficiary who succeeded to the property under decedent's will.[1]
   b. ☐ **(no will)** A person who succeeded to the property under Probate Code sections 6401 and 6402.

13. The specific property interest claimed by each petitioner in the real property ☐ and personal property ☐ is stated in Attachment 13 ☐ is as follows *(specify)*:

14. The names, relationships to decedent, ages, and residence or mailing addresses so far as known to or reasonably ascertainable by petitioner of (1) all persons named or checked in items 1, 9, and 10; (2) all other heirs of decedent; and (3) all devisees of decedent (persons designated in the will to receive any property) are listed in Attachment 14.

15. The names and addresses of all persons named as executors in decedent's will
   ☐ are listed below ☐ are listed in Attachment 15 ☐ No executor is named. ☐ There is no will.

16. ☐ Petitioner is the trustee of a trust that is a devisee under decedent's will. The names and addresses of all persons interested in the trust, as determined in cases of future interests under paragraphs (1), (2), or (3) of subdivision (a) of Probate Code section 15804, are listed in Attachment 16.

17. ☐ Decedent's estate was under a ☐ guardianship ☐ conservatorship at decedent's death. The names and addresses of all persons serving as guardian or conservator ☐ are listed below ☐ are listed in Attachment 17.

18. Number of pages attached: ______

Date: ____________________

(TYPE OR PRINT NAME OF ATTORNEY)	▶ (SIGNATURE OF ATTORNEY)*

* (Signature of all petitioners also required (Prob. Code, § 1020).)

I declare under penalty of perjury under the laws of the State of California that the foregoing is true and correct.

Date: ____________________

(TYPE OR PRINT NAME OF PETITIONER)	▶ (SIGNATURE OF PETITIONER) [2]
(TYPE OR PRINT NAME OF PETITIONER)	▶ (SIGNATURE OF PETITIONER) [2]

☐ SIGNATURE(S) OF ADDITIONAL PETITIONERS ATTACHED

[1] See Probate Code section 13152(c) for the requirement that a copy of the will be attached in certain instances. If required, include as Attachment 5 or 12a.

[2] Each person named in item 1 must sign.

DE-315

ATTORNEY OR PARTY WITHOUT ATTORNEY *(name, address, and State Bar number):*
After recording, return to:

TEL NO.: FAX NO.:
EMAIL ADDRESS:
ATTORNEY FOR *(name):*

SUPERIOR COURT OF CALIFORNIA, COUNTY OF
STREET ADDRESS:
MAILING ADDRESS:
CITY AND ZIP CODE:
BRANCH NAME:

FOR RECORDER'S USE ONLY

MATTER OF *(name):*

DECEDENT

CASE NUMBER:

ORDER DETERMINING SUCCESSION TO REAL PROPERTY
☐ **And Personal Property**
(Estates of $166,250 or Less)

FOR COURT USE ONLY

1. Date of hearing: Time:
 Dept./Room:
 Judicial Officer *(name):*

THE COURT FINDS

2. All notices required by law have been given.
3. Decedent died on *(date):*
 a. ☐ a resident of the California county named above.
 b. ☐ a nonresident of California and owned property in the county named above.
 c. ☐ intestate. ☐ testate.
4. At least 40 days have elapsed since the date of decedent's death.
5. a. ☐ No proceeding for the administration of decedent's estate is being conducted or has been conducted in California.
 b. ☐ Decedent's personal representative has filed a consent to use the procedure provided in Probate Code section 13150 et seq.
6. The gross value of decedent's real and personal property in California, excluding property described in Probate Code section 13050, did not exceed $166,250 as of the date of decedent's death.
7. Each petitioner is a successor of decedent (as defined in Probate Code section 13006) and a successor to decedent's interest in the real ☐ and personal property described in item 9a because each petitioner is:
 a. ☐ **(will)** a beneficiary who succeeded to the property under decedent's will.
 b. ☐ **(no will)** a person who succeeded to the property under Probate Code sections 6401 and 6402.

THE COURT FURTHER FINDS AND ORDERS

8. No administration of decedent's estate is necessary in California.
9. a. The real ☐ and personal property ☐ described in Attachment 9a ☐ described as follows is property of decedent passing to each petitioner *(give **legal description** of real property).*

 b. Each petitioner's **name** and specific property interest ☐ is stated in Attachment 9b. ☐ is as follows *(specify):*

10. ☐ Other orders are stated in Attachment 10.
11. Number of pages attached:

Date:

JUDICIAL OFFICER

☐ SIGNATURE FOLLOWS LAST ATTACHMENT

Form Adopted for Mandatory Use
Judicial Council of California
DE-315 [Rev. January 1, 2020]

ORDER DETERMINING SUCCESSION TO REAL PROPERTY
(Estates of $166,250 or Less)

Probate Code, § 13154
www.courts.ca.gov

Non–Judicial Council Forms

These forms are available as downloadable eForms at **www.nolo.com/back-of-book/PAE.html**

Who Inherits Under the Will?

Schedule of Assets

Notification by Trustee

Affidavit—Death of Transferor (TOD Deed)

Affidavit—Death of Joint Tenant

Affidavit for Collection of Personal Property Under California Probate Code §§ 13100–13106

Affidavit—Death of Trustee

Declaration for Collection of Compensation Owed to Deceased Spouse or Domestic Partner

Affidavit—Death of Spouse or Domestic Partner—Survivorship Community Property

Who Inherits Under the Will?

Beneficiaries Named in Will	Property Inherited

Schedule of Assets

Estate of ____, Deceased

Description of Assets	A Total Value of Asset on Date/Death	B How Is Asset Owned?	C Portion Owned by Decedent	D Value of Decedent's Interest	E Probate or Non-probate
1. Cash Items					
Cash in decedent's possession					
Uncashed checks payable to decedent					
2. Bank Accounts					
3. Real Property (common address, brief description)					
4. Securities Stock (name of company, type, and number of shares)					

	A	B	C	D	E
	Total Value of Asset on Date/Death	How Is Asset Owned?	Portion Owned by Decedent	Value of Decedent's Interest	Probate or Non-probate

Bonds (face amount)

U.S. Savings Bonds/Treasury Bills (series, amount, date of issue)

Mutual Funds (name of fund, number of shares)

5. **Insurance** (name of company, policy number, name of beneficiary, name of owner)

Policies on decedent's life

Policies owned by decedent on another

6. **Retirement and Death Benefits** (description, beneficiary, amount)

Employee benefits

Pension, profit-sharing, savings plans

Social Security/Railroad Retirement

Individual Retirement Accounts

	A Total Value of Asset on Date/Death	B How Is Asset Owned?	C Portion Owned by Decedent	D Value of Decedent's Interest	E Probate or Non-probate

7. Amounts Due the Decedent (name of payor, amount)

8. Promissory Note (name of payor, date, amount, balance)

9. Tangible Personal Property (household furniture, furnishings, personal effects, books, jewelry, artwork, valuable collections, antiques, etc.)

10. Automobiles (year, make, model)

11. Business Interests (names of partnerships or family corporations, brief descriptions)

12. Other Assets (copyrights, royalty interests, any other property not listed above)

Total Value of Decedent's Gross Estate ______________

Deductions (for federal estate tax purposes)

a. Personal debts owed by decedent at date of death

______________________________ ________

______________________________ ________

______________________________ ________

______________________________ ________

b. Mortgages/promissory notes due

______________________________ ________

______________________________ ________

______________________________ ________

______________________________ ________

______________________________ ________

c. Expenses of estate administration

______________________________ ________

______________________________ ________

______________________________ ________

______________________________ ________

d. Last illness expenses

______________________________ ________

______________________________ ________

______________________________ ________

______________________________ ________

______________________________ ________

______________________________ ________

e. Funeral expenses

______________________________ ________

______________________________ ________

______________________________ ________

f. Sales contracts (automobiles, furniture, television)

______________________________ ________

______________________________ ________

______________________________ ________

Total Deductions $________

Total Value of Decedent's Gross Estate (from previous page) $________

Total Deductions (from line above) ________

Value of Decedent's Net Estate $________

Notification by Trustee
(Probate Code Sec. 16061.7)

____

executed the ______________________________ Trust

in his/her/their capacity(ies) as Settlor(s) on ______________, hereinafter referred to as the "Trust."

1. The name, mailing address, and telephone number of each Trustee of the Trust is set forth below:

____

____

____

____

____

2. The address of the physical location where the principal place of administration of the Trust is located is:

____

____

____

____

____

3. The terms of the Trust require disclosure of the following information:

____

____

____

____

____

4. You are entitled, upon reasonable request to the Trustee, to receive from the Trustee a true and complete copy of the terms of the Trust.

5. **YOU MAY NOT BRING AN ACTION TO CONTEST THE TRUST MORE THAN 120 DAYS FROM THE DATE THIS NOTIFICATION BY THE TRUSTEE IS SERVED UPON YOU OR 60 DAYS FROM THE DATE ON WHICH A COPY OF THE TERMS OF THE TRUST IS MAILED OR PERSONALLY DELIVERED TO YOU DURING THAT 120-DAY PERIOD, WHICHEVER IS LATER.**

______________________ ______________________

Date Trustee

RECORDING REQUESTED BY

AND WHEN RECORDED MAIL DOCUMENT
AND TAX STATEMENT TO:

APN:
Commonly known as:

SPACE ABOVE THIS LINE FOR RECORDER'S USE

[*Include if applicable*: Exempt from SB2 fee per Gov. Code Sec. 27338.1(a)(2) because recorded in connection with a transfer of real property that is a residential dwelling to an owner-occupier.]

AFFIDAVIT – DEATH OF TRANSFEROR (TOD DEED)

____, of legal age, being first duly sworn, deposes and says:
__________________________, the decedent mentioned in the attached certified copy of Certificate of Death, is the same person as ____________________________, the transferor under the Revocable Transfer on Death Deed dated _________________________ and recorded on _______________________ as Instrument No. ____, of the Official Records of _____________________________ County, California, which named as beneficiary(ies) ______________________________________ and which transferred the following described property in ____________________________ County, California:

Assessor's Parcel No. ________________

Dated: ________________ ____
Signature

____
(Type or print name of person signing affidavit)

Certificate of Notary Public

A notary public or other officer completing this certificate verifies only the identity of the individual who signed the document to which this certificate is attached, and not the truthfulness, accuracy, or validity of that document.

State of California

County of ______________________________

Subscribed and sworn to (or affirmed) before me on this ______ day of ____________________, 20 ______

by____, proved to me on the basis of satisfactory evidence to be the person(s) who appeared before me.

[SEAL] ______________________________

Signature

RECORDING REQUESTED BY

AND WHEN RECORDED MAIL DOCUMENT
AND TAX STATEMENT TO:

APN:
Commonly known as:

SPACE ABOVE THIS LINE FOR RECORDER'S USE

[*Include if applicable*: Exempt from SB2 fee per Gov. Code Sec. 27338.1(a)(2) because recorded in connection with a transfer of real property that is a residential dwelling to an owner-occupier.]

AFFIDAVIT—DEATH OF JOINT TENANT

________________________________, of legal age, being first duly sworn, deposes and says:

That ____,
the decedent mentioned in the attached certified copy of Certificate of Death, is the same person as ____________________________________, named as one of the parties in that certain deed dated __________________, executed by ________________________________ to ____,
as joint tenants, recorded on ____________________________ as Instrument No. __________________________________, of Official Records of ____________________
County, California, covering the following described property situated in the City of ____________________,
County of ________________________, State of California:

Assessor's Parcel No. ____________________

Dated: __________________

____
Signature

____
(Type or print name of person signing affidavit)

Certificate of Notary Public

A notary public or other officer completing this certificate verifies only the identity of the individual who signed the document to which this certificate is attached, and not the truthfulness, accuracy, or validity of that document.

State of California

County of ___________________________________

Subscribed and sworn to (or affirmed) before me on this ______ day of ____________________, 20 _____ by_______________________________________, proved to me on the basis of satisfactory evidence to be the person(s) who appeared before me.

[SEAL] ______________________________________

Signature

Affidavit for Collection of Personal Property Under California Probate Code §§ 13100–13106

The undersigned state(s) as follows:

1. ______________________________ died on ____________, 20____ in the County of ______________________________, State of California.
2. At least 40 days have elapsed since the death of the decedent, as shown by the attached certified copy of the decedent's death certificate.
3. No proceeding is now being or has been conducted in California for administration of the decedent's estate.
4. The current gross fair market value of the decedent's real and personal property in California, excluding the property described in Section 13050 of the California Probate Code, does not exceed $166,250.
5. ☐ An inventory and appraisal of the real property included in the decedent's estate is attached *OR*
   ☐ There is no real property in the estate.
6. The following property is to be paid, transferred, or delivered to the undersigned under the provisions of California Probate Code Section 13100.
7. The successor(s) of the decedent, as defined in Probate Code Section 13006, is/are:
   ______________________________.
8. The undersigned ☐ is/are successor(s) of the decedent to the decedent's interest in the described property, or ☐ is/are authorized under California Probate Code Section 13051 to act on behalf of the successor(s) of the decedent with respect to the decedent's interest in the described property.
9. No other person has a superior right to the interest of the decedent in the described property.
10. The undersigned request(s) that the described property be paid, delivered, or transferred to the undersigned.

I/We declare under penalty of perjury under the laws of the State of California that the foregoing is true and correct.

Dated: ____________, 20______

______________________	______________________
Signature	Address
______________________	______________________
Signature	Address

(See reverse side for notary certificates)

Certificate of Notary Public

A notary public or other officer completing this certificate verifies only the identity of the individual who signed the document to which this certificate is attached, and not the truthfulness, accuracy, or validity of that document.

State of California

County of ___________________________________

Subscribed and sworn to (or affirmed) before me on this ______ day of ____________________, 20 ______

by_______________________________________, proved to me on the basis of satisfactory evidence to

be the person(s) who appeared before me.

[SEAL] ___________________________________

Signature

Certificate of Notary Public

A notary public or other officer completing this certificate verifies only the identity of the individual who signed the document to which this certificate is attached, and not the truthfulness, accuracy, or validity of that document.

State of California

County of ___________________________________

Subscribed and sworn to (or affirmed) before me on this ______ day of ____________________, 20 ______

by_______________________________________, proved to me on the basis of satisfactory evidence to

be the person(s) who appeared before me.

[SEAL] ___________________________________

Signature

RECORDING REQUESTED BY

AND WHEN RECORDED MAIL DOCUMENT
AND TAX STATEMENT TO:

APN:
Commonly known as:

SPACE ABOVE THIS LINE FOR RECORDER'S USE

AFFIDAVIT—DEATH OF TRUSTEE

The undersigned, being of legal age, being duly sworn, deposes and says:

That ____________________, the decedent mentioned in the attached certified copy of Certificate of Death, is the same person as ____________________, named as Trustee in that certain Declaration of Trust dated ____________________, executed by ____________________, as Trustor(s).

At the decedent's death, the decedent was the record owner, as Trustee of the ____________________, of real property commonly known as ____________________, which property was transferred to said trust and described in a deed recorded on ____________________ as Instrument No. ____________________, of Official Records of ____________________ County, State of California.

The legal description of said property is as follows:

Assessor's Parcel No. : ____________________

I, ____________________, am the named Successor Trustee under the above-referenced Trust, which was in effect at the time of the death of the decedent mentioned in Paragraph 1 above, and which has not been revoked, and I hereby consent to act as such. I declare under penalty of perjury, under the laws of the State of California, that the foregoing is true and correct.

Dated: ____________________

____
Signature

____
(Type or print name of successor trustee)

Certificate of Notary Public

A notary public or other officer completing this certificate verifies only the identity of the individual who signed the document to which this certificate is attached, and not the truthfulness, accuracy, or validity of that document.

State of California

County of ____________________________________

Subscribed and sworn to (or affirmed) before me on this ______ day of ____________________, 20 _____

by______________________________________, proved to me on the basis of satisfactory evidence to be the person(s) who appeared before me.

[SEAL] ____

Signature

Declaration for Collection of Compensation Owed to Deceased Spouse or Domestic Partner

(California Probate Code Sections 13600-13606)

I, ______________________________, declare as follows:

1. ______________________________ died on ______________ at ______________________ and at the time of death was a resident of California.

2. ☐ I am the surviving spouse of the decedent.

   ☐ I am the surviving domestic partner of the decedent.

   ☐ I am the guardian or conservator of the estate of the surviving spouse of the decedent.

   ☐ I am the guardian or conservator of the estate of the surviving domestic partner of the decedent.

3. The ______________________________ of the decedent is entitled to the earnings of the decedent under the decedent's will or by intestate succession and no one else has a superior right to the earnings.

4. No proceeding is now being or has been conducted in California for administration of the decedent's estate.

5. Sections 13600 to 13605, inclusive, of the California Probate Code require that the earnings of the decedent, including compensation for unused vacation, not in excess of sixteen thousand six hundred twenty-five dollars ($16,625) net, be paid promptly to me.

6. Neither the ______________________________ nor anyone acting on behalf of the ______________________________, has a pending request to collect compensation owed by another employer for personal services of the decedent under Sections 13600 to 13605, inclusive, of the California Probate Code.

7. Neither the ______________________________ nor anyone acting on behalf of the ______________________________ has collected any compensation owed by an employer for personal services of the decedent under Sections 13600 to 13605 of the California Probate Code [*add if applicable*: except the sum of ______________ dollars ($__________) that was collected from ______________________].

8. I request that I be paid the salary or other compensation owed by you for personal services of the decedent, including compensation for unused vacation, not to exceed sixteen thousand six hundred twenty-five dollars ($16,625) net [*add if applicable*: less the amount of ______________ dollars ($__________), that was previously collected].

I declare under penalty of perjury under the laws of the State of California that the foregoing is true and correct.

______________________   ______________________________

Date   Signature

RECORDING REQUESTED BY

AND WHEN RECORDED MAIL DOCUMENT
AND TAX STATEMENT TO:

APN:
Commonly known as:

SPACE ABOVE THIS LINE FOR RECORDER'S USE

[*Include if applicable*: Exempt from SB2 fee per Gov. Code Sec. 27338.1(a)(2) because recorded in connection with a transfer of real property that is a residential dwelling to an owner-occupier.]

AFFIDAVIT—DEATH OF SPOUSE OR DOMESTIC PARTNER—SURVIVORSHIP COMMUNITY PROPERTY

____, of legal age, being first duly sworn, deposes and says:

That ____, the decedent mentioned in the attached certified copy of Certificate of Death, is the same person as ____, named as one of the parties in the deed dated ________________________, executed by ____ to ____, as community property with right of survivorship, recorded on ______________________________ as Instrument No. ____, of Official Records of ____________________________________ County, California, covering the following described property situated in the City of ______________________________, County of ______________________________________, State of California:

Assessor's Parcel No. ______________________________

Dated: ____________________

____
Signature

____
(Type or print name of person signing affidavit)

Certificate of Notary Public

A notary public or other officer completing this certificate verifies only the identity of the individual who signed the document to which this certificate is attached, and not the truthfulness, accuracy, or validity of that document.

State of California

County of ____

Subscribed and sworn to (or affirmed) before me on this ______ day of ____________________, 20 ______

by____, proved to me on the basis of satisfactory evidence to be the person(s) who appeared before me.

[SEAL]

____
Signature

Index

A

B

C

D

E

F

G

H

I

J

K

L

M

N

O

P

T

U

V

W

Z